CW00972448

Manual of Heritage Management

Manual of Heritage Management

Edited by

Richard Harrison

Editorial Board

Neil Cossons
Patrick Greene
Terry Robinson
David Sekers
Rob Shorland-Ball
Michael Stratton

Published in association with the
Association of Independent Museums

Butterworth-Heinemann Ltd
Linacre House, Jordan Hill, Oxford OX2 8DP

 A member of the Reed Elsevier plc group

OXFORD   LONDON   BOSTON
MUNICH   NEW DELHI   SINGAPORE   SYDNEY
TOKYO   TORONTO   WELLINGTON

First published 1994

© Butterworth-Heinemann Ltd and The Association of Independent Museums 1994

All rights reserved. No part of this publication
may be reproduced in any material form (including
photocopying or storing in any medium by electronic
means and whether or not transiently or incidentally
to some other use of this publication) without the
written permission of the copyright holder except in
accordance with the provisions of the Copyright,
Designs and Patents Act 1988 or under the terms of a
licence issued by the Copyright Licensing Agency Ltd,
90 Tottenham Court Road, London, England W1P 9HE.
Applications for the copyright holder's written permission
to reproduce any part of this publication should be addressed
to the publishers

British Library Cataloguing in Publication Data

Manual of Heritage Management
  I. Harrison, Richard
  069.5

ISBN 0 7506 0822 6

Library of Congress Cataloguing in Publication Data

Manual of heritage management/edited by Richard Harrison.
  p.   cm.
  'Published in association with the Association of Indpendent Museums.'
  Includes bibliographical references and index.
  ISBN 0–75 06–0822–6
  1. Antiquities–Collection and preservation. 2. Great Britain –
  Antiquities – Collection and preservation. 3. Historic sites –
  Conservation and restoration. 4. Historic sites – Great Brtain –
  Conservation and restoration. 5. Cultural property, Protection of.
  6. Cultural property, Protection of – Great Britain. 7. Historic
  preservation. 8. Historic preservation–Great Britain.
  I. Harrison, Richard.
  CC135.M315   94–3941
  363.6'9–dc20   CIP

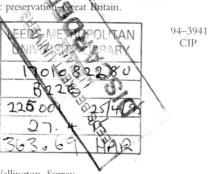

Typeset by TecSet Ltd, Wallington, Surrey
Printed and bound in Great Britain

Contents

Section Three: Funding and Operations Management   233

Section Co-ordinators: Rob Shorland-Ball and Terry Robinson

Preface

On behalf of the Editorial Board I would like to thank the very many people who have made this publication possible.

First and foremost the contributors who under the watchful eye of the Section Co-ordinators have collaborated to produce a manual which we intend will be useful to all those charged with managing the many and varied elements of the natural and historic environment.

The preparation of the Manual was in two stages. The first was writing a number of subject based chapters within the framework of five key areas of heritage management. The second was the collection of a number of case studies aimed at relating the subject matter of the individual chapters to practical experience in the field. The case studies were seen as an essential element in the structure of the Manual enabling it to be first and foremost a book which would be of practical value.

I am particularly grateful to the case study authors who so generously responded to requests for evidence of practical experience in many and varied aspects of heritage management.

The early gestation of the Manual was during a period of change at Butterworth Scientific (now Butterworth–Heinemann). Anne Berne, Senior Commissioning Editor of Butterworths Scientific saw it through its birth pangs and gave the Editorial Board a great deal of practical help. She was succeeded by Neil Warnock-Smith, Division Publisher, who with Angela Leopard, has brought the Manual to fruition.

My thanks are also due to the members of the Editorial Board under the chairmanship of Neil Cossons – Dr Patrick Greene, Terry Robinson, David Sekers, Rob Shorland-Ball, and Dr Michael Stratton (the last three of whom were also Section Co-ordinators) under whose direction I have tried to fulfill their original brief. Also to the other Section Co-ordinators, Victor Middleton, Graham Taylor, Ken Robinson and Dr David Uzzell. It was they who developed the brief for each section, were instrumental in selecting authors and who ensured that each section dealt comprehensively with its theme. There was also a third group of people who, with the Section Co-ordinators, gave a great deal of assistance with the case studies. They were chosen for their experience in specific areas of heritage management, and included: Jane Glaister, Professor Alan Patmore, Ian Parkin, Dr Marie Louise Stig Sorensen and Dr Christopher Young. I much appreciate their input.

Throughout what has proved to be a long period of development the Council of the Association of the Independent Museums has given every encouragement and support to me and my colleagues. For this we are very grateful.

Richard Harrison

Note

Each contribution reflects the opinion of the author, not the Board, and all sources have been quoted or referred to as far as known.

Contributors

Rosemary Allen, Headland Design Associates

Robert Baldwin, Nautical Museums Trust, Hastings

Sandra Bicknell, The Science Museum, London

Marion Blockley, Ironbridge Institute, University of Birmingham

John Bold, Royal Commission on the Historical Monuments of England, London

Lester Borley, Consultant

Philip Broadbent-Yale, National Trust

John Burnett, National Museums of Scotland, Edinburgh

Graham Carter, National Motor Museum, Beaulieu

Andrew Coleman, Wyre District Council

Neil Cossons, The Science Museum, London

Sir John Cox, Sound Alive Tours Ltd

Susan Denyer, The National Trust

Jonathan Drake, Heritage Policy, Southampton City Council

Paul Drury, English Heritage, London

Stephen Feber, Quarry Bank Mill, Styal

Alan Fishwick, Lake District National Park, Kendal

David Fleming, Tyne and Wear Museums

Laurie Friday, University of Cambridge

Colum Giles, Royal Commission on the Historical Monuments of England

Howard Giles, English Heritage, London

Brian Goodey, Joint Centre for Urban Design, Oxford Brookes University

Jonathan Griffin, English Heritage, London

Brian Griffiths, Faculty of Leisure and Tourism, Swansea Institute of Higher Education

Catherine Hall, Oakwell Hall Country Park

Geoffrey Halliday, University of Lancaster

Alf Hatton, Coventry Museums and Galleries

Richard Harrison, Consultant

Tony Hirst, The Boat Museum, Ellesmere Port

Mark Holloway, County Museums Service, Hampshire County Council

Karen Hull, Oxfordshire County Museum

Nicholas Johnson, Cornwall Archaeological Unit, Cornwall County Council

Arwel Jones, Mid Wales Festival of the Countryside

Suzanne Keene, The Science Museum, London

Lars-Åke Kvarning, The National Maritime Museums, Stockholm

Peter Lewis, Beamish, The North of England Open Air Museum

Christine McDonnell, York Archaeological Trust for Excavation and Research Ltd

Peter Middleton, L&R Leisure PLC, Liverpool

Victor T.C. Middleton, Oxford Brookes University and Ventures Consultancy Ltd

Roger Miles, The Natural History Museum, London

Sue Millar, National Maritime Museum, London

Ian Morrison, National Museums of Scotland

Sam Mullins, St Albans Museums

Rachel Newman, Lancaster University Archaeological Unit

Simon O'Connor-Thompson, Museum of London Archaeology Service

Richard Pailthorpe, Weald and Downland Museum

Alastair Penfold, County Museums Service, Hampshire County Council

Simon Rice-Oxley, The Visual Connection (TVC) Ltd

Gordon Riddle, Culzean Castle and Country Park, Maybole

Paul Risk, Stephen F. Austin State University, School of Forestry, Nacogcloches, Texas

Bob Roberts, Countryside Commission, Cheltenham

Kenneth Robinson, Montagu Ventures, Beaulieu

Terry Robinson, Countryside Commission, Cheltenham

Peter Rowsome, Museum of London Archaeology Service

Robert Scott, Manchester Museum of Science and Industry

Grahame Senior, Senior King Ltd

Adam Sharpe, Cornwall Archaeological Unit, Cornwall County Council

Brian Sparks, Hampshire and Wight Trust for Maritime Archaeology

Anthony Streeten, English Heritage, London

Michael Stratton, Ironbridge Institute, University of Birmingham

John Sutton, North York Moors National Park

Graham Taylor, National Parks Department, Northumberland County Council

David Uzzell, Department of Psychology, University of Surrey, Guildford

Giles Velarde, Consultant

G. J. O. Wallis, Dorothea Restorations

Paul Walshe, Countryside Commission, Cheltenham

Marion Wertheim, MEW Research

Sally Woodhead, The Young National Trust Theatre

Christopher Zeuner, Weald and Downland Open Air Museum, Chichester

Introduction

The *Manual of Heritage Management* is a companion volume to the *Manual of Curatorship* and is for the practical use of all those concerned with management of the natural and man-made heritage. Whilst many of the management issues related to museums are similar to those experienced by those administering country houses, ancient monuments, industrial sites, historical townscapes and countryside, this volume sets out to put these issues in the wider context.

The idea of writing a companion volume to the *Manual of Curatorship* was promoted by the Association of Independent Museums of which I have the honour to be President. AIM was formed in 1977 and brings together the significant number of museums which are in the independant sector. Its membership reflects a wider range of heritage interests than the traditional museum and it was for this reason that the Association sponsored the production of this manual.

In order to ensure that the contents of the Manual reflect best practice in each of the topics covered the Editorial Board, which was originally drawn from members of the AIM Council, was enlarged to be more representative of those working in the management of the man–made and natural environment.

The Manual is designed for use as a ready reference book. It is for this reason that it has two key elements – theoretical contributions written by leading authorities in their particular fields supported, where appropriate, by case studies related to the practical application of the theory in a wide range of real situations. Although based primarily, but not exclusively, on heritage management practice in the United Kingdom the Editorial Board is confident that the work has wide universal relevance.

The Manual is in five sections: Vision, Strategy and Corporate Planning; Conserving the Natural and Man-made Heritage; Funding and Operations Management; Interpretation and Presentation; and Marketing. Each section had its own Co-ordinator who was responsible for advising the Editorial Board on the appropriate author for each chapter, briefing them and undertaking the first, and most important stage of editing. They also played a key role in the choice of case studies. Several of them also contributed chapters to their own sections. The Co-ordinators were selected from people who had made an outstanding contribution in their own field and the success the Manual enjoys will be largely due to their efforts.

A General Editor was also appointed, whose key role to ensure that the concept for the manual developed by the Editorial Board was implemented and that when completed the sixty or so contributions formed a coherent whole.

Each section of the Manual is carefully structured in order to cover as many aspects of the overall topic as possible and takes into account the very wide market at which the Manual is aimed. Authors were selected with this in mind and as their brief focussed very much on the desire to make this a book which would be of benefit to practitioners in heritage and countryside management, they have drawn extensively on their own experience in a particular field of management.

The five sections of the Manual focus on what we believe are the major issues facing the heritage manager today – strategic planning as well as the day-to-day issues of management; the many aspects of managing the conservation of the heritage; how best to employ current thinking in interpretation and presentation and the all-important area of effective marketing.

Recognizing from the outset that the principal chapters of the Manual would tend to reflect philosophical as well as practical issues of management, we determined to illustrate as many of these as possible with case studies. Not all of the chapters required this form of elucidation but for each of those that did we have included one or more drawn from as wide a range of field experience as possible.

I am grateful to all the members of this team for their contribution and their time which was freely given.

Neil Cossons

but for each of those that did we have included one or more drawn from as wide a range of field experience as possible.

The final selection is not perhaps as comprehensive as one would wish but in projects of this kind there are always the constraints of availability of authors and, inevitably, time. As with the Sections we sought the assistance of a further range of specialists drawn form a broader range of disciplines than the section co-ordinates and they played a valuable role in assisting us to select topics and authors.

I am grateful to all the members of this team for their contribution and their time which was freely given.

As with all publications of this nature the manual reflects thinking and practice at a particular point in time and, in this case, the fairly extended period it has taken to bring the project to a conlusion. We are in a period of great change in many aspects of the management of our natural and man-made heritage with new challenges, opportunities and constraints as well as the development of new skills. With this in mind we see this edition regularly updated by the addition of new material and in particular by the inclusion of case studies which not only cover a wider range of experience but also reflect new thinking and attitudes.

As Chairman of the Editorial Board I also wish to make it clear that each contribution reflects the opinion of the author, not the Board, and to the best of our knowledge all sources have been quoted or referred to as far as known.

Neil Cossons

SECTION ONE

VISION, STRATEGY AND CORPORATE PLANNING

1

Vision, strategy and corporate planning: an overview

Victor Middleton

Like it or not, around the world in the 1990s heritage and management are inevitably and inextricably linked. For many it is a very uneasy marriage of interests. Few people involved with heritage resources consider themselves part of an *industry* in which the management practices developed in business and commerce can be readily applied. Nor is heritage an easily defined *market* with a clearly recognizable range of competing *products*. The organization and use of heritage resources and assets for profit are very much the exception, not the rule. Indeed, many believe that heritage and profit are not compatible, although revenue earning is increasingly seen to be important.

Heritage is a broad church comprising institutions which are primarily subsidized in the public sector, such as some national museums and galleries and most local authority museums; trusts such as the National Trust for Scotland, drawing on multiple funding sources and earned revenue; trusts for large and small independent museums; privately owned historic houses; gardens and nature reserves in a variety of ownerships; and organizations funded primarily through earned income from admissions and other sources, such as heritage centres.

Within the broad church the tenets of faith are widely agreed, although people working in one form of heritage, such as museums, typically have relatively few points of contact with people working in other forms, such as nature reserves. In practice, however, people recognize common interests without the need for precise definitions. The distinguishing characteristics which define heritage and bind it together are:

(1) a powerful underlying commitment and unifying set of attitudes to protect and conserve for posterity the objects, sites, flora and fauna, structures and other material evidence of a community's past and present;
(2) a shared perception of the intrinsic and cultural value of heritage and the wish to use it to communicate and interpret the past to present and future generations.

As this author put it, heritage communicates 'the natural and built environment of places and the origins and character of the human endeavour that brought civilisation in general, and localities in particular, to their present state' (Middleton, 1990).

The communication objectives for heritage resources almost always involve the provision of access and welcome for the public. Where resources are fragile or may be damaged by too many people, it may be necessary to restrict access. Restrictions limit, but do not alter, the principles of providing access. Establishing, operating and managing organizations to handle visits and to manage *public access* is the principal feature shared by all the heritage resources addressed in this manual. In the UK, as in other developed countries, there are several thousand organizations concerned with one or more aspects of heritage resources. Looked at from a management standpoint, although most do not consider themselves in this way, each of them in practice is operating or running a *business*. Notwithstanding the facts that most heritage organizations are small, that profit is seldom the motive, and that charging for admission may not apply, all are business entities with management needs. Most are independent and, typically in the early 1990s, have no management links with others.

Running a business means taking responsibility and being accountable for:

(1) planning and controlling the allocation of resources;
(2) managing the daily routine operations involved in providing visitor access and promoting awareness; and
(3) budgeting efficiently for costs and revenues.

By any definition these are business management tasks. In one form or another they are vital functions undertaken in every heritage institution. Yet as recently as the mid 1980s it was still exceptional for heritage sites and organizations outside the USA to devote much attention to business management issues or even to have drawn up written forward plans. By the early 1990s it is already rapidly becoming the exception not to have a corporate plan of some sort, although experience indicates that many such plans are superficial. They are of very dubious quality and value to the organizations that produce them. Most plans have been cobbled together more to convince outside organizations than to provide what Ambrose defines as 'a sense of purpose, a sense of direction, and a sense of achievement' (Ambrose, 1991). Few meet the practical criteria outlined in this section of the manual.

Adapting to survive: the message of Section One

As Griffin puts it in Chapter 5, 'Darwinian evolution works in business as in the animal world and demands that we adapt to survive'. Adapting to survive in the 1990s means understanding and practising management skills and using them first to help define a realistic future for heritage resources – *vision* – and secondly to achieve agreed goals in a period of rapid economic and social change. Section One aims to justify, explain and illustrate why and how growing professionalism in business management will increasingly affect all the forms of heritage noted earlier.

There is common agreement internationally that successful management is more a matter of attitudes than of techniques. Adopting and maintaining responsive, proactive, and outward looking attitudes in an organization is the vital responsibility of trustees and senior managers. If attitudes at senior level are responsive to changes in society and the public's needs, the management techniques will follow and departmental managers and supervisors will carry them out. Management techniques and managers can, of course, always be hired with the flourish of a cheque book. But, for better or worse, attitudes are organic within any organization and do not change quickly. Myopic attitudes or indifference on the part of managers will always outweigh the influence of the best intentions and techniques and may defeat the introduction of any management procedures.

This chapter explains why business management is increasingly relevant to all responsible for heritage resources. It is stressed that, although most modern management principles were developed in commercial organizations, there should be no confusion that management techniques are only or even especially appropriate to commercial operations. Management procedures are arguably even more necessary for the efficient conduct of non-profit organizations which lack the most powerful of all strategic levers for achieving efficiency and promoting change so far discovered – the need to satisfy customers in order to survive. Too often, from arboretums to zoos, attitudes

still prevail that business management is an 'unnatural practice' for non-commercial organizations. Its real value, in improving efficiency and in maintaining and developing heritage resources for the benefit of current users as well as for posterity, is still not understood. In particular, and stressing the need for positive attitudes, this chapter argues that the *process* of planning is much more important than the plan itself. The chapter examines the basic terms of management and describes what they mean in practice. It concludes with a summary of the strategic principles which are developed in the other chapters in this section.

Chapter 2 by Neil Cossons, Director of the Science Museum, London, draws on his experience in a wide range of heritage interests of what corporate plans are, why they matter, how they are drawn up and negotiated through an organization, and how they may be used as the framework for implementing agreed strategies. Cossons stresses the need for clear vision and leadership in heritage institutions of all sizes and the role that corporate plans may play in communicating *ownership* of vision and goals amongst staff. He explains how management techniques and planning concepts must be adapted or adjusted to the prevailing corporate culture of an institution, not crudely transferred from commercial organizations which normally operate with a very different ethos and culture.

Chapter 3 by Lester Borley outlines the practice of management in the National Trust of Scotland, of which he was the Director. Reflecting his responsibility for over 100 separate properties covering the natural and built heritage, Borley examines management and financial control procedures as they have developed and changed, especially in the last decade, in response to pressures on the organization. Partly financed by government, the Trust is not a commercial organization and Borley describes how it seeks to balance the constant demands of conservation against the needs for management accountability and revenue generation. His illustrations offer valuable supporting evidence of heritage management thinking in Scotland.

Chapter 4 by Peter Middleton is written from the standpoint of a consultancy, L&R Leisure PLC, which has achieved a national reputation not only for its consultancy activities but also for its management contracts of heritage operations on behalf of owners. L&R has developed particular skills in the systematic measurement and monitoring of performance in a continuously changing environment. Because it is invariably required to achieve revenue targets, within the overall constraint of an agreed heritage policy, it adopts a revenue rather than a cost orientation as the basis for budgeting and monitoring business operations. Also explained is the importance of targeting and monitoring performance at the margin using a combination of financial and non-financial measures.

Chapter 5 by Jonathan Griffin, Marketing Director of English Heritage, looks at management from a quite different aspect – that of consortia of heritage resources sharing common management services. Griffin believes that the future for many independently owned heritage resources lies in the development of functional networks for the sharing of management expertise using common procedures which enhance efficiency and achieve economies of scale without impairing the essential individuality of the constituent bodies. There is a good reason for believing that consortia formed for management purposes will develop throughout the 1990s and the chapter sets out the scope and rationale for this development, which all independent organizations should consider.

Three aspects of management strategy for heritage resources

A major communication problem exists with any word in everyday usage such as *management* in that everyone has their own definition. In heritage this is compounded by at least three different contexts, discussed below, in which management is applied. It is the third context which is the subject of Section One of the manual.

Managing the resource

Managing the resource, be it a collection, a historic house, or a nature reserve, is not surprisingly seen as the primary duty of management for heritage bodies. Knowledge and skills relevant to the resource, and a *passion* for its survival, are usually uppermost in the minds of trustees, owners, volunteers and employees responsible for it. Resource management skills are always capable of improvement – many examples are included in this manual – and they sometimes reflect decades of development. For as long as financial and other resources are adequate to ensure the survival of the institution, this inward looking preoccupation with managing the resource may not lead to overall management efficiency but it is unlikely to create major problems. Staff promotion and career progression in the heritage world is normally based on depth of knowledge and skills concerning the resource, often expressed through research and scholarship. Senior management posts in organizations responsible for heritage resources are, therefore, mostly filled by people whose experience and expertise derive essentially from a deep knowledge of the resource itself. In the early 1990s, although the position is now changing, remarkably few senior managers have even attended courses appropriate for broader management responsibilities inherent in controlling business operations. They are expected to acquire such organizational skills as they feel they need by a form of osmosis, or as a by-product of managing the resource and learning on the job.

Managing access

Increasingly in the last decade of the twentieth century, conservation aims mean that heritage resources have to be protected from a combination of misuse and overuse. In other words, public access to and use of heritage have to be controlled, influenced or constrained through a range of strategic and operational techniques which are covered elsewhere in this manual. Most of the principles and techniques of visitor management, in the modern form of influencing public access to and use of heritage resources, are already well established in the developed countries of North America, Western Europe, Australia and New Zealand, and Japan. In some of their forms, such as influencing access to museums and national parks, basic techniques have been practised for the last 100 years or so.

Managing organizations

Not yet well established for heritage resources, the management of organizations is a very different form of management from the previous two. It means the application of professionalism to planning, organizing and controlling the institutions and resources involved, perceived as business operations. This form of management is not to be confused or equated with commercial management practice or with management for profit. It is equally applicable to public sector and non-profit institutions.

The last 30 years have seen a world-wide revolution in the ways that businesses in general are managed. Stemming from developments originating in the USA, it is an accelerating revolution expanding from international commercial manufacturing industries and extending its influence more recently into the provision of services generally and into public sector and non-commercial operations too, for example education and health care services. The understanding of good practice in business management is still evolving and it is certain that the next decade will see further rapid developments, especially in organizations for which revenue earning is important but profit is not a primary or appropriate motive.

In this author's view, heritage organizations have to come to terms with a fundamental choice in the 1990s. Learn to use the new forms of business management, adapting the procedures as necessary to fit particular spheres of interest; or risk being left behind as other organizations respond more effectively to change. Apart from the loss of efficiency, at risk for many is the loss of existing visitor revenue to competitor organizations in the leisure, recreation and education fields. For some institutions, already teetering on a knife edge of survival, a fall in revenue will lead to collapse and the possible loss of heritage resources for ever.

There will always be a balance to be achieved in heritage between the energy expended on managing the resource and on managing access, and the effort put into business management procedures as outlined in this section of the manual. In the 1990s, achieving a working balance between the time and effort expended on these three aspects is the responsibility of trustees and senior managers. It is expected that the balance of effort will have to shift in favour of managing the organization as a business.

Heritage: a growth industry

As noted earlier, heritage is not an industry as economists define that term. Yet the various forms of heritage collectively present many of the characteristics of a market, with a large and growing public who are frequent visitors to heritage resources and who act as a market through their individual choices and preferences for what is provided by a growing range of competing organizations.

In developed countries there has been an extraordinary period of growth of interest in heritage. In part this reflects public interest and demand, in part the interests of supplying organizations dedicated to the conservation ideals noted earlier. The growth is a manifestation of relatively mature, educated and wealthy societies, able and willing to forgo some part of potential present consumption of resources for the sake of posterity. In recent years, it owes something also to the new environmental protection movement which is based on concepts of conservation and stewardship of natural resources. With very few checks, that interest has been growing for over 30 years. It is, however, all too easy to fall into the trap of assuming past growth trends will continue at a similar rate over the next decade or so, for the *same* presentation of the *existing* heritage resources.

Notwithstanding early 1990s experience of economic recession and its effect on visitor numbers and revenue, current forecasts suggest that there are convincing reasons to expect the *potential* demand for leisure and recreation to continue to grow throughout the 1990s. Public interest in heritage generally and other aspects of culture appear unlikely to diminish. But potential will not be converted into actual demand unless the necessary management skills are applied. There appears to be no reason to suppose that particular *current forms* of heritage, such as existing presentations of historic houses or of museum collections or of industrial archaeology, will enjoy continuously buoyant demand. Experience of leisure interests and common sense suggest that new forms of competition within and outside the heritage field will emerge to divert some potential demand in ways not now forseen. New forms of presentation to the public of existing heritage resources, and new forms of display

and interpretation, look certain to create new fashions to which managers will have to respond. The influence in the 1980s of the Jorvik exhibition in the UK, for example, is one illustration of that process. It does *not* mean, of course, that all heritage should follow the same fashion, which would be absurd and counterproductive. Monitoring and evaluation of visitor needs and expectations in order to enhance existing presentations are the necessary response.

Experience also suggests that management mistakes in presentation and display are relatively easy to hide when demand for what is available is growing strongly, because there is generally a shortage of capacity. In growth conditions the perceived need for improved management procedures at the strategic level is low. But when demand reaches a plateau or falls, or if capacity surges ahead of demand, weak management and poor presentation are likely to be increasingly exposed as more experienced visitors express their choices and preferences for other forms of heritage which better meet their interests.

Reasons why strategic business management is becoming more important

Noted below are some of the major economic and political events and issues of the last two decades which have given rise to current developments of more professional business management. Most of the events are international in their impact and affect heritage interests indirectly. Others, especially the growing sophistication of consumers and the importance of tourism markets, reflect international trends which have a direct impact on heritage provision. All the trends, however, have had a major impact on attitudes towards business management generally and on ways to improve its quality and effectiveness. It is the application of strategic management thinking and procedures to heritage resources which is of direct relevance to this section of the manual.

(1) Growing awareness of the powerful international impacts of late twentieth century economic and political events and trends and what it means to survive in a climate of constant change in the business environment. There has been a loss of faith in traditional (1960s) forms of long-term business planning based on forecasts. The most powerful changes resulted initially from the effects of the world-wide energy crisis of 1972–73, reinforced by the second crisis of 1979. International economic downturn and Middle East conflict in 1990–93 are just the latest examples of massive disruption to the overall climate for conducting business. There is no longer a condition of steady state from which to project the future. Massive shocks to the international system have revolutionized concepts and attitudes to strategic management in commercial and government sectors

generally, and influenced heritage organizations less directly.

(2) Recognition of the world-wide successes of Japanese enterprises with their participatory, consensus style of management and research-based quality control processes compared with traditional, more autocratic Western models in which senior management decisions are handed down for implementation through management hierarchies. 'Total quality management' concepts were barely mentioned until the mid 1980s; now it is almost impossible to avoid them.

(3) A sea change in the recognition of management deficiencies and the need for training at all levels from the mid 1980s onwards. Government and industry have recognized the need to secure greater management efficiency in commerce and industry and in the public sector.

(4) Response to the politically organized financial upheaval and squeeze on funding for local government and most public sector agencies, associated especially with the Reagan years in the USA and the Thatcher years in the UK. Those pressures have brought a previously unknown emphasis on performance measurement, management accountability and the operation of market economics in areas, including parts of heritage, traditionally associated with government subsidies to cover 'costs plus inflation'. Similar pressures can also be seen in developed countries around the globe, and are unlikely to relax in the 1990s.

(5) The emergence of more affluent and more demanding customers at all levels of society for goods and services as greater income, leisure time, education and media exposure have combined to make the public more aware of quality of provision. Improved quality demands are not of course restricted to the commercial sphere and are now being met in traditional public service provision.

(6) The growing internationalization of industry and commerce with ever larger conglomerate companies supplying common brands around the world for manufactured goods such as cars, audio equipment and soft drinks, and service products such as airline transport and fast-food restaurants. Although this trend may not appear directly relevant to heritage resources, the effects of international developments on management practices as well as on customer expectations should not be underrated. Some of the strategic implications for management and control in larger heritage organizations comprising multiple business operations, such as the National Trust for Scotland and English Heritage, are discussed in Chapters 3 and 5.

(7) A massive growth of supply or capacity in most forms of heritage provision in the period 1960–90, outstripping the growth in demand from the visiting public. This trend provokes and stimulates a previously unknown level of competition between organizations seeking to attract the same customers and forcing changes in the attitudes towards management in general and marketing in particular.

(8) Growing demand for travel and tourism is an important aspect in developing visitor demand for heritage. In some places, for example parts of London, Edinburgh, Paris and New York, tourists now form the largest sector of visits to heritage attractions. With the associated phenomenon of day visits involving long distances from home, the total so-called *tourism market* is often larger than the demand from a local community. Serving the public, a notion traditionally associated with serving a local community, in practice may increasingly mean serving the tourist market. The management and marketing implications of this are quite different. Of course, most heritage resources have a vital role to play within their local communities and must combine this role with that of visitor attraction for a transient population. In this author's view it is entirely appropriate that revenue earned from visitors should help to pay for local facilities.

(9) The emergence of relatively cheap and easy-to-use computers for information processing at a speed and with a level of detail which was unthinkable 25 years ago, shifting traditional planning procedures into a new dimension. Information technology has simplified and extended the possibilities for planning and for performance control and monitoring of organizations and provided managers with tools for better decision making in running a business which most heritage organizations have been slow to absorb. Some of the implications of this can be seen in Chapter 4.

(10) Emergence of *vision* as a concept to replace traditional analytical long-range planning forecasts. Vision or mission means a clearly focused view of the desired future for an organization, which determines the way that resources are allocated and controlled in the present. Heritage visions are much more likely to emerge from altruistic ideals and beliefs than from accountants' projections, but they must be articulated clearly so that all responsible for achieving the vision are clear about what is required of them and how they will know when they are achieving it.

To quote Sir John Harvey Jones (1987):

> Those of us that have worked in large organizations are uncomfortably aware that . . . instructions from the centre can almost always be circumvented if there is no belief in them further down the line . . . the problem has increasingly appeared to be how to develop planning processes which involve those who have to carry them out and thus acquire their commitment to success . . . [This] has to be done to a considerable extent by a shared vision of where each individual's responsibility fits into the overall pattern of direction in which the company is going. There is no question that the differentiation between successful and unsuccessful companies is a clear sense of mission on the part of the successful company.

Promoting unnatural practices

Using the word *industry* in its broadest sense, the following statement, written in 1960, may serve as a proper caution for those who believe that growth in the public demand for heritage will continue unabated. It also serves as a suitable introduction to the whole of Section One of this manual on the need to develop and communicate vision and effective business management principles within the heritage field.

> Every major industry was once a growth industry. But some that are now riding a wave of growth enthusiasm are very much in the shadow of decline. Others which are thought of as seasoned growth industries have actually stopped growing. In every case, the reason growth is threatened, slowed, or stopped is *not* because the market is saturated. It's because there has been a failure of management. (Levitt, 1960)

It is noteworthy that the cause of management failure which Levitt identified over 30 years ago as 'myopia' was not poor performance of departmental managers and supervisors. It was a direct failure of senior management at board level. The myopia was an inward looking focus on the operational requirements of long-established businesses, which failed to notice the speed and direction of change occurring in the world outside the businesses until it was too late to respond effectively. Their competitors and their (former) customers, by contrast, did respond. Generally, it was less a failure of the existing products in any technical performance sense, more a switch by customers to new or more competitive products which supplied their needs and interests more conveniently or at less cost for the same perceived benefits. The classic 1950s examples are the collapse of American railroad companies in an era of massive growth but *changing* demand for transport, and the failure of some major Hollywood film companies in an era of explosive growth for TV film material. In the UK, the loss of markets by most seaside resorts during the 1980s is a recent illustration of organizational myopia in the face of massive growth but changing needs in the demand for holidays. There are many examples. It is folly to suppose that heritage provision is immune from similar pressures.

Obviously, failure is much easier to see with all the advantages of hindsight and analysis. The requirement for surviving organizations is to make themselves aware of change while there is still time to do something about it. Awareness is built partly on market research information, commissioned to assist management decisions, but even more importantly it stems from an outward looking appreciation of events as noted earlier in this chapter. Outward looking, responsive organizations are not guaranteed to survive and prosper but it is certain that only luck will save the introspective laggards.

Paradoxically, the greater the preoccupation of managers in handling the day-to-day needs and crises of an organization, the more likely they are to fail because of changing circumstances going on around

them unnoticed. Whatever the depth and urgency of today's perceived problems, it is much more likely that vision and the solutions and opportunities for future growth will be detected outside the organization rather than within it.

Perhaps, above all, the failures identified by Levitt were failures to recognize that the good practice of management principles does not occur naturally. All management principles appear to be common sense when simply explained in the abstract. But assuredly they are always complex to implement, and only constant vigilance and management controls will ensure their continuous application after the initial introduction of new methods is implemented. Management principles must be seeded, nurtured and constantly tended by understanding senior managers or they will wither away – very naturally – before any worthwhile results are obtained. The greatest self-deception and the classic failure in the non-profit sector are to install the practices and procedures of management, and create the myths of management titles for staff, whilst failing to recognize that management is a continuous daily preoccupation that starts and finishes at the top. Management by lip-service was a very common phenomenon in heritage organizations in the 1980s.

If the directors and trustees of heritage resources do not understand the requirement for business management and have the attitudes and will to implement their vision, their organizations will be lucky indeed to achieve a secure future.

Whereas in the 1960s and 1970s management science was seen largely as a matter for ever more sophisticated techniques using the latest available quantitative tools and information technology to optimize decisions, the 1980s witnessed a massive switch to a growing appreciation of the value of visions and the people factor – human resource management, for those who prefer the jargon. What matters most about people is their attitudes to and motivation for the organization they serve and their understanding and belief in its future and their part in it. The greater the experience of change, the greater the need for clarity of vision to guide the organization's response.

Chapters 2 and 3 deal with some of the strategic issues of managing attitudes. Suffice it to say, in this chapter the effective implementation of strategic management is considered to be first and foremost about the attitudes of senior managers. A long way second, and sometimes barely relevant for smaller organizations, are the particular techniques with which the practice of management tends to be surrounded.

Usage of strategic management terms

Many readers of the manual will be only too aware of the confusion caused by the use of the same terms to mean different things. To some extent this confusion is just a fact of life, reflecting the relative novelty of the concepts within the heritage field, and it cannot be avoided altogether. Authors of management books and practitioners in particular tend to use the key terms in idiosyncratic ways to suit their own views and experience. There is no one authorized version which can be recommended.

To help clarify the worst of the potential confusion over strategic management jargon, this chapter offers here an interpretation of the meaning of five key terms to be found in Section One. It is recommended that these five should be used consistently within corporate plans. It is beyond the editor's control to ensure that the same terms are used by every author to mean exactly the same things throughout this book, and other usages will be encountered in other books.

It is commonly thought that only large organizations need to bother with the following terms. As most heritage organizations are very small, surely they can happily ignore them? Not so. The terms below are as applicable in principle to a museum run by volunteers as to the National Trust or a national park. Obviously, the larger the organization, the more effort is required to develop the concepts and communicate them through the organization, but they are not otherwise specific to big organizations.

Paradoxically, many of the modern procedures for strategic management are designed to help larger organizations think and act like smaller ones. Correctly applied, the concepts below may be used to identify and focus on the essentials which can be easily understood, cutting through and simplifying the inevitable complexity that surrounds the operations of any big institution. Complication is always the enemy of sound forward planning and should not be seen as a necessary part of it.

Forward or corporate plans refer to the management of an organization as a whole rather than any particular function within it. Corporate planning deals with the whole and the integration of the parts. In Section One, corporate issues are those which influence the longer run of two years or more ahead. The focus here is on business management, but corporate plans for heritage resources must relate to overall vision and goals for the resources at the centre of the organization's responsibilities. In the commercial world, corporate planning is often referred to as business planning; it usually means the same thing, but the former perhaps fits more comfortably with the non-commercial world of heritage.

Mission means the overall statement, aim or vision of an organization, identifying what it sees to be its core role, overall objectives and intended future position. A mission statement is usually a paragraph or two. The words 'policy', 'goal', or 'task' (with or without the adjective 'corporate') could be used to mean exactly the same thing, but these terms often also have other common uses which are not the same as 'mission'. The use of 'mission' is American in origin and is more widely used in that country as a management term. It nevertheless has acquired a fairly precise international meaning and it is always an endeavour to encapsulate in a few words the very essence of what a particular organization is aiming to achieve. The best mission statements are poetic in their simplicity and elegant choice of words. Always they express the fundamental criteria by which all strategic decisions must be assessed. A mission statement is a constant reminder of what the organization exists to achieve. It should be at the front of all forward or corporate plans and be understood by all staff in the organization, not just the managers. An example from English Heritage is shown as an appendix to this chapter.

Strategic objectives are specific and for larger organizations are likely to have multiple dimensions. They must be directly related to the mission statement and are typically related to selected aspects of an organization. They are often couched in terms of aspiration or very simple quantification and look forward to a desired achievement at least three years ahead. For example, a strategic objective may be 'to increase earned income from 25 to 40 per cent of annual revenue over five years'; or 'to complete a particular collection with a specified acquisitions policy'; or 'to undertake a major refurbishment programme or a management training programme for identified employees'. Strategies need to be *actionable* and *measurable*, which is why periods for completion and actual percentages (or volumes) should be specified, and why the objectives should relate to particular parts of the total organization. Without such specification, objectives may be no more than wishful thinking and useless for effective management purposes. In practice, the terms 'strategy' or 'strategies' is frequently used on its own to mean the same thing as strategic objectives. This is not necessarily wrong, but this author finds it less confusing to use the term 'strategic objectives' when that is what is meant, and to use the word 'strategy' on its own to mean an action programme as noted below.

Strategies comprise management action programmes stating how identified strategic objectives will be achieved. In this sense, strategies are means rather than ends. For the longer run of two to three years, strategies are likely to be set out only in broad, aggregated terms, but they are an essential element of any budgeting priorities and allocations which will run for several years. Most managers will find it less confusing if they reserve the term *targets* for use in their annual budgets, and specific short-run action programmes, such as a promotional campaign or a training schedule. In this sense, targets will always be subsets of strategies and will always be capable of measurement in terms of volumes, periods and personnel responsible.

Evaluation and control refers to ways in which an organization measures the extent to which it achieves or fails to meet its strategic objectives. Also known as *performance monitoring*, this is not just a matter of keeping records, vital though these are, but also a matter of how an organization is divided up functionally and administratively for the purpose of achieving efficiency in the use of resources. Examples are the deliberate division of a larger organization into cost and revenue centres and the systems which are designed into the day-to-day operations of a heritage attraction to make effective measurement of strategic objectives possible, as discussed in Chapter 4. Some of these systems are volume related, based on daily recording of visitors through ticketing and other transactions; some are financial, involving routine continuous tracking of money flows in different parts of the operation; some may involve personnel management procedures, or management by objectives. Some are based on information systems designed for management decision purposes and built into the strategic objectives noted earlier.

Process or plan?

The end product of forward planning is a written plan as discussed in Chapter 2. It usually involves management and staff in its preliminary stages, and is a document which boards of managers and trustees can debate before agreeing. But the plan is often less important than the process by which it evolves. A well drafted mission statement should be capable of lasting at least five years and possibly for several decades. Strategic objectives should also have a currency of several years, although the priorities allocated to them are likely to change as unforeseen and unforeseeable events occur and enforce change. Action programmes may have to change within days of being adopted.

In practice, then, some parts of a forward plan are likely to become obsolete within weeks of being written. But that is not important. What matters is that a plan reflects a process which managers and trustees understand and participate in as discussed in Chapter 2. A good plan is one in which those who have to implement it feel a sense of ownership; that comes only through direct participation in the drafting process. A good plan has clearly articulated goals, but flexible programmes always have to be adapted to changing circumstances.

Above all a good plan demonstrates the outward looking *attitudes* of senior management, stressed earlier as the most important single aspect of a well managed organization – in heritage or any other field. It not only expresses the positive attitudes but encapsulates the vital processes by which such attitudes are created, stimulated, sustained and refined.

Strategic management issues for heritage resources in the 1990s

'It is only by managing change and using it creatively that we will protect scholarship – not simply protect it but allow it to regenerate' (Cossons, 1991). This applies not only to scholarship, as Neil Cossons would agree, but to the protection of heritage resources themselves and their enhancement where possible for posterity. Putting more effort into managing change is not an *alternative* to effort in managing the resource itself; it is increasingly an essential condition for the survival of the resource. All the authors in Section One are fully aware that it is neither possible nor appropriate to apply commercial business management practices to heritage resources without adaptation. Mission statements or visions based on protection and conservation impose proper limits on the extent to which the resource itself can or should be modified or adapted in the interests of organizational efficiency or revenue generation. Apart from normal considerations of wear and tear on fragile and often unique resources, there are constraints on the use of heritage buildings, sites and collections which must always take precedence over business management considerations.

Within these broad and overriding constraints, however, there is an urgent need and immense scope to enhance the quality of heritage resources through the creative management of change and through the introduction of more effective business management procedures. Six particular issues for the 1990s are summarized from Section One; all of them are explained and illustrated in Chapters 2 to 5.

(1) Recognizing, through the formal adoption and operation of systematic strategic planning and monitoring procedures, that continuous change in the external environment affecting the future for heritage is now a normal experience and not exceptional. Planning processes are essential to enable managers and trustees to identify and devise creative responses to change while there is time to do so, without losing sight of the essential mission or vision.

(2) Recognizing that, with or without revenue objectives based on admission charges, achieving measurable satisfaction of increasingly sophisticated and frequent visitors to heritage is an essential strategic objective for sustainable heritage organizations.

(3) Accepting the need for setting measurable objectives and strategies, which reflect long-run mission statements, respond to identified change and visitor expectations, and aim to optimize the position for the heritage resource.

(4) Committing managers and trustees to the necessary disciplines of continuous systematic performance monitoring needed to assess the achievement of objectives on a daily, weekly and monthly basis. In practice this also means setting up information collection procedures which are a necessary requirement of monitoring and assessment, including the use of market research as necessary, for example to measure visitor satisfaction.

(5) Using, supporting and helping to create networks or consortia for heritage management purposes to contribute to the tasks above and share the expertise and costs, recognizing that, by the twenty-first century, small fully independent businesses operating on a stand alone basis will have become increasingly anachronistic.

(6) Accepting that, although they are simple enough to grasp as concepts, management procedures do not occur naturally and have to be carefully seeded and cultivated by senior staff. Relatively easy to introduce and operate for a month or so, management procedures are very much harder to implement and sustain with staff commitment over time. There are implications for staff training which have to be built into the processes.

Conclusion

For heritage 'Management is not an end in it-self . . . but the necessary practical means to achieve curatorially defined goals, recognising that public sector finance and private and other donations will never be sufficient to satisfy all needs' (Middleton, 1990).

In their different ways, all the chapters of Section One are concerned with achieving balance in heritage organizations in the allocation of available staff time and finances to the resource itself, to managing visitor access and revenue generation, and to managing the organization as a business. There are no simple formulas to apply, only a careful consideration of the issues facing each organization and selection from a range of well defined management principles and techniques. But if the precise recipe for the most appropriate balance is unique for each organization, the issues are essentially the same for all and the menu of management principles and techniques for devising solutions is accessible to all.

At the beginning of the 1990s there is an urgent need to adapt and transfer to heritage the management techniques and procedures which are already well developed in service sectors of the economy. The scope for improving the management of heritage resources is immense. It requires energy and commitment but it is an eminently worthwhile and achievable task, as the chapters in this section aim to show.

Appendix: English Heritage mission statement

The role of English Heritage is to bring about the long-term conservation and widespread understanding and enjoyment of the historic environment for the benefit of present and future generations, using expert advice, education, example, persuasion, intervention and financial support.

References

AMBROSE, T. (1991) 'Museum development planning – an introduction', in *The Forward Planning Handbook*, Museums and Galleries Commission, London

COSSONS, N. (1991) 'Scholarship or self-indulgence?', *Royal Society of Arts Journal*, February, 185.

HARVEY-JONES, SIR J. (1987) 'Introduction', in I. Ansoff, *Corporate Strategy* (2nd edn), Penguin, London

LEVITT, T. (1960) 'Marketing myopia', *Harvard Business Review*, July–August, 45–56

MIDDLETON, V. T. C. (1990) *New Visions for Independent Museums in the UK*, Association of Independent Museums, Chichester

2

Designing and implementing corporate plans

Neil Cossons

Planning and *management*, and the opaque language that in the business world tends to accompany both, can strike terror into the hearts of many who work in the museum and heritage field. Ask why, and the responses are often revealing. Most frequently there is the belief that planning and management are activities carried out by others elsewhere in the organization or, even more threatening, outside the organization altogether – for example in another part of a public authority. Some fear that the processes of planning and management are there to achieve economies, to make cuts in what is carried out in order to save money, and should therefore be resisted; others, that management is more or less synonymous with commercialization.

And yet in most museums a high proportion of the personnel are in effect *managers*. And if they are managers then they must, to a greater or lesser degree, be involved in planning too. Anybody who spends money should know how to manage those funds in the best manner possible, not only to get good value but to contribute effectively to achieving the objectives of the organization as a whole. Anybody who is responsible for staff, who are also of course an important resource, equally has an obligation to lead, involve and manage those staff in a manner that enables them to make an effective contribution. Here the need for good management is even greater as staff invariably represent the largest part of a museum's costs. And to do it badly is not only wasteful of resources, it leaves those people who are inadequately managed feeling demoralized and unwanted and therefore less able to make a full contribution to the jobs for which they are being paid and in which they have chosen to make their careers.

In order to manage effectively it is necessary to know what is to be achieved and to have an agreed sense of purpose and direction. That implies having a plan. This chapter is concerned with the development

of plans for museums. Many of the processes applicable to a museum can be used to equal effect in other heritage bodies, whether in the public or non-profit sectors, although it is important not to adopt uncritically the techniques and terminologies of one type of institution for use in another.

Why planning?

First, it is essential to understand the nature and managerial character or *culture* of an organization in order to establish the starting point for having a plan. Is it like a college and regulated by a body of fellows? Alternatively, is it like a cathedral with dean and chapter? Or, is there a company board, with a chairman, a chief executive and a series of managing directors? Analogies, generally speaking, are not easy to find because museums are by their nature singular institutions.

The prevailing cultural climate of a museum may be the most important asset it possesses. Equally, it can be a liability if change is desirable. The museum which has developed primarily as a research institution may display the organizational culture most frequently seen among groups of independent professionals. In management terms, the principal assumption of this culture is that the organization exists to help individuals achieve their own professional ambitions. Resources, facilities and administrative coordination are expected to be provided from some central source to support individual work programmes. In centrally managed organizations the opposite assumptions apply. Their organizational cultures validate the view that the individual is there to help the organization achieve *its* purpose.

The point here is to determine as a matter of policy what sort of culture the museum is to have and plan accordingly. The managerial approaches used by others can be examined, and in particular their processes of

planning, and then adapted to the needs of the organization concerned. It is also important to appreciate
that there may be sensitivities, on the part of staff or of
customers, if business techniques, approaches and language are directly transplanted into the museum environment. Equally, if culture *change* is one of the
objectives of management then borrowed language
can be used to great effect. Planning and organizational change often go hand in hand, but if the two
are to be consciously mixed then it is essential to
understand this at the outset.

Planning for improved effectiveness can help everybody in an organization. It should be something to
which everybody subscribes; there should in principle
be no losers.

Managing change, however, places different demands on an organization. Change must be expressed
in a forward plan and so it is easy for those of an
uncharitable disposition or who are resistant to change
to condemn the plan and the process of planning
which precedes it as a threat to them and, by implication, to the organization in which they work. Machia-
velli understood this when he noted that the reformer
has for enemies all those who gain from the existing
arrangements and only as the most lukewarm of friends
those who may benefit from the intended change. Far
better therefore to separate the business of organization
and managerial change from the process of corporate
planning. The plan may set out the direction in which
we want to travel and the means for getting there. The
detailed process of changing the organization to meet
those demands can follow on as a separate but related
initiative.

There is, invariably, much that can be learnt from
business techniques in a museum, but to apply them
does not mean that the museum is turning into a
commercial business, that its principles of public service are in any way being compromised, or that it is
being run for the purposes of profit. On the contrary,
to adopt sound management principles from one sector
and apply them in another can make good management sense. What is most important, however, is to
appreciate that adaptation is needed and that the culture of the museum itself may be as important and as
valid as the culture of the organization whose techniques are being borrowed.

A number of arguments have been mounted against
corporate plans for museums and heritage organizations. For example, in a museum where a high proportion of the budget is spent on staff and on the care of
enormous collections inherited from previous generations, and over which relatively little influence can be
exercised, is there any purpose in having a strategic
plan? Clearly the constraints on many museums are
considerable, particularly in terms of their collections
where disposal may not be an option. But the reason
for having a plan is to manage operation and development in an orderly fashion, even when the pace of

change is relatively slow. To say that a high proportion of the budget is spent on staff is to beg a number
of questions. Should the staff numbers be reduced
and those salaries turned into cash for use elsewhere?
If so, how and at what rate? Should the work that
those staff do or the way in which they do it change
in order that the museum can move forward? It is easy
to believe that planning is irrelevant because the constraints appear too burdensome. But effective corporate
planning demands a fundamental look at the nature of
the organization and a clear focus upon what it is there
for. Even in the most stable or lethargic of organizations there are choices to be made about the future,
options for how money should be spent and people
deployed. A forward plan produced as the result of a
formal planning process enables those options to be
examined, choices made and a sense of direction set
out for all to see.

Nor should one be inveigled into thinking that
corporate planning or strategic management are evils
forced on organizations by lack of adequate funding.
On the contrary, the need for sound planning and
management is even greater when resources are readily available. These are the times when the greatest
changes, and therefore the greatest mistakes, can
occur. Equally, it is very easy to make non-strategic
commitments of resources when times are good, only
to find that the pain of retrenchment when money
dries up is all the greater. The simple moral is that
irrespective of the economic circumstances in which
a museum finds itself, whether there are plenty of
certainties or uncertainties, the need to have a clear
vision of where the organization is going is imperative.

Vision and leadership

Another concern expressed about corporate plans is
that they too often lead to a consensus approach,
deadening creativity and eliminating opportunism.
Gordon Burrett (1985) summed up the relationship
between a plan and creativity:

> Vision, flair and opportunism are all prime essentials for
> the most successful museum and the director, the curator-
> ial staff and the trustees must conspire together to ensure
> that these qualities are kept alight. Good museums cannot
> be run by administrators or managers; thus, whilst there
> must be rules of the game, these should be very loosely
> drawn so that while they define broadly the aims of the
> museum they do not restrict the director to the extent that
> he cannot pursue an opportunity with confidence when
> he sees one. Clearly there has to be a dynamic balance
> between opportunism and an overall plan. If Govern-
> ment is going to be the major funder, then Government
> has to subscribe to some defined aims, to a plan, and not to
> paying for what the director or trustees happen to think
> they should be doing when they wake up in the morning
> in a certain mood. (When times are hard *more* courage is
> needed to take inspired action, develop bold policies, and

use resources more flexibly, but the inevitable tendency in these circumstances is of course to be cautious and conservative.)

Like all institutions, museums need leadership. Good planning can help develop good leadership. But the *style* of a museum is important, and it is therefore essential to decide whether it is better to have a focal point of leadership which is crisp and sharp, which can energize creativity, arouse enthusiasm and maintain morale, or whether consensus has to be the order of the day. Usually, it is some of each. Wallowing in consensus can produce very dull and boring results. Equally, following an eccentric leader who does not have the necessary management skills can be a dangerous path to tread. The mistakes can be expensive.

So, whatever the style of the organization the need for planning is still there. A good corporate plan can define the areas in which the museum would like to take initiatives even if the opportunities and resources are not yet available. Thus, when an opportunity does arise and it fits the objectives, the organization can move rapidly into gear to take advantage of it.

The purpose of a museum corporate plan

As Victor Middleton notes in Chapter 1, quoting Ambrose, the purpose of a corporate plan is to provide the museum and its staff with a sense of purpose (what are we here for), a sense of direction (where are we going?), and a sense of achievement (how well are we doing?).

But corporate plans are not always intended only for internal consumption. Many organizations, especially in the public sector, publish their corporate plans in order to tell the world at large about what they do and intend to do in the future. In other cases a plan may inform a government minister or the committee of a council as well as providing a framework for the internal management of the organization. A plan may also be an essential document when approaching external funding bodies for a grant or loan. These are not incompatible, but it is worth remembering that there are two objectives in mind when writing the plan.

What can cause complications is when a plan is also used as the principal mechanism for bidding for money. Ideally the two should be kept separate, the corporate plan informing – by defining objectives, establishing a programme for implementing them and setting out the resource implications – and the bid for money forming a separate document using the corporate plan as 'supporting evidence'.

In the case of the corporate plan of the National Museum of Science & Industry (NMSI) in Great Britain, for example, it is prepared to meet three needs:

(1) for the NMSI to set out clearly its corporate objectives and priorities and to understand the resource implications of fulfilling them;
(2) to provide the Secretary of State with a statement of the NMSI's objectives and strategic plan and their financial implications;
(3) to provide the Department of National Heritage with sufficient financial and planning information to evaluate the NMSI's grant-in-aid bid.

The statement of purpose, or mission statement

In setting out to develop a corporate plan an essential starting point is identifying and creating a sense of purpose and encapsulating that in a clear, simple and preferably short statement. It is not always easy to define and is all too often overlooked. But it is essential.

What are we here for? Most museums serve two major client groups: the collections, which have to be properly housed and cared for and on which the museum's wisdom and scholarship is founded; and the users of those collctions, who as general visitors, scholars, enquirers or educational groups require access in some form or other. So an initial statement of purpose might derive from the collections that the museum has, and the standard to which they should be kept, and could then proceed to the way in which they should be used, by whom and in what manner. By defining this sense of purpose it will be possible to build up a clear *statement of purpose*, often called a *mission statement*, which management and staff agree and which can be used to describe to the outside world the museum and what it does.

Here are two examples:

Hampshire County Museums Service (Southern England)
We aim to inspire and satisfy a deeper level of interest, enjoyment and understanding of Hampshire's heritage and environment by developing the full potential of the museum collections in our care and assisting other organizations with similar aims.
Beamish, the North of England Open Air Museum
An open air museum for the purpose of studying, collecting, preserving and exhibiting buildings, machinery, objects and information illustrating the development of industry and way of life in the north of England.

The Hampshire Museums Service is a local authority funded and controlled organization, while Beamish is an independent museum controlled by a trust. But each of them states, clearly and in language that most people can understand, the essential purpose of the organization. Sometimes a brief supporting explanation may help.

For example, in the case of the draft mission statement prepared by the Dundee Heritage Trust in Scotland for its Verdant Works project, some definition of the terms used was felt to be essential. The statement was to be read by people who would not necessarily have a clear understanding of what the word 'museum' might mean. So, the mission statement has a simple three-part explanatory note:

Verdant Works: draft mission statement
Develop and maintain a museum of broad appeal relating to the significance of Dundee's textile industries. Located at Verdant Works, the project includes restoration of its historic buildings and their supportive reuse.

Note
Museum: a museum is an institution which collects, documents, preserves, exhibits and interprets material evidence and associated information for the public benefit.
Textile: wool, linen, jute, man-made fibres, design, construction and contemporary uses.
Supportive reuses: revenue earning, cultural, historic and interpretive.

In all three examples, the mission statement forms a starting point for the corporate plan and is intended for external as well as internal consumption. In the cases of Hampshire and Beamish the collections are central to the core mission statement. At Verdant Works, where the intention is to develop and maintain a museum, this is then defined separately with an explicit statement of purpose.

Objectives and priorities

In support of the statement of purpose a series of aims and objectives can be defined. Appendices 1 and 2 set out respectively the role, corporate aims and objectives of English Heritage from the 1991–95 *Corporate Plan*, and the statement of purpose and values for the Museum of London from its *Forward Plan* for 1991–96. In each case the degree of detail is built up, from the general to the particular, to create as complete a picture as possible of the organization, its objectives, the activities that support those objectives, the resource implications of carrying them through and the order in which they will be carried out, that is the priorities.

To the summary of objectives a further level of detail has to be added. Each objective can be broken down into a series of discrete elements or programme areas to which costs can be attributed. The pattern of expenditure is now starting to become visible. If that expenditure can be set out in tabular form across, say, five financial years then a pretty complete picture will begin to emerge.

The format of a corporate plan

There is no set format for the structure and contents of a corporate plan. Each organization will develop its own to meet its own particular needs and in a form that it finds useful. Here is a set of headings under which a basic plan might be constructed, for a large heritage body such as a national or regional museum:

1 Statement of purpose or mission statement
   1.1 Supporting explanatory notes (if necessary)
2 Summary of objectives
3 Summary of progress against objectives since the last plan (with indications of performance against those objectives)
4 Programme areas
   4.1 Collections managements
   4.2 Research and scholarship
   4.3 Public services
   4.4 Marketing
   4.5 Museum management
5 Financial plan
   5.1 Summary of current position (with current and previous year's budget figures)
   5.2 Budget projections (set out year by year over the period of the plan)
   5.3 Fund-raising (with statement of current performance and targets year by year over the period of the plan)
6 Appendices
   6.1 Management structure
   6.2 Schedule of properties (with ownership status: freehold/lease/rent etc.)
   6.3 Notable additions to the collections
   6.4 Major events since last plan (exhibitions, new gallery openings etc.)

Each of the programme areas under heading (4) should if possible follow a common format, for example: statement of purpose; progress in the previous year; current position; objectives for the next five years, set out in priority order and stating resource implications and requirements. The common format not only acts as a helpful discipline for staff responsible for drafting plans, it also greatly assists in the process of comprehension by busy trustees or committee members, external bodies who need to know what is proposed and why, and by staff as a whole.

Appendix 3 sets out the table of contents from the beginning of the *Corporate Plan* for 1990–93 of the Otago Museum in New Zealand. The plan, which occupies just nine typed pages, sets out clearly the issues facing this medium-sized museum, and then lists the tasks that arise from them. The *Departmental Service Plan 1991–92* for the Department of Leisure and Arts of Oxfordshire County Council in England, set out in Appendix 4, establishes a framework of quality standards as a starting point. These apply throughout the County Council's activities and each department is required to develop its strategies accordingly. Whatever the shape and form of a museum plan, however, it must be readable, easy to understand and, if at all possible, inspire those who work in the organization to gather behind the objectives it sets out to achieve.

The planning process

How does a museum create its plan? Again, there are no set rules. Each museum will develop mechanisms that are appropriate to its own needs. In a small museum the whole plan might be written by one person, probably the director or curator in charge (let us for the purposes of this section call that person the director). The question of *ownership* is however important.

Ownership in this context means the sense of understanding, attachment and support which individuals generally in an organization feel for its corporate goals and objectives and the way that management is endeavouring to achieve them. If a plan is drawn up by a small team of experts or external consultants working in isolation from the rest of the organization, it may well provide an excellent analysis and contain well defined goals and objectives. But it is likely to be perceived by staff as an imposition and it may not secure their support. In such cases there will be a plan but no sense of ownership by the staff and sometimes, at worst, by the director.

The plan should be an expression of the director's view and vision as well as a statement of corporate activities. In most large organizations a team will be set up to develop and draft the plan, but whatever eventually emerges must carry the stamp of the director's inspiration and authority as well as enthusiastic involvement and support for the planning process.

Whether the plan is to be drawn up by one person or by a team it is useful to set out an order of procedure. This might be as follows:

(1) *Timetable and schedule for initiation and approvals*, including dates of key meetings at which drafts will need to be drawn up and submitted for formal approval).

(2) *Review of the current position*: (a) policies and purpose (b) current objectives (c) market review (who are the users and non-users?). Drawing on the knowledge and experience of staff, the review would then proceed to analyse the current position of the museum, item by item. In this way a qualitative picture could be built up which represents the starting point for the plan proper.

(3) *Drafting the corporate plan*. At this stage a series of headings, representing the contents of the plan, would be drawn up. A mission statement and a set of functional objectives would be defined which relate to the museum's overall policy statement. The key objectives that need to be met over the period of the plan would be identified, the priorities established, and the financial implications defined. It is at this stage that detailed financial analysis and planning is needed. Can the objectives be met through existing financial provision or is additional funding required? It is necessary to identify the various sources of funding, make predictions where necessary, and identify methods of income generation.

(4) *Gaining approval for the plan*. At this stage the complete plan should exist in draft form having absorbed as much as possible of staff knowledge and experience. The forward planning team in a large museum might then present it formally to the director and senior management team. In a smaller institution in which the plan would be largely written and devised by the director it might then be discussed with the chairman of trustees, before going to the next stage. Most museums will have formal procedures for the approval of the plan. Some may wish to circulate it quite widely in draft for comments from the staff of the museum. At the end of this period the plan will go, in draft, to the board of trustees or committee of management for formal approval. At this stage it will become the policy of the museum. Implementation follows.

(5) *Implementation*. The plan can now be presented to the staff and its specific objectives translated into targets for individuals or teams. For a large and complex plan, in a large institution, circulation of the full document may not be appropriate. However, either the document itself, or a well written and succinct résumé of it, should be in the hands of *all* members of staff within days of its formal approval by the museum's board. For a museum that uses team briefing this mechanism is particularly suitable for disseminating the contents of the plan and breaking it down into its various component parts to form the work programmes for individual members of staff.

(6) *Looking ahead to the next plan*. The essence of good corporate planning is that the process is rolled forward on an annual basis so that its topicality can be maintained, its objectives reviewed and updated, and a regular check carried out on progress against targets. Where a planning team exists they should not be stood down as soon as the plan has been adopted. Throughout the year data and other feedback must be collected, to monitor progress against the plan, and ease the compilation of the next one. It is much easier to collect data throughout the year to provide next year's analysis of the current position than to attempt to collect it retrospectively. Chapter 4, by Peter Middleton, offers valuable insights into how this may be achieved in practice.

The purpose of corporate planning is to provide a visible framework within which the museum as a whole can move forward. Its preparation requires realism so that the objectives which have been set are achievable. The plan also requires careful presentation so that the staff of the museum can both contribute to it and believe in it. In Chapter 1 Victor Middleton quoted Sir John Harvey-Jones in his introduction to the second edition of Igor Ansoff's classic, *Corporate Strategy*. It is worth restating part of that quote in this context too:

Those of us that have worked in large organizations are uncomfortably aware that one of the facts of decentralized leadership is that instructions from the centre can almost always be circumvented if there is no belief in them further down the line. No form of instruction can be sufficiently detailed that it cannot be evaded by someone who is determined not to follow it; the problem has increasingly appeared to be how to develop planning processes which involve those who have to carry them out and thus acquire their commitment to success and to following the plan as a part of the actual process of developing it.

The processes of consultation as a plan is prepared, and the degree of participation which staff can have in its preparation, are difficult to determine. In a museum, thickly populated with the individualist, the expert, the eccentric and the scholarly, the task of leadership is at once peculiarly privileged and singularly demanding. In many large museums there are often a wide variety of views on the direction in which the institution as a whole should be going. The curators may have one set of interests; those responsible for education or public services may well have another. The processes of preparing the plan in a large institution should, if at all possible, be spread fairly widely. Although the planning team itself might consist of no more than half a dozen people led by the director, they must be the right people so that they can be used as part of the information gathering process and perhaps to chair subgroups within the staff responsible for putting together detailed parts of the policy. Engaging people in the preparation of parts of the plan is a good way of giving them at least some degree of ownership. If that can then be followed by consultation at a broader level, using the whole draft plan, then most staff will recognize that they have had at least some opportunity to make an input.

But whatever the degree of consultation and participation, the final plan must be the clear and unequivocal statement of intent by the museum's director and management. Consultation almost inevitably flattens, taking away the sharp edges of policies, distributing the butter thinly over a large number of objectives when it perhaps should be concentrated thickly in a small number of core areas. So, in the event, the plan may well be something which the staff as a whole do not like. This does not mean it is a bad plan. It may then be a radical plan pointing a new direction for an institution that has perhaps lost its way. Corporate planning needs analysis. Analysis, if it is of good quality, is very revealing. And it is those revelations that are sometimes uncomfortable.

Finally, should all this appear daunting to a small organization with perhaps only one or two staff, it is worth making the point again that planning need not be threatening; and it can be of benefit to all sizes and types of institution. In many small and well run museums the plan is carried in the head of the person in charge. Don't let it stay there. Write it down. Once it is on paper, opportunities for improvement will immediately emerge. There may be little need to refer to

the plan thereafter, but in a year or so, when a new plan is being drawn up, the existing one will provide an invaluable point of reference and a measure of the progress that has been made in the intervening period. It is all too easy to be so close to an organization that change appears to take place at a frustratingly slow pace. A plan for the future is an excellent means of plotting a way forward, determining the rate of that progress and gauging success.

Appendix 1: the role, corporate aims and objectives of English Heritage, from the *Corporate Plan of English Heritage, 1991–95* vol. 1

The role of English Heritage is to bring about the long-term conservation and widespread understanding and enjoyment of the historic environment for the benefit of present and future generations using expert advice, education, example, persuasion, intervention and financial support.

Our aims are:

(1) to work with the public, private and voluntary sectors to increase resources for and commitment to conserving the historic environment;
(2) to ensure the flexible and responsible use of resources, taking account of long-term conservation priorities;
(3) to secure the best possible protection, care and use of the historic environment, and to ensure recording in cases of unavoidable loss;
(4) to establish high standards based on our own research and practical experience, and that of others, and to uphold those standards in our judgements and in the example we give;
(5) to give independent, authoritative information, advice and assistance reflecting the standards we have set;
(6) to help people to enjoy and understand the historic environment, and to see the need to protect it;
(7) to be open, responsive and fair in all our dealings;
(8) to attract and keep the best staff for the job and provide appropriate training and development to promote their effectiveness and job satisfaction;
(9) to manage our resources effectively, efficiently and economically.

The *key corporate objectives* for English Heritage for the *Corporate Plan* period have been revised since the last plan to take account of new and changing priorities. These are:

(1) to carry out work to improve our knowledge and understanding of the state of the historic environment in England; to evaluate this work periodically as a basis from which to assess more precisely the need for action;
(2) to maintain and present an efficiently managed estate of historic properties which provides a national

exemplar of good practice and continues to earn an increasing percentage of its total costs;

(3) to improve general understanding of the role we are playing in protecting the historic environment, particularly by informing people better what our aims and objectives are and what significant steps we take towards achieving them;

(4) to make more explicit to our own staff and others the standards to which we work with a view to strengthening both our internal competence and our external authority;

(5) to relocate our headquarters and the PIC regional teams as smoothly as possible, with particular attention to the organization's long-term efficiency and to the needs of all our staff.

Appendix 2: statement of purpose and values, from the *Forward Plan of the Museum of London, 1991–96*

The Museum of London's purpose is to make the history of London and its people, in all its diversity, intelligible to all. The Museum aims:

(1) to illuminate the past in such a way as to extend understanding in everyone who uses the Museum, from general visitor to researcher;

(2) to encourage as many, and as wide a range, of people as possible to use our services, through being responsive to their needs;

(3) to recognize that in a culturally diverse city there are many histories, each forming a valid strand in the identity of contemporary London;

(4) to promote opportunities for learning, entertainment and contemplation;

(5) to encourage and cooperate with other organizations concerned with the history of London;

(6) to relate London to other major cities in the world.

The Museum has a fundamental task, upon which all other activities are based: the formation and maintenance of a collection of objects and appropriate evidence related to a theme in London history. The collections are subject to continuous critical evaluation by posing essential questions:

(1) What is the capacity of these objects or data to evoke the past or present of London in the mind of the Museum user?

(2) What does the object or item of data itself say about London or its people?

(3) Either singly or severally, in a context either original or created in the Museum, can these objects and data provide opportunities for expanding understanding of London, when available to the Museum user?

The principal means by which the general user encounters the Museum's theme and collections are exhibitions, education programs, and publications. But these represent only a limited number of ways of looking at the history of London and its people. Therefore the resources of the Museum must be available through access to facilities for study and research.

Exhibitions, education programmes and publications must also be subject to continuous critical evaluation by posing essential questions:

(1) Have the objects and information been used in a way which is consistent with realizing their full potential while leaving the visitor free to ask questions? Is it consistent with our main purpose?

(2) Have we been objective in our exhibitions and publications, and ethical in our advertising and promotion?

(3) Have we reached the widest possible public in our approach?

(4) Have we maintained editorial independence?

Our public duty is to the collections and to accuracy; and, in its pursuit, to the effective use of all financial resources.

Appendix 3: table of contents, from the *Otago Museum Corporate Plan, 1990–93*

4.11 Complete registration of natural history material

4.12 Further development of cataloguing of Humanities Collection

4.13 Complete overdue maintenance of displays

4.14 Continue staff training needs assessment

4.15 Establish museum guide service as a first step towards a community engagement programme

4.16 Increase accessibility of museum library

4.17 Production of brochures and support literature

4.18 Complete Bird Hall displays

4.19 Plan redevelopment of Upper Fels

Appendix 4: *Departmental Service Plan, 1991–92*, Department of Leisure and Arts, Oxfordshire County Council

Introduction

The essential background to the Department of Leisure and Arts service planning continues to be provided by its *Service Philosophy and Policy Objects* of 1988 (which direct us to a unified department managed locally in the interests of the customer) and the County Council's QUEST programme, now in its second year.

The County Council is committed to the provision of high standards of service to the people of Oxfordshire. In 1991–92 this commitment is taking place against a background of budget reductions. In these circumstances it is all the more vital for the Department of Leisure and Arts to have a vision of where it wishes to be, and to agree action to get there. The Department has regularly to review and develop its services and the ways in which they are provided.

The QUEST programme is the focus of management action to achieve change and to give a sense of direction. It is a programme of action, but more than that it is the explicit statement of the key values that underpin all that the Department does:

QUality
Effectiveness
Service
To all

Quality is about achieving the required standards of service. In some areas it will be about setting higher standards than exist at present, and then achieving them.

Effectiveness is about maintaining agreed levels of service, the measurement of output and achieving more output for less input; in other words, 'working smarter, not harder.' It is about innovation and new ways of doing things. In 1991–92 it will be very important to do more with less.

Service to all is about putting customers first; serving the whole of Oxfordshire, not just the parts that it is easy to serve, and providing equal opportunities for people to use and benefit from our services. Some staff do not deal direct with the public but they also have customers to serve – schools, colleges, members, staff in other departments.

For all of us to accept the QUEST principles of quality services and minimum defined personal operating standards, the message must be that the Department of Leisure and Arts is public about its professional standards, is proud of them and adheres to them.

The ultimate objective of the QUEST programme, then, is to offer *quality services* that are *customer centred* and offer *value for money* to the chargepayers of Oxfordshire, in such a way as to achieve maximum access and optimum use. To achieve all this it is necessary at the outset for the Museum, Arts, Libraries and Leisure Committee to define the standard of service it expects the Department of Leisure and Arts to provide, and then for the Department to embody these in a customer charter for the people of Oxfordshire.

Service objectives and targets

Quality services

(1) To established standards of service for all activities of the Department (May 1991)

(2) To define the range and scale of services to be provided with static or declining resources (September 1991)

(3) To deploy resources to achieve higher-quality services for targeted customer groups (September 1991)

(4) To rationalize and integrate technical and support services to achieve maximum effectiveness to the public services of the Department of Leisure and Arts (review completed June 1991)

Customer-centred services

(1) To establish a framework of customer consultation and response, and surveys of use and non-use (July 1991: carried forward from 1990–91)

(2) To draw up a customer charter (August 1991: CF from 1990–91)

(3) To devolve the management of the Department of Leisure and Arts (completion October 1991: CF from 1990–91)

(4) To plan and implement a framework for integrated local management of the Department of Leisure and Arts public services (April 1992)

(5) To conclude the review of opening hours of all public services (September 1991: CF from 1990–91)

(6) To continue the programme for improving disabled access, external (including street) signing of buildings and facilities (CF from 1990–91)

(7) To continue the publication programme (all year: CF from 1990–91)

Value-for-money services

(1) To conduct service and budget reviews for: the directorate (May 1991); archives (September 1991); arts and recreation (May 1992)

(2) To establish internal service agreements for Department of Leisure and Arts technical and support

services, and for central support services (September 1991)

(3) To establish a policy and programme for income generation (November 1991: CF from 1990–91)

Individual projects of departmental management group

(1) To complete and open the Centre for Oxfordshire Studies (July 1991)

(2) To establish a joint reserve collection store (CF from 1990–91)

(3) To establish the means by which internal and external communications can be improved (CF from 1990–91)

(4) To plan and implement a delegated Department of Leisure and Arts education service to schools and colleges in Oxfordshire (April 1992)

(5) Delegation of budgets for the delivery of services to agreed standards and under revised financial regulations (completion October 1991)

(6) To plan replacement of libraries' computerized stock management system by a departmental system, to manage Department of Leisure and Arts materials in an integrated and accessible way (detailed project appraisal May 1991)

(7) To complete and open Woodcote Library (September 1991)

(8) To complete and open Wantage Library (April 1992)

(9) To complete and open Didcot Library (June 1992)

(10) To produce a draft arts strategy for Oxfordshire, including a review of policy, an audit of services currently provided and/or supported, and a plan for implementation (March 1992)

(11) To review and assess support for the cultural needs of black and Asian communities in Oxfordshire, including research into the range of cultural forms and traditions practised (March 1992)

(12) To produce an exhibition to promote countryside recreational opportunities provided by the Department to illustrate Department of Leisure and Arts Services of environmental recording and documentation (May 1992)

(13) To establish a business information service in conjunction with the Policy and Review Unit and other departments of the County Council (April 1992)

(14) To implement, under the contemporary documentation and collection policy, a project for 1991–92 based on Cowley, to record the car factory and social network associated with it (all year)

(15) To undertake the change in the Oxfordshire Countryside Project, by producing educational material contributing to collection of documentation (all year)

(16) Refurbishment of County Museum, Woodstock (all year)

(17) Achieve access for the disabled to the Museum of Oxford (April 1992)

References

BURRETT, G. (1985) 'Discussion' for Chapter XIV of *The Management of Change in Museums*, National Maritime Museum

HARVEY-JONES, SIR J. (1987) 'Introduction', in I. Ansoff, *Corporate Strategy* (2nd edn), Penguin, London

3

Managing strategies and financial considerations: historic properties

Lester Borley

This chapter considers strategies for the conservation and public presentation of long-established heritage property. Distinctions are made between the various types of property, and the institutional framework is described.

The work of the National Trust for Scotland is taken as a case study. Its aims and objectives are outlined, and the nature of the competition which it faces as a voluntary charitable body is explained. Its management structure, system of financial planning, setting of targets and phasing of activity are described. Particular reference is made to the management of fund-raising and appeals, and the provision of access for the public.

It will become apparent that a voluntary membership body has to act in a professional and businesslike way if it is to maintain its position as a private body working for the benefit of the nation.

The heritage business

The heritage business is an amorphous activity embracing many different properties and subjects which have become part of the business of leisure. Whilst rarely profitable in their own right, and often seen as loss-leaders for the tourism industry, heritage properties have inherent qualities which need protection and management, whether or not they are viable in the terms of other commercial visitor attractions, and require to be operated and managed in a businesslike way. To maintain their charitable status they must fulfil their stated objectives, which are monitored by the Charity Commissioners or by the Inland Revenue, in the case of properties in Scotland.

It is important to distingush between heritage properties and the many vistor attractions which have been created, especially since the Development of Tourism Act in 1969, which form part of the heritage business but which in themselves are usually interpretations of

aspects of social history, often based on collections brought together for the purpose. This chapter does not concern itself with such commercial properties, which are often managed in association with other visitor attractions.

Properties or subjects which may be considered part of the true heritage include stately homes, country houses and their estates, castles and mansion houses, cathedrals and historic churches, ancient monuments and natural landscapes of great scenic beauty (*Figure 3.1*). In their various ways they contribute to the nation's heritage, and have a fundamental value as reminders of the glories of the past and a prospect for the future. The need to sustain the national heritage is seen as part of our responsibility to the next generation. In France the word *patrimoine*, or patrimony, is often used as a better word for heritage, with its suggestion of inheritance. Definitions of the national heritage may vary widely, but a heritage subject concerns the nation in its collective sense rather than the benefit to a single person or family. Whilst the property might well be sustained by the efforts of one family, the fiscal regime introduced by successive governments defines that aspect of the heritage as having a greater than personal value, and thus is seen as desirable to sustain for future generations.

The institutional framework

The UK government has created several mechanisms for support for the heritage, notably through the functions of English Heritage, Historic Scotland and Cadw (Wales), which exist not only to own and manage property but also to help others, through financial aid and professional advice, to sustain properties in private ownership which are considered to be of varying degrees of national importance. The National Heritage Memorial Fund, and the national tourist

Figure 3.1 Crathes Castle: a sixteenth century castle near Aberdeen with a famous garden receiving over 100,000 visitors per year

manage several hundred properties of national importance. In addition there are associations of private owners, especially within the Historic Houses Association, which, whilst operating individually, gain much from collective action in terms of securing a better fiscal regime for heritage properties, particularly where private owners are encouraged to create maintenance funds or to achieve a legal status which avoids the debilitating effects of capital transfer tax. In some instances it suits the purpose of families to create a charitable trust for their property, if it is considered by the government to be of national importance.

It will be apparent from the above brief description of the institutional framework that there are many categories of ownership, control or management within the amorphous subject of the heritage.

The National Trust for Scotland

To understand the management and operation of heritage property it is perhaps useful to describe and discuss the operation of those in the care of the National Trust for Scotland. The concept of the protection of areas of national or regional significance first occurred in the USA in New England, with the establishment of the trustees of reservations in Massachusetts in 1891. This was a movement to protect relatively small areas of open country which were considered at risk during a considerable period of industrial expansion. The precedent established in the USA was followed soon after by the establishment of the National Trust in England in 1895, largely to secure the natural landscape of the Lake District, which was seen, 100 years ago, to be under potential threat. This was as much from changing methods of land use as from the needs of recreation in a compact area of high scenic value. The National Trust for Scotland, with similar objectives to its predecessors, came into being in 1931.

The purposes of the National Trust for Scotland are embodied in a subsequent Confirmation Act of Parliament in 1935 which says, in part, 'The National Trust for Scotland shall be established for the purposes of promoting the permanent preservation for the benefit of the nation of lands and buildings in Scotland of historic or national interest or natural beauty' (*Figure 3.2*). The Act also defines the protection of articles and objects of historic or national interest and the natural aspects and features of land and their related animal and plant life. The National Trust for Scotland is therefore unique in Scotland as having care for the heritage 'in the round', and is not limited to any one specialist area. Established as a charity, it was able to seek the support of members and others who chose to support its work through donations or voluntary effort. Its constitution provided from the very beginning for it to be directed by a Council which was partly elected and partly representative of a broad range of national bodies,

boards of the constituent countries of the United Kingdom, all have the power to grant-aid heritage subjects either for purchase, for endowment or for the improvement of presentation or facilitation for the public. In addition the nature conservancy councils and the countryside commissions help to sustain landscapes and natural history and scientific subjects which are considered important to the nation's heritage.

In the UK, local authorities also have a parallel responsibility for sustaining properties and subjects which are of regional or local importance. Because of the constraints on capital expenditure exercised by central government on local authorities, the properties in local authority ownership or control are quite often vested in separate charitable trusts, to facilitate their management, often in collaboration with other voluntary organizations. These hybrid mechanisms of ownership are increasing, as they can attract sponsorship and donations not normally available to local-authority-owned properties.

The National Trusts for England, Wales and Northern Ireland, and the National Trust for Scotland, which is a separate but similar body, between them

Figure 3.2 Souter Johnnie's Cottage, Kirkoswald, near Ayr: a re-created vernacular interior of the cottage which was the home of John Davidson, the original Souter Johnnie of Robert Burns's 'Tam o' Shanter'

which give authority to its deliberation of policy issues. An Executive Committee with a set of advisory committees exists to monitor the performance of the organization, whose day-to-day management is in the hands of a group of professionals, in some instances assisted by volunteers.

The principal aims of the Trust which are set down in the 1935 Act can be expanded into three main areas of equal importance:

(1) to influence and persuade others by example to share and support the Trust's aims and work;
(2) to own appropriate property – land, buildings and contents and other objects – to ensure their permanent preservation as far as possible for all time;
(3) to enable people to have access to its properties to see and experience them in ways which are consistent with their permanent preservation.

In meeting these aims the Trust always seeks to cooperate with and learn from others and endeavour to carry out the best current practice throughout its work. The aims are set down in a simple manner so as to be clear and concise. It follows from them that there are many functions which the Trust must perform in order to fulfil the aims.

Heritage organizations enjoying a charitable status have often been inspired by the commitment of members and volunteers who identify with its objectives and purposes. The ethos behind voluntary charitable organizations is a special aspect of life in the United Kingdom, and the commitment of individuals to the success of the national movement to protect the heritage will be seen later as contributing in no small measure to its financial and operating efficiency.

The properties of the National Trust for Scotland

Since 1931 the National Trust for Scotland has become responsible for the care of 120 different properties of varying nature and accessibility. They range in character from castles and large houses, countryside, gardens, historic sites, islands, museums, examples of social and industrial heritage and places associated with famous Scots (*Figure 3.2*). Overall the properties achieved 2 million visits from the public in 1992. The definition of the heritage is therefore very broad. The Confirmation Act of 1935 was not specific about the nation's heritage and the National Trust for Scotland has always been aware of the needs of the times, and

Figure 3.3 Pitmedden Garden, near Aberdeen, which is a re-creation of an original formal parterre of the 17th century: each summer 40,000 plants are bedded out to create a colourful spectacle which attracts 25,000 visitors

pragmatically taken into its care properties which might otherwise be at risk. This concept of a safety net means that the portfolio of properties in its care assumes a random pattern.

Perhaps the only thing most Trust properties have in common is that they operate at a deficit. Only four of the 120 properties of the National Trust for Scotland produce a surplus on their annual operating budget: Glencoe, Culloden, Inverewe and Threave. These are all served by recently built visitor centres, which do not suffer from the usual ailments of historic buildings such as dry rot, wet rot and nail sickness and the other myriad complaints which need constant maintenance, and which, as will be seen from *Figure 3.4*, absorb 81 per cent of the annual income of the National Trust for Scotland (£11.38 million in 1992).

The pie charts in the figure indicate the sources and the uses made of income for the year ended 31 October 1992. From this it can be seen that payments for admission by non-members contributed only 8 per cent (£1.084 million) of the income required. The net income from the trading company contribution provided a further 4 per cent (£484,000). The balance of 88 per cent of the income required therefore had to be found from other sources, including membership,

and that is the continuing challenge facing the National Trust for Scotland which shapes the strategies and objectives for the organization in meeting its obligations. It is a private body fulfilling a public role.

The nature of competition

At this point it is perhaps useful to consider the nature of the competition which the National Trust for Scotland faces in setting its strategies and meeting its targets.

Competition for visitors

The Scottish Tourist Board identifies and lists almost 1500 visitor attractions in Scotland which meet the needs not only of foreign visitors but also of domestic visitors, half of whom originate in Scotland, and in addition receive enormous numbers of day visits which are part of local leisure demand. The 1991 edition of the guide to *Museums and Art Galleries* lists 1300 properties throughout the United Kingdom, and the companion guide to *Historic Properties Open to the Public* lists a further 1300 properties. Of the 212 museums in Scotland listed in the first of these

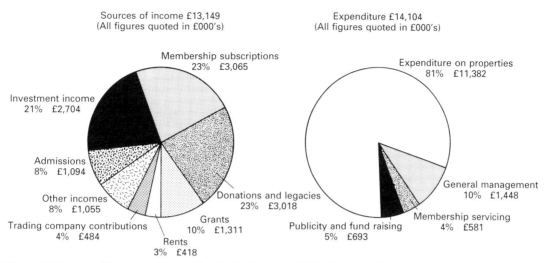

Figure 3.4 Sources of income and uses made of it in the year ended 31 October 1992

guides, 20 (10 per cent) are in the ownership of the National Trust for Scotland; and of the 128 historic houses in Scotland which are listed in the second guide, 37 (25 per cent) are in the ownership of the National Trust for Scotland. Historic Scotland, the executive agency of government, owns 330 monuments, 40 of which are of major interest, and the private owners in membership of the Historic Houses Association offer 36 houses in Scotland which may be visited by the public.

Thus if increased earnings from visitors is one of our management targets, it will be seen that there is a considerable amount of competition for the leisure time and spending of the general public. The National Trust for Scotland recorded almost 2 million visitors in 1992 to those properties where a record of attendance could be kept. Many of the properties are in remote, rural locations where high volumes can never be expected, and the basic cost of maintaining the property in good order and adequately staffed rarely makes it possible for visitor receipts alone to make more than a marginal contribution to the property budget.

Competition for membership support

The National Trust for Scotland was created in 1931 by the Association for the Protection of Rural Scotland, which in itself had been created by the Royal Incorporation of Architects in Scotland. In the last 40 years, with increasing wealth and leisure, the British public has espoused the cause of conservation and the nation's heritage, which has led to the establishment and growth of a large number of voluntary charitable bodies, often based upon a special interest.

In times of economic pressure people have to make choices between the many organizations which they perceive to be performing similar functions. There is therefore a need for the aims and objectives of the National Trust for Scotland to be clearly stated and an active campaign sustained to maintain the support and commitment of a loyal membership. By the end of 1993 there were 232,000 members, a doubling within ten years. The subscriptions from membership accounted for 23 per cent of the income (£3.06 million). Donations and legacies provided a further 23 per cent (£3.01 million), which is income directly related to the interest shown by members and other supporters in the work of the National Trust for Scotland. Members are serviced by a quarterly magazine *Heritage Scotland*, which with its full colour format has now become the largest circulation magazine in Scotland, and therefore constitutes a valuable advertising medium for others. The membership profile is not typical of the population at large, but tends towards the middle-aged with higher disposable incomes. This is usual for charitable conservation bodies. The profile of visitors to properties in the care of the National Trust for Scotland is closer to that of the population at large.

The cost of servicing members is £581,000 (4 per cent of the annual budget), and the majority of income from membership subscriptions can thus be devoted to the maintenance of properties. Visits by members to properties have grown to 50 per cent of the annual number recorded, compared with 33 per cent eight years ago. This reflects a growing interest and awareness of environmental matters, but also has been stimulated by improvement in the magazine and communication to members who are made more aware of developments and activities at properties

(*Figure 3.5*). In 1991, the Diamond Jubilee Year of the National Trust for Scotland, 1500 events were staged at Trust properties to encourage more interest from members and other visitors. A survey of membership reveals that free entry to properties is not the real motive for subscription, but the majority of members indicate that their subscription is seen as support for the work of conservation in general. Members make an average of three to four visits to properties per annum, and on that basis it would be cheaper for them to pay the normal price of admission per property, which bears out the research that the motive for membership has a deeper purpose.

Seventy per cent of new members join at properties, where the nature of the work of the organization is most apparent. The average length of membership is seven to eight years, and the last five years has seen a steady annual growth of more than 30,000 new members per annum, which more than compensates for the annual loss of members through retirement or other usual causes.

An overriding problem for all membership organizations active in conservation is that older people are attracted, and whilst young people as part of a family membership are encouraged to participate in the work of the Trust, the student age bracket (18–23) provides only 6 per cent of the total membership. This is compensated for to some extent by encouraging active support for maintenance projects through the NTS conservation volunteers.

Competition for financial sponsorship

Conservation bodies, such as the National Trust for Scotland, are not alone in seeking financial support within the wider community. The number of charities sponsoring special public appeals, often for famine relief or other natural disasters, taken with the well established charities with a social purpose, attract most individual giving. Cultural and arts-based organizations also need community support, particularly at a time when there is a decline in support in real terms from central and local government. Cultural activities have a great appeal for company sponsorship. The creation of trustee bodies to run national institutions such as museums, art galleries and botanical collections has also created further competition for scarce company sponsorship. An added complication for any charitable organization raising large sums of money in Scotland is that many corporate sponsorship decisions are taken by staff based in other countries.

Figure 3.5 Glencoe, site of the massacre in 1692 and a popular mountainous property in the Western Highlands of Scotland, offers scope for walks led by trained rangers

There is also the very important source of money which is available through statutory agencies of government, such as the tourist boards and the countryside agencies. Their resources are similarly under pressure from many applicants, and government policy, which reflects social and economic needs, often leads to the rewriting of the conditions of grant-aid with increasing frequency. The number of visitor attractions and other essential services which must seek public support has grown in the past twenty years, which also means that percentage levels of grant made available by statutory agencies have fallen in order to achieve a wider distribution of support for many worthwhile schemes.

The National Trust for Scotland has therefore to shape its strategies for sources of income from a wide field of potential supporters. Whilst it has established an investment portfolio which now contributes 21 per cent of its annual income (£2.70 million), it has to be active in all sorts of ways to sustain its annual income requirement.

Many organizations which are active in the politics of conservation are not managers of properties which require annual support. Others which manage commercially oriented visitor attractions in the heritage business have no long-term obligation to manage such facilities. The National Trust for Scotland was created to preserve the nation's heritage in perpetuity.

Properties of national importance are declared to be inalienable, which means they cannot be sold on to others. The National Trust for Scotland must therefore take a very long view of its statutory responsibility 'of promoting the permanent preservation for the benefit of the nation of lands and buildings in Scotland'.

The management structure

Having thus described the external environment in which the Trust must operate, we can proceed to describe in more detail the way it organizes itself to achieve its strategic objectives. To help shape these the Trust undertakes regular market research at its properties into the nature of its visitors and their needs and interests. It also researches the profile of its membership to obtain a clearer idea of those who are committed to its cause, and surveys the interests of the readership of its quarterly magazine. Without this information it would not be possible for strategic objectives to be sharply focused in the preparation of annual budgets and forward action plans.

Like most charitable organizations which start from small beginnings, the Trust found that the need for more formal management structures only gradually became apparent. The acquisition of properties, following a random pattern as previously described, poses different problems of management on a daily basis. In the 1930s the Trust acquired relatively small properties. Where any large building was involved it was usually placed in the guardianship of the Secretary

of State for Scotland, whose well funded executive agencies have managed such properties along with others which are of comparable national importance. In the post-war period, a combination of social change and economic pressure meant that a number of larger estates were placed at risk, and in the 1960s and 1970s the Trust became responsible for the ownership and future care of many more complex estates, buildings of great age and extensive land holdings.

The organization thus grew to meet the demands placed upon it. The early days of voluntary support had to be augmented by the recruitment of professional skills. In 1991 the National Trust for Scotland employed 340 full-time staff, 110 in headquarters and 230 in regional offices and properties. During the busy visitor season, from March to October, it employs a further 600 seasonal paid staff, but also has the benefit of a further 500 volunteers who act as guides at properties or give support in the management of events or other property services. A number of members give their time freely for practical projects involving the maintenance of countryside properties, organized in a series of work camps.

This voluntary commitment of time and effort remains one of the distinguishing features of the support for the National Trust for Scotland. Members of retirement age give their services in part because the work of the Trust enables them to connect with others of like mind.

In 1984 the structure of management of the Trust was reorganized to provide localized professional support for properties scattered throughout Scotland, which were grouped into five regions, each having approximately twenty properties and about an equal number of annual visitors to be managed. Small regional offices with administrative, factorial, surveying and publicity skills were established to provide local management support for the properties. This replaced the earlier practice whereby headquarters staff were allocated certain regional responsibilities.

Following the 1984 management reorganization, the headquarters staff were regrouped into four main divisions (*Figure 3.6*):

(1) Property Management Services, which covers a wide range of practical skills needed to help sustain properties;
(2) Marketing Services, which was responsible for all publicity and print production for all other divisions and regions;
(3) Financial Services, responsible for budget formulation and expenditure control;
(4) Administrative Services, responsible for procedures with regard to staff recruitment, training, conditions of employment and welfare.

In addition a small central unit managing external relations and central policy was established under the Director.

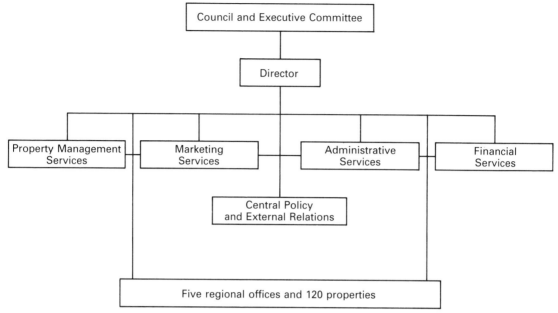

Figure 3.6 The National Trust for Scotland management structure plan reflects the need for a charitable organization to take a businesslike approach

A Management Group of seven senior executives, together with the regional representatives, meets monthly to act together for the supervision and management of resources. The annual budget process involves all staff and responsibility for expenditure is delegated well down the organization, which means that those who have proposed programmes of expenditure are accountable for their budget when approved. A monthly scrutiny of expenditure is achieved through the Management Group, with quarterly adjustments of budgets.

Financial planning

The figures in *Table 3.1* show how the various income levels are forecast. These are based on assumptions and past trends. Some costs will bear a higher rate of inflation than the national rate: this is particularly true of the building services industry, which is largely involved in the complex task of maintaining and restoring historic properties. An attempt is made to forecast for five years in detail, and to speculate on the tenth-year postion. The forecasting process is of course only as good as the accuracy of the assumptions made about the various levels of activity, which have to be based on past trends. It is essential to monitor the assumptions regularly. An unexpected economic recession, a change in the rate of VAT or the arrival of new legislation, both UK and EEC, can have a major effect on the Trust's forecasts and plans.

The annual net income from the trading company of £484,000 (4 per cent) in 1992 arises from a much greater gross trading figure, for which we are required by the Inland Revenue to establish a separate trading company. To avoid tax, the trading company covenants its profits to the National Trust for Scotland which, as a charity, is not taxed.

Figure 3.7 shows a three-year income comparison from 1988 to 1990, which indicates categories of income and emphasizes the unpredictable nature of legacies. Much of the freedom to act in an imaginative way will depend upon the amount of money which can be retained annually for future use. In 1990 this amounted to £3.4 million (27 per cent of income).

Setting targets

The primary objective is of course to manage the organization cost-efficiently, restraining a growth in permanent staff numbers by seeking voluntary support where appropriate or using outside consultants where the professional skills are only required on a short-term basis. In 1992 general management costs were held at 10 per cent of total expenditure (£1.448 million).

The cost of providing supporting facilities for visitors is small in comparison with the cost of maintaining the historic buildings. The programme of conservation of properties is grant-aided by Historic Scotland, the

Table 3.1 National Trust for Scotland: income and expenditure trends (£000 at 1990 values)

	Actual adjusted for inflation					Forecast at 1990 values					
	1986	*1987*	*1988*	*1989*	*1990*	*1991*	*1992*	*1993*	*1994*	*1995*	*2000*
Income											
Subscriptions											
Annual	1,528	1,763	1,907	2,164	2,196	2,328	2,467	2,615	2,772	2,939	3,933
Life	303	77	94	127	127	135	135	135	135	135	135
Donations											
General	90	71	71	29	20	50	50	50	50	50	50
Other funds	369	467	728	379	316	391	391	391	391	391	391
Investment income											
General	165	147	94	201	190	162	140	120	100	80	0
Specific	1,503	1,766	1,758	2,070	2,344	2,390	2,438	2,487	2,537	2,588	2,857
Legacies	869	948	800	1,253	2,555	1,285	1,285	1,285	1,285	1,285	1,285
Grants	860	698	956	1,180	809	1,273	1,273	1,273	1,273	1,273	1,273
Rents	314	344	320	319	296	296	296	296	296	296	296
Admissions	774	902	872	932	953	953	953	953	953	953	953
Trading company	484	708	612	813	581	664	664	664	664	664	664
Other receipts	337	528	420	601	621	547	547	547	547	547	547
Total income	7,596	8,419	8,632	10,014	11,008	10,474	10,639	10,816	11,003	11,201	12,384
Expenditure											
Properties											
Wages	1,325	1,416	1,561	1,702	1,820	1,880	1,942	2,006	2,072	2,141	2,518
Expenses of upkeep	3,388	3,896	4,103	4,836	4,373	4,846	4,986	5,006	5,047	5,090	5,306
Administration	865	907	927	1,057	1,084	1,106	1,128	1,150	1,173	1,197	1,321
Total property Expenditure	5,578	6,219	6,591	7,595	7,277	7,832	8,056	8,162	8,292	8,428	9,145
General management	1,934	1,919	1,990	2,016	2,200	2,275	2,320	2,366	2,414	2,462	2,718
Total expenditure	7,512	8,138	8,581	9,611	9,477	10,107	10,376	10,528	10,706	10,890	11,863
Surplus (deficit)	84	281	51	403	1,531	367	263	288	297	311	521
Inflation factor used (%)	32.2	26.6	19.0	10.9	—						

Countryside Commission for Scotland and other agencies as appropriate, each offering varying percentage levels of grant. Annual budgets are therefore based on a three-year programme which takes into account the fact that large restoration projects might be spread over several financial years. The programme of major repairs, improvements and developments (MRID) is the core of the budgeting process and requires inputs from the properties through the regional offices to headquarters.

Human nature being what it is, property and regional staff tend to be over-ambitious in the programmes of work which they wish to undertake, and a balance has to be struck between the resources allocated to properties within each of the five regions. In recent years 75 to 80 per cent of the budget bids have been met. A programme of conservation and restoration of the twenty major historic buildings in each region is based upon a rigorous quinquennial survey undertaken by consultant architects, and follows a work programme agreed with Historic Scotland which might take up to ten years to complete. The system of quinquennial survey introduced several years ago has provided an orderly and logical approach to the repair and maintenance of historic structures which, although expensive in their first years, should minimize the costs of maintenance in the longer term. Ideally the quinquennial review procedure should be followed for

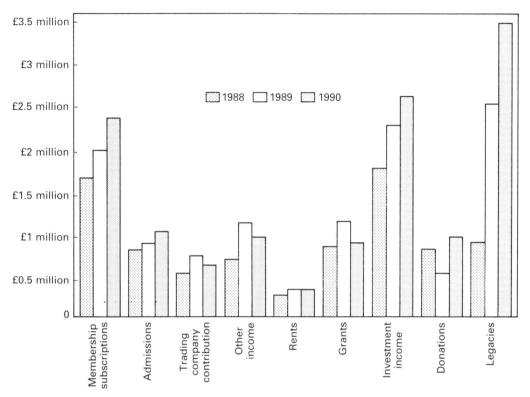

Figure 3.7 A three-year income comparison illustrates the fluctuating nature of certain categories, such as legacies and donations

all buildings and properties where repair and maintenance forms such a large part of the budget requirement.

Management plans

The wide range of professional skills involved in managing properties requires that there will be some common ground on which the various staff employed within each discipline can interact. There will always be creative tensions between staff at properties, at regional offices and at headquarters, and management plans reflect and state the common ground in order to create harmony and a sense of common purpose. Over the years it was possible for long-serving staff to feel intimately involved with properties in their care, and their knowledge of the idiosyncrasies of historic buildings and the planting and management of land was of inestimable value. The common ground was a consensus developed over many years.

Times change and so do staff, and the need for more streamlined management planning became apparent. The main reason for this was to formalize a five-year view about the management and marketing needs of properties, choosing between options for improvement or development, mindful of cost-efficiency and a competitive position within the leisure business. It has always been the Trust's aim to set high standards of maintenance and preservation and these standards have been emulated by others. The cost of such endeavour is high, and management planning enables staff to anticipate and justify expenditure on a programmed basis. This is especially important where grant-aid from government agencies has to be spread over many more applicants and where the inflation index for the building industry seems always to be above the average.

A growing public awareness of the countryside, with the consequent pressure for access, has also brought a need to know more about the ecology and archaeology of each property, both to protect rare sites and to use such knowledge to improve the experience for visitors.

Management planning is an integrated activity begun in the late 1980s, and by 1992 45 properties had been assessed or were in the final stages of the process. The remaining 75 properties are to be tackled in the next few years, by which time the first will need to be reviewed. The present target is to complete all management plans by 1996, and to finish their contributory ecological and archaeological surveys within the same timescale.

A good deal of time is required in the initial stages to audit each property comprehensively and to establish the facts and figures in a descriptive section. This covers a history of the property and its development, a statement of its physical resources and a detailed arrangement of information about its non-recreational land uses and its existing recreational uses.

It is important to have a statement of aims and objectives for each property. This, with the descriptive background, enables the prescription for improvements to the property to be set out clearly and a programme for further investment of money, manpower or other resources to be logically expressed.

The Headquarters Management Group uses the series of management plans as a set of objectives and prescriptions to justify the allocation of resources. The overriding investment is of course in the physical condition of the properties. The investment in marketing is a small proportion of the product investment. As noted earlier, the Trust is charged with maintaining its properties whether or not they actually receive visitors. The fact that they do attract about 2 million visitors per annum puts growing emphasis on the discipline of a management plan to maintain a balanced and systematic approach to the use of resources.

Public appeals for funds

The formulation of the five-year financial forecast assumes that all new properties taken into care will be fully financed with regard to the cost of acquisition, repair and the endowment of the inevitable deficit on annual running costs. If a major property of national importance is taken into care then the Trust has to seek support from other agencies such as the National Heritage Memorial Fund on purchase and endowment, and Historic Scotland and the Countryside Commission for Scotland on the repair and maintenance of facilities.

Sometimes the resources available from national agencies are inadequate to meet the whole cost and thus a public appeal has to be mounted. In recent years these have included raising public support for the restoration of the House of Dun in Angus, a 1730 villa by William Adam (*Figure 3.8*). The target for the appeal was £350,000, but £530,000 was raised towards the total cost of restoration of £1.5 million within the year. The restoration of a walled garden at Drum Castle to form a garden of historic roses of the seventeeth to twentieth centuries cost £75,000, and was raised by public subscription within three months. The largest appeal recently organized was for £2.5 million to restore 50 ancillary buildings of the eighteenth and nineteenth centuries in the 200 ha estate of Culzean Castle in Ayrshire. This target was reached within fifteen months, and the sum will be used to match resources from national agencies for

the restoration programme over a period of ten years. The adaptive use of these ancillary buildings for educational and other public use was stressed in the appeal.

In the case of each appeal a very careful analysis is made of likely sources of support from charitable trusts, commercial organizations, members' centres and individuals both in the United Kingdom and overseas. Targets are set for each category, and support from other charitable trusts is noteworthy. Commercial organizations tend to give less to capital programmes of restoration, preferring to be associated with the adaptive uses of properties or the creation of new public facilities. Much of the expenditure on the maintenance of properties is of course hidden from view, and in that sense offers less opportunity for a commercial organization to achieve public recognition for its philanthropy.

Successful fund-raising therefore depends upon an intelligent appreciation of the market-place to minimize the waste of time and effort. There is a large number of charitable trusts with stated objectives for various forms of assistance available to anyone seeking financial support, and time spent appraising the purposes of other charitable trusts is time well spent. Breaking down the total figure required into a package of smaller costed elements has proved effective in attracting support from many sources for whom the total sum needed would have been too daunting even to contemplate.

Needs of visitors

Whilst the overwhelming requirement for resources is for the maintenance of properties, there is also the requirement to provide access for the public, which in modern times implies a minimum level of visitor facilities. Eighty per cent of visitors to Trust properties arrive by car, reflecting the rural location of properties as much as the modern trend to use personal transport. Therefore access roads have to be adequate, and parking spaces for cars and the occasional coaches have to be sufficient for peak periods. Having travelled a journey of anything up to 80 km to reach a property, visitors require toilets. Moreover, because the property may be remote, it is usually desirable to provide a tearoom or restaurant according to the potential level of demand. A shop or smaller sales point is also expected by the public, which wishes to have a souvenir of a visit.

From the sources of income it has already been shown that the net return from the trading company contribution, at 5 per cent of total income, is a relatively small figure, but it arises from meeting the public's expectations. A property which does not provide adequate visitor facilities will probably suffer from the

Figure 3.8 Eighty-three per cent of income is spent on or allocated to the future maintenance of historic properties such as the House of Dun, near Montrose, a 1730 villa by William Adam restored in 1989

competition provided by those attractions which do take the trouble to assess and meet the public's needs.

The provision and upgrading of visitor facilities at National Trust for Scotland properties is subject to a three-year forward programme. It is also the practice of the Trust to review its interpretation and presentation techniques to ensure that they are kept up to date in terms of an increasing public awareness of changing media. A forward programme of reviewing five property presentations annually is therefore established, and over a period of ten years the interpretation and presentation of 50 of the Trust properties open to the public should be upgraded and new techniques of presentation introduced where appropriate.

When a property first comes into the care of the National Trust for Scotland, it is not usually possible or desirable to undertake a complete presentation. As the years pass, more of a property is brought into public view, which maintains the interest of members and repeat visitors. Attracting a local following to a

property, particularly in the early and late months of the season, is particularly important to help offset the costs of keeping a property adequately staffed and serviced.

Over the six- to eight-month opening period typical in Scotland, it is possible to distinguish between three phases of visiting. A good number of events are staged at properties in the spring months to attract local visitors. In the peak summer months events will continue but they are less necessary to stimulate visitor demand. In the last ten years the autumn opening period has seen a growth in second-holiday taking, and a different market of the middle-aged travelling without children has emerged. An overall marketing strategy for managing properties therefore has to take into account the changes in the pattern of visitors within the period of remaining open. In some cases it has proved possible to open for virtually the whole year, but this will only be true in Scotland of properties which are within easy reach of centres of population.

The future

In the 60 years of its existence the National Trust for Scotland has followed two distinct paths. The first has been to react to circumstances, to make pragmatic decisions on what might be regarded as important to Scotland's heritage, and to act as a safety net for properties of national importance which might otherwise be lost. This of course leads to a burden of financial responsibility which is the core of the strategy of fundraising. The second role has been one of information, especially in public awareness of environment issues, and a path-finding role in terms of anticipating the wider awareness of environmental issues among the general public.

This latter role requires far less financial resources, but does depend upon the experience gained in the management of the properties in the Trust's care. This experience helps to shape sensible policies for more general influence among other voluntary agencies, and owners of private property, where a balance between conservation and visitor access has to be found. There is a strong Scottish tradition of freedom of access, provided no damage is caused to private property, and this expectation has been met by the distribution of well managed properties, which act as points of attraction, fulfilling the needs of the public to explore the countryside or to learn more about the built heritage.

Despite the wildness of the landscape it is generally true that very little of the land surface of Scotland is true wilderness, and most of it has been affected by man in terms of the agriculture or other forms of land use. The distribution and pattern of human settlement in rural areas has fluctuated, and in many instances it is based on marginal existence. However a viable rural population is essential for a flourishing tourism and leisure industry. The properties of the National Trust for Scotland, which are often considerable employers of labour, clearly make a contribution to the social and economic stability of rural communities.

Because of the Trust's work with others in achieving a more effective fiscal regime, the owners of private property have a better chance of securing a stable future. This means that the National Trust for Scotland is less likely to be called upon to act as a safety net, but it takes a pragmatic view and will always respond to the national need. However this is costly in terms of national resources, and therefore the National Trust for Scotland is not an acquisitive body by nature, and seeks all possible ways short of ownership to ensure the future of properties of national importance.

What then might be seen as the primary role of the National Trust for Scotland in the future? There can be no doubt that with its present portfolio of 120 properties, covering such a wide spectrum of interest, the Trust can and should do more. This coincides with the growth in leisure, particularly for people taking early retirement, who have the energy and the time to satisfy their intellectual curiosity. Against this general awareness of environmental and conservation issues there will be scope for increasing the general knowledge of visitors to properties about conservation issues. With 2 million visitors to properties, this is clearly an important aspect of policy.

The Trust's properties have been used for many years for extramural studies, particularly for primary and secondary school students. A day spent in the countryside at an NTS property is often a moment of awakening for a city-based primary school child. Secondary school studies are now based upon modules of varying teaching disciplines, and it has been the practice to prepare classroom and property visit material matched to the needs of the curriculum. Studies in social history, the biosphere and aesthetics have thus been enhanced by the use of appropriate Trust properties. As every property is a reflection of historic and social development, any one of them is potentially a very good case study for educational and training purposes.

The universities have recognized the opportunity presented by the growing number of older people with more leisure time and disposable incomes by creating departments of continuing education, which was formerly known as extramural studies. This concept of education continuing for a lifetime presents a challenge and an opportunity for properties managed by heritage organizations, and should be an area of considerable potential.

Within the overall scope of teaching, very practical training in conservation skills is emerging. This is of direct benefit not only to young apprentices but also to those established in their professions, such as architecture or engineering, who can use the historic structures of NTS buildings, with all their conservation problems, to learn more about the techniques involved in restoration.

The greater number of visitors to Trust properties will of course continue to consist of those who are simply seeking a pleasant day's relaxation. An understanding of the historical and social importance of the properties will enhance their visit, and perhaps make them more interested in pursuing parallel interests in their leisure time.

Therefore the future for heritage properties is clearly one of producing added value, which is a very rich seam to be mined for many years ahead by those fortunate to administer properties of importance to the nation's heritage. Success in achieving our goals and strategic objectives and in evaluating the results of our policies will reflect the management efficiency which is essential for any charitable organization in the heritage business.

4

Measuring performance and contingency planning

Peter Middleton

Developing from the issues identified in Chapter 1, this chapter is about how to monitor and respond to *change*. Any heritage organization that operates as a business and trades with the public, whether it seeks to make profits or not, operates in a constantly changing environment. Tonight a water main may burst and flood the picture store in the basement. Next month you may get notice of a 20 per cent increase (or decrease) in grant, effective three months hence. Early next year the government may relax the rules on charitable giving. In a year's time, a major transport project may improve access – but unemployment might have doubled or interest rates halved.

Think for a moment about driving a car. You sit behind the wheel with an array of dials and digital displays in front of you. You look out of the windscreen at the front directly, and down the sides and out the back indirectly through mirrors. As you drive along, you pay a lot of attention to some dials and displays – the speedometer being an obvious example. You pay less continuous attention to the fuel gauge and almost no attention to the temperature gauge and the oil level and brake wear warning lights. No attention, that is, until something happens. Suddenly the engine oil level light comes on. You ignore it, and 100 km later your engine seizes up. You have no means of completing your journey – and you find yourself with a hefty bill.

Or suppose you are sitting in very slow moving traffic. The temperature gauge rises. You pay almost no attention, because soon the fan will cut in automatically and reduce the engine temperature. Time passes. The fan hasn't cut in! There is nothing for it but to turn off the engine and let it cool down. If you don't, the engine will overheat and you won't be able to drive.

If you have a car with a fuel efficiency display, it tells you how efficiently you are driving by measuring the consumption of fuel and averaging it out very quickly against your speed. If you accelerate sharply, the efficiency drops. If you are featherlight in touch, efficiency rises.

This simple, commonplace set of examples provides us with an everyday way of thinking about measuring performance, monitoring and contingency planning.

Successful organizations trading with the visiting public are outward looking, and constantly alert to opportunities and threats in the external environment. They monitor carefully identified variables and trends. They keep a weather eye on policy shifts that could affect them. They have prepared some contingency plans to combat hostile changes in circumstances. They are responsive and quick on their feet.

Reverting to the car analogy, successful businesses have dials and displays in their 'cars' that are easy to read (not too many, but ones that monitor the right variables). They have mechanisms to turn on warning lights to give advance notice of a bigger problem. They service their cars regularly; they monitor the car's health, the wear and performance of important parts. And when a warning light comes on, or a part fails unexpectedly, they have a contingency plan (hire a car, go to the garage, call in outside help) lined up to tackle the problem.

Most of us are reasonably good at keeping our cars on the road and preventing our engines seizing up. Modern cars are complex but these days are very reliable. The manufacturers have designed out many potential failure areas and given us lots of help to make our cars perform well and avoid problems. How good are heritage businesses at doing the same? Most are not as good as they could be: hence this chapter!

It is a crude generalization, but in the past many heritage organizations (especially in the public and not-for-profit sectors) perceived few external threats and tended to be inward looking. Now, many are subject to a wide range of external threats – even commercial heritage competitors, for heaven's sake!

Those that do prosper are the best equipped and organized to respond to both threats and opportunities.

Performance monitoring is part of business life

In commercial organizations that are revenue and customer oriented, the management focus tends to be on key financial ratios, profit targets, cash flow and the health of the balance sheet. If you look at the financial section of newspapers, you will find them peppered with performance jargon and shorthand. Manufacturer A's share price may have fallen from a high of 300p to 28p in two years; service sector business B has improved its balance sheet 50 per cent by a new acquisition; and so on. 'People' issues are now also given much more management attention, in manufacturing as well as service industries. So rates of staff turnover, standards of competency, performance appraisal and so on are now measures that many companies employ routinely. The newspapers, again, may record that retailer C has cut staff turnover from an all-time high of 30 per cent last year to under 15 per cent this year through the introduction of a bonus scheme linked to appraisals and of employee share options. Its annual report may proudly state that more than 10 per cent of all staff have acquired a new vocational qualification and that the company has achieved quality assurance validation under the appropriate British Standard.

The types of performance measures given as examples above may apply either to whole businesses or in the analysis of their component parts. Returning to our car analogy, we may be moving at the correct speed and not appear to be using too much petrol. But looking at how the fuel gauge drops in order to assess engine efficiency is a very crude measuring method. An electronic fuel consumption readout is much more precise. This is looking at one of a group of rates of utilization and reporting them in a way we can easily understand.

In business, we similarly need to break down the performance measures so that we can look at different parts of the operation. These may routinely include looking at costs separately from income; tracking or apportioning costs or income by function, department, section and so on; and analysing rates of consumption of materials, e.g. in manufacturing the raw materials used for processing.

By disaggregating a business in this way and monitoring key measures over time, we can build up a picture not only of the health of the business as a whole, but also of the way in which contributory parts either assist or hinder profitability.

In the non-commercial resource- and cost-oriented heritage sector, the management focus has tended in the past to be concerned with protection of assets, lack of resources, threats to funding, and balancing the demands of diverse professional interests, e.g. curatorial and marketing. Nonetheless, as explained by Victor Middleton in Chapter 1, this focus is increasingly turning to the monitoring of many of the same variables that the commercial world concentrates on.

Having established that heritage organizations have many of the same needs as any other business sector, from a monitoring and contingency planning standpoint, this chapter next explores the range of control and performance measures available and looks at their relevance.

Chapter 1 noted the growing requirement for heritage organizations to prepare corporate plans and then keep them updated. Implicit in the preparation and updating is the need for reliable data, consistent over time, and performance measures that find wide acceptability. Corporate planning *per se* is discussed in Chapter 2. Here we are concerned with measures that are strategically relevant – that is, relevant to the management task in the medium term (two to three years ahead).

Comparison measures in the heritage sector

In parallel with the growth of interest in corporate planning, government and industry bodies (especially in the museums sector) have encouraged the development of comparison measures, that is measures that enable comparison of efficiency, the use of resources etc. between different yet broadly comparable groups of organizations. Thus one may now find museum directors comparing notes on the percentage of their staff budget by value or the number of posts devoted to collections management or marketing. Whilst we are not directly concerned with this issue here, the body of knowledge that is being developed on this subject is helpful in providing measures that are useful *within* organizations as well as for comparing one with another.

Before we get into the detail, though, a few words of caution. Ames (1990), writing about the measuring of museums' merits, suggests that:

> There is little agreement even within a subject sector, i.e. history, art or science, as to which definable/measurable goals museums do or should have in common. To the extent such goals or values are concerned with quality and intangibles, they are difficult or impossible to measure. People who choose to devote their careers to the museum field are not often, by learning style or temperament, particularly inclined toward such a methodical and meticulous exercise. Those who think their institutions might not bear comparisons or meet standards easily, or do not care if they do, might be even less inclined.

In the business world, there are many examples of companies that plan well and monitor extensively yet fail to spot major market opportunities or threats and so go bust. Insight, experience, attitudes and luck all have a part to play. So those that set off to measure and monitor with zeal should be wary!

Pehaps the greatest spur in the public sector to setting up an effective performance monitoring system, however, is the encouragement (some might say pressure!) contained in the Audit Commission's (1991) report on the management of local authority museums and art galleries. Its Appendix B is specially relevant. The author does, however, detect a whiff of over-engineering in the museum world's sudden embrace of standard setting and performance monitoring. Large heritage organizations, in particular, should be careful not to develop such complex monitoring systems that:

(1) data collection and analysis become important activities in their own right, rather than a means to an end; and
(2) in the quest to monitor uniformly, sight is lost of the relatively small number of indicators that *really are* important.

Smaller organizations are less likely to fall into these traps. They simply don't have the time or resources to invest in these tasks, or the degree of complexity that warrants a substantial monitoring system. One of those phrases much loved by management gurus is worth remembering here: stick to the knitting!

Performance measures from a strategic standpoint

Since the standpoint of this chapter is a strategic one, we need to bear this in mind in addressing both the selection of performance measures and their use. The measures can be broadly divided into three groups:

(1) financial data
(2) non-financial data
(3) qualitative measures.

Financial performance measures

The relevance of any set of measures, whether financial or other, depends on two factors:

(1) how well they can be related back to the organization's stated strategic objectives (objectives which may often be only partially quantifiable);
(2) the degree of ownership amongst staff and directors/trustees of those objectives and hence of beliefs in reference to the measures as an aid to management decision making.

Let us take as an example a local authority managed museum which spends substantially above average on collections management. It is the only museum that this particular small authority has of its own. To the amenities committee that has responsibility for this museum, the fact that it spends x per cent more than average is of little interest. It costs $£Y$ to run, and that's that. Until, that is, there is a change of political power. The new council decides to hive off the museum into a trust and decrees that within three years it must recover 50 per cent of its present net cost from non-local-authority sources.

All of a sudden, the trustees (some of whom used to be members of the amenities committee) have a great deal of need for reliable performance measures. And, regrettable though it may be, the amount of money spent on collections management, over the next three years, may have to be reduced to compensate for the appointment of a commercial manager whose job it is to raise income. He or she will need measures of performance (e.g. success of fund-raising, shop sales etc.) that previously were not relevant, were not collected or were disaggregated (e.g. what little retail income was generated in the past was lumped in with donations and ticket income). For the next three years, performance against certain key measures will dictate whether this museum survives or not.

In this example, the measures being used are highly relevant to the objectives that the local authority gives to the new trust, and they are 'owned' by the trustees because if they do not pay attention to them, the museum will be on the road to ruin. Furthermore, the trustees have to learn to forecast what their performance will be in future years: it's no good the trust hitting its 50 per cent revenue generation target in the third year and promptly going bust in the fifth because it fails to take account of a slowdown in admissions growth caused by the arrival of a new competitor!

Here are some key overall financial performance measures for public and not-for-profit heritage organizations. Obviously, not all apply in every case:

(1) gross admissions revenue per annum;
(2) gross secondary spend (retail, catering) per annum;
(3) cost of retail, catering and other sales per annum;
(4) net contribution from retail, catering etc. per annum;
(5) gross income from other trading sources (e.g. conferences, services etc.) per annum;
(6) average admission receipt per person per annum;
(7) annual profit (deficit);
(8) cost of collections management per annum;
(9) cost of visitor services per annum;
(10) cost of marketing per head of admission per annum;
(11) gross annual income as a proportion of gross annual costs (or vice versa);
(12) cost of fund-raising as a proportion of funds raised per annum;
(13) cost of loans servicing as a proportion of total costs per annum;

(14) net monthly cash flow and cumulative monthly cash flow.

There are many other measures that can be devised, but from our own practical experience those above are some of the most useful. Even in this short list, questions of scope and definition arise. For example, for many institutions, the cost of collections management is borne across a number of budget heads. What proportion of the time (and therefore costs) of the director should be allocated to each, for example? In most cases, monitoring effort should be directed at changes in values of variables year by year or month by month (e.g. gross admissions revenue) or at changes in ratios between variables year by year. The UK leisure industry tends to talk about admission numbers to attractions. But a year-on-year rise or fall in admission *numbers* does not necessarily result in a directly proportional rise or fall in *revenues*. The latter depend upon pricing policies and the performance of secondary areas such as catering and retail.

For years, the transport sector has espoused staggered working hours because of the benefits of more evenly spread capacity utilization of trains, buses, motorways etc. The commercial leisure sector has been equally interested in reducing the peakiness of the conventional annual admissions profile. The not-for-profit sector has been much slower to realize the benefits achievable. But major museums like Ironbridge Gorge Museum have recognized that at peak periods the capacity to absorb the number of people who want to visit is constrained. Not only can the quality of the visitors' experience suffer, but the marginal cost of catering for periods of peak demand can be very high: for example, the cost of additional car parking for use on ten days a year can be very considerable.

From a strategic standpoint, therefore, heritage managers should be spending at least as much time thinking about the impact of changes in cost/income ratios and cost/admissions ratios as about aggregate visitor numbers. Ratios can be monitored and changes in management procedures can be made and evaluated. Aggregate numbers may have no more than historic interest in annual reports.

In the commercial sector, *margin control* is an important management task. A 1 per cent reduction in cost of sales (e.g. from more intelligent buying, faster stock turnover, less shrinkage etc.) can have a useful positive impact on the bottom line. A 5 per cent increase in revenue from a targeted segment (for example coach parties) can be measured and evaluated against the promotional cost incurred. Today it is quite common to hear directors of museums and managers of their commercial functions comparing notes on such variables; some comparison of performance in trading activities is now possible between groups of broadly similar institutions.

Ames (1990) has developed a comprehensive schedule of financial and non-financial numerical ratios for museums which can provide practitioners with some food for thought. For example, he suggests that in the USA each full-time equivalent (FTE) person wholly engaged in fund-raising should generate \$250,000–400,000 in revenue. If nothing else, such ratios make one think, even if to some they appear preposterous or open to varied interpretation.

Non-financial numerical measures

There is a wide range of non-financial numerical performance measures that are potentially as useful as financial ones. Key measures here include:

(1) visitor numbers by type (e.g. full-price adults, child admissions, school groups) as a proportion of total annual admissions;
(2) numbers of staff (expressed as FTEs) by functional category (e.g. sales, curatorial, finance);
(3) proportion of days open per annum with attendance of less than (say) 25 per cent of peak daily attendance;
(4) proportion of staff with less than one year's service and with more than five, ten and fifteen years' service;
(5) voluntary FTE staff as a percentage of total FTE staff;
(6) repeat visits as a proportion of total visits;
(7) visitors with journey time of up to 30, 60 and 90 minutes and of more than 90 minutes to site from home, holiday base etc.;
(8) customer complaints as a percentage of letters of compliment;
(9) average number of days taken to reply to customer letters.

The strategic importance of some of these ratios cannot be underestimated. Middleton (1990), writing about the outcome of the Association of Independent Museums' far-reaching assessment of the future for their members' organizations, notes that:

> Following a pattern which has changed remarkably slowly in the last quarter of a century, most museum buildings and collections are used intensively by visitors for little more than 25 days in a year. Even on those days, usage is typically concentrated into about five hours. For at least 150 days a year, most museums have very few paying users. This currently low level of revenue earning utilization from musuem assets looks astonishingly old fashioned in 1990 and is likely to become untenable in the next decade.

Brave would be the heritage attraction that set a target of increasing average daily attendance by (say) 30 per cent against a static total volume of admissions. But thinking about such a substantial change – which might be perceived as completely impossible – should provoke managers into at least addressing the issue of under-utilization. A 100 per cent increase in days on which say 25 people are admitted in January is perfectly feasible if targeted specifically.

As the commercial world becomes increasingly sophisticated in segmenting markets and tailoring products to suit them, so the notion of differential pricing over time for many visitor attractions is slowly gathering greater acceptance. If an attraction employs staff who work an eight-hour day and opens at 10 a.m., yet in winter few visitors other than groups arrive before midday, offering a substantially discounted admission price may be a worthwhile promotional device.

The monitoring of non-financial numerical variables is thus important in allowing informed debate on complex issues of this type. Indeed, it is the only way to establish if objectives and targets are being met.

Non-numerical measures

Non-numerical measures will always be the most troublesome because of the problem of definition. Any measure that is not easily quantifiable in a form that is universally understood (e.g. money, people, a ratio) presents difficulties. But that does not mean that measurement or assessment should not be attempted.

A visitor attraction might have an objective by ensuring that each of its visitors receives a warm and friendly greeting on arrival, and that the impression visitors form of the attraction within the first three minutes of contact with it is entirely favourable. We suspect that very few attractions have set such an objective, but from our own experience, it would be a very good thing if they did! This is essentially a *quality* objective and, slowly, British Standards for quality in

the leisure sector are creeping in. The number of hotels and local authority leisure centres that have been certified as having reached the appropriate British Standard (BS 5750) is evidence of this trend.

Visitor attractions, too, now have specified standards to aspire to. The ETB has published a National Code of Practice, and attractions that wish to benefit from tourist board promotions have to be able to meet the standards it lays down.

It is also very often the case that, for larger heritage organizations at least, apparently non-numerical objectives can in practice be quantified and monitored through market research surveys of samples of visitors. For example, most visitors will readily rate their *experience* of 'friendly' staff, 'interesting' displays, or 'good' signage on a scale of one to five. Provided that such research is repeated at regular intervals (using the same questions) it will be possible for managers to monitor visitor perceptions of the experience provided, and to respond as necessary.

From our strategic standpoint in this chapter, and from the personal experience of the author as a practitioner in the UK leisure industry, the achievement of quality objectives is the most important issue in any debate on non-numerical measures.

In the remaining sections of this chapter, we present a case study to illustrate some of the issues discussed above, consider contingency planning and opportunity and threat management, and offer concluding remarks.

Case study 4.1

Mersey Ferries

Peter Middleton

The leisure consulting company of which the author is a director, L&R Leisure PLC, has worked over a three-year period in helping to revitalize a loss making but famous utility transport operation – the Mersey Ferries. The ferries carry passengers across the River Mersey between Birkenhead and Liverpool in the UK. By the late 1980s the ferries had lost their mass-market commuter customer base owing to the impact of more convenient and competitive rail and road tunnels under the Mersey. Whilst the scale of the cross-river ferry service had been reduced as demand seeped away over a long period, the ferries remained protected both by ancient statute and by the affection of Merseysiders. The vessels themselves, some 30 years old, were a major part of the Mersey Ferries appeal.

The ferries operation is part of Merseyside's public transport undertaking, Merseytravel, and in 1989–90 ran at a net revenue cost of £2.4 million with income of only £0.6 million. The search for greater economy, set against the statutory backdrop and the emotional difficulty of seeking to abolish the service, led Merseytravel to look to the leisure side of the ferries operation for increased income.

Initial appraisal confirmed the demand and opportunity for the ferries as a leisure resource but concluded that pursuing this on the back of a low-price, low-quality utility business with a public sector, public transport culture would not achieve a change in the ferries' fortunes. Whilst Merseytravel as an organization strived to achieve high quality in all of its operations, the ferries business had become worn out. Although new investment could solve this deficiency, the culture of Merseytravel, as a public transport provider, was to do with fast, efficient mass transport at a competitive price that transport users would pay. In essence this was the culture of a utility business, not one focused on a leisure experience.

The reinvestment plan thus called for:

(1) a radical change in the culture of the ferries operation to a high-quality leisure- and service-oriented one;
(2) functional separation of the business from the rest of Merseytravel;
(3) the introduction of a new core product, namely a value-added leisure trip;
(4) a new focus on income generation as opposed to cost reduction;
(5) independent financial management with monthly management accounts, effective performance monitoring and departmental budgeting.

Whilst in the past Merseytravel's Ferries Division, as it then was, had its own divisional budget, its managers were unable to do much with the information it contained because it was produced infrequently and was regarded as inaccurate. By contrast, a mass of ticket income data was laboriously collected and manually processed, but the output was not used for any purpose save statistical reporting. It was not used as part of any coherent management decision making process.

In the past, the public transport culture of the business focused on passenger trips as the prime income variable, because passenger transport businesses exist to maximize the use of their services at least cost to the consumer. The new leisure-based business, however, was less interested in counting heads and more concerned with average income per person, the secondary spend, the perceived quality and value for money of the leisure experience, and customer feedback on the products offered. Thus the monitoring became more sophisticated and detailed, more important (in the sense that managers needed to shape the product to meet their leisure customers' wants as opposed to their previous transport customer needs), and more diverse (many more variables being tracked daily, weekly and monthly).

The contingency planning needs of the business also changed. Previously, contingency implied response to negative circumstances, the most usual being coping with abnormal passenger numbers if the alternative rail service failed for any reason. With a new set of leisure-based services contingency planning started to take on a new meaning. For example, it was considered how to respond to a spell of good weather by increasing the number of trips offered, how to arrange longer trips, and how to ensure that catering stock systems were able to react to rapid increases in demand. Attention was also given to how to respond to more medium-term opportunities such as visits to Liverpool by historic vessels and liners, themselves substantial incentives to take a ferry trip, and the potential threat that could arise from a rival operator.

Tables 4.1 and *4.2* illustrate two examples of the type of monitoring reports that Mersey Ferries now produces monthly to assess performance in its catering department and for river cruises. Note that, for ease of analysis, percentages are used as well as volume/cash measures, and that cumulative performance is expressed for the year to date (YTD), i.e. a measure of how the company is doing so far. Thus from a situation in 1989 where the ferries operation was static with

Table 4.1   Mersey Ferries Catering Department: income report

	Last month (£)	Actual YTD (£)	Target YTD (£)	Variance YTD (£)
Vessels (commuter)				
Vessels (MF cruises)				
Vessels (Corporate hire)				
Woodside Café:				
General catering				
Corporate hire				
Seacombe Restaurant:				
General catering				
Corporate hire				
Total income				

Table 4.2   Mersey Ferries cruises: ticket numbers and income report

	Last month	Actual YTD	Target YTD	Variance YTD (%)
MF Cruises (no.)				
Tickets sold (no.)				
Cruise ticket income (£)				
Corporate hire cruises (no.)				
Corporate hire charter fees income (£)				
Education groups:				
Groups (no.)				
People (no.)				
Income (£)				
Social groups etc.:				
Groups (no.)				
People (no.)				
Income (£)				
Total cruise income (£)				

long-established routines that had changed little in decades, the new business, within a year of its re-launch, has found itself with vastly changed needs for monitoring (both financial and non-financial) and greatly enhanced contingency planning and response mechanisms to meet its objectives to capture as much leisure income as possible.

Managers now collect as much if not more data than before, but there are crucial differences:

(1) The data is collected more rapidly (in some cases daily, e.g. numbers of cruise customers).
(2) The data is generally stored in computer files for ease of analysis and processing when making decisions.
(3) Monitoring reports on key variables are produced at least once a month and distributed to all team members to help them assess their performance.
(4) A summary monitoring report for the Mersey Ferries Management Group allows effective debate on performance to date, provides forecasts for the rest of the year, and enables management decisions to be based on up-to-date, reliable and relevant information.

Moving from an out dated, low-price transport operator to a high-quality, premium-priced leisure business has opened up a whole new way of perceiving the role of the ferries. What was seen as a problem of excess capacity, high fixed costs and declining income has been turned into an opportunity, in the medium to longer term, to significantly reduce the annual revenue losses.

Contingency planning

'Time spent in planning is seldom wasted'. This saying is invariably true, but oh, so often ignored! The corporate planning process, if properly adopted in a heritage organization, will force a degree of planning simply to arrive at a set of realistic forward objectives and strategies. Too frequently, however, once the corporate plan has been produced or updated, it goes on the shelf until the next prompt to review it.

In a world where external threats and opportunities abound, the responsive and successful organization has to do much more than plan forward effectively. It has to frequently ask itself 'what if' questions, challenge comfortable assumptions and be prepared to take decisive action when circumstances alter.

A classic case of inadequate contingency planning was evident amongst many heritage organizations during the late 1980s when withdrawal of Manpower Services Commission and Training Agency funding left many horribly exposed, having become used to substantial numbers of free or low-cost staff or special projects or support functions. Crisis planning with your back to the wall is rarely as effective as a well planned response worked out without the pressure of immediate danger.

Challenge funding in the arts sector is an example of a stimulus to positive contingency planning. Because such schemes are based on the premise of matching funding, they stimulate in arts clients some of the 'what ifs' that responsive contingency planning seeks to achieve.

In the financial sphere, sensitivity analysis is a useful tool to inform contingency and 'what if' discussions. Modern personal computers can easily, with a simple spreadsheet program, chart the impact of altering one key variable on the bottom line performance of the business. In an organization of any size, the manual alternative to this technique is, by comparison, often too time consuming to consider.

Such spreadsheets link together cost and income data using addition, subtraction, multiplication and division formulas. This means that if one wants to look at the effect on (say) the net contribution from catering arising from a specified percentage increase or decrease in admissions, one merely changes the admissions figure (or percentage) on the spreadsheet and all the other calculations change automatically to give a revised result.

Almost every business uses computers today, and many use spreadsheets. Once one has mastered the programs, they are marvellous tools. But be warned: garbage in, garbage out. One tiny unseen error in putting a formula into the spreadsheet, and the results may look right but be completely wrong! There is much scope for smaller organizations to join together in consortia to share financial systems, as noted in Chapter 5.

Management information systems

All of the performance measures discussed in this chapter are essentially ingredients in a management information system (MIS). This, although very grand sounding, is little more than a drawing together of the measures being used at any one time for monitoring purposes. The size and complexity of the organization and the range of measures being monitored will influence how sophisticated the MIS needs to be, how frequently it reports, who sees its output (i.e. the results) and who comments upon them. More important, however, than all of this is who *acts* upon the results of monitoring activities. All the care in the world lavished on building a complex, all-embracing MIS that tells you (almost!) everything is wasted unless it is easy to understand, relevant and helps with management day by day, month by month, year by year. So a final plea is made for relevance, simplicity, evaluation of outputs and the putting in hand of appropriate action.

Conclusions

This chapter has tried to present a practical case for performance monitoring in museums and other heritage organizations. As not-for-profit public sector and trust organizations strive for greater efficiency, seek more income, try to manage their collections better, so they will need performance measures to help them. In an uncertain world full of external threats and internal pressures, the ability to manage effectively depends on assembling the best available information to help take strategic decisions; resolve problems; plan for the future; respond to crises; limit the risk of failure; and maximize the potential to realize opportunites.

If this chapter gets you thinking about the adequacy, relevance or paucity of your present performance monitoring, it has served its purpose. And remember, be very selective in what you measure.

References

AMES, P. (1990) *Breaking New Ground: Measuring Museums' Merits: Museum Management and Curatorship*, Butterworth Heinemann

AUDIT COMMISSION (1991) *The Road to Wigan Pier? Managing Local Authority Museums and Art Galleries*, HMSO

MIDDLETON, V. T. C. (1990) *New Visions for Independent Museums in the UK*, Association of Independent Museums

5

Strategic linkages and networks

Jonathan Griffin

The problems facing museums and heritage attractions in the 1990s hardly need repetition. There is common ground that many of them are having to come to terms with serious financial problems as they enter their corporate middle age. Many will have to adapt to changing market conditions to ensure their survival.

Darwinian evolution works in business as in the animal world and demands that we adapt to survive if we are not to find ourselves overtaken by others. If we guess the future wrongly then we may adapt but find ourselves moving up an evolutionary dead end. Opting out of evolution is not an option. We cannot bury our heads and hope that the world will come round to our way of thinking. It is not enough to say that people 'should' care about this or that collection. We have to work at encouraging them.

If there were a universal panacea which would guarantee that any organization could effectively survive into the next generation we would have discovered it by now. Corporate plans, mission statements, aims, objectives and targets are means to try to reduce the risks involved. All require a vision of what the future will bring.

One of the tools potentially available to assist small and large organizations in this struggle for survival is the idea of management networks or consortia. These are not instant solutions which can be applied in all cases, nor are they easily established. There may be occasions when they are appropriate, others where they are not. The concept of networks is as much an attitude of mind as a contractual or voluntary obligation. They offer one practical way in which museums and heritage attractions can share costs and obtain information and management support.

Defining a network is difficult. Like many words, 'network' has become used in too many different contexts, from personal contacts to connections between computers; from working for the company from which you have just resigned, but on a self-employed basis, to a transport system. The common factors in all these are the concepts of mutual sharing and support leading to mutual benefit. Networks are cooperative and for the most part non-hierarchical. Within a heritage context, the concept of *networking* can be defined as looking for ways in which mutual benefit can be obtained by working more closely with other people or organizations in order to share information, business opportunities or skills.

Some networks will undoubtedly involve direct financial costs; others will involve only costs of time in meetings and other liaison. All should involve an identifiable, or where possible quantifiable, benefit. The latter may be measured in time or costs saved as well as in revenue earned through collaborative action.

There are similarities between networks and using consultants, but I see a difference in the sense that a network works within the mission statement of the organization and on a longer timescale. Networks are not short term but require commitment by all parties on a basis other than straight payment. They create an environment in which both parties can retain their independent identities. They are both a tool and a way of thinking.

The terms 'network' and 'consortium' are used interchangeably in most discussions about working together. I see little difference between the two, although consortia implies a slightly greater degree of financial interdependence. One can distinguish between *voluntary networks* formed by independently owned and managed institutions, and *consortia by ownership* which are networks of attractions or sites, grouped under common ownership and management. At first sight a large body such as English Heritage or the National Trust may appear to be one large organization, quite different in kind from the fairly loose networks currently formed by independent attractions, but closer examination will show that they exhibit many of the characteristics of networks, operating under an umbrella which is the parent organization.

To reduce confusion I shall use the word *consortium* throughout this chapter to imply partners coming together for management purposes whilst retaining their independence, and *group* to imply networks under a single ownership.

Defining the problem

We all believe that our particular museum or other heritage resource and its collection should survive and be available for people to see, learn from and enjoy. We believe in our collections and their benefit to present and future generations. Economists call this *existence value*. Most collections have been assembled through enormous amounts of money and hard work by dedicated people, but we are still unable to say what they are worth. In an effort to quantify this work, economists ask how much we are prepared to pay to ensure their continued existence. This is distinct from the concept of *option value* which asks how much we are prepared to pay to take up the option to use these collections. This is usually equated as the amount we are prepared to pay for access or to visit a heritage attraction.

It is important to distinguish these two values in our long-term planning. In reviewing our financial survival we need to be clear whether we are thinking of the survival of the collection as a collection, or of the option value to visit it at its present location. In English Heritage, as will become clear, we are constantly balancing the needs of the long-term conservation of the properties in our care against the needs of today's visitors; short-term financial benefits against long-term survival; existence value against option value. These are some of the hardest decisions we have to take.

Many different suggestions have been made as to how heritage resources should or could ensure their financial survival. By separating the existence and option values of collections I hope it is possible to examine some of the problems of survival more dispassionately and avoid some of the polarization of views which has dogged the question in the past. The central question is how we should achieve our survival into the next generation.

The exact meaning of the phrase 'small is beautiful' coined by Ernest Schumacher in his eponymous book published in 1973, has been much discussed in the business world. In many activities 'small' leads to simplicity and single-mindedness which often breeds success. What the idea appears to ignore, although Schumacher did not, is the benefits which can flow from its rival idea, 'economies of scale'. For several decades this has been the watchword of manufacturing, as opposed to service, industry, although the service sector has been vigorously pursuing scale in recent years, not least influenced by the opportunities presented by the single European market.

Greater size brings greater depth of expertise which can be shared. It also often brings more attenuated decision making which can create self-defeating bureaucracies. Smallness can bring clarity but can spread expertise too thinly.

The challenge for any organization is to balance these two ideas and to achieve both the benefits of smallness and the potential economies of large size. Many businesses operating in the service industry have run into problems trying to balance large size and a high quality of service. It is a characteristic of most service industries that the actual service is provided at the lowest level of the organization. As organizations grow in size, often by acquisition, they tend to lose sight of their customers and, although they may indeed obtain economies of scale, their level of service drops.

An example of size leading to a lack of service was British Airways, who instituted their 'Putting People First' campaign in the 1980s to try to re-create the personal level of service that their customers wanted. Many other large service companies have followed their path, not always as sensitively. Perhaps this is the thought behind the subtitle to Schumacher's book: 'A Study of Economics as if People Mattered'.

Small heritage resources do not have a unique set of problems. In practice they suffer many of the same problems as large organizations. It is a splendid paradox that large organizations often adopt structures and management styles designed to replicate those of small ones. The difference is that large organizations obtain some economies of scale which can only come through a sharing of resources. They may also waste the advantages in internal procedures. In addition, large organizations frequently have problems tackling the parts while keeping the whole in view.

The benefits of being big

Being large may bring an organization a number of management and operational benefits. These can be financial, marketing or in providing information. In financial areas large organizations can invest in different parts of their business at different times or they can balance peaks in one part of the business with troughs in other parts. This helps to create a more even cash flow and enables them to sustain short-run losses or to provide finance for the redevelopment of one part of a business with revenue generated by another.

In marketing terms, large organizations can bring together different elements to make the whole more than the sum of the parts. The rise in corporate advertising in recent years suggests that overall labelling or branding is seen as an increasingly important part of large-organization marketing. Someone who buys baby clothes is likely also to need baby foods. Loyalty can be all, as is evident in the car market where manufacturers attempt to recruit us for life.

Large organizations can share technology. There may be little apparent benefit in linking companies selling frozen peas and ice-cream until one realizes that both are operating fleets of frozen food lorries visiting the same shops around the country. Then it is clear that putting them together can reduce costs in transport, sales calls and computer hardware and software.

Large concerns can benefit from a much greater flow of information. Large numbers of people sharing information within the company means that research does not need to be replicated and specialist expertise can be shared.

Of course, all these apparent benefits are only worth having if the marginal cost of having them is less than the marginal benefit. There is no point in being a large company unless you can genuinely achieve these economies of scale.

But large organizations are changing. In his book *The Age of Unreason*, Professor Charles Handy describes a trend in big companies towards what he calls 'shamrock' organizations. These contain a much smaller core of highly skilled management and operations staff with a much larger penumbra of specialist organizations, temporary associate companies and part-time operational staff contributing to the main enterprise.

There are a variety of drives behind such changes. These include trends such as a desire to slim down traditional management bureaucracies to reduce costs and improve efficiency; the wish of people to take a greater hand in the development of their own careers; greater mobility between companies; reductions in working hours; the greater importance of service industries; and shorter working weeks. Information technology and demographic changes also contribute.

What is important is that such changes are leading large companies to think in terms of management networks. They are not just a tool for small organizations. If Charles Handy is right then there will be many more small units and individuals ready, willing and able to provide services on a more flexible basis than in the past. If so, then both large and small organizations should benefit. The 1990s are the decade to grasp this change.

Networking as a concept

The question for heritage resources is how to achieve some of these large-organization benefits from their particular perspective of relative smallness. How can they transfer the technology or thinking without incurring the high costs? This is the basis of networking. Networking need not compromise the mission statement, or lead to a loss of independence; it can be carried on in the background, out of sight of the customer. Working with others does not have to mean sacrifice of either identity or control.

Networks or consortia can result from what is sometimes called 'what if', 'why not' or 'upside-down' thinking, which challenges the historical approach and asks fundamental questions about the business one is actually in. It is an old saying in management that if you ask an Englishman why something is so, he will tell you the history; if you ask an American, he will tell you the reason. Sometimes our management is caught up in our pasts and not concerned with our futures.

Networks and consortia serve many different purposes and draw on the strengths and compensate for the weaknesses of a wide variety of small organizations. To understand the nature of networks and their benefits it will be helpful to look at a number of examples before pulling together the threads running through them.

Many networks are based on the sharing of professional knowledge and are concerned with the professional pursuit of the operations in question. Typically they are professional bodies or trade associations which are often the first way in which informal networks build up between organizations.

Knowledge-based networks

There is already a wide range of formal and less formal networks linking institutions for various purposes. Many of these started by sharing knowledge, rather than workloads, and this is often the starting point to successful networking.

The work of the Museums Association and of the Association of Independent Museums (AIM) is well known in the UK. These are primarily professional associations but there are also area museum councils (AMCs), country-wide museum consultative committees, and museum forums in some areas. These area-based organizations were developed primarily for exchange of information as linkages for curatorial purposes. To date, their functional role in providing management linkages has been limited, although there are indicators that this is changing.

It may be worth looking in more detail at two other trade associations to see how they have adapted and changed over time and in response to the changing needs of their members.

The National Federation of Zoological Gardens of Great Britain and Ireland, to give it its full title, was founded in 1966. The purposes were, and remain: 'To encourage the care and welfare of wild animals in captivity and the participation in the conservation of species; and to promote the education of the public in the natural world through the medium of zoos'.

The very title of the organization demonstrates that there was no marketing objective behind its formation. No advertisement could carry a name of twelve worlds, and its initials are no snappier. The Federation is a membership organization and includes the largest and smallest zoos and bird gardens in its membership. Its activities include seminars and trips designed to raise the professional standards of animal management.

Such activities are only the outward and visible sign of membership, however. Through membership, directors and curators are able to meet and discuss common problems, and over the last ten years the Federation has expanded its activities into marketing, conservation research and inter-zoo animal exchange. All these activities have come about because people met and identified mutual problems.

Through the Federation's work on animal exchange has come the radical idea of common ownership. Some leading zoos now hold herds of hoof stock in common ownership, exchanging animals to ensure a mixed bloodline and for the common good.

The Historic Houses Association is essentially a trade association which started out as a group of independent large houses working together on joint marketing promotions and exchanging experience on visitor management. In 1975 capital transfer tax was introduced and there was talk of a wealth tax. The Association swiftly took up the cause and fought the proposals. Taxation lobbying became its prime focus. This led to concern on many other matters to do with legislation and the Association now advises members on health and safety, employee law, sale room prices, and gardens and landscape management.

The Association has set up a membership scheme for the general public which, although less heavily promoted than those of the National Trust or English Heritage, provides admission benefits to its member properties.

Few people visiting a member's property would necessarily know that the house was in membership. Indeed, many properties are only open to the public in a very limited way. The Association's activity goes on behind the scenes and is dedicated to informing and assisting members in the business of managing their houses.

The promotional focus has not been lost. Eight of the larger houses, needing a heavier weight of marketing than some of the smaller could afford, have formed the Treasure Houses Group to provide an additional layer of promotion and secure the advantages of a marketing consortium.

Business–linked networks and consortia

There is a variety of different forms of business network. They are all concerned with enhancing the business in one way or another and as such tend to be more financially focused in their approach. They include networks whose prime purpose is related to marketing activities; networks designed to achieve cost reductions, perhaps through joint purchasing; and networks designed to increase management efficiency.

I draw a distinction between these three groups of networks and those which are consortia by common ownership. Prime examples of the latter are English Heritage and the National Trust. In this section we are looking at consortia of independent organizations.

Examples of business-linked networks are all over our high streets. The most obvious are the franchises such as McDonalds, Tie Rack, Kall Kwik or Body Shop. Less obvious are service industry franchises like Dyno-Rod. The chief characteristic of franchises like these is that their operations and marketing are run to such strict formulas that to the general public they appear like any other national chain store.

From a business point of view they serve both the franchisee and franchiser. They are a successful marketing front for local entrepreneurs while also being a way of buying chain store image and marketing for a small shop or service. There is a mutual benefit defined within formal contracts. They have the three main characteristics of a business network: joint marketing, purchasing and management economies. Because it suits their operations these examples also have standardized products but this is not an essential element for all forms of consortia.

A number of independent hotel networks in the UK are marketing and purchasing consortia. The best known are Best Western and Consort Hotels. Here the members are not strictly controlled as are franchisees. Operators jealously guards their independence and reject standardization of rooms and facilities. Through the setting and assessment of standards relating to quality and service, the group creates an overall image which can be effectively communicated to hotel users in a way which would never be possible for an individual hotel. Using a common corporate logo, the hotels are grouped into price and other categories which make sense to customers.

Behind the image visible to the customer lie many other benefits. For instance the group purchasing power is harnessed to provide real returns to the local manager, not only in terms of reduced costs but in providing a quality assurance that any item purchased is of a standard likely to be acceptable to the member. A Best Western manager does not have to spend hours researching the market for hard-wearing carpets. He has a reliable and independent adviser at the end of a telephone, as part of the membership service, free of charge. His choice of whisky and kitchen equipment is available at group discount rates. The hotels pay an annual membership subscription based on size and elect a board to conduct their corporate affairs.

Simple marketing networks also exist among visitor attractions. In recent years there has been a rapid growth in the number of cooperative marketing promotions of which the Cornwall Association of Tourist Attractions (CATA) is a good example. These promotions are now widespread with a multiplicity of different core themes. There are the geographic themes which, like CATA, are based on counties, such as DATA in Devon, and ESTAA in East Sussex. There are ones based on area themes like the Shakespeare Country Association of Tourist Attractions (SCATA), or Thomas Hardy's Wessex, Captain Cook Country, James Herriot Country, Catherine Cookson Country. Then there are subject themes such as Naval Heritage or Christian Heritage of Northumberland. However one views some of the rather artificial titles, the aims of providing a unifying theme to bring the parts together in the minds of prospective customers is clear.

Like most networks there are other benefits to membership. CATA has set the pace in providing inspections to back up membership and now runs a very effective mutual inspection system to ensure that all participant attractions meet certain basic standards of visitor welcome, cleanliness and facilities. Anyone not meeting the standards may be asked to leave the group. This helps to raise standards across Cornwall and to ensure that all members can confidently promote other attractions even if they are as diverse as a museum display, a bird park, a model village or a theme park.

Among museums there are many examples of networking for curatorial purposes and hundreds of joint brochure schemes. These are the forerunners of the more integrated management consortia identified in this chapter.

The savings which flow from cooperative leaflets are obvious. Distribution and origination accounts for a large proportion of the costs of getting promotional leaflets into the right hands. Cooperative leaflets effectively share these costs and, by cross-promotion at other attractions, ensure that leaflets get into the hands of people who are looking for things to do in the area.

Do cooperative promotions work? Clifford's Tower is the remains of a small keep set on top of a grass-covered motte in the middle of York. As the oldest main surviving evidence of York Castle, it looks out over what was once the bailey and is now a large car park in the centre of the city. On one side of the car park is the York Museum; on the other is the Coppergate shopping centre which is home to the Jorvik Viking Centre.

Until 1988 English Heritage produced its own leaflet for Clifford's Tower which featured a number of other English Heritage properties. That year we decided we would do better to put the same amount of money into the York City leaflet with a few other

attractions. Attendances increased by over 30 per cent in one year.

Were we just getting the overflow from the Jorvik Viking Centre's queues? Were there more people arriving in York? We cannot say for certain; but we do know that the growth in the number of visitors at Clifford's Tower was greater in percentage and absolute terms than the growth in visitors to York, to Jorvik or the Castle Museum. We made no other change to the promotional mix for Clifford's Tower during the period.

By promoting a small property like this alongside some of the major attractions of York we were able to raise the overall awareness for the keep. No one, surely, visits York just to see Clifford's Tower, but we increased the likelihood that they would do so while there.

Other operators who have learned the benefits of consortium operation well beyond promotion are the big boating holiday organizations like Hoseasons and Blakes. Hoseasons runs one of the most sophisticated booking systems for its members, who are able to hand over all management of the booking process to Hoseasons while they concentrate on running their boatyards.

Hoseasons provides services which now go well beyond the core conception of a centralized booking service. The most obvious benefit shows itself in the resolution of a crisis. If a boat breaks down in the wrong part of the Broads the nearest Hoseasons boatyard can help the customer get going again, while it is left to the association to sort out the paperwork out of sight of the customer.

Organizations which are consortia by ownership

There is clearly a difference between the business networks described and the truly single organization, but the distinction is not as clear as might appear at first sight. This is certainly true in the field of museums and heritage attractions, many of which still appear to be, and often are, independent operators.

Organizations such as Sea Life Centres, the Tussauds Group, the Science Museum, the Historic Royal Palaces Agency, the National Trust and English Heritage are all consortia by ownership. Each handles its portfolio of attractions differently but each benefits from an internal sharing of expertise, knowledge and cost savings. Each has a group organization with a core management team to support and communicate the operations and management at individual sites.

The Science Museum owns and manages museums on sites in London, York and Bradford accounting for around 50, 25 and 25 per cent of visitors respectively. It also has storage outstations around the country as well as depositing items on loan with other collections. Although the Museum is one body, each subsidiary museum has a separate management team whose work is coordinated from the South Kensington headquarters.

In every sense the museums can be thought of as a consortium of separate establishments dedicated to science and technology, railways and photography. Each has identified, and promotes to, its own target market. There is no national advertising campaign promoting the National Museum of Science and Industry. Each museum creates its own advertising and develops its own brand identity, reminding us that it is part of the National Museum. Cross-promotion between the museums takes place as for any network. Expertise is shared where necessary. Although they effectively form a group organization with an identifiable headquarters, the individual museums have retained their separate identities. Members of the public probably think first of the National Museum of Photography rather than of the Science Museum (Photography Museum).

The idea of extended museum consortia like this is replicated by other national museums such as the Tate, the National Portrait Gallery, the Victoria and Albert and the Royal Armouries, who are all keen to develop their reserve collections and wish to spread their activities out of the capital.

The National Trust and English Heritage are consortia in much the same way as the Science Museum. Although both are group organizations in their own right, they none the less exhibit all the attributes of extended networks. Both manage and present a range of historic properties or landscapes. The portfolios of both organizations are very mixed as different acquisition policies, legacies, bequests and some disposals have added, or occasionally removed, properties. They are in no sense the homogeneous collections which might have been built up by a commercial operator with different objectives. The network nature of each organization is shown in the very strong identities that it seeks to develop for its individual properties, or products, in its portfolios. Once again large organizations try to imitate smaller ones.

Although there is a definable English Heritage image to a property, in the same way that there is for a National Trust one, both seek to bring out the essential characters of the properties in question. The style of presentation required by a burial mound in Wiltshire is very different from that required for a ruined abbey in Yorkshire or a stately home in Essex. Conversely, both organizations aim to realize the economies of scale possible by brand marketing their properties.

Only about ten of the 120 properties of English Heritage at which an admission is charged actually produce annual revenues in excess of costs. The rest operate at a net cost. Of those ten, perhaps six or seven could stand on their own feet if they were not part of English Heritage. There is a rule of thumb that suggests that unless an attraction receives over 100,000 visitors each year it will not be able to afford full-time marketing support. Six of these ten properties exceed this figure, with Stonehenge receiving nearly three times as many visitors as the next busiest.

The benefits of marketing English Heritage as a brand are much the same as for marketing Heinz as 57 varieties. I doubt if the 56th and 57th selling product justify any advertising appropriation. The range is sold on the basis of the Heinz brand and on the strength of the leading, or flagship, product. In English Heritage we gain the benefits of geographical spread and variety of historic properties as well as fulfilling our aim of opening as many of our properties to the public as possible.

The smaller properties actually make a net loss as we are constrained by our desire to make them accessible to the public. By promoting them in a limited way, we help to build the total English Heritage product and reduce wear and tear on some of the flagship sites by encouraging people to discover new, more resilient, places to visit.

Each National Trust or English Heritage property gains marketing advantages by being part of a larger corporate entity. It also gains financial benefits as investment can be moved around within the organization. American fears about overseas travel following the 1986 bombing of Libya, and following the Gulf War of 1991, led to a downturn in the number of foreign visitors both to this country and to Stonehenge. Because we had properties all over the country the financial effects on our income were not as marked as they might have been had Stonehenge stood on its own. The same is true if there is a wet and windy summer in the south-east, or if, as is happening in many parts of the country, seaside resorts suffer a long-term decline.

Both the National Trust and English Heritage are structured along regional lines. The thirteen National Trust English regions and the five English Heritage regions have small teams which bring together key managers concerned with the day-to-day management of their properties. At the centres of both organizations are core staff or professional heads who set standards and monitor performance, determine overall specialist policies and provide high levels of expertise which cannot be broken down into smaller parts. Both organizations believe in pushing responsibility for decision making as far down the line as possible so that local decisions are made locally.

Information flows freely around such an organization. This helps to inform decision making and to reduce risk. There is always a danger that a complex organization will tend to grow towards being a bureaucracy in which the benefits of size are outweighed by the costs of liaison. No one has yet suggested a model for how to avoid this but the danger is something of which we are all aware. Organizational models are changing rapidly as the use of information technology assists the process of decentralization of control.

Running organizations with devolved management but with central core expertise or professional heads is bound to produce tensions or boundary disputes. The two organizations have different ways of resolving these in detail but both rely extensively on teamwork and the development of strong corporate spirit emanating from their mission statements or aims and objectives. Much time is taken up ensuring everyone is facing the same way and striving for the same goals. For those of us working in such an environment the results can often be very stimulating, resolving strongly held professional opinions in an atmosphere of cooperation.

Consortia by ownership provide a model of organization for groups of sites with common objectives, and there is considerable scope for exploring the extension of these organizations into the independent sector to bring the benefits of consortia to smaller organizations.

The role of information in consortia

Information is the most important commodity in a successful network. Without the open exchange of information and services an efficient network cannot exist. The services should lead to cost savings but information comes in many forms. Increasingly, the problem most of us face is that of dealing with too much, rather than too little, information.

In the days before photocopiers, pocket calculators and microcomputers, the process of corporate planning was fairly straightforward. Great leaders determined a direction and, through their vision, took their organizations forward. The influence of people like Frank Pick of London Transport, General Pitt Rivers, the first Chief Inspector of what is now English Heritage, or Octavia Hill of the National Trust, lasted for many years. They have become legends within their organizations and, in today's terminology, personified the culture or mission of their respective organizations.

Then came the advance of information technology and it became possible to assemble and manipulate figures and ideas with ease. Photocopiers meant that information could be swiftly and easily shared with others who were then able to contribute their analyses and views. This can lead to the democratization of decision making. Phrases like 'top-down' and 'bottom-up' became accepted business jargon as corporate plans were developed.

This change does not mean that great leaders no longer have a role; they still exist, although we may not recognize them in their lifetimes. The key change is that information sharing has not only become possible, but opened up the debate about the future to a much wider group within an organization. Planning

may well be no more than organized common sense, but there are now more minds involved.

The process of decision making is becoming a science in itself, and some of the research techniques of science are used to help guide future strategies. Inspiration is still critical, however, as Victor Middleton states: 'Research is not a substitute for flair and imagination; it is a fertile base on which creative talents thrive.'

Research is essential but it is the practical application of the information obtained which brings the real benefits. Research cannot look over the hill to see what will happen. It cannot even see the top of the hill clearly. It mostly looks back down the hill and gives you an idea of where you are now.

Research is one of the key benefits of networking as information can be both formal and informal. Keeping up to date is one of the most difficult problems for a busy manager. How often one cries out for a digest of articles, or legislation, or news. Networking can provide information and, with the present danger of information overload, provide a filter to separate the wheat from the chaff.

Information can be essential, necessary, useful or interesting. If it is none of these then it should be filtered out. It can be comfortable and help you sleep at night or it can give you nightmares. It can help you to enhance your profitability, or can be a luxury. It can help you avoid risks or save time. It can help to disguise what is actually going on. The hardest thing of all is to put a value on information and to quantify the costs and benefits of spending time in collecting it.

With the explosion in information systems and the growth in legislation, it is becoming more and more important to subcontract the work of filtering information. How many people managing an establishment with catering facilities can truly say that they are up to date with legislation? Is the same true for health and safety? How much better to subcontract this to specialists who can filter and advise, releasing the managers' energies for the core business.

Key features of successful consortia

What can we learn about networking from these examples? How can they help a museum or heritage attraction to take advantage of this tool?

First, every consortium should have clearly articulated objectives, its own mission statement, so that participants have no doubt for what they are paying. It is no good joining a network for the fringe benefits; this will only lead to disappointment.

Networks are not free. You have to be prepared to pay to join them in both cash and time. Every week we receive another offer from someone prepared to solve all our problems provided we pay a certain amount into some magic scheme. Each week we reject these. Networks need a wholehearted commitment by both sides to make them work. They cannot be treated on a payment and collect basis. They assume, and demand, input by the participants to the information flows. The act of faith is that the benefits should more than cover these costs, but this will seldom happen instantly.

The outputs come in various forms. The key objectives will spell out the primary outputs which are expected. These may be information exchange or cost sharing. If they are information-based networks then this should lead to the filter effect producing better quality, more timely and more relevant information to assist in decision making and to ensure that you are up to date with developments. If they are service-based networks then savings should accrue in costs or responsibilities.

There is a big difference between using a network and using consultants to solve a problem. In spite of their promised contributions, how many consultants actually sign up to your mission statement? How many really show long-term commitment to your aims and objectives? Many will be ready to give you advice, but will not participate in achieving the solution; others will want to implement their proposals on a narrow base.

For the most part, consultants can support short-term need or solve specific problems. Networking among partners with a vested interest is better related to long-term need.

The key to consortia networking is to work with people or organizations who are prepared to be as committed as permanent staff to the aims of your organization. They should be able to respond on their own initiative to changes in the business or curatorial environment, not wait to be asked. You should be able to feel that they are genuinely another arm of your organization. You must trust them and have confidence in them. Consortia are permanent relationships, not affairs. Above all there must be something in it for all parties other than just a fat cheque and another scalp on a curriculum vitae or list of clients.

Often the real benefits that flow from consortia operations are those for which you do not pay: the added value. These benefits may be the icing on the cake but they are the things which make the hard grind seem worth while. In many of the examples I have given, the original purpose of the consortium has grown into other areas and the informal exchange of ideas and needs has led to a more developed web of contacts and information links. The benefits of a friendly voice, of someone trying to achieve the same ends as you, at the other end of a telephone line when you have a crisis or problem, need no emphasis.

Networks do not have to be large scale; they may be no more than an agreement to share information or jointly employ part of a person. Large size is not necessary. The examples I have quoted are of large networks only because they are more visible and familiar.

Starting in management networking

There is no one formula for creating, using and sustaining consortia and networks. They are tools of thinking and approach, not patent medicines. It all depends on some careful and clear thinking about the particular circumstances and the business you are actually in.

Knowing what business you are in is one of the key elements of corporate planning, but too often we assume that what was right for yesterday is right for tomorrow. Too often we link the existence and option values of collections as if they were single activities. There is no reason in principle why the two elements cannot be handled separately. If the fundamental objective is to retain a collection as a unity, to retain its existence, then the option value elements might be treated in any number of ways. The collection could be exhibited free, given or lent to another heritage attraction, or put in store.

We also need to understand our business in other ways. The hospital director who was quoted as looking at his new hospital and saying 'what a pity we have to fill it with patients', was not only reflecting a sensitivity to his job, but also expressing the typical reaction of a perfectionist. It took British Rail many years to realize that it was in the business of moving people around the country and not of running a permanent way with neat timetables. When it finally came to terms with the presence and importance of passengers it changed our name from passengers to customers and installed lousspeakers in trains. These measures did not make the trains run on time, but British Rail had directed its investment towards satisfying the customer.

It is easy to mock British Rail, but I sometimes wonder whether, as managers of heritage attractions, we do not have the same myopia. Are we clear about the balance between option and existence values of our resources? Do we really know who our customers are? We sometimes assume that our visitors hunger and thirst after knowledge, that they are seekers after knowledge. Yet our research may well say that the prime reason for visiting is more to do with a day out than for the specific knowledge on offer. The day out may be a cultural one where informal learning is to take place, as opposed to one which consists of some sensory thrills like a theme park, but it is nonetheless a day out. It is this way of thinking that has led to shopping being a leisure pursuit, which has, in turn, spawned mixed developments like the Metro Centre in Newcastle which is a shopping mall with a theme park attached; the theme part element promotes the retail experience, and vice versa.

Starting in consortium networking requires some lateral or upside-down thinking. It needs the ability to think of connections between unlikely partners. Commercial wisdom might, for instance, suggest that you should not share information with your biggest rivals. But for the security and survival of both organizations this might be the best thing. You might both gain.

Again, you might look for other people with a similar problem. Technology transfer suggests that one should actively look outside the immediate nexus. A shop, a squash club and a heritage resource may have much more in common than appears at first sight; each can learn from the other. Sharing management skills may well produce new solutions and added value without compromising any of the partners. Joint purchasing, accountancy and staff training spring instantly to mind as starting points for such a network.

If Charles Handy is right about the changes taking place in large companies, then they will be looking for a much greater use of subcontracting in future. The subcontractors will have big-company skills and knowledge and will be looking for more opportunities to help others. They could be service providers to networks. Some traditional consultancy firms are moving directly into heritage operations as stake holders as well as management partners.

The heritage resource environment

It would be impossible to come up with a list of all the possible combinations for networks. The really creative networks will open new doors, working with partners outside the heritage business. What follows is a list of some possibilities.

Knowledge based

Skilled curatorial staff
It is already fairly common to share expertise with another heritage resource. This process is supported by the area museum councils and the Museums and Galleries Commission. Perhaps you have expertise that others need and vice versa.

Cleaning staff
Both skilled and unskilled cleaning could be provided by staff working for other organizations. The development of compulsory competitive tendering for local authorities in the UK has opened up this sphere.

Education staff
Skilled education staff may be shared with a neighbouring attraction, whether commercial or charitable. Joint staffing may lead to increased visitor numbers as educators can create mixed programmes to benefit both parties.

Travelling exhibitions
Sharing of resources, as some Area Museum Councils have shown, can be very effectively achieved by the creation of travelling exhibitions. Items which are not normally on display can be placed alongside objects from other collections to create a new exhibition which costs each party less than might otherwise be the case. It also adds value to both collections and makes a fresh heritage statement.

Purchasing and cost sharing

There are many opportunities for cost sharing through joint buying. Many of these will be most successful when they involve participants who are not heritage resources as they will help to bring commercial skills and high-volume demands.

Insurance, print, shop stock and catering items can all be bought effectively through extended networks of one form or another. Often heritage resources are prestige accounts and suppliers are keen to quote them as customers or to capture their business. This brings an added strength to the negotiations and benefits a heritage network.

Marketing

Market research
Research is typically expensive but is eminently suited to sharing. Information on visitors in a local area, on attitudes and intentions, can be provided by a network of interests working together. Costs can be shared equally between participants, related to the level of visitors at the participating attractions, or on the basis of buying questions in a survey.

Research sharing
Research information can also be exchanged free of charge on an 'honest broker' system with all sides contributing their data and receiving back in proportion to what they give. Some such networks maintain confidentiality and accumulate the information so that participants can obtain an overview without knowing the performance of the parts. In others the data are revealed openly to the participants.

Research analogues
In English Heritage we cannot afford to carry out research amongst the visitors to all our properties. Instead we carry out research at a carefully selected range of properties and use the results from the selected properties as analogues for others.

Advisory services
Advertising, public relations, design and marketing companies frequently specialize in particular fields and are keen to develop their expertise. Networks of non-competing attractions might profitably consider approaching professional advice companies together.

The agencies will welcome the savings in their research time that will flow from such relationships.

Cooperative promotions and referrals between partner sites
These are now becoming more and more the norm for the marketing of visitor attractions in this country. They are natural networks and provide a range of added-value services through the information flowing between members.

It is not always easy to decide whether to join a promotion based on the immediate locality or one based on the wider locality. One is often offered the opportunity to participate in promotions that draw together attractions in an area such as a district, a country or a tourist board region. Cost and the likely geographical size of the target market will help to resolve this.

Image generation
It is a strange economic principle that shops selling particular goods often do well when they are close to other shops selling the same things. By being together, the area gains authority which brings in additional customers. This is part of the thinking behind the growth in the number of shopping centres. Every other shop in Tottenham Court Road in London seems to be selling electronic goods, and the road therefore has a reputation as a good place to buy such goods.

Being close to, or promoting alongside, another heritage resource can have the same image benefits. Ironbridge actually consists of several museums each with its own specialist identity but, by working together under the Ironbridge image, the whole becomes more than the sum of the parts and Ironbridge gains authority as a place to visit.

Management efficiency

Cost savings can be obtained with relative ease in some administrative areas. Most heritage resources already buy in many of these services on a part-time basis but there is scope for extending these contracts to a wider client list and so creating a small network.

Statistics and ratios
An accountant who does the books for two attractions is professionally barred from sharing any knowledge gained from either party with the other. But, if the two organizations agree, then the data can be shared openly, leading to more information being available to each. This can lead to the creation of comparative ratios which can be used to help assess performance.

Financial systems
In the same way, it is possible to develop common financial systems which, if computers are available, can be run on the same machine, saving costs.

Bookings services
As an overlap with marketing activities, there is no reason why networks cannot run common booking services for groups and visitors, saving the need to provide backup staff support, ensuring a high standard of customer care and creating the opportunity for referrals and cross-promotion.

Distribution
The cooperative promotion schemes all achieve savings in print and distribution costs by creating a single leaflet. If budgets cannot be stretched to inclusion in a cooperative leaflet there is no reason why piggy-back mailing cannot lead to cost savings. Joining with a non-competitive organization to undertake a mailed promotion and sharing a list of addresses may save up to half the costs of a mailing. Some commercial companies may even be prepared to accept inserts at no charge as a form of sponsorship.

Professional advisory services
Other aspects of management services can be distinct from marketing ones. Catering and health and safety are fields full of traps for the unwary, with legislation changing all the time. Rather than buy in these services from a single specialist it will often be more cost-effective and efficient to buy them in from someone who is also supplying other heritage resources or attractions. They will only have to work out the implications of legislation once and can then advise all members of the network.

Crisis management
A Best Western manager faced with a chef who has suddenly gone sick just before a major event does not have to resort to the nearest agency chef who may know nothing of the hotel business. A phone call away is a colleague with an experienced under-chef who may relish the chance to stand in for a short period. The network provides the environment for such exchanges to take place.

Career development and training
Management courses are excellent ways of learning new management skills, but often the major benefit comes from looking objectively at the job one does on a daily basis from a different perspective. Equally valuable is the objectivity that comes from short-term secondments as both sides gain. The exchange of key staff for extended periods can lead to benefits for all. Networks can and should be providing such exchanges to help people grow and understand more about the jobs they do.

Other networks

Trade associations
As noted earlier, these exist in almost every sphere and provide networks of information, assistance and mutual

support. Often one can get more out of an evening chatting with others working in the same field than in any number of magazines, newsletters and management courses. It is of course important to pick the associations to suit the key purposes of the business.

The same informal contact can be obtained without the need for an association. By creating a local network, a group of attractions in an area can set up a quarterly meeting to talk over local problems, feeding in ideas from different disciplines and perspectives.

Additional revenue

Additional revenue may also be achieved through networking. Managers of one heritage resource may have a particular expertise which is useful to others. External consultancies can bring in much needed income and create new contacts which can benefit the resource itself.

One such network brings together a museum, a polytechnic and a college of further education, each contributing complementary skills. Together they are able to offer a comprehensive service to others.

Conclusions

The most challenging impetus to forming consortia comes from the realization that many heritage resources will never be able to survive alone, no matter how hard they try, and the acceptance that the future lies in some form of amalgamation. It is not axiomatic that amalgamation means the sacrifice of independence. A professional manager may be able to manage two or more heritage resources quite independently of each other, reporting to different groups of trustees.

A single management and administrative unit might manage all the option value requirements for several resources, leaving the existence or curatorial aspects to professional staff. Conversely, a single curatorial unit might manage the resources with separate business management units. The organizations will be united in the common aim of ensuring that their resources survive into the next generation. It is up to the business unit to help achieve this.

This is not a pipe dream. Consortia networks like this already exist. The horse-racing industry provides some good examples in the management of racecourses. Some of the largest and smallest racecourses are managed by the same teams, although the courses themselves have separate clerks of the course, market themselves separately and have separate boards of directors. At the extreme, one man is general manager at one racecourse, clerk of the course at two others, and a director at a third. Each racecourse is in separate ownership and has different long-term objectives. They range from one of the largest to one of the smallest. The team's skills and knowledge are available to all in the interest of enlarging the racing business.

Despite all the above it would be wrong to assume that networking is some new science of management. In many areas we are already well down the path and these examples will not be new to readers. It is the need to extend their use, especially for management purposes, which is important. Networking is not a universal panacea which will magically provide survival for a heritage resource. It is a way of thinking which assumes that there is more to be gained from working together, often with unexpected partners, than is lost by sharing information and resources, and making the initial commitment of time. The benefits of singleness are given up to the higher ideal and for the added benefits which flow from working together.

In some cases full integration of small organizations into a consortium by ownership will be the best answer, but competition must be retained if the resulting organization is to survive. Competitive pressure encourages efforts towards higher quality and lower prices. Provided these do not lead to extinction then this competition can do nothing but good in a business sense. Networks provide one way of spreading this risk by bringing in other expertise.

The future will depend on managers taking the initiative at local levels. Consortia networks cannot be imposed, only self-created and sustained. The opportunity is there if we are to ensure the survival of the resources in our care.

SECTION TWO

CONSERVING THE NATURAL AND MAN-MADE HERITAGE

6

Conserving the natural and man-made heritage

Michael Stratton and Graham Taylor

Section Two brings together chapters covering the conservation of the entire spectrum of what is now loosely termed 'our heritage', ranging from sites of ecological value to fine landscapes, historic buildings, archaeological sites and objects of cultural, scientific, industrial and artistic merit. Each aspect could be considered in a comparable way, stressing that in each case the heritage manager needs to identify the resource, understand how it was created and used, choose appropriate conservation techniques and liaise with appropriate bodies. While various disciplines often share common approaches, the expertise and technology involved, and the legislative and administrative contexts, are often very distinct. The approach of this section, therefore, is to focus on particular issues in the conservation of the natural and man-made heritage, highlighting contrasts in terms of administrative framework, policy objectives and methodology.

Several themes run through the contributions. All too often heritage managers have had to work within legal and administrative frameworks inherited from the Victorian period or the early twentieth century. For example, the systems of listed buildings and scheduled ancient monuments were not designed to reflect broader concerns for protecting urban and rural landscapes as the environment for local communities. Again, a growing interest in maritime archaeology has had to work with legislation more concerned with navigation and salvage than protecting historic vessels and their contents.

There has been a great flowering of public interest in our history and environment. This has led to a climate of support from within local and national government, generating a rapid expansion in the number of professionals, more money for conservation and a series of legislative and policy developments to tip the balance in favour of conserving our heritage. The social climate now demands that the public has access to the natural and man-made heritage. Those involved in farming or nature conservation have to accept that the countryside is a living and working environment for a whole community. Graham Taylor (Chapter 11) charts the evolution of conservation of the natural environment from a preoccupation with very special sites and the containment of urban and industrial development towards the integration of conservation and rural land use and development.

Political and ethical issues have to be taken on board even in such areas as recording and conservation. Short-term policy decisions, based on narrow academic criteria, have to be replaced by longer-term strategies that can be justified to political masters and to be public. The necessity to stand back and think through what should be recorded and preserved is forcing professionals to work from first principles. Such a theoretical approach is presented by Jonathan Drake (Chapter 9) in relation to artefacts and by Anthony Streeten (Chapter 12) in outlining the rationale behind the Monuments Protection Programme. Alan Fishwick (Chapter 7) describes how recording and defining the natural environment now underpins management decisions and how information technology assists in the process.

The defining of policy objectives is made more complex by the fact that traditional compartmentalizations in terms of academic discipline, distinguishing between archaeology, historic buildings and decorative art, and between museums and other institutions, can no longer be entirely adhered to. It has to be accepted that objects can be quite justifiably looked at in different sorts of ways by different professionals and different groups of the public. At the same time these groups also approach the heritage with different aims and there is a need for conflicting demands to be reconciled through conscious decision making, such as between the requirements of conservation and display for important and vulnerable objects. Suzanne Keene (Chapter 17) highlights the potential of a systems approach for resolving such problems in relation to museum conservation.

7

Defining and recording the resource: the natural environment

Alan Fishwick

Naturalness

The geology and broad sweep of the physical land-scape apart, little if any of Britain's surface can be claimed to be natural in the sense of unmodified by the activities of humans or their livestock. Even in the remoter uplands it is unusual to walk far without encountering obvious signs of use in tracks, walls and fences, while the tutored eye may also be able to discern the legacy of ancient cairns and cultivation marks. There are however areas of the countryside, both large and small, where, despite the long history of occupation, the vegetation is composed of native species, has a composition and structure regarded as similar to natural (unmodified) types, and supports populations of native animals. These areas are widely accepted as *semi-natural* and form the principal focus for nature conservation in Britain.

The concept of naturalness also features prominently in landscape conservation, and the term *natural beauty* has achieved common currency, in particular, through its use in national park and countryside legislation. In this context artefacts such as walls, hedges and verna-cular buildings, together with the more intensively managed land and semi-natural areas, are all accepted as contributing to the natural landscape.

The effective conservation of the landscape, its wild-life and natural resources has to be achieved as part of the social and economic development of any area. A mix of statutory processes and formal designations is applied, and a variety of incentives and voluntary efforts are used. Policies have to be shaped and justi-fied, and decisions have to be made about priorities and allocations of resources. Good information is essential. The conservation interest has to be identi-fied, described and classified and its importance assessed. An understanding of the processes and changes taking place in the natural environment is needed also, to ensure appropriate protection and management, and to assess the environmental impacts of development and other changes.

All these considerations apply at a wide range of scales and levels of significance, from the small site or feature (uncultivated field corner, hedgerow, pond) regarded by the county wildlife trust's member as of local importance, to the occurrence of a rare species or hundreds of square kilometres of beautiful countryside judged by very different criteria to be of national or international importance. An integrating methodology is required to bring some semblance of order to this diverse area of study, and to provide a means of relat-ing apparently disparate survey data to ensure appro-priate use is made of existing and new information. Systems thinking provides one way forward.

Systems thinking

The geographical work of Chorley and Kennedy (1971) provides a useful reference point: systems can be identified at all scales of magnitude and degrees of complexity, and the world can be viewed as compris-ing sets of interlinked systems which are nested into each other to form a systems hierarchy. Landscape and wildlife habitats can be viewed as a set of systems, defined at different scales in relation to different cri-teria, but interlocking to form a related whole, with current processes and changes superimposed on the evidence of the past.

The objectives of any particular study will determine the survey methodology. When one is evaluating the natural environment, subdivisions ought logically to rest on physical parameters. Some do, for example studies within river catchments; for others, such as the assessment of populations of migratory birds, it is essential to distinguish the geographic ranges of differ-ent populations of the same species to enable reason-able conclusions to be drawn. However, the reality of statutory responsibilities and decision making means that very often administrative boundaries and functions determine the purpose, extent and content of any study.

Figure 7.1 provides an example of how a systems framework can be applied to draw out the potential interrelationships between different surveys that have been undertaken in Cumbria. They relate to a mix of physically and administratively defined units. In the following sections these examples are placed in the context of some of the main national approaches to recording and evaluating components of the natural environment. The discussion starts with species, and moves on to consider vegetation communities and the selection of sites of special scientific interest. Approaches to mapping habitats and features of the landscape are then introduced before the scope of landscape assessment is briefly described. The penultimate section outlines the land classification system developed by the Institute of Terrestrial Ecology which has attempted to integrate landscape and ecological surveys at regional and national levels. The concluding section identifies current changes which are likely to influence the recording of the natural environment and the availability of data in the future.

The recording of species

Surveys to compile maps of the distribution of plants throughout Britain began in earnest in the 1950s through the efforts of the Botanical Society of the British Isles, and provided the foundation for the National Biological Records Centre and the network of county recorders. The work resulted in the publication of the *Atlas of the British Flora* (Perring and Walters, 1962) and subsequent systematic recording and comparative studies underpin the *Red Data Book* lists of rare and threatened species (Perring and Farrel, 1983). Botanical recording is well established in Cumbria (Case study 7.1) and similar approaches to data collection and handling are established in many counties. At a national level a coordinating Commision for Biological Recording has been established to oversee the operation of the national network of recorders and maintain liaison with users; an Environmental Information Centre has been set up at the Institute of Ecology's station at Monk's Wood; and the context for the information is being developed through a national map of land cover (Wyatt, 1992).

Distribution maps of any species are vital to establish assessment criteria, and to determine the status of species identified in any local study. Information about changes in populations will identify those which are particularly vulnerable. Nationally rare species of vascular plant are defined as those occurring in 1–15 national grid squares of side 10 kilometres and nationally scarce species are those occurring in 16–100 such grid squares. The *Red Data Book* uses these species data to list extinct, endangered, vulnerable and rare species. The lists in turn provided information to construct the Schedule of Protected Plants in the Wildlife and Countryside Act 1981.

Recording at national and wider scales is not confined to vascular plants. It is important not to overlook components of the natural environment such as fish (Maitland, 1985). The systematic monitoring of birds is well established. For example, annual counts of wildfowl and waders are organized by the Wildfowl and Wetlands Trust and the British Trust for Ornithology. Criteria have been agreed through international conventions, such as the Ramsar Convention on the protection of wetlands, against which to assess site records. For example, any site regularly holding 20,000 waterfowl, or 1 per cent of the individuals in a population of one species or subspecies, is considered internationally important (Stroud *et al.*, 1990). Other criteria embodied in the convention cover representative or unique habitats and assemblages of rare, vulnerable or endangered species.

The 1 per cent threshold is also applied to national populations to assess importance of sites. The Royal Society for the Protection of Birds and the Nature Conservancy Council (now reorganized) have developed the '*Red Data Book* approach' for birds in Britain (Bibby *et al.*, 1989). They have identified 117 species as being most in need of conservation attention on the basis of criteria such as international significance, rarity and vulnerability to threats, particularly habitat loss. Local surveys of birds and breeding sites (Cumbria Naturalists Union, 1991; Lake District National Park Authority, 1990) contribute to the stock of national knowledge, while the RSPB is converting its research findings on the interrelationships between species and habitats into species action plans which will be used to determine priorities for the organization's future work (Porter *et al.*, 1990).

In the Lake District, counts of wintering wildfowl undertaken for national surveys (which are published annually, e.g. Kirby *et al.*, 1991), the occurrence of rare fish, systematic surveys of aquatic plants (Stokoe, 1983) and lakeshore habitats, and changes in water chemistry (Carrick and Sutcliffe, 1982), all contributed to an assessment of the conservation importance of the lakes undertaken by the National Park Authority to formulate strategic policies for their conservation and recreational use (Lake District National Park Authority, 1986a). Wherever possible national criteria for particular conservation interests were used in the evaluation, and regard was paid to the way in which high landscape and wildlife conservation values converged in semi-natural lake marginal habitats.

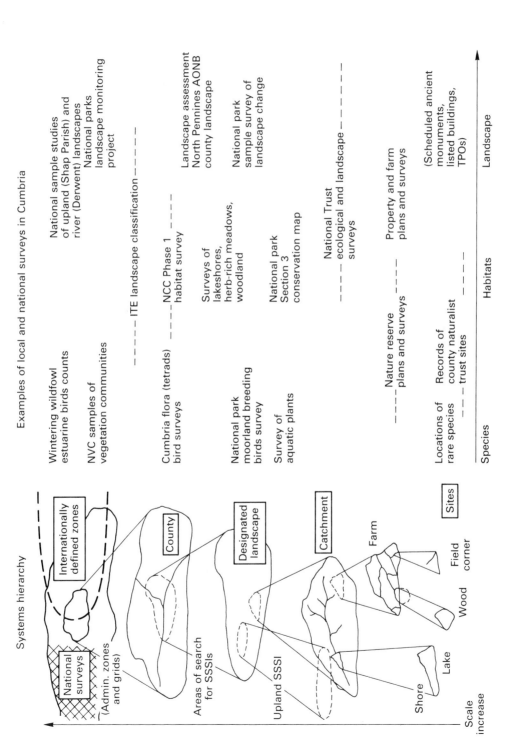

Figure 7.1 Systems framework: relations between surveys in Cumbria

The classification of vegetation communities

Numerous attempts have been made to extract objectively defined vegetation communities from the apparent kaleidescopic variety of semi-natural habitats. The lack of consensus on an overall classification of the different vegetation communities presented problems to the then Natural Conservancy Council when selecting habitats for its review of nature conservation in the 1970s, and led to the commissioning of a major study to define a national vegetation classification (NVC). The first three volumes of this work, which cover major natural, semi-natural and artificial habitats, have been published (Rodwell, 1991a; 1991b; 1992).

To establish the classification, samples were obtained from homogeneous stands of vegetation, either directly in the field or from existing studies. In the field work, species lists for vascular plants, bryophytes and macrolichens were recorded from quadrats and linear strips (10–30 m) where necessary (e.g. hedgerows, streams, ditches), and abundance was assessed using the Domin scale (an·assessment of percentage cover). Quadrat size depended on structural variations in plant communities, but was generally 2×2 m for short herbaceous vegetation and dwarf shrub heaths; 4×4 m for tall open herb communities, shrub heaths and low woodland field layers; 10×10 m for species-poor or very tall herbaceous plants, woodland field layer and dense scrub; and 50×50 m for sparse scrub woodland canopy and understorey. Standard recording sheets are used which also require basic data on slope, aspect, altitude and soils. A variety of statistical and mathematical techniques were used to examine the relationships between samples and define the communities which make up the classification.

Over 30,000 samples were used to develop the NVC and these have been coded into a computerized database. The Unit of Vegetation Science at Lancaster University is now developing a national vegetation database to which will be added new survey data as they are made available. It will be possible to search the database to retrieve samples by specifying one or more of a variety of attributes: grid reference, district council area, physical attributes, or plant species. A computer programme (MATCH) has been developed which performs a statistical comparison between new samples of vegetation and profiles of all the NVC communities and subcommunities. This ranks the ten closest matches to the new samples and lists the species under- or overrepresented in the samples compared with the most similar amongst the NVC vegetation. The Unit of Vegetation Science is developing vocational training in the survey methodology, data processing and applications of the NVC.

The classification consists of more than 250 communities. The field methods provide a standardized approach to detailed vegetation recording, and the classification offers a means of describing vegetation communities. The approach does however require a considerable amount of botanical expertise and time, and consequently may be inappropriate or impractical for some studies. Undoubtedly the relationships between the NVC and other methodologies will be the subject of investigation, as will methods for matching new samples with existing classes. Some already well established methodologies are likely to be retained for some purposes.

Woodlands provide an example of a habitat which has been recorded from a number of different perspectives. The Peterkin classification for woodlands was derived from a record of tree and shrub species and the structural types (standards, coppice, shrubs, saplings) in which the species occurred, together with a list of vascular plants and information on soils (Peterkin, 1981). Twelve stand groups were identified on the presence and absence of thirteen tree and shrubs species, and subtypes within the groups were defined to accommodate samples which did not fit, using the full range of composition and site characteristics.

Kirby (1982) has illustrated how Peterkin's stand type methodology can be applied to the mapping, comparison and evaluation of woodland types in the Duddon Valley. The Lake District National Park Authority (1986b) has also used the method as a basis for an ecological description of woodlands which it owns, and a tool for determining and guiding management policies. In this context the Peterkin classification has the advantage that many of the characteristic tree groupings can be readily recognized by staff working on the ground.

Historical maps have been used to compile county inventories of ancient semi-natural woodland (Kirby *et al.*, 1984; Whitbread, 1985), and evidence of the longevity of woodland cover also may be deciphered from botanical evidence. For example the presence of small-leaved lime (*Tilia cordata*) is regarded as a good indicator of ancient woodland sites in the Lake District (Piggott and Huntley, 1980), while particular interest has been attched to the oakwoods found at high altitude (Yapp, 1953). The huge volume of documentary evidence that exists in estate and other records is also capable of shedding light on the influence of management on the present pattern and structure of woodland communities (Satchel, 1989) and in so doing provides a context for future management. The problem is the amount of time to research, collate and interpret such information.

The identification of special sites for wildlife conservation

The recording and evaluation of species and habitats is fundamental to wildlife conservation. The identification and scheduling of sites representing all major types of natural and semi-natural habitats have been a cornerstone of wildlife conservation policy in Britain, and are paralleled by a comparable approach to the documentation and designation of geological and physiographic features. The publication of *A Natural Conservation Review* (Ratcliffe, 1977) represented a milestone in elucidating the science and subjectivity involved in the assessment of importance for nature conservation and the selection of sites of special scientific interest (SSSIs).

The approach followed in the *Review* has been consolidated in *Guidelines for the Selection of Biological SSSIs* (Nature Conservancy Council, 1989) which provides an invaluable account of the rationale, operational methods and criteria adopted (principally naturalness, diversity, typicalness and size, supplemented by provisions for rare species and for animal assemblages such as sea-bird colonies). It is a basic principle of site selection that the series of SSSIs should contain adequate representation of the country-wide variation in natural and semi-natural ecosystem types. The pragmatic solution to achieve this has been to adopt administrative 'areas of search' (Cumbria is divided into three such areas) and to select the best examples of particular habitats in these areas.

It is common practice for local wildlife trusts and local authorities to identify sites of wildlife importance which are not of sufficient quality to be scheduled as SSSIs, but which are considered to have a local significance. This practice is also being advocated for geological sites through the concept of regionally important geological/geomorphological sites (RIGs: Nature Conservancy Council, 1990a). In this case the selection of sites is related to factors such as value for schools and further study, historical value, and aesthetic value.

The degree to which standardized criteria have been developed to identify 'local' biological sites varies from county to county, but generally they will be judged important for one or more of the criteria used to identify SSSIs. The rationale behind the identification of these sites is important if their recognition is to influence decisions on development and land use change. The Local Government Conservation Initiative (Collis and Tyldesley, 1993) is playing an important role in promoting standards for the recording, evaluation and selection of these non-statutory 'sites of importance for nature conservation' to ensure the case for their conservation can be properly justified.

Mapping wildlife habitats in the wider countryside

The view has become prevalent that safeguarding key sites does not satisfy the total requirements for wildlife conservation or meet public aspirations, and that there

is a need to conserve a much greater part of the national capital of wildlife which occurs in the wider countryside. Survey and recording has to take account of the substantially larger area to be covered. Cumbria was one of the areas in which the then Nature Conservancy Council developed its Phase 1 survey to meet this need (Nature Conservancy Council, 1990b) and the Lake District is one of five pilot areas chosen by English Nature to develop its 'natural areas' concept. This aims to characterize the different nature conservation interests and potential in distinctive tracts of the English countryside (English Nature, 1993).

The objective of the Phase 1 survey of Cumbria was to provide a complete and up-to-date record of wildlife habitats in the county, including information on their extent, location and conservation value (Kelly and Perry, 1990). This was achieved by comprehensive field mapping at the 1:10,000 scale of all units of land use and semi-natural habitat greater than 0.25 ha. The information is presented on colour-coded maps supported by brief descriptive notes summarizing the interest of particular sites. The survey has been supplied to the National Park Authority and is used, together with more detailed surveys of specific habitats such as herb-rich meadows, to help assess planning applications and agricultural and forestry proposals.

The mapping system was developed through the practical application of broad land use and ecological definitions in the field, and was preferred to the interpretation of aerial photographs because more account can be taken of the plant and animal species present and the ecological characteristics that cannot be detected through conventional air-photo interpretation. One of the advantages of the approach is that it is not too demanding in terms of ecological knowledge, but it is labour intensive and the Cumbria survey depended to a considerable extent on government job creation schemes for its implementation. Because the maps are drawn manually, measurement of habitats is also laborious, but it is possible to reproduce and store the maps fairly cheaply by copying them using colour microfiche. Some authorities (e.g. Wigan Metropolitan Borough Council) have digitized their Phase 1 surveys and consequently handle the maps on computer.

Mapping landscape features and change

There are broad similarities between the Phase 1 surveys described above and work in the national parks to map landscape features. The National Parks Landscape Monitoring Project completed by Silsoe College (Countryside Commission, 1991) is the first comprehensive survey of the landscapes of the parks and assessment of how they have changed in the last fifteen years. The study provides an example of the use of air-photo interpretation to quantify the extent of land cover types and a selection of point and linear features. A spatial analysis software package (SPANS) running on a personal computer was used for much of the data processing, and enabled results to be expressed in both tabular and map form at a variety of different scales; for example the parks as a whole, individual parks, and parishes.

In the Lake District, panchromatic aerial photographs between 1:18,000 and 1:25,000 in scale from the early 1970s and late 1980s with backup colour for the 1980s were used for the project. The categories interpreted and compared for the two dates included nine linear features, mainly types of field boundaries; four point features, such as groups of trees and ponds; and 38 land cover types, distinguishing areas of moor and heath, woodlands, agro-pastoral land, water and wetland, rock and coast, and developed land. The classification was developed from an earlier national sample study of landscape change (Hunting Surveys and Consultants, 1986) and reflected the practical constraints of the use of aerial photographs. Data on point and linear features are expressed per kilometre square, while land cover types have been digitized from 1:10,000 map overlays.

Neither the condition nor the quality of landscape features can be assessed from this type and scale of photography, and the ecological content of the definitions used falls short of those employed in the Phase 1 field surveys. However, although the labour demands for the interpretation of aerial photographs and the data transfer to computer are high (21 person months for interpretation and 6 person months for data input to the computer for the Lake District: C. Bird, personal communication), those for the former are substantially less than are required for field survey, and the computerization enables huge gains in the ease of data processing and handling.

The landscape survey of the national parks provides basic information on the distribution and extent of landscape features and cover types. The results pose questions about the impact and desirability of the changes that have occurred. The information can be used to assist policy development, or to provide the context for more detailed studies such as the sample surveys of the condition of boundaries and fields which have been undertaken in the Lake District (Lake District National Park Authority, 1989). It provides a baseline against which to monitor change, but with additional information and appropriate parameters the modelling capabilities of SPANS can be used to explore future landscapes and to try to assess the most likely consequences of new pressures for change.

The demands for information about the distribution of particular land cover types and for up-to-date information to monitor the way they are changing has led to the increasing use of satellite imagery as a data source. The distribution of heather in the Lake District recorded as part of a national survey (Bunce, 1988) accords reasonably well with other surveys, such as those undertaken to meet the requirements of Section 3 of the Wildlife and Countryside (Amendment) Act 1985 (Lake District National Park Authority, 1988), but other studies undertaken in the area (Chisholm and Pope, 1988; Taylor, 1989) have identified a number of limitations in applying current images and technologies. These include the difficulties of obtaining cloud-free images, the less well defined land parcels in the uplands and the difficulty of discriminating between some land cover types. Some classifications are undertaken using automated techniques; in others the image is assessed visually in much the same way as the visual interpretation of an aerial photograph. The first digital land cover map of Great Britain, created from Landsat satellite images from the period 1988-91 was launched in 1993 (Fuller and Groom, 1993). It comprises a basic set of 25 cover types such as inland water, urban and arable land and semi-natural vegetation, and the data is being used in a variety of environmental studies.

Landscape assessment

Surveys of the component features of the landscape may form part of the studies of the character and quality of an area. Landscape assessment is the umbrella term which has come to encompass the survey and research activities associated with the description, analysis, classification and evaluation of landscape. Attempts to classify landscape at the county scale gained impetus in Britain in the early 1970s through the preparation of the then new structure plans. A great deal of effort was applied to develop objective methods of classification, and arguments centred on the appropriate survey unit (the national 1 km grid square figuring prominently) and the relative worth of public and professional opinion. Current practice has been reviewed for the Countryside Commission by the Landscape Research Group (1988).

The scope of such work is considerable, and in Cumbria ranges from academic debate on the interrelationships between art, literature and the appreciation of landscape, as exemplified by the symposium and exhibition on 'The Discovery of the Lake District' at the V&A in 1984 (Countryside Commission and Victoria and Albert Museum, 1986), to pragmatic plans for individual farms such as were prepared for Dobcross Hall Farm near Carlisle (Countryside Commission, 1984) as part of the Demonstration Farms Project (Cobham *et al.*, 1984). National studies on moorland change based on cartographic evidence (Parry *et al.*, 1982), on changing upland landscapes (Allaby, 1983) and on the landscapes along rivers (Travers and Morgan, 1987) have also included parts of the county.

In recent years the impact of changes in agriculture has been a focus of debate, initially because the pressures for modernization threatened valued habitats and features of the landscape. Attention is currently concentrated on the impacts of measures to reduce production and on schemes to support environmentally sensitive farming in the interests of landscape conservation. Specific approaches, along the lines of work on the Demonstration Farms Project, have been developed to identify the importance of landscape and wildlife features at the farm scale and form a basis for action (e.g. Farming, Forestry and Wildlife Advisory Group for Scotland, 1990), while the Ministry of Agriculture has had to develop landscape mapping and monitoring systems for evaluating the effectiveness of the designation of environmentally sensitive areas (Ministry of Agriculture, Fisheries and Food, 1991). In the Lake District the National Trust has taken a lead in elucidating the historic farmed landscapes in its care to underpin future management decisions (Case study 7.2).

The Countryside Commission, which has a remit to conserve the natural beauty of the countryside and to improve and extend opportunities for its enjoyment by the public, has published the approach that it takes to landscape assessment in three key areas of public policy: the selection of special areas and the determination of their boundaries (e.g. areas of outstanding natural beauty, inheritance tax exemption cases); investment decisions (e.g. for grant-aided projects and land acquisitions); and environmental impact analysis (Countryside Commission, 1987). The approach is demonstrated by the Land Use Consultants' (1991) study of the North Pennines Area of Outstanding Natural Beauty and it is also being used by Cumbria County Council to define and describe landscape areas of 'county importance' for the review of the structure plan (Cumbria County Council, 1992).

The North Pennines landscape is described by reference to the forces shaping the landscape, both historically and at present, and in terms of the special features that are typical of the area and the way the landscape has been perceived over the years. The area is divided into a number of recognizable landscape types which are strongly related to topography: moorland ridges, summits and plateau, and the components of the Dales. The special character and quality of the area which make it of national importance are drawn out of this analysis. This last aspect of the work depends on the individual merits of the area, and in that respect there are differences with say the assessment of sites of special scientific interest which can draw on national databases for their justification.

The Countryside Commission have, however, piloted an experimental classification scheme in the South West region, intended as a precursor to a 'new map of England', which will identify and describe areas of landscape with a coherent identity

and character (Countryside Commission, 1994). The Commission is working with English Nature to ensure work on 'natural areas' and the 'new map' is complimentary.

Land classification

National surveys of topography, geology and soils provide a wealth of specialized information on the natural resources of Britain. The Institute of Terrestrial Ecology (ITE) has developed a more general approach to land classification as a basis for national and regional surveys of rural land use changes, landscape and ecology (Bunce and Heal, 1984).

Work in Cumbria (Bunce and Smith, 1978) was part of ITE's early investigations into the application of multivariate methods of regional ecological surveys. Attributes from Ordnance Survey maps, together with information on the geology, were recorded for a sample of 1 km grid squares, and these were differentiated into sixteen classes. The main attributes distinguishing between classes were then used to classify other grid squares. The resulting distribution maps related well to recognizable geomorphological features but suggested other patterns not readily apparent from direct observation. Surveys of vegetation within each of the land classes showed a strong association with the land classes which gave support to the use of the land classification, for example, to structure sampling frameworks for more detailed investigations.

This methodology has not been pursued by local authorities in Cumbria, probably because other sources of information have been available and much decision making and policy formulation have been done at a more detailed scale of resolution. In the different circumstances of the Highlands of Scotland, the Regional Council has applied it to provide a stratified sample frame for more detailed surveys (e.g. amenity woodland survey) and modelling work, as well as to form the basis of a 1 km square database for environmental features in the region (Claridge, 1988). At a national level ITE has applied a wider range of parameters than were used in its Cumbria study (climatic, topographic, human artefacts from Ordnance Suvey maps, geology, soils) and the ensuing classification has underpinned an impressive range of applications (Institute of Terrestrial Ecology, 1991a), including work on landscape (Barr *et al.*, 1986) and wide-ranging assessments of the ecological consequences of land use changes (Institute of Terrestrial Ecology, 1991b).

ITE's countryside survey, 1990, combines detailed recording of species and landscape features with land cover maps derived from satellite imagery. The data collected, which includes freshwater macro-invertebrate assemblages, forms the initial building blocks for a computerized database for each 1 km square in

Great Britain. This Countryside Information System has been designed to integrate the countryside survey data with other national datasets to improve access to information for both policy and research functions (*Barr et al.*, 1993).

Conclusions

The surveys considered here demonstrate that there are significant overlaps between surveys of landscape and wildlife. They also draw attention to the way in which the natural heritage and the cultural heritage are often inseparable, both in concept and in reality. A number of current developments appear likely to cause a further evaluation of traditional demarcations between different disciplines, and to bring about greater integration of information from the natural and cultural environments. Initiatives are also being taken to try to standardize survey methodologies, and this work is likely to gain in momentum as European environmental legislation requires more comparisons across national borders.

At the institutional level, the merging of the countryside and wildlife conservation agencies in Wales and Scotland is likely to bring some rationalization of survey work, the integration of existing datasets, and an examination of the spatial and functional relationships between statutory designations for different purposes. At the policy level the government has reacted to public concern about the environment with *This Common Inheritance* (Department of the Environment, 1990) and in enacting European Community legislation giving public rights of access to environmental information held by public authorities (Department of the Environment, 1992a). Local authorities are attempting environmental audits (Lancashire County Council, 1991), while the Natural Environment Research Council has launched the Environment Change Network, a multi-agency research programme to establish a national network of sites (including Moorhouse National Nature Reserve in Cumbria) to provide long-term monitoring of a wide range of physical, chemical and biological variables. In the national parks the government (Department of the Environment, 1992b) has responded to the recommendations of the Edwards Committee (Edwards, 1991) and proposed that the purposes of the parks should refer explicitly to wildlife and cultural heritage, and that parks should develop environmental inventories to enable the state of the parks to be monitored to assist policy making.

Developments in information technology will assist the process of data integration and the interrogation of different data sets to tackle specific problems. Cheap and powerful computers, the availability of proprietary software to create flexible relational databases, and the development of more specialized packages for digital mapping and spatial analysis are providing considerable potential to store, manipulate and use environmental data. Portable computers will be used more frequently for recording data in the field. The work reviewed here provides examples of the way that individual projects have begun to use these capabilities.

There are, however, significant difficulties to overcome to make full use of these facilities. Much survey work is still labour intensive and very costly. A great deal of existing environmental data is stored on paper maps and the costs of transferring these into digital formats that can be handled by computer are also considerable. The quality of data is very variable, and the different scales at which data are assembled means that their integration is far from straightforward. Inter-relationships between point, gridded and continuously mapped data can be complex to unravel, and are complicated by the fact that different surveys use different definitions for habitats, land cover types and landscape features. Even when data are already stored on computer there may be some problems in transferring data from one system to another because of the different formats that have been used in compiling the information for particular systems. Equally, public agencies and research institutes are expected to generate more income, and data are a potential source of revenue. In consequence significant additional costs are likely to be incurred in obtaining and maintaining datasets through the payment of licence and copyright fees, and the running of specialized computer systems.

There seems little doubt that these wider issues of the integration of conservation objectives and environmental data will begin to feature more prominently in a literature that, despite the work of ITE, has previously generally concentrated on survey methodologies in separate disciplines. But finally it should not be forgotten that, in the context of heritage management, recording and evaluation are a means to an end, and the real concern is how data can be used effectively to influence decisions about the future.

Useful addresses

Biological Records Centre, Environmental Information Centre, Institute of Terrestrial Ecology, Monks Wood Experimental Station, Abbots Ripton, Huntingdon, Cambridgeshire, PE17 2LS

The Environmental Change Network (ECN), Institute of Terrestrial Ecology, Merlewood Research Station, Grange-over-Sands, Cumbria, LA11 6JU

Unit of Vegetation Science, Institute of Environmental and Biological Sciences, Lancaster University, Lancaster, LA1 4YQ

The Royal Society for Nature Conservation, The Green, Nettleham, Lincoln, LN2 2NR

The British Trust for Ornithology, The Nunnery, Nunnery Place, Thetford, Norfolk, IP24 2PU

The Wildlife and Wetlands Trust, Slimbridge, Gloucester, GL2 7BT

References

ALLABY, M. (1983) *The Changing Uplands*, CCP 153, Countryside Commission

BARR, C., BENEFIELD, C., BUNCE, R., RIDSDALE, H. and WHITTAKER, M. (1986) *Landscape Changes in Britain*, Institute of Terrestrial Ecology

BARR, C. J., BUNCE, R. G., CLARKE, R. T., FULLER, R. M., FURSE, M. T., GILLESPIE, M. K., GROOM, G. B., HALLAM, C. J., HORNUNG, M., HOWARD, D. C., and NESS, M. J. (1993) *Countryside Survey 1900 Main Report*, Countryside 1990 series, vol. 2, Institute of Freshwater Ecology and Institute of Terrestrial Ecology

BIBBY, C., HOUSDEN, S., PORTER, R., and thomas, g.. (1989) 'Bird conservation strategy', in J. Cadbury and M. Everett (eds), *RSPB Conservation review* no. 3, royal Society for the Protection of Birds

BUNCE, R. G. (1988) *The Distribution and Status of Heather in England and Wales*, report to the Department of the Environment. Institute of Terrestrial Ecology, Grange-over-Sands

BUNCE, R. G. and HEAL, O. W. (1984) 'Landscape evaluation and the impact of changing land use on the rural environment: the problem and approach', in R. Roberts and T. Roberts (eds), *Planning and Ecology*, Chapman and Hall, London

BUNCE, R. G. and SMITH, R. S. (1978) *An Ecological Survey of Cumbria*, Cumbria County Council and Lake District Special Planning Board

CARRICK, T. R. AND SUTCLIFFE, D. W. (1982) *Concentrations of Major Ions in Lakes and Tarns of the English Lake District (1953–78)*, Occasional Publication no. 16, Freshwater Biological Association, Windermere

CHISHOLM, N. W. and POPE, B. A. (1988) 'Remote sensing inputs into a vegetation database on an upland national park', in Curtis (ed.), *Operational and Classification Problems in the Use of Remote Sensing for Monitoring and Inventory of Projected Landscapes*, Proceedings of the EARSel Workshop, Directorate General for Science Research and Development EC.

CHORLEY, R. J. and KENNEDY, B. A. (1971) *Physical Geography: a Systems Approach*, Prentice-Hall, London

CLARIDGE, C. J. (1988) 'The approach adopted by Highland Regional Council', in R. G. H. Bunce and C. J. Barr (eds), *Information for Forward Planning*, ITE Symposium no. 21, Institute of Terrestrial Ecology

COBHAM, R., MATTHEWS, R., MCNAB, A., STEPHENSON, E. and SLATTER, M. (1984) *Agricultural Landscapes: Demonstration Farms*, CCP 170, Countryside Commission

COLLIS, I. and TYLDESLEY, D. (1993) *Natural Assets; Non-statutory sites of importance for nature conservation*, The Local Government Nature Conservation Initiative

COUNTRYSIDE COMMISSION (1984) *Demonstration Farms Project, Dobcross Hall: Farming with Conservation*, CCP 178

COUNTRYSIDE COMMISSION (1987) *Landscape Assessment: a Countryside Commission Approach*, CCD 18

COUNTRYSIDE COMMISSION (1991) *Landscape Change in the National Parks*, CCP 359

COUNTRYSIDE COMMISION (1993) *Landscape Assessment Guidance*, CCP 423

COUNTRYSIDE COMMISSION (1994) *The New Map of England: A celebration of the south west landscape*, CCP 444 and *The New Map of England: A directory of regional landscapes - results of a pilot study in south western England*, CCP 445

COUNTRYSIDE COMMISSION AND VICTORIA AND ALBERT MUSEUM (1986) *The Lake District: a Sort of National Property*, papers presented to a symposium at the Victoria and Albert Museum, CCP 194

CUMBRIA COUNTY COUNCIL (1992) *Assesment of County Landscapes*, Technical Paper no. 4, in support of the Cumbria and Lake District Joint Structure Plan

CUMBRIA NATURALISTS UNION (1991) *Birds in Cumbria*

DEPARTMENT OF THE ENVIRONMENT (1990) *This Common Inheritance*, HMSO, London

DEPARTMENT OF THE ENVIRONMENT (1992a) *Freedom of Access to Information on the Environment: Guidance on the Implementation of the Environmental Information Regulations 1992 in Great Britain*

DEPARTMENT OF THE ENVIRONMENT (1992b) *Fit for the Future: a Statement by the Government on Policies for the National Parks*

EDWARDS, R. (1991) *Fit for the Future: Report of the National Parks Review Panel*, CCP 334, Countryside Commission

ENGLISH NATURE (1993) *Natural Areas: Setting nature conservation objectives*, a consultation paper, English Nature, Peterborough

FARMING, FORESTRY AND WILDLIFE ADVISORY GROUP FOR SCOTLAND (1990) *Conservation on Farms: Case Studies of Good Practice in Scotland*, Countryside Commission for Scotland and Nature Conservancy Council

FULLER, R. and GROOM, G. (1993) *The Land Cover Map of Great Britain*, GIS Europe, October

HUNTING SURVEYS AND CONSULTANTS (1986) *Monitoring Landscape Change*, Department of the Environment and the Countryside Commission

INSTITUTE OF TERRESTRIAL ECOLOGY (1991a) *Bibliography: Publications Arising from Studies Using the ITE Land Classification*

INSTITUTE OF TERRESTRIAL ECOLOGY (1991b) *Bibliography: Reports Arising from the Project 'Ecological Consequences of Land Use Change (ECOLUC)'*

KELLY, P. G. and PERRY, K. A. (1990) *Wildlife Habitat in Cumbria*, Research and Survey in Nature Conservation, no. 30, Nature Conservancy Council

KIRBY, K.J. (1982) 'The broadleaved woodlands of the Duddon Valley (Cumbria)', *Quarterly Journal of Forestry* 76, 83–91

KIRBY, J. S., FERNS, J. R., WATERS, R. J. and PRYS-JONES, R. P. (1991) *Wildfowl and Wader Counts 1990–1991*, The Wildfowl and Wetlands Trust

KIRBY, K. J., PETERKEN, G. F., SPENCER, J. W. and WALKER, G. J. (1984) *Inventories of Ancient Semi-Natural Woodland*, Focus on Nature Conservation, no. 6, Nature Conservancy Council

LAKE DISTRICT NATIONAL PARK AUTHORITY (1986a) 'The Lakes and Tarns: Their Conservation and Recreational Use', *The Lake District National Park Plan*, Chapter 15

LAKE DISTRICT NATIONAL PARK AUTHORITY (1986b) *Rusland Woods: Management Plan*, unpublished report

LAKE DISTRICT NATIONAL PARK AUTHORITY (1988) 'The Section 3 conservation map', *The Lake District National Park Plan*, Chapter 9 (revised)

LAKE DISTRICT NATIONAL PARK AUTHORITY (1989) *A Sample Survey of Recent Changes in the Enclosed Landscapes of the National Park*, unpublished report

LAKE DISTRICT NATIONAL PARK AUTHORITY (1990) *A Survey of Moorland Breeding Birds in the Lake District National Park*, unpublished report

LANCASHIRE COUNTY COUNCIL (1991) *Lancashire: A Green Audit*

LANDSCAPE RESEARCH GROUP (1988) *A Review of Recent Practice and Research in Landscape Assessment*, CCD 25, Countryside Commission

LAND USE CONSULTANTS (1991) *The North Pennines Landscape*, CCP 318, Countryside Commission

MINISTRY OF AGRICULTURE, FISHERIES AND FOOD (1991) *The Pennine Dales Environmentally Sensitive Area. Report of Monitoring 1991*, ESA Monitoring Report no. 1

MAITLAND, P. S. (1985) 'Criteria for the selection of important sites for freshwater fish in the British Isles', *Biological Conservation*, **31**, 335–353

NATURE CONSERVANCY COUNCIL (1989) *Guidelines for the Selection of Biological SSSIs*

NATURE CONSERVANCY COUNCIL (1990a) *Earth Science Conservation in Great Britain: a Strategy*

NATURE CONSERVANCY COUNCIL (1990b) *Handbook for Phase 1 Habitat Survey: a Technique for Environmental Audit*, field manual

PARRY, M. L., BRUCE, A., and HARKNESS, C. (1982) *Changes in the Extent of Moorland and Roughland in the Lake District National Park*, Surveys of Moorland and Roughland Change no. 10, Department of Geography, University of Birmingham

PERRING, F. H. and FARREL, L. (1983) *British Red Data Books. Vol. 1: Vascular Plants*, 2nd edn, Royal Society for Nature Conservation, Lincoln

PERRING. F. H. and WALTERS, S. M. (1962) *Atlas of the British Flora*, Nelson, London

PETERKIN, G. (1981) *Woodland Conservation and Management*, Chapman and Hall

PIGGOTT, C. D. and HUNTLEY, J. P. (1980) 'Factors controlling the distribution of *Tilia cordata* at the northern limits of its geographical range. II: History in north-west England. *New Phytologist*, **84**, 145–164

PORTER, R., BIBBY, C., ELLIOT, G., HOUSDEN, S., THOMAS. G. and WILLIAMS, G. (1990) 'Species action plans for birds', in J. Cadbury (ed.), *RSPB Conservation Review*, no. 4

RATCLIFFE, D. (ed.) (1977) *A Nature Conservation Review*, 2 vols, Cambridge University Press, Cambridge

RODWELL, J. S., (ed.) (1991a) *British Plant Communities. Vol. 1: Woodlands and Scrub*, Cambridge University Press, Cambridge

RODWELL, J. S. (ed.) (1991b) *British Plant Communities. Vol. 2: Mires and Heaths*, Cambridge University Press, Cambridge

RODWELL, J. S. (ed.) (1992) *British Plant Communities. Vol. 3: Grassland and Montane Vegetation*, Cambridge University Press, Cambridge

SATCHEL, J. E. (1989) 'The history of woodlands in Cumbria', in J. K. Adamson (ed.), *Cumbrian Woodlands: Past, Present and Future*, Institute of Terrestrial Ecology Symposium no. 25, HMSO, London

STOKOE, R. (1983) *Aquatic Macrophytes in the Tarns and Lakes of Cumbria*, Occasional Publication no. 18, Freshwater Biological Association

STROUD, D. A., MUDGE, G. P. and PIENKOWSKI, M. W. (1990) *Protecting Internationally Important Bird Sites: a Review of the EEC Special Protection Area Network in Great Britain*, Nature Conservancy Council

TAYLOR, J. (1989) *Evaluation of Spot Satellite Images for Measurement of Landscape Features*, unpublished report to the Countryside Commission, Cranfield Institute of Technology, Bedford

TRAVERS MORGAN (1987) *Changing River Landscapes: a Study of River Valley Landscapes*, CCP 238, Countryside Commission

WHITBREAD, A. M. (1985) *Cumbria Inventory of Ancient Woodland* (provisional), unpublished report, Nature Conservancy Council

WYATT, B. K. (1992) 'Resources for documenting changes in species and habitats', in P. T. Harding (ed.), *Biological Recording of Changes in British Wildlife*, Institute of Terrestrial Ecology Symposium no. 26, HMSO, London

YAPP, W. B. (1953) 'The high-level woods of the English Lake District', *North Western Naturalist*, **24**, 188–207, 370–383

Case study 7.1

The Cumbria flora

Geoffrey Halliday

Work on a new flora of vascular plants for Cumbria began in 1974 in response to the need for information for conservation purposes in the newly formed county. Recording, coordinated by Dr G. Halliday at Lancaster University, has been based on the tetrad (2 × 2 km square) and each of the 1760 units has been visited at least twice. A checklist of the known flora was published (Halliday, 1978) to assist the volunteer recorders, some 30 of whom have been active at any one time. Given the scale of the survey there is inevitably some unevenness in the depth of coverage because of the distribution and interests of the volunteer recorders. The records are, nevertheless, an invaluable source of information on the occurrence and distribution of species in the county and they also contribute to national surveys. For example bog rosemary (*Andromeda polifolia*) has been shown to be relatively widespread in Cumbria, and as a result can no longer be considered a national rarity.

It is possible to search the database in a flexible way. Species can be listed that occur along, say, the corridor for a proposed pipeline or road. A mapping package developed by Malloch (1988) assists effective presentation of data and can also be used as an aid to interpretation. *Figure 7.2* illustrates the distribution of *Minuartia verna* (spring sandwort), an upland species mainly associated with the limestones of the Pennines and north of Morecambe Bay, but also occurring on the more base-rich rocks of the eastern Lake District fells. *Figure 7.3* shows the way in which combinations of species can be mapped to identify the likely distribution of particular habitats. In this case upland basic flushes are indicated by the occurrence of at least five of the following species: *Carex dioica* (dioecious sedge), *Carex hostiana* (tawny sedge), *Carex lepidocarpa* (long-stalked yellow sedge), *Eleocharis pauciflora* (spike rush), *Eriophorum latifolium* (broad-leaved cotton grass), *Euphrasia scottica* (slender Scottish eyebright), *Pinguicula vulgaris* (common butterwort) and *Selaginella selaginoides* (lesser clubmoss).

Reference

HALLIDAY, G. (1978) *Flowering Plants and Ferns of Cumbria: a Checklist for Westmorland, Furness and Cumberland*, Occasional Paper no. 4, Centre for North West Regional Studies, University of Lancaster

MALLOCH, A. J. C. (1988) *Vespan II: A computer package to handle and analyse multivariate species data and handle and display species distribution data*, University of Lancaster

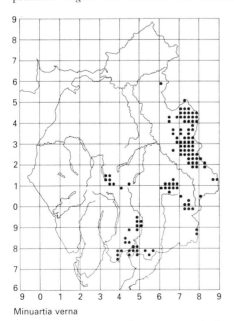

Minuartia verna

Figure 7.2 Distribution of *Minuartia verna* in Cumbria

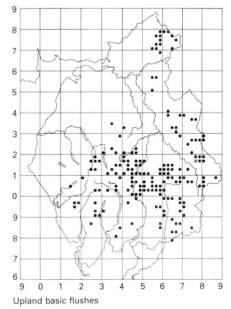

Upland basic flushes

Figure 7.3 Distribution of upland basic flushes in Cumbria indicated by species combinations

Case study 7.2

Deciphering historic handscapes in Great Langdale

Susan Denyer

The National Trust has embarked on a detailed appraisal of the historic landscapes in its charge in the Lake District. Great Langdale was the first valley to be surveyed with the intention of providing land managers with information to assess the implications of changes and to guide their decisions. The approach is akin to that which might be taken to record an archaeological site or historic building. Two surveyors and an archivist undertook the work, which has yielded a new understanding of the way that the pattern of landscape elements – the walls, the farmsteads, the hedgerows and the trees – has evolved.

The field work recorded the present-day elements of the landscape in great detail. Walls were examined metre by metre for construction styles and features such as rabbit smots (traps) and hogg holes (to allow the passage of sheep). Cultivation marks, every path and hedge, and the foundations of buildings long since disappeared have been mapped. But the understanding of the landscape has come from integrating the field evidence with information gleaned from interviews with the farming community, old paintings, prints and photographs, as well as documentary evidence.

A grant of land by William de Lancaster to Conishead Priory in about 1216 refers to 'the inclosed land of Great Langden' and provides evidence of a single enclosure of the valley floor, later known as the 'ring garth'. Field patterns can be related to the ring garth (*Figure 7.4*). It is thought that most cultivation in the Middle Ages was within this wall on the valley floor, and irregular fields around farms are probably medieval. Intakes on the fellside outside the wall were rare before the sixteenth century, but in the seventeenth century became common. Some remains of abandoned farmsteads can be linked to the amalgamation of small tenements in the eighteenth century, and many buildings on remote pastures were peat huts where fuel cut on the fells was stored to dry before being taken to the farmstead (Hall, 1991).

Reference

HALL, M. (1991) 'Every last hogg hole', *Country Life*, May

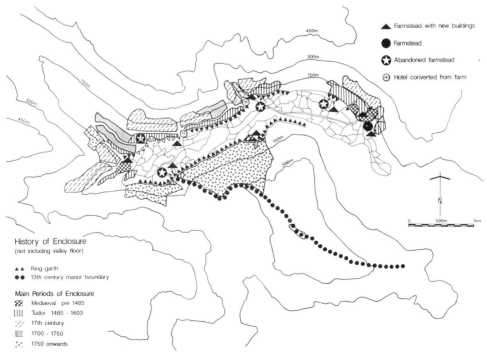

Figure 7.4 Field patterns related to medieval ring garth in Langdale

Case study 7.3

The development of the Hadrian's Wall National Trail

Andrew Coleman

The concept of a 130 km national trail along Hadrian's Wall had been brewing over a considerable number of years, in response in part to the needs and aspirations of visitors to 'walk the Wall', and in part to the desire of the many interested organizations and affected land-owners to provide a safe and properly managed long-distance footpath along the course of Hadrian's Wall. At present access on foot is restricted to 60 per cent of the Wall, links between the main fort sites are poor, and walkers are forced to walk many miles along dangerous and busy roads. This in turn has resulted in a diminished experience for visitors and has led to some problems of trespass and unmanaged access.

The seed for the trail was born from a number of detailed studies of the Wall corridor (*DART Report*, 1976; *Strategy for Hadrian's Wall*, 1984), and more fully developed as a feasibility study by the Countryside Commission in 1985. Following this and a review of its policies on national trails, the Commission decided to undertake a detailed and rigorous study to plan the development of the national trail through the appointment of a project officer in 1989, and to submit these findings in a report to the Secretary of State for his approval.

The project presented a quite unique opportunity and challenge: how to create a new trail along an internationally recognized ancient monument, one of Britain's finest archaeological and historical features, designated a world heritage site in 1987 (one of only fourteen in the UK), whilst at the same time recognizing the overriding need to safeguard and conserve the resource – the monument itself (the linear frontier and earthworks and their associated features) and the landscape through which it passes. Clearly there was a need for a carefully planned proactive approach that would enable the Commission to assess and analyse the potential impact of the proposed national trail on the archaeological heritage of Hadrian's Wall. This would mean finding a way to fully understand the nature of the resource. Complementary to this was the need to provide accurate and reliable information about the physical condition of the proposed route, the characteristics of the terrain and existing facilities across the route, and the costs of its creation and long-term management which would constitute an essential part of the Commission's statutory report to the Secretary of State.

A three-stage approach was decided upon, dividing the research work into clearly identifiable areas which would best utilize the countryside skills and tools developed within the Commission, whilst bringing in specialist archaeological advice from English Heritage, the Royal Commission on the Historic Monuments of England and independent consultants.

Stage 1 comprised a detailed field survey undertaken in 1991 by two trained graduates. First they were to establish the exact position of the route, its physical condition, and the character of the terrain over which the trail was proposed. This was called a base-line condition survey and used an established methodology previous developed by the Commission which had been used successfully on other national trails and was adapted and modified to suit the special needs of this case. This involved surveying and then mapping the alignment of the proposed route on 1:10,000 OS base maps and recording detailed information about the route using pro formas, backed up by notes and photographs. The route was divided into varying sections of between 20 and 500 metres, for which detailed information about the terrain, its land use, soil type, slope, drainage etc., was recorded, and along which the vegetation and soil loss of the path surface were carefully measured. Information was also gathered wherever a crossing point was met, e.g. field boundary, road or river, and the condition and need for new gates, stiles, bridges etc. were similarly recorded. All recordings were uniquely identified and cross-referenced to the maps.

Once completed, the mass of survey data for the 130 km route was carefully transferred and stored on to a computer database for ease of retrieval and handling to draw out the overall summary figures needed. These results gave for the first time a strategic picture across the whole route of what creating the route would entail, showing its overall condition, highlighting the most vulnerable areas, and providing a shopping list of work required to establish the route on the ground. Importantly it also provided a baseline – an accurate record of the present condition against which change could be measured over time.

Stage 2 involved a desk study to determine the exact position of some 1814 archaeological features identified by the Royal Commission on the Historic Monuments of England to achieve their precise location in relation to the line of the proposed route. This was achieved using large-scale 1:2500 OS maps for the entire route.

At this point, it became evident that there was a lack of accurate information about the condition and sensitivity of archaeological features where these were already crossed by public footpaths along the line of the Wall, particularly through the most visited central section of Northumberland National Park. Reapirs to the archaeology normally only occur after significant visible evidence of damage is found, and inevitably mean that management action is normally both expensive and reactive. English Heritage, the principal custodians of the Wall, understood the opportunity and need for such information, which would enable them to improve monitoring of archaeological features and act speedily upon changes before they become serious. Thus a partnership was entered into between English Heritage and the Countryside Commission to jointly fund the third stage of the research and share its findings.

For stage 3, then, a joint brief was developed and the research was undertaken by Environmental Resources Ltd to draw upon their archaeological expertise. The study was underpinned by the information already obtained from the baseline condition survey, the detailed map records on the proximity of known archaeological features, and a range of visitor statistics across the Wall corridor. The brief was to draw together the information gathered to provide a complete picture of the potential interaction between the proposed route, the archaeology and the likely users of the trail. A model was developed that classified archaeological features in relation to their sensitivity to visitor pressure, taking into account the intrinsic vulnerability of each archaeological feature, the landform characteristics and the visitor distribution patterns, both existing and forecast. An additional weighting was deliberately given to the archaeological component, reflecting the importance of the monument and the need to safeguard its integrity.

The results of the model enabled the two organizations to locate and identify the distribution of key sensitive archaeological sites across the route and respond to a range of management options. These included major or minor rerouting of the trail, protection of archeological features using a range of appropriate surface treatments, and specified routine monitoring. The single most important management prescription would be a commitment to a long-term management strategy to provide adequate maintenance over the years ahead.

In conclusion, the research formed a critical part in the planning and evolution of the Hadrian's Wall National Trail, shaping and developing the route and setting the standards for its creation on the ground. The results of both the condition survey and the impact assessment study clearly demonstrate the suitability of the route to be developed as a national trail, and provide the foundations for informed and responsible management in the future.

References

DARTINGTON AMENITY RESEARCH TRUST (1976) *The Hadrian's Wall strategy for conservation and visitor services*, Countryside Commission, CCP 98
HADRIAN'S WALL CONSULTATIVE COMMITTEE (1984) *The strategy for Hadrian's Wall*, Countryside Commission
COUNTRYSIDE COMMISSION (1992 unpub.) *Hadrian's Wall proposed National Trail baseline condition survey*
NORTHERN ENVIRONMENTAL CONSULTANTS LTD (1992 unpub.) *Assessment of the impact on archaeology of the proposed Hadrian's Wall National Trail*, Countryside Commission

Case study 7.4

Hawkstone Park, Shropshire

Paul Walshe

When the merits of a particular candidate for promotion to general were put to Napoleon Bonaparte, he would say: 'Yes, but is he lucky?' Napoleon knew that luck favoured the well prepared. Hawkstone has been lucky. After a century of neglect and decay it was bought as the adjunct to a hotel by an owner who hadn't realized that in buying a hotel he had bought what had been the finest late eighteenth century 'sublime' landscape in the country. It has now been restored and opened to the public. Hawkstone was lucky but it had been well prepared for its luck.

Hawkstone, a seat in North Shropshire, was purchased in 1556 by Sir Rowland Hill, merchant, philanthropist and the first Protestant Lord Mayor of London. It remained in the Hill family – alternately Rowlands and Richards – for 350 years. Its golden years were those of the eighteenth century and the early part of the nineteenth century, when a new hall was built; the River Hawk, a 3 km long lake, was constructed under the direction of the landscape designer William Emes; and the red standstone cliffs rising suddenly and dramatically out of the North Shropshire plain were developed for their picturesque and sublime qualities. Miles of paths and steps cut into the sandstone took you on long walks to explore these hills linked by stone and rustic wooden bridges.

On your route you visited the Raven's Shelf and the Awful Precipice, climbed up the Deep Cleft and entered the dark Tunnel to feel you way to the Grotto, sat on the Rustic Sofa ('made of various sorts of curious moss') or rested a while in the Vis-à-Vis before travelling on to see the Scene in Switzerland to gaze on the Ship's Beak, the Fox's Knob and other extraordinary rock shapes. Refreshed at the Gingerbread Hall, you set out on the Walk to Renard's Banqueting House, entered St Francis's Cave, saw the White Tower and the Obelisk with the statue of Sir Rowland Hill at the top, and eagerly approached the Hermit's Summer Residence anxious to converse with the hermit. At first hermits were employed, but so many were lost to the seductive charms of the local milkmaids or to the 'damps' that an automaton was installed. The voice and the movement of the hermit were provided by the guides. Visitors were 'amazed' at the personal knowledge the venerable hermit had of them. Fazed by the hermit, you walked on to visit the Vineyard, the Tower Glen, the Glen, the Urn, the turrets of the medieval Red Castle, the Giant's Well, the Stone Lion in his steel barred den, the Menagerie and the Greenhouse. Sated, you sat and gazed on the

Grand Valley, the Gulp, the Elysian Hill and the Scene in Otaheite. Exhausted, you returned to the Hawkstone Inn which had been built in the late eighteenth century to accommodate the visitors who flocked to take in these delights, the 'antiquities' of Hawkstone.

However, when the third Viscount Hill inherited in 1875 his father's spending had so undermined the family's finances that in 1894 the estate was declared bankrupt, and the contents of the hall were sold by public auction. Over the next 30 years the hall, the inn and the land – parcelled up into 22 ownerships – were sold. The 'antiquities', neglected and vandalized, crumbled and sank under the weight of enveloping rhododendrons. The human cries of fright, alarm and wonder gave way to the staccato calling of jackdaws nesting in the ruins of the White Tower and the Red Castle.

Lord Gibson, then Chairman of the National Trust, came across this slumbering masterpiece in the early 1980s and wrote to Jennifer Jenkins, then Chair of the Historic Buildings Council, asking if any help could be offered to the owners of the park so that a future could be secured for this extraordinary landscape. Derek Sherborne, the HBC's Chief Inspector, and myself, then the Countryside Commission's Landscape Architect, visited Hawkstone and between us we offered generous grants towards its restoration. However, we quickly realized that simply to offer grant-aid was not enough. The implications of restoration needed to be known by the owners and local people. The means of managing the restored landscape and ensuring its economic viability needed to be known. The park was in a number of ownerships and a mechanism for coordinating a restoration programme did not exist. The owners were businessmen, farmers, hoteliers and, at Hawkstone Hall, a religious order running a pastoral centre. They had neither the time nor the skills to put together a practical restoration package.

But we believed we could provide the time and the skills necessary to help local people find the way to breathe new life into this landscape so that it would continue to live for them and for their children. In December 1985 the Commission called a meeting of owners, local people and representatives of local people at Hawkstone Hall under the chairmanship of Jeremy Benson, Commissioner of English Heritage. At that meeting it was agreed that consultants should be appointed to produce a practical, historically authentic and realistic restoration plan and that, very importantly, they should work closely with, indeed work to, the owners and local people. An advisory committee of owners, local people and their representatives was set up at that meeting. Presentations were made to this committee throughout the management plan production process – presentations on the surveys, the restoration options, the access options and the draft and final costed proposals.

The cost of the consultants was born equally by Shropshire County Council and the Countryside Commission with no strings attached. We had no guarantees and expected no guarantees that anything constructive would come out of the exercise. We simply believed that Hawkstone was such an important landscape that the effort to try to restore it and open it once again to the public had to be made. Importantly we didn't believe that the consultants' job ended with the completion of an agreed restoration and management plan. They were employed to attempt to see the project through to implementation, and to this end the restoration and management plan was seen and attractively presented as a sales document. The property at the heart of the restoration was the Hawkstone Park Hotel. We convinced its owners to accept the restoration proposals and persuaded them to lease the historic landscape to a local trust we would set up. They sold the hotel to Pavilion Leisure. We persuaded them to join us in setting up a charitable trust for the historic landscape. We took them, representatives of the committee and the consultants to Liverpool to make a slide presentation to the Charity Commissioners. No one had ever taken the trouble to go to Liverpool and make a presentation to them before.

They were enchanted by Hawkstone, and ours became one of the fastest charities ever created.

In the September that the Hawkstone Charitable Trust came into being, we heard the hotel was sold yet again – to the Barclay brothers. I sent them our sales document: the restoration and management plan. They telephoned. They were amazed: they hadn't realized they'd bought such a landscape with the hotel. Would I meet them at their London hotel, the Howard, on the Thames by Waterloo Bridge? When we met they said they were astounded by the report. Would we mind if they restored the landscape? They'd use our consultants and follow the restoration and management plan to the letter. Having thought about it, I said no, we didn't mind. We notice, they went on, that you have gone to much trouble to put a package of grants together for the restoration – central and local government – and this was much appreciated; but would we mind if they paid for the restoration themselves? They found this so much more straightforward. Again, after some thought, I said no, we didn't mind. Lastly, they said, we had set out a ten-year restoration programme, and they fully understood the funding reasons behind this; but would we mind if they restored it in two years? And to this request too – after some careful thought – I said no, we wouldn't mind. True to their word, the Barclays restored Hawkstone in two years. Hawkstone was extremely lucky. It started with a philanthropic owner and again, when it needed to, it fell into the hands of a philanthropic owner. Only this last time it had been well prepared for its luck.

Case study 7.5

Landscape change

Bob Roberts

The Countryside Commission and the Department of the Environment have been gathering information on landscape change in England and Wales using the consultants Hunting Technical Services. Two linked studies have been completed, one looking at the extent of features like farmed land, woodland and semi-natural vegetation around 1947, 1969 and 1980, and the other looking at linear features such as hedges, walls and fences at the same dates and in 1985. This is the first time that national figures have been available for the wide range of features that make up the whole landscape.

As simple before-and-after measurement might sometimes disguise quite considerable change in the distribution of features, the Countryside Commission set out to reveal these hidden changes. Our information identified not only change in the area of features (like woodland and farmland), but also the extent to which original cover has been replaced by new, and the nature of exchanges between different features.

For instance, we found that, although the total area of broad-leaved woodland in 1980 was about 23 per cent less than in 1947, about 40 per cent of the 1947 broad-leaves had disappeared by 1980, with newly developed woodland making up the rest of the 1980 count (*Figure 7.5*). Some other interesting facts that emerged are illustrated in *Figures 7.6–7.9*.

Such a survey raises questions as well as answering them. It was designed to produce some straightforward facts on what is happening, rather than why, and we hope to go on to investigate the mechanisms of change, at the same time improving monitoring techniques so that we can keep our information up to date.

However, now we have a good factual base to start from, we are far better equipped to study the causes of change, and find practical ways of ensuring that the continuing evolution of our landscape creates rather than destroys pleasant and enjoyable places.

It was clear from the start that linear features such as hedges and walls, and area features such as woodland, heath and permanent grass, would have to be examined separately because of the different scales of photograph required for each.

The team working on linear features interpreted aerial photographs covering 140 sample sites, each measuring $12 \, km^2$. The sample was carefully structured so that it was representative of every sort of landscape, with at least two and up to four samples in each county. For each site, the team examined aerial photographs taken around 1950, 1970, 1980 and 1985, measuring the length of every hedge, ditch, bank and woodland edge, and noting the changes that had taken place.

The area features interpreters (inevitably, the A-team!) looked at a total of 707 sites, again carefully structured, and including the 140 linear feature sites mentioned above. This time the boundaries of more than 30 different types of landscape feature, like moorland, lowland heath, and different sorts of farmland and woodland, were recorded over sites of about $5 \, km^2$ in extent. There were at least ten sites in each county, with more in counties with particularly complex soil patterns. About 2.5 per cent of the total area of England and Wales was interpreted in this way, using aerial photographs from about 1950, 1970 and 1980. By recording the boundaries of each feature on a computer, it was possible to calculate their total extent at each target date, and the net gains and losses that occurred in between.

Although interpreting and digitizing more than 3000 aerial photographs kept four members of the A-team fully occupied for two years, generating a mountain of interpretation overlays, computer tapes and disks and printout paper along the way, their results were inevitably summarized on little more than a sheet of paper!

Monitoring work

Aerial photographs, Landsat satellite data and field observation have been the three vital ingredients of the Monitoring Landscape Change project. By using the best attributes of all three, and integrating the different sorts of data, it was possible to identify changes in the landscape of England and Wales, both nationally and regionally.

Truth checking

Interpretation of aerial photographs is as much of an art as a science, and photographs can be misleading. For example, in spring, growing crops can look very similar to permanent grass. To check how accurately features have been identified from the photographs, we carried out detailed field investigations at 350 sites. This 'truth checking' showed that most features were interpreted with an accuracy of well over 90 per cent.

But perhaps the most exciting and novel aspect of the work was using images from the Landsat satellite to calculate the current distribution of major landscape features. These data, mainly from satellite orbits in 1984, are a census of the complete land surface of England and Wales based on more than 3000 million separate pieces of information, each relating to an area about 30 metres square on the ground.

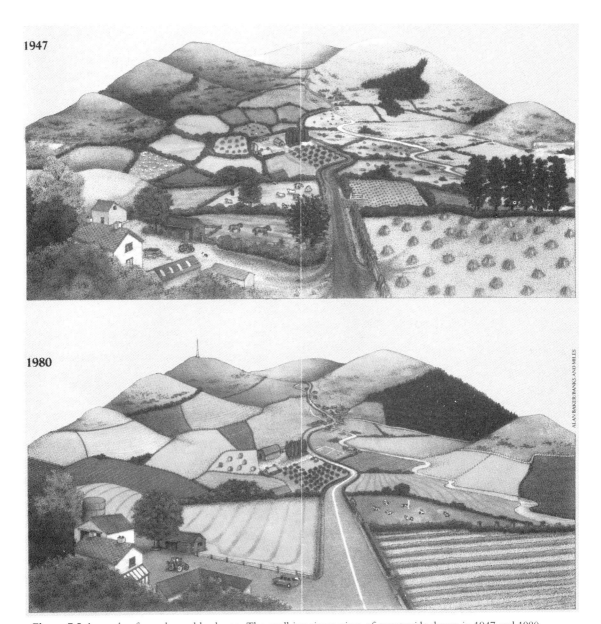

Figure 7.5 A sample of our changed landscape. The small imaginary piece of countryside shown in 1947 and 1980 illustrates some of the major changes quantified in the study. Of course, change occurs at different rates in different places, and our illustration should not be considered as typical of everywhere, but it does sum up the general changes we measured. The overall increase in woodland is largely in coniferous trees (from 0.7 per cent of the land surface up to 2.7 per cent) rather than broad leaves (down from 5.6 to 4.2 per cent). There is a general increase in field size, a conversion of semi-natural landscapes like moorland to coniferous woodland and agricultural land, and an increase in developed land including roads and towns. All forms of grassland have decreased. Farmed land remains at about 72 per cent of the land surface, but cropped land increased from 27 per cent in 1947 to 35 per cent in 1980

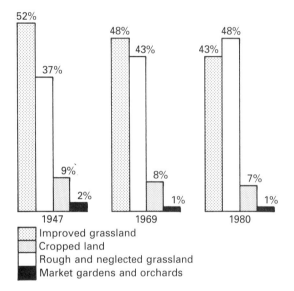

Improved grassland
Cropped land
Rough and neglected grassland
Market gardens and orchards

Figure 7.6 Composition of farmland in England and Wales. The proportion of the land surface that is farmed altered very little during the survey period (72.7 per cent in 1947 to 71.8 per cent in 1980). However, within this category significant changes took place. Most noticeably, cropped (i.e. cultivated) land increased from about 37 per cent of all farmland in 1947 to more than 48 per cent in 1980. We also know that about a fifth of the land identified as cultivated in 1947 was under a different use (usually grassland) when surveyed in 1980. So the simple increase in the area of cultivated land actually masks more considerable changes in the farmland category

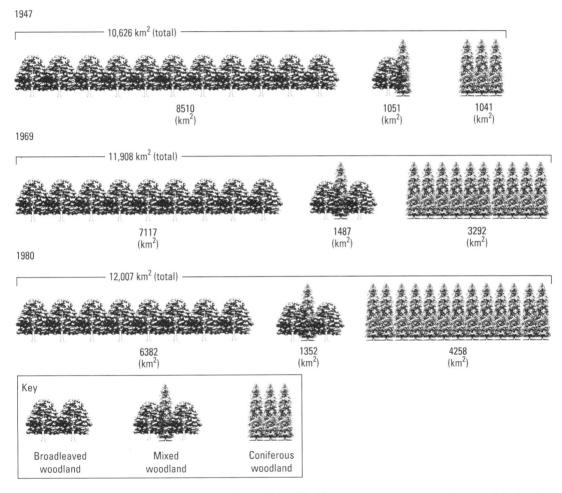

Figure 7.7 Composition of woodland in England and Wales. Woodland and forest cover generally increased during the survey period, from 7 per cent of the land surface in 1947 to 7.9 per cent in 1980. The area of coniferous woodland increased more than two and a half times. However, some 40 per cent of the broad-leaved woodland present in 1947 had disappeared by 1980, though the total area of broad leaves was only down by 25 per cent because of the planting of new woodland

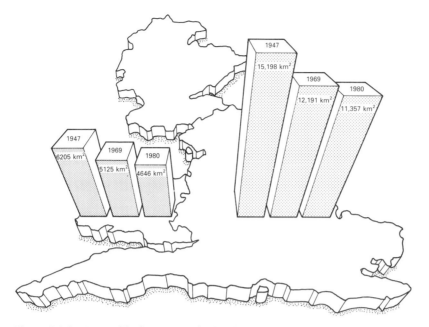

Figure 7.8 Semi-natural landscape in England and Wales. The area of semi-natural landscape (heath, moor, bog, bracken, gorse, wetlands, bare rock and sand) fell by just over a quarter between 1947 and 1980. Although England has more of this landscape than Wales in absolute area, semi-natural landscape covers a greater proportion of the land surface in Wales. So the figures for Wales show a decreased from 29.8 per cent cover in 1947 to 22.4 per cent in 1980, whereas England's cover fell from 11.7 per cent in 1947 to 8.8 per cent in 1980

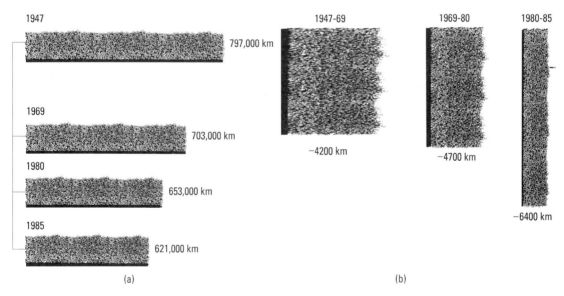

Figure 7.9 Hedgerows in England and Wales: (a) absolute lengths (b) annual rate of change (loss). The absolute length of hedgerows in England and Wales diminished by about 306,000 km (about 22 per cent of their 1947 extent) during the survey period. The rate of loss accelerated from about 4200 km per year during the early survey period to about 6400 km per year in the 1980s. The greatest rates of recent loss are in East Anglia and the East Midlands. The overall length of walls, banks and open ditches also diminished during the survey period by between 7 and 15 per cent. Although fences increased by some 13 per cent, the much greater loss of other linear features, and in particular hedges, means that field sizes have generally increased

8

Defining and recording the resource: the built environment

John Bold

Field recording of buildings and sites, and the cataloguing of the records made, are complementary activities which should be managed in a unitary, mutually informing manner. For professional and financial reasons this unity is not easily achieved. A professional distinction tends to be drawn, mistakenly, between the pioneering act of discovery on site and the office-based curation and cataloguing of the records made, too often perceived as unexcitingly passive.

The nature of both public and private sector funding compounds this mistaken distinction by providing finance more readily for short-term goal-oriented activities of the recording type than for the long-term cataloguing of the results. Since the requirements of cataloguing should in fact be an important element in determining the extent and levels of recording, the whole process runs the risk of being compromised. The growing influence of private funding further tilts the balance in causing organizations to be more and more influenced by the individual client; overall aims and objectives for the greater good may thereby be threatened.

The key issue to be resolved by heritage recording bodies is the balance between the maintenance of an infrastructure for the long-term development of the national record, and the pursuit of shorter-term publicly and privately funded recording activities that complement it. This however may not present a real dilemma. The nature and extent of funding, whether long or short term, is itself a product of the changing social, economic and political environment, and in the fullness of time that which we may now castigate as short term, opportunisitic and chaotic may come to be seen as fundamental to the historic process of cultural change. The residual record will then be recognized as an artefact geared to the needs of its time in much the same way as the making of the record is acknowledged to be indispensable for our present purposes. This may be small consolation to those locked into the apparently interminable corporate planning and bidding processes.

The record in context

The recording of buildings is a political act, conditioned by perceptions of historical significance and informed by the making of choices; it is an exercise incomplete until the record made is in the public domain, accessible to all potential users. Availability of a record is the only absolute requirement of the recording procedure; it profits no one if a few inchoate notes, soon incomprehensible even to their compiler, sit unremarked in a private filing cabinet.

Recording itself admits of no absolutes; it is a selective process. The reason for recording individual buildings, their importance and quality, the resources deployed, the capabilities and enthusiasms of the person making the record, all vary – and in so doing bear on the nature of the record made. A summary analysis, a brief description with a snapshot or a lengthy report accompanied by detailed photographs and measured drawings may all be of value depending upon the circumstances in which the record was made and the purposes for which it was made. None of these will be of any lasting value, however, unless good observation, sound knowledge of the subject and analytical intelligence have been brought to bear on the process of recording. Questions must be posed, hypotheses constructed and answers sought. The results must then be presented in a form which others can test; this is a process analogous to that employed by the natural scientist. Without analysis, we have a mere inventory of phenomena – the 'raw incomplete language' to which Primo Levi (1989, p. 103) has referred in discussing chemical formulas, which tells us nothing about structures or relationships but 'works as if a typographer extracted from his type font the letters, e, a, c, r and claimed that he had in this way expressed the word care'.

It is incumbent upon all who are engaged in the recording of buildings to attempt to ensure that their records have a utility beyond their own immediate needs. It is important therefore that the parameters of their activities are defined – the levels of recording activity, the time spent, the aim of the survey – to enable the users to judge the assumptions made and the successes and failures of the enterprise. Such definition is especially incumbent upon those who work in the public sector.

The role of RCHME

The Royal Commission on the Historical Monuments of England is the primary public sector recording body, the national body of survey and record, engaged since its foundation in 1908 on the recording of archaeological sites and historic buildings and making that information publicly available. Over the years RCHME has increased the range of both date and type of building recorded and of the levels of record made. Beginning with a terminal date of 1700, first extended formally to 1714, then in effect to 1850, RCHME now admits of no cut-off date. Recording effort, which was originally concentrated on the ecclesiastical and domestic, now includes the institutional and, increasingly, the industrial, potentially one of the most significant groups of all.

RCHME has also taken on a succession of additional responsibilities. Having worked closely with the National Buildings Record since 1946, RCHME took responsibility for it in 1963. Responsibility for the Industrial Monuments Survey followed in 1981, for the archaeological recording and mapping functions of the Ordnance Survey in 1983, and for the Survey of London in 1986. These extra tasks brought additional funding and, more significantly in the longer term, new ideas concerning what constitutes an acceptable level of record and a less exclusive view of which buildings ought to be recorded.

RCHME began life with the injunction laid upon it not only to record buildings but also to 'specify those which seem most worthy of preservation'. This last function now carries less force following the postwar introduction and development of the listing programme, now administered by English Heritage on behalf of the Department of National Heritage, but the principle which underpins RCHME's activities remains the same: that of gathering evidence in order to facilitate the making of judgements of relative value. In the words of RCHME's Royal Warrant, admirable in its catholicity, the task is to identify those monuments and constructions 'illustrative of the contemporary culture, civilisation and conditions of life of the people of England'. Identification and historical evaluation are necessary functions in any society which

values its history and culture, for it is only by assessing what exists and by analysing and explaining its development that we can move forward on the basis of commonly understood and agreed assumptions. Knowledge and understanding must precede decision making, otherwise decisions become arbitrary and uninformed. The recording of buildings and the dissemination of those records is indispensable not only for informing the planning process and for the quotidian decision making within local authorities on alteration, restoration or demolition of a particular building, but also, more broadly, for providing a basis of understanding of groups of buildings within a typological or geographical framework; and more broadly still for supplying the building evidence which, together with the economic, social, political and artistic, contributes a vital component of our overall historical understanding and perspective. Recording and the dissemination of records are educative, informing procedures.

Levels of record

The range of possible responses to recording needs has prompted RCHME to clarify its procedures for users of its material and to guide those who deposit their work in the national archive by defining four levels of record for architectural recording (RCHME, 1991). These rise from a simple description and 35 mm photograph at level 1 to a detailed analysis of the building in its context, involving documentary research and numerous drawings and professional photographs, at level 4. These levels are not intended to be exclusive. They do not for instance take account of photogrammetric survey, a technique which has become indispensable, when allied with historical analysis, for the very detailed recording of particularly complex buildings which are to undergo thorough restoration or reconstruction. At all levels, including those above level 4, choices are made and the recorder must attempt to come to terms with the built evidence by judicious selection and by arguing for its significance. The recorder is never merely an eye; the record presents, at best, a critically filtered reality. There is a school of thought prevalent among adherents to the concept of the total record that more and more detailed records are axiomatically more and more valuable. The total record however is a chimera, and it is often the case that the Mies van der Rohe dictum 'less is more' is as applicable to the recording of a building as it is to its designing. For even photogrammetry, that apparently wholly reflective exercise, is selective, involving interpretation and analysis in determining which elements of the original photographs should be transposed on to the drawing and which rejected as insignificant. At all times in recording it is the significant which must be identified, and the recorder must vary his or her view of relative significance according to the purposes for which the survey is being made. All elements of a record – report, drawings, photographs, technical analyses – should be complementary. The written report itself is the key, providing description and analysis, elucidating all other elements.

The stimulus for recording

Statutory obligations for recording

In a country with more than half a million listed buildings, protected under a succession of Town and Country Planning Acts – most recently the Planning (Listed Buildings and Conservation Areas) Act 1990 – the limited resources available for recording must be deployed with circumspection. Excluding London, for which special arrangements are made, there are at least 8000 applications per year for consent to alter or demolish listed buildings. RCHME has the statutory right to record in all these listed building consent cases. Its resources however allow it to record analytically only about 300–350 of these in detail although many more are photographed and all are logged. Others are recorded by county archaeological units or other special interest organizations and groups. RCHME's national responsibility and national coverage enable it to record far more of the buildings threatened than any other body.

However, much goes unrecorded, and many hard choices have to be made both of buildings to be investigated and of the appropriate level of record. Many considerations are brought to bear: the national or local significance of the building, in so far as it is possible to adduce this prior to actually visiting and recording; the quality of any available record held either in the National Monuments Record or elsewhere; the degree of threat to the building; the extent to which the making of a record would contribute more generally to an increase in knowledge of a building type or the architecture of a particular region; and, most mundanely, the availability of appropriate trained staff. A threatened Georgian house in an area rich in Georgian development is often less likely to be recorded than a comparable house in a predominantly nineteenth century environment because as one of a group an individual threat is of less significance to the total stock, and moreover it is quite possible that there is a better non-threatened survivor next door. This crude and expedient rule of thumb carries with it the danger that, by the time due notice has been taken, all the most typical Georgian houses with their original internal arrangement surviving will have been lost, whereas all those in less obviously Georgian centres will have been sedulously recorded; a balance must be struck. There is an element of exaggeration in this example, but it has been deliberately chosen to make the point because the Georgian house is an artefact with which most feel familiar and this is paradoxically the greatest threat to its understanding.

Although the use of listed building consent is an invaluable mechanism, the use of the statutory procedures alone as a trigger for recording is relatively arbitrary. Other sources of information, in particular local and county planning authorities and recording groups with local knowledge, should be used to supplement listed building consent information. The quality and extent of RCHME's recording and the overall deployment of its resources have been considerably improved by these contacts.

RCHME records buildings under threat; English Heritage often funds the recording of exceptional buildings as part of its grant-in-aid programme; county archaeological units also record buildings under threat and, increasingly, seek funds for recording buildings which are to be redeveloped. Most of these records are eventually available in the national archive, which as a result is inevitably in part an *ad hoc* selection, many of its contents being based on expediency and immediate need rather than on any longer-term consideration either of absolute value or of comprehensiveness. The records held are, equally inevitably, variable in quality and in content.

Thematic surveys

It is for reasons of value and comprehensiveness that RCHME has in recent years attempted to carry out selective thematic surveys of types of building about which knowledge is limited, for both statutory and academic purposes. There can be no consensus for either in circumstances of ignorance, and we are still remarkably ill informed abut many well known building types. It has been shown recently, for example, that most academic assumptions about the country house in the late seventeenth and early eighteenth centuries have been based on a sample of the same most familiar 200 houses (Saumarez Smith, 1988). In order to provide a more comprehensive basis for the understanding of buildings which are similarly or even less adequately understood, many more thematic surveys are needed. The study of vernacular architecture for example on a thematic and regional basis has made immeasurable progress over the last twenty years through the publication of such exemplary analyses, based upon detailed surveys, as Eric Mercer's *English Vernacular Houses* (1975) and Barry Harrison and Barbara Hutton's *Vernacular Houses in North Yorkshire and Cleveland* (1984).

RCHME has also carried out surveys of housing and textile mills in Yorkshire, of medieval houses in Kent, and national surveys of hospitals and farmsteads. In the cases of mills and hospitals in particular the absence of a consensus view on their relative historical importance has proved a great impediment to those charged with deciding the fate of individual buildings and sites.

Perceptions of what is important change, but the achievement of a total survey of all buildings of interest in any large group is unlikely. For this reason relatively rapid selective surveys, followed by detailed analysis of a few particularly significant examples, are carried out by RCHME to provide a representative selection which will have an exemplifying utility beyond the purely local level. No national body can expect to serve all purposes by posing and answering all possible questions. Rather it can define the parameters of the subject and point the way for future detailed work which can be carried out by others at regional and local level. Such work could be most usefully coordinated nationally in order to ensure common standards and prevent duplication. In the absence of resources to record all buildings of interest this is the most effective means of gathering information and accumulating knowledge on our rich architectural heritage.

The funding of the archive

In defining levels and subject areas of recording it is easy to overlook the resources required for making available to as wide a public as possible the results of the work. Records of buildings, whether photographic, graphic or written, are not mere arcana for a specialist audience. They are vital elements in educating the public in our history and in helping to shape planning decisions that affect our environment. All too often financial provision for the care and dissemination of records is overlooked. They pile up, inaccessible and unindexed, in dusty storerooms, deteriorating through an absence of professional indexing and proper curatorial care. Such records might just as well have never been made. The problem is not merely one of resources, which in the public sector seem doomed to be limited, but also one of methodology and attitude. The archive must be taken into account by the recorder and vice versa. Levels of cataloguing require just as much definition as levels of recording: the one impacts upon the other. Certain information must be recorded in the field in order to satisfy cataloguing needs. These requirements help to impose a discipline and consistency upon the recording process.

Data standards

Experience and wide consultation with users of its records has enabled RCHME, in association with English Heritage, to identify those vital fields of information which should form a core data standard for architectural records. This is not just a cataloguing tool but has been informed by the functional needs of an overall recording policy, ranging from the initial site visit to the record in use. The need for such a standard has been prompted by the proliferation of computerized cataloguing systems and the accompanying realization that greater speed of access to information within individual collections will have as its corollary relative inaccessibility between collections unless common standards of accessioning and interrogation of information are formulated. An agreed core data standard providing guidelines for locational, typological and dating information will be an invaluable aid to researchers not only within national collections in England but also, it is anticipated, internationally. It will also regularize the recording and cataloguing procedures in use and save separate organizations the trouble of inventing individual solutions to common problems.

In England, the computerization of architectural records, including the computerization of the statutory lists of historic buildings, is regarded by many as a desideratum for proper management of the country's building stock. Quantification and comparative judgements of value are notoriously difficult within the confines of a paper-based system. Furthermore, current methods of record management within those systems are duplicative and costly. Computerization of the statutory lists and the equivalent amount of associated information which is centrally held will provide us with the nearest we are likely to get to an accessible, comprehensive archive of information on the built heritage. The process of computerizing information on buildings is costly: it is time consuming and requires specialist staff and expensive equipment. However, costs are relative; although a computerization programme would cost over £3 million (the same as RCHME's total annual architectural budget), at less than £10 per building this would be a very small additional cost to that of visiting, identifying and recording buildings in the first place. If the saving in time and effort to all those county and local authorities who maintain duplicate paper records is also taken into account then the cost of an efficient system, readily accessible and compiled to a common standard, becomes nugatory.

Survey and record: public and private funding

It has been a great failure of all recording and protective agencies that full costings for the care of buildings and the necessary associated record keeping have not been made from the beginning of any programme. If they had then perhaps the programmes could never have been begun at all since it is a feature of public sector funding that it is piecemeal and variable, and government commitment to a coherent long-term programme is notoriously elusive. Government accounting systems militate against long-term planning in favour of short-term expediency, a pragmatic system which requires an equivalent response if the public is to receive the best possible service. The temptation in seeking funding is to cost the ground breaking, record making parts of the operation and make appropriate bids, leaving the prosaic archive or publication elements to later years and subsequent bids. The consequence is clear: the record is made and remains in the drawer. As the number of records piles up, so the cost of dealing with them properly increases and the likelihood of securing funding declines because the allocation of resources is always relative. If £1000 is available and the choice is to visit and record a house which will be demolished next week, or to use the money for cataloguing 100 records which will still be there in a fortnight, it would be unusual for the money to be spent on the latter even though the long-term benefit might well be the greater by so doing. The ideal solution to this particular problem is to cost the whole exercise of recording and archiving from beginning to end on a year-by-year basis and to divide up the work accordingly, not allowing backlogs of material to accrue: a counsel of perfection, perhaps, but a fundamentally important objective nevertheless.

Increasingly, national and local organizations are being encouraged to seek funding from the private sector to supplement their basic income from the public purse. This particular route, already being navigated by the museums, is fraught with danger because it encourages the short-term attractive project rather than the duller, more worthy long-term programme, the one-off recording rather than the cataloguing of backlogs; and furthermore it encourages recording bodies to research and investigate buildings on the basis of available finance rather than academic or statutory imperatives. Record making should always be in tune with the overall interests of the organization. There is much to be said in favour of owners of buildings contributing to the costs of recording but only if such record making is organizationally relevant and is carried out in an intellectually independent and impartial manner. Private funding should be a bonus, enabling a more substantial coverage or a more contextual study than would be possible on core funding alone. It should not be allowed to distort the wider aims of a recording body such as RCHME, founded to provide a public service, which properly depends on central funding in order to fulfil its duties and proper investment to take full advantage of new technologies whose benefit is long term rather than immediate.

New technologies

All concerned with recording and with the archiving of information on historic buildings must appreciate that, although new technologies will create greater opportunities, they do not represent panaceas. Cataloguing is fundamentally labour intensive whether on card index or database; advanced imaging presupposes a sophisticated level of cataloguing in order to achieve successful retrieval. In field recording the use of electronic distance measuring followed by computer-aided drafting to produce the drawn results of the surveys requires a high level of expertise and investment. The danger inherent in the use of new and complex technologies is twofold. Firstly they may give the impression, as increased automation always tends to do, that the relatively less expert will be able to produce an aparently more polished piece of work, probably at greater speed than before, as if we could all be Tolstoys if we had word processors. Secondly the mere capacity, exciting though the prospect might be, to record the hitherto unrecordable large site or to draw the hitherto undrawable may encourage recording in order to fulfil the potential of the systems in use rather than the requirements of the recording body or the user of the information.

There is an element of determinism in the application of new technologies which too often causes means to become ends. The systems we use should all be geared towards providing a better service to users rather than becoming ends in themselves. The purpose of a body of survey and record is to provide information on the built heritage to as many users as possible, as swiftly and accurately as human ingenuity will permit. The needs of the user should be paramount.

No recording body would refuse additional funding to improve its equipment and refine its performance, but all concerned must recognize that the first priority in the recording and making available of information is intelligent thought. In quantifying the resources required to do the job it must not be forgotten that this is the rarest and most expensive commodity of all.

Conclusion

RCHME has a pivotal role to play in the compilation of the national record of the built heritage, not only in recording and archiving but also in articulating, academically and functionally, the desirable levels of record and of information retrievability. RCHME has developed the infrastructure necessary for it to record and curate, setting levels for recording, standards for cataloguing, and mechanisms for the management, integration and dissemination of information. It also has a continuing academic, political and advisory role in determining what should be recorded in the longer and shorter terms to meet changing historical and socio-economic criteria. This broad view of past achievements and future possibilities will inform RCHME's task of reconciling the superficially conflicting requirements of short-term projects and long-term programmes to provide a service for all who require information on the built environment.

References

HARRISON, B. and HUTTON, B. (1984) *Vernacular Houses in North Yorkshire and Cleveland*, John Donald Publishers Ltd

LEVI, P. (1989) *Other People's Trades*, Abacus, 103

MERCER, E. (1975) *English Vernacular Houses*, Royal Commission on the Historical Monuments of England, HMSO

RCHME (1991) *Recording Historic Buildings: a Descriptive Specification*, Royal Commission on the Historical Monuments of England

SAUMAREZ, SMITH, C. (1988) 'Supply and demand in English country house building 1660–1740', *Oxford Art Journal*, **11**(2), 3–9

Case study 8.1

Billingsgate Roman Bath House

Simon O'Connor-Thompson and Peter Rowsome

The Billingsgate Roman Bath House Project concerns the conservation, archaeological investigation and presentation of the remains of a Roman building of winged-corridor design with an associated but structurally independent bath suite. The remains are located at 100 Lower Thames Street, London EC3.

The project demonstrates to a peculiar degree the problems that can be encountered in trying to conserve and comprehend important archaeological remains in a dynamic urban context.

Background

The freehold of the site is owned by the Corporation of London, the local authority for the city of London. Roman remains were first discovered at the site during the construction of the Coal Exchange in 1848, when part of a Roman bath house was preserved and displayed within the basement of the new building. Further excavation work in 1859 revealed more of the bath as well as an associated building to the north and east. Following the Ancient Monuments Act of 1882 the site was amongst the first in London to be scheduled.

As a result of the widening of Lower Thames Street and the resultant demolition of the Coal Exchange, a large part of the Roman monument was investigated between 1967 and 1970. The bath suite was re-excavated and parts of the east and north wings of the surrounding Roman building were investigated. However the archaeological remains were retained within a purpose-built basement for eventual public display. Development of an adjacent site in 1974 led to the investigation of part of the western area of the monument, and in 1975 limited excavation work was also carried out at the extant northern end of the Roman building's east wing.

For the most part the 1967–75 excavation had finished with the exposure of the structural elements of the masonry building and roughly contemporary external surfaces. However in many places sondage trenches had been cut to much lower levels, and parts of a sequence pre-dating the construction of the main masonry building phase had been exposed. It was also the case that small areas of deposits post-dating the winged-corridor building and bath had survived, particularly at the northern end of the building's east wing.

Recent work

The need to maintain the monument and protect it from decay led to the Corporation of London's decision in 1987 to commission the compilation of a detailed record of the site. This work was carried out by one of the Museum of London Archaeology Service's predecessors – the Department of Urban Archaeology. Initially a survey recorded the state of the visible monument. More extensive archaeological recording and limited excavation took place in 1989–90 in conjunction with conservation work by Nimbus Conservation Group and environmental monitoring by Ridout Associates.

The 1989–90 site work called for close cooperation between the archaeologists, conservators and other professionals involved in the project. The masonry, walls and floors of the Roman building had been consolidated and sealed by the Ministry of Public Buildings and Works following the 1967–70 excavations, and it subsequently became clear that the materials and practices used at that time were unsympathetic to the monument and inappropriate for the site conditions. The conservation work by Nimbus was designed to stabilize the deteriorating condition of the remains and to correct earlier conservation errors so that a clear and proper presentation of the site would be possible.

Methodology

A system of work was developed in order to ensure that a full record was made of the site, whilst also recording the conservation process itself. The order of work generally involved an initial archaeological record being made (including a description, a scaled plan, and as necessary an elevation and a photograph). This formed a pre-conservation record of the remains. Modern concrete and intrusive or damaging repairs to the Roman remains were then identified, recorded and removed. This was followed by further archaeological recording of the then exposed Roman remains, prior to Nimbus completing the conservation process. At times this order of work included limited archaeological excavation which also enhanced the presentation of the monument. Nimbus adopted the archaeological planning grid and context numbering system in order to cross-reference their work and records with the archaeological record.

The method of work adopted by the archaeologists (pre- and post-conservation recording) and conservators (initial cleaning, removal of unsympathetic materials, modern conservation) meant that many features or areas requiring conservation were returned to many times during the course of the work.

The Corporation of London, through its Historic Buildings Architect, promoted discussion between Nimbus, the Museum archaeologists and English Heritage as to the best method of display of internal and external areas and floor levels within the monument. During the excavation and conservation programme, samples of mortars used by Nimbus were collected for future reference.

The main programme of archaeological and conservation work was concluded in September 1990. Those parts of the site which were considered unsuitable for exposure or public presentation were covered, where necessary, with a geo-textile membrane and then buried with washed salt-free sand.

Post-excavation

The large number of excavations at the site and the changes in archaeological technique which have taken place over the past 150 years are reflected in the variable nature of the archive. The site work can be broadly categorized as antiquarian observations, Guildhall Museum and other rescue excavations, and more recently the controlled survey of the site and the excavation of restricted areas to answer specific questions.

The incremental archaeological investigation of the site has created a patchwork of contiguous and overlapping excavation areas recording to different depths and widely varying methods. A further category of record resulted from the 1989–90 work – the records of the conservation process itself as undertaken by Nimbus.

The net effect has been to create a series of interdependent sets of data which are inseparable in the development of a comprehensive site narrative. Reconciliation of the site sequence and finds groups from all of the phases of excavation is considered an absolute prerequisite to full site assessment. The substantial and detailed archaeological record produced during the 1989–90 work now forms the essential set of control data for the analysis of all earlier excavation records.

The 1989–90 stratigraphic record is made up of 1234 individual contexts (record sheets), associated 1:20 scale plans, 1:10 scale section and elevation drawings and other records forming a standard Museum of London field record. Timber and masonry record forms, environmental sampling registers and photographic records were maintained according to established practice.

Research aims

Excavation

The 1987–90 archaeological work was designed in part to record the Roman remains before and after the conservation process and in part to enhance or clarify aspects of the visible remains for public display. It was also hoped that excavation of certain deposits would help to secure the dating sequence, and thus the phasing of the site.

Post-excavation

The approach to the assessment takes into account the number of excavations at the site and the absence of a single, standard recording system. Among the academic research aims can be included the need to develop a detailed and securely dated structural sequence for the winged-corridor building and associated bathing suite from construction to final abandonment and demolition, as well as to investigate in detail the changing function of the bath and winged building in all their phases, and the likely form that their association took. Was the building a private or a commercial establishment?

Special considerations

Since the Roman building and bath might eventually form part of a public display and exhibition, the current post-excavation work endeavours to anticipate the needs of the Corporation of London, architects, conservators, designers, other professionals and statutory bodies who will be involved in any future design brief for the display of the remains. Consequently a number of more detailed research aims are being framed which will contribute to the informative display of the remains:

(1) To research the likely overall appearance of the original buildings, drawing on evidence in the building material and stratigraphic record, and on the much wider study area of Roman architecture and construction techniques. Did the bathing suite have a pitched or vaulted roof? Other areas of enquiry concern the likely height and roof-line of the main building's wings, and evidence for two- and three-winged urban buildings. Was the physical proximity of the winged-corridor building and bath a product of their function, or might it indicate that the wider area was densely occupied in the later Roman period?

(2) To consider the internal appearance of the various rooms within the bath suite and east wing of the building. Can this be derived from plaster and other materials recovered during excavation?

(3) To compile site data for inclusion in a management (conservation) manual as an aid to future display, and

to inform any further or continuing conservation work which may be necessary.

Postscript

There is a shadow hanging over the mid-term future of the project in the shape of the office block that now stands empty above the viewing chamber in which the remains are preserved. Until the future of this building is determined – which may mean demolition and rebuild at some future date – the Roman remains are less likely to be generally accessible to the public.

Case study 8.2

The assessment of Cornish mine engine houses

Nicholas Johnson and Adam Sharpe

The Cornish beam-engine house (*Figure 8.1*) is a most evocative symbol. It is an icon both of past greatness, when Cornwall was the world centre for metal mining, and of that most modern of issues – conservation and green tourism.

Nearly 3000 engines were erected in the county from the early decades of the eighteenth century. Beam engines, used for pumping, winding and stamping, have an extraordinarily long technological life. In Cornwall, their use lasted from at least the 1720s up to 1959. The buildings that housed them conform to a general design with an infinite variety of differences of detail. Perhaps as many as 2500 engine houses were constructed in the county, and approximately 240 survive in a more or less recognizable form. They are important buildings and deserve protection.

Over the last decade the Cornwall Archaeological Unit has been endeavouring to identify, characterize, protect and conserve historic mining remains. In order to develop a management and protection policy and programme for engine houses, the Unit has developed a standard assessment technique. This has been carried out during surveys of the Central Mining District (Camborne-Redruth-Gwennap mines) and the St Just Mining District. Out of a total of over 1000 recorded engine houses that were constructed in the two areas, 116 surviving houses were assessed. A full description of both these surveys (Sharpe *et al.*, 1991; Sharpe *et al.*, 1992) and others have been published by the Unit.

Survey method

The surveys involved the four stages outlined in the Secretary of State's guidance to local authorities in Planning Policy Guidance Note no. 16, *Archaeology and Planning* (1992). These stages are as follows.

Figure 8.1 Pascoe's pumping engine, South Frances mine, Treskillard, Cornwall (courtesy Cornwall Archaeological Unit)

Appraisal

A thorough search is made of maps, mine plans, and documentary sources to identify the sites of all engine houses constructed.

Assessment

(1) A field visit is made to confirm whether or not an engine house still survives. If the house is substantially intact, it is described.
(2) A thesaurus of structural and technical terms has been developed so that descriptions are consistent (*Figure 8.2*). Each engine house is described using a standardized two-page multiple-choice checklist (*Figure 8.3*), recording the overall dimensions, the construction materials used and the features found in each house as well as assessing the condition and the necessary required management works. The form also provides for rapid sketch elevations and a plan of the site.
(3) Each site is photographed and a taped description is recorded for future reference.

Evaluation

In order to protect and conserve these structure it is necessary to value and prioritize them.

Value scoring

The value of each site has been evaluated using a modified form of English Heritage's Monument Protection Programme (MPP) scoring system. There are two main evaluation types:

Monument importance value (MIV) This assesses the importance of individual structures as examples of their class. Thus the more complete is a structure, the better it is documented, the greater is its potential for amenity, and the higher the number of other sites relating to the industry in its proximity, the higher will be its value. The criteria are as follows. The individual category scores are squared and the totals are added together to give the MIV.

Group value (association)	1 low; 2 medium; 3 high
Survival	1 poor; 2 medium; 3 good
Archaeological potential	1 low; 2 medium; 3 high
Documentation (archaeological)	1 poor; 2 medium; 3 good
Documentation (historical)	1 poor; 2 medium; 3 good
Diversity (features)	1 low; 2 medium; 3 high
Group value (clustering)	1 isolated; 2 clustered
Amenity value	1 low; 2 medium; 3 high

Site management appraisal value (SMAV) This assesses the condition of structures, that is the urgency of any work required. Unlike assessment for scheduled monument status where sites with good condition and high potential are preferred, here we are looking for sites that have high potential but are in need of management work. The scorings on which the calculations have been based are arranged to reflect this:

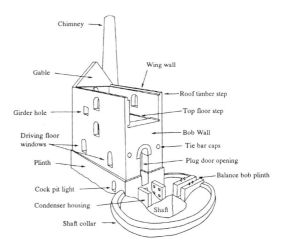

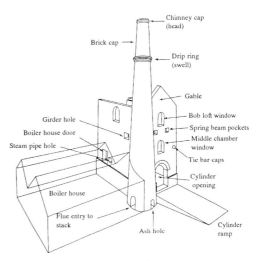

Figure 8.2 Guide to the naming of pumping engine house external features. (a) front elevation; (b) rear elevation

some are used in the reverse way to that in MPP. The scores are calculated in the same way as for MIV.

State	1 good; 2 medium; 3 poor
Stability	1 stable; 2 deteriorating; 3 unstable
Structural fragility	1 fragile; 2 average; 3 robust
Vulnerability (threat)	1 safe; 2 vulnerable; 3 threatened
Conservation value (present)	1 poor; 2 limited; 3 good; 4 important
Conservation value (potential)	1 poor potential; 2 some potential; 3 good; 4 important

MINE NAME: *Wheal Peevor*   **HOUSE NAME**: *60"/70"* **CONSTRUCTION DATE**: *1872*
NGR: *SW 707 442*   **CAU PRN N°**: *19208.02*
PARISH: *Redruth*   **LISTED/SCHEDULED (N°)**: *Scheduled/Listed Grade 2*
OWNER: *ECCI*   **ADDRESS**: *John Keay House, St.Austell*
OCCUPIER: **ADDRESS**:
RECORDER: *A.Sharpe*   **DATE**: *14-5-91*
PHOTOS TAKEN DURING VISIT: <u>Colour Slide</u>/Print; <u>B&W Print</u>; Polaroid

---

CONSTRUCTION
FUNCTION: <u>Pumping</u>/Winding/Stamping/Crushing/Man Engine/Multiple/Other

OUTSIDE LENGTH: *9.2m (6.8m internal)* **OUTSIDE WIDTH**: *6.85m (4.05m)* **HEIGHT**: *12.5m*
BOB WALL CONSTRUCTION: <u>Granite</u>/Killas/<u>Squared</u>/Random <u>stonework</u>
BOB WALL THICKNESS: *1.65m*   **QUOINS**: Yes/No/<u>Granite</u>/Killas
FRONT DOORWAY (plug door): **HEIGHT**: *5.08m* **WIDTH**: *1.42m* **SHAPE**: Square/<u>Arch head</u>
REAR DOOR (cylinder arch): **HEIGHT**: *2.72m* **WIDTH**: *2.46m* **SHAPE**: Square/<u>Arch head</u>
CONSTRUCTION OF OTHER WALLS: Granite/<u>Killas</u>/Squared/<u>Random stonework</u>
OTHER WALLS THICKNESS: *0.95m*   **QUOINS**: <u>Yes</u>/No/<u>Granite</u>/Killas

WINDOW SHAPE: Square/<u>Round</u>/Gothic/Slit/Other
WINDOW HEAD TYPE: Wood/Stone Lintel/<u>Brick</u>/Stone <u>Arch</u>/Lost
FRAMES EXTANT: Yes/<u>No</u>   **MATERIAL**: Wood/Metal/<u>Unknown</u>
NUMBER OF WINDOWS: OFFSIDE *5*   NEARSIDE *0*   REAR *2* FRONT *0*
OTHER OPENINGS IN WALLS: <u>Main Girder</u>/<u>Spring Beams</u>/<u>Boiler House</u>/Other Door/<u>Steam</u>
                              <u>Pipe Hole</u>/Other (Cataract Pit entry)

ROOF EXTANT: Yes/<u>No</u>   **METALWORK INTACT**: <u>Yes</u>/No <u>Cast-iron fitting</u>
STACK EXTANT: <u>Yes</u>/No/Partial   **STACK POSITION**: <u>Attached</u>/Distant/None/Unknown
STACK SHAPE: <u>Round</u>/Square/Both/Other   **STACK MATERIAL**: <u>Stone</u>/Brick
UPPER PART OF STACK: Stone/<u>Brick</u>/Lost   **LIGHTNING CONDUCTOR**: Yes/<u>No</u>
INTERNAL PLASTERING EXTANT: Yes/<u>No</u>/Traces **INDICATIONS OF FITTINGS**: Yes/<u>No</u>
ARCHITECTURAL FEATURES: <u>Tie Bars</u>/Fancy Detailing/Name/Date Stone/Other
BRICKS: Named: Yes/No/<u>Red</u>/White **BEDSTONE**: <u>Yes</u>/No **CYLINDER DIA.**: (holes): *N/A*
BALANCE BOB: <u>Plinth</u>/Pit/No   **LOADING**: Flywheel/Stamps/Other/<u>No</u> **SLOTS (N°)**:*N/R*

BOILER HOUSE EXTANT: <u>Yes</u>/No/Not Found   **LOCATION**:Offside/<u>Nearside</u>/Rear/Detached
DIMENSIONS OF BOILERHOUSE: **LENGTH**: *15.0m* **WIDTH**: *6.0m* **HEIGHT**: *2.5m max.*
BOILER POND LOCATED: Yes/No/<u>Not Found</u>   **DIMENSIONS**: *N/A*

SHAFT POSITION: <u>Near</u>/Distant/Not Known/Not Relevant
SHAFT CONDITION: <u>Open</u>/Choked/Capped/Not Known
EVIDENCE FOR RE-USE OF THE BUILDING: *None*

SITE FORMAT: Single Building/<u>Group</u>
OTHER STRUCTURES NEARBY: *Whim, stamps, floors*

Figure 8.3 Part of an engine house multiple-choice checklist for use in the field, shown completed

The scoring system tends to favour the better preserved later engine houses. The scores do not always reflect historical or technical significance (i.e. whether the engine is an early Newcomen atmospheric engine or a much later type). A comments box is appended so that such factors are available for consideration.

Works assessment
Each building was assessed for repairs necessary and average costs involved. The following categories were used:

Category 0   An engine house in very good overall condition, requiring wall cappings, lightning conductor (as applicable) and other minor works including pointing, grouting and local rebuilding. No emergency works required. Expenditure less than £15,000 excluding any shaft treatment.
Category 1   An engine house as in category 0 but requiring some emergency work. Expenditure less than £15,000 excluding any shaft treatment.
Category 2   An engine house which, apart from maintenance works as in category 0, is showing signs of instability or is liable to movement and collapse of part of the structure. Elements of the structure are unstable or liable to storm

MINE NAME: **LEVANT**　　　PRN: **SW33SE/39/2ind**
HOUSE NAME: **Engine Shaft pumping engine**　CONSTRUCTION DATE: **1835**
FUNCTION: **Pumping**　ENGINE SIZE: **40"/45" cylinder diameter**　BEDSTONE: **Removed**
KB REF NO: **E1376**　　　NGR: **SW 3683 3451**　　　PROTECTION: **Listed Grade 2**
OWNER: **Robens Estate**
FOUNDRY: **Harvey**

MIV	SMAV	MIV + SMAV	Comments
39	29	68	Some early features. Important within context. Considerable amenity potential.

Type	Func	Age	Op
🏭	〜	E	Sa

Description

Despite its larger size, this engine house is rather overshadowed by the attention paid to its neighbouring whim engine house on Skip Shaft, and yet of all the surviving engine houses in West Penwith, this is one of the oldest. The site has been well-photographed; Trounson, for example (Trounson, 1982) includes a series of archive photographs (most dating from the last decades of the 19th century) which taken together show all four elevations of the engine house. The house was built in 1835 for a 40" Harvey-built engine, was re-cylindered to 45" in 1872 with another Harvey-built engine, and in 1891 was given a new beam after the breakage of the old one.

The building is of average proportions (though perhaps a little more square in plan at 8.2m x 5.9m than houses of later build), the build is of granite throughout. Squared blocks were used for the whole of the bob wall, which is of more than average thickness (at 1.5m, a house of later date would have had a bob wall nearer 1.2m thick for an engine of this size), whilst on the side and rear walls granite was used only for quoins and to frame wall openings. Following earlier practice, the lower two thirds of the walls (the main load-bearing portion) was built considerably more massively than the upper storey, and as well as the internal step at upper floor level (a feature which persisted in the build of later houses), the external face has a pronounced (double) step at this point to reduce wall thickness above. Despite the relatively massive build of the shell of the engine house, it was felt necessary to add a series of (three) tie bars across the inner and outer faces of the bob wall. These were probably added retrospectively, once the engine had begun work.

The wall openings show features transitional between early and developed practice - some have plain granite and timber lintels, whilst others have brick or stone arched heads. The plug door opening is an imposing arch headed feature, the arch being constructed of stone voussoirs. Below the level of the cylinder plat it is slightly reduced in width. In the rear wall, the cylinder doorway is a broad (1.56m wide x 2.1m high) granite lintelled opening. Only one course of stonework separated the lintel of this feature from the cill of the middle floor window, also granite lintelled, which is set rather low on the elevation. The upper floor window, also granite lintelled, is set high in the gable. This aperture is infilled with a modern plank screen. On the offside wall there is a single window at middle floor level at the centreline of the elevation. This has an arched head of three courses of flush-laid brick headers both internally and externally. Stone has been lost from its cill. The main

Figure 8.4 Part of an engine house report summarizing both descriptive detail and management recommendations (pictograms explained in *Figure 8.5*)

damage. Expenditure £15,000–£25,000 excluding any shaft treatment.

Category 3　An engine house which has suffered major structure movements and is in danger of a significant collapse of a major portion. The structure requires extensive repair and remedial works if it is to be preserved in its current form. Remedial works exceeding £25,000 excluding any shaft treatment.

Report

The final report (*Figures 8.4, 8.5*) summarizes the type and condition of the engine house, the engine type, function and date, and the management needs.

Mitigation

(1) The reports contain sufficient detail for any listing and scheduling proposals. A programme of listing and scheduling is now in progress.

(2) A priority list for capital works has been drawn up on the basis of the MIV plus SMAV scores, modified to take into account the availability of grant-aid and the owner's requirements. Action is now under way in the Central Mining District to implement this programme of works (Mineral Tramways Project: Kerrier Groundwork Trust) and elsewhere in the county.

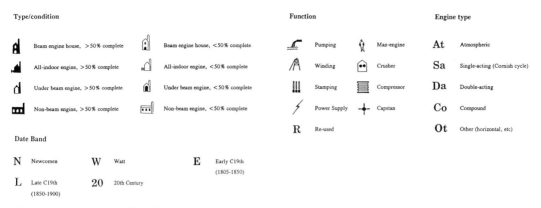

Figure 8.5 Pictograms used to describe engine houses and engines in the survey reports

Conclusions

It is intended that all engine houses in Cornwall will eventually be examined in this way. The Unit believes that this methodology is relevant to a wide range of closely defined monuments, structures and buildings. It is particularly applicable to historic industrial sites. As long as there is room for professional judgement and that this is given due weight in any evaluation procedure, it is possible and desirable to quantify value and priority.

References

SHARPE, A., LEWIS, R. and MASSIE, C. (1991) *Engine House Assessment – Mineral Tramways Project*, Cornwall Archaeological Unit

SHARPE, A., EDWARDS, T. and SPARROW, C. (1992) *St Just. An Archaeological Survey of the Mining District. Vols I and II*, Cornwall Archaeological Unit

Case study 8.3

Piel Castle, Cumbria

Rachel Newman

Piel Castle stands on a low mound of boulder clay at the southern end of the tidal Piel Island, guarding the mouth of the harbour at Barrow-in-Furness on the northern side of Morecambe Bay. It was built by Furness Abbey, perhaps as a refuge from the marauding Scots, or more probably as a warehouse and customs post to regulate the thriving trade along the coast and with Ireland. A licence to crenellate 'their dwelling-house of Fotheray' (Calendar of Patent Rolls, 1 Edward III) was granted in 1327, which implies that a building already existed on the site; indeed, some have suggested that the island was fortified as early as the twelfth century (Curwen, 1910, p. 271).

Documentary references to the castle are not frequent, but it appears to have decayed by the early fifteenth century, when some refurbishment probably took place. However, by the Dissolution of Furness Abbey in 1537 it was reported that the structure was in bad repair. There is no record of any further refortification. The gradual ruination of the fabric can be charted in various prints, which demonstrate that the east wall of the keep collapsed on to the beach in the early nineteenth century. This decay was partially halted later in that century by the construction of sea defences, which slowed the erosion around the south and east sides of the castle, and by a relatively thorough scheme of consolidation, particularly in the keep. The castle was taken into guardianship by the state in 1919.

A project of excavation and survey was undertaken in the deteriorating weather conditions of the autumns of 1983 and 1984 by the Lancaster University Archaeological Unit to record and analyse the monument in advance of a major programme of repair and consolidation organized by English Heritage from 1987 to 1991. This programme was designed to retard the slow erosion of the fabric, to stabilize the monument for the next half century and to deter vandalism. This project formed the first in a series of fabric surveys by the Unit on behalf of English Heritage, involving properties in its care and in connection with grants to owners of other ancient monuments. During the course of this, the methodology by which such surveys have been performed has been developed by the Unit at a rapid pace so that the use of a computer-aided design (CAD) system in connection with photogrammetric plots is now standard practice.

Small-scale excavations were undertaken in 1983 at selected points within the various elements of the monument, with the aim of establishing whether any important archaeological deposits would be disturbed by the scaffolding constructed for the consolidation work. This involved the total excavation of the interiors of the surviving perimeter towers and the inner north-western tower, as well as a section excavated from beyond the gate into the inner bailey, through the western and central compartments of the keep. All the excavations proved that the site had been cleared of debris, probably during the Duke of Buccleuch's consolidation works in the 1870s. Little trace of floor levels survived and, indeed, few traces of the medieval occupation were recovered. The excavations demonstrated that the monument had been altered during the occupation of the site, although it seemed that there had never been intensive medieval activity, whilst they also served to confirm that no significant archaeological deposits would be disturbed by the subsequent consolidation.

Every standing wall of the castle was surveyed both internally and externally in the autumn of 1984 in order that a full understanding of the fabric of the monument should be gained prior to consolidation. Parts of the east wall of the keep and the southern curtain wall have collapsed on to the beach, and these have been recorded. Partially rectified photographs were supplied for the 1984 survey, and these produced basic information for external walls, although the difficulties of photographing elevations on the edge of the island introduced a significant error into many of the montages. This information was grafted on to a survey of each elevation using a theodolite and lap-top Epson HX-20 microcomputer. The theodolite was set up at right angles to a chosen identifiable point on the elevation to be surveyed (the reference point). The horizontal and vertical angles for each point of detail were read and this information was fed into the computer, which produced x and y coordinates for each point relative to the reference point. The program calculated the coordinates at 1:50, which was the scale of the archive drawings, and at 1:1, which allowed a check on the accuracy of the survey data by means of taping the distance between any two points and comparing the measurement with the computed data. The accuracy of this method primarily depends on the wall being in a regular and vertical plane and, furthermore, the theodolite needs to be sited at a reasonable distance from the elevation, not always possible in the cramped spaces of some interiors, otherwise the size of the vertical angle to a given point tends to introduce an element of distortion. The surveyed points were recorded on a photograph or a sketch of the wall. After accurate plotting of these selected points, supplementary detail was added on site, and a written description of each elevation was made. This noted features of particular interest and also produced an approximate chronology for the monument.

Annotated archive drawings were produced, in a form which enabled their reduction to an A3 copy from which the architect designing the specification for repairs and consolidation could work. The castle had been constructed largely of roughly coursed rounded stones, clearly collected from the surrounding beaches. Most of these had been worked to produce an approximately smooth surface and many internal walls retained traces of plastering. All architectural detail, such as door and window surrounds and the quoining at the corners of structures, was constructed of red sandstone ashlar, almost certainly quarried in the precinct of Furness Abbey. This had generally been worked to a high quality and had frequently been a target for robbing; it was also more subject to erosion than the beach stones, many of which were granite. The specification for the fabric survey took account of the essentially random nature of the construction of the walls and therefore only architectural detail was drawn stone by stone, although particular note was made of putlog holes and possible building lifts, which should not be obscured by the consolidation processes. Areas of vegetation and exposed core material which would need attention were also highlighted.

The consolidation work, which was undertaken by John Laing Stonemasonry from a purpose-made compound next to the castle, concentrated on the keep and inner bailey. The Unit maintained a regular presence on site, which allowed the recording of elements not visible during the original survey. These were primarily at a high level, and therefore accessible only from scaffolding, such as wall tops, intramural passages, particularly connected with garderobes, and details of windows, such as the positioning of glazing bars and shutters. These were added, where appropriate, to the original annotated drawings, or supplementary drawings were created at a scale of 1:50, with some details at 1:20. In addition, several more lengthy watching briefs were maintained when vegetation was being stripped, or on the one occasion when underpinning proved necessary. An as-built record was compiled by the English Heritage clerk of works for the site, which, with the fabric survey, will form the basic site archive. This is particularly important in areas where decayed fabric has been rebuilt completely, as in the western keep, to prevent unauthorized access to the monument. Regular monthly site project meetings

were held between the contractor, the architect, the English Heritage clerk of works and the Unit, which assessed progress, discussed the forthcoming work programme and highlighted any particular archaeological constraints to the work.

The project was made much more difficult by the consistent prescription by administrators of autumn and winter field seasons, which meant that both recording and consolidation work was frequently hampered by cold and bad light internally and by appalling weather, particularly high winds, externally. Although overnight stays on the island were made regularly, the timetable was dictated by the tides and the light, which often did not coincide by significant amounts. Despite this, the fabric of the keep and inner bailey has been well consolidated, and emergency repairs have been undertaken on the south-western and north-eastern outer towers. Much information has been gained about the history of the castle, which has proved to be much more complex than might have been assumed from first glance, although the standard of preservation below ground has been shown to be poor. The continuous close contact with the monument over a number of years produced a wealth of detail which perhaps would not have been so evident in a more rapid survey. The castle clearly was not constructed in a single phase, although the construction techniques used made it extremely difficult to dissect, and there is evidence that changes in design, particularly the incorporation of buttresses to the keep, were made during the main building programme. The gatehouse to the keep had also obviously been modified. In addition, much was learnt in terms of methodology, which has been put to good use by the Unit on subsequent occasions, allowing the refining of techniques beyond all recognition. The results of the excavation and initial analysis have been published (Newman, 1987) and it is intended to publish in the near future the information gained during the consolidation works. The archive will be deposited with the Cumbria Archive Service once this final report has been completed.

References

Calendar of Patent Rolls, 1 Edward III

CURWEN, J. F. (1910) 'Piel Castle, Lancashire', *Transactions of the Cumberland and Westmorland Antiquarian and Archaeological Society*, new series, **10**, 271–287

NEWMAN, R. M. (1987) 'Excavations and survey at Piel Castle, near Barrow-in-Furness, Cumbria', *Transactions of the Cumberland and Westmorland Antiquarian and Archaeological Society*, new series, **87**, 101–16

Case study 8.4

Project work in Staithes

John Sutton

Staithes is a small fishing village situated on the York-shire Coast, to the north of Whitby. The old part of the village consists of around 250 houses, mainly from the seventeenth, eighteenth and nineteenth centuries. The buildings are grouped tightly around small yards and strung along narrow streets and passageways. It is a very compact village, originally confined in site to a steep-sided valley and a ledge at the foot of the coastal cliffs (*Figures 8.6, 8.7*). A more recent part of Staithes is situated just inland. Here the buildings are mainly in brick, in contrast to the predominance of stone in the old village.

The village has a fascinating history which includes tales of smuggling, links with Captain Cook and tragic losses of life in the fishing·community. Staithes seems to have been at its peak in the late 1800s. A largely self-sufficient community was involved in lobster, crab and line fishing, with ironstone and associated workings providing employment just inland. The village was on a railway, with its own station. The railway sent fresh fish to London three times a week and it brought goods into the village, including the Welsh slate still evident on many of the roofs. Artists were attracted to the village, notably the Staithes Group, who were active in the area over several decades.

A century later, the picture is very different. The railway has gone, there are only three boats fishing full-time, the local economy is depressed and the only major source of employment is the nearby Boulby potash mine. Many villagers have moved to housing in the newer part of Staithes and some of their former homes have become holiday cottages or second homes. These often stand empty for much of the year, giving the village a feeling of neglect. Despite this apparent decline, Staithes still has great character and retains an air of individuality. In particular, there is

Figure 8.6 Staithes: village setting

Figure 8.7 Staithes: building group

a local determination that the village should remain a living, working place, and not merely an attractive cluster of weekend and holiday homes.

It was against this background that a number of authorities and agencies held a series of meetings in the late 1980s. Some attended with the aim of putting together a coordinated package of improvements; integrated projects had been shown to work elsewhere and Staithes seemed to be an ideal location for such an approach. The scheme that emerged was more basic than this, but it did have the advantage of a long-term commitment. Agreement had been reached on the benefits of enhancing the village environment and on the importance of developing projects in partnership with the local community. It was on this basis that the scheme moved forward, involving a group comprising the North York Moors National Park, Scarborough Borough Council, Hinderwell Parish Council and the Yorkshire Rural Community Council.

Village enhancement schemes

The National Park Authority had expertise in environmental improvement schemes and so took a lead in this field. The old village of Staithes had been designated a conservation area in 1972 and a town scheme had been operating since 1983. With the cooperation of English Heritage, the scheme was expanded to cover virtually all the properties within the conservation area, about 100 of which are listed. The budget was increased and grants were offered at 50 per cent towards approved works, to encourage a better take-up. The Borough Council also offers house renovation grants and occasionally the town scheme provides top-up funding towards appropriate materials and fittings. By late 1992, around £100,000 had been paid in grants towards building restoration.

The network of passages, steps and narrow streets weaving through the village adds greatly to its interest and character. These features have been the main focus for work carried out through the National Park's village improvement scheme, re-laying existing materials where possible and elsewhere using appropriate materials such as Yorkstone flags, sandstone and, occasionally, whinstone setts. Initially, this work was carried out by a community programme team. The supervisor was a local man with a good range of skills and a keen interest in the work. This helped to ensure a high standard of work and a steady improvement took place in the village over a period of several years. When the community programme ceased in 1989, there was a significant drop in the number of enhancement schemes undertaken. Contractors have been used since, although sometimes with disappointing results, and a team funded by the North Yorkshire Training and Enterprise Council has also carried out some projects in the village. Over £30,000 has been spent on village improvements, most of which has been material costs.

These schemes have brought a definite improvement to the village. New pantile roofs are probably the most noticeable feature when looking down on Staithes from the cliffs. Walking through the streets, the attention to detail in the buildings and streetscape becomes more apparent. The distinctiveness of Staithes has been respected in these schemes, with the effort being concentrated on enhancing the existing character of the place, and avoiding any temptation to try to modify that character.

Involving the local community

Community involvement was seen as the other major element in the revitalization of Staithes as a living, working village. The Parish Council has been involved from the outset, both in the detailing of the village improvement schemes and also in discussions on wider issues. In order to gain insight into the views of residents, the Rural Community Council helped to conduct a village appraisal in 1989. This highlighted a number of key issues and, perhaps more significantly, showed villagers' concerns for the future. The views also helped to confirm the validity of the original aims set by the project group.

It was recognized that further work with the community would need the commitment of a considerable amount of staff time. Progress was therefore limited until the National Park appointed a community liaison officer in early 1992. The officer took on a role of guiding and enabling – listening to what people had to say, suggesting ideas and taking a lead on improvement projects where necessary. Although there had been a delay in following on from the village appraisal, this approach was well received and a good working relationship soon developed.

The present situation

The local community has become increasingly involved in developing new projects. Meetings are very informal and there is an emphasis on encouraging participation. One of the effects of this approach has been a shift in focus, with people wanting to look at the village as a whole. It is recognized that further enhancement schemes are still needed in the conservation area, but it has also become apparent that some worthwhile improvements could be carried out on the approaches into the village. Social and economic benefits are seen as being closely tied to environmental improvements. An example is the main village car park, which occupies a central location on land once crossed by the railway. By bringing together local people and various professionals, issues such as tourism, car park security, a children's play area and visitor information are being worked into a comprehensive improvement scheme. A similar approach is planned for major streetscape improvements in the conservation area.

Looking ahead

The long-term benefits of the project work in Staithes will be centred on the physical improvements in the historic village. Also of importance, although less tangible, will be the valuable process of different organizations and local people working together in a partnership. Local involvement, raising confidence and the actual achievements on the ground are inseparable elements in such a project and these are the measures by which success will be judged. If Staithes can remain a living, working place, retaining some of its character and traditions from the past, matched with an optimism for the future, then the project will have achieved its main aims.

Case study 8.5

The RCHME/WYAS survey of Yorkshire textile mills

Colum Giles

In 1984 the Royal Commission on the Historical Monuments of England and the West Yorkshire Archaeology Service began a survey of textile mills in Yorkshire. The archive resulting from the survey is available for public consultation in the National Monuments Record (NMR), curated by RCHME, and in 1992 the findings were published (Giles and Goodall, 1992). This case study explains the background to the survey, and describes the aims and methods employed and the results achieved.

The Yorkshire Textile Mills Survey was a collaborative venture between a national body (RCHME) and a local agency (WYAS). Both parties, and consequently the public, benefited from the pooling of resources, and the archive, held centrally in the NMR and locally in the WYAS Sites and Monuments Record, was made more easily accessible for use both to the organizations involved in the work and to members of the public.

Reasons for survey

There were a number of reasons for the decision to study textile miles rather than another category of building. The most important was the threat posed to mills by redundancy. Many mills were no longer being used for their original purpose, and in others the older parts of the complexes were being left empty in favour of modern buildings more suited to contemporary working practices. Some mills were abandoned completely, with little prospect of an economic new use being found, and many complexes, especially those on valuable urban sites, were threatened with complete demolition. A report (Tym and Partners, 1984) put forward the idea of central and local government agencies encouraging demolition through grant-aiding. The report suggested that the existence of large numbers of redundant industrial buildings deflated property values and acted as a disincentive to new investment. Their clearance was seen as one means of attracting new industries to replace the region's traditional economic base. The Royal Commission recognized that the rate at which mills would be lost, already rapid at the time that the survey was being considered, would accelerate if this became official policy, with the obvious consequence that many mills would be swept away with no record having been made of them.

Another powerful incentive to study textile mills was provided by the lack of understanding of their historical significance. There were a small number of pioneering published studies of mill architecture, and a few individuals with a great knowledge of the industry and its buildings. In key areas, however, people who on a daily basis had to make decisions about the value of individual mill sites lacked clear guidance about the significance of what they were obliged to assess. Some of these people were deciding whether or not mills should be demolished, and while an appreciation of the historical importance of a particular site might not necessarily affect the outcome of deliberations, it serves everyone's purpose if decisions are based on the best possible quality of information. This clearly was not happening in many instances.

The poor understanding of mill architecture was as apparent at the national as at the local level. English Heritage's resurvey of buildings of special historic or architectural importance was launched in the early 1980s, but few of the listers on the ground had either the detailed knowledge necessary for an appreciation of mill building, or the resources to allow them to acquire this. As a result, formal architectural and aesthetic criteria, imported from the study of other types of building, were commonly applied to mills and to industrial monuments in general. More appropriate criteria, such as the way in which the form of some buildings reflected their function, and the way in which the site worked as a whole, were frequently neglected. The result was that the new lists omitted much that had significance for the development of the industry and its buildings.

That the textile mills of Yorkshire were an important class of monument, and therefore worthy of study, was widely accepted. The physical presence in the local landscape of multi-storey mills and great expanses of sheds alone gave them prominence, and it was incontrovertible that their historical role in the development of the area gave mills a regional significance as a building type. To some extent, the popular image of the area was one formed by the mills and by the industries and infrastructure which had developed around them.

Survey aims and methods

The philosophy underlying the survey gave the Royal Commission a number of objectives. Most importantly, its work had to attempt to provide a better understanding of the significance of mill building, allowing interested parties – developers, planners, historians and so on – to make informed judgements about either individual sites or the class of monument as a whole. The means to this end were the compilation of an archive for public consultation and the publication of the survey findings. These two aspects could provide both detailed information on particular mills and a general overview outlining the development of the industry's buildings.

The survey was divided into a number of distinct phases. First, a rapid survey of all sites identified from early twentieth century map sources allowed the degree of survival to be established. This stage of the survey produced RCHME level 1 records (RCHME, 1991), with all extant sites noted and photographed both from the ground and from the air. A total of nearly 2000 sites were recorded by a team of two field workers in less than nine months. This archive was then assessed, and 150 sites were selected for more detailed recording (RCHME level 3). The chosen sites covered the major themes of importance, including date of construction, branch of the industry, function (that is, whether a spinning mill, weaving mill and so on), and type of power employed. These sites were then recorded by combining the evidence of field work with that drawn from documentary sources. Usually a team of two field workers spent up to a day at each site. Return visits by graphics officers and photographers produced measured survey drawings and publication photography respectively. The archive which resulted from this stage of the survey provided the evidence for the last stage, the preparation of a publication outlining the survey's findings.

The survey, including research, field work and the preparation of material for publication, lasted for about six years. It was staffed by two investigators responsible for the project design, report writing and preparation of publication text, by a graphics officer responsible for survey work (assisted by a contract post) and for book illustrations, and a research assistant who provided the documentary evidence incorporated into the archive. In addition the survey made significant demands on RCHME's photographers and on the Air Photo Unit, and depended heavily upon administrative support during the survey and on editorial staff during the preparation of the publication.

The results of the survey

The survey had a number of results, some direct and obvious, others less so. The archive of sites is accessible for public use in the National Monuments Record and in the West Yorkshire Archaeology Service. It has been used most often for planning purposes, on the occasion of an application to alter or demolish a Yorkshire mill. It is also a resource which will prove useful for the purposes of historical research.

The publication resulting from the survey is available, and the expectation is that its analysis of the changing form of mill buildings and mill complexes will have an impact in various fields. Its method of approaching the study of large industrial complexes, with its emphasis on the functional aspects of industrial architecture and on the importance of the relationship between buildings, is one which can usefully be applied more widely, alongside the more conventional structural and aesthetic lines of enquiry. The working methods and the results can also act as an exemplar, showing other agencies what can be achieved. This in fact has already taken place, for soon after the beginning of the Yorkshire survey RCHME entered into partnership with the local authorities of Greater Manchester to conduct a similar survey there. An existing survey of mills in east Cheshire also received RCHME support during its course and in the preparation of a publication. Three published volumes on the textile mills of the north of England represent a substantial contribution to the study of industrial buildings (Giles and Goodall, 1992; Williams and Farnie, 1992; Calladine and Fricker, 1993).

On a practical level, the techniques used to record the mills and present the findings should influence the way in which other agencies approach the recording of industrial complexes. For example, the use of aerial photographs enhances the archive considerably, for aerial views allow an overall assessment of a site which is beyond the means of either ground-level photography or block plans. In the published work, graphic illustration played a crucial role in conveying understanding of the sites described. Phased evolution diagrams, block plans, cut-away views and reconstructions allowed the reader to grasp important concepts – site development, the relationship between buildings and machinery, the way in which power was distributed through a site and so on – in a clear and attractive presentation, allowing the buildings, often recorded as empty shells, to show the ways in which they had evolved and functioned as industrial structures.

It is to be hoped that RCHME's work will have an effect on heritage management by means of its impact on the planning process. The knowledge gained by RCHME staff was recognized by English Heritage, which commissioned the preparation of a set of guidelines for the listing of textile mills. In these guidelines, it was argued that more appropriate criteria should be applied in the assessment of mills for listing purposes. Above all it is hoped that, while unable to record all mills to an equal level of detail, RCHME has by its survey work and publication provided a broad context against which individual mill buildings and complexes may be judged. It is in this key role of conveying understanding that RCHME's educative function is most clearly manifested.

References

CALLADINE, A. and FRICKER J. (1993) *East Cheshire Textile Mills*, RCHME

GILES, C. and GOODALL, I. H. (1992) *Yorkshire Textile Mills 1770–1930*, HMSO

RCHME (1991) *Recording Historic Buildings: a Descriptive Specification* (2nd edn), Royal Commission on the Historical Monuments of England

TYM, ROGER and PARTNERS (1984) *Mills in the 80s: a Study of the Reuse of Old Industrial Buildings in Greater Manchester and West Yorkshire*, Greater Manchester and West Yorkshire Metropolitan County Councils

WILLIAMS, M. and FARNIE, D. A. (1992) *Cotton Mills in Greater Manchester*, Carnegie Publishing Ltd

9

Defining and recording the resource: artefacts

Jonathan Drake

> Artefact. Also arte-, 1821 [f. arti-, comb. f. L. ars, art- + *factus*, pa. ppl. *facere* make]. An artificial product.
> *Shorter Oxford Dictionary on Historical Principles*

Artefacts are a uniquely powerful means of conveying information about our heritage to present and future generations. They provide evidence of human activity from periods without surviving structures or landscapes. They offer a concrete link with the experience of individuals in the past. They are the source of detailed information to interpret townscape and countryside; they complement and contextualize oral testimony recalling vanishing societies and industries.

At the same time, the ways in which this information is encoded in artefacts, and the processes by which it is apprehended by an audience, are alike highly complex. Paradoxically, there is at once a vast number of artefacts surviving today while at the same time those artefacts are a minute and often unrepresentative sample of those in use in the past.

Artefact management is thus an important but difficult part of the heritage manager's job, and one which must be founded on an understanding of the resource. This chapter seeks to plot a path through the minefield by examining what artefacts really are, highlighting the range of items which count as artefacts and showing how they carry information. It suggests how artefacts can be acquired and recorded so as to maximize their usefulness now and in the future; it looks at what artefacts represent and at the resource available to us in relation to what has been lost. Finally, the implications for managing artefacts and presenting them to the public are explored.

What is an artefact?

Artefacts are anything constructed or selected and hence given meaning by human choice. They are not simply the 'artificial products' of the dictionary definition. The term encompasses a far wider range of objects, a substantial proportion of which are not the result of a manufacturing process, but have been instead simply removed in some way from their natural context by human agency. Such artefacts are often physically unchanged: neither the late Iron Age slingstones found at Maiden Castle by Sir Mortimer Wheeler (1943), nor the many natural objects collected and arranged at Kettle's Yard in Cambridge by Jim Ede (1984), are altered from their natural state. Although there is no question that such objects have a meaning, it is one which is wholly dependent on their selection, location and juxtaposition. Likewise, the same object can be given a range of very different meanings by its selection for a number of purposes. Indeed, the Kettle's Yard stones are in material and form identical to those excavated by Wheeler at the great hill fort (which, so the story goes, were themselves topped up from Chesil Beach when all the genuine slingstones from the site had been sold as souvenirs!).

What counts as an artefact?

Artefacts comprise metal, stone, organic materials like bone and wood, ceramics, glass, plastic and other synthetic materials. All the different classes of material found in museums of human history are included, as well as a vast range of other categories selected and/or modified by human action. There are high-status, highly specific objects which are often relatively easy to identify and attribute, if not to interpret, and also the plain and simple. Generally speaking, the higher-status and more unusual material is preferentially preserved, leaving the material evidence for commonplace human activities underrepresented. In addition, where it exists, the latter is often less easy to identify or to understand, since it is less differentiated: a poor household will have only one kind of spoon, used for many purposes, while a rich merchant might have six different types, each characteristic of a particular use.

I do not, however, intend to discuss all classes of artefact in detail; there are too many, and most have well established literatures of their own which describe their nature and range. Instead, I want to highlight a number of kinds of materials which are not in general regarded as artefacts in the usual sense of the term, and consequently are managed in isolation. The essence of heritage management should be to integrate the different parts of the resource, and the same principles can and should be applied to all artefacts falling within the broad definition I have proposed above.

Contemporary illustrations or representations are a good example of such concealed artefacts. Representations are themselves artefacts, and also function as surrogates for the artefacts they record, which are in many cases absent from the material record owing to loss or decay. They also provide evidence for processes and human actions which are not explained fully, if at all, by surviving artefacts. These records or representations, while appearing to be more intelligible than other types of artefact, are usually just as encoded. What they record is not easily interpreted; nor is the reason for their production.

Archives are another type of artefact which present similar difficulties in interpretation. In the same way, what they do *not* describe is often as significant as their overt subject matter. The nature of the record (clay tablet, tally stick, pipe roll, government *Blue Book* etc.), its physical characteristics, and the content of the setting down of the information, carry as much data as the words themselves. Treating them simply as written sources of information not only ignores their inherent bias, but also fails to make use of the considerable body of non-verbal data they carry.

It is tempting to assume that pictorial records and archives complement other artefacts. However, the same selection processes which result in the invisibility or unintelligibility of particular activities or human actions in the material record are just as germane here. The low status and the commonplace are very often equally unrepresented both in the material record and in contemporary illustrations and written sources. In general, therefore, the availability of one class of artefact cannot be regarded as a substitute for others, nor can a simple process of aggregating all available artefacts be relied upon to produce a complete impression of a given culture.

The potency and cultural significance of *art objects* has tended to set them apart from artefacts in general – so much so that they are often not regarded as artefacts at all. Yet they are capable of functioning at several levels simultaneously. At the simplest, they furnish a period room, or complete an assemblage of artefacts characteristic of a particular culture. At another, they can be treated as illustrations providing a record or representation of human activity, which can be used to illuminate the context or guide the interpretation of another artefact, or to describe activity for which there are no other material correlates. Art objects are, however, most important as evidence of values, preoccupations and attitudes, an encapsulation of the world-view of the patron, the artist and the age in which they lived. Other artefacts carry some of this information, but less accessibly; since it was not the prime reason for their creation, this part of their meaning is more deeply encoded, and less complete.

At the same time, this is not to argue that the interpretation of works of art is unambiguous, or that is is easy to apprehend what a contemporary audience would have understood from them. The values attributed to them in their social context are not fixed and absolute, but are fluctuating and conditional – both between different social groups, and over time. To this extent, the visual image is not a mere representation of reality, but a symbolic system (Gombrich, 1972), which may offer more information about the deeper spiritual, social and political aspects of the past precisely *because* it is not a simple representation of human action.

The changes which have taken place in art since the late nineteenth century have reduced the extent to which art objects are useful artefacts for the elucidation of the collective preoccupations of society, at least at a surface level. They now have more to do with the artist's exploration of individual ideas and of the medium itself – though these changes themselves offer a revealing commentary on the recent past.

On a less elevated plane, there is a further class of material which should be treated as an artefact, since it is also the product of human actions and decisions. *Environmental evidence* – soils, pollen cores, faecal material and so on – furnishes information about the lives of humans in the past, and their impact on the landscape in which they lived. A medieval latrine in Worcester (Greig, 1981), for example, produced objects and residues which revealed details of diet, refuse disposal, wild and cultivated plants, and the types of insects and parasites coexisting with the human population.

Finally, artefacts also include complex *assemblies* of other individual artefacts – particularly machines and structures. The individual components are intelligible only as parts of a greater whole: the piece of *Lorica segmentata* in a suit of Roman armour, the brake van at the end of its rake of wagons. Hence, although each individual part has its own context of production and use, there are strong arguments for treating the complete assembly as the artefact in order to understand its function and significance. Indeed, without necessarily adopting a quasi-mechanical or systems model for the operation of society, there is a real sense in which successively greater levels of insight into the human past depend on progressively aggregating artefacts into ever more complex assemblies.

Ultimately, therefore, *landscapes* are artefacts, shaped by the interaction between nature and human choice, explaining and explained by all the combinations of lesser artefacts which they comprise. In this way, most of what I discuss in this chapter concerning the information content, meaning and management of artefacts can and should be applied to the buildings and landscapes dealt with elsewhere in this volume.

How do artefacts carry information?

Artefacts are shaped by human decisions. What they are made of, how the raw material is processed, what shape and finish it is given, all provide information about choices made in the past. To these should be added the changes which occur during the life of the artefact – both in its original context of use, and also in its subsequent secondary existence after disposal, whether actually thrown away or retained in some kind of collection or hoard. This immediately begs important questions about authenticity: if genuine artefacts are defined as those in an original and unaltered state, very few examples would be available to use, and the amount of data at our disposal would be drastically reduced.

George Washington's axe is notorious (Hayton, 1986), with its two new heads and three new handles. But what about the steam locomotive *Mallard*, which broke the rail speed record in 1938? Is it any less authentic because it is now fitted with what is probably its fifth boiler since that record-breaking run (Shorland-Ball, 1990)? Is a painting any less authentic because, like Peake's 1610 portrait of Henry, Prince of Wales, the original background, a formal mannerist wall, was replaced in the late seventeenth century by a romantic Titianesque landscape, and an allegorical figure of Father Time was obliterated altogether (Savill, 1985)? Likewise, is a Chinese export porcelain bowl less genuine because it had silver-gilt mounts added to it when it arrived in England in about 1580 (Lang, 1985)?

In most if not all cases, it is precisely such *modifications* which convey the most useful information. The portrait of the Prince of Wales reveals evidence of changing taste, and the way in which works of art were repainted to conform with that taste. *Mallard*'s history tells us how rapidly steam boilers wear out – and also suggests that even though the locomotive was of immense significance, after 1938 it was worked as hard as any of its less romantic fellows. The Chinese bowl highlights interesting contrasts between approaches to decoration in two very different societies, and is also a neat demonstration of the literal repackaging of exotic artefacts as part of their appropriation by a different culture. Other, more homely examples (the adaptation of farm carts to enable them to be drawn behind tractors in many parts of the world during the early to mid twentieth century) can reveal the practical impact and absorption of technical change.

Although only indirectly the product of explicit human intention, *patterns of wear* are another important source of information. Their analysis is often the only means of determining the use to which an object was put. For example, through microwear studies it has proved possible to suggest whether flint blades were used for cutting meat or hides, working bone, or harvesting cereals (Sieveking and Newcomer, 1986).

Repairs in response to wear or damage also carry useful data about artefacts and the people who used them. Holes have been found in many prehistoric pots, drilled after firing in order to permit the repair of cracks by the insertion of bindings. This suggests that such vessels were expensive to procure, meriting the effort of first aid, and that whatever their function, cracks did not impair their usefulness.

Traces of decay are likewise informative. Particular organisms which attack timber live only in the intertidal zone – so the evidence of their characteristic burrows can be used to infer the waterline of a timber vessel. Similarly, the remains of nematode worms preserved in the corrosion products on the reverse of a Saxon brooch revealed the types of organism feeding on corpses in the sixth century AD (Platt, 1980).

Traditionally, museums have sought pure and unaltered artefacts. They have a place, but acquisition policies should give equal value to the battered, repaired and reused examples which have much greater potential information content. Interpreting this evidence is important too: traces of soot on a cooking pot, or paint worn off machinery by the pressure of a human hand, powerfully evoke the context in which the artefacts were used. Conservation practice must take these factors into account: over-restoration not only destroys evidence, but also increases the already considerable difficulty of conveying a persuasive impression of conditions in the past.

Modification, wear, repair and decay are all intrinsic to the individual artefact. A great deal of the information carried by artefacts is, however, *extrinsic* or contextual. In the extreme case, like the flint pebbles from Maiden Castle, Kettle's Yard and Chesil Beach, *all* the information is of this kind. Provenance is equally important to works of art and to archaeological material: not only does it convey considerable data itself, but it also critically affects the significance of the intrinsic characteristics of the artefact. For example, the Arretine pottery discovered by Mortimer Wheeler in 1944 was itself quite ordinary; what was remarkable was its find spot, at Arikamedu on the southern coast of India, clear evidence of Roman trade routes reaching the subcontinent (Hawkes, 1982). In England in the 1760s, on the other hand, the ninth Duke of Norfolk completed his 'set' of ancestors by buying old portraits and renaming them (Robinson, 1986), thus arbitrarily changing their provenance for dynastic reasons.

The recording and acquisition of artefacts

Recording and acquiring artefacts are two aspects of the same process: the recovery and retention of data about the past derived from the material record. This process has been pursued in different ways, but its analysis in these terms helps to unite the various approaches explored over the last 100 years, and provides a basis for its management in the future.

The importance of contextual information places a premium on the satisfactory recording of artefacts and their provenance, since it cannot be subsequently reconstructed from the artefact alone. In general, artefacts have been recorded via acquisition (including excavation, purchase, accident and so on) and curation: documentation (see Chapter 10) has normally been an adjunct to the possession of the concrete object. Over the last 100 years, the steady increase in categories of information recorded about the past has been accompanied by a commensurate increase in the types of artefact deemed worth collecting. For example, a Roman villa site outside Ipswich, excavated at various times since 1893, demonstrates how at first only mosaics, coins, glass, bronze and fine ceramics were retained by the archaeologist. In the inter-war period, coarse pottery, iron and worked bone were added; in the 1950s, animal bone and selected building material; and most recently, in 1990, mortar and soil samples, cess material and carbonized seeds (Drake, 1981; Plouviez, personal communication).

This process has been intensified by the development of new methods of analysis, which have subdivided classes of artefacts previously regarded as uniform. Three or four production centres were thought to account for the Samian ware found at the Roman town of Colchester: now, inductively coupled plasma (ICP) spectrometry suggests that there were up to eleven (Hart *et al.*, 1987). In the same way, New Hall porcelain has been separated into factories A, B, X and Y (Holgate, 1971). Furthermore, following the Samdok (1980) contemporary collecting initiative in Sweden, objects which were previously regarded as too recent now warrant collection, up to and including the artefacts of the present day. Southampton Museums collections, for example, contain badges, leaflets and tape recordings of council meetings relating to the anti-poll-tax campaign of 1990 – which also illustrates another trend, the acquisition of ephemera.

Curating artefact collections is vastly expensive, whether they be the charming but bizarre cabinets of curiosities (see for example Alexander, 1979) which mainly serve to illustrate the obsessions of those who assembled them, or the rapidly expanding archaeological and social history collections which are the product of the current search for completeness. For this reason, the management of acquisition, principally via explicit *acquisition policies*, has been a growing focus of museum attention, and is a cornerstone of the Museums and Galleries Commission's (1989) registration scheme. By setting minimum standards for the care of collections, and demanding that acquisition takes into account the institution's ability to achieve them, the scheme provides a framework for rational decision making. The status of Registration as a test for grant eligibility, and the Audit Commission's (1991) endorsement of it, should help ensure that artefact acquisition becomes progressively more closely related to curatorial resources and the public service objectives of the individual museum or heritage centre.

Tying acquisition to particular goals in this way also takes into account that it is impossible to collect the entire assemblage of artefacts associated with a particular culture. It is hence impossible to acquire material to satisfy the totality of possible heritage management goals, whether of research, preservation or presentation. It is therefore inevitable that acquisition is problem oriented, and it is better that the objectives and assumptions governing it be made clear, so that it does not continue to masquerade as a neutral process.

Just as the prevailing interest in animals, plants, landscapes and buildings has been biased towards the rare, the grand and the spectacular (King and Clifford, 1987), so in the acquisition of artefacts the everyday objects used by people in the past still tend to be underrepresented. In the more distant periods of human history, this problem has been ameliorated by the extent to which the survival of *any* material object is unusual, and its recovery makes an obvious gain for the stock of available information. By contrast, the ordinary artefacts of the last 200 years have been greatly neglected. Acquisition policies must take into account these common products of the era of industrialization, which are of much greater relevance for understanding society as a whole, and the lot of the majority of individuals, than the first, the biggest and the best. The *unusual* object is precisely that, and its irrelevance to the generality of human existence is excerbated by the extent to which contemporary records focus on it and the activity it represents, as noted above.

Mass-produced artefacts are a particular problem: social history collections have tended to ignore them, or else to retain only a few examples, so that the representation of different artefacts is in inverse proportion to their frequency in society. Notwithstanding the practical difficulties, it would be more representative of a specific period to collect every category in quantities directly proportional to its frequency of occurrence, rather than to select one example of everything. Furthermore, the opportunities for collecting inexorably rise with increasing social and technolgical change (Audit Commission, 1991); so to the challenge of managing the acquisition of examples of artefact types with a very wide currency must be added the rapidity with which they are replaced with more modern substitutes, and wholly new categories are added.

The solution lies in addressing and questioning the nature of acquisition and its goals. In broad terms, acquisition is a means of preserving and making available artefacts, their provenance, and the information they carry. Acquisition in terms of physical ownership and curation of the object by a heritage management institution is not automatically the most effective way of achieving these ends, and alternative strategies should always be considered. Private collections already in aggregate hold the bulk of extant artefacts, although biased towards certain fashionable or idiosyncratic categories. Particularly if the increasing commercial value of provenance and the growing interest in history can be drawn together, it may be that some kinds of artefacts can be safely entrusted to the care of private individuals. The crucial weakness, of course, is the difficulty of securing public access and ensuring the curation of the material and its provenance in the long term. However, it would be worth exploring guardianship arrangements based on a development of the British government's scheme for acceptance in lieu of tax (Museums and Galleries Commission, 1990), although public ownership of a proportion of each artefact category will always be necessary as a safeguard for both the objects and the associated contextual information.

More practically, the acquisition process should be seen as a range of options related to the relevance of the artefact, its characteristics, whether other institutions hold equivalent and accessible examples, and especially the goals of the body considering acquisition. At the simplest level, acquisition can consist of noting the existence of a particular class of artefact in a particular location, forming a gazetteer-like database similar to the archaeological sites and monuments records. This might be appropriate if the artefact type is well known and represented in satisfactory type series held in public collections. Beyond this non-intensive record come increasingly detailed recording methods, from simple pro forma descriptions and individual record photographs, through measured drawings, technical specifications and analyses, to film and sound. These techniques can be deployed to deal with artefacts which are within the scope of the acquisition policy, but which are too big or too expensive (a ship, for example), too fragile (food, perhaps), or not collectable at all (the process by which an object is made or used).

The acquisition of concrete artefacts forms the other end of this continuum, from evocative or totemic parts (a locomotive nameplate) to the artefact itself, and finally its physical context (maybe a canal boat

moored at the wharf from which it traded). The most cost-effective response can be selected from within this progressively more expensive repertoire, which closely relates the means of acquisition to the purpose for which it is undertaken. Such a model for decision making is comparable to that increasingly used by archaeologists in assessing the intervention appropriate to a given site and the threat posed to it. Just as full excavation is the counsel of last resort, so too should be the acquisition of the artefact and its context.

In parenthesis, it is worth noting a further parallel with field archaeology. In the same way that amenity value can influence a decision to schedule an ancient monument, an artefact's potential value for public presentation may make it worth acquiring even if it is not particularly endangered, or has little intrinsic research or curatorial importance.

The curation of collections

Acquisition, whether of the artefact itself or of information about it, once embarked upon brings with it the burden of curation. The various aspects of the curatorial process are widely accessible via museological publications, including the *Manual of Curatorship* (Thompson, 1992) and the many works listed in it. I do not, therefore, need to attempt to cover this wide subject here, but it is important to emphasize that the curatorial role does not exist independently. Its function is to manage objects and their provenance so that they are available for use whether in museums or elsewhere, and the heritage manager must understand its complexities and responsibilities. Artefacts represent specific management problems, especially those of security, environmental control and conservation. Artefactual research, exhaustively explored by Thompson's (1992) contributors, is of particular importance. If pursued according to purely academic agendas it may seem remote from the priorities of heritage management, but it is nevertheless an essential tool. It serves to uncover information, to facilitate interpretation, to support authenticity, even to sustain illusion. The successful employment of artefacts for *any* purpose is dependent on the effectiveness of the research carried out on them, and decisions about their management can only sensibly be made on the basis of the information that research provides. Research must therefore be actively managed so that it supports the decision making process and facilitates the use of artefacts to best effect.

What relationship do the artefacts at our disposal bear to the past?

One of the principal factors influencing the insight into human behaviour obtainable from artefacts is the relationship of the sample we now have to the activity it represents. There are at least five major problems or processes distancing us from the past, which can be summarized as follows:

(1) The material record for any period does not represent the entirety of activity at that time; not all activities have material corollaries.

(2) Many activities are represented by artefacts insufficiently durable to enter the material record unless in very exceptional circumstances.

(3) Many categories of material are in some way recycled when the artefacts which they comprise wear out or become obsolete – by reuse, by melting down or by being burnt as fuel, for example.

(4) Once artefacts enter the material record (whether in archaeological deposits, or in some way collected or hoarded) they are subject to all kinds of decay and loss – through the processes of decomposition and decay, through further selection via subsequent human activity, or by activities resulting in their disposal beyond the reach of the modern observer (like refuse disposal for landfill).

(5) Finally, the process of recovery or acquisition, by its methods, its search area, and the availability of time, money and technology, can never recover all that is theoretically available. In addition, it will inevitably be biased in particular ways related to the implicit and explicit assumptions governing it.

The visible effects on the artefacts which *are* accessible to the modern observer do give some indication of the selection processes which have taken place. It is, however, inevitable that survival to the present day almost guarantees that the artefacts at our disposal are in a real sense exceptional. Conveying this information to an audience is difficult and inevitably exposes the temporary and uncertain character of our explanation of the past. All the same, the public prefer sharing the process of interpretation to being blinded by seamless science: carried out imaginatively, this approach offers a genuine opportunity for participation which enhances rather than diminishes the experience of history.

What do artefacts represent?

Artefacts and their associated contextual information are evidence of social systems and their interrelation. They are therefore a route to the understanding of human life in the past, providing insight into the significance and the values inherent in human activity. Artefacts offer not merely technical explication and historical description, but also an opportunity to investigate the choices made by our predecessors.

They are *not*, however, what the positivist New Archaeologists memorably called a complete 'fossil record of the actual operation of an extinct society' (Binford, 1968). By reconstructing all the physical constraints and material objects associated with a given society, the cultural frame of reference will, they believe, be automatically and completely

revealed. This mechanistic view is still implicit in many approaches to the past, probably because concrete artefacts are seen on a common-sense basis as objective entities. However, this objectivity is not transferable to the meanings of the artefacts. The approach also ignores the role of perception and the non-material components of the society being studied, and hence runs the risk of confusing the correlation and association of artefacts with causality. We cannot be sure that the function and significance attributable to an artefact in use today can be reliably extended to a similar object in use in the past. Neither can we easily transfer interpretations derived from historical or anthropological observations to other socieities. It has been demonstrated, for example, that anthropology can provide at least two mutually contradictory explanations for pretty well any assemblage of artefacts associated with human burial (Ucko, 1969).

Nevertheless, we are wholly reliant on our inferential processes, our ability to 'read' objects and their context. Modern values inevitably inform the processes we apply to artefacts in an effort to bring us closer to their meaning, and hence serve as mediating factors which further distance us from them. Even the superficially simple activities of cataloguing, or arranging objects in a display, are inevitably founded on assumptions and interpretations, and hence reify them.

Although ostensibly explaining human history, artefacts in this way tell us far more about the present. Exhibited objects act less to preserve or articulate a particular past, and more to promote new values based on or legitimized by a transformed conception or representation of the past. A seminal event in the history of archaeology illustrates the point. C. J. Thomsen, the Curator of Copenhagen University Museum, in 1816–18 categorized the collection in his care into stone, bronze and iron (Klindt-Jensen, 1975). This organization of the physical objects was intimately bound up with Thomsen's chronological and developmental interpretation of Scandinavian prehistory which his display illustrated. It is still a familiar framework today, so much so that Thomsen's division of prehistory into the neolithic, the Bronze Age and the Iron Age is rarely identified as an interpretative schema, albeit one supported by a great deal of evidence! Rather differently, and much more recently, work in Southampton and elsewhere has shown how nineteenth and twentieth century views about women's roles in society have been reflected in museums' interpretation of the artefacts and activities associated with women in the past (Jones, 1991).

What do artefacts mean to the public?

When, after the long chain of production, use, survival, acquisition and research, the artefact is finally selected for exhibition, what does it convey to the public? The meaning of artefacts on display, whether in a museum, a heritage centre or a reconstructed setting, is dependent on a complex set of interactions. Artefacts do not have fixed meanings; like words in a sentence, their significance depends on their context, their order, their juxtaposition with others, and the knowledge of the audience. Over twenty years ago, investigations into the effectiveness of US government exhibitions showed the importance of four main factors: the nature of the object, the mode of display, the extent and type of supporting material, and the background (intellectual, educational and social) of the visitor (Shettel, 1973). These constitute a presentational package with a powerful semiotic value. Indeed, as far as the audience is concerned, it is this package which is the artefact they see, and not the artefact itself.

Underlying the use of artefacts in any type of public display are the same Renaissance humanist assumptions which were the foundation of the earliest public museums: that objects are intrinsically intelligible and that, through their study, information is gained both about the object and about its context of production and use. However, the most superficial analysis of the audience shows that such assumptions must be wrong: 90 per cent of the visitors to the National Railway Museum in York are not railway enthusiasts and have little previous knowledge of the subject (Shorland-Ball, 1990) or of the artefacts on show.

At the same time, in museums, heritage centres and historic houses, the trend is towards unlabelled displays, and especially towards reconstructions. Immediately, the managers of these displays are making considerable assumptions about the representational value of the artefacts, and about the uniformitarian nature of their meaning. However, the viewer's understanding is strongly dependent on his/her past experience and knowledge. As a direct result of the wide use of historical images in the media, films and advertising, most people associate characteristic values and meanings with particular artefacts. Milk churns, beer barrels, errand bicycles and flat caps are used to promote the old-fashioned quality of butter, beer and bread, and by extension evoke a pre-war or perhaps nineteenth century idyll. Objects which have been appropriated in this way and are used in displays about the past bring with them the context of 'Hovis Country' – not the social context in which they furnished the far from idyllic lives of real people.

The nature of the visitor's understanding is also affected by the *overall* context of his/her experience. Blist's Hill at the Ironbridge Gorge Museum may faithfully group artefacts in ways closely similar to original assemblages, and may (arguably less successfully) group the buildings in which those assemblages are placed into a typical late nineteenth century

Shropshire townscape, but the overall effect is compromised by the absence of the noise, atmosphere and population of that place and time. It is probably for this reason that the Jorvik Viking Centre in York has been so successful in giving the visitor an *impression* of life in the past, by total immersion in sounds, smells and light as well as the physical reconstruction.

This in turn alerts us to a particular problem: the extent to which a high degree of realism, or the appearance of realism, is a source of power and persuasion. The more a room setting in the Museum of London, or a National Trust house, or an English Civil War re-enactment gives the impression of completeness, the more likely the visitor is to assume that he/she is seeing history as it really was. The idea that authenticity increases in direct proportion to the number of original artefacts displayed echoes the German nineteenth century historian Ranke, who believed that by the scientific assembly of enormous numbers of facts, one could apprehend 'wie es eigentlich gewsen' – how it really happened. The danger is that such displays appear to be unmediated (D. Haraway, quoted in Jordanova, 1989); the role of the heritage manager and the other specialists involved being invisible, the interpretative burden of their work is masked.

Not that this is an argument against placing artefacts in appropriate settings for explanatory purposes. It is rather that there is a particular difficulty in presenting an effective impression of the past, while at the same time making clear that it *is* just an impression, and that more than one interpretation is possible. Labels and explanatory panels are of course not necessarily a solution: often they are a vehicle for the curator's erudition, fulfilling with their technicalities and accession codes the same role as the critical apparatus of references and bibliography in a learned paper. Even where they are more comprehensible, they are still regarded as holy writ by the public, their ability to convince demonstrating how much of the audience's attention is directed at the label, and how little at the artefact (Phillips, 1986).

Public presentation and the threat to artefacts

Parts of a historic landscape may be sacrificed, for example to construct facilities to serve those coming to view the landscape, as at Stonehenge – and buildings may be adapted for reuse, hence, losing parts of their original structure. Artefacts, on the other hand, are generally regarded as inviolate once acquired, because of a combination of curatorial values and the greater practicality of retaining an artefact entire and unaltered. Few heritage managers would be happy with the way the Miami Rock and Roll Car Museum has taken 1950s' convertibles and cut them up to form booths and tables for its café!

Nonetheless, the use of artefacts in displays about the past always carries with it the risk of their destruction. In the first place, preparing artefacts for exhibition often changes them by removing evidence of the objects' use or history. Cleaning a bronze axe head may remove mineralized traces of the wood it was used to cut in the first millennium BC. Three thousand years younger, Claes Oldenburg's giant upholstered Hamburger, an icon of the 1960s' focus on the art of common objects, has now been restored as if it were the high art its creator rejected, so that it is 'as shiny and new as a Bonwit Teller Christmas package' (Amaya, 1984).

Once on display, artefacts inevitably suffer – whether from renewed exposure to environment fluctuations and natural decay, or from the impact of the public, closely paralleling the damage suffered by historic landscapes and structures as a direct result of their popularity. Picture researchers handling engravings in the British Museum have caused noticeable deterioration (Wilson, 1989). Working displays have proved a powerful way to convey information about how machines operated, what they were for, and what it was like to use them, but they have also shown the adverse effects for the historic machines themselves. If wear can be confined to parts already replaced many times during the life of an artefact – bearings, for example – their continued replacement need not be a great concern. However, replacement of original parts, and modifications to suit modern safety standards, are surely less acceptable: though does removing the asbestos lagging from a 1930 tug tender de-authenticate it? In these instances, as with Stephenson's *Rocket*, and even the cave paintings at Lascaux, it may be preferable to construct a replica. It may be possible, too, with smaller artefacts, to have touchable or working facsimiles beside cased and protected originals.

In the final analysis, the heritage manager must assess the value (and especially the rarity) of the artefact against the benefits obtained by its display and the concomitant risk of damage. Making objects accessible to the public today must be allowed to compete with the long-term demands of preservation for posterity, although the unique trustee role of the public collection does impose an unavoidable responsibility to curate some examples of every artefact category in perpetuity.

The exploitation of artefacts

Despite the manifold difficulties of acquisition, curation, interpretation and display, artefacts constitute a very powerful means of investigating and presenting the human past. It is for this reason that museums and heritage centres have developed a range of techniques for the exhibition of objects, which have succeeded to varying degrees in overcoming such problems. At one extreme artefacts can be isolated in glass cases, using selectivity to effectively direct attention at particular characteristics and information. At the other the near complete reconstruction will provide context and explanation without recourse to words, but in a much less focused way. It is not even necessary for the artefacts themselves to be directly on show. In the Jorvik Viking Centre, a very large number of replicas are deployed in the ride through reconstructed Viking York. The genuine objects appear in the baldly named Artefact Hall, where they serve to validate the reconstruction offered next door. Elsewhere, artefacts can be used solely as prototypes without being displayed at all, as at Dorchester, where the Tutankhamun Experience consists entirely of facsimiles.

The effectiveness of artefacts in transmitting particular ideas and values is further attested by their growing commercial role. Both the meaning directly apprehended by the audience, and the transfer effects where that meaning influences the impression given by the goods and services with which the artefacts are associated, have been manipulated in this way. Many shops and restaurants now use artefacts for shop fitting. Laura Ashley, the clothing and interior design chain, uses nineteenth century furniture to create an ambience for the display of its fabrics and papers. TGI Fridays, a group of fast-food restaurants, uses an eclectic mixture of hunting, sporting and motoring objects to sustain an image redolent of the 1950s and the outdoor life, to differentiate themselves from their competitors in the crowded 'themed destination' catering market. At Brewers' Quay in Weymouth, the Timewalk juxtaposes a walk-through heritage centre (genuine objects and replicas in historical tableaux) with an accompanying retail mall in a converted Victorian brewery, where artefacts are used to carry the impression of quality and authenticity into the shops themselves.

Commercial interest can increase the cost and rarity of artefacts, but it has potential benefits for the heritage manager with attractive collections. Artefacts are a valuable source of design – whether for direct reproduction or for adaptation. The Victoria and Albert Museum was established in 1851 to provide inspiration to designers and manufacturers. It continues to exploit its collections in this way, both for financial gain and to encourage people to visit the museum to see the originals (Elkan, 1990). Heritage managers should not, however, see such collections as a licence to print money; considerable effort is needed to secure good returns, and products worthy of the originals (Breuer, 1990).

Conclusion

I have tried to show the complexity of artefacts and their interpretation, and how those complexities can and should be incorporated into the management of the resource. The heritage manager will need access to artefact specialists, but must use their advice in such a way as to steer a path between curation for its own sake, and the use of objects as decoration. Artefacts must be integrated with the rest of the heritage resource, so that the different elements can support and explain each other. Only from this basis can landscapes, structures and objects be managed intelligently, the priorities and problems inherent in each informing decisions about them all. The varying perspectives that the different resources offer permit the creation of an exciting, an attractive and above all a critical impression of the past, representing something of the complexity of human existence. As the means by which individuals and societies adapt and give meaning to their environment, artefacts help define people's identity, and hence their heritage. The display of artefacts to the modern public thus affords a glimpse of the life of their predecessors, and an opportunity for engagement with it. Museums and heritage centres are theatres providing a dramatization of history in which the artefacts are more than mere props: they are the understudies for the missing human actors.

References

ALEXANDER, E. P. (1979) *Museums in Motion*, AASLH, Nashville, Tennessee

AMAYA, M. (1984) 'Blam: at the Whitney', *Studio*, **179**(1007), 54–55.

AUDIT COMMISSION (1991) *The Road to Wigan Pier? Managing Local Authority Museums and Art Galleries*, HMSO, London

BINFORD, L. R. (1968) 'Archaeological perspectives', in S. R. Binford and L. R. Binford (eds), *New Perspectives in Archaeology*, Chicago, 5–32

BREUER, D. (1990) 'Licensing and retailing in Brighton', *Museum Development*, October

DRAKE, J. C. (1981) *Castle Hill Roman Villa*, BA thesis, Department of Archaeology and Anthropology, University of Cambridge

EDE, H. S. (Jim) (1984) *A Way of Life: Kettle's Yard*, Cambridge University Press, Cambridge, 17–18, 46–47

ELKAN, J. (1990) 'Licensing: the V and A experience', *Museum Development*, August

GOMBRICH, E. H. (1972) 'The visual image', *Scientific American*, **227**(3), 82–96

GREIG, J. (1981) 'The investigation of a medieval barrel-latrine from Worcester', *Journal of Archaeological Science*, no. 8, 265–282

HART, F. A., STOREY, J. M. V., ADAMS, S. J., SYMONDS, R. P. and WALSH, J. N. (1987) 'An analytical study using induc-tively coupled plasma (ICP) spectrometry, of Samian and colour-coated wares from the Roman town at Colchester, together with related continental Samian wares', *Journal of Archaeological Science*, no. 14, 577–598

HAYTON, B. J. (1986) 'George Washington's axe', *AIM Journal*, **9**(6), 3

HAWKES, J. (1982) *Mortimer Wheeler, Adventurer in Archaeology*, Weidenfeld and Nicholson, London, 239

HOLGATE, D. (1971) *New Hall and its Imitators*, Faber and Faber, London

JONES, S. (1991) 'The female perspective', *Museums Journal*, February, 24–27

JORDANOVA, L. (1989) 'Objects of knowledge: a historical perspective on museums', in P. Vergo (ed.), *Museology*, Reaktion Books, London, 22–40

KING, A. and CLIFFORD, S. (1987) *Holding your Ground*, Wildwood Press, Aldershot

KLINDT-JENSEN, A. (175) *A History of Scandinavian Archaeology*, Thames and Hudson, London

LANG, G. (1985) 'Triumph of the Baroque: porcelain', in G. Jackson-Stops (ed.), *The Treasure Houses of Britain*, Yale University Press, London, 209

MUSEUMS AND GALLERIES COMMISSION (1989) *Guidelines for a Registration Scheme for Museums in the United Kingdom*, London

MUSEUMS AND GALLERIES COMMISSION (1990) *Acceptance in Lieu*, London

PHILLIPS, D. (1986) *Don't Trust the Label*, Arts Council, London, 5–13

PLATT, H. M. (1980) 'Preserved worms on an Anglo-Saxon brooch', *Journal of Archaeological Science*, no. 7, 287–288

ROBINSON, J. M. (1986) 'Ancestral piety', in D. Garstang (ed.), *The British Face: a View of Portraiture 1625–1850*, Colnaghi, London, 11–13

SAMDOK (1980) *Today for Tomorrow*, Nordiska Museet, Stockholm

SAVILL, R. (1985) 'The Jacobean long gallery', in G. Jackson-Stops (ed.), *The Treasure Houses of Britain*, Yale University Press, London, 132–133

SHETTEL, H. H. (1973) 'Exhibits: art form or educational medium?', *Museum News*, no. 52/1

SHORLAND-BALL, R. (1990) *The National Railway Museum*, unpublished lecture to the Southampton University Industrial Archaeology Group

SIEVEKING G. de G. and NEWCOMER, H. H. (eds) (1986) *The Human Uses of Flint and Chert*, Cambridge University Press, Cambridge

THOMPSON, JOHN M. A. (1992) *Manual of Curatorship* (2nd edn), Museums Association, Butterworth Heinemann, Oxford

UCKO, P. J. (1969) 'Ethnography and archaeological interpretation of funerary remains', *World Archaeology*, no. I

WHEELER, R. E. M. (1943) *Maiden Castle, Dorset*, Society of Antiquaries of London Research Committee Report, London

WILSON, D. M. (1989) *The British Museum: Purpose and Politics*, British Museum Publications, London

Case study 9.1

The York Archaeological Trust

Christine McDonnell

The York Archaeological Trust for Excavation and Research was set up in 1972 as a charity dedicated to educating the public in archaeology. The results of its excavations are published in separate parts, or fascicules, making up a series of twenty volumes of *The Archaeology of York*. The Trust's collection currently consists of archaeological material recovered from over 140 excavations in York and from a small number in North Yorkshire. In addition, there are growing ethnological, teaching and reference collections and groups of replica objects.

Over 140,000 small finds are housed in environmentally controlled storage at the Trust's Archaeological Resource Centre and a further 6150 boxes of bulk finds, over 8000 samples for environmental analysis, and a number of structural timbers and architectural fragments are stored in a modern warehouse on the outskirts of York. Some 770 Viking objects are on permanent display at the Trust's Jorvik Viking Centre. Other finds from Trust excavations are on permanent display at the Yorkshire Museum. Collections handling areas and temporary storage facilities are available at the Resource Centre, at the Pottery Studios, and at a Finds Processing Area situated adjacent to the Trust's Conservation Laboratories which augments handling facilities on site.

The Trust considers the preservation, documentation, interpretation and management of this primary source to be of the highest importance. For these reasons it employs a team of conservators, researchers and curators. Also for this reason it adopted a computerized recording system as early as 1975.

Collections management begins on site with efficient processing and documentation. Although handling techniques differ for different categories of finds, the principles of good management remain the same and the Trust follows codes of practice established by the Museums and Galleries Commission (1987; 1992).

Material is initially sorted into two main groups, bulk finds and small finds. Pottery and tile, animal and human bone are washed: all but the animal bone is marked; and all are documented, bagged and boxed by context and transferred to the store. Structural timbers, environmental samples and architectural fragments are allocated additional accession numbers, recorded and removed to the store or Conservation Laboratories as appropriate. Small finds, that is objects, part objects and evidence of manufacturing activities, of metal, fired clay, stone, osseous and organic materials, are divided into material type and placed in the appropriate environmental conditions. Each small find is assigned a unique number, and data are entered into a day book and recorded on the computerized recording system. The Trust has used the Yorkshire Museum's accession system from the outset.

The purpose of the Trust's collections management system is not only to ensure that finds are curated and maintained in optimum conditions from the point of their discovery, but also to allow their efficient and rapid publication. The key is the computerized system which allows an integrated approach to all these.

The Trust's original system, an adaptation of that used by the Museum Documentation Association (MDA), made use of the mainframe facilities at the University of York. In the early 1980s, however, the Trust took advantage of the radical advances offered by the new microcomputers and, taking the existing system as a starting point, developed the considerably more sophisticated Computerized Integrated Finds Record (CIFR). CIFR forms the core of the networked finds management system, which provides a complete vertical integration of data from site to publication on the one hand, and from site to the store or permanent display on the other. Essentially, it has three main elements: it is a collections documentation and accounting tool; it allows for effective care of the collection both in store and on display; and it is a research system with a series of automated analytical tools.

There are two separate databases, one for small finds and one for bulk finds, environmental samples, architectural fragments and structural timbers. Each excavation has its own file on the network. Entries are made by context for bulk finds and by object for small finds. Data are entered at the earliest possible opportunity, that is as soon as the material has been excavated. Subsequently, as material passes through each element of the research design, the record is corrected, updated, expanded and eventually completed. Analytical results and treatments, and recommendations for handling, storage and display, are added by conservators. Catalogue entries are added by the Trust's artefact researchers. Databases are indexed on all the major fields and have indexed glossaries. A complex find facility allows searches on complicated combinations of data and key words and report generation.

CIFR is complemented on the network by computer-aided design (CAD) and statistical packages, and word processing facilities. This set-up is further complemented by the Trust's Context Recording System

(CRS), from which phasing information is lifted, and the editorial department's desk-top publishing arrangements. In addition to CIFR there is a separate pottery database, also with report forms and highly flexible complex find facilities, which records ware type, fabrics, forms and quantities.

The Trust has a dynamic collection, with an estimated 40,000 object movements a year. Prior to CIFR this represented the updating of eight written records for the curators alone. By allowing the automation in the three key areas of collections care, storage and research, the Trust has eliminated the enormous amounts of work generated by the performance of repetitive tasks. Thus it has avoided much of the expensive rekeying of data, the generation of hand-written lists, rewriting and re-editing.

That the York Archaeological Trust has chosen to continue to use CIFR rather than the MDA's Modes should not be seen as a criticism of that system. CIFR shares a commonality of standards with Modes and although different needs require different responses, the principles of good practice remain the same.

Obviously, high standards in documentation are of little use if not accompanied by rigorously enforced standards in collections handling, storage and security. Whether related to the environmental and physical safeguarding of the finds or to recorded data, security is of the highest priority. All buildings are inspected by the Security Adviser of the Museums and Galleries Commission. Access to material is strictly regulated. Rights on the network are password limited. Tape backups are made nightly and monthly tapes are archived. A network-specific virus detection package is updated monthly. Paper records and X-radiographs are copied and archived and all the records in the York Archaeological Trust's archive are microfiched by the National Monuments Record.

In the nine years 1983–92 the Trust published over 7000 finds, in contrast to the previous eleven years when only approximately 700 were published. In part this reflects the increase in the number of staff, but it also reflects gains in efficiency in fascicule production owing to the improved access to data and the elimination of many repetitive tasks which computerization has allowed.

And what of the future? Increased efficiency generates increased demands and we must update if we are to meet these demands. New developments such as the adoption of a synthetic approach to material culture require new tools. The Trust is not alone in having to work within closely controlled budgets, which means waiting for equipment replacement and valuable programming time. However, a multiple finds database to aid the research and analysis of large quantities of vessel and window glass, metal working slag, leather and plaster and a more sophisticated version of the bulk finds element of CIFR – are in production. Key images will shortly be added via an existing facility. The reason that the Trust chose to spend relatively large sums on developing an integrated finds recording system in the past, and the reason it will continue to do so, is that to increase efficiency is to improve the quality of work and thus produce a more erudite and swift response to the management of the heritage.

References

ENGLISH HERITAGE (1991) *Management of Archaeological Projects*

MUSEUMS ASSOCATION (1987) *Code of Practice for Museum Authorities*

MUSEUMS ASSOCIATION (1992) *Standards in the Museum Care of Archaeological Collections*

Case study 9.2

County collections and their management

Alastair Penfold and Mark Holloway

Effective collections management has become closely associated with possible changes which may become necessary as a result of impending local government reform. This is especially relevant in Hampshire where a centralized museum organization is responsible for delivering a local service in various sites throughout the county. Many of these central functions can only be fully expressed if the core function of collections management is working properly. This case study describes some of the stages necessary for an effective collections management overhaul of a county collection.

Over the course of its history Hampshire County Council Museums Service has acquired several important social and local history collections assembled by former town museums prior to their absorption into the county service. These collections were typical of their period and contained a wide range of material, from local memorabilia and ethnology to fine and decorative art. The Museums Service has just completed a comprehensive redisplay programme for all its major sites, incorporating material from its principal collections including social and local history. While every effort was made to use as many objects as possible, it was inevitable that many remained in store at museum headquarters.

The opportunity of rehousing these reserve collections in more environmentally suitable buildings, combined with the introduction of a fully computerized documentation system based on the Museum Documentation Association (MDA) Modes program, has provided an ideal opportunity to really get to grips with collections management and planning. Incentives to do so have been greatly strengthened by recent educational reforms, with their emphasis on the handling of objects, and impending local government reform. Although Hampshire Museums Service has a good record for delivering a county service at local level, increased efficiency in collections management can only enhance and strengthen its reputation and hopefully ensure its long-term survival whatever the future may hold in store.

The collection, which consisted of approximately 7500 items, was housed in two separate, poorly equipped buildings. Material was stored on open shelves or in cardboard boxes, and was arranged by museum of origin rather than by type or material. This rather bizarre method of storage had resulted over the years in considerable duplication of basic types of social history items, including the inevitable sewing machines, gas masks and cast iron mangles.

The aim of the re-storage programme was to transform the social history stores from inadequate and poorly accessible buildings containing numerous small uncatalogued collections into well organized environmentally controlled areas suitable for the storage and long-term management of a comprehensive county-based social history collection. Work began in July 1992 and was completed in January 1993. The programme is best summarized under the following two headings.

Planning and preparation

A detailed plan outlining the aims of the project, costings and staff requirements was prepared well in advance to enable adequate time for recruitment of two short-term contract staff and delivery of racking and storage boxes. The project was costed out at £7500 including materials and wages.

Long-term objectives identified at the beginning of the planning stage included better access to collections through improved documentation and storage, which would in turn lead to increased use for educational handling and temporary exhibition purposes. Improved physical storage would also allow for a more planned and sustainable approach to the conservation of material required for these purposes.

The project was approached from the outset as a joint venture between members of the curatorial and conservation teams. This team approach was essential to the success of the scheme and has been continued as part of the long-term collections management of key collections within the service.

The physical upgrading of storage areas necessitated the use of a temporary holding area while essential building work was carried out. The move involved a slight reduction in total storage space and it was therefore considered essential to maximize the use of all available space. Industrial warehousing methods were thought most appropriate, especially as there was a glut of cheap equipment available on the second-hand market.

A second-hand battery-operated fork-lift truck was acquired for £1500 together with used industrial-grade slot-in Dexion racking and Euro wooden pallets, again second-hand at £2 each. Appropriately sized stackable plastic boxes and trays were ordered from a local firm, prices ranging from £8 to £20 depending on size. All boxes and trays fit on to the pallets with sufficient clearance for handling etc. They also stack on top of one another to maximize racking space (*Figures 9.1, 9.2, 9.3*). A large supply of plastic tags and ties was also acquired. Two temporary staff (both former volunteers) were recruited in June/July 1992.

Procedure

All existing boxes and shelf contents were examined *in situ* and given temporary labels detailing the type of contents, i.e. lighting equipment, kitchen utensils etc., loosely based on the Social History and Industrial Classification (SHIC) system.

An action list was drawn up for members of the team to begin work on particular categories of material. Great care was taken to ensure that details from old box lids and labels were properly recorded and attached to the relevant object before reboxing. A temporary record form was devised for the purpose which was especially useful when dealing with mixed

Figure 9.3 Storage area, Hampshire Museums Service

uncatalogued collections. Trestle tables were put up in each store for basic sorting work.

Once grouped into basic types, material was examined for first-aid conservation requirements and treated if necessary.

After the basic sorting had been completed, material was entered on to computer using the Modes program (*Figure 9.4*). Entry on to computer was initially confined to high-priority categories of material. Low-priority items including craft tools were not listed individually. Analysis of the resulting entries has allowed an up-to-date and accurate assessment of the social history collection and its contents, and the collecting policy has been amended to reflect these findings.

All material was wrapped or bagged before final packing in plastic boxes or trays and palleted and racked. A rack/store location list marked the completion of the

Figure 9.1 Storage area, Hampshire Museums Service

Figure 9.2 Storage area, Hampshire Museums Service

Figure 9.4 Entering materials data on computer, Hampshire Museums Service

project. Each box was given a number which was keyed to a pallet, a level and a bay of racking.

Conclusion

The project is fulfilling all expectations with regard to increased accessibility as expressed through improved temporary exhibitions and the establishment of educational handling collections. The Museums Service is now in the position of knowing what it has, where it came from, where it is now and what it wants to acquire in the future. As a result of the project, a disposal policy is being implemented in accordance with Museum Association guidelines.

Case study 9.3

Tyne and Wear Museums History Department

David Fleming

Museum collections come in a variety of guises – artefacts large and small, photographs, documents, film, video, sound recordings, buildings – but the principles governing their assembly and management are constant. Ignoring the principles inevitably results in the chaos endured too often by museums: poorly documented collections in inadequate storage, with insufficient staff and financial resources to care for or use the collections properly.

The collection management policy is the document wherein the museum sets out precisely what collections it intends to assemble, how it intends to look after them, and even how it may dispose of them. Such written policies are largely a recent phenomenon, and in established museums often they address retrospectively the problems created in earlier years by undisciplined collecting. In new museums the policies offer hope of avoiding such problems by strictly limiting the sphere of collecting. The collecting policy sets limits which render future sound management achievable, which prevent the museum being overwhelmed by collections with which it cannot cope. It is the keystone of the wider-ranging collection management policy.

Tyne and Wear Museums is a hybrid organization, the collecting responsibilities of which cover a host of subject areas and a geographical locality which is largely urban in nature. The origins of some of the collections lie in the early nineteenth century; others have begun to be assembled much more recently.

Purpose of the collecting policy

In setting up a History Department, Tyne and Wear Museums has aimed to bring order to areas of collecting which were afflicted by lack of direction, exacerbated by the complexity of the service's funding structure. We needed clearer responsibilites, clearer line management, and collecting policies which respected thematic and geographical boundaries.

In formulating the current collecting policies, we face the familiar issue of patterns of collecting which have already been set, for better or worse. Our collections have both strong and comprehensive areas, as well as weak areas and gaps. They are a mixture of the specialist and the diverse, and of the local, regional, national and international. In writing our collecting policies, our curators have had to assess strengths and weaknesses and, where necessary, place limits on collecting where there may have been none before.

We have had to reassess our aims, and to assess what resources might be available to care for and use the collections. Our collecting policies will not work if we cannot make realistic forecasts for the collections' welfare needs, and, in a deteriorating financial climate, we have to be extremely vigilant about taking on more than we can cope with.

Assessing the collections

In assessing our 'history' collections we begin by classifying them vertically, i.e. by identifying broad groups of activity. Currently these are: costume and textiles, maritime history, social history, and science and industry. Everything we collect within the History Department has to fall under at least one of these headings. A logical next stage is then to classify the collections horizontally, i.e. by identifying to which of our five funding local authorities the various items belong. Thus, we find that Newcastle and Sunderland have strong maritime collections, Newcastle has strong costume and science and industry collections, while Gateshead, North Tyneside and South Tyneside are actually thin in all areas. None of the districts has very strong social history collections overall, although there are pockets of excellence.

Reassessing the collecting areas

Next, the aims of the component museums and districts need to be matched to the existing collections. It is quite possible, indeed probable, that current aims and perceived future needs will be different from those of our predecessors, especially in the light of our assessment of the financial climate. The kind of factors we have to consider are the forthcoming Fashion Gallery in Newcastle (despite there being a large collection there has only been the opportunity for limited display), which is a priority development; or the proposed National Shipbuilding Museum in South Tyneside; or the top priority social/industrial gallery in Gateshead. Such developments encourage proactive collecting in areas deemed important in a district's history, compared with passive collecting which is unlikely to be representative of anything.

Display and interpretative requirements are only one issue, albeit an important one. What about documentation resources, storage and conservation requirements, the availability of curatorial time to do *anything* with existing or newly acquired collections?

This is where the wider-ranging collection management policy, itself a component of a corporate plan, comes into play, because it is here that realism may overwhelm aspiration.

Tyne and Wear Museums are, for example, making good progress with computerizing item documentation, at a predictable rate. The time will come, therefore, when this work will be complete. There is at present, then, no problem with this aspect of the collecting process. On the other hand, we do not have infinite numbers of curators to produce item data, so this is a crucial factor in deciding an acceptable rate of new acquisitions. Moreover, conservation is expensive and time consuming, with huge backlogs of remedial work already outstanding. Furthermore, good-quality storage is at a premium, and is especially difficult to find (and afford) for large industrial items such as marine engines, locomotives or road transport.

It is impossible to overstress the rigour which must be attached to writing the collection policy. Even now, policies which are in essence meaningless are still being produced by reputable museums, as an exercise which seems designed to give the curators total *carte blanche*. Some such policies embody all the past's bad practices while being designed to satisfy the Museums and Galleries Commission's registration requirements.

Results

The results of our analyses of needs matched to resources are still being realized. Collecting in the area of social history, traditionally our weakest, has accelerated, with improved storage to match and major displays on the way. Storage needs for maritime and science and industry collections are under close scrutiny, and in the latter area idiosyncratic collecting has been terminated. Major new displays are planned here too. So far there has been little change as far as the costume and textiles collections are concerned, although here again the future display potential and storage needs are now part of our policy analysis.

A most beneficial effect of having produced collections assessments, and reassessing collecting areas, is that there has been a painless growth of an attitude wherein any lack of discipline is seen as positively harmful to our museums. The days of heads in the sand, of squirrelling away collections regardless of the museums' abilities to fund their care and use, seem to be over.

10

Defining and recording the resource: documentation

John Burnett and Ian Morrison

Documentation lies at the heart of the curator's life. The curator, as against the conservator, spends far less time in handling objects than in handling information about them. Although museums are distinguished from other similar institutions, such as libraries and archive repositories, by the fact that they hold collections of objects, curators in museums spend most of their working lives generating and manipulating information.

Museum documentation is a practical subject. It may be defined as the creation and maintenance of a system or systems for handling information concerning collections. The creation (or refining) of the system should always be the most difficult part of documentation: once created, the system should be easy to maintain and use. It should be practical and workable.

Documentation should be distinguished from the processes of handling subject information – such as the identification of specimens or the ascribing of provenances – which is a matter for scientific research or curatorship. In the real world, the same individual is often responsible for carrying out both types of action. The distinction, however, remains. For example, in cataloguing a plate, the judgement that the picture on it is of the London International Exhibition of 1862 is a matter of curatorial skill, as is the decision to interpret 'DM & SS' on its rear as the mark of David Methven and Sons of Kirkcaldy. The structuring of that information into a standard format which is consistent with the records for other items in the collection is part of the activity of documentation.

Since documentation is a practical subject it is rather difficult to discuss it in the abstract, but one other way of conceiving documentation in a particular institution can be mentioned. A documentation system can be thought of as a related group of blocks of structured information, in which the links between the various blocks are almost as important as the information in each block.

Take the case of an imaginary industrial museum. The central blocks in its documentation system – which will often be thought of as 'the documentation' – is its accessions ledger, in which items are listed in the order in which they arrive on the premises, and the associated card index which files the names of donors. But there are many other blocks of information which should be related to these core units. Correspondence relating to acquisition and conservation is filed in filing cabinets, cross-referred to the central ledger by accession number. Each object may also have a file of its own which may contain all sorts of material: photographs of the object at work, technical drawings, press reports of its removal to the museum, and so on. The accession number again acts as the link between this file and the ledger. There is also a card file which contains information on the firms who have made or used items in the collection: this assembles all of this kind of information in one place, and it removes the need to record the firms' histories in other parts of the documentation. The documentation system can also be made more efficient by clarifying its relationship with outside sources of information – perhaps published biographies of local industrialists, or local archives. Each of these can be thought of as blocks in the information system, even if they are not in the museum, since references are made to them in documentation in the museum, and they are a part of the understanding of the collections.

From the point of view of management, one of the chief characteristics of documentation is that it can soak up large amounts of staff time. Good documentation is expensive because it needs to be based on careful planning and consideration of the museum's aims, and it takes time to build up a body of accurate data. Bad documentation is expensive because it involves the curator, and perhaps others, in unstructured searching. This absorbs more time and makes it impossible to exploit fully the information concealed within the documentation. It is therefore essential to be quite clear about the aims of documentation, and to involve the highest level of management, and possibly funding or grant-giving bodies, in clarifying these aims and accepting the consequent cost, and particularly the cost in staff time.

It is particularly important to think about issues in documentation in relation to broader policy questions. There is a small but good book by Elizabeth Orna (1987) on this subject. Another booklet (Burnett and Morrison, 1991) gives some practical ideas about how to think about documentation and its aims. The Museum Documentation Association has published a short but very good basic textbook on the practice of documentation (Holm, 1991). There is also a useful section on documentation in a handbook on museum planning (Ambrose and Runyard, 1991).

Functions of documentation

The documentation of collections has five types of function:

(1) formal functions (e.g. accounting for the objects);
(2) collections management;
(3) documentation management;
(4) retrieval of information about the object itself;
(5) public service.

Each is closely linked to the others.

Formal functions

The most important function of documentation for most kinds of material is evidence of transfer of title. An institution which cannot demonstrate that it owns the objects in its collections is in a very vulnerable position.

Equally important in the minds of funding bodies is the need for a museum to be able to account for its holdings. Sometimes an insurer will insist on adequate documentation before the risk of covering a collection is accepted. This basic need to show that assets are being handled responsibly, which is taken for granted in manufacturing industry and the retail trade, is wrongly regarded by much of the heritage sector as being an unnecessary chore. Auditing should be the confirmation that the job of collections management is being well done.

Collections management

Collections management information includes all of the information about the administrative and other processes which institutions apply to objects, covering

(1) acquisition;
(2) movement within the institution;
(3) loans from and to the institution;
(4) conservation;
(5) photography;
(6) disposal.

Documentation management

Documentation can consume large quantities of staff time and so needs to be managed with care, not least by the staff who are working on it. A documentation system should be able to produce simple statistics, such as number of records created and number of items uncatalogued, broken down according to the various areas of the collections, so that effort can be applied where it is most needed.

Retrieval of information about the object itself

In order to prepare exhibitions and publications, and to carry out any kind of research, it has to be possible to find objects which are of a particular type or material, or which come from a particular area, or were made at a particular date. The range of possible questions and information which might be relevant in their answers is enormous. Discipline and clear thinking are vital in this area.

Public service

Heritage bodies exist to give the public a service. Documentation can do this directly or indirectly. Indirectly, it enables the staff to prepare exhibitions and answer enquiries. It can also allow the public to have direct access to information. This may be at a simple level, such as having files or captioned photographs through which visitors can browse. Increasingly, however, information technology is having an impact on this function. The Microgallery at the National Gallery in London shows what can be done with huge financial resources. Other museums are experimenting with simpler projects and it is likely that this will be a major area for development in the next ten years.

Documentation of different kinds of material

Different kinds of material – books, museum objects, data on geological sites, or whatever – need different kinds of documentation. There are two reasons.

First, the material varies in how much it tells us about itself. An archaeological training is needed to catalogue a collection of neolithic material, but a book tells us explicitly much about its content and circumstances of production.

Second, the information is used in different ways. Books are normally sought by author, title or subject. In handling fossils, the stratigraphic context is extremely important, and there are international conventions for naming species. Only in recent years have conventions been outlined for naming various kinds of building or archaeological site. These differences represent the various ways in which information is used by different professional and scholarly communities.

Although most heritage bodies focus on a particular type of material, they should also be aware of the issues involved in handling other types. Many bodies have supporting material of other kinds: almost every museum, for example, has its own library and archive, no matter how small. It is very rare for a body to operate with no relation to any other bodies which operate in the same subject area but hold different kinds of material, or even the same kind of material, but for a different purpose – in the way that some museums conceive their biological collections as being only for taxonomic purposes, whilst others place a heavy emphasis on ecology.

Entry and exit documentation

Every object entering or leaving a museum should be recorded at the time of entry or exit in a consistent way. Many museums use entry and exit forms for this purpose. Serially numbered multi–part pre-printed carbonless forms can be purchased from the Museum Documentation Association, or an in-house design could be implemented. The minimum information required on an entry form is a unique identification number, a brief description of the object, the name and address of the depositor (and owner if that is different), the date of entry, the reason for entry (identification, proposed gift, loan for exhibition etc.), and the signatures of the depositor, the owner and the museum representative. The requirements of exit forms are similar. This is the most fundamental level of documentation in a museum.

Accessioning

Accessioning, or registering, is the act of formally adding new acquisitions to the collection. The primary purpose of an accession record is to provide evidence of a change of ownership of the items from the source to the museum. Accessioning should take place as soon as possible after receipt. The stages involved in accessioning a group of items are as follows:

Register entry   Basic details of source, identification and history are recorded in a secure and permanent register.
Numbering   Each item is allocated a unique number and is marked or labelled accordingly.
Acknowledgement   In most cases of gift or bequest, an acknowledgement letter is sent to the source of the items.
Transfer of title   A further form may be required to complete the formal transfer of title to the objects, particularly in the case of valuable or significant items.

The first two stages are the minimum requirements of the Museums and Galleries Commission's registration scheme for museums. The register itself may be the traditional bound ledger or a computerized equivalent. In the latter case it is recommended that printout is obtained on a regular basis and bound in a secure and permanent fashion. A copy should be kept at a separate location for security. The *accession number* of each object should be unique to that object and distinct from any entry number.

The technique for physically marking an object with its accession number will vary according to its physical nature. Tie-on labels are simple to apply in most cases but have a habit of becoming dissociated from the objects. On the other hand, more permanent and secure marks may have aesthetic or conservation drawbacks.

The commonest technique, suitable for a wide range of objects, is to use varnished drawing ink on a base coat. Conservators currently recommend that the base coat should be 20 per cent Paraloid B72 in acetone (e.g. 20 g B72 to 100 ml acetone). The upper protective varnish layer can be the same solution. When using these or similar substances, be aware of the Control of Substances Hazardous to Health (COSHH) Regulations, and particularly the risks associated with the use of acetone. If in doubt about the suitability of any particular technique, consult a conservator.

The description in the accession record should contain the minimum number of words to express what the object is and why it is interesting: '26 photographs of the interior of St Mary's Church, 1920–40', or 'mercury thermometer signed *Alexander Wilson 1759*', or 'tweed cap worn by Lloyd George'. For some kinds of object some further information may be essential because they are needed to make a certain identification, such as the weight of a gemstone or the dimensions of a painting.

Cataloguing

The purpose of cataloguing is to record details which might be required for any purpose, from preparing a display to satisfying an academic query. Important information is often impossible to obtain from the object itself. Most museums have large numbers of objects whose origins cannot be identified because associated data have been lost, or never recorded.

On the other hand, many documentation projects in museums have failed as a result of attempting to record too much about each object. Even with an automated system, some information is best kept in paper form, such as original manuscript material, plans and drawings. Much tedious descriptive effort can be avoided by using photographs. In the past some museums have even gone to the lengths of asking curators to write a description which would enable readers to re-create the object before their eyes. This is going too far, given the possibility of looking at the object itself, or at a photograph. It is vital to assess which types of information are going to be needed for retrieval purposes, and to ensure that these are recorded consistently and that they are comprehensively indexed. Many museums find that indexes of associated names and places are the most used.

Catalogue information is held in a file of records, normally one per object. A record is subdivided into a set of fields, each of which holds a discrete piece of information, for example a donor or date of manufacture. The fields may be arranged as boxes on a card or as a series of data entry screens on a computer. This structured information is essential for efficient retrieval.

It is also useful to have an unstructured area on the card or computer database for general information which does not fit into the standard fields. An example might be comments on why the object was acquired. Sophisticated computer systems may even be able to retrieve information in this free-text form.

Museum catalogue records usually include details of the current location of objects. This information, which may change much more frequently than descriptive or provenance details, must be recorded and kept up to date. It may be difficult to achieve this with a manual system and this requirement can be one of the most powerful justifications for considering a computer system. Sometimes current location information is kept separately.

If catalogue records contain sensitive information such as personal details, vulnerable site data, valuations or storage locations, security must be considered. A lockable cabinet may be adequate for a card-based system, and strict control of access to computer systems is essential.

Classification and terminology control

The Bible tells us that God named the animals on the fifth day, and it was Aristotle who first classified them and so introduced the idea of relating objects to one another by their similarities. There were various subsequent attempts to organize the tangible world, some of them quite successful: in their different areas the names of Linnaeus and Melvil Dewey are still remembered. Although archaeologists were already making attempts to classify artefacts in the eighteenth century, two centuries have not brought a great measure of agreement. Nor has the museum community achieved much more. At a conference in Cambridge in 1987 it was accepted that the issue is of great importance, but no collective way forward was identified (Roberts, 1990). In some subject areas, curators have developed classification schemes which work well

enough in practice, even if some parts of them may look arbitrary or even bizarre. Examples are the Social History and Industrial Classification (SHIC Working Party, 1983), the American *Nomenclature* (Blackaby *et al.*, 1988), which covers a similar area, and the ICOM (1982) costume vocabulary. There is also a useful guide to the different ways of recording place names (Museum Documentation Association, 1991a).

There are world-wide conventions on the naming of scientific specimens, including animals, plants and fossils. Those who are not biologists should be aware that the unambiguous name of a plant or animal is always its scientific name: *Quercus robur* is much more specific than oak.

Numbering systems

The choice of method used to number items in a collection or archive is apparently a simple issue: keep it that way. Numbering systems should be simple and immediately understood. It is dangerous to build any kind of meaning into a number, except perhaps the year of acquisition of the item. A number of the form 1990.1, with a running number within each year, is unlikely to pose problems in the future. Numbering systems which include information about the objects are vulnerable to change. One national museum based the numbers given to its collection of ship models on the year of launch of the original vessel on which the model was based. In time, models were reidentified, dates of launch were found to be dates of fitting out, and opinions as to the likely dates of some types – 'a Venetian galley of the 1540s' – changed, and the whole collection had to be renumbered. Numbers which include a classification are similarly dangerous. Whatever benefit they may have appeared to have before computerized record keeping has now vanished.

The variety of museum objects

The data which describe artefacts and scientific specimens are different from one another. The data which a museum can usefully hold on various kinds of artefact may also vary. For archaeological material it can be important to know exactly where it came from – the exact point in space, if possible to the nearest centimetre. More modern material, however, is more likely to have a rich background of associations – makers, owners, users, events, places and dates relating to all of them. For particular purposes it may be necessary to record other types of data, such as dimensions of objects when planning a reorganization of storage. For certain types of object, schemes for standardizing naming or description have been produced (see below).

It is sometimes said that certain kinds of collection are self-documenting. This misleading term means that because of the existence of conventions it is possible to organize the storage of insects, shells, coins or stamps in such a way that someone familiar with the subject can locate material which they want to see. For example, coins are normally arranged by country, monarch, metal, denomination and date.

The age of a collection can sometimes pose a problem, particularly in a field such as archaeology. A century ago curators were using object names which are now considered incorrect. Two centuries ago some scholars still regarded flint arrowheads as 'elf bolts'. Antique language should be preserved as an aid to understanding collections as collections (Burnett and Clarke, 1989). Particularly in older institutions with complex histories, some study of museum history may explain oddness in the record keeping, and provide a starting point for planning for the future (Burnett, 1991).

The purposes of documentation, too, can vary. The extreme case of an exhibition catalogue is the type produced to accompany large temporary exhibitions of paintings. An examination of such a catalogue (Sutton, 1984) reveals these characteristics. All 127 paintings exhibited are described in detail, illustrated in colour, and discussed at some length. There is a biography of each artist, 75 pages of introductory essays, and a bibliography containing 1200 items. This lavish production is in fact playing a number of roles at once: catalogue, textbook, photographic archive and bibliography. Its success is partly due to the understanding in the art world of the requirements for this kind of production. A photocopied list of items in a collection of local history photographs can be just as successful if care is taken to define exactly when people are going to use it, and what the reader will want to learn from it.

Books and other published material

The museum library is a resource which is used primarily to increase the understanding of the museum's holdings, buildings and site. To do this it may contain material which does not refer directly to the museum but provides contextual background. This may be a sizeable addition. The library may have the secondary function of providing information which is needed for non-curatorial purposes: trade directories, directories of grant-giving bodies, market research publications and current affairs material.

The size and content of the library will depend on a number of factors:

(1) whether its users are seen as being the staff, researchers, the general public, or a combination of them;
(2) availability of other libraries nearby;
(3) subject matter;
(4) age of the institution;
(5) funding.

The different types of publication which may be found in a museum library are:

(1) catalogues of museum collections and special exhibitions;
(2) monographs;
(3) periodicals;
(4) bibliographies;
(5) trade and/or street directories;
(6) local and/or national newspapers.

It is valuable to see the library as being a core function within the museum, even if its operation is only part of the job of a member of staff. The library is a resource, and it needs to be managed. This approach also provides a focus for two other desirable activities. One is the creation of newspaper cuttings files which relate to the museum, or its subject, or both. The other is the maintenance of an awareness of the range of information sources, within and outside the museum, which may be useful to the people who use the library.

A museum library may represent a significant continuing cost apart from staff time. Books are being published in greater and greater numbers every year, periodical subscriptions rise faster than inflation, and periodicals may need to be bound.

Archives and photographs

In the context of a museum, it is simplest to think of the term 'archive' as covering manuscript material, ephemera, photographs, and other material which does not fit comfortably into that museum's collections or library. Handling archives will fall to the curator or librarian except in the largest institutions – but whether or not there is a specialist available, they do introduce particular issues. The profession of archivist is older than that of curator, and there is a mass of expertise in storage and conservation on which museums can draw. Record offices and other archive repositories are normally willing to offer advice to other bodies who have archive holdings but no specialist staff.

Photographs often pose a large and difficult problem. Even small museums can easily find themselves with thousands of photographs. Unless they have very specific subjects, for example portraits or machines, they are impossible to describe. A good photograph of an interior or a street scene contains dozens of points of interest. Is there time to identify all of them? Is there somebody who has the necessary knowledge? In most cases the first step will be to make outline records and to return to a detailed examination of the photographic archive when resources permit.

The cost of maintaining an archive is chiefly the cost of storage, which can be enormous. There are high staff costs in accessioning and repairing backlogs in documentation. A significant number of users of an archive can also put pressure on staff time, and will require accommodation.

Information technology

Hardware

The key item of hardware for most museums is the personal computer (PC). First introduced in the late 1970s, the PC has changed working life in Western civilization. In the mid 1980s there were two important developments which were not recognized by many users.

First, since the IBM PC became a world standard there has been a wide choice of machines between which information can be moved easily, and 'PC' has now come to mean the IBM PC and its clones. A small museum can buy one brand of PC, and then another three years later, and experience no difficulties. (Beginners should be warned to avoid non-PCs – often the cheapest machines – which are still resolutely non-conformist). Second, the power of machines became such that there was no longer a need to buy the most powerful machine you could afford, which would be the least inadequate one. The correct machine can now be purchased on the basis of the software which is going to be run and the amount of information which the machine is going to have to hold. Costs keep falling: you should not have to pay more than £1000 for a PC.

Small portable computers are now being sold in large quantities. They offer the same performance as a desk-top PC, but are slightly more expensive. Their other drawbacks are that the keyboard is inevitably cramped, and the screen – unless you spend a lot of money – is not as bright and clear as a larger machine.

The other piece of essential hardware is the printer. Engineers have invented a host of ways of making ink marks on a piece paper, and printers vary greatly in the amount of noise they make, the quality of their printing, their speed and their cost. The best advice is to see what other people are using. Costs are between £250 and £1600.

Software

The most common types of PC software are word processors, databases, and spreadsheets and accounting packages.

Word processors are widely familiar, and have nearly consigned the typewriter to the scrapheap; shareholders in Remington Rand may have noticed. They make possible the input, layout and manipulation of text with a flexibility which the typewriter

cannot emulate. The most widely sold word processing packages in the UK in 1991 were Wordperfect, Word and Wordstar. Every office will benefit from having a word processor. Their extension, with far more power to create elaborate layouts, is the desktop publishing (DTP) package. DTP is likely to be a liability in the hands of those without training in graphic design: it can take a long time to learn, and in unskilled hands can produce horrible results.

Databases handle packages of information rather than continuous text. They can be thought of as holding information in a huge set of pigeon-holes. In a museum database, each object relates to a row of holes (a record), and each hole may or may not hold information. Each column (a field) is devoted to a particular type of information: the accession number, the donor's name, or whatever. A database creates a structure of this kind and makes it possible to retrieve the information quickly. There is a catch. Whereas a word processor can be used as soon as it is loaded into a computer, a database has to be set up to do exactly what is needed of it.

The most commonly purchased database package in 1991 was Dataease. Among other widely sold products are Foxbase, Paradox and DBase. It is now quite easy to transfer data from one database to another, and there is a case for beginners to start by buying a cheap and easily learned database, and progressing later to one of those mentioned above.

Archaeologists have applied a wide range of statistical methods to their research, and inevitably computing, with its power to handle large quantities of data and to present the results graphically – and thus make it easier to spot patterns – has been successfully applied to many problems (Lock and Wilcock, 1987).

The law

In using computers, two legal issues should be borne in mind. The first is the Data Protection Act 1984. If you keep information on individuals on a computer – even if it is nothing more than a mailing list – then you are required to register. Sometimes registration has been carried out by a parent body such as a local authority, but it may have failed to register the museum's particular use of the information. The Data Protection Registrar can be contact at Springfield House, Water Lane, Wilmslow, Cheshire, SK9 5AX (telephone 0625 535777).

It is both illegal and irresponsible to use pirated computer software. PC software is normally licensed for use on one machine only, and its unauthorized duplication (except as a backup in case of a failure) is in breach of the Copyright Act 1990: this is known as piracy. Successful prosecutions have been made under the 1990 Act. Pirated software is the chief source of computer viruses which can destroy data and computer programs. Beware.

Some thoughts for the future

The largest change in the use of computers in museums in the next decade will be easy to miss. Curators will become more and more comfortable with the idea of using computers for a wide variety of taks. At the same time software will become easier to use: barriers will be falling everywhere. Computer imaging will become much more important than it is now, but the need for the skill of the photographer to create good-quality images may limit progress in all but the wealthiest institutions. Progress in imaging may be chiefly based on collections of old photographs. The ability of telecommunications to allow museums to have access to one another's data will be realized to an extent, but the costs and lack of standardization may limit progress. Sharing information between museums will slowly become more important (Roberts, 1992). The greatest brake on progress, however, will be the incompleteness of the information which museums hold about their own collections. The world of industry and commerce will drive technology forward, but museums must look to their own resources to create databases of good-quality information concerning their own collections.

Technology and prices change so quickly that it is difficult to give advice on reading matter on computers and information technology. There is one excellent article on the messy reality of museum automation which, despite being over ten years old, has not dated (Sarasan, 1981). The Museum Documentation Association (1991b) publishes a guide to software in use in museums in the United Kingdom.

Staff, experience and management

Museum documentation is still a comparatively new subject, and it has progressed by drawing on many ideas which have been developed in the world of libraries. Staff who have come to museums with library experience have been important. However, at the same time as museum documenation has been developing, librarianship has become less well defined and there is now a pool of expertise in general skills of information handling. By employment, consultancy or free advice, museums should draw on the professional knowledge which has been built up.

In a practical subject like documentation there is no substitute for experience. Experience can be drawn on in a number of ways. There are a number of good written accounts of successful projects. In a field which is being changed so rapidly by automation, it is definitely best to look for recently published material. The Museum Documentation Association has issued a number of collections of papers given at their conferences which contain much food for though (Light *et al.*, 1986; Roberts, 1988), and there are a few articles in periodicals. *Computers in the History of Art* is the most useful source at present. Its content is wider than its name would suggest. The reader should always be aware that accounts of this kind tend to emphasize the successful parts of the work they discuss.

For an honest view of pitfalls, it is best to visit institutions which are similar to your own, and which operate documentation systems which are comparable with your system – or the system you would like to have. Training courses, seminars and professional meetings can also be very valuable for finding out what is going on, especially since documentation is an activity which is less conspicuous in print than it should be. For museums, advisory visits are carried out by the Museum Documentation Association, by area museum councils and (in Scotland) by the National Museums of Scotland. For a project of any size, consideration should be given to employing a consultant, though it may be easier to make this decision than to find a suitably qualified person.

The generalization which underlies the above paragraphs is that a large quantity of thought should go into planning and designing any change – such as automation – to a documentation system. When one of the present authors joined the National Museums of Scotland in 1986 he had first to examine the existing, and very diverse, manual documentation systems. With the aid of a consultant with substantial experience of large databases a study of the software available was carried out: this involved a thorough study of the literature, hours on the phone, a dozen visits to the south of England and finally ten days in North America. We believed that it was essential to see our chosen software being used in an environment similar to our own; in other words, we were drawing in a very specific way on experience built up in another part of the museum community. Once software and hardware had been selected, the software was tested for several months using 43,000 records generously lent to us by the Historic New Orleans Collection. Thus we had established our own basis of experience before we reached the irrevocable point of having to pay for the software.

The basic skills are not always quite as simple, or as basic, as they may seem. For a retrospective project – one in which a body of existing information is going to be reworked, almost certainly by inputting it to a computer – there should be someone available who understands the structuring of information, such as a person with a background in librarianship. Training and day-to-day (or hour-by-hour) management of staff who are inexperienced in documentation can be vital. The comparative failure of many UK government funded training schemes which focused on documentation illustrates this point.

Volunteers should be managed with care. Particularly if they have a knowledge of the subject matter of the museum, volunteers can have a role in producing information, say by cataloguing photographs. They do not often have the professional background to be able to present this information in the consistent form which will be needed for an information system. A significant management input is needed if volunteers are to be deployed effectively in documentation.

Given that all work in documentation is labour intensive, this is emphatically true of the input of records. Experience shows that it cannot be done particularly quickly: trained workers can input seven records per hour when the records contain an average of 1000 characters. This figure is dependent on a number of factors, including the intelligibility of the old record (it is not wise to be optimistic) and the quality and consistency of the handwriting. Input almost inevitably involves a restructuring of the data and is far more than copy typing. A good level of concentration is needed to do it well, and if work of good quality is to be produced then breaks of adequate length must be provided. If input can be mixed with another kind of work, so much the better.

Unlike many other aspects of museum work, it is possible to quantify most types of documentary activity. The numbers of objects and records in a museum should always be known, but often are not. These numbers can then be used to generate numerical information for planning – and seeking funding for – further documentary, conservation or other work.

Afterword

Documentation is important. The issue for the future, however, is information rather than documentation. Information is a key resource in museums, as important as objects or other kinds of evidence. We are moving into an information society, in which management, museum practice and the possibilities for earning revenue will focus increasingly on making knowledge accessible.

References

AMBROSE, T. and RUNYARD, S. (eds) (1991) *Forward Planning: a Handbook of Business, Corporate and Development Planning for Museums and Galleries*, Museums and Galleries Commission, London

BLACKABY, J. R., GREENO, P. and the NOMENCLATURE COMMITTEE (1988) *The Revised Nomenclature for Museum Cataloguing*, American Association for State and Local History, Nashville, TN

BURNETT, J. (1991) 'Collections, information and computers in the National Museums of Scotland', *Proceedings of the Society of Antiquaries of Scotland*

BURNETT, J. and CLARKE, D. V. (1989) 'The role of older descriptions and identifications of objects in a museum database', *International Journal of Museum Management and Curatorship*, **8**, 431–434

BURNETT, J. and MORRISON, I. (1991) *Wimps. worms and Winchesters* (2nd edn), Information Series no. 14, National Museums of Scotland, Edinburgh

HOLM, S. (1991) *Facts and Artefacts: How to Document a Museum Collection*, Museum Documentation Association, Cambridge

ICOM (1982) 'International Committee for the Museums and Collections of Costume: vocabulary of basic terms for cataloguing costume', *Waffen- und Kostümkunde*, **24**, 119–152

LIGHT, R. B., ROBERTS, D. A. and STEWART, J. D. (eds) (1986) *Museum Documentation Systems: Developments and Applications*, Butterworths, London

LOCK, G. and WILCOCK, J. (1987) *Computer Archaeology*, Shire, Princes Risborough

MUSEUM DOCUMENTATION ASSOCIATION (1991a) *Place Name Recording Guidelines*, Museum Documentation Association, Cambridge

MUSEUM DOCUMENTATION ASSOCATION (1991b) *WHO is using WHAT software for documentation WHERE*, Museum Documentation Association, Cambridge

ORNA, E. (1987) *Information Policies for Museums*, Occasional Papers no. 10, Museum Documentation Association, Cambridge

ROBERTS, D. A. (ed.) (1988) *Collections Management for Museums*, Documentation Association, Cambridge

ROBERTS, D. (ed.) (1990) *Terminology for Museums*, Museum Documentation Association, Cambridge

ROBERTS, D. A. (ed.) (1992) *Sharing the Information Resources of Museums*, Museum Documentation Association, Cambridge

SARASAN, L. (1981) 'Why museum computer projects fail', *Museum News*, **59**(4), 40–49

SHIC WORKING PARTY (1983) *Social History and Industrial Classification*, Centre for English Cultural Tradition and Language, University of Sheffield

SUTTON, P. C. (ed.) (1984) *Masters of Seventeenth-Century Dutch Genre Painting*, Philadelphia Museum of Art, Philadelphia

Case study 10.1

Bennie Museum, Bathgate

John Burnett and Ian Morrison

The Bennie Museum in Bathgate, West Lothian, is an excellent example of how a very small museum, with a little professional input, can plan the effective use of new technology. It can now provide a better service with a reduced workload on individual volunteers.

The Bennie Museum originated from a community effort to save two cottages owned by the Bennie family from demolition. Collecting started in 1980 and the museum opened in May 1989, with around 3000 objects, mainly of local historical interest. Since then the acquisition rate has increased to around 1000 objects per annum, mostly outright donations. This is expected to stabilize. All work is done by volunteers, though advice has been taken from the Scottish Museums Council, the National Museums of Scotland and the Museum Documentation Association. The management committee includes a professional curatorial adviser with extensive experience of documentation in small museums.

The entry system is based on a simple receipt book. Up to 1991 the objects were catalogued on MDA 'museum object' cards and indexes were created by simple name, Social History and Industrial Classification (SHIC) and donor, as soon as possible after entry. The manual system met the museum's documentation requirements up to the date of opening but after that it became increasingly difficult to maintain.

In autumn 1990 the decision was taken to buy a computer for word processing and documentation. The software being used initially is the Museum Inventory System (MIS). This provides a basic inventory of the collections and also acts as an automated index to the existing manual documentation. Initial input of records, directly from the cards, was completed in less than six months, largely by the voluntary custodians, many of whom had not used a keyboard before, let alone a computer.

The idea of using volunteers for data input is fraught with potential difficulties, particularly regarding consistency. In this case there was no other viable option and there are two advantages. One is that the custodians now have an excellent grasp of the scope of the collections. The second is that they provide a direct link between visitors and the information which would otherwise be buried in the catalogues.

Case study 10.2

Highland Folk Museum, Kingussie

John Burnett and Ian Morrison

The Highland Folk Museum was founded in 1934 and contains extensive collections of buildings, objects, photographs, books, archives and audio tapes illustrating the life and work of the Highlands. From 1934 until 1976 various catalogues were prepared. The original listings gave a simple name, one dimension, provenance if available, and donor. For many years even less was recorded about new acquisitions. In some cases the same accession number was used twice, causing much confusion. While under joint university control, parts of the collection were transferred to the Marischal Museum at Aberdeen.

The transfer of records to MDA 'history artefact' cards, which began in 1976, was a slow process as objects were reaccessioned and renumbered, if necessary, at the same time. Most of this work was done through Manpower Services Commission schemes. About 10 per cent of the collection had been catalogued to 1989. A further 15–20 per cent had been photographed and skeleton MDA cards prepared. Most of the remainder is covered by store lists which have at least an accession number.

The manual system is built around the National Museum of Antiquities of Scotland (NMAS) classification scheme and the MDA cards are stored in this order. This classification is also used for the library, archive and slide library. There are indexes by surname, for donors and associated people, place name and simple name.

The acquisition of a collection of 140,000 glass negatives from a photographer's studio in Inverness was the last straw for attempts at manual cataloguing. It was obvious that an automated system was the only way to deal with such a large collection of images. An application written in the Dataflex database management system has been developed by Regional Council Information Technology staff. The Social History and Industrial Classification (SHIC) is used, and any objects or people of interest in the photographs are recorded. This provides sufficient information to answer (in the affirmative) questions such as: 'Do you have any pictures of Irish wolfhounds in the Highlands?'

A microcomputer is used with the Museum Inventory System (MIS) to provide a basic record of all artefacts. A variant, MISBOOK, is used for the library. The resulting databases are fully compatible with dBASE III Plus, which is used to flesh out the records if necessary.

There are plans to integrate museum databases, library catalogues and archive records and make them accessible, with other local authority information, to anyone across the extensive telecommunications links now being developed throughout Highland Region. This network will also permit museums to exchange information and might act as a prototype for a nationwide system.

11

The legislation and institutional context: the countryside

Graham Taylor

As we shall see in Chapter 15, conserving the natural and man-made environment in the countryside is very much about managing for multiple objectives. In Britain, a long-settled and crowded island, there are very few areas of truly natural vegetation and few areas where there is a sense of wilderness. Although we are concerned with managing a living system it is one in which man plays an integral part. Indeed part of the dilemma in conservation is that much of the valued habitat for wildlife is the result of traditional farming practice which often is no longer carried out. Equally, for many people part of the pleasure of visiting the countryside lies in its purposeful use for agriculture, and being able to experience a contrasting way of life to their own is very attractive to visiting city dwellers.

The British have a deep, powerful and sentimental attraction to the countryside. The countryside is a theme in literature, painting and music and it is used in advertising. A home in the country is an ambition of many urban people. Alongside the growth of support for rural conservation, largely among urban people, have run two themes: first the profound technological changes in agriculture and forestry over the past 40 years which have led to extensive changes in both the natural and man-made elements of the rural landscape; and secondly the changes in the rural population and its economy which have gradually integrated town and country socially and economically. This is the context for the complex legislative and institutional arrangements for conservation which have evolved in Britain.

The changing style of conservation and countryside management

The post-war period has seen unprecedented changes in rural industries and rural society. Not surprisingly

conservation practice has also undergone a parallel evolution.

What we shall see in the rest of this chapter is a series of developments which might be said to fall into phases:

(1) A reliance on *designation and regulations* in the immediate post-war period. Conservation would be achieved through the planning system and the national parks, national nature reserves and other designations. Agriculture was seen as a stable influence.
(2) The evolution of *countryside management* from the late 1960s where public bodies deployed staff to conserve the landscape and resolve access problems in certain areas which were seen to be under pressure, such as national parks and urban fringe.
(3) A period of *confrontation with agricultural development* in the 1970s and early 1980s which followed the industrialization of agriculture and the landscape and habitat loss which were a consequence.
(4) A new period of *partnership with agriculture* in which conservation objectives and practical mechanisms to achive them have been incorporated into agricultural policy. This period began in about 1985 and is still developing.

A brief history

There is no intention, in a practical manual such as this, to chart in detail the long history of wildlife conservation and the protection of the amenity of the countryside (there are many excellent accounts: Blunden and Curry, 1990), but a history of the last 50 years is helpful to an understanding of the way the current systems work. A convenient starting point is the wartime Committee on Land Utilisation in Rural Areas, chaired by Lord Justice Scott, which reported in 1942. This report was crucially influential on post-war thinking on the protection of the countryside.

128

The Committee believed that the rural community was essentially an agricultural community and that a prosperous agriculture would maintain both the rural community and the landscape. The assumption was a benign, unchanging agriculture, in tune with its environment. Equally the Committee saw the main threats to the countryside, apart from government neglect of agriculture, as urban and industrial development. The post-war preoccupations with urban containment, the creation of national parks and nature reserves and state support for agriculture derive from this analysis.

Subsequent events have not however confirmed the Scott Committee's analysis. Even by 1942 the rural population was no longer largely an agricultural one, and, to remain prosperous, farms have become more industrial, have amalgamated and have had to specialize in arable, dairy or beef and sheep production. Agriculture has shed over 75 per cent of its labour and altered much of the lowland countryside, sometimes dramatically. The long-term process of rural depopulation was countered and more recently reversed by the in-migration of more prosperous retired people and commuters with very different expectations, particularly of an unchanging countryside. What is more, in the early 1990s the prospects for agriculture are more uncertain than at any time in the post-war period, while public support for conservation and the desire for public access to the countryside for recreation have never been greater.

The legislation and the bodies which implement it

Town and country planning

A key foundation of post-war conservation has been planning policy. Town and country planning comprises two principal components:

(1) *development plans*, which are prepared by local authories in response to changing social and economic factors and which indicate how land might be developed and used;
(2) *development control*, by which all development must receive the consent of the appropriate local government planning authority, taking into account the development plan and other factors.

Currently, the basic Act of Parliament covering planning is the Town and Country Planning Act 1990. The full scope of the duties of the planning authorities is the subject of several useful textbooks (e.g. Heap, 1991).

Of the development plans, structure plans provide a strategic framework for developing in a county and are prepared by county councils. District-wide local plans relate to actual areas of land, indicating what type of land use or development would be acceptable in those locations. The local plan is prepared by the district council and must conform to the structure plan.

Both types of plan have to take account of central government policy as set out in Planning Policy Guidance Notes (PPGs) issued and revised periodically by government. The Secretary of State (for Environment or Wales) must approve the development plans.

District councils handle most planning applications and certain other categories such as mineral extraction proposals are a county council responsibility. However in the national parks the national park authority is the planning authority. The process of development control is now to be led by the development plan. Provided a development conforms with the plan it should normally be approved.

The foundation of current planning law was the Town and Country Planning Act 1947 which established the principles. It also required the production of an official definition of what constitutes 'development', the General Development Order. It has been revised periodically, most recently in 1988. It also lists those activities which are exempted. In the spirit of the Scott Report, most agricultural and forestry activities are exempt. An exception is that farmers and foresters are required to consult the planning authority on the design, appearance and siting of farm buildings and farm and forest roads. At the same time planning policy allowed development on agricultural land (other than for agriculture and forestry) only in exceptional circumstances.

The effect of the town and country planning policy has been to prevent sporadic development in the open countryside, to contain the growth of towns and to restrict the growth of villages. To that extent the countryside has been protected from change. The primacy given to agriculture in the use of rural land was removed in 1987, other than on the very best soils. The government has made clear that this is not intended to lead to wholesale development in the countryside (Department of the Environment and Welsh Office, 1992).

Agriculture and forestry

The second plank of post-war rural policy has been the promotion of agricultural efficiency. Both under the Agriculture Act 1947 and, since entry into the European Union (EU), under the Common Agricultural Policy (CAP), the aim has been to raise farm incomes, stabilize prices and maintain secure supplies. In both regimes greater efficiency has been a major objective. The CAP comprises two main components:

(1) *the guarantee sector*, which is concerned with maintaining production at a desirable level through systems of price support, import control on non-EU foodstuffs and intervention on products in surplus in order to dispose of them and thereby maintain the price farmers receive;

(2) *the guidance sector*, which is a system of grants and subsidies to encourage particular types of innovation, diversification, the retention of farming communities in less favoured areas (usually upland areas) and, more recently, conservation of the fabric of the farmed landscape.

The effect of these policy instruments over more than 40 years has been to transform lowland agriculture into a highly capitalized, low-labour industry of high-input/high-output specialized sectors – arable, dairy etc. The effect on the uplands, poorer agriculturally and with fewer opportunities to diversify, has probably been that many more farming families remain in the hills than otherwise. The systems of production in the uplands remain less changed than in the lowlands and, while production has increased, chiefly in sheep, and more intensive grassland management in particular has led to quite widespread vegetation change, the landscape remains less altered than parts of the lowlands.

Domestic agricultural policies are drafted and promoted by the Ministry of Agriculture, Fisheries and Food (MAFF) which also handles the grants and manages the guarantee sector mechanisms. An arm largely independent of the EU, the Agricultural Development Advisory Service (ADAS), is responsible for technical advice and the development and promotion of good practice by research and advice. ADAS has encouraged diversification of farm businesses and promoted conservation on farms, for which some grants are available for activities which fit in with farm practice. However, ADAS has had to retrench recently as the steam has gone out of agricultural development with the growth of surpluses in many commodities.

Forestry policy is the responsibility of the Forestry Commission which now has two distinct organizations to carry out its two functions. Best known is its role as the state forestry company, the Forest Enterprise, owning and managing mainly large commercial softwood plantations. These are chiefly in the hills of the north of England, in Wales and in Scotland. The Forestry Commission is also the Forest Authority, the part of the agency responsible for promoting new planting through grants, controlling the retention of woodlands by issuing felling licences, and promoting good practice by research and advice. The Commission has done much to encourage public enjoyment of its forests and, despite the controversial nature of much of its planting, enjoys a good reputation. The new emphasis in policy on broad-leaved production is welcomed by nature and landscape conservationists.

Tax incentives have historically been a major tool for promoting forestry policy but these were removed from foresty planting in the budget of 1988, ending a controversial period of unsatisfactory planting. The grants and tax incentives led to planting on low-cost land, often in remote areas, for example wetlands of ecological interest, with little prospect of truly commercial production. There is also now a very strong and explicit presumption against softwood (conifer) planting in the hills of England following a statement of policy by the Secretary of State for the Environment in 1988.

Rural development and tourism

A minority of rural people now work in agriculture and forestry, and the promotion of more diverse rural employment, of rural shops, transport and other services, and of housing have been other objectives of government policy. The responsible agencies (the government departments and local authorities apart) are the Rural Development Commission in England, the Welsh Development Agency and the Development Board for Rural Wales (Mid Wales Development) and in Scotland the Highland and Islands Development Board. Each country also has national tourist boards and in England there are regional tourist boards which do research, promote areas as destinations and support development in particular localities.

The significance for heritage managers of these active development agencies is twofold. First they encourage and guide development and can be very influential on the pace and scale of economic growth in an area. Potentially this is two edged: it can help to change an area in ways which threaten the integrity of towns, villages and individual buildings; but it can also help to give new life to communities, and to find new uses for redundant buildings (as can farm diversification) and therefore retain them for the future. Development can also help sustain the viability of local shops and services which are of value to visitors coming to enjoy the rural heritage as well as to residents.

Secondly they may have grants to assist the more commercial aspects of heritage conservation and interpretation. This can be an important part of developing the tourism infrastructure and of creating rural employment.

Landscape, nature conservation and public enjoyment of the countryside: the immediate post-war structure and practice

After planning, agriculture and other aspects of rural development, conservation is the final plank of post-war rural policy. It was set firmly within the thinking and framework of the legislation which we have described above. Most rural land has no other safeguard than the protection from intrusive urban and industrial development given by planning policy. A small proportion receives additional protection through one of several conservation designations. Most of the designations, applying in the main to land in *private ownership* it must be stressed, are designed to influence their management. The designations of greatest significance are made by national conservation agencies, but the planning authorities are also able to define areas of great landscape value and other local land categories where stricter standards of development might apply.

In the development of thinking about conservation during the war and immediately afterwards, a divide grew up between landscape conservation and nature conservation. Landscape conservation also intertwined with public enjoyment and owes its origins to three strands of thought:

(1) The notion of natural beauty influenced by the romantic painters and poets, developed during the nineteenth century. This led to the formation of voluntary amenity bodies, such as the National Trust and the Council for the Protection of Rural England, which exist either to hold land or to campaign for the protection of the countryside.
(2) The desire of the people of a largely urban society to get out into the countryside and the campaigns for freedom of access, particularly to the hills.
(3) The international concept of national parks, starting in the United States but becoming a world-wide movement.

The government commissioned John Dower, a wartime civil servant, to draw these threads together and describe how they might apply in Britain (Dower, 1945).

Natural history has a long and distinguished record in Britain, but the drive for a separate organization for nature conservation in Britain grew out of the concern for recognition of the significance of the work of the emerging discipline of ecology. In particular new insights pointed to the need for the systematic protection of important, representative habitats through the creation of nature reserves and based on a rigorous science base.

When the post-war government established expert committees to prepare for legislation to protect the countryside, it was persuaded to divide the issues of landscape conservation and public enjoyment from those of nature conservation. The resulting legislation, the National Parks and Access to the Countryside Act 1949, therefore provided for the following (references are to the Act):

(1) National parks to be designated by a National Parks Commission (Part II) to care for what John Dower has defined as 'extensive areas of beautiful and relatively wild country in which for the nation's benefit and by appropriate national decision and action
   (a) the characteristic landscape beauty is strictly preserved;
   (b) access and facilities for public open-air enjoyment are amply provided;
   (c) wildlife and buildings and places of architectural and historic interest are suitably protected;

(d) established farming use is effectively maintained'.
(2) Access to the countryside to be secured by a more systematic recording of public rights of way on definitive maps prepared by the highway authorities (Part IV); through promotion by the National Parks Commission of long-distance paths (Sections 51–55); and by securing access to open country by means of access agreements. Various subsequent highways and countryside Acts have developed and consolidated the law relating to public rights of way. Some twelve long-distance paths or national trails now exist and more are planned.
(3) Nature conservation was recognized as a function of national government and a new agency, the Nature Conservancy, was established with a research arm and a regionalized executive arm (Part III). The latter was to hold and manage national nature reserves and to declare land in the ownership and management of others as sites of special scientific interest and to notify the local planning authority of them as worthy of special care.

The new government agency, the National Parks Commission, was to designate national parks and also areas of outstanding natural beauty (AONBs) which were intended to have the same status in terms of landscape quality but without the recreational potential and purpose.

Ten national parks were established between 1951 and 1957, most governed by a special county council committee, or a joint committee where the park fell into several counties. The family of national parks has been joined by the Norfolk and Suffolk Broads, and the government has committed itself to equivalent status for the New Forest. Two, the Peak District and the Lake District, were and are independent planning boards. The national park authorities are thus within local government. Two-thirds of the members are appointed by the county councils, with district council representation, and one-third are appointed by the Secretary of State for the Environment or for Wales. In 1974, as a result of a review by an expert committee under Lord Sandford, the national parks were greatly strengthened by being given a chief officer and a specialized team of staff; a firmer policy framework; and new financial arrangements. Additional money is provided to the authorities by a 75 per cent grant for national park work through the National Park Supplementary Grant from the Department of the Environment. The Countryside Commission commissioned a further review of national parks by a panel under Professor Ron Edwards which reported in January 1991. The government has committed itself to making all national park authorities independent bodies, but still within the local government framework. Legislation on that and national park purposes is expected in the 1994–95 parliamentary session (Department of the Environment, 1992).

Scotland was not covered by the national park provisions, although a report from the Countryside

Commission for Scotland on the mountain areas of Scotland proposes the designation of four areas as national parks.

Later a third planning *definition*, heritage coasts, was devised to bring recognition to the finest undeveloped coast. The areas were chosen by the National Parks Commission, later the Countryside Commission, but are adopted by the local authorities.

The Nature Conservancy covered the whole of Great Britain, with advisory committees for each country. Later the Conservancy became a committee of the Natural Environment Research Council (1965–73) and in 1973 it became the Nature Conservancy Council. At that point the NCC became divorced from its ecological research base which was only partly replaced by the establishment of a chief scientist's team. The Nature Conservancy Council has since been reorganized into agencies for Scotland, Wales and England (see later).

Response to social and agricultural change in the post-war era

Beginning in the 1950s the new prosperity of the urban population led to greater leisure time, higher disposable income and rapidly increasing car ownership. Visiting the countryside for recreation grew rapidly without adequate provision, leading to great concern over localized damage and fears for the future. The response was a White Paper *Leisure in the Countryside* in 1966 and the Countryside Act of 1968 for England and Wales. This broadened the remit of the National Parks Commission which became the Countryside Commission. It was to promote landscape conservation and public enjoyment across the whole countryside. The principal developments in the late 1960s and early 1970s were country parks and picnic sites. The Countryside Commission for Scotland with an equivalent role and purposes was established by the Countryside (Scotland) Act of 1967.

The new Commissions' means of achieving the development of the new countryside recreation sites and of promoting new ideas like environmental interpretation was a combination of advice, based upon research and experiment, and grant-aid. This growth of provision for recreation led to the establishment of a new professionalism and a more critical view of performance, in particular of the national parks. The committee under the Junior Environment Minister, Lord Sandford, reported formally in 1974 but it anticipated many of its findings by securing in the Local Government Act of 1972 provision for a new, more capable form of national park authority.

In the 1970s official research began to confirm the nature and extent of change in the landscape and loss of wildlife habitats as a result of agricultural development. There were deep divisions between the voluntary conservation bodies on the one hand, and the Ministry of Agriculture and farming interests on the other, about the significance of change and the need to place restrictions on agriculture in the interests of conservation. The Countryside Commission appeared to accept the inevitability of change and promoted the concept of 'new agricultural landscapes', different from but perhaps as diverse and satisfying as those lost.

It was the issue of moorland reclamation, in particular in the national parks, which finally united voluntary and official conservation bodies. Operations such as ploughing and reseeding with more productive grasses were grant-aided by MAFF and allowed increased stocking with the added incentive of additional hill farming subsidies. The loss of heather moorland on Exmoor had been well documented over a period of twenty years. The proportion of the park covered by heather moorland had fallen from one-third to one-quarter, fragmenting the moorland block and eroding the sense of limitless space which was the principal reason for designation. The argument on Exmoor was the trigger for the development of the general arguments about moorland reclamation. The debate led to the establishment of several central policy principles of the government's approach which became incorporated in the Wildlife and Countryside Act 1981. Those principles, bitterly opposed by voluntary conservation interests, were:

Voluntary principle Rather than compulsion, advice and grants to landowners and farmers would achieve the objectives of conservation.
Compensation The Act gave the national park authorities and the Nature Conservancy Council (NCC) the power to object to the giving of agricultural grants. If they sustained their objection and ministers supported it they would be required to offer compensation for *profits forgone* by way of a voluntary but legally binding management agreement.
No reserve powers If the farmer or landowner chooses to decline the management agreement and proceed (without grant) then the authority cannot prevent the operation proceeding.

The operation of the spirit of the voluntary principle underlying the Act has been greatly assisted by several other provisions and operations related to agricultural grant regimes:

(1) The NCC was required under the Act to renotify the owners of all the sites of special scientific interest, over 3000 then and now over 5500, representing around 8 per cent of the land surface of Great Britain. The NCC was also required to consult the owners and occupiers and to notify them of 'potentially damaging operations'. A partnership over management, with financially attractive management agreements, has gradually been built up between NCC and farmers, but the administrative cost has been very large and the work has been a preoccupation of the NCC over many years.

(2) Farmers seeking MAFF grants were required from 1980 to consult the national park authorities on their plans. This process has triggered a dialogue with farmers, supported by a range of discretionary grants and truly voluntary management agreements, often with public access provisions. In the following ten years relationships improved very markedly between the parks and farmers.

(3) Despite the power to object to the payment of grants by MAFF, no 'profit foregone' compensatory agreement under the Act as a result of an objection has ever been concluded. The national park authorities have gone to great lengths to avoid the potential conflicts. The informal approach has been assisted by the government's willingness to fund truly voluntary management agreements by both NCC and the NPAs. The improvement grants which created the pressures for development have mainly been phased out.

Other provisions of the 1981 Act covered wildlife protection, mainly birds and endangered species; and the opportunity was taken to make several nature conservation, countryside and national parks provisions and provisions on rights of way, notably on the definitive map. The Countryside Commission also became a grant-in-aid body, independent of the civil service.

In the following ten years, the public's support for wildlife and countryside conservation has continued its growth, with membership of voluntary conservation bodies increasing several fold during the 1980s. The greening of public opinion and the consequent greening of politics has led to the incorporation of references to conservation into new areas of public policy affecting the countryside. The gradual greening of agricultural policy is worth remarking. Some examples will suffice:

(1) A special experiment was instituted in the Norfolk and Suffolk Broads to prevent reclamation of grazing marshes to cereal production, the Broads Grazing Marsh Conservation Scheme. Instead of management agreements it offered standard payments, on a voluntary basis, of £123 per hectare per annum, reflecting the different in return on the two enterprises. The scheme began in January 1985 administered by the Countryside Commission in association with MAFF but was handed over to MAFF entirely after three years.

(2) The Broads scheme led to environmentally sensitive areas (ESAs) begun in 1987, which offer standard payments on an area basis to farmers who volunteer to adopt 'traditional' farming methods in order, for example, to preserve herb-rich hay meadows and maintain stone walls. ESAs operate under EC legislation and a major expansion is planned during 1994.

(3) A package of grants for farm conservation and farm diversification was introduced by MAFF in 1987 under the title 'Alternative Land Use and Rural Enterprise'.

(4) All capital grants for reclamation of moorland were withdrawn from 1984.

(5) National park farm conservation schemes were operational in most parks from the late 1980s.

(6) A countryside stewardship scheme was set up to 'purchase' environmental benefits from farmers who farm in an environmentally friendly way.

The climate of conflict and mutual distrust between conservationists and the farming community, although not entirely forgotten, has been transformed in the past ten years. One remaining factor should be mentioned and that is the decline in real farm incomes in the past decade which has taken the steam out of some development plans and undermined business confidence. Especially in the uplands the prospects are now very uncertain for the typical family farm, and countryside interests are now concerned for the sustainability of traditional farming and the landscapes it created and maintained. Because of the lack of diversification opportunities, upland farmers are very vulnerable to reductions in prices or in subsidies for sheep and beef.

Meanwhile the Countryside Commission had also developed, experimentally, the concept of countryside management which aims to achieve several public benefits simultaneously on private land: amenity and conservation, eyesore removal and better public access. The pilot experiments began in the early 1970s in the Lake District and Snowdonia National Parks as the Upland Management Experiments (UMEx) and were joined by more in three heritage coasts and in the urban fringe countryside. The experiments allowed the Commission to demonstrate the essential elements of the approach, which were to employ a project officer with: a brief to develop an action plan for landscape and access improvement; the discretion to negotiate informal local solutions to local problems; the ability to liaise with others on problems beyond his or her scope; and a budget to carry out works directly. Countryside management is now firmly established in the local government approach to promoting conservation and public enjoyment of the local countryside. It has also been developed a stage further through the Groundwork approach. This links informal countryside management to economic regeneration and has also sought to involve the private sector and to engage the local community generally as a major player.

Reorganization of conservation agencies

A recent development is the reorganization of the countryside agencies. The proposals, announced without consultation by the Secretaries of State for Environment, Scotland and Wales in July 1989, became law in the Environmental Protection Act 1990. They are:

(1) the creation of a Countryside Council for Wales combining the functions of the Countryside Commission and NCC from April 1991;
(2) the creation of a Nature Conservancy Council for England, English Nature, in April 1991;
(3) the establishment of a Nature Conservancy Council for Scotland in April 1991 and its combination with the Countryside Commission for Scotland to form Scottish Natural Heritage in April 1992.

The separation of landscape and nature conservation is regarded by some people as an artificial and distracting issue. However Britain is not alone in the developed world in organizing its conservation activities in this way. Be that as it may, some would say that the opportunity has been missed to prepare a new integrated brief for the Scottish and Welsh combined agencies. At the time of writing the Government is considering amalgamating the Countryside Commission and English Nature under a new integrated brief.

Fiscal legislation and conservation

To assist the conservation of the national heritage, capital taxation legislation gives conditional exemption from tax for land and other property of heritage quality. These fiscal incentives for conservation cover:

(1) pictures, books, works of art etc. of scientific, historic or artistic merit in their own right;
(2) land of outstanding scenic, historic or scientific (nature conservation) interest;
(3) buildings of outstanding historic or architectural interest.
(4) land essential for the protection of the character and amenities of a building qualifying under 3;
(5) objects historically associated with a building qualifying under 3.

All property is assessed in terms of national importance, and the Inland Revenue Capital Taxes Office (CTO) relies on the official agencies – the Countryside Commission, the nature conservancy councils and their successors, the Forestry Commission, and English Heritage – for advice on whether the property qualifies.

The reliefs available are from *inheritance tax*, which is charged when property changes ownership by way of bequest; and from *capital gains tax*, which is charged when property passes by way of gift or is sold. Certain gifts are also chargeable to inheritance tax when the donor dies within the subsequent seven years.

Owners whose land qualifies can apply for tax exemption provided they are prepared to give undertakings to conserve the land and allow reasonable public access. This is the meaning of the term 'conditional exemption'. These conditions can be contained in a management plan at the time of a 'chargeable event' such as a death. It is also possible to obtain informal advice in advance from the expert advisory agencies to enable the owners to maintain the heritage quality of their property so that it will qualify in due course, or indeed to improve it. Relief on non-heritage property is also possible if it is set aside to provide income for the maintenance of heritage property – a type of maintenance fund.

If owners are not able or willing to continue to maintain heritage property, other fiscal reliefs are possible: gifts to charity for national purposes for public benefit; private treaty sales to bodies approved by the Inland Revenue; and acceptance of a property in lieu of tax. A fuller description of all of these reliefs is contained in the Inland Revenue's memorandum *Capital Taxation and the National Heritage* (1986).

The effect of all these is first to leave property in private hands, but protected by the potential loss of tax relief if it is neglected, damaged or disposed of; and secondly to assist the acquisition by conservation bodies of heritage properties at less than full market price or even at no cost.

The voluntary sector

So far we have considered mainly the official side of conservation. In practice voluntary bodies play a major part, described in more detail in Chapter 18. They tend to play a complementary role to central and local government and to the official agencies. They operate by:

(1) lobbying and campaigning for legislative or policy change or for resources to be given to official bodies;
(2) acting as agents for official bodies in carrying out duties placed on government;
(3) providing advice and expertise to official bodies;
(4) holding land and managing it for public benefit and operating visitor facilities;
(5) raising money to support conservation;
(6) promoting understanding of the heritage through information and education work;
(7) providing an outlet for volunteers' energy, expertise and commitment by way of practical work, education, environmental interpretation and so on.

References

BLUNDEN, J. and CURRY, N. (1990) *A People's Charter*, HMSO, London

DEPARTMENT OF THE ENVIRONMENT (1988) *General Development Order 1988*, HMSO, London

DEPARTMENT OF THE ENVIRONMENT (1992) *Fit for the Future: Statement on Policies for the National Parks*, London

DEPARTMENT OF THE ENVIRONMENT AND WELSH OFFICE (1992) *The Countryside and the Rural Economy*, Planning Policy Guidance Note no. 7, HMSO, London

DOWER, J. (1945) *National Parks in England and Wales*, Cmnd 6628, HMSO, London

EDWARDS, PROF. R. (1991) *Fit for the Future: Report of the National Parks Review Panel*, Countryside Commission, Cheltenham

HEAP, SIR D. (1991) *An Outline of Planning Law* (10th edn), Sweet and Maxwell, London

INLAND REVENUE (1986) *Capital Taxation and the National Heritage*, Inland Revenue, London

MINISTRY OF LAND AND NATURAL RESOURCES AND WELSH OFFICE (1996) *Leisure in the Countryside, England and Wales*, Cmnd 2928, HMSO, London

SANDFORD, LORD (CHAIRMAN) (1974) *Report of the National Parks Policy Review Committee*, HMSO, London

SCOTT, MR JUSTICE (CHAIRMAN) (1942) *Report of the Committee on Land Utilisation in Rural Areas*, Cmnd 6378, HMSO, London

Case study 11.1

Wicken Fen: the management of a nature reserve

Laurie Friday

Wicken Fen is one of the oldest nature reserves in Britain. In represents one of the last remnants of the fenland that once covered hundreds of square kilometres of the shallow basin south of the Wash. Wicken Fen has largely survived drainage and conversion to arable because its species richness and value as a habitat remnant were recognized at the turn of the century by entomologists, who bought parcels of land and placed them under the care and protection of the National Trust. Wicken Fen has been managed by the National Trust ever since and, in 1993, has been designated a National Nature Reserve.

The reserve comprises about 245 ha (605 acres) divided into three distinctly different areas (*Figure 11.1*):

The Sedge Fen (133 ha), the largest remaining and least drained fragment of the original fenland, with a diverse patchwork of habitats: open water, sedge, herbaceous fen ('litter'), droves, fen scrub ('carr').
St Edmund's Fen (22 ha), which is largely undrained, but is overgrown with fen carr.
Adventurers' Fen (including the Charles Raven Reserve) (89 ha), which was drained in the seventeenth and nineteenth centuries and was dug for peat ('turf') until about 1920. It was drained again during the Second World War and returned to the Trust in 1952.

The National Trust owns some peripheral land which is managed in various ways, including hay meadow; wet rough grassland; native broad-leaf planted woodland; and arable (which lies outside the reserve). It also owns a number of buildings on the reserve, close to the entrance, and in Lode Lane.

The reserve is open to the public. Facilities include a car park, public conveniences, a boarded walkway and interpretative displays. There is an active education programme.

Main features of Wicken Fen and their implications for management

The water table and its control

All stages of the succession from open water to woodland can be seen at Wicken Fen: open water; reedswamp; sedge and herbaceous fen; carr; and woodland. The stage found in any one place on the Fen depends partly on the height of the water table, and this depends on the distance of the plot from the nearest open water, the season, and the height of water in the

adjoining lode and ditch system (which depends in part on the height of the retaining banks) (*Figure 11.2*). The banks surrounding the Fen have recently been water-proofed to prevent water seeping out on to the lower-lying adjacent farmland.

Water quality

The water that supports the fen communities at Wicken is derived from rainfall and from drainage from the chalk uplands to the south. The Fen receives water from agricultural surroundings, which is potentially enriched with nutrients, particularly nitrogen and phosphorus, and contaminated with pesticides. Water from these sources is likely to have a detrimental effect on freshwater life and, if flooding occurs, on the fen vegetation. Some of the internal ditches and ponds are protected from this danger, being cut off from outside waters and receiving input only from rainfall or from water percolating through peat.

Management practices, especially cutting regimes

The different terrestrial plant communities, and to a large extent the landscape, owe their existence to different types of management, some of which have been carried on for centuries, and their frequency. Some of these practices lapsed in the early years of this century and have only recently been revived as part of the management of the reserve.

The various management practices have produced a wide range of habitat types within a comparatively small area on the Fen (*Figure 11.3*):

(1) *sedge, litter fields* and *droves*, mown in various cycles;
(2) *reedbeds*, some cropped;
(3) *carr* and incipient *woodland*, where cutting has lapsed;
(4) *open water*, all man-made, including ditches, dykes, meres and ponds; the ditches are cleared in short lengths on a long rotation;
(5) *turf diggings*, old and new.

Peat

The substratum is predominantly sedge peat of slightly alkaline pH and rich in bases. It is maintained by being kept waterlogged, which prevents the decomposition of the organic matter. If the Fen became drier, the surface peat would begin to waste away by oxidation, as it has in the surrounding drained farmland. The shrinkage of the surrounding land has created severe

Figure 11.1 Wicken Fen nature reserve

Figure 11.2 Lode, Wicken Fen

problems in maintaining high water levels on the Fen. As the peat wastes, nutrients are released and the pH of subsequent drainage water is lowered. This effect is seen in places on the Fen where raised topography has produced local acidification, and this is reflected in the flora.

The management plan

The management of the reserve is carried out by the Fen staff, under the Head Warden, according to a management plan. This plan is drawn up and amended every five years by the Secretary of the Local Management Committee under the guidance of the National Trust through its Land Agent. The management plan summarizes the aims and objectives of management as follows:

(1) The maintenance of historic and present diversity is vital to the continuing interest of the property.

(2) The effective maintenance of water levels underlies the Fen's ecology and is crucial for the success of all other management practices.

(3) The diversity of the Fen's flora, fauna and landscape is largely dependent on the maintenance of all stages in the succession from open water, through

reedswamp, herbaceous vegetation (sedge and litter) and scrub (carr), to woodland. The representation of these different communities on the Fen depends on relative water and land levels, and on the continuation of traditional cropping practices.

(4) Management for the production of traditional crops must be continued. The main traditional crops are sedge and litter. Other crops, such as reed and turf, may also be taken for conservation or demonstration purposes (but see 10 below). Marketing of the crops will be pursued where possible.

(5) The relatively small area of sedge should be maintained and, if possible, increased by upgrading of litter fields to sedge fields by cutting early in the year or not at all or by clearance of carr where much sedge is present.

(6) Diversity in the litter fields should be encouraged by a programme of cutting at different times of the year, and at different frequencies.

(7) Small-scale turf digging should be maintained for demonstration and to re-create former low-pH habitats.

(8) Droves and paths have considerable natural history interest as well as a utilitarian function. Management should therefore attempt to strike a balance between preserving their natural history interest and allowing access to Fen staff, machinery and visitors as appropriate.

138

Figure 11.3 Mixed habitats, Wicken Fen

(9) Lodes and dykes have considerable natural history interest, part of which stems from patterns of management. A balance needs to be struck between the need to keep dykes open and the preservation of that natural history interest dependent on well developed vegetation. This is best achieved by clearance at rather longer intervals than would be appropriate in agricultural land, by clearing only short stretches at a time, and by leaving some ditches to undergo succession to dryness. These waterways have reversed their role in that they are now seen as a way of getting water into the fen and keeping it wet, rather than as a way of draining it.

(10) Reed is a traditional crop in the fens but not, on a large scale, at Wicken. Its harvesting conflicts to some extent with the natural history interest of the reedbeds but it produces valuable income and maintains and demonstrates a traditional fenland activity. It should continue, subject to measures to safeguard the fauna of the reedbeds.

(11) Carr is a relatively recent phenomenon at Wicken. Clearance of carr to produce more extensive sedge and litter fields is desirable. Carr, however, is of considerable ornithological, entomological and botanical interest and its complete clearance, even if possible, is undesirable. Carr cover of 40–50 per cent is a reasonable aim, with at least some of the residual area in large blocks. A range of ages of carr should be created and maintained.

(12) Trees and woodland have developed largely because of past drying of the Fen. Recently, however, higher water levels appear to have caused the death of many trees. This process should be monitored. Trees should be managed with regard to their value to the landscape and nature conservation, but also with public safety in mind. Dead wood is a vital habitat for many species, including some rare ones, and should therefore be retained in some areas of the Fen.

(13) The ponds in the area of the old brickworks are of great interest to freshwater biologists and should be preserved from disturbance and pollution.

(14) Adventurers' Fen has not yet realized its potential as a wetland reserve. The development of a management plan for Adventurers' Fen of the same order of completeness as for the remainder of the Fen is a subject to be addressed by the Management Committee in the near future.

(15) Marginal areas of the Trust's land should be managed in a way that is sympathetic to the ecological and landscape characteristics of the SSSI and to provide an agricultural rental income where appropriate. They should be maintained and, as opportunity allows, extended to act as a buffer between the Fen and the surrounding land.

(16) The Sedge Fen (excluding Verrall's Fen), and the part of Little Breed Fen south of Sedge Fen Drove, should be regarded as areas generally open to visitors when the state of the paths permits.

(17) Verrall's Fen and St Edmund's Fen should be open to visitors at all times but this is not publicized and visitors are not specifically encouraged to go there.

(18) Those parts of the Charles Raven Reserve away from public footpaths and paths giving access to hides should be closed to visitors, except by special permission or in escorted groups. This is to minimize disturbance to birds.

(19) The boardwalk is to be maintained and possibly extended, where appropriate, to prevent damage to paths in wet conditions and to provide convenient access for less able visitors.

(20) Interpretation of the points of interest of the Fen should make full use of trail guides, illustrated colour guides and other material. The displays in and around the William Thorpe Building and the Fen Cottage should be maintained.

(21) An education programme will be positively pursued at the Fen. Use by educational parties of the parts of the Fen to which there is general access should be encouraged, subject to suitable safeguards. Activities such as insect sweeping and pond dipping should be confined to the area set aside for this adjacent to St Edmund's Fen.

(22) The Trust's properties in Lode Lane should be maintained in a fit condition and used for appropriate purposes. Artefacts and buildings of local social and historical significance should be conserved and displayed.

(23) Reseach and monitoring of the flora, fauna, water quality and hydrological state of the Fen should be an integral part of active management.

(24) The Fen's archives should be maintained.

(25) Wicken Fen was, and is, the habitat of several rare species. These should be conserved in the national interest. This involves specific management for certain surviving species (such as *Viola persicifolia*) and may involve the reintroduction of species which have become extinct locally in recent years, such as the Fen Ragwort (*Senecio paludosus*) and the Swallowtail and Large Copper butterflies. Reintroduction should be carried out only when research has shown that conditions are satisfactory for their release and survival. Management of these key species may sometimes require that specific practices be carried out in localized areas, and these may be allowed to override the normal prescription for the compartment, but each case should be considered individually.

(26) The landscape of Wicken Fen, which results from the traditional management of sedge, litter, lodes and ditches, and the presence of buildings such as the Fen Cottage and Windpump, should be maintained and protected from all forms of pollution, including noise and visual intrusion.

(27) Equipment, workshop facilities and staffing levels are to be maintained, within the finance available to manage the reserve, to realize the objectives and work programme outlined in the management plan.

(28) Financial management will be organized so as to secure sufficient resources and income.

Case study 11.2

Details of objection to planning application adjoining SSSI

Philip Broadbent-Yale

The following is a description of the steps taken, in particular the legal and statutory planning issues, which were raised in a successful objection by the National Trust to a planning application adjoining Wicken Fen. Case Study 11.1 describes the Fen and the reasons for National Trust ownership, and provides the background to why we raised such a strong case against the development which we believed was inappropriate and potentially damaging.

The main proposals of the scheme which were submitted by agents for the adjoining owner to the local planning authority in December 1991 was for the creation of a recreational lake on 109 ha of grade 1 and 2 farmland immediately adjoining the Fen. The development involved stripping topsoil, creating earth embankments between 2.4 and 4 metres high, and flooding the area to a depth of 2 m to provide two lakes, one of which was to be used for fishing and sailing and the other for rowing, water-skiing and jet-skis. There was also ancillary development proposed for 100 floating cottages, a clubhouse and a peatland study centre. The visitor use was predicted at a peak of 290 cars per hour.

Our response to the planning authority took the form of a detailed objection to the actual application and its supporting report. We took into account Local Plan policies and statements (LPPS and LPS), appropriate Department of the Environment Planning Policy Guidance Notes (PPGs), and comments from relevant authorities, namely the Ministry of Agriculture, Fisheries and Food (MAFF), the National Rivers Authority (NRA), the Internal Drainage Board (IDB) and the Agricultural Development and Advisory Service (ADAS).

Objection

The following is a condensed version of our actual objection. Headings and paragraph numbers refer to the application submitted by agents acting for the developer.

Site description

Eighty per cent of the subject land is classified as grade 1 or 2.

We have seen an ADAS report dated 18 December 1991 which indicates that this application would 'constitute the irreversible loss of best and most versatile agricultural land . . . of grades 1 and 2'. East Cambridgeshire District Council (ECDC) LPP 47 indicates a presumption against development on grade 1 and 2 land, particularly where it is irreversible.

DoE PPG 7 of January 1992 states that 'considerable weight should be given to protecting such land [grades 1 and 2] against development, because of its special importance'.

The scheme proposes development involving considerable earth movement to extract clay subsoil to construct dams up to 4 m tall; construction of clubhouse facilities; car parks to accommodate 290 cars per hour; and possible sale of topsoil from site. This amounts to irreversible development and is contrary to local and DoE policy.

1.5 One of the main features of the area, and part of its beauty and charm, is the flatness of the fens. The proposals would create considerable intrusion with the construction of 4 m high banks, clubhouse facility with balcony, and alien tree planting in what is currently an open, rural, agricultural landscape. The development is alien to the sense of place.

There is also considerable historic interest in the area. Reach Lode has historic significance with its link as an access when the village of Reach was a port. An archaeological scatter site has been identified and a Saxon funeral urn was found which is now in the Archaeology and Anthropology Museum in Cambridge. The potential for other archaeological remains or evidence of settlements is likely in the area and this would be irreparably damaged with the scale of earth movement proposed.

2.7 LPS 6.18 refers to landowners having a statutory requirement to keep public rights of way open. The scheme proposes the closure of a public road by flooding. We would object to the closure of this public highway.

The footpaths at the top of the lode banks *must* be retained, not *could* be.

What is presently a pleasant countryside walk along a tranquil lode bank will be disturbed by noise from water-ski power boats, jet-skis and sail boats all moving at considerable speed compared with the restfulness of the present environment.

1.9 The site is presently visible from the footpaths on National Trust land, as well as from other non-Trust areas. The proposal to raise the level of the site and to flood it to a depth of over 2 m effectively makes the site considerably more visible in the surrounding countryside and particularly from Wicken Fen immediately to the north. The intrusion of sails and new buildings will be considerable.

1.10 LPP 159 clearly states that 'Development which *could be* considered *detrimental to* the interests of *Wicken Fen and its users* will not be permitted' – the Wicken Fen Safeguarding Area (WFSA).

DoE Circular 1/92 dated 2 January 1992 requests 'English Nature to give priority to defining consultation areas around sites of international importance' and for 'wetland sites, it may extend as far as the 2 km maximum'. The Circular also goes on to refer to the need for rigorous environmental assessment for sites identified in the Nature Conservation Review. Wicken Fen is such a site and English Nature would seek to establish it as a national nature reserve if the National Trust were not responsible for the site.

The proposal includes significant development within the WFSA. The proposals are only an outline application and could well change by the detail stage and at future expansion of the site. The National Trust feels very strongly that a site which we have protected for over 90 years and which we are charged with protecting for the nation in perpetuity *could be* detrimentally damaged. The application is therefore contrary to the Local Plan and to the DoE Circular and should be refused.

Peatland Study Centre

Suggesting the development of a study centre is ironic in view of the destruction of the peat resource in this proposal.

Wicken Fen already has a well established information centre at the William Thorpe Building with a thriving educational programme, 35,000 visitors per annum, professional/qualified staff, volunteer work base and ideal habitat for conservation, education and scientific research. Visitors come for the peace, quiet and natural landscape and researchers value very highly the lack of disturbance at the site.

The value of the Fen for research is shown by the bibliography for Wicken Fen which amounts to over 650 references to articles written about the habitats, flora and fauna of the property. For instance Dr N. B. Davies of the Department of Zoology at Cambridge University is using Burwell Lode, along what would be the complete northern boundary of the proposed site, as one of the main sites for his ongoing study of cuckoos as parasites of reed warblers. This is widely acknowledged in the zoological scientific world as a pioneering study and has achieved cover page status

in one of the world's foremost scientific journals, *Science*, and has recently appeared in *Scientific American*.

Such high-profile studies show the importance of Wicken Fen. It would be inappropriate to permit development which could damage the Fen, or to try and re-create facilities within the development area which could hope to provide the standard of the internationally respected habitats that already exist at Wicken Fen.

LPP 98 states that 'tourist facilities will be . . . subject to environmental and nature conservation considerations.' This ancillary development is inappropriate to the area.

Club facilities

4.1–4.2 These are all commercial ancillary activities contrary to LPP 98.

4.3 Reference to a balcony will mean that the building will be highly visible at lode bank level. Lighting at night will create light pollution owing to the open nature of the surrounding area, will be visually intrusive and will be disturbing to wildlife. Indeed the survival of moths may be affected and the research on these species certainly would be affected. The night-time walks at Wicken for interested visitors and scientific research rely on the darkness of the surrounding area for their success, and this would be compromised by exposed lighting and flood lighting at such a facility.

The fishermen's cottages

We would be concerned that future intensification of use could lead to these cottages being permanently occupied. Indeed the proposal contains no mention of a need for a permanent residence for a site manager which we would anticipate being an early request.

Water sports

The sails on the boats will be highly visible, owing to their bright colours, and their rapid movement will create an even greater sense of intrusion.

The Trust would be concerned that fish introduced to the proposed lakes could be transferred to the lode system and thence into Wicken Fen itself. Certain species could be deleterious to existing water life. Invasive plant species could also be introduced to the waters and spread to the Fen.

6.3 Noise travels far on the Fens owing to their open nature. The noise from a high-speed powered boat or jet-ski is totally out of keeping with the area and would be extremely intrusive for existing visitors to the area. The noise from jet-skis is particularly annoying as it is tonal and unsteady. The application only refers to a protective screen against Burwell Village. They have failed to consider any protection for Wicken Fen or Wicken Village which in fact are closer.

The main usage, and therefore intrusion, will be at weekends which is when visitors to Wicken Fen come to enjoy the peace and solitude of the place.

Conservation and lanscape

7.1 Owing to the significance of Wicken Fen, the National Trust strongly request a full environmental assessment study of the proposal before any consideration is given to this application. Changes to water tables, noise and landscape would be unacceptable for such an important SSSI and that is why the wording of the WFSA is so specific. There have been sightings of otters on the banks immediately adjoining the proposed development, and the disturbance proposed might prevent them recolonizing the area. The National Trust is also aware of at least one rare species, for which records are available, whose habitat would be directly affected by the proposals.

Proposals to plant

Cotoneaster, lilac and conifer are unsuitable species not naturally occurring in this area. We would be concerned that exotic trees, shrubs, etc. might be planted which could invade Wicken Fen. Planting of inappropriate species as proposed will make the area look manicured rather than natural.

The footpath leading north to Wicken Fen is statutory footpath no. 9 and therefore access is not difficult over Burwell Lode. This could have the highly detrimental effect of increasing access to a presently undisturbed area of the Fen.

Water-related issues

Water supply and control
8.1 It is not totally clear from the description whether the water will come from the high-level system of the lodes overseen by the NRA or from the low-level system overseen by the Internal Drainage Board. If it is the former, any reduction in flow of water in the lodes owing to water being taken into the proposed reservoir is likely to reduce the lodes' biological interest. The National Trust would have considerable concern as the lode system links directly into the Fen. If the latter, we would ask for clarification from the IDB that there would be sufficient water to provide the volume required to fill the proposed lake.

The water in the low-level system is nitrate, phosphate and pesticide rich and if there is no outflow from the proposed lake this could lead to a build-up in pollution. It could also create an algal bloom problem on the surface which would not be conducive to enjoyment of water sports.

Considerable clarification is required on these points and they should be the subject of an environmental assessment statement.

Navigation
8.5 LPP 95 indicates a presumption against 'intensification of existing uses' on the lodes.

Noise and traffic impacts

9.1 Farm machinery is normally used during the week and has a low, constant tone. The main use for these facilities would be at weekends when powered boats and jet-skis would introduce different noise of considerable change and tone which could be intrusive. This is just when most visitors to Wicken Fen are coming to enjoy the presently undisturbed property.

9.4 It is not clear from their description whether the banks will be 4 metres above water level or 4 metres above base level. If the former, it will be a significant scar on the open landscape; if the latter, it would appear to be an ineffective noise barrier. The two banks proposed will run parallel to each other and will therefore channel noise south and north. The latter directly towards Wicken Village.

Accessibility
9.5 'The site is remote.' The National Trust does not wish to see this changed to the extent that this development proposes.

LPS 6.17 refers to old mineral workings being used for water recreation sites. There are gravel workings at Mepal within the ECDC area and further afield at St Ives, and the National Trust seek clarification as to whether the developer has considered making use of these areas which are being encouraged by the planning authority.

LPS 6.15 refers to noisy recreational sites being located against existing noise generators such as main roads. The National Trust supports such guidelines. This application clearly will be contrary to these.

LPS 6.15 also refers to the ECDC wishing to see sites appropriately located to overcome problems of unauthorized use. With public footpaths crossing the centre of the site and also round the complete perimeter of the western lake, this imposes considerable problems for controlling unauthorized use.

Traffic generation
9.7 A rate of 290 vehicles an hour implies one every 14 seconds. The National Trust hope that ECDC would give detailed consideration as to whether the road junctions and infrastructure in the immediate area could cope with this level of usage, whether the 2.5 km of single-track access road is sufficient in case of emergencies, and also whether this level of usage is

appropriate for what is presently an undisturbed rural location.

The National Trust would be concerned that users may try to enter the proposed site by other means, e.g. along Harrison's Drove to the north of the site, leading to policing problems and increased entry into the south-east corner of Wicken Fen.

9.8   If there are 100 cars already parked for residents of the floating cottages and a further 290 cars per hour arriving, this will require an extensive car park area. This would be clearly seen from public footpaths in the area.

Employment generation

10.1–10.2   The planning authority should require the developers to indicate how many of the 30 jobs claimed to be created on the site will be available for employment of the local community.

Agricultural considerations

11.1–11.10   We have already commented in some detail at paragraph 1.1. If this scheme is being developed as a farm diversification project, we wonder whether the planning authority has been satisfied as to the financial viability of the scheme. The proposals in fact cast doubt on the viability by introducing suggestions for a further application to sell topsoil off the site with up to twenty lorry movements a day for three years, and the use of the lake for fish farming. These are already significantly altering the nature of the scheme. The latter proposal could cause pollution problems and would not be compatible with their objective for conservation management of the edges.

Development in the countryside

12.1   Clearly from what we have said above there are numerous contradictions between the arguments the developers have used in their application and the policies contained in the Local Plan. The National Trust believes that the Local Plan policies support our position for:

(i)   protection for Wicken Fen – LPP 50, LPP 52 and special protection under LPP 159;
(ii)   location of noisy recreational pursuits alongside existing noise generators – LPS 6.15;
(iii)   a presumption against development of grade 1 and 2 agricultural land – LPP 47;
(iv)   a presumption against development which is not in keeping with the surrounding area – LPP 54;
(v)   a presumption against development which does not provide significant improvements to the landscape and environmental quality of the area – LPP 57.

12.6   They fail to comment at this point about the use of jet-skis, whereas in Annexe 2 they refer to demands for the 'new growing sport of jet-skiing'. The National Trust would be extremely concerned about future intensification of use of the lakes and how they would be policed to prevent such additional inappropriate use.

12.7   The statements here show how the developers are trying to manipulate the application. They clearly wish to draw people from much further afield than the local area (paragraph 12.4), and with 290 vehicles per hour they are clearly looking for a significant influx of people from outside the area.

The National Trust strongly believes that this remote rural site is not appropriate and that disused mineral workings adjoining main roads would be considerably better for this scale and type of development which is clearly what the Local Plan is seeking (LPS 6.17). If users of the proposed facilities are prepared to travel from afar then they would also travel to another, more suitable, alternative site.

Tourism developments

13.2   LPP 96 refers to LPS 6.22 which seeks to harness 'existing small sites in the area' to build into the Fenland Interpretation Strategy Initiative. They are not seeking a major study centre. With accommodation already being provided at Wicken Fen in the William Thorpe Building for interpretation and education, the National Trust does not believe that the area requires further such accommodation (see Annexe 4 for article on education at the Fen). It is purely being promoted within this scheme to disguise the commercial element of the development.

Future management

15.1   Paragraph 3 of the developer's agents' covering letter clearly shows that they have not yet approached potential operators. The National Trust therefore finds it difficult to see how the agents can say it will be managed by an experienced operator. We are concerned as to the safeguards for the future standard of management, control of water quality, control of noise and prevention of intensification of use.

Conclusion

Within one week of us submitting this detailed objection, the developer withdrew his application on the basis that he would prepare a full environmental assessment statement. The National Trust, in conjunction with the Countryside Commission and English Nature, subsequently prepared a detailed requirement of the points which we would require the EAS to cover. This we submitted to the planning authority and the developer. The Fen was designated a National Nature Reserve in 1993. We have subsequently heard no further from the developer.

144

Case study 11.3

The heather moorland of the Exmoor National Park

Graham Taylor

Exmoor National Park is in the south-west of England and, compared with other predominantly moorland areas, the temperatures are higher and the growing conditions for grasses, even cereals, are more favourable. Therefore, despite the designation of the area as a national park because of its moorland, farmers were keen to exploit these climatic advantages by improving the pasture by ploughing up and reseeding with more productive species of grass. The incentive of improved grazing was also fuelled by agricultural grants. This led to a loss of moorland under the plough, and it fell from about one-third of the area of the park in 1954 to about one-quarter today.

The 1970s were still the era of expanding agricultural output through high commodity prices and grants, in this case, for ploughing, drainage, fencing, roads and new buildings. All upland farmers were eligible. A voluntary understanding between the farming interests and the Exmoor National Park Authority (NPA) was proving ineffectual and the voluntary conservation lobby, together with the NPA, the Countryside Commision and the Nature Conservancy Council, persuaded the government to hold an enquiry conducted by Lord Porchester in 1977. The developments over the following fifteen years mirror the changing attitudes and policy towards conservation and agriculture. Porchester proposed the creation of two maps, the first identifying the extent of the moorland and the second showing those tracts important to the character of the area to be conserved, if possible, for all time.

None of this had the force of law and there were to be challenges. But out of the disputes emerged, in 1980, a compromise. It involved a voluntary arrangement with special funding from the Department of the Environment meeting 90 per cent of the costs of compensating the farmer for the loss of income if he were prevented from improving an area of moorland. Thus the principle of compensating farmers for profits forgone was established and it was incorporated in the Wildlife and Countryside Act 1981 for both landscape and wildlife conservation. The legislation allowed for any local authority to conclude voluntary agreements and for national park authorities and the Nature Conservancy Council to follow a particular procedure if they formally objected to improvements to land in national parks and sites of special scientific interest. Since Porchester less than 50 hectares of moorland has been improved without the agreement of the

NPA. The reason is only partly the protective regime. More important in recent years has been the withdrawal of grants for improvement and a fall in commodity prices and therefore farm income. There is a reluctance to invest at times of uncertainty. In parallel with this has grown a greater financial and staffing capacity in the NPA to negotiate and fund practical and positive conservation work.

In 1991 the Exmoor NPA acquired the moorland holdings of the Fortescue Estate, some 1500 hectares (actually 1477 hectares of moorland and 231 of pasture, most of which it is planned to revert to moorland) and a key component of the mosaic of moorland and in-bye farmland in the Park. It is managed by being let on a long-term grazing licence to the former owners so that the established relationship between the farms and the moorland is maintained. The NPA is now anxious that agricultural support for the uplands should not be cut too far and so remove all incentive to manage the farms traditionally. Continuing to graze the moorland is essential to maintain its existing vegetation and with it the character of the Park.

In 1991 the NPA also developed and launched a new Farm Conservation Scheme, to be funded through its own resources. The scheme offers two tiers of area payments based on the conservation value of the land and for following agreed prescriptions, for example reduced grazing levels. Linear-based payments are made for the maintenance of traditional field boundaries (walls and hedges) and rights of way. Optional capital payments for woodland management and improving the infrastructure of the farmed landscape, e.g. to rebuild walls, are also agreed as part of a whole-farm plan.

Ironically, shortly after the launch of the NPA's scheme, the Ministry of Agriculture, Fisheries and Food (MAFF) announced a three-fold increase in the area covered by its environmentally sensitive area (ESA) designations. Among the new areas was to be Exmoor. The ESA concept is closely parallel to the Exmoor NPA scheme but is separately and more generously funded. The NPA is delighted and the indications are that their scheme has been influential in the design of MAFF's ESA prescriptions.

The irony could not be more complete. The original position was that agriculture was antagonistic to conservation because of the single-minded purpose and structure of agricultural support. In order to counter one form of public support for agricultural production, the NPA had to compensate the farmer for not damaging another public interest (this is the opposite of the 'polluter pays' principle). Now the form of farm support is geared to rewarding farmers for delivering environmental goods. A new agricultural commodity has been born.

Case study 11.4

East Durham Groundwork Trust

Graham Taylor

The Groundwork movement grew out of the experiments in countryside management by the Countryside Commission in the 1970s. The Commission ran a competition, the Urban Fringe Experiment or UFEX80, to choose a town or city to test the principles on a much larger scale. St Helens Metropolitan District Council won but a new principle was also to be tested at the request of the Secretary of State for the Environment. Instead of being local authority led the new Groundwork project would be a trust managed by a board drawn from the public, voluntary and commercial sectors and operating as an independent body.

The East Durham Groundwork Trust was one of a number of new trusts set up in 1986 under the umbrella of the Groundwork Foundation – the body which assists the establishment of new trusts and promotes the development of a movement now 28 trusts strong.

The EDGT is based on Easington district, much scarred by mining and where environmental and economic regeneration are clearly interlinked. The District Councils of Easington, Sedgefield and the City of Durham, the County Council, and representatives from local industry, Business in the Community and the Durham Wildlife Trust make up the board. The aims are principally those of improving the living environment and restoring the working environment, but as a means to those ends as well as an end in itself the Trust has developed an impressive environmental education and interpretation component to its work. It draws on strong links with British Coal and other local industry for support and contacts, as well as receiving substantial sponsorship and income from undertaking environmental work on commercial property. The trading arm is a company which covenants its profits to the Trust.

Examples of cross-sectoral involvement and the multiple benefits include the following.

Seaton Holme

This is a grade 1 listed building, dating from the thirteenth century, which was in a deplorable condition having been left empty for nine years. A partnership between the Trust and the local Parish Council, in conjunction with the County Council and sponsored by a variety of interests, has rescued the building from further deterioration.

The partnership has raised the £500,000 required to completely renovate the building and provide the following facilities:

(1) a visitor discovery centre for East Durham;
(2) a gallery for touring art exhibitions;
(3) a function room with catering facilities for weddings, business training etc.;
(4) the village library;
(5) office facilities for the Groundwork Trust, the Parish Council and to let.

Seaham Harbour Coastal Centre

The Old Seafarers Mission overlooking Seaham Harbour has been converted to serve as an environmental field centre by a partnership between the Seaham Harbour Dock Company, Durham County Council, the Countryside Commission and the Groundwork Trust. The capital costs of conversion were provided through the Dock Company, grant-aided by the Countryside Commission. Durham County Council's Education Department has seconded a teacher to manage the Centre, working to a small management committee.

This unique facility is now receiving over 5000 organized visitors per year which are mainly made up of school and adult interest groups. The Centre provides an excellent base for studying the coast, the environment and industry past and present.

Easington Colliery Community Link Scheme

Following a generous offer of sponsorship from British Coal's Deep Mines Division the Trust has developed a local countryside Community Link Scheme in Easington Colliery, sponsored by the Countryside Commission and others. The Trust employs a community landscape architect who has been working in the colliery to identify improvement schemes with local people, secure funding and oversee implementation, involving locals in every stage of the project.

Schemes completed so far are as follows:

Seaside Lane A very prominent landscaped pocket park in the heart of the settlement. The £35,000 cost was provided by British Coal and the Parish Council.

Station Road   Comprehensive landscaping on the approach to the colliery, paid for by British Coal, the County Council and the Parish Council.

School nature garden   A pond and micro-environment sponsored by British Coal and English Nature.

Window-box campaign   Hundreds of window-boxes provided to residents, particularly pensioners, paid for by British Coal and constructed by Easington Unemployment Committee.

Many other schemes will be developed over the time-scale of the project.

12

The legislation and institutional context: the built environment

Anthony Streeten

Human influence on the landscape of Britain spans a period of over 400,000 years. The natural and man-made environments thus share a substantial common inheritance. Protection and management of the cultural heritage depend upon the meticulous understanding of landscape form and development, based upon careful observation, recording and research. Databases are fundamental to the definition of conservation policies, derived from critical judgements of that which deserves protection on account of its importance, or special significance. Since there are no absolute measures of importance, legislation has been shaped by the attitudes of successive generations towards conservation. There is every expectation that future legislation will continue this response to changing perceptions and priorities.

Approaches to the classification of sites and monuments, coupled with the complexities of land ownership and the often competing demands for land use, have led to a narrow definition of conservation priorities concentrated selectively upon the components of a historic landscape rather than upon appreciation of its totality. This in turn has exercised a profound influence over legislation and conservation policy, with a familiar emphasis on 'buildings', 'sites' and 'monuments'. Despite obvious imperfections and increasing endeavours towards a more integrated approach, the traces of past human activity – buildings, ruins, earthworks and buried remains – provide a necessary and convenient framework for considering management of the historic environment.

In this chapter we shall examine how those with responsibility for the management of historic buildings, monuments and landscapes can apply relevant legislation for the fulfilment of conservation objectives and in particular how they can seek guidance or even financial assistance from the appropriate agencies. Successful conservation initiatives invariably rely upon managerial skills and knowledge of statutory and other

procedures in order to develop partnerships and funding packages. Balancing conservation requirements with financial realities demands clear judgement which will stand up to scrutiny within the statutory process. The first step is to understand the formalities and to know where to obtain advice.

Legislative controls are exercised at the levels of both national and local government, with a corresponding network of local, specialist and national agencies concerned with protection and management of the heritage. The Secretaries of State for National Heritage and for the Environment (and their counterparts in Scotland and Wales) undertake specific functions in relation to the historic environment, and the Department of the Environment has wider responsibilities with respect to forward planning and development control exercised by local planning authorities comprising the English district councils, county councils and metropolitan boroughs, together with some national parks and urban development corporations. In England, too, many duties for the protection and management of the historic environment are delegated with necessary financial provision to English Heritage (Historic Buildings and Monuments Commission for England), while national responsibilities for compiling, coordinating and maintaining heritage databases are fulfilled by the Royal Commission on the Historical Monuments of England. There are analogous arrangements in Wales and Scotland with CADW: Welsh Historic Monuments, which is an executive agency within the Welsh Office and Historic Scotland, and there are separate Scottish and Welsh Royal Commissions.

Apart from the relatively few buildings and monuments owned or maintained by national and local agencies, successive legislation has been framed in recognition of the principle that first responsibility for custody of the heritage should remain with landowners. Legislation thus provides mechanisms both for control and for assistance – whether in the form of advice, or financial or other resources. A common theme among all statutory designations and controls is the desirability of obtaining informed opinion. Professional and voluntary bodies therefore have a key role in furthering the objectives of conservation, and appropriate specialists are identified for formal consultation within the various statutory processes.

The range of disciplines relevant to understanding the historic environment – encompassing for example archaeology, landscape history, architectural history and industrual archaeology – finds no direct correlation with specific aspects of the legislation intended to safeguard the cultural heritage. Instead, the framework for protection and management is derived from patchwork of cumulative legislation, interpreted in light of public acceptance and reinforced by case precedent. Current legislation, however, is concer exclusively with physical features of the historic environment. There is no statutory recognition for the former processes of agriculture or industry which have shaped the landscape or might indeed yet be capable of sustaining its traditional management for the future.

Legislation

Among the current English legislation relating specifically to protection and management of the cultural heritage, two enactments cover the principal designations of ancient monuments, areas of archaeological importance, listed buildings and conservation areas. The Ancient Monuments and Archaeological Areas Act 1979 (as amended by the National Heritage Act 1983) has superseded previous legislation relating to ancient monuments, the antecedents of which extend as far back as 1882. Meanwhile, the Planning (Listed Buildings and Conservation Areas) Act 1990 has re-enacted more recent provisions of the town and country planning legislation affecting buildings and areas of special architectural or historic interest. Government advice in PPG 15: *Historic Buildings and Conservation Areas*, replacing Circular 8/87 provides detailed guidance on interpretation and identifies other statutory powers, including those relating to grants for the repair of historic buildings. Grant-giving powers are derived from the Historic Buildings and Ancient Monuments Act 1953, while the establishment of English Heritage was enacted by the National Heritage Act 1983.

Matters affecting the historic environment are also governed by the Town and Country Planning Act 1990. Related government guidance in PPG 16 *Archaeology and Planning* reinforces archaeological issues as a material consideration in planning decisions. It details preferred procedures for archaeological assessment and the preservation of important remains affected by development proposals. Certain large or environmentally sensitive projects which require plan-

exemption in plan...
the case of ecclesiastical exemption...
ing controls, the Care of Churches and Ecclesiastical Jurisdiction Measure 1991 prescribes that a faculty be issued by the chancellor of the diocese – or under delegated powers by the archdeacon – for defined works affecting places of worship and churchyards belonging to the Church of England. This does not apply to cathedrals or to non-Anglican churches; ecclesiastical exemption is to become available to other denominations and faiths with similar systems of control approved by the Secretary of State for National Heritage. Anglican cathedrals are subject to the Care of Cathedrals Measure 1990, and all ecclesiastical property is subject to the normal requirements of planning permission.

Conservation of the historic environment also benefits from legislation covering the variety of protective and indicative landscape designations such as national parks, areas of oustanding natural beauty, sites of special scientific interest, evironmentally sensitive areas and others. For the present purpose, however, it is convenient to consider separately the procedures for designation and the practical arrangements for protection and management of the cultural heritage.

Selection and statutory designations

Statutory control for the historic environment is concerned principally with protecting the historic fabric and the setting of buildings, ruins, earthworks and buried archaeological remains. The former are usually listed while the last two categories can only be scheduled, although there is a significant overlap in the designations for buildings and ruins. Certain historic engineering structures are scheduled rather than listed, while roofed buildings in use are rarely scheduled and those which are may be recommended for

being carried out by
both listed and sched-

ing of ancient monuments
ken by the relevant Secretary
otland and Wales, after consul-
utory advisers. The Secretary of
ty under the 1990 Act to list build-
onsidered to be of special architectural
nterest, again having taken statutory
the case of buildings situated in England,
lish Heritage. Local authorities have a duty to
te conservation areas, although such designa-
may also be made by the Secretary of State.
eas of archaeological importance (AAIs), however,
are generally designated by the Secretary of State,
although they may, with his approval, be designated
by local authorities. Current practice relating to the
designation of AAIs is summarized below.

Scheduled monuments

In 1983, the Secretary of State published non-statutory
criteria to assist with the definition of nationally important monuments suitable for statutory protection. Most
fall into the categories of ruins, earthworks and buried
remains. Unlike listed buildings, scheduled monuments are not graded but are selected as the most
important examples from among the known sites
registered principally in county sites and monuments
records. Scheduled monuments rank broadly in importance with grade I and II* listed buildings. The discretionary criteria used for selection comprise: period,
rarity, documentation, group value, survival/condi-
tion, fragility/vulnerability, diversity and potential. A
convenient explanation of these terms appears in PPG
16, but it should be noted that buildings in ecclesiastical use and those used as dwelling houses cannot be
scheduled.

The selection of monuments for scheduling has been
carried out since 1882, partly during recent decades as
a strategic response to identified threats and more
recently in the context of thematic assessments for
particular groups or classes of monument. Most scheduling recommendations originate from English Heritage and in 1986 the Monuments Protection
Programme was initiated to embark upon a systematic
review of the statutory protection for ancient monuments. Estimates at that time indicated that the 13,000
or so scheduled monuments represented only a proportion of the known archaeological sites believed to
be of national importance. The Monuments Protection Programme is expected to increase the number of
scheduled monuments up to the end of the century, in
order to ensure statutory protection for a representative
sample of the most important and best preserved of the
nation's monuments.

The formal recognition of importance conferred by
scheduled status is often perceived as a prerequisite for
successful conservation initiatives. In practice, however, statutory protection frequently has greater relevance as a safeguard in the longer term rather than as a
catalyst for meeting immediate management needs.
Since the importance of a monument can best be
judged in relation to others of its class, the initial
assessments are made generally using data from county
sites and monument records. The first stage of selection
is thus to ensure that accurate and retrievable documentation is available; only rarely and as a procedure of
last resort will scheduling be considered as an *ad hoc*
reaction to specific threats.

Areas of archaeological importance

There are no formal criteria for the designation of
AAIs, although procedures are prescribed for statutory
advice before designation. Part II of the 1979 Act
merely authorizes the designation of those areas
which appear to merit treatment as such for legislative
purposes. In practice, the five areas designated up to
1990 have been confined to the historic town centres
of Canterbury, Chester, Exeter, Hereford and York.

Listed buildings

Buildings of special architectural or historic interest fall
into certain categories based upon date and upon the
value of specific examples within types: those showing
technological innovation or virtuosity; those having
significant historical associations; and buildings with
group value.

Principles of selection for the lists have been
approved by the Secretary of State as follows:

(1) All buildings built before 1700 which survive in
anything like their original condition are listed.
(2) Most buildings of 1700 to 1840 are listed, though
selection is necessary.
(3) Between 1840 and 1914 only buildings of definite
quality and character are listed, and the selection is
designed to include the principal works of the principal architects.
(4) After 1939, a few outstanding buildings are listed,
but since 1988 it has been prescribed that only buildings over 10 years old can be listed.

The buildings are classified in grades to show their
relative importance as follows:

Grade I These are buildings of exceptional interest (only
about 2 per cent of listed buildings so far are in this grade).
Grade II * These are particularly important buildings of
more than special interest (some 4 per cent of listed buildings).
Grade II These are buildings of special interest, which warrant every effort being made to preserve them.

The task of revising the lists of historic buildings, which have been published by the Secretary of State for the guidance of local planning authorities since 1947, began in the late 1960s in areas perceived to be of greatest sensitivity, often in towns and cities. During the 1980s, however, geographical coverage was completed through an accelerated and intensified programme of fieldwork. The opportunities for coordinated assessment during this accelerated resurvey nevertheless highlighted the need for selective reappraisal of certain lists compiled during the 1970s. This has led to a further phase of list review intended to validate and expand the selection of listed buildings in some towns and cities, especially where industrial buildings are poorly represented in the statutory lists.

The need for *ad hoc* and temporary listing through building preservation notices has been reduced significantly as a consequence of systematic fieldwork. Certificates of immunity from listing (valid for a period of five years) may also be granted by the Secretary of State for National Heritage following a definitive assessment of a particular building. In exceptional cases, buildings may be delisted if they are subsequently demonstrated not to be of special architectural or historic interest. All requests for listing, immunity certificates and delisting are addressed to the Department of National Heritage.

Conservation areas

The 1990 Act contains a statutory definition for the purposes of designating conservation areas considered to be of 'special architectural or historic interest, the character or appearance of which it is desirable to preserve or enhance'. Conservation areas are often centred on listed buildings but not always. They are used primarily for historic settlements, but among the examples of rural designation the Swaledale Conservation Area is intended to promote and encourage management of this distinctive landscape characterized by dry-stone field walls and barns. The identification of areas suitable for designation is often carried out in conjunction with the preparation of development plans.

Designation of constraints

The designations of scheduled monuments, listed buildings, conservation areas and areas of archaeological importance are registered as local land charges. There are, however, significant variations in the principles of identification. Conservation areas and areas of archaeological importance are defined on statutory maps. Scheduled monuments are identified by their schedule entry which generally includes a small-scale maplet for identification. Listed buildings, however, are identified by their address, assisted by a brief description, and are usually denoted on maps held in England by English Heritage and the relevant local

planning authority. Only in the case of listed buildings does the statutory protection extend to the curtilage of the listed structure.

It is the duty of English Heritage and its counterparts to publish lists of scheduled ancient monuments. These are arranged by district within counties. The Secretary of State for National Heritage publishes lists of historic buildings arranged by civil parish within local authority areas. English Heritage has also published an index to all conservation areas designated up to 1989. Publicly accessible copies of these documents are available in the National Monuments Record of the English Royal Commission, which also contains photographs of many listed buildings taken during the accelerated re-survey and on other occasions. English Heritage maintains the Register of Parks and Gardens which is an advisory document, not entailing additional statutory controls, for the guidance of planning authorities and others.

Statutory consents and controls

Provisions relating to areas of archaeological importance, listed buildings and conservation areas are generally exercised through local planning authorities, while matters relating to scheduled monuments are handled by the Secretary of State for National Heritage. In the case of buildings which are both scheduled and listed, the requirements of scheduling take precedence. While there is a requirement for public advertisement of most applications made under the 1990 Act, there are no similar requirements under the 1979 Act.

Scheduled monuments

Works affecting scheduled monuments are controlled under the 1979 Act, which defines as an offence unauthorized works and wilful damage to a scheduled monument. It further stipulates the requirement to obtain scheduled monument consent for:

(1) any works resulting in the demolition or destruction of or any damage to a scheduled monument;
(2) any works for the purpose of removing or repairing a scheduled monument or any part of it or of making any alterations or additions thereto; and
(3) any flooding or tipping operations on land on or under which there is a scheduled monument.

Applications for scheduled monument consent are determined by the Secretary of State for National Heritage, but in accordance with the National Heritage Act 1983 he is required to consult with the Historic Buildings and Monuments Commission for England (English Heritage) before granting consent. English Heritage thus provides necessary professional and technical advice to assess the implications of proposed schemes. Internal procedures for 'scheduled monument clearance' apply to Crown property. Before taking a final decision, the Secretary of State may in exceptional cases call a public local inquiry and will in any event communicate his intentions to the applicant, inviting either acceptance of the intended decision or a request for a hearing, before his decision is finalized. Certain limited categories of work are authorized under the Ancient Monuments (Class Consents) Orders 1981 and 1984. These include certain agricultural and forestry operations, coal mining, certain works executed by the British Waterways Board, the repair or maintenance of machinery, essential works for the purposes of health and safety, and works carried out by English Heritage. With these exceptions, scheduled monument consents may be withheld, granted unconditionally or granted subject to conditions. Compensation may only be claimed in the exceptional circumstances of modification, revocation or the refusal of consent for certain works authorized by a planning permission which had been granted before scheduling or which had been otherwise authorized under the General Development Order. Compensation may also be payable if the proposed works do not require planning permission because they do not constitute development. In the event of planning applications affecting a monument which is already scheduled, local authorities in England are required under the General Development Order to consult English Heritage.

An advisory leaflet is available from the Department of National Heritage. In addition English Heritage has issued guidance notes on the preparation of scheduled monument consent applications relating to works of repair, archaeological excavations and development affecting a scheduled monument. Preliminary consultation with the relevant English Heritage inspector of ancient monuments is often recommended before submission of a formal application.

Areas of archaeological importance

The designation of AAIs under Part II of the 1979 Act carries no presumption of preservation, but the legislation does prescribe procedures for the observation and, where necessary, prior investigation of groundworks within the specified areas. Potential developers are required to give six weeks' notice to the relevant planning authority of any intention to disturb the ground, tip on it or flood it. The investigating authority for the area (usually the relevant archaeological unit) then has the power to enter the site and carry out excavations for a period of up to four and a half months, if required, before development may proceed.

By 1990 five areas of archaeological importance had been designated, covering historic town centres. Since PPG 16 had been framed to deal with archaeological considerations more comprehensively than the provi-

sions for AAIs would allow, however, the decision was taken to suspend any further designations pending a review of effectiveness for planning policies and procedures.

Listed buildings

Buildings included on the statutory lists are subject to additional planning controls defined in the 1990 Act and exercised through the listed building consent procedures. The demolition of a listed building, or the alteration or extension of a listed building affecting its character as one of special architectural or historic interest, can be authorized only by a specific grant of listed building consent, although there are specific health and safety provisions. Unlike scheduled monument consent, however, listed building consent is not required for works of repair and certain like-for-like replacement. PPG 15 provides guidance on definitions.

Unlike decisions affecting scheduled ancient monuments, listed building consents remain the primary responsibility of local planning authorities. However, for buildings situated in England, the Secretary of State for the Environment has directed that English Heritage should be notified of all applications for listed building consent to alter, extend or demolish any grade I or II* building and for specified works of demolition affecting Grade II buildings. Procedures for statutory consultation with specified amenity societies apply to all applications for the demolition of a listed building, irrespective of its grade. Local authorities intending to grant consent for the demolition of any listed building and for all works affecting grade I and II* buildings are also required to notify the Secretary of State to enable him to decide whether or not he should call in the application for his own determination. The Secretary of State is advised on these decisions by English Heritage. Modified procedures apply within Greater London where English Heritage exercises certain additional functions with regard to listed buildings. The 1990 Act provides that Crown buildings may be listed and that departments will consult the local planning authority about any proposals to alter, demolish or extend a building of special architectural or historic interest. Local authorities are also required to make all of their own applications to the Secretary of State, although regulations require applications by county councils to be sent to the Department of the Environment via the district council.

Listed building consents may be withheld, granted unconditionally or granted subject to conditions. Special provisions apply in the exceptional cases of compensation payable under the 1990 Act for the refusal, revocation, or conditional granting of consent. An important distinction compared with ancient monuments, however, is the provision for an owner to serve on the relevant local authority a listed buildings purchase notice if he can claim, among other things, that the land has become 'incapable of reasonably beneficial use'.

Ecclesiastical exemption from listed building controls applies to works of alteration, extension and partial demolition, being authorized instead for the Church of England under procedures defined in the Care of Churches and Ecclesiastical Jurisdiction Measure 1991. Listed building consent is, however, required for the complete demolition of a listed church, except in the case of a Church of England scheme made under the Pastoral Measure 1983. In the case of demolitions under the Pastoral Measure, the Secretary of State for the Environment is invited by the Church Commissioners to consider – in the light of reasoned objections – the need for a non-statutory public local inquiry. Listed building consent may, however, be required in the normal way where a church of the Church of England is to be transferred to secular use in accordance with a redundancy scheme.

Quite apart from the procedures for listed building consent, local authorities are required under the 1990 Act, when considering planning applications affecting a listed building, to have special regard for the desirability of preserving the structure and its setting. In exceptional cases when a local authority has issued a direction under Article 4 of the General Development Order, planning permission may also be required for works which would otherwise have constituted permitted development. The effect of the proposed development on a listed building and its setting can then be taken into account by the authority when considering the application. Local authorities are required to notify English Heritage of any planning application which affects the fabric or setting of a grade I or II★ listed building.

Conservation areas

Similar provisions apply following the designation of a conservation area, since the 1990 Act requires that special attention must be paid to the desirability of preserving or enhancing the area in the exercise of any planning and related powers. Local authorities intending to issue an Article 4 direction affecting unlisted structures within a conservation area are however required to obtain prior approval from the Secretary of State for the Environment, although Government proposals will allow councils a greater degree of control over minor development without having to obtain ministerial permission.

Conservation area consent is required for the demolition of any building within a conservation area, and the Secretary of State for the Environment has directed that all planning applications relating to development proposals above a certain size affecting the character or appearance of any conservation area should be notified to English Heritage. Local authorities are also encouraged to set up conservation area advisory committees and many have specialist conservation officers within their planning departments.

Management of the historic environment

Statutory controls are themselves an important instrument of management for the historic environment, but central government, local authorities, national agencies, amenity societies and others have specific powers and responsibilities with regard to conservation. It is appropriate to consider the respective roles of the principal institutions in England.

Central government

The Department of National Heritage is the government department with responsibility for heritage policy. In addition to responsibilities for the legislative framework of planning controls and statutory protection for the heritage, government maintains the occupied royal palaces and historic buildings of the civil estate. Through the Historic Royal Palaces Agency it maintains, manages and opens to the public the Tower of London, Hampton Court Palace, Kensington Palace, Kew Palace and the Banqueting House. Many other duties including the distribution of grants are delegated to agencies sponsored by government, including English Heritage and its counterparts, the royal commissions, the National Heritage Memorial Fund and the Churches Conservation Trust. Government fiscal policy towards taxation relief benefits both the natural and the cultural heritage (see Chapter 11).

Local government

As well as their responsibilities for development control, local planning authorities exercise important influence over conservation of the historic environment through development plans and related policies. Advice is often sought from national agencies such as English Heritage, through Conservation Area Parnership[and under the Faculty Jurisdiction Rules 1992 local authorities are themselves notified of certain works affecting the architectural or archaeological interest of historic churches. Local authorities also maintian historic buildings and monuments in their own care or use, and provide important technical, information and advisory services, including sites and monuments records. They are also empowered to make discretionary grants or loans towards the costs of repair to buildings of architectural or historic interest (whether or not they are listed). Such resources may be directed towards town schemes in selected conservation areas for which funding is shared with English Heritage through Conservation Area Partnerships. Local authorities may also enter management agreements for the benefit of conserving and facilitating public access to ancient monuments and adjoining land. Under the 1979 Act they are also empowered to make discretionary grants towards the costs of preservation, maintenance and management of any ancient monument, and to incur expenditure on archaeological investigation and publication.

An important provision of the legislation relating to listed buildings – not paralleled in the 1979 Act – is the power of local authorities to carry out urgent works of preservation and to serve repairs notices on the owners of listed buildings which have fallen into a serious state of disrepair. The formalities include separate procedures for carrying out emergency repairs, the costs of which may be recovered from the owner, and the serving of a repairs notice as a preliminary to compulsory acquisition. This can be a worthwhile means of achieving positive benefits since local authorities may then be able to negotiate acquisition by a suitable owner – sometimes a buildings preservation trust – who will be able to undertake the repairs and put the buildings to beneficial use.

English Heritage

The general duties of English Heritage – defined for statutory purposes as the Historic Buildings and Monuments Commission for England – are so far as practicable:

(1) to secure the preservation of ancient monuments and historic buildings situated in England;
(2) to promote the preservation and enhancement of the character of conservation areas situated in England;
(3) to promote the public's enjoyment of, and advance their knowledge of, ancient monuments and historic buildings situated in England and their preservation.

In addition to statutory advice on scheduling and listing and related matters, English Heritage maintains, manages and opens to the public some 400 historic properties.

It is empowered under the 1953 Act to make discretionary grants for the repair of buildings of outstanding architectural or historic interest, their historically associated contents and parks, and historically associated land, with special provision for churches and cathedrals. Expenditure can also be incurred under the 1990 Act where it will make a significant contribution towards preserving or enhancing the character or appearance of a conservation area (including grants towards the repair of buildings covered by a town scheme). The 1979 Act facilitates discretionary grant towards the costs of preservation, maintenance and management of any ancient monument, and expenditure may be incurred for the purposes of archaeological investigation and publication. Like local authorities, English Heritage may enter management agreements for the benefit of preserva-

tion and public access to ancient monuments and adjoining land. Grants may also be made for the acquisition of ancient monuments and for the acquisition of buildings of outstanding achitectural or historic interest, the latter being confined to local authorities and the National Trust outside conservation areas. English Heritage has wider grant-giving powers in London.

Research and advisory services include building conservation, the Ancient Monuments Laboratory and the Central Archaeology Service. Among special initiatives are the Register of Historic Parks and Gardens and the preparation of advisory lists of buildings at risk, while English Heritage also maintains management records for scheduled monuments and listed buildings. Academic and specialist publications include technical handbooks, archaeological reports and the *Conservation Bulletin*. A series of advisory leaflets includes, amongst others, guidance on the principles of repair for historic structures, the appropriate treatment of historic farm buildings, new works affecting historic churches, archaeological policies in development plans and conservation area practice.

Royal Commissions on (Ancient and) Historical Monuments

The Royal Commissions for England, Scotland and Wales are responsible for identifying and recording ancient monuments and historic buildings. The English Royal Commission maintains the National Archaeological Record and the National Monuments Record, and has national responsibility for the oversight of local sites and monuments records. Surveys comprise building recording (notably for buildings threatened with demolition or alteration), topographical field survey and aerial photography. The Royal Commission also provides archaeological information for Ordnance Survey maps and is responsible for the Survey of London. Publications include inventories, syntheses and surveys, as well as short books on particular subjects.

Royal Fine Art Commission

The Commission influences both public and private bodies to achieve the highest standards of architectural design, through consultation during the preparation of schemes and within the planning process. A recurrent concern is to achieve the best contemporary design appropriate to the setting of a historic environment.

Church of England

Informed advice on the appropriate treatment of historic churches comes in the first instance from diocesan advisory committees, and there are arrangements for notification of certain works to English Heritage, local authorities and the relevant national amenity society. It is also a requirement of English Heritage grants for historic churches that consultation should take place with English Heritage concerning any future alterations to churches which have previously received financial assistance for repairs. Advisory literature is published by the Council for the Care of Churches. Grants for specific purposes are also administered by the Council for the Care of Churches, which can make grants for contents but not for repairs to historic fabric, and by the Historic Churches Preservation Trust, which can make grants for repairs but not for contents.

There is a separate Cathedrals Fabric Commission for England, and the Care of Cathedrals Measure 1990 prescribes procedures for consultation with English Heritage, the amenity societies and local planning authorities about works affecting the archaeology, fabric and furnishings of cathedrals and their precincts. Permission for such works must be obtained either from the Cathedrals Fabric Commission or from a fabric advisory committee established for the relevant cathedral.

Churches which are no longer in regular use as a place of worship may be subject to a formal declaration of redundancy under the Pastoral Measure. In the first instance, the diocese requests advice from the Council for the Care of Churches. Decisions are taken by the Church Commissioners; procedures for advice on the historic interest and architectural quality of the building are obtained from the Advisory Board for Redundant Churches, which also provides advice on historical and architectural matters when a redundancy scheme is being prepared for eventual disposal of the building either for another use or by demolition. Redundant churches of greatest historic, architectural or archaeological interest may be vested in the Churches Conservation Trust (see below).

National Heritage Memorial Fund

Established in 1980, the Fund is able to make grants or loans towards acquisition, maintenance or preservation for the most outstanding examples of the nation's heritage.

Churches Conservation Trust (formerly Redundant Churches Fund)

The Trust cares for some 290 Anglican 'churches in retirement' which are of historical, architectural or archaeological interest; funding is provided jointly by the Department of National Heritage and the Church Commissioners.

National Trust

The National Trust is the largest private landowner in Britain and includes among its duties the preservation of places of historical interest for the benefit of the nation. It is an independent charitable organization set up under its own Act of Parliament which has acquired and now cares for and opens to visitors over 200 historic buildings and monuments.

Civic Trust and building preservation trusts

The Civic Trust is concerned with developing and promoting high standards in planning, design, restoration and new building. A separate Council of Management run in association with the Civic Trust administers the Architectural Heritage Fund which provides one source of loan capital for local building preservation trusts. These are invariably of charitable status and may be set up specifically to deal with one building or a particular locality. At a national level, the Buildings at Risk Trust encourages the use of revolving funds to achieve successive conservation projects, while the Landmark Trust has rescued over 250 buildings and structures at risk by assuring their future use and maintenance as holiday accommodation.

Professional bodies, specialist and amenity societies

Among numerous local and national amenity societies, the following receive statutory notice of all applications for consent to demolish a listed building: the Ancient Monuments Society, the Council for British Archaeology, the Georgian Group, the Society for the Protection of Ancient Buildings, the Victorian Society and the Royal Commission on the Historical Monuments of England.

Specialist period societies range in the scope of their interest from the Prehistoric Sociey to the Association for Industrial Archaeology and the Twentieth Century Society, while another organization, SAVE Britain's Heritage, campaigns for historic buildings at risk. The Garden History Society and the Association of Gardens Trusts have responsibilities towards historic parks and gardens. The Theatres Trust owns the freehold of three London theatres and at a national level is consulted formally under the terms of the General Development Order on planning applications which affect theatres. Professional interests in the heritage include the Royal Institute of British Architects, the Royal Town Planning Institute and the Institute of Field Archaeologists.

Countryside interests

National organizations whose primary concerns are not related directly to the cultural heritage nevertheless make a significant contribution to conservation of the historic environment. Many sites of special scientific interest and nature reserves designated by the nature conservancy councils – in England known as English nature – have features of archaeological interest, while the responsibilities of the Countryside Commission for Countryside Stewardship and public access to the countryside complements the role of English Heritage with regard to the cultural heritage. The special planning procedures for national parks ensure the integration of professional archaeological advice into planning decisions and landscape management. Since the introduction of environmentally sensitive areas in 1986, management prescriptions in these areas have also included the protection of historic features from potentially damaging land uses, and a more recent enhancement of the scheme makes provision for optional conservations plans. The responsibilities of the National Rivers Authority have far-reaching consequences for the archaeology of river valleys and for the built environment and archaeological potential of rivers themselves. Coordination of these and other related interests presents a significant organizational challenge.

Conclusions

Protection of the historic environment is by no means synonymous with its preservation. The conservation of both buildings and monuments often depends upon their continued use and always relies upon their effective management. Legislation provides a framework for determining the appropriate balance between economically sustainable land uses and the needs of conservation. The various national, local and specialist institutions have defined roles which contribute both to decisions and to beneficial management of the historic environment.

One of the opportunities now to be grasped is the characterisation of historic landscapes whose importance may be greater than the value of their individual features. Government has indicated the scope for advisory registers, but the challenge is to harness existing resources to the benefit of landscape management and conservation both generally as well as in areas of greatest importance and value. As we have seen in Chapter 11, agricultural policy and related schemes can play an important part in encouraging appropriate management for the natural and man-made environment, but the continued commitment of landowners and the voluntary sector is essential. For the purposes of both designation and enforcement, the statutory framework depends ultimately upon public acceptance of its objectives.

Select list of relevant legislation and guidance

Historic Buildings and Ancient Monuments Act 1953
Local Authorities (Historic Buildings) Act 1962
European Communities Act 1972
Ancient Monuments and Archaeological Areas Act 1979
National Heritage Act 1980
National Heritage Act 1983
Local Government Act 1985
Housing and Planning Act 1986
Water Act 1989
Town and Country Planning Act 1990
Planning (Listed Buildings and Conservation Areas) Act 1990
Pastoral Measure 1983

Care of Cathedrals Measure 1990
Care of Churches and Ecclesiastical Jurisdiction Measure 1991
Town and Country Planning General Regulations 1976 (Statutory Instruments 1976 no. 1419)
Ancient Monuments (Applications for Scheduled Monument Consent) Regulations 1981 (Statutory Instruments 1981 no. 1301)
Ancient Monuments (Class Consents) Order 1981 (Statutory Instruments 1981 no. 1302)
Ancient Monuments (Class Consents) (Amendment) Order 1984 (Statutory Instruments 1984 no. 222)
Areas of Archaeological Importance (Notification of Operations) (Exemption) Order 1984 (Statutory Instruments 1984 no. 1286)
Town and Country Planning (Assessment of Environmental Effects) Regulations 1988 (Statutory Instruments 1988 no. 1199)
Town and Country Planning General Development Order 1988 (Statutory Instruments 1988 no. 1813)
Planning (Listed Buildings and Conservation Areas) Regulations 1990 (Statutory Instruments 1990 no. 1519)
Faculty Jurisdiction Rules 1992
Circular 8/84: Establishment of the Historic Buildings and Monuments Commission for England
Circular 18/84: Crown Land and Crown Development
Circular 8/87: Historic Buildings and Conservation Areas – Policy and Procedures
Circular 15/90: Consolidation of the Town and Country Planning Legislation
PPG16 1990: Planning Policy Guidance Note no. 16: Archaeology and Planning
PPG 15 (consultation draft, 1993): Planning Policy Guidance Note no. 15: Historic Buildings and Conservation Areas

Bibliography

DARVILL, T., SAUNDERS, A. and STARTIN, W. (1987) 'A question of national importance: approaches to the evaluation of ancient monuments for the Monuments Protection Programme in England', *Antiquity*, **61**, 393–408
DEPARTMENT OF THE ENVIRONMENT (1990) *Environment in Trust: the Heritage of England and Wales*
FORTLAGE, C. A. (1990) *Environmental Assessment: a Practical Guide*, Gower, Aldershot
MYNORS, C. (1989) *Listed Buildings and Conservation Areas*, Longman, London
ROSS, M. (1990) *Planning and the Heritage: Policy and Procedures*, Spon, London
SAUNDERS, A. D. (1983) 'A century of ancient monuments legislation 1882–1982', *Antiquaries Journal*, **63**(1), 11–33
SUDDARDS, R. W. (1988) *Listed Buildings: the Law and Practice*, Sweet and Maxwell, London
WALKER, R. (1988) *The Cambridgeshire Guide to Historic Buildings Law*, Cambridgeshire County Council

13

The legislation and institutional context: museums

Alf Hatton

The current legal and political structure of museums in the UK is affected by a certain feeling of imminent change, coupled naturally with an uncertainty about the outcome of that change and its effects on museums and their employees. This is more often voiced in terms of the dangers to the resource, or the collections that museums hold and seek to continue accumulating, than in terms of the loss to the users and beneficiaries of those collections.

The present situation of museums is also affected to a very large degree by its own roots. It is thus absolutely imperative that any description of that structure is set against a background of the evolving social role of museums as institutions. Indeed, it can be argued that this is where we will find the origins to which many of the legal and political changes now emerging can be traced. Often it is stated quite plainly that changes in society are at hand and lately that the pace of change is quickening. This is a general hypothesis put forward most forcibly by Toffler (1970), but it has its museological proponents as well (e.g. Singleton, 1979, p. 11).

There are most certainly antecedents to the museum as a social institution in the form in which we experience it today (Alexander, 1979, pp. 6–8; Lewis, 1984, p. 5) – at least four and probably more. Alexander (1979, p. viii) discusses six museum types, and Burcaw (1983, p. 9) lists seven in terms of their social function. Weil (1983, pp. 32–51) expands this to fifteen, considering only art museums. The most immediate predecessor is, of course, the simple collection itself, the *cabinetti* and *Wunderkammer* described elsewhere (e.g. Alexander, 1979, p. 8; Lewis, 1984, p. 10). As direct evidence of the collection as a root of contemporary museums, most often UK museums have been founded upon a collection established by an individual: 36 per cent in the case of local authority museums, but 65 and 60 per cent respectively for the nationals and independents (Prince and Higgins-McLoughlin, 1987, p. 47).

Traditionally, museums have been classified by the academic category into which their principal collections have fallen (e.g. Alexander, 1979, p. vii; Prince and Higgins-McLoughlin, 1987, p. 40), and this traditional classification still persists. The other principal means of classification has been by funding and governing body type (most notably Prince and Higgins-McLoughlin, 1987). Indeed, some of the most significant results of this study were the inconsistencies of practice across the national, local authority and 'other' (as defined) types.

Neither of these traditional classifications of museums has great value to the modern heritage manager. A more useful analytical model might be based upon size of budget, size and levels of staff, capital asset values (excluding collections), and so on, along lines more commonly used in business. These factors in combination will have a critical effect on the nature, style and responsibilities of management, overshadowing issues arising from the nature of the founding collections or the main sources of funding.

Each museum, in a variety of classes, by such an analysis would more usefully be compared with other non-profit[1] organizations with similar aims and objectives in protecting, preserving and interpreting the heritage. Thus, a small community museum might be better compared with a local wildlife trust, a medium-sized or county-wide grouping of local government museums might be better compared with an administration area in either English Heritage or the National Trust, and so on.

The social function of museums

The museum role can be defined principally as preserving the past in some form, for some public use, and the current UK definition follows this pattern (Museums Association, 1994, p. 403). However, other stated social purposes for museums have included: *preservation* as a discrete act in its own right (e.g. Cannon-Brookes, 1984, p. 116); a *non-verbal reality model* (Cameron, 1971, p. 15; and among many others, Radley, 1990, pp. 46 ff.); *treasure, fetish* and *symbolic roles* (Alexander, 1979, p. 88; Meyer, 1979, p. 18; Weil, 1983, pp. 31–55); *informal* and *unstructured education* (Ripley, 1969, p. 85; Chadwick, 1980; and Brown, 1987, p. 9); *sanitization* of the *past*(s) (Green, 1985, p. 6);[2] and even the *arbiter elegantiarum* (Strong, 1986, p. 19). Indeed, although museums have been said to contribute 'relatively little to our practical welfare', they have consistently been alleged to provide 'a vital symbolic role' (Elliott, 1987, p. 7a). Even the Audit Commission (1991), in its report on local authority museums and art galleries (LAMGs), allowed for several different mission statements at local level, and the Office of Arts and Libraries (OAL, 1991: now part of the Department of National Heritage), also in a recent report, acknowledges both variation between institutions and to an extent within them for national museums and galleries (NMGs).

The Audit Commission report suggests local authorities need to consider why they are supporting museums: to conserve things for future generations? to improve the quality of life? to aid economic development or encourage tourism? to help people's education? It concluded that if an authority is supporting several museums, each may have its separate purpose (dare one say market niche?). Thus ultimately judgement as to performance may need to be set against several base criteria. The Audit Commission also concluded that authorities should consider which people it is trying to serve: local residents, a regional population, a wider national or even international tourist market, ethnic minorities, or schoolchildren? Again, responses to this would significantly differ depending on perceptions of, and stated aims on, purpose. It raises the possibility in the future of segmenting the market for museums, something the majority in the UK have singularly failed to do, mostly from a perfectly understandable adherence to a philosophical belief in 'equity' (Flynn, 1990, p. 114) as public sector or public sector derived organizations. This reluctance may also have something to do with a simple lack of a marketing attitude amongst museums generally.

These two reports represent a logical extrapolation of earlier recognition and a line of development in museum management, and public sector management in general, that museums (and other public institutions) must be scrutinized through concepts such as *value for money* (Robertson, 1985, pp. 127–8), *cost-effectiveness* and *profitability*.

The OAL report listed several policy concerns for NMGs: the level of access to, and use of, services provided by NMGs to their client groups; standard or quality of service provided generally; standards of display and of scholarly activity; management, safekeeping

and development of collections for present use and for posterity; management of buildings; generation of additional resources from the private sector; and encouragement of greater financial self-reliance. Access, use, services, standards, quality, of service generally, in display and scholarly activity, in safekeeping and development of collections for present use and for posterity, without exception all impinge on perceptions of museum role.

Preservation as a primary function, indeed role, of museums is enshrined in the professional Code of Practice in the UK (Museums Association, 1994), with the public utility ensuing from this activity very much an afterthought, at least in terms of the UK's basic working definition of a museum. As recently as 1989, Wilson wrote that collections and scholarship were what prevented the British Museum from being a 'junkyard of curiosities' (1989, p. 24). Yet where Wilson and Worcester (1988, p. 37) provide some evidence that museums and historical matters are of great importance in the cultural life of the UK, there is other evidence that social class is a factor in museum visiting, e.g. in Merriman (1989a, pp. 149–71). The precise reasons why museums exist in society, and why people value and visit them, have rarely been tested; Chadwick (1980) and Merriman (1989b) are two immensely valuable exceptions.

One is bound to note, however, that *statements of purpose* are more often a description of *what* museums do, possbly even *how*, but not *why*, whereas the more esoteric claims tend to try to answer the question 'why'. It can be argued, and has been (Cameron, 1971, p. 16), that at any rate conceptually, the 'why' of museums' existence is where the modern museum's difficulties lie; it represents the ideals and values of an individual, but it is contemporarily funded by the great majority of us through taxation in one form or another throughout the developed world.

The origins of the modern museum lie also in diverse social functions: votive offerings, the spoils of war, the treasure house, a place where relaxation and *musing* can take place, literally *re-creation*, and the academic/scholastic library. Some of this diversity is still at work in the minds of those who run museums, to the extent that there is often polarized debate over the precise social role museums play; in marketing terms, there is an *undifferentiated product range*. Many museums espoused specifically educational aims at their inception. Indeed, education is often still posited as *the* alternative to all the other primary purposes that museum staffs have claimed as their insititutions' *raison d'être*.

There are also most definitely non-European social institutions in all cultures which fulfil the museum role as defined above (see Ripley, 1969, p. 19; Layton, 1989). What museums in particular have been slow to realize is that 'pre-museum' relationships with the past continue to exist within the societies of the developed world. Probably, the least likely outcome of an innate need to deal with the past is the museum, except in so much as Western societies seem to share a proclivity to institutionalize their group behaviours.

There are non-museum institutions of considerable size in the UK which also deal with various aspects of the past: English Heritage, its Scottish and Welsh equivalents, the National Trust, its Scottish equivalent, the private owners in the Historic Houses Association. In no sense, then, could museums be said to have attained a monopoly over the collection of physical and some other remnants of the past, its preservation and its management, although they have come close with those aspects of the past that could be termed the 'movable heritage'.

The museums we consider here, then, are essentially an outcome of Western technological and democratic, social development, and in particular the municipal legislation of the nineteenth century. They became visitor centres of the arts and culture, which were to bring refinement to the lower orders by some osmotic process or by simple association. That is to say, museums are an institutionalized form of social behaviour, specific to the Western technologically defined nations.

The scale of the evidence is stunning: one museum per 38,000 head of population in nineteen industrialized nations, as opposed to one per 3 million in the low-income countries (de la Torre, 1984, p. 51). There is also the oft' quoted one museum per fortnight being established, although warning bells have been sounded at last that this may not be good for the nation's longer-term economic health (White, 1983; Hewison, 1987). One wonders also about the psychological health of a nation so apparently besotted with its own past. De La Torre's (1984) evidence provides the clearest indication possible that musuems, as we understand them in the developed Western societies, are an unambiguous product of the *economic system* which spawned them. Taborsky supports this view, noting that social systems other than Western ones have heritage preservation mechanisms (1982, p. 339) and that museums in the Western social systems are not 'causal agents' for heritage preservation (p. 341).

In short, the museum concept, as we know it, is still fairly new by any historical timescale. Legal and political structures, therefore, have to be seen in the light of issues ensuing from both their long- and short-term histories, as much as from changing demands on museums, and certainly in balance to changes demanded from within themselves as institutions.

The legal and political structure

There has never been a proper overall structure acceptable to the museum profession (Cheetham, 1966, pp. 167–74; 1968, pp. 70–3), but the legal and political structure within which museums actually exist falls approximately at present into three neat sectors according to the nature of their governing body, one of the two traditional means of classifying museums in the UK: local government, national museums, and independent and other museums.[3]

The local government sector of UK museums and galleries accounts for slightly over one-third of the UK museum population (Prince and Higgins-McLoughlin, 1987, pp. 28–9). Ipswich Borough Museums and Galleries would be an example. The independent museums (for instance the Ironbridge Gorge Museum), including company museums (for example the Bass Museum of Brewing), individually owned museums etc., account for over 44 per cent, whereas the nationals (e.g. The British Museum, the Natural History Museum, the Victoria and Albert Museum, the Royal Armouries), including the few remaining government departmental museums, account for the remainder.

As Prince and Higgins-McLoughlin indicate (1987, p. 28), just over half of local authority museums are already in multi-functional leisure or recreation departments. As they indicate, this has an effect on the future of museums in that the level of employment of the chief museum officer, and consequently the level at which his/her professional and technical advice is heard, is downgraded considerably (p. 32).

Significantly, the largest single category is voluntarily run museums, and, noticeably, those directly controlled by government are decreasing in number. Inevitably, this last group includes the majority of the large museums, mostly in London, and is significant in a number of ways. Firstly, they take up the largest share of public expenditure on museums (Audit Commission, 1991, p. 5: £100 million as opposed to £90 million on LAMGs). Secondly, they are concentrated in the south: 60 per cent of national and governmental museums (Prince and Higgins-McLoughlin, 1987, p. 23). Finally, they are few in number (see Bourn, 1988, p. 1 for the principal NMGs comparatively audited). Yet they curate probably the most significant collection holdings in most of the academic disciplines by which museums are often traditionally classified.

They are only marginally more cost-effective from a net expenditure per visit (or unit of service) perspective (Audit Commission, 1991, p. 5): £4.20 per visit as opposed to £4.50 amongst local government museums. Clearly, however, from the point of view of economies of scale and high standards of scholarship, this concentration of heritage would appear to be effective. There is as yet no commonly agreed test of that effectiveness, or indeed of the many other facets of museum operation, though there has been considerable interest since 1990 in performance measurement, performance indicators, and standards.

A change easy to detect, and already well under way among the nationals, is towards a kind of independence, a trustee status, whereby direct control by government departments ostensibly ceases, and the proportion of direct funding by government decreases as independence brings with it the necessity for seeking alternative sources.

All of these museums, despite their differences in size, date of origin, funding, internal organization etc., almost without exception have been founded with the traditional museum *raison d'être* as being 'an institution which collects, preserves, displays . . . for the public benefit' (Museums Associations, 1994, p. 403).

Museums in the independent sector in the UK owe their very establishment and expansion over the last two decades to the importation of the US model of capital fund-raising, and various reports have made much of their greater success in such activities (e.g. Hale, 1987, p. 44), at a time when there was no formal requirement or incentive for other categories of museum to emulate their example. Interestingly, a recent report (Middleton, 1990) suggests that market saturation has occurred and that many of these independent museums, whilst successful in setting up and running to date, are unlikely to go on being so. Museum closures are forecast[5]. It may also be that some of the independents are rapidly approaching the end of their 'product life cycle', and, uncushioned by direct public financing, may have failed to plan vigorously for continued repeat visits through either diversification or product redevelopment.

Though not overt at present, there is certainly an awareness in the last remaining directly funded sector, local government museums, that some form of arm's-length management will be on the agenda for them in the next decade. Compulsory competitive tendering (CCT) and privatization have already affected related leisure services within local authorities, such as sports centres and swimming pools, and the restructuring of the public sector in other areas, e.g. education and health, is well under way with a marked effect on their management. It thus seems logical to expect further effects of this sort on museums.

Within the local government sector, some museums and galleries lost departmental status during the last attempt at reform in April 1974, the local government reorganization. Organizationally they became divisions or sections of the newly created leisure, culture, or recreation and amenities departments. Other recreational services, such as parks, swimming pools and play areas, were also amalgamated at this time into the new multi-role departments. This was in spite of the process being viewed as unwise by management consultants in at least one large museum service (Cossons, 1970, p. 111), and being actually staved off in the case of that service. This reorganization, as far as museums are concerned, has been noted as 'divisive' (Loughborough, 1978, p. 165) and costly (Robertson, 1985, p. 126) in that it has produced no economies of scale or savings, or indeed identifiable benefits to the community. It remains to be seen whether current trends do produce economies of scale, greater efficiency and greater financial self-sufficiency, or simply a shrinkage in supply to cope with static or falling demand.

Indeed, Robertson (1985) has argued convincingly that increased central management costs are one of the reasons for the growing trend towards the imposition of admission charges against a long-standing tradition of free entry to local museums in this century. This was recognized in the Audit Commission's report (1991, p. 40) in that museums should be able to negotiate charges for central services, i.e. not be charged for those they do not need – a possible end to central establishment charges! It would be fairer to add that this may also be due to the increasingly difficult financial problems of local authorities, and the prevailing political perception of their profiligacy, not necessarily borne out by some evidence (Flynn, 1990, p. 24).

Neither the 1974 organizational change, nor the latest trends, have been perceived by a large proportion of museums staff as a positive step in enhancing their ability to carry out what they regard as their principal function: the collection, documentation and preservation of the past.

Museums, then, are no strangers to political swings and roundabouts, and this can in no small part be due to a certain vagueness and reluctance on the part of their staffs to agree a single overriding social purpose, other than collection *per se*. That this is unsatisfactory and incomplete, from the point of view of social benefits, is evidenced by the growing demands on museums by the general public. Though still, proportionately, a small section of the UK populace use museums at all, let alone regularly, there is demand for museum services.

This susceptibility, in the absence of a unified view of social purpose, has even led to political dimensions affecting staff carrying out their work (see Kirby, 1988, pp. 89). The political dimension has even occasionally spilled over into the national press, as in the case of Glasgow (e.g. Rafferty, 1990). It is even possible, without implying any political viewpoint held by individual museum professionals, to see certain museums as being in the vanguard of the present government's pursuit of 'fiscally sound' policies, e.g. the Science Museum, because of their grasping the nettle of dealing with the changing circumstances they find themselves in, whilst not protesting, at any rate too publicly, about those changes. Other museums, e.g. the various labour and social history museums, would seem to be on the fringe of current developments in museums, and thus might be seen as quietly antipathetic to those trends.

Museum constituencies

Another way of looking at museums in the UK is to look at them in terms of the constituencies involved. There can be said to be four main ones: the collections; the governors; the staff; and the users. It would be grossly untrue to suggest that these are in any way equal partners, but it would be true to say that each of the four exerts its own influence over the management of museums. It is the differentials between those counterpoised influences that explain in part some of the issues currently being dealt with.

The collections

A collection-related issue is that many museums exist in buildings from the nineteenth century or before: half were built before 1850, and a further half of these before 1750 (Prince and Higgins-McLoughlin, 1987, p. 35). However, as many as three-quarters of museums have in fact been established since World War II (p. 26). Clearly one function of the modern public museum in the UK *de facto* has been to provide a continuing life for *buildings* that might legitimately be considered part of the heritage in their own right.

Another collection issue is that, through decades of copious collecting across all the traditional collecting subjects, often of material not relevant specifically to the immediate area surrounding the museum, museum decision makers have perpetuated a central role in their thinking for the *encyclopaedic model* (Lewis, 1984, p. 11; Greenhalgh, 1989, p. 89). This is a common enough situation and has presented the twentieth century with seemingly almost unmanageable collections (Brears, 1984, p. 7). It has often been referred to as an *embarras de richesse* (e.g. Meyer, 1979, p. 197). It seems to be endemic to the beast, and has been stated as one cause, in general terms, of many early museums' current problems, where fashion, and indeed scholarship, have since made some collections almost redundant in terms of the current public usages of such museums (e.g. Parr, 1950, p. 165 and 1963, p. 23 for biological collections; and Ames, 1986, p. 28 for ethnographic collections).

This over-concentration in museums on collecting and collections has quite recently been analysed, and it has been shown to equate to two-thirds of the total operating costs of the sample group of museums, or alternatively £118/m^2 out of £172/m^2 (Lord *et al.*, 1989a, p. 33). This is, to say the least, of some concern. Elsewhere, they indicate a figure of 80 per cent of collections in store, as opposed to 20 per cent on display (Lord *et al.*, 1989b, p. xvi). Greenhill some time earlier noted this question of the proportions of activities museums undertake as being a fundamental issue (1977, p.123).

However, the third factor in this attribution of museum problems to their history was that in the period of municipal museum growth in the nineteenth century, when many current local museums were being established, there was no agreed structure for municipal museums. In consequence, there is an uneven spread of both museums, as social institutions, over the country, and of collections in terms of the opportunities for use that they can generate. The uneven choices exercised by museum authorities also mean that standards vary enormously in collection size and management, public facilities and services, and quality of experience. This serendipitous distribution can in no way be described as providing a nation-wide museum service.

Rationalization of collections, in the absence of any comprehensive structure for cooperation on deaccessioning of collections, is just not a feature of museum operation at present (Devonshire, 1989, p. 37). Even if only as a way of redressing the balance of activity which has been called into question, and lately been analysed quantitatively for the first time (Lord *et al.*, 1989a), for example, in the area of collections in store (80 per cent of collections in store, with only 20 per cent on permanent display), this would seem to be a case of collective *problem avoidance*. Where 70 per cent of museums surveyed have collecting policies, only 49.2 per cent have disposals policies. Most strikingly, where average purchase acquisition costs for collections amounted to only 2.5 per cent of operating costs, this rises to 38 per cent when the ongoing costs of maintaining objects in the collections was added, and a staggering almost 70 per cent when indirect costs were apportioned (Lord *et al.*, 1989a, pp. xxii–xxiii).

Rationalization seems to be feared as a step towards general disposals of collections, either as a short-term response to a cash crisis, or as an undoing of the very basis of museums as warehouses where artefacts are kept and preserved *in perpetuity*. The depth to which this is felt is expressed in adherence to the Cottlesloe principle (Babbidge, 1991), and to the extent that action was taken in 1991 by the Museums and Galleries Commission to blacklist Derbyshire County Council for the sale of two Lowry paintings from its collections. This lack of willingness to rationalize may have been, and may still be, due to awareness of the vagaries of fashion in both collecting and rationalization, and the regrettable destruction of collections which took place immediately after World War II (Brears, 1984, p. 18). Recently, Wilson has defended the case against disposals vigorously (1989, p. 25).

That museums have over-collected, and often in the face of static if not declining levels of resources, regardless of arguments about the adequacy of levels of resources in general, has contributed to museum problems in two ways. Firstly, it has continued to exacerbate collection management demands on resources. Far more devastatingly, it has meant that the museums profession has externalized the problem as someone else's, thus avoiding any attempt at resolution. This has been described as a sure way to avoid strategic decisions by accumulating objectives (Kovach, 1989, pp. 142–3).

The governors

The governors of museums vary almost as much as the museums themselves and their collections. Within the local government sector there are elected members, each representing his/her own ward within a defined geographic area, on an elected and politically driven council covering the larger geographic area. This larger unit of administration varies from county councils to metropolitan districts, London boroughs and shire districts. The City of London stands apart from these categories as a special case, whereas the other categories are the British attempt in England and Wales to differentiate between urban and rural geographic areas, with their differing environments and presumably public service needs.

The shire counties represent a second tier above metropolitan and shire districts, but there is discussion about the need for this second tier, or a second tier at all. The 'upper' level may be abolished in some areas as part of the latest review of local government. This is important, as a number of the largest and most all-embracing museum services actually come under the shires, and certainly, within the local authority sector, most of the existing museum directors of chief officer rank are county-level employees. Their abolition, if threatened, could undo much work done of the most comprehensive nature by these widely based museum services, some of which must have contributed to efficiency by economy of scale.

It also has to be pointed out that Scotland, though within the British administrative system, has different legal and local authority structures, which in so far as they affect museum work, appear to produce a more cohesive network across the Scottish nation. Scotland has many significant administrative differences from England and Wales, based ultimately on a different basis for its legal code.

Elected members are in effect local politicians who, once elected, are then allotted to certain committees. Each committee will have a different remit, but most often the one dealing with museums will have composite responsibilities covering a variety of other leisure and cultural activities. Often at the county level of administration, the commitee is also focused on related activities such as archives. At district level the museum element makes an often unhappy bedfellow with sports centres, parks, theatres and even crematoria.

Amongst independent museums, there is a direct analogy with the private foundation boards that are common in many fields in the USA – what has been called the third, the non-profit or not-for-profit sector (see note 1). Though the term 'non-profit' has a specific legal and fiscal definition in the USA, there, and even more so now in the UK, it is becoming less precisely applied, often simply to mean those enterprises that fall outside the direct control of the public sector, but do not have as a mission the creation and distribution of a profit. As such, the UK use of the term is beginning to mean a curious but appropriate nexus of some public organizations, some voluntary ones, and of course the independents when it comes to museums. The problems and special circumstances of such museums, as organizations, vary little from other such organizations: charities; independent schools; independent hospitals; wildlife trusts; and so on. Little use has yet been made within museums of the experience built up in these areas to ease transition to such status, let alone to plan growth and sustained development, where a museum is already independent.

The staff

Collections are the central resource of museums, and have had considerable, if not total, influence over past and present museum policy, and thus resource allocation. It is hardly surprising therefore that there has been a dominance of curators as opposed to designers, educationalists and other communicators in staff structures, in terms of both numbers and tenure of key positions.

All the staff of museums, of course, exert an enormous influence on the general management of museums and their ability to change directions, to be flexible, and to meet changing demands on them. This is not unusual: all employees exert an influence on their employer's ability to take and implement decisions; the earlier twentieth century history of British industrial relations should demonstrate that. Nor is this unusual because so many museums, even independents, are closely linked to, and even dependent on, significant levels of support directly from the public sector. The influence of staff over corporate goals is especially prevalent in the public sector where there is a high proportion of professionals.

There is evidence (Drucker, 1955, pp. 326–7) that wherever professionals are the main labour currency in an organization, they will exert a greater than normal influence, but not through direct industrial action or negotiation. This is a common feature of the public sector, in that in hospitals, for instance, consultants have exerted enormous influence, and in general, medical staffs continue to exert powerful influences over the health service. Similarly, teachers within the school system exert what might be described as the most significant influence. What is interesting is that both of these parts of the public sector (and many others) have been undergoing radical restructuring over the past decade or more, within the general policies of the government. Whether one agrees with their policies, and whether or not one chooses to believe that the government's motivation is economy and efficiency, as opposed to straightforward cost cutting for its own sake, it is a fact that the government has been seeking to change the way the public sector is managed.

Museums have begun to feel the effects of this with, first of all, trustee status for some NMGs, and most recently the publication of reports by the OAL (1991) and the Audit Commission (1991). The former is based on work at the Natural History Museum, the National Gallery and the Science Museum, and sets out the government's needs for performance measurement in the NMGs, and the latter describes the same process and new forms of management accountability for LAMGs.

For museums, the problem of professional influence over general management has been identified before: 'Too often, museum staff feel that the custodial function is justification enough for public acceptance. They lose sight of the institution's larger social role' (Dickenson, 1988, p. 149). It is of course a problem of a generational change expected of museums, but which they are in the main as yet ill equipped to answer. Museums grew up as collections, largely idiosyncratically in terms of their distribution throughout the UK, but also in terms of their subsequent collecting. This has meant, some might say not unreasonably, that the key decision makers have been curators, or former curators, at best. But both Greenhill (1984, p. 4) and Hale (1987, p. 20) thought this was a problem. What Burns describes as the 'cult of the curator' (197, p. 213) has applied, and collections and collection issues continue to dominate in thinking, activity and of course finance.

It would not be unfair to say that the majority of curatorial staff are, in the museological sense, *object oriented* rather than *people oriented* – a not unreasonable stance, perhaps, given their precise role in the museum, and the backlogs of collection management work that exist. The real issue is, however, how long museums can go on being entirely object centred in their key decision making activity, and how long those key decision maker posts can continue to be dominated by object-centred thinkers, when all the evidence is that the public, the funders, and large swathes of museum staffs (including many object-centred curators) actually want museums to change.

We may be seeing the evolution of the museum, as a heritage agency, away from its original, predominantly object-collecting base. No doubt museums and any successor agencies will continue to have that unique feature of educating through artefacts, but their *modus operandi* will change as new technology presses the pace of the public's information needs, and their outputs and formats will change in response

to the diversification of public demand. This can only mean more generalist training and education for the key museum decision makers. Thus, in future, training provision will evolve which emphasizes museology or the museum as a whole, as opposed to narrower constructs of curatorship and the rather specialized management needs of museums. There should then be consequent changes in the dominance of curators in those key roles.

Fopp has identified the need for managerial training for museum leaders (1986, p. 187), putting the change in identified training needs down to a change in the public's awareness of museums. Of course, the Hale Report also made extensive reference to the need for management training, in particular the idea of museum professionals being trained to work as part of a team (1987, p. 50), rather than as just a bunch of specialists who work in the same building. It is this specific aspect of museum education and training that needs to be urgently addressed, to produce rounded museologists, as an awareness of management training needs has now belatedly taken root. It is clearly an aspect of 'museumness' wherever these institutions occur since, outside the UK, Tyler has also noted the rise in popularity of management courses for museums personnel in Canada (1984, p. 25).

But even in as specific and technical an area to museums as collection management, UK museums do not necessarily have a good record. For instance, where the nationals are concerned, Bourn records approximations of 30 years' conservation work needed at the British Museum (1988, p. 12). Each of the NMGs included in the report had some similar, almost inconceivable, conservation targets. In terms of object records, as a linchpin to wider access to data, the NMGs were better (pp. 14–15). Other UK museums, though, have been slow in the area of computerization of records (Roberts, 1986). This seems to be in the nature of the institution, as there is evidence of a similar situation in Canada (Homulos and Sutyla, 1988).

When Bourn (1988) was published and first read, a number of former and practising curators and directors felt that the survey described an all too common situation. Opinions as to its causes, of course, differed. Many alleged the usual cause as being underresourcing of museums in general. There is abundant truth in that statement, but there are additional contributing factors. Given the dominance of curatorially trained personnel in decision making positions, since the majority of the most senior, if not all, managerial posts in museums are traditionally held by those with a curatorial background (Hale, 1987, p. 20), in a strictly theoretical management sense the decision makers could be said to have been too *task oriented* as opposed to *goal oriented*. It has even been suggested that a personality profile different from that of an object-centred one is required for museum management:

There is really no competition between this sort of person and the traditional curator. The man or woman with the cast of mind which enables them to become the greatest authority on earth on a mini subject is not attracted by this sort of career or vice versa. . . . Potential managers are not to be found amongst those who live in an ivory tower of specialisation, too narrow-minded to assimilate the museum's aims, policies and priorities as a whole, or to appreciate the relevance of other departments' work to their own. (Greenhill, 1984, pp. 43, 44)

Greenhill went as far as to point out that museum management is not a 'spare-time job for any curator' (1984, p. 67). His view finds support in a significant office holder of the Museums and Galleries Commission itself (Longman, 1987, p. 78); and again suggesting it is common to museums anywhere, its counterpart in the USA was expressed by Black (1984, pp. 28–30).

Even such a noted scholar-director as Sir Roy Strong, a former director of the Victoria and Albert, has accepted that traditional academic disciplines may not provide an appropriate background for museum management (1988, p. 18). In larger museums (where a curatorial discipline is represented by more than one professional member of staff), this philosophy can be extremely divisive: 'United we stand and divided we fall is an all too true adage, and yet how rarely one ever encounters a truly united museum with a staff all pulling in the same direction' (Strong, 1986, p. 19). This demonstrates that a very narrow definition of the role of museums is still at work in the eyes of curators, and when management is applied, sometimes by forces external to the museum, there results what Scown-Geary (personal communication) has called *corporate sabotage*.[4]

It is also tempting to try to explain the apparent conflict in terms of *individual* or *personal goals* competing with *organization goals* (see Boot *et al.*, 1977, p. 148). This is not unique to museums, or the public sector. As Drucker states of the private sector:

> And what distinguishes the professional employee from the non-professional workers, whether skilled or unskilled? It is primarily that he is a professional, that is, that his work, its standards, its goals, its vision, are set by the standards, *the goals*, the vision of a profession, that in other words, they *are determined outside the enterprise*. (Drucker, 1955, pp. 326–7, my emphasis)

Others have sought to explain the problem from a different angle from that of a theoretical management approach. Ettema (1987, p. 62) for instance, sees it in a historical context, where social historians have joined more traditional curatorial specialists in natural history, archaeology and the decorative arts 'in place for several generations'.

The users

It is useful to examine this constituency from two angles: firstly, the evidence of a product(s) or service(s) provided by museums; and, secondly, the evidence of what it is that users actually want from museums: 'One of the ways in which museums demonstrate to society the value and worth of the collections they hold and the activities that they undertake on and around them is by quoting the number of visitors they attract' (Prince and Higgins-McLoughlin, 1987, p. 135). Users tend to be the as yet only *quantified* and *publicized* demonstration of museum value and worth, the other frequently quoted one being *purchase prices* for spectacular works of art or antiquity. Both impressions may contribute to a confused or skewed perception, in all constituencies, over concepts of museum social purpose. Where performance has been measured at all, i.e. visitor figures, it can only have served to confirm perceptions of the museum concept's outdatedness, since it states loudly that the museum is a visitor centre of sorts, an 'attraction'. Hale even described the competitive influence of the media in this respect (1987, p. 20).

Although Robertson, rightly, calls into account visitor figures as an indicator of the value of a museum (1985, p. 128), one might be left to assume, from the evidence, that those in charge of the UK's museums were not in fact interested in who uses their museums, let alone why. As Prince and Higgins-McLoughlin show (1987, p. 132), the majority, close to 70 per cent in each sector as they define them, had *never* undertaken a visitor survey. As they say: 'This is highly significant in terms of museums often-stated public roles and expectations' (pp. 132–3). It is difficult not to agree with Doughty's statement (1968), as quoted by Hudson (1975, p.109): 'In its affected self-esteem the profession has not lost touch with its public – it simply never found it, or even attempted to . . . If this arrogance continues it is difficult to see how museums can find their place in society or serve a useful purpose as display centres.'

Cossons warned of the need for reliable, across-the-board, quantitative data a decade and a half earlier (1970, p. 112). Yet even as recently as 1985, Drew was able to state that nobody knew how many museums there were in the UK (1985, p. 115). More telling still, Cannon-Brookes puts the counterpoint view, warning of the dangers of attempting to reconcile 'conventional management theory evolved for the market-place with the non-quantifiable dimensions of museum collections and their spiritual resources' (1989, p. 133). That changing demands on museums would, in time, catalyse changes within the museums was also predicted: simply the application of management technique in seeking to define objectives for museums would in itself cause a probing of 'basic assumptions on which museums have existed in the past' (Cossons, 1970, pp. 112–13).

The Audit Commission report, however, plainly states the *consumer's right* to be addressed fully as a constituency, in concluding as it does that as a result of concentrating on conservation rather than balancing between 'the twin causes of conservation and exhibition . . . some local authority museums are worthy but dull' (Audit Commission, 1991, p. 6). The OAL report (1991, pp. 7–8) also addresses the same issues *vis-à-vis* the NMGs (see above). In bringing the needs of the museum consumer into the open, Ames has argued:

> The traditional museum with its purified versions of Disneyland is still very much in vogue, however, even though it is becoming evident that such museums serve a limited clientele (the higher education strata). Though ostensibly designed to serve the public, these large museums, it seems to me, are a more accurate reflection of the interests and aspirations of the *museums profession*. (Ames, 1986, p. x, my emphasis)

Thompson noted the shift away from 'an imperialistic view of man towards a domestic one' (1978, p. 2) in the growth of folk museums, and Foster (1979, p. 56) saw these, and open-air museums, as responding to increased leisure. If one accepts Bennett's view of museums in the late nineteenth century as materializing and thus supporting 'the power of the ruling classes' (1988, p. 64), it is small wonder that the UK's more traditional museums have had difficulty in continuing to justify themselves.

The evidence is, however, accruing steadily for the public's awareness of the value of museums as a leisure activity, and, fortunately, not just through quotations of ever increasing numbers of visits without analysis of why such increases have occurred and what they represent. Chadwick's survey in Derby, Nottingham and Leicester found that most people used museums for enjoyment and that museums helped people make advantageous use of leisure time (1980, p. 45), a clear indication that, though unarguably leisure, museums were seen as beneficial leisure rather than as a simple alternative to the most common forms of leisure: TV, public houses, and so on. MORI, in a focused survey on one museum, and an unusual one in a number of ways, the Royal Armouries, found that one in three of those surveyed had visited historical monuments or local museums, whilst a quarter had visited major national museums or art galleries (1985, p. 1). The Armouries is unusual in being a national museum, one of the smallest of them, and located in a world renowned monument – the Tower of London – which must skew any generalizations drawn on Armouries-specific research.

Merriman also found survey evidence of the public's demand for a museum product(s):

Contrary to those who might see museums and visiting heritage as a refuge for those with unfavourable views of present-day society, who are nostalgic for yesteryear, the survey shows that the more positive (i.e. favourable) one's views are of contemporary society, the more one is likely to visit museums. (1989, p. 158)

Elsewhere, he provides evidence that 47 per cent is a likely proportion of the British population visiting a museum or art gallery once a year (1989b, p. 155).

Though by no means exhaustive, this evidence, combined with obvious signs of the public's rapidly changing tastes in leisure, all indicate that in future no museum in the UK can afford past complacency in terms of user research and matching outputs to consumer demand. This is no different in a national museum or a local community museum: what will differ is the outcome of such consideration, and obviously the potential of the individual museums themselves, which of course will remain as varied as the present day. It is an argument for more specific *market niching* by all museums, and a move away from the generic museum model inherited from the last century.

Peters and Waterman advocate 'sticking to the knitting' (1982, p. 15), i.e. not getting into other types of business, but staying in your own. It may be then that several species of museum will evolve, as each decides which business it is in. Rather than the more diffuse present museum concept, at least three discrete businesses may emerge: conservation, education and leisure.

Some facts and figures

Local authority expenditure on museums and galleries in the UK is almost the same as for NMGs (Audit Commission, 1991, p. 1), but is spread across some 650 LMAGs which attract about 20 million visits per annum (p. 5). As noted earlier, they cost some £90 million p.a. for those directly administered, with a further £6 million p.a. on other LMAGs through grants, some of that to independent museums, of course. Although NMGs cost more (£100 million), and there are less of them, they get more visits, and thus cost marginally less per visit: for example an NMG visit cost £4.20 net expenditure, whereas an LAMG visit cost 4.50 net, in the early 1990s.

Over 40 per cent of LAMGs have been set up in the last two decades (p. 10) about a quarter of the total between 1971 and 1980, with a further 120 since 1981. This is part of that general increase, the 'museum a fortnight' often cited: 'The growth in the number of museums *may* reflect an increased interest in conserving the heritage and providing a sense of place and continuity at a time of great social and technological change' (p. 10, my emphasis). Equally, of course, it could merely reflect success on the part of museum professionals in lobbying for a worthy cause, a direct example of their influence in policy making in heritage in the UK. The factors which have made it possible are also very complex: trends in leisure, individual and family mobility, social expectations, increased education possibly, and increased disposable income certainly.

It would appear that local authority expenditure (p. 10) has increased in real terms since 1980 despite the loss of some large museums, e.g. the now National Museums and Galleries of Merseyside, previously under the local authority as a county service. County councils spend £13 million, the City of London £4 million, the metropolitan districts £29 million, the London boroughs £5 million, and the shire districts £43 million. This grand total may not in fact be excessive: it depends on the comparator used. In comparison with the NMGs, it may seem good value; it certainly spreads wider over the population as a whole, but of course much thinner. In comparison with the National Trust's tax exemption deals to house owners, and its sheer size and volume of resources in capital financial terms, the amount spent on LMAGs is probably insignificant, and similarly if compared with English Heritage's capital assets.

It does compare with the National Trust's net revenue expenditure of £71 million in 1990 (Baring, 1991, p. 32). As an observation on the trend towards 'greater self-reliance', it can be seen that those LAMGs that do charge for admission recover an average 22 per cent of expenditure by that means, compared with 11 per cent for those that do not (Audit Commission, 1991, p. 25). By contrast, the National Trust achieved just under 11 per cent of its gross income from admissions (Baring, 1991). The Trust's most significant single source of income was in fact membership fees, at 40.46 per cent of its gross revenue. Is there a lesson for both government and museums to be learned here?

Compared with these, we have Hewison's calculations (1987, p. 27) that the National Trust is the biggest landowner in the UK after the state. Taking his figures for the Department of the Environment's work in 1986–87 on the *built heritage*, English Tourist Board heritage project grants in 1985–86, and the estimated expenditure of local authorities in 1985–86, you reach a credible total of approximately £150 million being spent on various forms of heritage and environmental preservation. Hewison (1987, p. 27) also points out that earnings from overseas visitors to Britain amounted to £5473 million in 1985–86, and £110 million by visitors to historic houses and gardens (not all of whom are from overseas), about 40 per cent of which do not charge for admission. This contrasts sharply with figures on earned income for museums (Prince and Higgins-McLoughlin, 1987, pp. 156–7), where the majority gross less than £2500 p.a., with only half of the nationals reaching a figure of £100,000 or more.

Thus, the proportion of earned overseas income from museums is likely to be minuscule.

The point is, though, that all these heritage agencies are probably underfinanced, but in a revenue sense only. Bound by the nature of their business as non-profit, they are thus unable to release or convert some of those capital assets to finance revenue developments, as a straight profit making business would.

Conclusions

This last concern, the move towards imposing a greater financial self-reliance on museums, has great significance indeed, and should not be seen as a simple but reasonable response to demonstrably poor performance in the past. It is clearly a trend towards increased independence from the public sector sources of finance as the sole or main provider.

It is clear that museums in the UK are at something of a crossroads. Assuming a continuation of the trends in demand, and of the present government's general policies, choices about social role and hence programming priorities are going to have to be made. Were the present main opposition to regain power, it has to be said that they are unlikely to make their first act of government a doubling of museum expenditure. Museums simply do not occupy a central political role; nor has a museum issue ever won or lost either a local or a national election.

The problem of choice has been long understood: Coffey (1961, p. 28) says that the great debate between research and scholarship on the one hand, and education and popularism on the other, is due to lack of professionalism in museums. In other words, both sets of protagonists identify with either scholarship or popular education, but not museums. Parr supported this view, asking 'Is there a museum profession?' (1960), and later labelled the problem 'a plurality of professions' (1964). This problem of a lack of museologists has also been more recently revived (Washburn, 1985, p. 18). Drew, a significant Chairman in the Museums and Galleries Commission's change of gear in the 1980s, doubted that 'a profession . . . as fragmented . . . can hope to be taken all that seriously' (1985, p. 116).

The dichotomy in the present museum situation was related by Ripley (1969, p. 51) to questions of purpose and role.

All of these science and art museums and the related fields of history and anthropology began to show signs, which became so evident in the twentieth century, of division of goals, of cross-purposes . . . With the development of museums as great public institutions there came a fuzziness about their purpose. This has bedevilled the inhabitants of museums ever since.

In simpler, management-oriented terms, Weil (1983, p. 50) sees it as a failure at the very beginning of the management process, the failure to be specific about goals:

> No museums can play all these different roles all at once. To try to be everything is to wind up being nothing. Each museum must choose which roles to emphasize, and this choice, in turn, may depend on the museum's own resources, the changing needs of the community, the particular interests of the museum's staff and trustees, and the level and type of activity in other museums of the area.

The current trend towards recognizing the economic aspects of museums, so unwelcome amongst museum professionals as anathema to their perceptions of museum purpose, was recognized by 1979, when Lickorish pointed out that:

> Tourism, embracing the longer visits away from home, makes a major contribution to many service industries and the leisure trades . . . Tourism and its major service trades represent a growth business. Most experts forecast continued expansion in the 1980s. Since leisure time will grow, cultural activities and serious pastimes will appeal more because they offer great personal satisfaction. (1979, p. 117).

Specifically, he recognized the effect of museums in *indirect economic impact*:

> Although there are no official figures, recent studies have suggested that 1–1.5 million jobs depend on visitor spending. Visitor patronage brings prosperity to regions which may have few other economic resources, and supports services and amenities which the local residents alone could not afford. (p. 117)

More recently, economic impact (see Myerscough, 1988, p. 3 for a definition) surveys from the UK (Myerscough, 1988) and the USA (Bloom and Powell, 1984, p. 21) have demonstrated the positive economic benefits of the museum in urban renewal schemes, as well as tourism. Museums, therefore, clearly have something more tangible to offer *politically* than rather vague contributions to the quality of life.

The UK evidence in Myerscough's major studies (Myerscough, 1988, p. 13) show a comparably substantial impact in the UK. Of 132 million admissions during 1984–85 to museums, galleries and heritage attractions together, museums and galleries took 73 million of the total, exceeding theatre, concert and cinema visiting. This equates to an estimated consumer spending of £52 million during 1985–86 (p. 19), i.e. just 12 per cent of the total £433 million, with museums and galleries representing just over 6 per cent of that sector's total. Here, then, is the evidence for a much better performance in income generation on the part of museums: that they should capture only 6 per cent of the disposable income of over half of the market (55 per cent), and at the same time lose out on the other additional benefits that successful trading can bring, noted by Sekers (1985, p. 132).

However, the downside is also coming to our notice: Norwich (1991, pp. 45–52) has cited the dangers of 'tourism pollution' for museums amongst cities, gardens and areas of outstanding natural beauty, and predicts the need to limit what might now, with hindsight, be considered excessive promotion of heritage in general. In terms of museums, it has to be said that some of the most crowded days, certainly at national honeypots in London such as the British Museum, and at the better marketed museums outside London such as the Merseyside Maritime Museum, leave a lot to be desired in the way of the museum experience. Whilst arguing for a diversification of that ill defined museum experience, generating a wide and continuously reviewed product range in the future, I would personally argue for a marketing and demarketing imperative: some of those products can and should be charged for, itself a disincentive to uncontrolled demand, especially when supply is controlled by resources. It may also mean marketing some museum products some of the time, instead of trying to market all of them all of the time.

There needs also to be a clearer statement of purpose, museum by museum, as called for in reports such as the Audit Commission's (1990), for without such, corporate objectives can only vaguely be discerned, and very rarely achieved. An underachieving museum affords no one any benefit at all. The degree of variance in stated social purpose in the literature is extremely wide, with often vehement argument at either end of a spectrum or continuum of social roles postulated by the profession and by museum supporters. The debate often also appears polarized in the UK.

The evidence of museum activity, however, to support such a wide panorama of social efficacy in the UK is sadly not yet there. Users of museums have simply not been asked, consulted or tested as to their needs and wants; indeed, neither has the museums' ability to provide such diverse services and products as are assumed to be desirable and achievable been fully tested. Whilst there is evidence of a growing awareness of the need for social relevance in the literature, particularly in the 1980s, neither is this absolutely fresh (rather it is an intensification of a debate on museums existing since at least the nineteenth century), nor is it matched by evidence of significant changes in traditional museum activity or emphases within such activities (Prince and Higgins-McLoughlin, 1987, p. 119).

It might be that in the future museums are able to be categorized by their missions and objectives: visitor centres versus research centres, educational facilities versus information centres, and so on. That is, managements might take the line that one or perhaps two of these various social roles represents a feasible, achievable objective, but not all, thus avoiding the classic museum dilemma of attempting all at once, and singularly failing in some whilst underachieving in all.

The picture that emerges is that the overall operational philosophy of museums in general is both a little one-sided, probably as a function of the history and growth of museums and their general philosophy, and a little introverted, in the sense that usage of the museum resource is counted as almost a by-product rather than a *raison d'être* or primary purpose, or even an equal part of a balanced system. Critics of the current museum dilemma between collections and utilization, such as Norwich, and there are many, tend to err on the side of caution in favour of restricted usage, to preserve the resource, and hence vote for preservation as a primary *raison d'être*.

However, it does have to be asked whether this imbalance of activity is necessarily uniquely typical of museums as institutions which were either established within the public sector, or adopted by it and subsequently managed within that sector's prevailing structures, working methods and philosophies. Also, can other predominantly Victorian concepts still with us be said to be any more flexible?

Secondly, it is clear that whilst museums in general cannot claim excellence in their management of themselves as institutions (Greenhill, 1984, p. 41; Hale, 1987, p. 20), and patently need to improve in order to win a larger share of resources and maintain their existence against increasing competition, neither can this be said to be uniquely typical of museums. Indeed, it could and has been said that this is not all that different from the situation in management altogether, and not just British management:

In marked contrast to the prevailing wisdom today, management theorists of the first sixty years of this century did not worry about the environment, competition, the marketplace, or anything else external to the organization. They had a closed system view of the world. That view, myopic as it now seems, centered on what ought to be done to optimize resource application by taking into account only what went on inside a company. It didn't really change much until almost 1960, when theorists began to acknowledge that internal organization dynamics were shaped by external events. Explicitly taking into account the *effects of external forces* on the organization's internal workings, then, launched the 'open system' era. (Peters and Waterman, 1982, p. 91, my emphasis).

Ettema's analysis of this central issue in museums (1987, pp. 62–3) is that diametrically opposed *formalist* and *analytical* schools have:

generated two competing approaches to the problem of linking artefacts and education. These approaches do not represent self-conscious schools of thought so much as perspectives or tendencies of thought, frequently based on unexamined assumptions about what history is and what it is for. They are ideas of which museum professionals partake to greater or lesser degrees, yet the profession as a whole increasingly *divides* itself along the lines of these perspectives. (my emphasis)

Hence, perhaps the profession's own schism as to purpose, role and function, and its adherence to older, essentially Victorian, ideals of museum social role, may have contributed to the development and dominance of leisure, even tourism, at the present time. That is to say, without a basic philosophical structure which defines tangible, current returns from their activities as an integral part of their make-up, rather than as some by-product, museums may well have allowed themselves to become 'a place to go' (Mead, 1970, p. 23). These issues could be boiled down to a simple test of whether museums serve the community as a whole, or some narrower elite, be it the academic, the artistic or the cultural, or even the most privileged of the museums world, the staff themselves, furthering their own personal erudition.

Perhaps museums are just very poor at communicating their aims and objectives, so that some see museums as tourist or entertainment facilities, and others see them as research centres. Are these roles indeed mutually exclusive?

Notes

1 'Non-profit' or 'not-for-profit' has a specific meaning in the USA, defined by law. Kovach (1989, pp. 149–56) explains the differences between museums with this status in the USA and 'for-profit', i.e. meaning businesses. 'Non-profit' must not be automatically assumed to be synonymous with public museums, which can also be 'non-business' but may well not have the legal tax-exempt status that 'non-profit' implies. The term is growing in use in the UK, tending to be synonymous with 'independents' in the case of museums and with 'charitable trusts' in general.
2 To be fair, Green (1985), in questioning the cordon sanitaire in relation to social history, and especially contemporary social history, was complaining that this was part of the reifying effect of museums. It could, however, equally be postulated as a social function, albeit unconscious and maybe even desirable, since it is a clear, measurable effect, unlike the many other postulated social functions.
3 Further destructuring of the public sector in the UK in the run-up to the twenty-first century may produce a move towards the more management-oriented classification suggested above.
4 Corporate sabotage was the term used by T. Scown-Geary, former marketing manager to the British Museum (Natural History), during private discussion in February 1987, to describe the attitudes of staff in more traditional functions which seemed tacitly to undermine agreed corporate policy.
5 Chatterley Whitfield Mining Museum is the likely first casualty as it went into voluntary liquidation in August 1993. The exact causes are not known at this point in time, but failure to achieve significant visitor volume may be one, suggesting that Middleton's (1990) view of market saturation may be accurate.

References

ALEXANDER, E. P. (1979) *Museums in Motion*, American Association for State and Local History, Nashville, TN

AMES, M. M. (1986) *Museums, The Public and Anthropology*, University of British Columbia and Concept Publishing, New Delhi

AUDIT COMMISSION (1991) *The Road to Wigan Pier? Managing Local Authority Museums and Art Galleries*, HMSO, London

BABBIDGE, A. (1991) 'Legal, decent and honest?', *Museums Journal*, **91**(9), 32–33

BARING, N. '1990 finances', *The National Trust Magazine*, **63** (summer), 31–33

BENNETT, T. (1988) 'Museums and "the people"', in R. Lumley (ed.), *The Museum Time-Machine*, Comedia (Routledge), London, 63–85

BLACK, C. (1984) 'The nature of leadership', *Museum News*, **62** (5), 28–30

BLOOM, J. N. and POWELL, E. A. (eds) (1984) *Museums for a New Century*, Report of the Commission on Museums for a New Century, American Association of Museums, Washington, DC

BOOT, R. L., COWLING, A. G. and STANWORTH, M. J. J. K. (1977) *Behavioural Sciences for Managers*, Edward Arnold, London

BOURN, J. (1988) *Management of the Collections of the English National Museums and Galleries*, Report of the Comptroller and Auditor General, National Audit Office and HMSO, London

BREARS, P. (1984) 'Temples of the muses: the Yorkshire philosophical museums 1820–50', *Museums Journal*, **84**(1), 3–20

BROWN, L. (1987) 'New needs in adult and community education', in T. Ambrose (ed.), *Education in Museums: Museums in Education*, Scottish Museums Council and HMSO, Edinburgh

BURCAW, G. E. (1987) *An Introduction to Museum Work* (2nd edn), American Association for State and Local History, Nashville, TN

BURNS, W. A. (1971) 'The curator-as-canary', *Curator*, **xiv**(3), 213–220

CAMERON, D. F. (1971) 'The museum: a temple or a forum?', *Curator*, **XIV**(1), 11–24

CANNON-BROOKES, P. (1984) 'The nature of museum collections', in J. M. A. Thompson (ed.), *Manual of Curatorship*, Butterworths, London, 115–116

CANNON-BROOKES, P. (1989) 'Editorial: management, professionalism and the archival function of museums', *International Journal of Museum Management and Curatorship*, **8**(2), 131–135

CHADWICK, A. (1980) *The Role of the Museum and Art Gallery in Community Education*, Department of Adult Education, University of Nottingham

CHEETHAM, F. W. (1966) 'Towards a national museum service', *Museums Journal*, **66**(3), 167–174

CHEETHAM, F. W. (1968) 'A national museum service for Britain', *Museums Journal*, **68**(2), 70–73

COFFEY, K. (1961) 'Operation of the industrial museum', *Museum News*, October, 26–29

COSSONS, N. (1970) 'McKinsey and the museum', in S. P. Osmond, N. Cossons, and N. I. Ambercrombie (eds), 'Session 4: Recruitment, training and management in the museum profession', *Museums Journal*, **70**(3), 110–113

DE LA TORRE, M. (1984) 'Museum financing in the developing countries', in A. Bochi and S. de Valance (eds), *Museums for a Developing World: ICOM 1983*, Proceedings of the 13th General Conference and 14th General Assembly of the International Council of Museums, London, 24 July to 2 August, International Council of Museums, Paris

DEVONSHIRE, A. (1989) *Attempting the Impossible? The Rationalisation of Museums Collections*, unpublished MA museum studies dissertation, Institute of Archaeology, University College London

DICKENSON, V. (1988) *Management Development for Canadian Museums*, Information Services, Communications Canada, Ottawa

DOUGHTY, P. S. (1968) 'The public of Ulster museum: a statistical survey', *Museums Journal*, no. 1, 16–25, and no. 2, 47–53

DREW, SIR A. (1985) 'The Presidential Address', *Museums Journal*, **83**(3), 115–118

DRUCKER, P. F. (1955) *The Practice of Management*, paperback edn 1989, Heinemann, Oxford

ELLIOTT, D. (1987) 'Medium for what?', in 'The museum as medium', *Museums Journal*, **87**(2), 77–83

ETTEMA, M. J. (1987) 'History museums and the culture of materialism', in J. Blatti (ed.), *Past Meets Present: Essays about Historic Interpretation and Public Audiences*, Smithsonian Institution Press, Washington, DC, 62–85

FLYNN, N. (1990) *Public Sector Management*, Harvester Wheatsheaf, London

FOPP, M. (1986) 'The science of management', *Museums Journal*, **85**(4), 187–189

FOSTER, R. (1979) 'The changing philosophy of museums', *Museums Journal*, **79** (2), 54–57

GREEN, O. (1985) 'Our recent past: the black hole in museum collections', *Museums Journal*, **85**(1), 5–7

GREENHALGH, P. (1989) 'Education, entertainment and politics: lessons from the great exhibitions', in P. Vergo (ed.), *The New Museology*, Reaktion Books, London, 74–98

GREENHILL, B. (1977) 'New patterns in museum management', *Museums Journal*, **77**(3), 123–125

GREENHILL, B. (1984) 'Museum Management', in A. Bochi and S. de Valence (eds), *Museums for a Developing World: ICOM 1983*, Proceedings of the 13th General Conference and 14th General Assembly of the International Council of Museums, London, 24 July to 2 August, International Council of Museums, Paris

HALE, SIR J. (ed.) (1987) *Museum Professional Training and Career Structure*, Report by a Working Party, HMSO for Museums and Galleries Commission, London

HEWISON, R. (1987) *The Heritage Industry: Britain in a Climate of Decline*, Methuen, London

HOMULOS, P. and SUTYLA, C. (1988) *Information Management Needs in Canadian Museums*, background paper for Museum Policy Working Group, Information Services, Communications Canada, Ottawa

HUDSON, K. (1975) *A Social History of Museums*, Macmillan, London

KIRBY, S. (1988) 'Policy and politics: charges, sponsorship, and bias', in R. Lumley (ed.), *The Museum Time-Machine*, Routledge, London, 89–101

KOVACH, C. (1989) 'Strategic management for museums', *International Journal of Museum Management and Curatorship*, **8**(2), 149–156

LAYTON, R. (ed.) (1989) *Who Needs the Past?*, Unwin Hyman, London

LEWIS, G. D. (1984) 'Collections, collectors and museums: a brief world survey', in J. M. A. Thompson (ed.), *Manual of Curatorship*, Butterworths, London, 23–27

LICKORISH, L. J. (1979) 'The value of museums to the economy', *Museums Journal*, **73**(3), 117–118

LONGMAN, P. (1979) 'Dead arts and sacred cows', in 'The museum as medium', *Musuems Journal*, **87**(2), 77–83

LORD, B., LORD, G. D. AND NICKS, J. (1989b) *The Cost of Collecting: Collection Management in UK Museums. A Report Commissioned by the Office of Arts and Libraries*, HMSO, London

LOUGHBOROUGH, B. (1978) 'The effects of local government reorganisation', *Museums Journal*, **77**(4), 165–168

MEAD, M. (1970) 'Museums in a media-saturated world', *Museum News*, **49**(1), 23–25

MERRIMAN, N. (1989a) 'Museum visiting as a cultural phenomenon', in F. Vergo (ed.), *The New Museology*, Reaktion books, London, 149–171

MERRIMAN, N. (1989b) 'The social basis of museum and heritage visiting', in S. Pearce (ed.), *Museum Studies in Material Culture*, Leicester University Press, London, 153–171

MEYER, K. E. (1979) *The Art Museum: Money, Power, Ethics*, Twentieth Century Foundation, New York

MIDDLETON, V. (1990) *New Visions for Independent Museums in the UK*, Association of Independent Museums, Chichester

MORI (1985) *Attitudes to Museums and the Armouries*, Market Research and Opinion International, London

MUSEUMS ASSOCIATION (1994) *Museums Yearbook* (annual), Museums Association of Great Britain, London

MYERSCOUGH, J. (1988) *The Economic Importance of the Arts in Britain*, Policy Studies Institute, London

NORWICH, J. J. (1991) 'Tourism pollution', *Museum Management and Curatorship*, **10**(1), 45–52

OAL (1991) *Report on the Development of Performance Indicators for the National Museums and Galleries*, Office of Arts and Libraries, London

PARR, A. E. (1950) 'Museums of nature and man', *Museums Journal*, **50**(8), 165–171

PARR, A. E. (1960) 'Is there a museum profession?', *Curator*, **3**(2), 101–106

PARR, A. E. (1963) 'The functions of a museum: research centres or show places?', *Curator*, **6**(i), 20–31

PARR, A. E. (1964) 'A purality of professions', *Curator*, **7**(4), 287–295

PETERS, T. J. and WATERMAN, R. H. (1982) *In Search of Excellence*, Harpers and Row and Warner Books, New York

PRINCE, D. R. and HIGGINS-MCLOUGHLIN, R. H. (1987) *Museums UK: the Findings of the Museum Database Project*, Museums Association and Butterworths, London

RADLEY, A. (1990) 'Artefacts, memory and a sense of the past', in D. Middleton and D. Edwards (eds), *Collective Remembering*, Sage, London, 46–59

RAFFERTY, J. (1990) 'A palace where the King is merely the curator', *The Independent*, 12 September, 18

RIPLEY, D. (1969) *The Sacred Grove: Essays on Museums*, Simon and Schuster, New York

ROBERTS, D. A. (1986) *The State of Documentation in Non-National Museums in South-Eastern England*, Occasional Paper no. 9, Museums Documentation Association, Cambridge

ROBERTSON, I. (1985) 'Financing museums: the view of the professional', *Museums Journal*, **85**(3), 125–129

SEKERS, D. (1989) 'Financing museums through commercial activities', in I. Robertson, H. T. Hirst, D. Boston and D. Sekers (eds), 'Discussion group 1: Sources of income for museums', *Museums Journal*, **85**(3), 131–133

SINGLETON, H. R. (1979) 'Museums in a changing world', *Museums Journal*, **79**(1), 11–12

STRONG, SIR R. (1986) 'Museum public relations: observations of a director', in C. Bellow (ed.), *Public View: the ICOM Handbook of Museum Public Relations*, International Council of Museums, Paris, 11–16

STRONG, SIR R. (1988) 'Scholar or salesman? The curator of the future', *Muse*, **VI**(2), 16–26

TABORSKY, E. (1982) 'The sociostructural role of museums', *International Journal of Museum Management and Curatorship*, **1**, 339–345

THOMPSON, G. B. (1978) 'A museum's role in a changing society', *Museums Journal*, **78**(1), 2–3

TOFFLER, A. (1970) *Future Shock*, Pan, London

TYLER, B. (1984) 'Goldfish, piranhas and the three As of professional development', *Muse*, **II**(3), 24–27

WASHBURN, W. (1985) 'Professionalising the muses', *Museum News*, **64**(2), 18–25

WEIL, S. E. (ed.) (1983) *Beauty and the Beasts*, Smithsonian Institution, Washington, DC

WHITE, D. (1983) 'Is Britain becoming one big museum', *New Society*, 20 October, 96

WILSON, SIR D. M. (1989) *The British Museum: Purpose and Politics*, British Museum, London

WILSON, G. and WORCESTER, R. M. (1988) 'The role of research in the planning process of the Royal Armouries', *Museums Journal*, **88**(1), 37–40

14

The legislation and institutional context: the maritime heritage

Robert Baldwin

> Thus should man at once lose half his inheritance if the Art of Navigation did not enable him to manage this untamed beast [the sea], and with the bridle of the wind, and the saddle of his shipping, to make him servicable. Now for the services of the sea they are innumerable. It is our great purveyor of the world's commodities . . . the sea yields the Action to the bodie, Meditation to the Mind, the World to the World by the Art of Arts, Navigation.
>
> Samuel Purchas, *His Pilgrims*, 1625

The United Kingdom's extensive maritime heritage makes it an important, unique and controversial issue. It is the product of our successfully meeting the evolving challenge of waterborne transport over 4000 years. The management of that heritage is a huge task, falling in part outside the conventional scope dealt with by museums or archaeologists or those involved in conservation of historical buildings and natural environments. It is thus important for the heritage manager not only to realize the opportunities for museum coverage, ship preservation, and marine archaeology, but also to grasp that significant parts of that heritage are not attended to adequately because of legislation designed for the days when Britain saw its future more in terms of regulating a vast, flourishing merchant marine.

Alongside the introduction of free-trade doctrines which cut the scope for smuggling and allowed British shipping and ports to grow rapidly in the nineteenth century, various abuses of these opportunities became evident, such as the well known coffin ships. Thus it became necessary to regulate the shipowner, the shipmaster, the crew, the pilots, the harbour and dock authorities, and the conduct of ancillary occupations like marine insurance and salvage. A succession of Merchant Shipping Acts from 1835 to 1913 addressed such problems, but now constitute, especially in respect of their provisions about salvage, an unfortunate incubus to the effectual preservation of the marine heritage. In the nineteenth century there were hundreds of shipwrecks and strandings each year around British coasts (*Figure 14.1*). This led to the formation of the Royal National Lifeboat Institution and to the growth of salvage operations by towage firms anxious to reap more benefit from their investment in steam

tugs. Unfortunately the same legislation and opportunism has encouraged the treasure hunter by creating a market in addition to the enduring allure of underwater finds. However, these treasure hunters can often become involved in painstaking historical research, thereby presenting the heritage manager with an opportunity to reform and educate them as to the real significance of their mutual concern.

The nature of that maritime heritage has been formed by Britain's island character and long coastline, comprising many natural harbours, navigable rivers, and convenient beaches and landing sites. That heritage is found not just in the form of ancient ports and shipping, but in a huge range of surviving written and printed records (now mostly in official repositories) and in public and private collections of artefacts, souvenirs and heirlooms. That heritage is also to be found in the survival of many ancillary marine trades and traditional practical skills. Significantly, and now materially threatened, there is also the underwater environment, and its intrinsic archaeological potential. The latter contains much of the best evidence about the nature of ancient shipping and cargoes as well as revealing the form of post-medieval trade with a far-flung empire serviced very largely by British ships. Yet, offshore, rather less than effectual protection is afforded to our marine heritage.

The dangers emanate also from commercial gravel extraction, dredging, longshore drift, uncontrolled dumping and even from fishing and crabbing by modern trawlers. European fishery limits of 5 km for registered coastal fishing craft, and an 80 km exclusion zone for non-EC fishing vessels, provide but limited protection for this traditional activity and associated fish stocks. However, such limits do

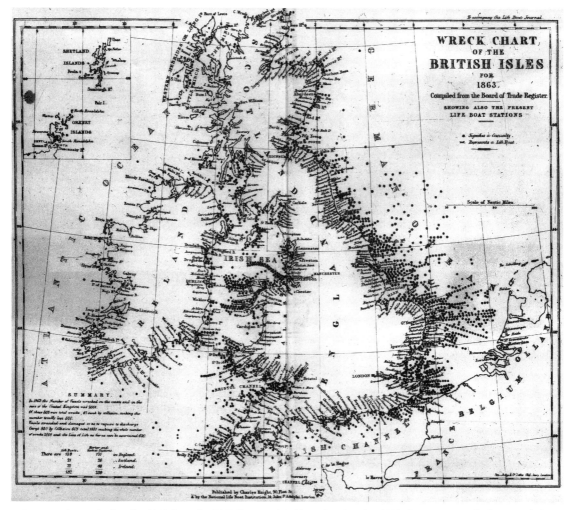

Figure 14.1 Wreck chart for 1863 from the RNLI's journal *Lifeboat*, showing that 2001 ships were wrecked or stranded, and 507 were total losses (courtesy National Maritime Museum)

increase the incidence of inshore damage by some specialized types of trawl which scrape the seabed bare of mollusca, crustaceans and fish, and can destroy the closely associated marine archaeology in the process.

This is an area where knowledge of the law is important, albeit the law offers truly effectual safeguards to only a few protected offshore archaeological sites. The duty of care thus poses regulatory and educational challenges to the heritage manager beyond simply arranging storage, conservation and access to publicly held collections and repositories. In responding to such popular interest, informed guidance becomes a major part of this duty of management.

Historical background

The final severance of Britain's land link with the continent of Europe about 5000 BC ensured that its

communication and trade with the rest of the world would rely on maritime capability. In the fourth millennium BC the villagers of Skara Brae, Orkney, clearly ate cod and kept larders of shellfish – evidence that marine activity characterized their coast dwelling life. By that date ship construction had begun in the eastern Mediterranean. Ship models from Merimida Beni Salaam in Egypt predate even the Badarian models made c. 5500–4000 BC. Twelve boat burials discovered at Abydos and Saqqara in 1991 provide evidence for planked boat construction by Egyptian shipwrights about 3000 BC as did Cheops large craft buried about 2650 BC and found in 600 parts in 1954.

No European evidence of large boats pre-dates the five large planked boats found at North Ferriby on the Humber which date from c. 1500 BC. Their cargo carrying capacity provides evidence of deliberately developed boatbuilding skills, trade, and a safe landing site – in other words the ancient antecedents of the concept we know today as a port. A sewn wooden boat, also dated by radiocarbon methods to about 1500 BC and found directly beneath a Roman wharf at Dover in October 1992, shows that similar construction methods certainly sustained sea travel (*Figure 14.2*).

Thereafter maritime trade and associated naval activity have been an important sector of the British economy. The influence of immigrants, and the inevitable international transfer of ideas, have had a major effect on its changing form. As an island people living by trade, it is not surprising that marine activity has formed a significant part of our heritage.

Five hundred years ago the achievements of Christopher Columbus, and then John and Sebastian Cabot, helped open European minds to the opportunities of a world beyond the traditional confines of medieval European trade. Such trans-oceanic crossings would require appropriate sailing ships and a knowledge of navigation and charts. During Queen Elizabeth I's reign (1558–1603) England became concerned with oceanic trade and tried to start colonies and trading outposts in America and Asia. Later, the requirement to sustain those links safely, and to protect the realm from invasion, necessitated constant naval protection and led to many naval battles with rival powers in the Stuart and Georgian eras.

Underlying both requirements was the great scientific challenge of determining longitude at sea. The work of the Royal Observatory at Greenwich, founded in 1675, and the development of Harrison's chronometers had, by the 1760s, solved this problem. That new technical competence underpinned the scientific achievements of Captain Cook charting Australasian and polar regions on three voyages of

scientific exploration completed between 1768 and 1780. Thereafter Britain remained pre-eminent in marine science and hydrography. Her shipowners were able to utilize that knowledge to sustain the world's largest merchant fleet and navy, while improving the design of sailing ships and meeting the new challenge in naval architecture – the construction of coal fired iron steamships. Thousands of these ships kept her new dock systems busy as Britain became the workshop of the world in the era 1790–1890. The creative vision of men like Isambard Kingdom Brunel, John Scott Russell and Sir Francis Beaufort helped make commercial fortunes for shipowners like Samuel Cunard and Alfred Holt.

Meanwhile the laying of an extensive British undersea telegraphic cable system enabled Victorian shipowners better to match their steamships to available cargoes. The exploitation of Marconi's discovery of radio waves transformed ship-to-shore communications to make the marine insurance and shipbroking functions of the City of London pre-eminent. In the 1890s the steam turbine opened the possibility of fast and luxury oceanic travel by liner. With the unfortunate demise of the SS *United States* (1952) the last of the historic Blue Riband holders is the RMS *Queen Mary* (1936), now preserved at Long Beach, California. Following World War II and the development of inter-modal containers, there has been a big reduction in the size of the British merchant marine and in the Royal Navy. The loss of the Baltic Exchange buildings and a new building for Lloyd's emphasize changes which have accompanied a huge growth in world trade, the majority of which is still carried by sea, albeit with many fewer ships and mariners.

In meeting future challenges in our use of resources and to sustain trading success and tourism, we must recognize our responsibility to protect the most important elements of our seafaring heritage. In this context it is possible to see five important themes in our nautical heritage as a major seapower, and to resource it accordingly. Those themes are:

Figure 14.2 Excavation beneath the A20 at Dover Harbour in October 1992 revealed a wooden boat dating from about 1500 BC. Marine achaeologists carefully surveyed and saved her timbers for study and display at Dover (courtesy V. Fenwick)

(1) the development of boat and shipbuilding skills; here evidence exists in the archaeological record and in ever more sophisticated written and model forms;
(2) the development of passage making skills into navigational sciences that could sustain world-wide trade and naval ambitions;
(3) the development of ports and an infrastructure of skills, brokerage and nautical instruction that could sustain and change maritime enterprise;
(4) the evidence of seafaring ways of life, of social and family traditions and artefacts closely associated with maritime endeavour and, increasingly, leisure;
(5) the study of the oceanic and underwater environment including hydrography, oceanography and marine archaeology.

History of concern for the marine heritage

The management of this heritage is a huge task, which inevitably is spread over many institutions. These include museums such as the National Maritime Museum, the National Museums on Merseyside, the Imperial War Museum, the Science Museum, the British Museum (Natural History), the National Trust and many local museums and county record offices. Working institutions, notably the Royal Navy, Lloyd's of London, the Royal Institute of Naval Architects, the Institute of Marine Engineers, the Royal Institute of Navigation, and various port and harbour authorities have also played significant parts. But the Ports Act, 1990, by allocating much of the income which Trinity House of Deptford Strand had enjoyed since 1514 to port and harbour authorities, has put the integrity of their library and collections of artifacts at risk. Recently, their archives have been lodged with other major marine archives at the Guildhall Library. Thus even new legislation may not always be framed with the nautical heritage in mind.

Yet, concern to preserve significant items of Britain's maritime heritage was evident in an early seventeenth century attempt to preserve the *Golden Hind* at Deptford, an effort which was effectual until about 1662. Individuals like Samuel Pepys (1633–1703) ensured the preservation of important early records such as those he bequeathed to Magdalene College, Cambridge. Buildings from the naval dockyards that he did so much to organize also survive, albeit that the naval dockyards at Chatham, Portsmouth and Plymouth better represent the technological demands of the Georgian and Victorian navies.

The Hakluyt society, founded in 1846, greatly stimulated scholarly awareness of our maritime achievements. Its example was followed in 1893 by the Navy Records Society, and in 1910 by the Society for Nautical Research. City record offices in London, Bristol and Chester have carefully preserved important maritime, customs and commercial records from the twelfth century onwards. The records of the Royal Observatory, founded at Greenwich to solve the problem of determining longitude at sea, which run from 1675, are now available in Cambridge University Library, while the Public Record Office holds much about the medieval and Tudor antecedents of the Royal Navy and about the Royal Navy itself from 1660 onwards. The huge shipping and warehousing archives of the English East India Companies who conducted a monopolistic trade with the East from 1600 to 1833 can be found as part of the Oriental and India Office Collections of the King's Manuscripts at the British Library, while other significant maritime records are in the British Library Map and Manuscript Rooms. More can be discovered by consulting the Royal Commission on Historical Manuscripts which maintains a comprehensive and increasingly computerized directory of the holdings of all record repositories in Great Britain, and publishes a useful list of addresses.

The Ordnance Survey's *Map of Maritime England*, published in 1982, identified over 700 landward maritime heritage sites. Precise coverage of individual sites, museums and characteristic regional identities can be found in the National Maritime Museum *Guide to Maritime Britain* (1990). Worthwhile details of the natural coastal heritage are given in Robert Hallman's *Coastal Britain* (1984). In pursuit of particular inquiries, the *Libraries, Museums and Art Galleries Yearbook* and the *Museum Association's Yearbook* will be invaluable. The county sites and monuments records offer increasing potential for maritime matters. The Society of Genealogists Reference Library is open to non-members interested in that resource. Like the Transport History Trust, it holds lists of professional research workers who will undertake specialized studies on a fee-paid basis.

Scope for museum coverage

Today, the Admirality's technical shipping archive started in 1720, and a ship model collection dating from the 1650s, plus the contents of the Greenwich Hospital Collection and the Royal Naval Museum, Greenwich, and much from the former Royal United Services Museum, are to be found within the National Maritime Museum at Greenwich. Before 1934 preservation of the maritime heritage lacked such a focus of activity, except for the collections of the Royal School of Naval Architecture, established in South Kensington in 1864 by transferring models from Somerset House where they had been since 1780. With the very significant exception of HMS *Victory*, built at Chatham in 1765 and retained at Portsmouth until she became a primary focus for the Society for Nautical Research in the 1920s, only the Science Museum offered such a focus. Although the Science Museum still has a superb ship model collection and a fine collection of items illustrating marine technology and propulsion and much accumulated expertise, it is to the National Maritime Museum, founded by Act of Parliament in 1934, that one must look for comprehensive collections of ship models and small boats, ships' draughts and plans, hydrographic charts, navigational instruments, maritime antiquities, uniforms and pictures, prints and drawings. It has inherited a reference library from the Society for Nautical Research, and a large manuscript collection of personal papers, naval records, records of maritime businesses, and a very significant part of the official documentation of merchant seamen's careers from the General Registry of Seamen. The Museum and its Maritime Information Centre are devoted to preserving Britain's maritime collections. Other centres of expertise are to be found in museums at Liverpool, Portsmouth, Chatham, London, Bristol, Southampton, Newcastle, Hull, Cardiff, Belfast, Glasgow, Troon and Aberdeen.

Many older local authority museums hold personal collections of international significance: for example Hastings Museum, founded in 1892, holds items gathered on Lady Brassey's famous Pacific cruises on the steam yacht *Sunbeam*. Local historical societies have often secured important maritime collections for independent local museums. In consequence it is often possible to harness local trusts, and so the enthusiasm of children and adults, and local authorities to achieve this, for example, the Fisheries Museum at Anstruther and the Shipwreck Heritage Centre at Hastings, opened in 1987. On a large scale the Mary Rose Trust was able to appeal to a national audience partly because of the prospect of raising the ship so as to secure her future in a museum context. Other significant examples of the harnessing of local enthusiasm are to be seen at Barrow-in-Furness and Charlestown. In the Channel Islands the local businesses and historical societies have played important roles, culminating in the new Maritime Museum opened in Guernsey in June 1991. Such new institutions can offer considerable educational benefits to future generations. New charitable trusts have been created to preserve specific collections relating to seafaring, fishing communities, marine archaeology, or even specific historic ships. They have taken advantage of government funds available from training and employment creation in times of economic depression – times when many privately owned marine artefacts are discarded.

Securing particular items for museums, particularly complete vessels, can be expensive in terms of both purchase and conservation, but careful planning of cash flows, taking full advantage of the tax and estate duty concessions offered by the Inland Revenue and Customs and Excise, can make a significant contribution. The Fund for the Preservation of Scientific and Technological Material, the National Art Collections Fund or the National Heritage Memorial Fund can help supplement such flows. There remains, however, considerable scope to acquire important and relevant items without significant cost. Favourable opportunities to collect items of more modern technological significance may occur as whole technologies are superseded by new ones. The Paddle Steamer Preservation Society took such an opportunity to operate PS *Waverley* commercially on coastal cruises.

At Greenwich in 1989 it was agreed amongst all the museums involved to attempt a coordinated national approach towards maritime collecting policy to make best use of available resources, since the definition of collecting policy was soon to become a formal requirement under the registration guidelines of the Museums and Galleries Commission.

Local authority planning powers have, since 1948, contributed significantly to the preservation of port areas like the Cinque Ports and the waterfronts at Liverpool, Berwick, Bucklers Hard, Glasgow, Dundee, Aberdeen, Stromness and Lerwick. These areas almost always include a museum element as part of the interpretation of the area, the best examples being the very fine displays at the Albert Dock, Liverpool, and the whaling displays, fishing archives and tradition of curatorship established in the grand former offices of the Hull Docks Authority at Kingston upon Hull. These are prime sites whose attractiveness will ensure that they become popular tourist resorts. Consequently partnerships with local authorities, national museums, and quangos like English Heritage, the English Tourist Board, the Scottish Development Agency, the Highlands and Islands Development Board, the Welsh Office and the Northern Ireland Office have often been effective, establishing museum sites like the Welsh Industrial and Maritime Museum in Cardiff and Swansea Docks. Dockland development corporations have helped fund the major collections of cargo handling equipment, including tugs and lighters assembled by the Museum of London and by the National Museums on Merseyside.

Ministry of Defence endowments have secured, through specially endowed trusts, the preservation of unique buildings and public access to them within the historic dockyards at Chatham and Portsmouth. Public access now also seems assured to the Royal William Victualling Yard at Plymouth. Museums and interpretative displays established thereabouts have flourished, with nearby use of waterfront historic buildings for ship preservation. Ministry of Defence funding also sustains the finest hydrographic records in the world through the office of the Hydrographer of the Navy at Taunton. Public records in their care include original surveys by Greenvile Collins and James Cook, as well as world-wide surveys and wreck records comprising both historic and current data. The Hydrographer's divestment of oceanographic functions to the Institute of Oceanography at Wormley in 1950 means that new EC regulations enforcing a duty to provide such oceanographic and historical data for environmental studies apply at both Taunton and Wormley. Future heritage managers are likely to find the Hydrographer's detailed surveys and profiles of the world's coasts, and even individual Victorian harbour buildings and lighthouses, to be of inestimable value, especially where there is no other comparable record like the Ordnance Survey's. Thus the first large-scale map, plus charts and profiles of Hong Kong were compiled by naval hydrographers in the 1840s.

Ship preservation

Despite the long-standing success of the project to keep USS *Constitution* (1797) afloat in Boston Navy yard, the great turning point in this respect was the public outrage which followed the deliberate sinking off Portsmouth of the HMS *Implacable* on 2 December 1949. HMS *Implacable* was built for the French Navy in 1800 as the *Dougay Trouin*. This 74-gun two-decker was, like HMS *Victory* (1765), a survivor from the Battle of Trafalgar in 1805.

The *Cutty Sark*, rescued from Portugal by the Cutty Sark Preservation Society in 1952, was the first beneficiary of the new climate, opening to the public in 1957 (*Figure 14.3*). The Cutty Sark Maritime Trust was founded in 1969 to share the experience gained in restoring the *Cutty Sark*. Popularly known as the Maritime Trust, it has helped to save and restore other sailing ships of historical and technical importance, including *Barnabas* (1881) and *Softwing* (1910), both in sailing condition at Falmouth; *Blossom* (1887),

Peggy (1890) and *Elswick II* (1930) at the Tyne and Wear Museum; the *Kindly Light* (1911) at Cardiff, and *Provident* (1924) at Brixham. Other vessels preserved out of water include the *Kathleen and May* 1900 in St Mary Overy Dock, London, *Gipsy Moth IV* (1966) at Greenwich, and *Lively Lady* (1948) at Portsmouth. Their steamships include, *Lydia Eva* (1930) at Great Yarmouth, *Robin* (1890) and *Portwey* (1927) in London. Other vessels under restoration include HMS *Gannet* (1878) and HSL (S) 376 at Chatham, the latter an 1889 tender to the Royal Yacht at Gosport, *Ellen* (1889) at Falmouth, and the dinghy *Hope* (1914). Their biggest project is RRS *Discovery*, currently under restoration as part of a major exhibition about polar research in Dundee. The Trust's purpose is not to collect ships but to foster their

(a)   (b)

Figure 14.3 (a) The clipper, *Cutty Sark*, built in 1869, was restored by Captain Dowman of Falmouth in 1922–38. Brought ashore at Greenwich in 1952, she has since attracted over 13 million paying visitors (courtesy Maritime Trust). (b) The Maritime Trust's historic steam vessel, *Robin*, built in London in 1890, now lies alongside the Grade I listed warehouses of India Dock, London built in 1802. Appropriate re-use of this site is a major future challenge (Courtesy of R.C.D. Baldwin)

preservation, for it is seen that these vessels can provide education and an inspiration to future generations. In consequence several restored ships have been handed on to the care of other institutions.

Two other truly significant preserved iron ships are I.K. Brunel's *Great Britain* (1843) at Bristol and HMS *Warrior* (1860) now at Portsmouth. English Heritage, the National Heritage Memorial Fund and the Fund for Scientific and Technological Material have helped preserve and restore these and other important ships through trusts dedicated to the particular ships. Major achievements are the preservation of HMS *Cavalier* (1944) at Brighton, HMS *Chrysanthemum* (1918), HMS *President* (1918), HQS *Wellington* (1934) and HMS *Belfast* (1938) in London and HMS *Caroline* (1914) in Belfast, and the submarine *Holland 1* (1901) at Gosport. A private trust has secured the preservation in working condition of the famous J class yacht *Velsheda*. Major challenges for the future include HMS *Unicorn* (1824) at Dundee, the CS *John W. Mackay* (1922, but the last of the steam cable ships), and the return and restoration of the four-masted *County of Peebles* (1875) from Punta Arenas, Chile, to join other preserved ships, notably *Carrick* (1864), in Glasgow. These important British achievements are just part of a huge international effort devoted since the 1950s to ship preservation, which can be grasped by consulting the *International Register of Historic Ships* by Norman Brouwer. This lists over 700 ships, but is currently being updated to include many Eastern European ships.

There are canal museums at Stoke Bruerne, Gloucester, and Ellesmere Port which include preserved canal boats. The large boat collection afloat at Exeter Maritime Museum may survive despite its financial difficulties. Many small and traditional sailing craft are to be found, sometimes working, in coastal and riverine locations. The Windermere Steamboat Museum at Bowness houses a unique collection assembled by G. Pattison, and includes *Dolly*, the oldest mechanically powered boat in the world. The most extensive small-boat collection in Europe is gathered at Douarnenez, in Brittany. The finest British collection of Roman and medieval ships and cargo handling equipment is at the Museum of London, owing to twenty years of carefully concerted waterfront and industrial archaeology.

At the International Congress of Maritime Museums in Amsterdam, held in the autumn of 1992, the work of the new UK National Advisory Committee on Ship Preservation was described. It is advised in turn by a technical subcommittee of naval architects to ensure the best use of the very limited financial resources and skills available. Judgement about the feasibility of preserving historic ships is wisely left to experienced and qualified naval architects. Until 1993 the National Maritime Museum retained a Naval Architect who was regularly consulted by the national grant-giving agen-

cies. His wealth of professional experience was available to advise on most related matters, including the formal expectations of Lloyd's Register and other ship classification societies, and the requirements set down by the Department of Transport. In future the Nautical Institute and the Institute of Marine Engineers may proffer such help, as may more locally available members of the Royal Institution of Naval Architects.

Ship preservation depends in part on keeping alive various traditional skills, particularly those associated with wooden boatbuilding and cordage manufacture. Notable ventures here are the restoration of Brunel's block mills at Portsmouth and the retention of the ropery at Chatham which remains operational with machinery dating back to 1811. The potential of the Georgian timber seasoning sheds at Chatham is likewise obvious. Organization of the international tall ships gatherings and the experience of sail training has kept traditional skills of ship handling alive, and secured an increase in the number of sailable tall ships. In England the Sail Training Association and others have fostered the experience for young people from all walks of life. The Thames Traditional Boat Society has also provided a forum for private wooden boat-owning enthusiasts. *Classic Boat* has become the magazine representing the considerable practical enthusiasm of this sector, who gather for an annual Wooden Boat Show at the National Maritime Museum, Greenwich, and at the Mariners Museum, Newport News, Virginia.

Marine archaeology

The importance of underwater wreck sites lies in the self-contained nature of the community of a ship at the moment of its loss, and in the curious fact that only misadventure has preserved a ship whose working sisters have been scrapped. Such ships might be anywhere in the world, perhaps even lying in international waters. Sometimes they may be in waters where there is no effectual legal protection. Significant sites are very numerous, because organic material often survives well in underwater sites. Such sites are much at risk from worm action and tidal scouring, and from the consequences of new sea defences, groynes, and outfalls. Apart from modern fishing methods, mineral extraction, and commercial salvage, simple treasure hunting or pillage by unscrupulous or unknowing divers take further toll. Sites can even be endangered by abandoned archaeological activity and associated piling, as the example of the VOC *Amsterdam* (1748) is revealing. The *Amsterdam*'s accessibility at low tide also illustrates further legal problems if ownership and access to vessels falls across the low-water mark, for national and local jurisdictions, entail separate sets of obligations (*Figure 14.4*).

Figure 14.4 A view taken in 1984 of VOC *Amsterdam*, wrecked near Hastings in 1749, illustrates why historic shipwrecks require controlled access to secure future archaeological opportunities (courtesy of R.C.D. Baldwin)

Her example also illustrates the damage caused by the unrestricted use of mechanical excavators in 1969–70, and the problems associated with securing the long-term finance necessary to undertake a complete archaeological excavation of so large a vessel as a Dutch East Indiaman. There are even worse problems associated with the wreck site of the English East India-man *Admiral Gardner*, which suffered seriously from damage done by the mechanical grabs used to recover her cargo, as have other East Indiamen wrecked in international waters, or off coasts where there is no effective or scrupulous archaeological control. The Foreign and Commonwealth Office is now consider-ing how to use its residual interest in English East Indiamen around the world, so as to protect those wrecks from depredation.

Ministry of Defence officials have tried to protect ships of the Royal Navy and ships taken as historical prizes from similar depredation, especially if they are war graves, but they have no formal archaeological remit. They have therefore normally only handed over such shipwrecks to archaeological trusts whom they judge able to undertake the responsibilities of owner-ship, like the Mary Rose Trust and the Warship Anne Trust. The Anglo-Russian Diplomatic Protocol under which 1187 gold bars were recovered in 1981 and 1986

from HMS *Edinburgh*, lost in 1942, provides a contrast that illustrates the nature of commercial salvage.

All this is despite the fact that the activities of hydrographic surveyors in the service of the Royal Navy did much to establish the basis of modern archaeology between 1810 and 1870. While the Ancient Monuments Act of 1882 only envisaged controlling landward archaeological sites, the Ancient Monuments and Archaeological Areas Act of 1979 did envisage the marine context. It did not materially change the formal emphasis, but it provided for finds of interest to be taken into the temporary custody of museums and for some control over the export of items recovered from the soil or seabed of Britain unless they had been buried there for less than 50 years. In consequence museums have to be satisfied the law is being complied with, and not being used to encourage the deliberate damage of archaeological sites protected by law. Museums have consequently been reluctant to take a positive role, but this is chan-ging thanks to the influence of the Nautical Archae-ology Society, the Mary Rose Trust, the Isle of Wight Archaeological Trust and the Nautical Museums Trust, all of which have been involved in seeking preserva-tion and interpretation of this heritage. So a Joint National Archaeology Policy Committee comprising the National Maritime Museum, the Institute of Field

Archaeologists, the Society for Nautical Research, the Council of British Archaeology and the Nautical Archaeology Society was formed to seek administrative and legislative reforms for the marine heritage.

The central management problem remains that the principal legal provisions were formed to regulate commercial salvage when the discipline of archaeology was still in its infancy, and nobody anticipated that the technology would exist to conduct archaeological recording of wreck sites. The Merchant Shipping Acts of 1894 and 1913 are now to a significant extent

Figure 14.5 Items recovered from the *Mary Rose* included a wooden tig, a pewter jug, wooden dishes, combs, a manicure set and various items of cutlery

in conflict with the ethos of the later Protection of Wrecks Act 1973. The latter Act, which transformed attitudes, was framed in the light of a spectacular popular success in terms of marine archaeology, namely the rediscovery in 1971 of the *Mary Rose* (1509), later put on view in Portsmouth Dockyard (*Figure 14.5*). However it took the evident need to protect various Armada wrecks, and the Sussex wrecks of HMS *Anne* (lost in 1692) and VOC *Amsterdam*, to secure the legislative change.

The Protection of Wrecks Act 1973 set out a basis for the designation of a historic wreck site 'on account of the historical, archaeological or artistic importance of the vessel, or any objects contained in it or formerly contained in it which may be lying on the sea bed'. The procedure involves consideration by the Advisory Committee on Historic Wreck Sites before the Secretary of State for Environment can designate such a site by statutory instrument. Within the designated area it is an offence to tamper with, damage, remove or salve any part of the wrecked vessel, or to obstruct access without a specific licence. The Advisory Committee determines the conditions and restrictions necessary to protect the archaeological value of the site, or to secure its thorough archaeological survey. The Archaeological

Diving Unit at St Andrews University has a limited capability to investigate, record and monitor such sites on behalf of that committee.

If anyone undertakes any wreck site survey, they must notify and hand over any artefacts raised to the Receiver of Wreck of the Department of Transport because Part IX of the Merchant Shipping Act 1894, slightly amended by the Merchant Shipping Act 1906, still applies. However, Section 53 of the Archaeological Areas Act remains largely unused as a means of protecting wreck sites, although the Secretary of State did designate one highly dangerous wreck site, the SS *Richard Montgomery* (1944) near Sheerness. The locations of all such designated sites are initially advertised in the press and *Notices to Mariners*, and where practicable on the largest-scale Admiralty chart of the area. Booklet NP96 on the work of the Hydrographic Office's Wreck Section gives further guidance and advice to those who encounter shipwrecks and aircraft that have crashed into the sea.

Some sites, notably those off the Isle of Wight, are further protected by the Coastal Protection Act 1949, under which local district authorities who actually took up powers to control seabed extraction up to 5 km from the low-water mark can regulate archaeological activity too. Protection for aircraft lost at sea is afforded by the Protection of Military Remains Act 1986. In Northern Ireland the Historic Monuments Act 1971 applies instead of the above mentioned 1979 Act, while in Guernsey the Wreck and Salvage (Vessels and Aircraft) (Bailiwick of Guernsey) Law 1986 has helped secure the recording of the Roman merchantman located at the entrance of St Peter Port harbour.

The formal handover of responsibilities for historic shipwrecks from the Department of Transport to the Secretary of State for Environment (who already formally held responsibilities for landward sites) left some problems created by the Department of Transport *Historic Wrecks Guidance Note to Receivers of Wreck* of 1986, which followed three seemingly worthwhile principles, namely:

(1) that artefacts from historic wrecks should remain accessible to the general public;
(2) that such collections should remain together;
(3) that items of particular interest should be offered first to national museums, and then to local museums.

But the Merchant Shipping (Fees) 1980 Regulations have sometimes frustrated the best of intentions, because in the process of administering a salvage award the Receiver of Wreck is required to deduct his expenses and 7.5 per cent from any salvage award paid to the salvor (or finder). If the owner does not make a claim, the Receiver of Wreck is then obliged to dispose of unwanted items. This does much to ensure that historical finds of significance still have to be sold, a course which perhaps puts locally recovered items beyond the financial means of local museums.

In the international context some of the best heritage practice is to be found in Western Australia. There the international value and nature of their maritime heritage in wreck sites is fully recognized in law, and evident in their successful museum practice (see J. Green, *Navigators and Shipwrecks, Australia's Heritage*, 1985). A conference held in Vancouver in 1983 entitled *Nautical Archaeology, Progress and Public Responsibility*, later published in 1984, included an international survey of the law and nautical archaeology by P. J. O'Keefe. The Historic American Buildings Survey published *Guidelines for Recording Historic Ships* in 1988, the same year as Unesco published a *Code of Practice for Scientific Diving*.

British achievements in the management of our archaeological heritage are rather eclipsed by those of the state governments of Western Australia and British Columbia. Since 1959 the latter state alone has created 28 marine parks of special interest between Discovery Island and the Queen Charlotte Islands, including the vast 8500 ha site of Desolation Sound, and other historic sites designated as natural heritage sites. The Curatorial Division of the Canadian National Parks Service acted in conjunction with the Royal British Columbian Museum to secure the archaeological heritage of these areas and the many west coast shipwreck sites, but in a way that encourages seaborne access and respectful and informed public appreciation. Similar ideas have informed the legal changes passed in the United States in 1990 to protect sites of special marine archaeological significance.

In Britain the National Maritime Museum has reduced its marine archaeology unit to one part-time non-diving archaeologist. However, the Nautical Archaeology Society now offers a preliminary education and training course in conjunction with the British Sub Aqua Club. The Council for British Archaeology has drawn attention to the best international practice and sought to get an agreed European Convention adopted in respect of shipwreck sites of historical significance, but it has been dogged by problems arising in the Mediterranean and the Aegean. The Universities at St Andrews and Bangor offer postgraduate MA and MSc courses in marine archaeology with well informed staff and conservation facilities. Courses in maritime history can be found in syllabuses taught at London, Hull, Liverpool, Durham and Bangor Universities, while naval architecture and marine engineering are taught at Glasgow and Newcastle Universities. The Warsash College of Nautical Studies at Southampton University provides a range of maritime teaching for those engaged in shipping and for those wanting training in marine management, maritime leisure management and oceanography. The Marine Society, founded in 1756, extends similar scope to serving British mariners through its training college at Greenhithe and through shipboard library services.

Following the publication of the report of the Joint National Archaeology Policy Committee in May 1989, entitled *Heritage at Sea*, the government proposed improvements under the provisions of a White Paper *This Common Inheritance* published in 1990. It envisaged transfer of certain functions from the Department of Transport to ensure that the responsibility for historic wreck site designation is discharged by the Secretary of State for Environment, or by the corresponding agencies in Scotland, Northern Ireland and Wales. In consequence the Royal Commission for Historic Monuments has begun to compile and pay for a central register of historic wreck sites, initially utilizing Hydrographic Office data. The logic should be that coastal marine sites will be treated on an equal basis with land sites of archaeological importance, but there has been delay in reallocating resources accordingly. This situation should change as Kent, East Sussex and Hampshire are now systematically recording historic underwater sites.

The National Maritime Museum holds records of 4000 British wrecks and nearly 10,000 world-wide, and operates at Valhalla on Tresco in the Scilly Isles a small museum devoted to the heritage of local shipwrecks based on a collection of salvaged figureheads. The Hydrographic Office of the Ministry of Defence holds well over 100,000 wreck records but the archaeological information they contain is often just incidental. They have successfully cooperated with county archaeologists in the Isle of Wight, East Sussex, Dyfed, Essex, Kent, Hampshire and Shetland to add many underwater sites to those county site and monument records. It is to be hoped that this will be extended with the financial support of the Royal Commission on Historic Monuments to other coastal counties during the 1990s.

Hampshire and Dorset County Councils have produced sensible strategies for taking further their responsibility in these areas, and they enjoy the support of the Association of County Archaeological Officers and the Institute of Field Archaeologists. In this way it is to be hoped that other underwater sites will be added both to the National Archaeological Record and to the county sites and monuments records. Thereafter the scope for training archaeologists and historians, educating divers, and improving the surveying, excavation and conservation of sites with endangered elements can be put on a sounder basis. Identification of wreck sites using public records should also be improved. Up to 1993 there were just 42 British wreck sites identified as Historic Wreck Sites.

The Nautical Archaeology Society undertakes such surveys and runs training programmes in the techniques of underwater archaeology, as well as organizing conferences and the publication of the *International Journal of Nautical Archaeology* – the foremost journal of its kind in the world. Another charity, Marine Archaeological Surveys, helps in this work and in active surveying with the help of members of the Nautical Archaeology Society. Another body which has played a significant role is the Nautical Museums Trust, which was founded in 1982 to preserve the maritime heritage in shipwrecks and make the results of research on them available to the public. It has since opened the Shipwreck Heritage Centre at Hastings to interpret one of richest displays of wreck sites visible at low tide in Europe, and lobbied to protect similar sites. It has been active in pressing for the creation of a limited number of maritime heritage parks. The special powers conferred on the county in 1949 are being wisely exploited by the Isle of Wight Trust for Maritime Archaeology, and the Isle of Wight Planning and Cultural Services Department.

In 1992 marine archaeologists showed the potential of cooperation with the new National Rivers Authority in saving the Rye barge *Primrose* (*c.* 1890). At Hartlepool the county has managed to coordinate the industrial archaeology of the harbour with archaeological recording and restoration of the *Foudroyant*, built at Bombay in 1817, and the planning of an expanded maritime museum. Policy for many sites in the north of England has become much clearer following publication late in 1992 of a study by Alison Gale for the North of England Museums Service entitled *Catching the Tide*. In West Wales, two small underwater sites of especial natural interest have actually been designated marine parks, and another covering the Menai Strait was announced to Parliament in 1994 as 'virtually agreed'. These agreements follow the model of similar primacy for the natural and archaeological context at historic sites in care of the National Parks Service in Canada and the USA and the examples of the Great Lakes in particular. The International Conference of Maritime Museums will surely take note of these precedents in its consideration of our international important marine heritage.

General conclusions

A hugely positive change has come to pass in attitude towards the maritime heritage in the last 50 years as a strictly commercial and industrial view of the sea has given way to the present balance. There is now more available for public appreciation, and yet much more could still be done in many seaside towns and villages. A basic golden rule of heritage management applies to our archaeological record: do not encourage the disturbance or salvage from sites that might be important to our marine heritage. However, if precise records of a wreck's location in terms of latitude and longitude, or in terms of radio navigation coordinates or grid references can be offered in conjunction with positive identification of a historic site, the data may well be of value to the compilation of a nation-wide marine site and monuments record. There is plenty of historical research and conservation work still to be done on existing maritime collections and ships. Those who have the time, energy and skill could well be directed towards existing institutions and societies who rarely have enough volunteers and members to meet all the demands of conserving our vast maritime heritage for the future. As the numbers of professional mariners decrease, technical questions about ship handling and navigation will increase; today much of that curiosity is proving to be genealogical, historical or related to natural history.

The interested public may seek extramural university courses, or educational events arranged by museums and societies. Genuine researchers are generally better directed in the first instance to local archival and historical sources and then to the counsels of experienced curators, rather than diving untrained into ecologically and the archaeologically frail marine contexts with all their associated conservation challenges. Encouragement ought to be given to heritage managers and curators to build relationships of trust and understanding with those interested in our maritime heritage, whether ashore or underwater. Good working relationships with divers, deployed with an informed corpus of specialist knowledge, should secure the practical protection of our underwater heritage. The major challenge of securing a coherent future will rest on the heritage manager's application of cost/benefit analysis to both the natural history and the shipborne elements of our maritime heritage.

Useful addresses

Archaeological Diving and Advisory Unit, c/o St Andrews University, St Andrews, fife, Scotland. Te. 0334 629 19

British Library, Bloomsbury, London, WC1 3DG. Tel. 071 636 1544 except, Oriental and India Office Collections, Blackfriars Road, London, SE1. Tel. 071 412 7873

CADW, Welsh Historic Monuments Executive Agency, Brunel House, 2 Fitzallan Street, Cardiff, CF2 1HY. Tel. 0222 465 511

Chatham Historic Dockyard, Chatham, Kent. Tel. 0634 812551

Department of Environment for Northern Ireland, National Monuments and Buildings Branch, 533 Hill Street, Belfast, BT1 2LA. Tel. 031 244 3108

Glasgow Museum of Transport, 25 Albert Drive, Glasgow. Tel. 041 423 8000

Guildhall Library, Aldermanbury, London, EC2 Tel. 071 606 3030

Historic Scotland, 20 Brandon Street, Edinburgh, EH1 5RA. Tel. 031 244 3108

HMS Victory and Royal Naval Museum, HM Naval Base, Portsmouth, Hampshire. Tel. 0705 22351

Hydrographic Office, Ministry of Defence (Navy), Taunton, Somerset, TA1 2DN. Tel. 0823 337900

Maritime Museum of East Anglia, Marine Parade, Great Yarmouth. Tel. 0493 2267

Museum of London, 150 London Wall, London, EC2Y 4HN. Tel. 071 600 3699 (or 071 538 0209 for Port of London Library)

Museums and Galleries Commission, 16 Queen Anne's Gate, London, SW1H 9AA. Tel. 072 233 4200

National Maritime Museum, Park Row, Greenwich, London, SE10 9NF. Tel. 081 858 4422

National Museum of Science & Industry, Exhibition Road, London, SW7 2DD. Tel. 071 938 8000

National Museums on Merseyside, Maritime Museum, Albert Dock, Liverpool, L3 4AA. Tel. 051 207 0001

National Register of Archives, Quality Court, London, WC2. Tel. 071 242 1198

Nautical Archaeology Society, c/o Institute of Archaeology, 31–34 Gordon Square, London, WC1H OPY

Nautical Museums Trust, Shipwreck Heritage Centre, Rock A Nore, Hastings, East Sussex. Tel. 0424 437452

Public Records Office, Ruskin Avenue, Kew. Tel. 081 878 3444

Receiver of Wreck, Marine Emergency Administration Division, Department of Transport, Spring Place, 105 Cromwell Road, Southampton, SO1 0ZD. Tel. 0703 329 100

Royal Institution of Naval Architects, 10 Upper Belgrave Square, London, SW1X 8BQ. Tel. 071 235 4622

The Salvage Association, Bankside House, Leadenhall Street, London, EC3A 4AA. Tel. 071 623 1299

Scottish Fisheries Museum, St Ayles, Harbourhead, Anstruther, Fife, Scotland. Tel. 0333 310628

Town Docks Museum, Queen Victoria Square, Kingston upon Hull, Humberside. Tel. 0482 224316

Welsh Industrial and Maritime Museum, Bute Street, Docks, Cardiff. Tel. 0222 371805

Windermere Steamboat Museum, Rayrigg Road, Bowness, Cumbria. Tel. 09662 2117

Bibliography

General British naval and mercantile history

ALBION, R. G. (1975) *Naval and Maritime History: an Annotated Bibliography*, David and Charles, Newton Abbot

BALDWIN, P. (1991) 'Trans-oceanic Commerce', *RSA Journal*, October

BALDWIN, R. C. D. (1994) 'The fate of Trinity House's Library and Archives', *Map Collector*, No. 67

BARNABY, K. C. (1948) *Basic Naval Architecture*, Hutchinson, London

BEAVIS, L. R. W. (1986) *Passage from Sail to Steam*, Vancouver Maritime Museum and University of Washington State Press, Seattle

BURWASH, D. (1969) *English Merchant Shipping, 1460–1540*, David and Charles, Newton Abbot

CAMERON, A. and FARNDON, R. (1984) *Scenes from Sea and City, Lloyd's List 1734–1984*, Lloyd's List, London

COLLEGE, J. C. (1969) *Ships of the Royal Navy: An Historical Index*, David and Charles, Newton Abbot (Revised 1990)

CORLETT, E. (1975) *The Iron Ship*, Moonraker Press, Bradford-on-Avon

DAVIES, R. (1972) *The Rise of the English Merchant Shipping Industry in the Seventeenth and Eighteenth Centuries*, David and Charles, Newton Abbot

FRANCIS, C. and TUTE, W. (1981) *The Commanding Sea*, BBC and Pelham Books, London

GENEALOGICAL SOCIETY, (1986) *My Ancestor was a Merchant Seaman*, London

HALLMAN, R. (1984) *Coastal Britain*, Batsford, London

HARLAND, J. (1984) *Seamanship in the Age of Sail*, Conway Maritime Press, London

HEWSON, J. B. (1983) *A History of the Practice of Navigation*, Brown and Ferguson, Glasgow

HOUSE OF LORDS SELECT COMMITTEE ON SCIENCE AND TECHNOLOGY, (1992) *Safety Aspects of Ship Design and Technology*, H.L. Paper 30.1, HMSO, London

JONES, G. (1987) *A History of the Vikings*, Oxford University Press, Oxford

KEAY, J. (1991) *The Honourable Company. A History of the English East India Company*, Harper Collins, London

KEMP, P. (1976) *The Oxford Companion to Ships and the Sea*, Oxford University Press, Oxford

LANDSTROM, B. (1976) *The Ship*, Allen and Unwin, London

LARKIN, D. and SPECTRE, P. H. (1991) *Wooden Ship: the Art, History and Revival of Wooden Shipbuilding*, Houghton Mifflin, Boston, Mass

LAVERY, B. (1990) *The Arming and Fitting of Ships of War, 1660–1815*, Conway Maritime Press, London

LOADES, D. M. (1992) *The Tudor Navy*, Scholar Press, Aldershot

MCCONNELL, A. (1982) *No Sea too Deep: The History of Oceanographic Instruments*, Adam Hilger, Bristol

MacGREGOR, D. R. (1988) *Fast Sailing Ships: their Design and Construction, 1775–1875*, Conway Maritime Press

MARCUS, G. J. (1975) *Heart of Oak: A Survey of British Sea Power in the Georgian Era*, Oxford University Press, Oxford

PARRY, J. H. (1971) *Trade and Dominion*, Wiedenfield and Nicholson, London

QUINN, D. B. and RYAN, A. N. (1983) *England's Sea Empire, 1550–1642*, Allen and Unwin

REDIKER, M. (1987) *Between the Devil and the Deep Blue Sea: Merchant Seamen, Pirates and the Anglo-American World*, Cambridge University Press, Cambridge

RITCHIE, G. S. (1967) *The Admiralty Chart, British Naval Hydrography in the Nineteenth Century*, Hollis and Carter, London

REYNOLDS, C. G. (1976) *The Command of the Sea – The History and Strategy of Maritime Empires*, J. Hale, London

RODGER, N. A. M. (1986) *Naval Records for the Genealogist*, HMSO, London

RODGER, N. A. M. (1986) *The Wooden World*, Collins, London

ROSE, S. (1982) *The Navy of the Lancastrian Kings*, Allen and Unwin, London

SHAW, B. (1992) 'Shipping and the Future of Europe', *RSA Journal*

VINSON, S. (1994) *Egyptian Boats and Ships*, Shire Publications, Princes Risborough

WHEATLEY, K. (1990) *The National Maritime Museum Guide to Maritime Britain*, Webb and Bower, London

WILLIAMS, J. E. D. (1992) *From Sails to Satellites – the Origin and Development of Navigational Science*, Oxford Science Publications, Clarendon Press, Oxford

'Mariners Mirror', *Journal of the Society for Nautical Research*

Maritime museums and ship preservation

BOUDRIOT, J. (1983/84) *Monuments Historiques Grand Larges*, No. 130, Cnmh, Paris

BROUWER, N. J. (1985) *International Register of Historic Ships*, Anthony Nelson

BURTON, A. (1982) *The Past Afloat*, Andre Deutsch, London

KENTLEY, E. and SPENCE, D. (eds) (1990) *The National Maritime Museum: the Collections*, Scala Press, London

LAMBERT, A. (1987) *Warrior: Restoring the World's First Ironclad*, Conway Maritime, London

NEILL, P. (1988) *Maritime America, Art and Artifacts from America's Great Nautical Collections*, Balsam Press, New York

STAMMERS, M. K. and HEAL, V. (1988) *Discovering Maritime Museums and Historic Ships*, Shire Publications, Princes Risborough

Marine archaeology

ANDERSON, R. K. (1988) *Guidelines for Recording Historic Ships*, Historic American Buildings Survey and National Parks Service, Washington D.C.

CHETTLEBURGH, P. (1985) *An Explorer's Guide to the Maritime Parks of British Columbia*, Maclean Hunter, Vancouver

COLLINGS, P. (1988) *The Illustrated Directory of North East Shipwecks*, Collings and Brodie, Chester-le-Street

DRAPER, S. (1992) *Shipwrecks*, National Maritime Museum, Greenwich

FERGUSON, D. M. (1985) *The Wrecks of Scapa Flow*, Orkney Press, Stromness

FITZHUGH, W. W. and OLIN, J. (1993) *Archaeology of the Frobisher Voyages*, Smithsonian Institute Press, Washington, D.C.

GREEN, J. (1985) *Navigators and Shipwrecks*, Australia's Heritage, Australia Press, Perth

GREENHILL, B. (1976) *Archaeology of the Boat*, A & C Black, London

DEPARTMENT OF ENVIRONMENT (1990) *Government Response to Heritage at Sea*, DOE, 17 December

HOCKING, C. (1969) *Dictionary of Marine Disasters, 1824–1962* (2 vols), Lloyd's Register of Shipping, Crawley

HOOKE, N. (1989) *Modern Shipping Disasters, 1963–87*, Lloyd's of London Press, Colchester

HYDROGRAPHIC OFFICE (1993) *N.P.96*, Wrecks Section, Taunton

HUTCHINSON, G. (1989) *Heritage at Sea: Proposals for a Better Protection of Archaeological Sites Underwater*, Joint National Archaeology Policy Committee, National Maritime Museum, Greenwich

LANGLEY, S. B. M., O'KEEFE, P. J. O. and UNGER, R. (1984) *Nautical Archaeology—Progress and Public Responsibility*, B.A.R. International Series, 220

MARSDEN, P. (1985) *The Wreck of the Amsterdam*, Hutchinson, London

MARSDEN, P. (1988) *Shipwrecks of South East England*, Batsford, London

MEDLAND, J. C. (1986) *Shipwrecks of the Isle of Wight*, IWCP, Freshwater

MILNE, G. (1984) *The Roman Port of London*, Batsford, London

MILNE, G. and HOBLEY, B. (1981) *Waterfront Archaeology in Britain and Northern Europe*, Council of British Archaeology Research Report, London

WILLIAMS, D. L. (1992) *Salvage*, Ian Allen, Hampton Court

International Journal of Nautical Archaeology, Academic Press, London

Maritime communities

BALDWIN, R. C. D. (1992) 'The London Operations of the East India Company', *South Asia Library Group Newsletter*, No. 39

BENHAM, H. (1980) *The Salvagers*, Essex County Newspapers, Colchester

CARR, R. M. J. (1986) *Dockland: An Illustrated Historical Survey of Life and Work in East London*, North East London Polytechnic and Thames and Hudson, London

COAD, J. (1989) *The Royal Dockyards, Architecture and Engineering Works of the Sailing Navy, 1690–1850*, Scholar Press/Royal Commission on Historical Monuments, Aldershot

EVANS, E. S. P. (1978) *Buildings of Liverpool*, Heritage Bureau, Liverpool

JEFFREYS, D. E. (1978) *Maritime Memories of Cardiff*, Starling Press, Newport

LENMAN, B. (1975) *From Esk to Tweed: Harbours Ships and Men of the East Coast of Scotland*, Blackie, Glasgow

MOSS, M. and HUME, J. (1977) *Workshop of the British Empire*, Heinemann, London

RITCHIE, A. (1985) *Exploring Scotland's Heritage*, RCAHM (Scotland), HMSO

Legal and environmental matters

ARCHAEOLOGICAL DIVING UNIT (1994) *A list of sites and publications related to historic wreck sites designated under the Protection of Wrecks Act 1973*, St Andrew's University, St Andrew's

BRITISH STANDARDS INSTITUTE, (1989) *Recommendations for the storage and exhibition of archival documents*, BSI, London

CHARITIES AID FOUNDATION (1993) *Directory of Grant-making Trusts*, CAF, Pembury

CLIFFORD CHANCE, (1991) *Environmental Law Guide*, Lloyds of London Press, Colchester

DARLING, G. (1993) *LOF 90 and the New Salvage Convention*, Lloyds of London Press, Colchester

DONALDSON (1994) *Safer Ships, Cleaner Seas - Report of Lord Donaldson's inquiry into the prevention of pollution from merchant shipping presented to Parliament by the Secretary of State for Transport*, Cmnd 2560, May, HMSO, London

DOUGLAS, R. P. A. (1993) *The Law of Harbours and Pilotage*, Lloyds of London Press, Colchester

FISHER, J. and LOCKLEY (1954) *Sea-Birds, New Naturalist Series*, Vol. 28, Collins, London

FORRESTER, S. (1989) *Environmental grants; A guide to grants available for the environment from the Government, companies and charitable trusts*, A Directory of Social Change Publication

GOLDREIN, J. (1993) *Ship Sale and Purchase*, Lloyds of London Press, Colchester

HETHERINGTON, J. A. and SHEPHERD, J. G. (1975) *Observations on the use of cost-benefit analysis in the control of radioactive waste disposal*, Technical Report 17, MAFF, Fisheries Radiobiological Laboratory, Lowestoft

DEPARTMENT OF ENVIRONMENT. (1991) *This Common Inheritance*, A White Paper, HMSO, London

KINNE, O. (1977) *Marine Ecology*, (5 vols) John Wiley, Chichester

LEE, A. J. and RAMSTER, J. W. (1981) *Atlas of the Seas around the British Isles*, MAFF and British Oceanographic Data Centre, Bidston

MUSEUMS AND GALLERIES COMMISSION (1990) *Guidelines for a Registration Scheme for Museums in the United Kingdom*, MGC, London

MEESON, N. (1993) *Admiralty Jurisdiction and Practice*, Lloyds of London Press, Colchester

SEAWARD, D. R. (1982) *Sea Area Atlas of the Marine Molluscs of Britain and Ireland*, Conchology Trust and the Nature Conservancy Council, London

STARKE, J. G. (1994) *Introduction to International Law*, (11th edition) Butterworths, London

Case study 14.1

The Hampshire and Wight Trust for Maritime Archaeology

Brian Sparks

Against the background of the *Mary Rose* and other work in the area during the early and mid 1980s, the Isle of Wight set up a Maritime Heritage Project which concentrated on the Yarmouth Roads wreck site. This protected site is believed to contain the wreck of the sixteenth century merchant carrack *Santa Lucia*.

In 1990 the Isle of Wight Trust for Maritime Archaeology was formed. At about the same time, the County Archaeologist for Hampshire prepared a report on maritime archaeology in Hampshire which led to a seminar being held in the Royal Naval Museum in April 1991, with representation from both sides of the Solent.

With the backing of both County Councils, the joint Hampshire and Wight Trust for Maritime Archaeology was formally launched in June 1991. Four months later a Director was appointed and an office was set up on the Highfield campus of the University of Southampton. On the Island, the Trust inherited a Maritime Heritage Exhibition at Fort Victoria, a boat and some equipment. Mooring and workshop facilities have been made available at Fishbourne Quay, IoW.

Details of the Trust

Policies

The Trust's Memorandum of Association has an objective of 'the advancement of education of the public in maritime archaeology and heritage'. The last word gives the Trust a wide remit. The policies cover research, education and coordination.

Organization

The Chairman of the Trust is the Chairman of the Management Committee. This committee deals with the wider aspects of the Trust's business such as fund-raising, publicity, budgets, exhibitions and administration. The Archaeological Working Group oversees the Trust's archaeological programme. In addition to the Director, the Trust currently employs a Field Officer and a Research Assistant. Secretarial and administrative tasks are shared between these employees.

Area of operation

This covers Sea Area Wight and the immediate coastal hinterlands of Hampshire and the Isle of Wight.

Archaeological programme

The Working Group recommended and the Management Committee subsequently endorsed the need for a structured approach to the archaeological programme, which took full recognition of the work that had already been completed or was being progressed by other authorities in the area. It was agreed that the Trust should adopt a balance between ship and non-ship activity. Bearing in mind the Trust's overall objective, it was decided that the drowned river valley of the Solent and its associated superb anchorage would be an appropriate theme for the initial core programme.

Projects

Research project: maritime archaeology and commercial surveys

While the relationship between developers and archaeologists on land is becoming well defined, stewardship of the marine environment has barely started. In parallel with work being done by the Joint Nautical Archaeology Policy Committee on developing a code of practice for seabed developers, Sarah Draper, the Trust's Field Officer, is undertaking a twelve-month research project (June 1992 to May 1993) which aims to develop procedures for managing the archaeological resource by examining the survey work currently undertaken by users of the marine environment.

All offshore activities organizations have been identified, contact has been established with the majority and information on legislative constraints has been collated.

In conjunction with the Oceanography Department, University of Southampton, a sub-bottom profiler and associated remote sensing survey equipment was trialled in 1992, resulting in the acquisition of a large volume of data which will be used later in the project to assess the potential for current survey practice to identify maritime archaeological sites.

This project is being part-funded by the Department of National Heritage and the Crown Estate.

Quarr/Wootton site

In 1981 some finds of Roman pottery were observed on Wootton beach on the north-west coast of the Isle of Wight. In 1984 and 1985 these were followed by quantities of Roman and medieval ceramics which had been recently disturbed by coastal processes. In 1991 the Isle of Wight County Archaeological Unit completed an assessment of the intertidal archaeology of the beach. A detailed archaeological survey of 5 km of coast is now being carried out.

The Trust is involved with the offshore dimension of this site and tasks will include:

(1) an underwater evaluation of the topography of Ryde Middle and Brambles paleoshoals to investigate the general character of Roman and medieval scatters and to compare the strewn material with the intertidal assemblage;
(2) a near shore evaluation of the submerged peat deposit and man-made structures off Wootton/Quarr beaches to compare the quality and intertidal dimensions of this neolithic, Bronze Age and Roman site;
(3) an underwater survey and sampling of the submerged paeloenvironmental deposits at Bouldner to obtain sea-level chronological data for the project.

The Needles wreck site (HMS *Pomone*)

The aim of the current work on this protected wreck site is to produce a detailed topographical survey in order to model and analyse the environmental mechanisms and their interaction with the ship. This will build on the considerable progress that has already been made in interpreting the distribution of various classes of material from the wreck. As a great deal is already known about the original vessel, understanding the distribution processes will provide a valuable control for other sites where the subject is not as well known.

Diving took place on this site in September and November 1992 and in 1993 and initiated work on the installation and fixing of survey points for the construction of the computerized topographical survey. As the survey will make use of several techniques, the current work on this site offers a good opportunity for training under the Nautical Archaeology Society's training scheme.

In an area with other unprotected wrecks close by, illicit diving is a threat to this site.

Base chart of the Solent

Hampshire County Council and the Royal Commission on the Historical Monuments of England grant-aided a temporary post for the Trust to translate the maritime archaeological information received from the RCHME into the Hampshire Sites and Monuments Record.

The data has enabled the production of a distribution map/chart of all known underwater archaeological sites in the Solent and Wight areas. Sites for future projects can be identified and the data compared with those held, for example, by the Crown Estate Commissioners.

Langstone Harbour

Hampshire County Council, the Trust Wessex Archaeology and the University of Portsmouth are undertaking an appraisal of foreshore and estuarine archaeological sites along the Hampshire coast. Because of the density of known discoveries of prehistoric and Roman material from the Langstone Harbour fringes, combined with local interest in sea-level and coastal changes, the following programme of work is planned over a period of three years:

(1) a detailed archaeological survey of the northern Langstone Harbour area and its islands;
(2) a core sampling programme of the harbour sediments;
(3) a survey of documentary and map sources to provide data on historically attested coastal changes;
(4) an appraisal of recent data from development sites, air photographs etc. to record recent changes in the coast/harbour geomorphology.

As data are collected they will be used to build up a series of geographical information system models by the Department of Geography, University of Portsmouth.

Mixon site

Claims by Hume Wallace that stones from the submerged Mixon reef, off Selsey Bill, were used in the construction of Roman buildings in the region, and that there were remains of a defensive wall on the rock outcrop, resulted in samples of the rock being collected in September 1992 for analysis at the University of Southampton.

Yarmouth Roads wreck site

Following work carried out by the Isle of Wight Maritime Heritage Project, the Trust is assisting with the preparation of a final report on this important protected wreck site.

It is hoped that publication of the evaluation work from the Yarmouth Roads wreck site monitoring programme will enable the Trust to demonstrate the need to preserve *in situ* submerged historic monuments of the Solent area.

Exhibitions

The Trust inherited a Maritime Heritage Exhibition at Fort Victoria, Isle of Wight, and has been able to make some modest improvements to it.

The Trust's triple-panel display has been exhibited at various locations where it has aroused interest in the work of the Trust and maritime archaeology in general.

Liaison and coordination

In order to achieve its objectives as an enabling umbrella organization, the Trust liaises with a large number of authorities and individuals both locally and nationally. These include:

Department of National Heritage
Dorset County Council
Hampshire County Council
Isle of Wight County Council
Local city and borough councils
Mary Rose Trust
Royal Naval Museum
West Sussex County Council
University of Southampton

University of Portsmouth
Council for British Archaeology, Wessex Region
Nautical Archaeology Society
Royal Commission on the Historical Monuments of England
Society for Nautical Research
Standing Committee on Problems Affecting the Coastline
Isle of Wight Training and Enterprise Council
Crown Estate
National Maritime Museum
English Heritage
Archaeological Diving Unit
Severn Estuary Levels Research Committee
Solent Forum

and a large number of private sector companies with an interest in the marine environment.

Case study 14.2

The warship *Vasa* and Swedish maritime archaeology

Lars-Åke Kvarning

The Baltic Sea has a very special quality of interest for maritime archaeology. The salinity is low, which makes it impossible for the shipworm *Teredo navalis* to live there. This of course has been well known to marine biologists, but the private researcher Anders Franzén was the first to realize what it meant for ship historians. The Baltic is the only sea where fleets of big ships have been sailing through the centuries and where sunken ships can be preserved for very long periods. Franzén devoted his research work to locating lost men-of-war from the sixteenth and seventeenth centuries.

In 1956 he found the royal warship *Vasa* which had capsized on her maiden voyage on 10 August 1628 –

still in Stockholm harbour waters. The salvage work that led to the raising of the ship in 1961 caught the interest of the whole world. Under close surveillance from the national and international media, this huge man-of-war was lifted from the seabed, where it had been lying at 32 metres for 333 years (*Figure 14.6*). The hull was still in one piece, even though the sterncastle and the beakhead had been broken. The objects registered when the salvage and the excavation were over numbered 24,000, of which 12,000 were constructional parts that were to go back into the ship during restoration.

A salvage operation like this had never been carried out, and it resulted in the oldest fully identified and

Figure 14.6 On 24 April 1961 the warship *Vasa* breaks the surface after 333 years lost, raised by the two pontoons *Oden* and *Frigg*. The world's press, radio and TV followed this unique event (Photo courtesy Vasa Museum, Stockholm)

complete ship in the world. First it was necessary to find a method of preserving the huge mass of water-logged wood, as this had never been done before. Those appointed responsible for the preservation found a Swedish patent owned by the forest company Mo and Domsjö using polyethylene glycol. This substance and the method used by the *Vasa* preservation department have since become the standard treatment in many cases of waterlogged wood.

A temporary museum was built where the public could see the ship and follow the preservation and also the restoration that started very soon after the salvage (*Figure 14.7*). It was a combined workshop and museum and it very soon became the most visited museum in Scandinavia. In 1990 the temporary arrangements were replaced by a permanent Vasa Museum where this imposing warship can be seen in a huge hall with surrounding exhibitions that place the ship in its context (*Figures 14.8, 14.9*).

One thing is certain: the *Vasa* adventure has had an enormous impact on maritime archaeology in Sweden. And yet the *Vasa* project did not have much to do with underwater archaeology. It was more of a very special and very delicate salvage operation followed by an archaeological excavation when the ship was out of the water. The part of the operation that came closest to underwater archaeology as we know it today was the thorough search of the seabed around the place where the *Vasa* had been standing on the bottom, to recover everything that had come loose from the ship during the centuries – among other things the majority of the 700 sculptures and ornate details that had been fixed to the outside of the ship.

Up to this point underwater archaeology in Sweden had not been an organized discipline but rather the bringing up of objects and parts from shipwrecks for commercial reasons, the main interest in salvaging these items being to sell them to museums or to private collectors. Furthermore there was no law to protect our underwater heritage when it came to shipwrecks. The existing law of 1942 protecting all land sites of ancient monuments only extended to old harbour constructions, man-made underwater barriers

Figure 14.7 View of the lower gun deck towards the bow of the *Vasa* after excavation. The mud that was in the ship is taken out and the decks are washed. Along the starboard side a gun carriage is lashed in front of each gun port. Through the square-shaped holes in the foreground, light and air were let down to the lower decks. The huge horitzontal beam in the background is the bitt around which the anchor cable was lashed.

Figure 14.8 The early seventeenth century warship *Vasa* in her new museum, where she can be experienced at seven levels from the keel up to the sterncastle. Several exhibitions surround the ship: 'Salvaging the *Vasa* ', 'His Majesty's Ship', 'Three Masters — Three Styles', (the carvers that made her decorations), 'Life on Board,' 'Sweden 1628' and the 'Computer Adventure' (allowing visitors to use a computer in experimenting with and exploring the ship) (photo: Gunnel Ilonen, Vasa Museum, Stockholm)

Figure 14.9 Starboard side of the royal warship *Vasa*. The different stairs lead to the wheelhouse and the two cabins. Rising behind is the high stern (photo: Hans Hammerskiöld for the Vasa Museum, Stockholm)

etc. The interest in shipwrecks caused by the salvaging of the *Vasa* and the growing interest in scuba diving made it necessary to consider some sort of law for the protection of shipwrecks.

In 1967 and 1971 additions were made to the law of 1942 protecting ancient monuments so that its protection of land sites also applied to shipwrecks 'if 100 years or more can be assumed to have passed since the ship was wrecked, and also to objects found in or close to such a wreck and connected to it'. The law was later revised and from 1 January 1989 it says: 'Also shipwrecks are ancient monuments if 100 years or more can be assumed to have passed since the ship was wrecked.' This means that – as on land – you cannot move, take away, excavate, cover or in any other way change or damage wrecks.

The right to make decisions concerning ancient monuments like shipwrecks was at the same time transferred from the Central Board of National Antiquities to the county administrations. The Central Board of National Antiquities retains its supervising role, and the National Maritime Museum remains the body for submissions and expert advice. It might also be worth mentioning that consent to investigate a shipwreck or any other underwater monument will only be given to institutions with knowledge in marine archaeology and other experts. Private divers can obtain permission to perform some investigations after a special examination. All investigations in Sweden are made in consultation with and under the surveillance of the Maritime Museum.

During the 1970s the Maritime Museum found it necessary to concentrate its maritime archaeological work on developing techniques for different underwater activities. One was to develop techniques for underwater archaeological excavations in order to bring them to the same scientific and technical level as the excavation of land sites, and also to see that they resulted in all the necessary documentation of results to make them accessible and useful for the future handling of the material. Another interesting field was to develop a good technique for documenting the wrecks of ships and boats, making it possible to analyse and interpret the remains in order to identify their construction and to carry out any necessary reconstruction. This of course is of great interest in the Baltic, where shipwrecks are often well preserved.

When the addition to the law of ancient monuments concerning shipwrecks was passed in 1967, the Maritime Museum at the same time took on the responsibility of compiling a register of all known shipwrecks older than 100 years and also all known ship losses around the Swedish coast. These registers are developed by recording reports from investigations, searches and surveys and also from reports on shipwrecks and ship losses in old newspapers etc. The collective name is the Swedish Maritime Archaeological Register. Today it holds information on more than

1000 shipwrecks and other maritime monuments and it also contains more than 10,000 particulars on ship losses in earlier times. Much of this is the result of research work carried out by the Maritime Museum, but much information about shipwrecks comes from scuba divers, with whom the Museum has good co-operation.

Information and education for those interested in maritime archaeology started in the 1960s, and scuba divers in particular have taken a big interest in these matters. The broadening of their views and their knowledge has been most important and educational courses have been a tradition in the Museum since then. This means that there has been and still is a fruitful connection between the divers and the Museum, which has been very important for the registration and description of underwater finds (*Figure 14.10*).

After the salvage of the *Vasa* there was an increased consciousness of the value of maritime archaeology, of the potential knowledge base in this new branch of archaeology. It was clear that there was an urgent need for trained marine archaeologists, a profession that did not exist until then. University courses in maritime archaeology at the Institution for Archaeology of the University of Stockholm started in 1975 in cooperation with the Maritime Museum, which

Figure 14.10 Wreck of paddle steamer *Eric Nordevall*, launched 1832 and lost 1856 in Lake Vättern in Sweden: depth at the wreck site is 45 metres (photo: K. Halt)

provides the lecturer and administrator for this education. A series of research projects mapping and exploring our maritime society is undertaken. This is the only university education in maritime archaeology that exists in Sweden, and there are few such courses world-wide.

15

Conservation techniques: nature conservation and countryside management

Graham Taylor

Britain, with its long history of occupation and traditional land uses, possesses landscapes and habitats of great diversity and beauty. The consequences of this are that conservation of the countryside and of wildlife is largely dependent on the activities of landowners and farmers and that, while taking land into protective ownership and management has its place, it is insufficient as a strategy for conservation.

In Chapter 11 the importance of public policy for agriculture and forestry and of planning policy in shaping the countryside was emphasized. In this chapter, the practical aspects of conservation are discussed, particularly the options available to practitioners in conservation.

A scientific basis for nature conservation

All plants and animals are relatively limited in their distribution. Evolution has led to a great diversity of species, each adapted to a particular type of location, its habitat. The climate, the soils, the effects of other species and the management practices of human beings all interact to create a complex set of habitats with characteristic assemblages of species of plants and the animals which depend upon them.

The science which aims to understand the relationships between living organisms and their physical and biological environment, ecology, is a relatively new science which came to maturity in the 1930s and 1940s. The practical application of the knowledge gained from the science of ecology helps to give a more rigorous science base to nature conservation in three ways:

(1) Through analysis, description and classification of habitats it is possible to identify particular rare or important examples which may then, if appropriate, be given a designation such as a site of special scientific interest.
(2) By an understanding of the processes which create or maintain a habitat it is possible to identify operations or influences which could damage or alter the habitat. In this way it is possible to notify owners of undesirable practices.
(3) The same sort of knowledge can be used to improve the diversity of habitats, to restore damage or even to create habitats.

It has to be admitted that knowledge of habitat management remains imperfect and probably always will. Also, it is important to emphasize that ecological knowledge is not the sole requirement for determining conservation strategies. There will always be an element of judgement and subjectivity. Nature conservation may have a scientific basis but the value of a habitat or the desirability of its conservation are judgements. This only serves to emphasize the need for rigorous analysis.

Responding to change: the options

It follows from the man-made origin of so many of our landscapes and habitats that it is changes in the traditional management which will usually trigger intervention for conservation purposes. The loss of habitats and the removal of landscape features such as hedgerows have become apparent from national surveys, alerting policy makers to serious trends. But at a more local level information on, for example, the loss of traditional hay meadows can lead to practical action too.

A small proportion of the countryside has the added protection of designation as sites of special scientific interest, but for the most part the regulation of activity in the countryside is limited. Most land management activities in farming and forestry do not qualify as development under the planning regulations.

So far, recourse to the law to prevent change has played a very modest role in preventing change. At the time of writing the government has tentatively proposed a last-resort power to prevent the removal of hedgerows. That power would be linked to an incentive payment scheme to keep the hedgerows in good order. As with any publicly funded conservation scheme, resources are bound to be limited, and so practitioners will need to discriminate between cases.

There are, essentially, five possible responses to undesirable change brought about by changing agricultural or other practices:

(1) to react creatively in order to turn change to the advantage of conservation;
(2) to offer advice to farmers and others in order to counter change;
(3) to offer selective incentives to farmers to discourage some changes and encourage other positive conservation activities;
(4) to acquire particularly important properties;
(5) to accept it, which is often the only practical response.

A creative approach to nature conservation

If regulation by public bodies is relatively restricted in its value in conserving landscapes and habitats, and persuasion and support to landowners rather more valuable, how do conservation bodies achieve influence?

In the past decade or so some nature conservationists have specialized in using the engine of change, particularly in the urban environment, to help create opportunities to further conservation. Four types of opportunity will serve to illustrate the approach:

Temporary open space   Major urban building projects often take many years to complete. During that time open space created by demolition can be rapidly developed, by agreement with the owners, to provide pocket urban wildlife habitats. Water bodies are particularly rapidly colonized and wild flower meadows and scrubland can be created in a year or two. Urban wildlife groups exist in London, Birmingham and other cities and they make use of these sites to increase environmental awareness through education and volunteering. Sometimes permanent urban wildlife parks can be created to which local people become very attached.
Net environmental benefit or planning gain   When land is taken for development, planning authorities often seek some compensating benefit. This may be a contribution to the cost of new roads or a community facility somehow associated with the development. It can also involve setting aside land to create new habitats to compensate for those lost or to enhance the area. A new science park in Crewe is greatly enhanced by attractive water bodies and other skillfully designed habitats which set off the high-tech industrial units.
Restoration   If development must take place, then restoration to a beneficial new conservation (or recreation) use has many

attractions. In Gloucester and Wiltshire the Cotswold Water Park is the legacy of a major gravel extraction industry. In Northumberland, open-cast coal mining has created two country parks and several valuable wildlife reserves.
Partnerships and sponsorships   Developers, especially those with a long-term involvement in an area, may well be receptive to ideas about improving their operations to make them 'greener', providing their employees with benefits and serving the wider community. Advice, sponsorship and help in kind can all be forthcoming.

Examples of all these approaches have been found in the recent garden festivals, where wildlife trusts and other conservation bodies have capitalized on the opportunities presented by the drive for redevelopment and the shop window that the festivals provided.

The need for clarity of purpose: management plans

Given the diversity of landscape and habitats within even small areas of the countryside, it is essential to both characterize the resource – landscape, vegetation, animal populations – and understand the management which brought it into being or maintains it. (The techniques for this were explained in Chapter 7.) Only then can the strategy for dealing with change effectively be determined.

Most national conservation agencies have a more or less clear strategy backed up by increasingly thorough surveys. The nature conservation agencies have the benefit of a nature conservation review and numerous surveys of vegetation. The Countryside Commission for England has carried out sample surveys for its project Monitoring Landscape Change, and national surveys of countryside recreation have been repeated at intervals to guide its policy development in recreation policy.

At a more local level, the authorities responsible have been required since 1974 to prepare national park plans to guide their own activities but, more particularly, to enable them to devise ways to influence others in their stewardship of the parks. Clarity of view is needed about the character and quality of the landscape, about the desired objectives for conservation of the area and about the means to achieve them. This is not always straightforward or simple.

At the individual site level, plans can be either simple – a fence to exclude sheep and allow natural regeneration of woodland – or complex. The 1981 Wildlife and Countryside Act, in requiring the nature Conservancy Council (as it then was) to renotify the owners/occupiers of sites of special scientific interest (SSSIs) of their scheduling, also required the notification of a list of potentially damaging operations upon which the owner would need to consult the Council before carrying out any of them. But of course this assumes a detailed understanding of the ecological consequences of sometimes subtle changes including abandonment of traditional management practices.

The renotification process is now largely complete but has been a massive operation which has concentrated resources on a small fraction, albeit an important one, of the countryside. But since wildlife populations cannot survive in islands in the countryside, what of the wider landscape?

Creating awareness and understanding

In the 1970s, when agricultural policy was dedicated to production as the overriding objective, the first priority for conservationists was to draw attention to the loss of habitat and damage to the farmed landscape and historic features. These consequences had gone largely unacknowledged publicly or in government policy and the agricultural industry was generally unaware of how it might compensate for the changes.

The New Agricultural Landscapes initiative by the Countryside Commission consisted of research initiatives to establish the extent of change, practical demonstration projects – Demonstration Farms and the New Agricultural Landscape Projects – and grant-aid for tree planting and the maintenance and creation of landscape features on the farm. Also, and very significantly, it involved in the 1980s support for the farming and wildlife advisory groups (FWAGs) as a means of extending awareness among farmers. It remains important, even though agricultural policy has significantly changed, that farmers and land occupiers are offered sound technical information and advice in a form which allows them to appreciate the value, in conservation terms, of their land and the ways in which their activities might affect it. The voluntary sector – FWAGs, the wildlife trusts and so on – are well placed to contribute.

Offering incentives: grant-aid and management agreements

Awareness and understanding are essential conditions for successful partnership with the farming community in the conservation of the wider countryside. The government's preferred voluntary approach and the economic realities of farming mean that advice and financial incentives are the principal tools for the conservation agencies and local authorities. In a number of areas this will be supplemented by the authorities' own direct practical countryside management schemes.

Grant-aid

Grant-aid programmes target limited funding on the positive work the grant-aiding body has identified as important. Because grant-aid schemes usually entail a contribution from the farmer, he has to see some personal benefit in the work, whether it be enjoyment of his own farm or practical benefit to his farming. Grant schemes tend to be confined therefore to items such as amenity tree planting or woodland management, or as a top-up grant to bridge the gap between the costs of the normal farming option and the preferred method. Thus, national park authorities (NPAs) are now able to top up Ministry of Agriculture grants to encourage the use of traditional materials in new farm buildings, to build or repair dry-stone walls rather than put up wire fences, and so on.

Management agreements and plans

Management agreements can cover a much wider range of activities and circumstances. The current interest in management agreements stems from the provisions of the Wildlife and Countryside Act 1981, which was itself a response to loss of habitat and landscape change as a result of agricultural development. Management agreements need not, however, be triggered by a threat and can be positive and inventive. Increasingly they have become a means of retaining particular habitats and landscapes made rarer by modern agriculture. At their simplest they are a legally binding agreement for a period, usually 25 years, between a public agency or local authority and an owner or tenant. The owner or farmer contracts to follow a very specific management prescription, the effect of which is usually to add to his costs. The public will pay a financial consideration to reflect work done or the profits forgone. More elaborate schemes involve removal of stock at certain times of the year, sharing of the costs of new buildings for winter housing of stock to prevent over-grazing, and so on. Maintenance of public access provision can be negotiated in addition.

For the authorities spending public money it is necessary to be clear not only about the value in terms of conservation or public enjoyment, but to be able to show that the sums of money involved are reasonable from the farmer's point of view. Land agency skills as well as ecological knowledge are needed, together with the legal advice to conclude a watertight agreement.

A recent development in some national parks has been the conclusion of *whole-farm management plans*. These are moving towards a full partnership with the farmer in which the NPA defines the desired end product in terms of habitat and landscape and the farmer contracts to either modify his practices or allow the NPA to do work. The trend is clear that land of conservation value may well attract supplementary income for the farmer and create local employment. In these uncertain times, farmers are now quite receptive to this approach. It can be combined with applications for assistance under, for example, the

Countryside Stewardship Scheme administered by the Countryside Commission.

Countryside management

Countryside management, pioneered in the early 1970s in the uplands and urban fringe, has become commonplace. In the basic schemes, teams of practical field staff or self-employed craftsmen led by a project officer undertake small-scale conservation and access work on private land and at little or no cost to the owner. Tree planting, eyesore removal, permissive paths and rights of way restoration, the creation of circular walks with interpretative leaflets, and programmes of guided walks and wayside information panels are among the options. The funding and leadership are typically from one or more local authorities, but steering is generally by a group drawn more widely to embrace local landowning and farming, wildlife and amenity interests.

The experience of all countryside services, of which those in the national parks are some of the best developed, is that the presence of field staff, in particular *ranger services*, is a most effective means of communication with the community. Rangers, often supervising estate staff or as part of a countryside management service, enable the authority to offer a channel for information and advice which will help to raise the awareness and understanding mentioned earlier, and provide a means of communication in the other direction. Often it will be the role of the ranger, as the lubricant between the farmers and the visitor, which will initiate contact. Once made, however, the contact can enable the farm liaison staff, ecologist, historic buildings adviser and, via other agencies and authorities, other advisers to channel their advice to the farmer or landowner. The national parks are providing almost a broker service for other people's schemes, a 'one-stop shop' for advice to members of the farming community.

In these ways an effective partnership between the rural community and the public agencies can be built up. It would be premature to signal the end of hostilities between the authorities and elements of the rural community while the authorities have to carry out development control work. This still dominates the agenda of some national park authority meetings, and remains an important means of preventing undesirable development. However, there has been a significant shift of emphasis from regulation to partnership.

Land acquisition

There is now a consensus that as much as possible should be done to enable land to continue in traditional ownership and management. However, in the last resort it is possible to acquire particularly important properties if there is a threat or if it presents a desirable opportunity to achieve public access or secure control of a strategic piece of country. In terms of public access to the countryside, the feeling seems to be that we have probably almost completed the national programme of country park development and that, in any event, the emphasis has shifted to access to the wider countryside as the public's confidence in using the countryside has grown.

Land acquisition for conservation carries a management cost and may deflect the organization from a more significant role, perhaps in influencing the management of the wider countryside. The message is clear: be sure that an opportunity to purchase fits within a clear strategy for conservation or public access, and be clear on your objectives. Even if acquisition is not your objective, change of ownership can be an opportunity to influence the future management of a piece of land; new owners are often open to information and advice from conservation interests about the management and potential of the land.

If bringing land into protective ownership by a conservation body is the desired option then sources of public and charitable funding need to be explored. The National Heritage Memorial Fund, the Countryside Commission, English Nature, Scottish Natural Heritage, the Countryside Council for Wales and local authorities can all offer grants. Public sources will probably ask the district valuer (DV) to advise them on the appropriate value and their grant will be based on that. You may lose the grant altogether if you pay an inflated price: remember that the commercial value of conservation sites is often quite low and the authorities will be mindful of that and of the danger of inflating the market for land of conservation value. The DV's valuation will help in private treaty or auction sales to put a ceiling on the price. Sometimes negotiation and patience reveal the true price aspiration of the owner. Public funding authorities also expect a management plan to be drawn up and will often apply conditions which restrict the use of the land.

Money, manpower and expertise

The acquisition of land clearly focuses an organization's attention on the issues of what manpower and skills it requires. With the acquisition of land may arise liabilities and obligations: tenants whose livelihoods depend on that land, obligations to neighbours with stock regarding fences, weeds, access etc., and maintenance costs. All these are discussed in detail elsewhere in this volume, but suffice it to say that the cost needs to be allowed for in planning for the management of the site and arrangements must be made to acquire the necessary legal and property management advice and, perhaps, estate work skills.

The practical work can be contracted out or, in some cases, may be suited to volunteers. Much can be done by volunteers (see earlier) in surveying the resources of the site, undertaking practical work or providing visitor services in the wider countryside. This approach is often very economical, but not always. Volunteers certainly need to be managed, however.

Money for development and management, in particular the desirability of attracting other people's resources, is always a problem. Grant-aid is available from the Countryside Commission, the Countryside Council for Wales and other countryside agencies, but they have their own priorities. It is therefore a partnership based on mutual benefit. The same applies to sponsorship. Donations and appeals, legacies and other fund-raising activities are dealt with in detail elsewhere. Attracting financial support and dealing with donors, sponsors and other partners is a skilled job in itself.

The scene is constantly changing. New schemes now exist which could provide an alternative means to achieving your purposes, such as the Countryside Commission's Countryside Stewardship Scheme. This is an important national pilot scheme which aims to achieve the retention of, or re-creation in some cases, of selected landscapes and habitats in the wider countryside rather than just in designated landscapes or wildlife sites. Farmers and *other landowners* enter into ten-year agreements to manage their land in environmentally friendly ways. The package of measures is chosen to fit the circumstances. In return landowners are paid standard amounts for carrying out management of the land according to a prescription from a menu of options. The uplands, chalk and limestone areas, waterside, coastal areas and lowland heath and historic landscapes are covered. There are also payments for access.

It pays to keep up to date on the schemes available and to talk to the promoters, who may be more flexible than you think!

Having said all that, the most precious sites and the most evocative and inspiring scenery may be best protected in the ownership of a public body or the National Trust.

Conclusion

We appear to be moving into an era when conservation and public enjoyment of the wider countryside are seen as objectives of public policy for land use alongside the traditional ones of farming, forestry etc. Multiple land use as a fact has been with us for a very long time, but with the downturn in farm incomes it is being seen by farmers as a potential source of farm income, to set alongside the value of the farm produce. We are not at the point where conservation and access form an integral part of farm support, but already there are a whole range of experimental approaches, supporting traditional farm management practices and conservation on the farm, and reflecting current public interest and concern.

For practitioners in conservation a sound appreciation of the value of the area for conservation, clarity in planning and a solid relationship with the land occupiers, based on understanding and trust, will be essential whatever the next steps. The conservation of both the finest and most characteristic of our landscapes and the habitats of many of our most familiar plants and animals depends very largely upon the continuation of traditional patterns of farming.

16

Conservation techniques: the built environment

Paul Drury

There is perhaps no one thing, which the most Polite part of mankind have more universally agreed in; than the Value they have ever set upon the Remains of distant Times. Nor amongst the Severall kinds of those Antiquitys, are there any so much regarded, as those of Buildings; Some for their Magnificence, or Curious Workmanship; And others; as they move more lively and pleasing Reflections (than History their Aid can do) on the Persons who have Inhabited them; On the Remarkable things which have been transacted in them, Or the extraordinary Occasions of Erecting them.

Letter from John Vanbrugh to the Duchess of Marlborough, 11 June 1709, in G. Webb,
The Complete Works of Sir John Vanbrugh

The nature of the inheritance

With a few trifling exceptions, mere ornaments in the landscape or monuments in cities, buildings are and were designed primarily to serve a purpose. The 'conditions of well building' were set out by Sir Henry Wotton in 1624 as 'commoditie, firmeness and delight'. 'Commoditie' may often be accompanied by 'firmeness', and sometimes by 'delight', but unlike the latter, at least, it can be defined by 'performance criteria': that is minimum standards, which of course change through time, but which must continue to be met if a building is to be of beneficial use and thus justify its maintenance rather than its replacement or abandonment. Thus our inheritance of historic buildings and areas has been shaped not only by the obvious criterion of durability, but also substantially by the less obvious one of adaptability. The types which have survived best were designed for uses which remain as valid as when they were conceived, and for which the performance criteria have changed in ways which historic buildings can accommodate. For example, houses built for the middle ranks of society from the late medieval period onwards remain in great numbers; those of the lowest levels of society built more than 150 years ago have largely disappeared; and those of the upper levels, country houses, have suffered disproportionate reduction over what is, historically, a very brief period – the half century from about 1925 to 1975.

The more specialized the plan and form of a building, the less likely it is to survive the next phase of technological or social innovation which makes that purpose obsolete. Early cotton mills or warehouses, for example, offer extensive open-plan areas of well lit space, and so adapt for many purposes. On the other hand, cinemas, or industrial-scale breweries and gas works, are hard to adapt to any other purpose, and so relatively few are surviving the social and technological changes which have made their original purpose largely or wholly obsolete. Given that only an infinitesimally small proportion of historic buildings and virtually no historic areas have been or are likely to be preserved as monuments, that is as sterile objects whose sole purpose is academic and didactic (and perhaps to stir the emotions), it is clear that historic buildings and areas must adapt to survive. Queen Street Mill, Burnley, may survive as a weaving shed in the form of a subsidized 'living museum', but its numerous contemporaries must justify their continued existence by their adaptability to contemporary needs. Moreover, before the introduction of protective legislation, buildings would tend to be adapted only where the result could realize the latent value of the site on which it stood: many areas of our historic towns and cities were thus rebuilt on a much greater scale in the nineteenth and twentieth centuries, as site or location value increased significantly in relation to the value of the existing buildings.

Our inheritance of historic buildings and areas influences the present, but contemporary needs also influence, and change, those buildings and areas. To have survived into the era of legislation which inhibits their loss, they must have been capable of beneficial use, and what might be termed 'constructive reinterpretation', by each generation since they were built. Those that were not have perished. One is tempted to draw an analogy with drama or opera: the works which have survived in the repertory are those capable of enriching the experience of succeeding generations, through reinterpretations which make them accessible to contemporary audiences. Sometimes this process goes too far, and the result is merely novel, or even ridiculous. The analogy holds with historic buildings, but with one essential difference. The text of a great play or the score of an opera passes to the next generation undamaged by such endeavour. The fabric of a building or town is usually irrevocably damaged by inept reinterpretations. A historic façade stuck to the front of an office building, its scale grossly inflated, upwards and outwards, beyond any conceivable relation to the retained element, is perhaps the most common equivalent of 'men in dinner jackets carrying spears'.

The recognition that most historic buildings and areas have changed with each generation, and must continue to change to survive, is fundamental to an understanding of the concept, processes and results of endeavours to conserve them. Historically, some have changed to ruins, which themselves have survived through inertia or the fact that the cost of removing them was greater than the benefit of doing so. This is especially true of military works: castles have survived beyond the period when they could realistically be adapted to meet current performance criteria for either citadels or houses, and often a later 'sympathetic new use' as prisons, largely because, despite sometimes central urban locations, the combination of massive structure and awkward earthworks often made their demolition unattractive. When the means of easily dealing with them became available, antiquarian concern was such that the survivors were scheduled as ancient monuments. More recently, many World War II concrete defences have survived simply because the cost of their demolition exceeded the benefits, and they too are now taking their place on the schedule, at a time when, ironically, the inherent weakness of ferro-concrete construction is demonstrating the essential impermanence of all but the most massive.

Conservation of historic buildings and areas is therefore different in nature from the conservation of, say, a museum artefact. With the latter the aim is wholly to suspend or reverse the natural processes of decay. With most buildings and areas, the aim cannot be preservation as such, but adaptation to suit contemporary needs in ways which build upon rather than detract from their inherent qualities, character and associations. The process is a dynamic one: the legacy of the past should enrich and give depth to the present, not be seen as a negative constraint, whilst the fusion of past and present can sometimes be highly creative in its tension (see, for example,

Cantacuzino, 1989). However, where the survival of historic buildings demands major capital investment, even the existence of protective legislation will tend to help only those on the margin of commercial viability unless there is massive public subsidy available, which is not the case in Britain.

Why do we seek to conserve historic buildings and areas?

Approaches to the conservation of the built environment must be based on an understanding of why we value historic buildings, monuments and areas, and of what qualities we seek particularly to retain. It will immediately be obvious that the consensus view, if there is such a thing, of the answers to both questions has changed radically through time, and thus is likely to continue to change in the future, particularly at a time when conservation and environment are major political issues. John Harvey (1972, Chapter I) provides a thoughtful introduction to the subject.

Some few buildings are generally accepted as great works of art, as expressions of the spirit of mankind or of a nation or a faith. These, together with many others, also impart a sense of permanence, at least in relation to the span of human life; they give a sense of stability and provide points of reference in a rapidly changing world. Most buildings constructed before the middle of the nineteenth century, when the developing railway network allowed the cheap transport of mass-produced materials over great distances, achieved a consonance with their locality. Both the vernacular, and to a lesser extent the polite, building of every geographic region was a product of its social structure, local materials and wider cultural influences, giving a clear regional identity. Moreover, most of them will be aesthetically pleasing, whether through the harmony of the vernacular refined over time, or the calculated proportions of Georgian building. The patina of age tends, too, to enhance the appearance of natural materials, especially stone and brick, and this, particularly, emphasizes to most people the importance of old buildings in giving a sense of continuity in a changing world.

The built environment is, of course, also a historic document, which can provide information about the past which is not available from any other source. This is true not only of architectural history but also of social and economic history, and evidence from this source is increasingly used in these fields. It remains true that the origins and architectural development of many important buildings, particularly country houses, has yet to be understood at anything more than the most superficial level, making detailed recording and interpretation particularly important (ICOMOS, 1990).

Increasingly, the value of conservation is seen in the context of contributing to tourism, a major element of the national economy. However, there is a problem in this: save for buildings which directly attract paying visitors, those who bear most of the costs of conservation – building owners and occupiers – do not share in any direct sense in the gains. Even at a more general level, the value which they contribute to society and the economy as a whole is hardly likely to be reflected in the modest tax concessions available to historic building owners (VAT relief on alterations to some listed buildings, conditional inheritance tax exemption) and the limited grants available from public funds.

Assessment

Proposals for conservation, indeed the decision about what elements of the built environment to conserve, should begin with an assessment of the origins and development of the structure or area, and its relative importance both as a whole and in its constituent parts. In the case of historic areas, this should encompass the development of the street and tenement pattern, the inherent historic interest and architectural quality of the extant buildings, and the townscape quality of the place (English Heritage, 1993). For individual structures, it is necessary clearly to understand the original form of the building and the succession of later developments and modifications. In the case of, say, a Georgian terraced house, this will often be a relatively simple and straightforward process, which should be within the capabilities of any architect, building surveyor or conservation officer. By contrast, understanding a complex urban timber-framed building which has evolved over six centuries, or an industrial building which has undergone many changes in a century to accommodate rapidly changing requirements, will generally need specialist expertise, and even the basic story may not be recoverable without some physical opening up, accompanied by documentary research.

Approaches to conservation

Attitudes to conservation have tended to polarize, most notably between those who seek to restore buildings to some real (or imagined) pristine state, and those who seek to undertake only minimal repairs to delay the progress of decay. The latter view has been championed by the Society for the Protection of Ancient Buildings (SPAB), founded by William Morris in 1877 and set out in his manifesto (printed in, for example, Harvey, 1972, pp. 210–12), in reaction to the ruthless reconstruction and reworking of so many medieval churches in the name of restoration. Debates purely at the level of philosophy can and do still occur in the case of a very small number of buildings which are essentially monuments, whose use (if any) is ritual or ceremonial. However, in most cases the need for

the building to serve a useful purpose, to earn its living, has a major influence on decisions.

Before the rise of the conservation ethos, decisions about whether to reuse buildings, to adapt them to changing circumstances, or to build anew, tended to be based on practical considerations: was it easier and more economic to adapt than to rebuild in order to achieve a building which met its user's requirements and exploited the value of the site? This judgement was, of course, subject, in the case of polite buildings, to questions about the aesthetic and/or symbolic value of the existing buildings. Having made the decision, the result would generally be carried through in such a way that the new was visually integrated with the old. Now, with statutory protection, there is often little choice but to adapt, and moreover in such a way that a line is drawn between the elements of the building which are perceived as having architectural or historic interest and anything which is done subsequently. The implication is that such later work is of less value; indeed it may specifically be seen as being transient, i.e. reversible, when some golden age dawns and the building once again can be used as it was when it was first constructed.

There is no doubt that where fine historic spaces must be subdivided, this should be seen as a short-term expedient readily capable of being reversed. However, to insist in all cases on a distinction between old work and new, rather than to allow their integration into a single coherent whole, can be at odds with the accretive unity which is the essence of the character of many historic buildings, especially houses both grand and vernacular. To do otherwise than continue the process of accretive adaptation, making some changes in the style of adjacent work, and perhaps some in a contemporary style, is often to introduce a note of discord which is wholly at variance with the essential character of the building and the influences which formed it. To argue that such changes falsify the history of the building is not necessarily sustainable. To the trained observer, such changes will always be detectable at close quarters; indeed it is their very complexity, and the skill with which elements were blended together, which makes unravelling the development of many country houses such a fascinating exercise. If historic precedent is modified, it should be to ensure that in continuing in the tradition of development, existing work of quality and importance of any period is not destroyed to make way for new; and that the changes should be adequately recorded (ICOMOS, 1990). There is, and has always been, a place for counterpoint and contrast; but it should not be a universal solution, imposed to the detriment of the ensemble.

The present appearance of historic buildings is often the result of a long period of change and adaptation, as well as weathering and inevitable natural decay. In some cases, at a point in this pattern of change the building will have ceased to be treated with any particular concern for its structural or visual integrity, for example when a terrace of houses becomes engulfed in a factory, or a Norman keep becomes a coke store, as happened at Canterbury Castle. An important issue is the extent to which restoration to some earlier phase in a building's development, which is perceived to be of greater value – aesthetic, didactic or historic – than the building in its current state, is acceptable or even desirable. The strict SPAB view is that all previous alterations are part of the building's history and should be maintained: 'preserve as found'. This at least avoids the subjective judgement involved in adopting any other course, but save for some very few monuments selected for preservation as historic documents alone, without contemporary use, it will generally neither be possible nor, in the writer's opinion, desirable. A subjective judgement is unavoidable – but it must be based on objective fact.

As a general rule, it may be reasonable to suggest that restoration to the last period of considered change may be justified. By this is meant a phase of adaptation which, although probably in the style of its own day, was undertaken with obvious regard for both the final appearance of the building and the integrity of its structure. Two provisos are, even so, necessary: firstly, that any work removed is in itself of no quality or significance, architectural or historic; and secondly, that speculative restoration is avoided. For example, a sixteenth century timber-framed building may have been refronted in brick in the eighteenth century, and some of its sash windows crudely replaced with standard steel casements in the 1950s, following wartime bomb damage. Reinstatement of sashes to the original pattern, preserved in the majority of openings, would be desirable in restoring the sense of unity and harmony to the front, and in enhancing the building's contribution to the appearance of its context. Removing the Georgian front and speculatively reconstructing a timber-framed front based on a few surviving timbers would generally be considered unacceptable: it would involve loss of an element of intrinsic quality, and wholesale speculation, producing a new 'old' building. Yet such schemes are still carried out, based on the perceived greater interest of the earlier structure because of its age, and on the 'need' to restore structural integrity to the timber-framed building. In practice, of course, such judgements, even if financial considerations are not involved, are usually less clear-cut. What if the Georgian brick front, never well attached to the framing, is about to fall away, necessitating either its total rebuilding or its removal? Or what if it is not a front, but the expedient under-building of a few bays of a jettied storey?

In summary, there should be a presumption against the restoration of a building to some earlier period of its development, expedient damage or loss excepted, if only because judgement of what is historically important or aesthetically pleasing changes from generation to generation. Who now would not wish to have seen the evidence retained from the clothier William Bell's house created within the church of the Blackfriars at Gloucester after the Reformation, rather than its ruthless destruction by the Ministry of Works to lay bare the medieval work?

The extension of old buildings is a particularly contentious issue (official policy advice for England is set out in Department of the Environment, 1994). There are some which, because of their unity of form and composition, cannot be the subject of addition without prejudice to their character and integrity, and are of such importance that this should be preserved. Extensions to lodges, garden temples, and indeed medieval churches (English Heritage, undated) are very rarely successful. There is general agreement that extensions should be subservient in scale and sympathetic in form, massing and detailing to the original building, although we should note in passing that many cherished historic buildings disregard this maxim by encapsulating an earlier and more modest structure. There is general acceptance that extensions should be clearly distinguishable as such, rather than seeking precisely to match the original. Where the existing building consists of a number of discrete elements, all readily assignable to a particular period, there is merit in continuing the tradition. Where all melds into a unified whole, there is also merit in continuing that tradition: the 'Surrey style' provides a good example of this, and the case is forcefully argued by Gradidge (1991, Chapter 2). The modern counterpoint can also be successful; what is to be avoided above all is the thin weak pastiche of historic style, which neither blends with the old nor has any intrinsic character of its own.

Conservation of historic buildings also depends on sympathetic use. Generally the best use for a building will be the one for which it was built, unless the performance criteria for that use have changed so much that major reconstruction would be entailed to keep it in that use. Successful conservation always depends on a use or uses consistent with the historic form, character and structural capacity of the building. As a general rule, the more specialized the building form, the more contrived become attempts to conserve, which can often destroy that which they set out to save. Churches, for example, present particular problems: even removal of the principal fittings can be a major loss. Subdivision of the internal space in a transparent fashion, for example as offices on mezzanine floors, can be successful and has the advantage of being reversible, whilst conversion to cellular housing is likely at most to preserve the structure as an element in the landscape, assuming that this can be achieved without the insertion of a plethora of rooflights and new windows.

The suitability of the spaces within a historic building for a new use is but one issue. Compliance with structural performance requirements (for example floor loadings), Building Regulations, the demands of the fire officer and the insertion of services may require the effective reconstruction of the building, resulting in a complete loss of that very character and authenticity which it was sought to conserve. In considering schemes for conversion, it is essential that all these issues are considered at the outset. Seemingly innocuous schemes, once accepted in principle, are effectively unstoppable. The standard requirements of institutional investors are often excessively generous even in new buildings, and should not be imposed unthinkingly on historic ones. Office floor loadings provide a good illustration of this: $2.5 \, \mathrm{kN/m^2}$ is adequate despite institutional demands for $5 \, \mathrm{kN/m^2}$ (Mason, 1992).

Repair

The repair of listed buildings, rather than their alteration, extension or demolition, does not require listed building consent, on the basis that such work, which is assumed to use like-for-like materials and techniques, will not affect their character. Yet it is the repair and maintenance of historic buildings which is responsible for more destruction of historic fabric and character than alteration works for which consent is sought and granted. Traditional natural materials on roofs are stripped and replaced by artificial substitutes; walls are sandblasted clean and repointed in cement mortar; joinery is replaced with crude reflections of the original. Inside, the pernicious process of stripping out reduces the buildings to a masonry or timber shell which is then lined out with 'olde worlde' materials in place of the real thing.

Principles for the repair of historic buildings have been set out by Brereton (1991). The purpose of repair is to restrain the processes of decay, without damaging the character of buildings or monuments, altering the features which give them their historic or architectural importance, or unnecessarily disturbing or destroying historic fabric. Repair work should be kept to the minimum necessary to stabilize and conserve buildings and monuments, with the aim of achieving a sufficiently sound structural condition to ensure their long-term survival. The authenticity of a historic building depends crucially upon the integrity of its fabric; therefore any unnecessary replacement of historic fabric, no matter how carefully done, will adversely affect its appearance, seriously diminish its authenticity, and significantly reduce its value as a historic document.

A strategy for repair must begin with a clear understanding of the historic development of the building, based if necessary on archaeological and architectural investigation, documentary research, recording and interpretation of the structure in question, and its assessment in a wider context. Recording and understanding will, with complex buildings, need to continue during the course of repairs. Arrangements should be made for the subsequent preservation and updating of all records.

The detailed design of repairs should always be preceded by long-term observation of structural defects, and an investigation of the nature and condition of the materials of the building and of the causes, processes and rates of decay. If decayed fabric is replaced without first carrying out such an investigation, problems are likely to recur.

Repair techniques should match or be compatible with existing materials and methods of construction, in order to preserve the appearance and historic integrity of the building, and to ensure that the work has an appropriate life. Exceptions should only be considered where the existing fabric has failed because of inherent defects of design or specification, rather than because of neglect of maintenance, or because it has completed its expected life. New methods and techniques should only be used where they have proved themselves over a sufficient period, and where traditional alternatives cannot be identified.

Repairs should be honestly executed, with no attempt at disguise, but equally must not be unnecessarily obtrusive or unsympathetic in appearance. Most importantly, a historic building should be regularly monitored and maintained, under specialist professional oversight.

The heritage manager and the historic built environment

Whilst the management of the historic build environment can readily be discussed at the general level, every case is unique, and it is impossible to lay down simple rules for dealing with historic buildings and areas. However, the following key points should be in the manager's mind:

(1) Begin any appraisal or management strategy with a professional assessment of the architectural and historic interest of the place, as a whole and in its constituent parts. This should include documentary research, analysis of the fabric of the buildings (which is the *primary* document for their history) and comparative study to place the buildings in their national (or wider) context. This provides the essential basis of knowledge to devise or reappraise a conservation strategy.

(2) Recognize that any change of use, but particularly the preservation of a building as a monument, will significantly change its nature.

(3) Employ professional advisers experienced in understanding and conserving historic structures.

(4) Eschew 'restorations' to some perceived earlier, more 'important' or more 'perfect' phase in the

history of the place, other than in some exceptional cases which do *not* involve speculative restoration.

(5) In alteration and repair, seek to retain as much historic fabric as possible, avoiding drastic renewal.

Note

This contribution was written when the author was in private practice, and the views expressed in it are not necessarily those of English Heritage.

References

BRERETON, C. (1991) *The Repair of Historic Buildings: Advice on Principles and Methods*, English Heritage, London

CANTACUZINO, S. (1989) *Re/Architecture: Old buildings/New Uses*, Thames & Hudson, London

DEPARTMENT OF THE ENVIRONMENT (1994) *Planning Policy Guidance 15*: Historic buildings and Conservation Areas

ENGLISH HERITAGE (undated) *New Work in Historic Churches*, London

ENGLISH HERITAGE (1993) *Conservation Area Practice*, London

GRADIDGE, R. (1991) *The Surrey Style*, Surrey Historic Buildings Trust, Kingston upon Thames

HARVEY, J. (1972) *Conservation of Buildings*, Batsford, London

ICOMOS (1990) *Guide to Recording Historic Buildings*, Butterworths, London

MASON, J. (1992) 'Floor loads', *Architect's Journal*, 28 August, 43–45

WEBB, G. (ed.) (1927) *The Complete Works of Sir John Vanbrugh. The Letters*

WOTTON, H. (1962) *The Elements of Architecture*, London

Case study 16.1

Marsh Windmill, Thornton, near Blackpool

G. J. O. Wallis

Marsh Windmill is a late nineteenth century tower mill retaining virtually all its early machinery listed grade II. Following deterioration of external timberwork, the fan stage, sails and cap covering were renewed during the early twentieth century, but more deep-seated problems caused by water entering the timber cap frame and supporting structure in the tower were not treated at that time.

By 1989 the mill had passed into the care of Wyre Borough Council who recognized its potential for attracting visitors from nearby Blackpool. They constructed a new shopping 'village' nearby, and funded full restoration of the mill as its centrepiece.

Figure 16.1

The contract

The structure was inspected in detail by a specialist consultant millwright, and his repairs specification was incorporated into a standard JCT intermediate

Figure 16.2

Figure 16.3

form of contract. Competitive tenders were sought from three carefully selected specialist companies of millwrights, and a contract was let to Dorothea Restorations Ltd of Bristol and Stockport.

The work comprised:

(1) craning of 7 m diameter cap, covering, frame, windshaft and fan framing to ground level; supply and installation of a temporary cap;
(2) location of large sections of new and second-hand pitch pine and oak;

Figure 16.4

(3) reconstruction of complete cap frame, fan frame, fan and timber-boarded roof;
(4) repairs to tower masonry; supply and erection of new oak curb to carry the rotating cap;
(5) repairs to cap winding mechanism and internal milling machinery;
(6) re-erection and commissioning of all millwork, including new sails;
(7) painting of all exterior timberwork.

The method of working was at the contractor's discretion, work being supervised by the Borough Council architect.

As repairs to millwork proceeded, and the contractor's capability was proven, additional work normally outside the scope of a millwright was ordered through Dorothea who acted as main contractor, including application of a new proprietary masonry coating to tower walls. Dorothea also supplied a new oak reefing stage and a lightning conductor system.

Works were substantially completed in a period of eighteen months.

Conservation policy

The conservation policy originated from, or was influenced by, four bodies:

(1) The specialist consultant, a millwright known for capable and consistent implementation of the conservation philosophy of the Society for the Protection of Ancient Buildings. This established a sound basis for the contract, ensuring preservation of as much existing material as practicable.
(2) English Heritage, whose inspector ensured correct use of grant monies for preservation as a primary aim, and faithful replication only where unavoidable owing to advanced decay or loss of material.
(3) The 'client' – the supervising architect, Wyre Borough Council.
(4) The contractor, Dorothea Restorations Ltd, who have published their conservation policy. Most day-to-day decisions on the extent and nature of restoration/replication work was made by the contractor's site supervisor and job manager in conjunction with the client.

Materials and techniques

Dorothea's policy was to employ modern equipment as necessary and appropriate to ensure fast and safe working, whilst retaining as much of the mill's original materials as possible. Where new parts had to be made they were constructed of traditional materials by traditional techniques wherever possible, replica parts being exact copies of originals. Redundant parts were stored in the mill.

Detailed colour photographic records were kept at all stages, and a video record was taken of the whole contract. Commissioned by the client, video footage was subsequently incorporated into an introductory presentation for visitors to the mill.

Materials for repairs included use of:

(1) specially imported and selected Honduras pitch pine 380 mm square for new shears (cap main frames);
(2) selected second-hand pitch pine (former Lancashire mill roof beams) for replica fan shears and other joinery;
(3) sand-cast iron and bronze for new parts, cast in the traditional manner from either originals or new wooden patterns;
(4) selected English oak for curbs, beams, boards, pegs, etc., originally of that timber;
(5) traditional lead flashings and bituminous seal coats to roof boarding;
(6) thinly sawn red cedar boarding to sail shutters;
(7) retention and repair of original wooden parts where feasible, by scarf repairs/strapping etc.

Modern materials were employed:

(1) for shafts, links and other working parts to which subsequent access for maintenance would be difficult or dangerous;
(2) painting metal and woodwork;
(3) lightning conductor air and ground terminations.

Full use was made of tubular scaffolds, powered hand and machine tools, and mobile cranes. During erection of four sails, each weighing 2 tonnes, *two* cranes were used, the second being required to provide access for an operative. The operation was completed within one working day, and provided a good photo-opportunity for the client's public relations needs.

Subsequent work

During 1990, the mill was operated on many occasions by wind power. Unfortunately, even on the Fylde coast, it was discovered that the wind direction and power were not sufficiently consistent for commercial needs – a problem well known to traditional wind-millers. Accordingly, in 1991 a design and build contract was offered to Dorothea to supply and fit an electric motor drive to the sails. The company

adopted the following brief for equipment in accordance with its published conservation policy.

The equipment must:

(1) not permanently alter existing traditional mill machinery or structure;
(2) be capable of disconnection from millwork to allow wind powering;
(3) be removable if no longer required;
(4) be as unobtrusive and quiet as possible in operation;
(5) be easily started and stopped (at the touch of a button);
(6) be safe in operation;
(7) be fail-safe;
(8) not be a significant fire risk;
(9) be durable;
(10) be easily maintained.

This demanding brief was fulfilled by use of a compact drive package located between two grain bins on the mill's dust floor. The millwork was driven by a 600 mm diameter nylon spur gear driving on to the great spur wheel under the floor. Thus new machinery was distributed on two levels as unobtrusive locations, without modification to original machinery. One locked start switch was provided, together with a series of emergency stop buttons on all floors containing moving machinery. Moving machinery was guided and operators were provided with clear written operating and maintenance instructions and with training.

Conclusions

The conservation project was ambitious and complex. Its success was due principally to:

(1) common understanding of and agreement on conservation policy by the consultant, the grant-aiding body, the client and contractor;
(2) good working relationship between client's supervising officer and contractor's supervisor;
(3) resources and expertise of the contractor;
(4) diligent preparation and management of the contract by the client, incorporating carefully selected professionals at each stage, and ensuring adequate funding to achieve a good standard of conservation and subsequent maintenance.

17

Conservation techniques: museum collections

Suzanne Keene

The organization of conservation and preservation in many institutions today is based on a variety of assumptions and views, some overtly expressed and acknowledged, some barely recognized. Yet all the activities which museums and similar organizations undertake are based on their collections; hence, the preservation function is fundamental to all other museum activities. In this chapter, I attempt to take a fresh view of the preservation function of museums. To achieve this, preservation is examined by means of three analytical questions:

Does the concept of preservation differ from museum to museum? Experience of working with different institutions, and with different types of collection, suggests that the purpose for which collections are held, and hence what is meant by their preservation, differs a great deal.
What is the theoretical system which would be needed to undertake preservation in a logical world? Although all museums do preserve their collections, analysing this as a functional part of a wider system helps in understanding what processes go towards building this function.
Do the system and what happens in the real world of museums coincide? The processes identified in the analysis are discussed in terms of what happens, or should or could happen, in actuality.

Preservation and museum policies

The greatest influence on the degree and manner in which collections are preserved is the purpose of the institution itself. The preservation, or conservation, of museum collections is undertaken for a reason. That reason must be predicated on the purpose of the institution holding them. But do museums have a single purpose?

Two major functions are always cited in the statutes or other instruments establishing museums: to preserve and care for collections; and to display them and use them in other ways to entertain, educate and enlighten

(ICOM, undated). These functions are contradictory, since it is almost impossible to establish optimum conditions for preservation during display or use. Every museum therefore has to strike its own balance. The establishment of this balance will have profound effects on the museum's preservation function.

There is a wide spectrum of types of museum, from art galleries where the aesthetic is all, to farm or industrial museums where the ethic is to preserve and demonstrate the function of the object as well as simply to use it as a passive source of information.

Paradigms for museums

An important role of the national museums in Britain is to act as centres of excellence and sources of expert advice, to show other museums what they should be aiming at. In a sense, they are paradigms which set the standards and limits of museumship.

Three of the national museums in particular strike one as being as different as they could possibly be. These are the Science Museum, the Natural History Museum, and the National Gallery. If they are indeed paradigms, then a close examination of their roles may shed light on some of the contradictions to be found in other less specialized museums.

The Science Museum is used as the example for museums of industry and machinery (e.g. P. Greene, 1990, internal Museum of London seminar), where public enlightenment through the active demonstration of how objects function is the paramount objective.

The National Gallery is the picture museum *par excellence*. Here, art and the aesthetic experience reign; the object must speak for itself and it must be in such condition that nothing will interfere with the viewer's experience.

The Natural History Museum stands as an exemplar for museum collections of natural objects. In spite of its truly enormous holdings of objects, many of its displays use not objects but graphics, or three-dimensional constructions and educational computer screens, along with other interactive devices to put across concepts. But it is a great research institution as well as a museum, and its activities go far beyond and have a deeper significance than its public displays (Radford, 1990).

What are the differences that make these three institutions stand out from each other, and from the other national museums? One fundamental difference is the size of their collections. At the two extremes, the Natural History Museum holds about 65 million objects and the National Gallery holds some 2200. There is naturally an inverse ratio between the size of the collections and the proportion on display, with the National Gallery having all its pictures on display, and the Natural History Museum less than 0.1 per cent of its objects in its public galleries.

Do the differing functions of the museums determine their purpose for holding objects? Do they have to be as they are? One could envisage a museum of natural history which held and exhibited only a few key objects. An art gallery, if it had sufficient funds, could acquire and store an enormous archive of European painting, or could set out to represent the social, technical and ideas history which produced its works of art. The differences then are not inherent in the type of collection: they must arise from differences in the reasons for holding collections, derived of course from the museums' various fundamental purposes.

Can these three museums be envisaged as being at the points of a triangle (*Figure 17.1*)? Can other museums be described in terms of the coordinates of the diagram? Indeed, other museums or types of collection do seem to share more or less of the characteristics of the museums at the points of the triangle.

For example, archaeological collections are like natural history collections and like archives of documents: the objects are being kept as a source of scientifically valid evidence about the past. In the early days of Rescue, the archaeological pressure group, the destruction of sites without excavation was often compared to tearing up historical manuscripts. Archaeological objects represent the last physical remnants of 'manuscripts' which have been destroyed through excavation. For both natural history and archaeological objects, as for archives, their context is all-important. Just as unbroken ownership must be demonstrable for documents in an archive (BS 5454: 1989), so the connection of object and context must be unimpeachable for these collections to be of use as evidence. If conservation treatments or other physical intervention alter the nature of the object then its worth *as evidence* is severely diminished.

Similar to picture collections are, of course, other art collections: works of art on paper, and sculpture. Collections of furniture and other objects meant to be enjoyed because of their appearance share a prime purpose of display for appreciation.

Collections where demonstration is the objective include many of those in agricultural, industrial and transport museums. One might add to these the buildings themselves, since many historical buildings which exist in a museum context are certainly used to demonstrate a past way of life and function. Particularly good examples are those at the Welsh National Folk Museum (St Fagans) and of course National Trust properties.

Effects on museum management

The divergent uses which museums make of their collections have, of course, far-reaching consequences for the preservation of the collections and the nature of the conservation activities devoted to them.

Although those who run museums are obviously aware that there are differences between them, there is little acknowledgment of the fundamental nature of the divergence. Only very recently has the Science Museum offered for public debate, albeit among fellow professionals, its policy of what is described as the destruction of evidence by demonstrating objects (Mann, 1989). Discussions of what museums are tend to view museums as being of one general type (Hebditch, 1990; Weil, 1983). Certainly the public is not aware of the difference in approach, as was well demonstrated in the Auditor General's report which castigated museums for not showing a greater proportion of their collections (Comptroller and Auditor General, 1988).

Most museums do not, of course, conform closely to any one of the three paradigms which have been identified. They will be somewhere in the middle of the triangle. Nothing in a museum collection was

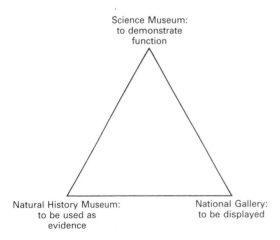

Science Museum:
to demonstrate
function

Natural History Museum:
to be used as
evidence

National Gallery:
to be displayed

Figure 17.1 The purposes for which museum collections are held

actually designed to be there (except possibly by hopeful or well known artists). Especially in the case of local history or social history museums, different parts of their collections will follow different models, or be expected to serve more than one purpose at once. The various curators responsible for the different collections will tend to base their approach on that of their role model, the corresponding national museum. These in turn influence specialist training courses where they exist. It is not surprising that the individuals concerned, such as art and archaeology curators, often find difficulty in sharing a common approach within one institution. There is likely to be fundamental (and possibly unrecognized) disagreement on what a proper museum ought to be doing. Curators as individuals sometimes of course feel torn between restoring the functionality of an object and preserving its true nature as evidence of past technology (e.g. Swade, 1990).

Effects on collections preservation

The effects of the demonstration approach on the preservation of collections, if by 'collections' is meant assemblages of real historic objects, has been well explored (Mann, 1989). It might be questioned whether if objects are likely to end up partly or even entirely as replicas it would not be better to resolve the dilemma by building accurate replicas in the first place. There are other possible ways of resolving it. In the Welsh National Folk Museum, the approach is said to be to retain and not use the most perfect example of the object, and to designate other similar objects specifically for use (R. Child, 1988, personal communication).

The effects of the display approach can be equally destructive. Objects can only be displayed if they are lit. The progress of fading and other damage due to light is normally not perceptible by eye, because it happens slowly, and we cannot retain accurate memories of past images against which to compare changes. There has been much intensive scientific work on the effects of light, but to many art curators the question is beside the point, because as far as they are concerned the collections are not there to be preserved for nebulous future generations; they are there to be displayed and appreciated. But the image which is the point of the display is almost certain to be drastically altered if it is exposed to sufficient light energy. Can this be irrelevant?

When the purpose of a collection is to be an archive for use in perpetuity then policies which promote its preservation are most likely to be adopted. Problems are likely to arise because such collections – natural history specimens, paper or archaeology archives – are likely to be numerically very large. They take much up-front investment in organizing and inventorying them, and are expensive in storage materials, which must all be of archival quality. Once organized, however, they require little upkeep, and because the aim is to maintain them as unchanged evidence they require minimal remedial conservation treatment.

The users of museums

So far only the attitudes of the holders of the collections, the museum professionals, have been discussed. But what about the users – the public? On analysis, museums have an astonishing variety of uses (*Figure 17.2*). Obviously, some of them will want to benefit from the collections in one way, some in another (*Figure 17.3*). Scholars will want to use the collections as evidence; film producers will be after objects for demonstration. The question is whether the short-term wishes of one particular set of users, or indeed museum professionals, should override the needs of other future possible users. Does this matter? Museum people are fond of quoting Maynard Keynes, 'in the end we are all dead'; but the point about institutions is that they have a life beyond that of their employees.

The public is becoming both more and less sophisticated in its use of museums. On the one hand, the success of exhibitions such as *Art in the Making* (National Gallery, series, 1989 and ongoing) and *Fake!* (British Museum, 1990) shows that substantial numbers of people want and enjoy an extremely detailed, accurate, academic and scientific treatment of objects (MacGregor, 1990). This can only be provided by preserving objects as evidence; in the case of *Fake!*, real fakes! On the other hand, the growth of simulated historical experience exhibits within and outside museums, and the healthy attendance figures at the Science Museum and similar demonstration museums, indicates the reverse: that many people want history primarily as entertainment. Perhaps the truth is that more people are visiting museums more often, and they want a wide range of education and entertainment, which is being provided by all these different museums.

Changing taste

It seems a pity, however, that approaches seem to be so compartmentalized between different types of collection, and in particular that many types of museum find it so difficult to contemplate the maintenance of collections as permanent archives. This may be changing, as the National Audit Office and the Museums and Galleries Commission force a greater accountability for the collections as a publicly owned resource. The standards which are being developed in connection with museum registration will not allow the neglect of the preservation function of museums, which has been brought about in part by some of these interpretations of their role. Curators are also coming to terms with a plurality of views at the highest levels of

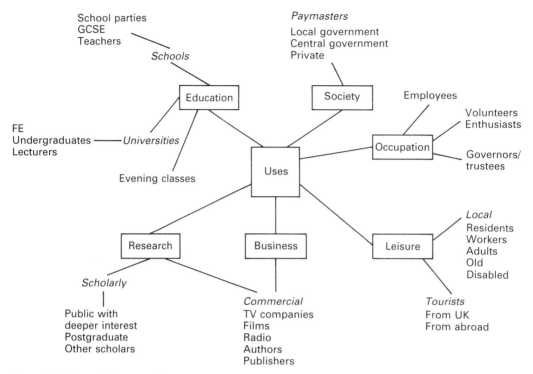

Figure 17.2 Some of the users of museums

museum management, as conservators on the one hand and exhibitions and marketing specialists on the other increasingly demand and find a voice in policy development.

The public response to the recent report by the Comptroller and Auditor General on the collections

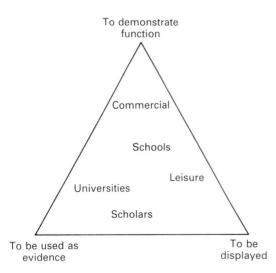

Figure 17.3 Museum users and their interest in collections

of the English national museums, and the ensuing sitting of the Public Accounts Committee, elicited a remarkable amount of press comment (a typical headline 'Arts for oblivion', gives the flavour), echoing – with probably more vehemence than felt by the average member of the public – the censure expressed in the public reports. It seems likely that the debate about the natural environment – at the core of which is the need to live within the limits of a fixed resource – strikes chords when the maintenance of museum collections is discussed. The public seems to perceive museums as above all places where a resource, objects, is properly looked after: so in museums at least there should be no need to worry about using up a finite resource. Witness the surprise and sometimes dismay expressed by people visiting typical stores on museum open days. In truth, museums are mostly no better at looking after their possessions than are private individuals; indeed, they are often far worse. Most museums could find examples of objects that were in excellent condition when first acquired, which have since suffered severe deterioration in overcrowded and unsuitable stores: ethnographic collections are especially vulnerable.

In America, as so often, the debate on the importance of caring for collections is far advanced, and has occasionally been pursued in the courts. It is being demonstrated there that concepts such as 'due care', 'fiduciary responsibility' and 'standards in the industry' can be applied just as well to the responsibility of museums to preserve their collections as to the activities of many other institutions (Ulberg and Lind, 1989; Weil, 1983).

A systems view

It is easy to slip into thinking of the conservation of museum collections as 'what conservators do'. However, the rise of collections management as a distinct function within museums reflects a useful trend towards thinking in broader terms about how collections can be preserved. But it is still difficult to free one's thoughts from preconceptions based on one's institution as currently organized.

A tool which is often used in management studies to assist a fresh view is the systems approach (Handy, 1981). Common to the many variations on this is the concept of an organization as a grouping of interrelated and interdependent components or subsystems, which have some common, overarching purpose. So-called open systems, such as museums, respond to pressures and influences from outside their boundaries. The systems approach to management, used wisely, can be 'a means of understanding situations' (Vickers, 1981).

A particular branch of systems studies, the soft systems methodology, is especially useful when looking at complex organizational situations – and museums are nothing if not complex. The general approach here is first, to describe the real-life situation in detail; then, to leave the real world and think in highly abstract terms; and finally, to compare the abstraction with the reality in order to highlight contradictions. The methodology was developed by Checkland (1981) and is well explained in Naughton (1983). A condensation is described here of this process as applied to museums (Keene, 1993).

What we need to do, therefore, is to describe a notional museum in systems terms, and see what this tells us about the preservation of the collections. This approach can equally be applied to an individual institution, which will have its own particular purpose. Such a museum system is shown in its real-world context in *Figure 17.4*.

The real world

In fact, the first stage in a full soft systems analysis is to sketch a diagrammatic 'rich picture'. This is an annotated cartoon-like depiction of the situation being investigated. On this occasion, however, we will take the rich picture to have been conjured up by the discussion above of museum roles and paradigms. The first step here, then, is a root definition: a precise description of the processes which are fundamental to the organization, or the part of the organization, in

Figure 17.4 A public museum system and its context

question. A passable root definition of a museum might be:

Root definition of a museum system   A system in which professionals are employed to collect, preserve and research objects which are of value to people because of their historic, scientific or aesthetic qualities, and to use them as a source of evidence and in the transmission of ideas, concepts and insights through displays, publishing, lecturing or other public events.

Systems abstractions

Now we must pass into the abstract domain of systems, and imagine one or more relevant systems. A relevant system describes the process which is essential to the aspect of the organization that one is interested in. If the preservation of the collections is what we are leading to, then this is the focal point on this occasion.

It is very helpful to think first about a completely different sort of system. What are the basic processes in a factory making shoes or any other commodity for sale, for example (*Figure 17.5*)? Here, the physical goods are brought in as raw materials, are worked so as to transform them into finished products, and

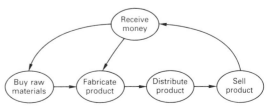

Figure 17.5 A relevant system for a production company

eventually pass out of the system to be sold, to provide money to keep the system working.

In contrast, the root definition of a museum said that its collections are to be preserved within the system. They form the non-renewable resource to be used not for making something different, but for putting across ideas and concepts, and transmitting these to the public. An abstract view of the process that would be needed in such a system might look like *Figure 17.6.* Though they are very broad approximations to reality, the contrast between the production company and the museum is clear. Readers might like to try sketching out relevant systems for other allied systems: a library, for instance; or a site of special scientific interest.

While the root definition was a concise description of what a museum is, the relevant system is a description of the theoretical system which would need to exist in order for an organization with that root definition to function. The relevant system needs to be described in words:

A relevant system for museums A system in which a non-renewable, intrinsically valuable resource is acquired, maintained and enhanced for the future, and used and reused without deterioration, in conjunction with knowledge and ideas, to transmit and present evidence for ideas, concepts and insights about culture or history to the general public.

Has the definition of the relevant system changed our view of museums? It has drawn out the fundamental reason for holding collections, and shown that the functions of preserving the collections, and synthesizing and transmitting ideas and concepts, are distinct and separate: in real life these are too often blended into a sort of surrogate ownership of objects. It has also shown us that while the collections must be maintained, because they are non-renewable, and must be the real thing, because they are the basis for ideas and concepts, they are primarily there as a basis, not as an end in themselves. This will give both curators and conservators pause for thought.

The preservation subsystem

The abstraction of the museum relevant system helps to define the relevant system that is needed for the care of the collections: the conservation subsystem.

A relevant system for conservation A subsystem to maintain a non-renewable resource for use as evidence for, or the transmission of, ideas and concepts.

The absolute essence of this system, viewing only its inputs and outputs, is abstract indeed. From this, we can draw up an additional relevant system (*Figure 17.7*):

A second relevant system for conservation To transform or maintain collections or objects in a certain condition C1 into collections of objects in a condition C2, which must be the same or better than condition C1.

This sharpens up our definition, getting to the heart of exactly what is preservation. If collections are to be preserved then clearly condition C2 must not be worse than condition C1, although the definition of

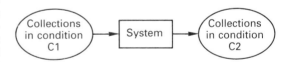

Figure 17.7 The second relevant system for conservation

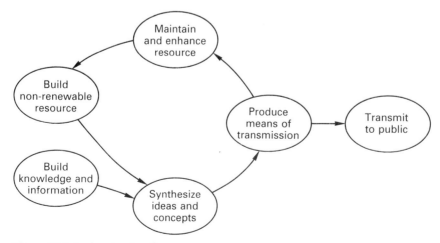

Figure 17.6 A relevant system for a musuem

these conditions (in terms of policies and objectives) would leave a good deal of scope to any individual museum.

Root definition of the conservation subsystem

Working backwards now, we need a root definition for the conservation subsystem. It must relate closely to the root definition for the museum, and take account of the relevant systems described above. A working approximation can be:

Root definition of a subsystem for conservation A subsystem in which professionals maintain and enhance the historical integrity and physical condition of museum collections, by setting standards, monitoring conditions, eliminating causes of deterioration, remedying past deterioration, and preparing objects so that they can be used effectively and without being damaged.

Conceptual model

Once again in the abstract systems world, the next stage in this analysis is to make a conceptual model, which draws on the root definition and shows all the processes which are essential to the operation of the system. The root definition may well have been redrafted in the light of the relevant system. Here, the conceptual model (*Figure 17.8*) will be restricted to the preservation subsystem. The processes which have been distinguished by means of the conceptual model – that is, processes *internal* to the conservation model – are as follows:

(1) set standards for condition, use, storage etc;
(2) monitor condition of collections;
(3) reduce risks and causes of deterioration;
(4) remedy deterioration;
(5) prepare objects for use.
(6) plan and monitor subsystems activities;

The subsystem must also be effective, and contribute to the purposes of the wider system. Therefore, it also contributes to and receives input from subsystems outside it. Its major interactions with processes *external* to the conservation model are:

(1) set policies for, monitor and control this and other subsystems;
(2) provide resources and monitor effective use;
(3) build knowledge relating to collections;
(4) produce media for communication, in which the objects play the central role.

Real world and systems compared

Now the real world, even if only a generalization, can be compared with the systems view set out above. The

system processes will be taken one at a time, those external to the conservation system first.

Processes external to the conservation system

Set policies for the use and maintenance of the collections
Discussed above is the importance to collections preservation of the policies of the whole institution for what use is made of the collections. Wherever possible, nationally or internationally, recognized standards should be referred to and used.

Policies relating to the preservation of the collections must cover:

The balance of the display, demonstration, and archive functions of the institution These may differ for different collections.
What is acceptable use of the collections Some policies on these lines have been established for particular types of object: musical instruments, for example (International Committee for Musical Instrument Collections, 1986); the collections of the Science Museum (Mann, 1989); the care and use of places (Australia ICOMOS, undated).
Collecting and acquisition If too many objects are collected to be maintained within the resources available, then standards agreed for the condition of the collections will not be met.
The respective roles of specialist staff Greenhill has proposed that the curator speaks for the past of the object and the conservator for its future, and that it is the task of management to balance these two views in the interests of the institution (Greenhill, 1983). It is important for the welfare of the institution and its collections that both views are heard, rather than taking it for granted that one should always prevail. The new museum profession, collections management, also plays a vital role in maintaining the physical resource and making it accessible for use: these functions are only really effectively performed if they are centralized.

Policies must of course be clearly and explicitly communicated to the members of the organization, and their implementation monitored. If policies are not succeeding, then it must be considered whether they need adjustment or alteration.They may have been unrealistic in view of the resources available; or they may not have been closely enough targeted towards the central purpose of the organization; or circumstances may have changed.

But in real life, how many institutions have explicit conservation policies? Very few, we may suspect. A lot of often counter-productive discussion might be saved if more institutions had them. The key to developing and monitoring such policies can only be wide involvement in their formulation. Perhaps a good idea would be for institutions to set up internal conservation panels, with a periodically changing membership. These might even include members of the institution's governing body.

Provide resources and monitor effective use
Resources for all activities include staff, finance, space, and equipment and materials. The factor which should

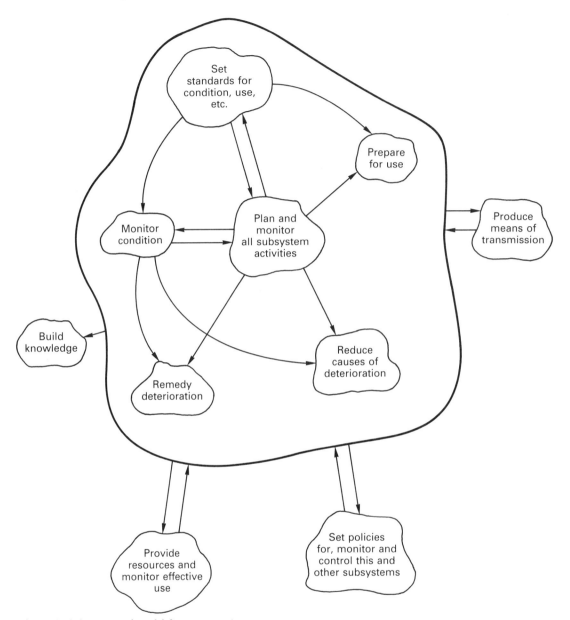

Figure 17.8 A conceptual model for a conservation system

determine the allocation of resources is whether they are adequate to ensure that the policies set above are met. If they are not, then either policies must be adjusted or else resources increased; otherwise, disillusionment and demotivation among staff will be the inevitable consequence.

Space is required both for stores and for work. These need to be kept separate. Collections, objects and people can all be endangered if there is inadequate or unsuitable space.
Finance   The need for this is self-evident.

Equipment and materials must be adequate both for active conservation work and for the proper storage of objects. There are numerous examples of staff being employed without the resources being available for them to do an effective job.
Staff   It is the responsibility of management to ensure that staff with the right expertise and skills are appointed. This is possibly more important for conservation than for any other museum activity, because active conservation treatment, and the effects of passive mistreatment or neglect, are usually irreversible. Poor quality in any other activity can often be corrected subsequently, except perhaps in the documentation

of the provenance of the object. As well as qualified conservation staff, there need to be technical staff who can do a lot of the mundane but essential housekeeping tasks associated with the care of collections. It is not sensible to employ someone with a higher degree to put objects in boxes, for example.

Monitoring the effective use of resources is important. In real life, it must be part of the planning and monitoring process in the conservation system itself to provide information on how resources have been used, and what work has been done.

Build knowledge relating to collections and objects
Treatment often involves the most detailed examination of an object that is ever likely to occur. It may involve scientific examination, and it is always an opportunity for systematic observation. The information so gained is too often confined to a conservation treatment record. Instead, it must be added to the commonly available pool of information about the object.

In real life, conservation and curatorial information systems need to be unified, whether on paper or computerized. Curators could usefully be more aware of the possibilities and limitations of scientific and conservation examination, and articles and publications about objects should wherever relevant include a conservation or scientific contribution.

Produce media for communication
This means transmitting ideas and concepts by means of objects. The internal process of preparing objects will usually be driven by the needs of the external process of producing media. The systems view has pointed up the importance of not letting this take over all resources for conservation.

Processes internal to the conservation system

Set standards for collections condition
It is important to define what is considered acceptable condition for objects and collections. Apart from pictures, it is unlikely that the aim will be perfect display conditions for all objects; indeed, this might well conflict with archive functions. As a minimum, objects in collections should be in a stable condition, that is, not deteriorating; otherwise, there is little point in having them. In other words, condition C2 must not be worse than condition C1.

In real life, this needs to be spelt out as part of the conservation policy.

Monitor condition of collections
Museums cannot know if they are succeeding in maintaining their collections unless some sort of audit is conducted periodically. This will help both accountability and the formation of strategies for improving the care of the collections.

In real life, it is not necessary to examine every individual object; statistical sampling techniques can be used so that only a proportion of objects needs to be inspected. Of course, the method used and the data collected must be the same if results from surveys at different dates are to be compared. Surveys are best done by conservators and curators working together. Too many data are extremely difficult to make sense of, so the purpose of the survey needs to be carefully thought out, and a pilot must be undertaken, analysed and reported beforehand.

Reduce risks and causes of deterioration
In the wrong conditions, whole collections can be destroyed in a short time; in the right ones, collections can be preserved so that they need virtually no remedial work or maintenance. The eighteenth century Chinese bed at Calke Abbey looks as fresh as the day it was made, because it had never been unpacked, and the crates had remained in an equable environment.

The *risks* include those of disaster, fire and flood, as well as those of crime such as theft or vandalism. To reduce these, the institution must spend time and energy on imagining how they might occur, on measures to counter the possibilities, and on drawing up plans to mitigate their effects should they happen. The *causes of deterioration* fall into two broad categories: environmental, from inappropriate humidity or temperature, or pollutant gases or dirt, or pests; and physical, from bad handling, insufficient support, overcrowded storage, or during transport.

Much has been written about preventive conservation and the museum environment (most importantly, Thompson, 1986). The difficult part is to make sure that this well rehearsed and readily available knowledge is applied with common sense and judgement, and incorporated into what museums actually do.

In practice, an absolute prerequisite for success is to incorporate preservation and conservation considerations into the first – planning and specification – stages of every project or activity. Indeed, a formal conservation impact statement perhaps ought to be drawn up. Every activity involving objects should have access to conservation advice – preferably by means of a conservator on its core team, who attends its meetings. Otherwise there is the severe risk of having to change specifications, plans or even structures at a late stage, which is expensive both financially and in relations between staff or contractors. But we are all only human, and still things will not always go right. A willingness to think around problems and to compromise will always be necessary.

Some new thinking about environmental standards may help here (Michalski, 1990). There are many different standards for environments said to be beneficial for different types of object, but in fact little information on how much benefit is gained by creating *nearly* the right conditions. For instance, if it can be considered acceptable for humidity to rise above 60 per cent during two or three weeks of the year, this may save tens of thousands of pounds on plant.

'Greener' methods which concentrate on cost-effective modifications to the building structure, such as insulation, may be both more effective and also much cheaper than the mechanical systems loved by services engineers (Staniforth, 1987; Padfield and Jensen, 1990). For example, the Koblenz Federal Archive is housed in a new building having many of the physical characteristics of a castle! One can only urge consultation with other institutions known to have tackled the same problems: money for travel to visit such places will be very well spent.

Light levels often cause the most conflict in museums. The standards of 50 and 200 lux for sensitive and less sensitive objects are those usually adhered to. However, another way of expressing these is as 200 kilolux hours per year and 650 kilolux hours per year respectively (Thompson, 1986). This means that in certain circumstances the standards can still be met if objects are displayed at say two or three times the normal standard, provided that they are only on display for a short period. If a watercolour spends nine out of ten years in store, then it may be reasonable to display it at 100 lux during a six-month exhibition. This will not cause more fading than displaying it at 50 lux for a year. The difficulties here are that few museums have the effective record and management systems that would allow the cumulative light exposure of an object to be logged over any period; that temporary exhibitions often turn into permanent displays; and that an object once displayed often becomes more sought after in future exhibitions.

The *responsibility* for general preservative measures is often ill defined. Conservators may be responsible for environmental specification and monitoring, but not for organizing its control; stores and storage may well be split between several different curators; security is usually divided between curators and buildings maintenance; responsibility for packing and transport is not attributed at all; and so on.

In actual practice, there needs to be one person at a senior level with delegated general responsibility for the physical welfare of objects. This may be a senior manager; it is increasingly often the head of conservation. The person will probably not control all the staff involved in objects, but he/she must have the authority to see that problems are rectified.

There must be appropriate *procedures, standards and guidelines*. Risks can only be effectively controlled if people are aware that they exist, and know how to avoid them. The museum needs practical, well understood policies and guidelines for handling and using objects, as the basis for standard procedures that everyone understands. Some formal training needs to be provided too. Standard specifications for areas such as storage equipment and materials, and for display design, can save hours of work.

Remedy deterioration

In an important sense, to have to treat an object is to admit failure in other parts of the subsystem. When objects are treated, what is done is extremely important, because they are the basis on which all other museum activities are based. If work is wrongly done it can irredeemably compromise the object's historic nature.

There are two important questions to be resolved here. The first, referring to the setting of standards, is what the general approach to treatment should be: minimalist, with work being oriented towards remedying damage or deterioration and making the object strong enough for use; or restorative, aimed at the restoration of the object's supposed former appearance or function. The second question is whether the most effective treatments are being used, and whether recent advances in understanding deterioration and developing treatments are being taken account of. This can probably only be promoted by making sure that conservators, and curators if possible, attend conferences and refresher courses, which are in plentiful supply.

It must be established *who decides* what should be done to objects. The roles of curators and conservators need to be clarified. It was proposed some years ago that curators should decide 'what' should be done, conservators 'how' (Cannon-Brooks, 1976). This is impractical. It is conservators who actually do the work, and hence have all the power in any real sense. There are probably as many instances of conservators doing far more to an object than curators would have wished as of curators insisting on work which conservators consider unethical. It is essential for managers in charge of both to give a strong lead; to ensure that debate takes place; and to enlist both sides in articulating a policy framework for what work should be done.

Opinion in general is moving strongly towards minimalism in work on objects in museums, for both ethical and financial reasons. Of course there will be some objects so damaged as to need virtual remaking. But it should be considered carefully whether it is actually worth it, if what results is a virtual replica. If parts are replaced, for instance tool handles, the question of whether they are distressed to make them seem old or not must be tackled. Sometimes when touring museums one gets the feeling that no one in the past ever used anything new at all! If objects are to be 'the real thing', it may be best to be honest about restoration. The greatest exception to this is in picture conservation, where every effort is usually made to disguise any replacement of losses. Again, this is in fact a matter of taste, and examination of conserved wall paintings in Italy, for example, will show a wide range of approaches to restored losses.

In real life, there are plenty of examples of curators and conservators working very closely together while an object is conserved, to produce a result that is more than the sum of its parts. For example, the cleaning and investigation of the Winchester Reliquary, excavated in 1976, was a process of discovery for curator, conservator and archaeologist alike (Hinton *et al.*, 1981). The conservation of the Blackett Baby House, an eighteenth century miniature house, showed all the dolls' dresses and furnishings such as the window curtains and bed hangings to have the same constructions and fixings as their real, full-size counterparts – of great interest to costume and furniture historians (Museum of London object). The exhibition series *Art in the Making*, referred to above, fully demonstrates the value of a collaborative approach to examining and conserving pictures.

However, it is not easy to ensure adequate consultation, especially when conservation work is primarily for exhibitions, when both curators and conservators have tight deadlines, and because of the sheer number of objects that are conserved. Some institutions have written treatment proposals, agreed by curator and conservator. While essential for really large and complex projects, this will not of itself promote discussion. Real communication may be most usefully addressed by the conservation panel suggested above.

It is only when objects are conserved in institutions such as museums that really close collaboration like this is possible, and these institutions have a special responsibility to make sure that this happens.

Prepare objects for use
Preparing objects for use means cleaning, mounting, supporting and sometimes restoring them to make them presentable and understandable while on display. This is usually the top priority work of conservation staff. Unfortunately, the objects selected for exhibition tend to be those in the best condition, and so there is little gain interms of the condition of the collection as a whole. Logging the condition of objects treated, and the purpose for which the conservation was done, can give rise to some enlightening management information.

Plan, monitor and control all subsection activities
Like the need for finance, the need for this is self-evident, but it is considerably more difficult to put into practice. However, progress towards proper care of the collections will not happen unless work, budgeting and staff management are properly planned and controlled. This is not the place to discuss these matters in detail, but the need for a unified museum work plan and schedule must be stressed.

Real museum systems

The systems world is very logical. In it, a museum would identify where it fits in the triangle (*Figure 17.1*); accurately define its systems, including the subsystems relating to the preservation of its collections; and establish objectives, policies and structures accordingly. The real world, however, is more accurately described as, in another systems term, a mess: a tangle of string with the ends buried inside it. Why is this?

Museums are just like other institutions: they are composed of people. People at work are not just concerned with the purpose of their job, and how to do it most effectively. Work, as those without it well know, is about more than earning a living. People's view of themselves, society's view of them, their sense of achievement, their power to determine what happens to them and in the world, are all heavily bound up in their work. The operation of systems in museums is, in reality, a matter of how people behave.

The role played by curators in relation to other professionals is central to these systems. Burrett, talking of his Raynor scrutiny of the Victoria and Albert and Science Museums (Burrett, 1985), mentions 'keeper barons'. In recent years, as museums have grown and their public has become more discerning and demanding, many different professions have taken on much more prominent roles. The curator, defined in the *OED* as 'person in charge, manager; keeper or custodian of museum', is now just one professional among others, and these others are taking part in directing the play when they were only meant to shift the scenery.

Like Greenhill before him, Burrett goes on to address the actual issue before us: 'preserving the existence of museum objects'. The physical security of the collections has, he says, a strong claim to priority over all other museum activities, and no museum manager would dare publicly to dissent from this. 'But this principle is not in fact reflected even imperfectly in the actual policies of many, if any, museums . . . adequate conservation . . . can and should be given a much higher priority even to the extent of overriding the curatorial interest in some situations.'

But the two separate major functions of museums – to preserve the collections, and to display and use them – have probably never been so strongly emphasized and at the same time so sharply opposed. Squeezes on museum finance have forced the marketing and display elements of organizations to the fore, since it is perceived that the collections are a resource to be exploited.

The responses of some major museums highlight this ambiguity of objective. Some institutions such as the Royal Scottish Museum have responded by placing their conservation departments within their public service division, and it is likely that the processes of preparing for use and of remedying deterioration will predominate in this organizational climate. Other major museums, such as of course the Victoria and Albert, but also the National Maritime, the Museum of London and others, are redefining the role of curators more generally, separating responsibility for the physical care and management of the collections from the role of synthesizing ideas and concepts. As Burrett recommends, museums are 'bringing to management, including policy-making, the full weight of the museum's professionalism', and recognizing that 'a much greater degree of collegiate management is required'. In the national museums on Merseyside, the head of conservation is part of the most senior management group, reporting to the director. At the same time, the functional analysis being undertaken by people in museums themselves for the Museums Training Institute's scheme of qualification is, if it achieves nothing else, assisting redefinition of who does what in museums.

These changes are in effect making museum systems more like the one proposed in this analysis (especially *Figures 17.6* and *17.8*). In time, we shall judge if the analysis was correct.

Acknowledgements

My thanks go to Alf Hatton, of the Ironbridge Institute, for reading and commenting on the precursor of this chapter and encouraging this approach. I am grateful to Gail Ham, of Coopers Lybrand Deloitte, for sparking off thoughts about museum paradigms, and to Derek Keene of the University of London Centre for Metropolitan History, who helped me to pursue them. Max Hebditch made invaluable comments on the chapter.

References

AUSTRALIA ICOMOS (undated) *The Australia ICOMOS Charter for the Conservation of Places of Cultural Significance* (The Burra Charter)

BS 5454: 1989 'The storage and exhibition of archival documents', British Standards Institution, Milton Keynes

BURRETT, G. (1985) 'After Raynor', in *The Management of Change in Museums*, National Maritime Museum, London

CANNON-BROOKS, P. (1976) 'The art curator and the conservator', *Museums Journal*, **75**, 161–162

CHECKLAND, P. (1981) *Systems Thinking, Systems Practice*, Wiley, Chichester

COMPTROLLER AND AUDITOR GENERAL (1988) *Management of the Collections of the English National Museums and Galleries*, National Audit Office Report, HMSO, London

GREENHILL, B. (1983) 'Museum management', in *Proceedings of the 13th General Conference*, ICOM

HANDY, C. B. (1981) *Understanding Organisations*, Penguin, Harmondsworth

HEBDITCH, M. (1990) 'Why do we preserve objects?', in *Managing Conservation*, conference papers, United Kingdom Institute of Conservation

HINTON, D. A., KEENE, S. and QUALMANN, K. E. (1981) 'The Winchester reliquary', *Medieval Archaeology*, **XXV**, 45–77

ICOM (undated) *Statutes*, ICOM, Paris

INTERNATIONAL COMMITTEE FOR MUSICAL INSTRUMENT COLLECTIONS (1986) 'Recommendations for regulating the access to musical instruments in public collections', *ICOM News*, **39**(3), 5–8

KEENE, S. (1993) *Information for Managing Conservation*, PhD thesis, University College London

MANN, P. R. (1989) 'Working exhibits and the destruction of evidence', *Journal of Museum Management and Curatorship*, **8**, 369–387

MACGREGOR, N. (1990) 'Museums for their own sake', *The Guardian*, 11 October

MICHALSKI, S. (1990) 'Towards specific lighting guidelines', in *Proceedings of the 9th Triennial Meeting of the ICOM Committee for Conservation*, ICOM, Los Angeles

NAUGHTON, J. (1983) 'Soft systems analysis: an introductory guide', in *Complexity, Management and Change: Applying a Systems Approach*, course T310 Block 4, Open University, Milton Keynes

PADFIELD, T. and JENSEN, P. (1990) 'Low energy control in museum stores', in *Proceedings of the 9th Triennial Meeting of the ICOM Committee for Conservation*, ICOM, Los Angeles

RADFORD, T. (1990) 'Cut down to skeleton staff', *The Guardian*, 16 May

STANIFORTH, S. (1987) 'Temperature and relative humidity measurement and control in National Trust houses', in *Proceedings of the 8th Triennial Meeting of the ICOM Committee for Conservation*, ICOM, Los Angeles

SWADE, D. (1990) 'Computer conservation and curatorship', *Resurrection*, **1**(1), British Computer Society

THOMPSON, G. (1986) *Museum Environment*, Butterworths, London

ULBERG, A. D. and LIND, R. C. JR. (1989) 'Consider the potential liability of failing to conserve collections', *Museum News*, January/February

VICKERS, G. (1981) 'The poverty of problem solving', *Journal of Applied Systems Analysis*, **8**. Reprinted in Mayon-White, B. (ed.) (1986) *Planning and Managing Change*, Harper and Row in association with the Open University, London

WEIL, S. E. (1983) *Beauty and the Beasts*, Smithsonian Institution Press, Washington, DC

Case study 17.1

Collections conservation in Oxfordshire

Karen Hull

Oxfordshire Museums underwent internal reorganization during 1992. As part of the County Council Department of Leisure and Arts, museums along with libraries, archives, countryside and arts were integrated into five geographic areas. Curators became museum officers and spread throughout the areas as part of area teams, managed locally. Site managers take responsibility for museum buildings, thus in theory releasing museum officers for greater involvement with their local publics *and* maintaining a central county-wide role with collections. The system is still developing and is not yet fully staffed.

Museum collections management was retained centrally to give support to the branch museums and museum officers and to manage the county-wide collections. The Collections Management Team comprises: Collections Manager; Conservation Manager, Senior Conservator and Conservation Officers; Keeper of Collections, Registrar and Photographer; Collection Management Assistant and Curatorial Trainee.

A Professional Services Team headed by the County Museums Officer monitors policy and professional performance measures. The team includes Senior Museum Officers and other related county-wide heads, i.e. Archives, Centre for Oxfordshire Studies and the Development Officer of Cogges Manor Farm Museum.

The first task of the new Collections Management Team has been to move the county's reserve collections to the new joint store. This purpose-built building provides 1700 square metres of storage and work space including a laboratory, a workshop and a documentation/research room. The move has provided a real knowledge of the objects, as staff document, photograph and pack the social history collections. A full inventory is being created for the first time of archaeological, social history and large agricultural collections. At the same time, the collecting policy is being reviewed, and a collection management policy written. Fundamental questions are being tackled head on. Oxfordshire Museums' statement of aims promises to: 'provide services which create an understanding and appreciation of Oxfordshire's heritage and environment by developing the full potential of the collections within their care and by working with other organizations with similar aims (Museums Arts Libraries Leisure, March 1992).

As we understand our collections better, the task of collections management becomes clear. We must maintain a creative tension between caring for our collections and developing their full potential. Access and accountability are high on the agenda of the Department of Leisure and Arts. The collections, or non-renewable resources, are there as a basis for the conversations we can build between the objects and the public. It is in those conversations that we are able to gather more information and interpretations and add more layers of understanding to the past and the present.

This case study looks at some of the methods used in Oxfordshire to use collections and to monitor and maintain the tensions that are inherent within active collections management. Using the terminology of Suzanne Keene's Chapter 17, the relevant system to *our* real world, although still developing, has a number of key points. It is, at heart, a system of involvement.

Setting a policy

The policy of involvement begins with the team itself – valuing individuals and the skills they bring. Team building has been a rewarding exercise. We began by asking ourselves why we work in museums and by sharing individual notions of what a museum was for! From this dialogue we built a statement of purpose for collections management; 'To care for, develop and give access to Oxfordshire's collections'. We shall repeat this exercise as experience and personnel change.

As a direct outcome of our first discussions, conservation officers are now involved in a newly created Accessions Group to which all new acquisitions are brought and questioned. Exhibition planning and redisplay also include conservation staff at the first stage rather than the last. A preventive conservation programme is under way which encourages museum officers and site staff to be involved with monitoring and prevention and at the same time providing a 'flying squad' help service for general housework and maintenance to stores and displays.

The revision of the collecting policy is involving all curatorial staff and will layer the collections, again in close discussion with conservators. Layering will place some objects in the 'permanent archive' category, with 'handling' collections at the other extreme.

Accountability brings with it a tighter discipline on collecting, and in Oxfordshire we are placing a greater emphasis on recording, particularly of contemporary issues. This pulls the museum photographer firmly out of the role of supporting technician into recorder and creator of small two-dimensional exhibitions.

Providing resources

Oxfordshire is indeed fortunate to have a new purpose-built store which provides $1700\,\mathrm{m}^2$ of environmentally controlled space. Laboratory, workshop, sensitive stores and research space are included within the building, which will provide the base for conservation, care, documentation, research and access. Even so, as revenue budgets diminish the value of the team skills rises. The Collections Management Team is supplemented by the county-wide team of museum officers who hold specialisms related to the strengths of the collections, i.e. archaeology, social history, natural history etc. It is in those complementary skills and a common sense of purpose that our real resources lie, and unlike the collections these resources need constant encouragement and renewal. Collections management is as much about people management as it is about objects.

Clearly communicating the enthusiasm and expertise of the museum staff is the best route to a greater public understanding of the collections.

Producing media and communications

Oxfordshire's policy of access to the reserve collections is benefited hugely by all the collections being under one roof for the first time.

Research facilities and regular public open days will be part of the store's life. Documentation is the beginning (and often the end!) of accessibility. In Oxfordshire, Modes and Modes Plus and a full photographic record of the social history collections support the availability of the objects themselves. We are about to tackle the task of layering the access to collections as part of the revised collecting policy.

An integrated computer system is planned to link museums' object information, potentially, with the sites and monuments record, the local studies collections and the archives. All those resources would then be available through both museum and library service points.

Other media for communication are as follows.

Flying objects

Purpose built and designed by the conservation section, flying objects (FOs) are cased in a dual-role carry/display unit. Security, stability and ultraviolet protection are integral to the design. The objects are chosen from the reserve collection to travel to non-museum venues with two clear objectives. First, they make contact with and give opportunities for conversations between museum officers and non-museum visitors. Secondly, the objects advertise the core work of museums, carrying a simple statement of why we collect. At the time of writing, the prototype is being tested. We hope to have created ten FOs by the end of 1994.

Museum boxes

The museum box scheme began in the late 1980s as part of reminiscence work. In 1991, with the help of grant-aid from the Area Museum Service and help in kind from the charity Link Age, 26 boxes were produced using handling material. The boxes are themed on topics such as 'A Day at the Seaside' and 'Washday'. A pilot scheme was set up in cooperation with Oxfordshire County Council's Department of Social Services. Two members of staff from each day-care or residential centre for the elderly attended a training day and follow-up session after their first loan of a box. The training built up personal contact and understanding of the museum service and the collections involved. This involvement has not only meant a greater respect for the objects and their safety – which had been a real problem with earlier users – but also helped with evaluation and monitoring. The scheme is about to widen to the private sector and the popularity of the boxes could easily overtake use.

Alert maps

The collections and records associated with the natural history collections are currently being prepared for use within the planning process of local government. Information on habitats and species will provide a centralized biological database and create alert maps for use throughout the county in planning policy in reference to nature conservation.

Inputting, as ever, is a problem, but the end product will apply a wonderful and previously unsung resource to an area of real need.

Exhibitions

Oxfordshire Museums no longer has a designer post, so members of the Collection Management Team are acquiring DTP and display skills to support museum officers in generating small local exhibitions and to help repair permanent displays. Future county-wide exhibitions will be a mixture of contemporary issue and collection-based displays, with the greater emphasis on collections. Museums are historically weak at selling their core activities. We have a policy of reversing that professional trait!

Build knowledge

Most of these media for communication do encourage the conversations referred to earlier. The Change

Project is another new venture aiming to build our knowledge as well as share our own. We hope to establish a network of recorders – recording change throughout the county in a variety of media that will transfer into the collections, i.e. photographs, oral recordings etc. So many local projects produce material that is enjoyed for a brief while and then lost. The Change Project hopes to involve the people of Oxfordshire in what we do and museums in what local societies and schools are interested in.

Another aspect of building knowledge will be realized in combining the conservation records of condition, treatments etc. with the curatorial documentation. Group discussion and teamwork too gives a much richer mix to the background and understanding of the collections. This can only benefit the interpretation.

Research is given high priority in the collections management policy but, as with so many museum services, allocating sufficient time is a real problem. The public service role within the Department of Leisure and Arts is understandably strong. Research still bears the stamp of the ivory tower – and yet must be recognized as fundamental to every other area of our work.

Monitoring

Monitoring in terms of conservation practice is a continuous task involving not simply conservators but all curatorial and site staff. Observation and responsibility for monitoring are central planks of the preventive conservation programme and are included in in-house training for all levels of staff, particularly museum assistants and attendants. The preventive conservation programme uses a cross-section of the Collections Management Team to systematically deal with gallery problems and storage areas in the branch museums. The main reserve store has full air handling but will need constant watch as the new building settles.

Setting standards of environmental control will be comparatively easy in the main store – but our branch museums, in unsuitable and various buildings, will rely heavily on the training we can give to staff *in situ* and the resources available centrally for building maintenance and repair.

Monitoring our own performance is easier and is encouraged within the management systems of service planning: a yearly exercise and staff appraisals. Like most museums, Oxfordshire's danger lies in trying to tackle too much.

A system of involvement with collections brings with it the tensions of care versus use, which can only be managed creatively by the staff respecting conflicting disciplines, by debate and by constant reference to the aims of the service.

Oxfordshire's practice affirms the paragraph at the end of Chapter 17: real museum systems are built of people.

18

Working with other interests: the natural heritage

Graham Taylor

The themes of previous chapters have emphasized that the conservation of the natural environment frequently requires a collaborative approach. Whether developing a site explicitly for conservation or promoting greater awareness of the need for conservation of the wider countryside, few practitioners can operate in isolation.

Information and advice

The starting point for any countryside conservation or recreation initiative has to be an understanding of the resource, as described in Chapter 7. Information will be held by government conservation agencies (Countryside Commission, Countryside Council for Wales, English Nature, Scottish Natural Heritage) on the conservation status, and often they will have detailed survey information useful for management purposes. Designation on landscape or scientific grounds is important because it may unlock advice, influence and resources.

The voluntary conservation bodies such as county conservation trusts are likely to have information on sites which are of nature conservation interest, even if not of sufficiently high quality to justify designation as sites of special scientific interest (SSSIs).

Other sources of data are museums, which frequently house biological records centres, and local and national park authorities who as planning authorities maintain their own records and can assist with other information.

Consents

The national conservation agencies and local planning authorities are important collaborators because consent may be needed to do work, especially on sensitive sites such as SSSIs. If there is a changed use of land it may require planning consent, usually from the local district council. The planning authorities will also be able to advise on the need for other consents such as from the National Rivers Authority if the development is likely to affect drainage or water courses. The lesson is to talk to everyone who is likely to need to be consulted, and to talk early on in the process so that both parties are able to influence events without pressure.

Achieving influence

Local authorities can help in many ways and open doors which might otherwise be obstacles, especially to voluntary groups. But even national government agencies find it helpful to use existing networks and channels of communication. For example the National Farmers' Union has an intimate knowledge of the farming community and can provide advice on how to approach groups or individual farmers. Parish councils can be very helpful with information and in effecting introductions and undertaking voluntary work.

Resources

Voluntary bodies are likely to require financial support, and grant-aid is frequently instrumental in getting even modest schemes off the ground. The support of the local authorities can be influential in attracting grant-aid from bodies like the Countryside Commission. In other cases the support of the conservation agencies can be instrumental in attracting grants from the National Heritage Memorial Fund, and local authorities can advise and assist in attracting European funding in those areas where such funds are available. Sponsorship and help in kind from commercial sources is also increasingly helpful to conservation bodies.

Putting the scheme together

In the process of consulting with the many interest groups involved in the countryside, practitioners should keep in mind the potential for collaborative ventures. The primary consideration should be to achieve the objectives of the scheme. In large schemes the aim might well be to divide the tasks and responsibilities according to the capacity of the partners. For example, a voluntary wildlife group might have identified an important woodland on a farm requiring management. The options of acquisition by the wildlife group or a voluntary management agreement between the farmer and the local authority present very different issues.

Acquisition by another body, perhaps a national voluntary conservation organization with greater access to funds and management expertise, might be preferable. This can leave the local group to provide volunteers or arrange public access events to promote public awareness and understanding.

Protective ownership of small sites, valuable though that may be in some cases, is only one part of a strategy for conservation of the countryside. Owners, once informed, are often quite proud to be host to rare species or managers of important landscapes. Advice may be readily taken or agreement given to voluntary help with management. In this process, the help of the National Farmers' Union and the Country Landowners' Association at the regional or county level should be sought.

Promotional campaigns, to encourage habitat or species protection for example, can attract sponsorship and help in kind because of the high profile they present. Again public sector bodies may be able to complement sponsorship money raised by voluntary bodies. Similarly, promotion of public awareness and enjoyment of the countryside can attract support from several sectors. However, voluntary bodies should be thorough in their planning if they open sites to the public. Again, consult the appropriate authorities, including the Health and Safety Executive if any risks are involved to visitors, employees or volunteers.

Case study 18.1

The Mid Wales Festival of the Countryside

Arwel Jones

The Festival of the Countryside is a region-wide programme of tourism and recreational events which involves a wide range of organizations, including: a rural development agency, the Development Board for Rural Wales (DBRW); conservation bodies such as the Countryside Council for Wales and the Montgomeryshire, Dyfed and North Wales Wildlife Trusts; tourism organizations such as the Wales Tourist Board, Mid Wales Tourism Ltd and Heart of Wales Tourism Association; and many local and community groups.

The initiative was launched in 1985 as a contribution towards the World Conservation Strategy, under the direction of CYNEFIN, a Welsh conservation foundation. It is a coordinated attempt at sustainable, environmentally sensitive tourism development and marketing over an area of $7700\,\text{km}^2$, some 40 per cent of the land surface of Wales.

The purpose of the Festival

Aims

The main aims of the Festival are:

Environmental education To convey, in an interesting and coherent way, the messages of the countryside and of conservation.
Enjoying the countryside To satisfy the varied recreational demands of residents and tourists.
Socio-economic To stimulate the rural economy and boost revenue for providers of rural attractions.

Objectives

Detailed objectives include:

(1) improving access to the countryside whilst protecting the most sensitive and fragile areas of mid Wales;
(2) increasing public awareness of natural history, rural issues, historical and cultural dimensions of mid Wales;
(3) putting agriculture and other rural industries in context and encouraging the purchase and use of rural foods and crafts;
(4) encouraging the use of public transport;
(5) creating jobs and economic benefit;
(6) providing a single, comprehensive and integrated programme of events, activities and attractions in the mid Wales countryside;
(7) involving a wide range of organizations, groups and individuals in the development, planning, delivery and review of the programme;

(8) bringing in well known personalities to boost local events and maintain a high profile for the Festival as a whole;
(9) promoting environmental education through walks, talks, lectures, exhibitions, leaflets and other means;
(10) encouraging the establishment of local festivals as part of the main programme;
(11) promoting participation in environmentally acceptable sports;
(12) providing publicity and public relations support to event organizers;
(13) acting as a funding broker, identifying and providing grant-aid, fees and other sources of income where possible;
(14) providing professional support and backup to event organizers;
(15) stimulating a range of related publications, including leaflets, booklets, catalogues and books.

How this is achieved

A key factor is that of partnership. In addition to the organizations mentioned above, every local authority in mid Wales has become actively involved in the Festival, largely through a funding partnership with the Countryside Council for Wales, and formerly through the Countryside Commission Office for Wales. These include Gwynedd, Dyfed and Powys County Councils, Brecknock Borough Council, and Ceredigion, Meirionnydd, Montgomeryshire and Radnorshire District Councils. The region's two National Park Authorities, Snowdonia and the Brecon Beacons, contribute events and ideas. Various commercial sponsors have also been secured.

A significant body of events has developed during the Festival's eight years of operation, some 600 in total each year, many of which are of an innovative nature (*Figures 18.1, 18.2*). The Festival's team of four (two full-time) people acts as the central coordinator by:

(1) directly organizing key events;
(2) working with others to develop and establish new events;
(3) identifying opportunities for innovation;
(4) pulling together and marketing the overall programme;
(5) providing a year-round support and advisory service.

The programme includes rural activities grouped together under the following themes:

Figure 18.1 Mid Wales Festival Director and David Bellamy review the programme

Nature and wildlife These include nature reserve visits, bird and mammal watching and natural history courses.

Walks and guides A range of guided and self-guided walks.

Rural rides Narrow-gauge railway trips, white water rafting, pony trekking and mountain biking.

History and industry Visits to working farms, forests, reservoirs, markets and water mills, castles and other historic sites.

Arts and crafts Art, sculpture and photographic exhibitions and visits to craft workshops.

Eating out Carefully selected quality cafés and restaurants which offer regional cuisine.

The programme is also subdivided by area and by frequency of event (daily, weekly or less frequently).

The main promotional vehicle is a free magazine, with an annual print run of approximately 120,000, which is widely distributed throughout the region and beyond, by direct delivery to tourist information centres and other outlets, and by mail order. Specific local posters and handbills are often also produced. The team issues regular media releases, events diaries and special itineraries for journalists, and liaises closely with television, radio and press contacts.

The Festival has become a local development agent for DBRW, administering a significant social development budget to enable community groups and other organizations to develop innovative activities. A Farming Festival has been organized by the Dolgellau and District Tourism Association, a Countryside Fair is run jointly by Aberystwyth Town Council and the local branch of Friends of the Earth, and an annual village exhibition is organized by the Llandinam Community Group. Other sponsored organizations have included

Figure 18.2 The Royal Welsh Show, one of the many events in the Festival programme

the Montgomeryshire Wildlife Trust, the Ramblers and the RSPB.

In addition, CYNEFIN has been appointed a rural arts agent by the Calouste Gulbenkian Foundation, with a budget for the development of community arts and cultural activity.

An important step was the 1989 publication of the *Mid Wales Companion*, a 220 page softback guide to the landscape, wildlife, history and culture of mid Wales, written by Moira K. Stone for CYNEFIN and published by Anthony Nelson Ltd. The book was designed to complement the Festival and provide more in-depth information for those wishing to explore the region in detail (*Figure 18.3*). Careful attention was paid to the selection of sites mentioned in the text and to the significance of local culture and the Welsh language. A series of treasure trails using clues from the *Companian* has been developed as a spin-off.

During 1991, a skills and needs survey of the Festival's contributing organizations and individuals revealed that most felt their strengths lay in their experience, their professionalism, and their understanding and love of their subject and area. Perceived weaknesses, however, lay in marketing and in business and organizational skills. With this in mind, a weekend seminar was run in 1992 to address these needs, supported by the EC and Powys Training and Enterprise Council. Further training events are planned.

Results and benefits

The Festival has now become an integral and respected part of the tourism landscape of mid Wales. It has succeeded in creating a high profile 'green' image for the region whilst maintaining a sensitive approach to development. By consulting with partners and regularly reviewing activities, a working balance has been achieved between the needs of economic development and the conservation of the region's natural resources. Thus far, serious conflict has been avoided.

The Festival team is often consulted by national and regional organizations on responsible tourism issues, and the initiative has become well recognized at home and abroad. For example, the Festival received the British Tourist Authority's 'Come to Britain' award for public enterprise in 1985 and was highly commended at the first 'Tourism for Tomorrow' awards sponsored by the TV programme 'Wish You Were Here' and the BTA in 1990. It was identified as an exemplary project in a German soft tourism publication entitled *Mehr Wissen – Mehr Handeln*, and came sixth throughout Europe in a rural tourism competition organized by Euroter in 1991.

In 1985, the Festival attracted 90,000 known participants. By 1992 this had grown to 280,000, and there were a further 600,000 estimated attendances at related

Figure 18.3 Researching the *Mid Wales Companion*

commercial attractions. This is estimated to be worth over £5 million to the regional economy, based on an average spend per participant per night of £20 (using official UK tourist statistics).

Future plans

These include:

(1) developing an extended programme to include autumn and winter activities;
(2) working with the accommodation sector – in particular farmhouse groups – to establish new green tourism packages;
(3) building on international links, e.g. with the Instituto de Desarrollo Comunitario de Galicia in northern Spain and with the Gîtes organization in Brittany;
(4) producing a handbook based on the Festival's experience in events development, animation and community involvement. This initiative is part-funded by the European Commission, and English, French and German language versions are planned.

Reference

STONE, M. K. (1989) *Mid Wales Companion*, CYNEFIN, Anthony Nelson Ltd

19

Working with other interests: the built environment and museums

Michael Stratton

Heritage managers cannot solve every problem unaided; they need to network with organizations who can advise them over specific issues and concerning possible sources of financial support. This chapter takes up some of the themes considered in Section Two and identifies bodies that might be able to offer expertise or grants. The most important organizations in the United States are also identified, and a broad indication is given as regards the structure of architectural conservation and museums in Europe.

Buildings: defining and recording the resource

Before embarking on any recording project it is worth examining whether there are any drawings by the architect or by historians. The first port of call is the National Monuments Record, holding the work of the Royal Commission as well as a range of drawing and photographic records. The RCHME is responsible for the Survey of London which researches the architectural and historical development of London, parish by parish. The Royal Institute of British Architects has a massive collection of architects' drawings, while the Public Record Office at Kew also has many drawings within its archives. The national monuments archives for Scotland and Wales should be consulted as appropriate. There are also bodies with comparable remits in Ulster and Eire. The Conway Library within the Courtauld Institute of Art holds a library of around 800,000 photographs of European buildings and a collection of architectural drawings.

Many county and city records offices hold underused collections of deposited building plans, showing the layout and elevations of properties erected from the late nineteenth century. Bound volumes list the submissions in chronological sequence and provide a register for the bundles of drawings. Sadly some councils chose to edit, microfiche or simply destroy these invaluable records of urban development.

If it proves necessary to implement a recording programme, it is worth contacting the royal commissions, though they are tied, for the most part, to recording structures that are to be demolished, or threatened with major alterations, or to regional or thematic surveys covering particular types of building. English Heritage also undertakes some recording work.

The level and techniques of recording must be appropriate to the site and the circumstance. In the case of complex elevations it is worth examining the potential of photogrammetry through contacting the Institute of Advanced Architectural Studies. Some counties have archaeology units that may be able to assist with recording. County archaeology units may be directly funded by the county council with additional staff earning their keep through contracts, typically funded by developers. Smaller units may only have one core funded post, the county archaeologist, with the other staff being on short-term contracts. Most units are now only able to undertake outside work on a contract basis. Several universities have departments with appropriate skills; it may be worth encouraging students, whether individual or as part of a field project, to take on a particular project. In the 1970s and 1980s it was possible to establish recording and excavation teams with government funding through employment training schemes; such projects may still be practicable in urban and industrial areas with high unemployment.

Archaeological excavation is being used more selectively as a research process, owing to the expense and the destruction involved. The main national body for archaeology in Britain is the Council for British Archaeology, which is working to promote archaeology in education, heighten public consciousness towards the archaeological heritage and promote appropriate policies of conservation and research. The Institute of Field Archaeologists is attempting to bring some minimum standard into play amongst the recorders and excavators at work across the country. Those involved in leading teams of archaeologists may benefit from contact with the Standing Conference of Archaeological Unit Managers.

The national recording body for the United States is the Historic American Buildings Survey (HABS), based in Washington. It is paralleled by the Historic American Engineering Record (HAER) concerned with industrial sites. Some European countries have national agencies involved in recording. The main body in France is the Inventaire Général, a research and documentation department initiated in 1964 and linked to the heritage section of the Ministry of Culture. The Inventaire also supports individual or group research projects. Recording work is also undertaken by the ministries of culture in other countries, such as Greece. Elsewhere, e.g. in Germany, projects are more likely to be initiated on a regional basis.

The amateur has played a key role in British preservation and much can be achieved through encouraging specialist groups to undertake inventories or recording. The Friends of Cast Iron, based in New York and led by the indefatigable Margot Gayle, proved to be a most effective organization in promoting the protection of a particular type of building. Gayle's success in preserving American iron architecture encouraged the formation of comparable groups, such as the Friends of Terracotta or, in Britain, the Tiles and Architectural Ceramics Society. Letterboxes, pillboxes, follies and fountains are all the subject of societies only too keen to add to their inventories and to offer advice.

Buildings: the legislation and institutional context

In Chapter 12, Anthony Streeten has considered the main bodies involved in building conservation and the way in which the legislation operates. The conservation cause can usually be furthered, especially if the case goes to public inquiry, by liaison with as many groups and individuals as time permits. English Heritage is sponsored by the Department of the Environment to protect the historic environment, and to grant-aid to local authorities and individuals. The equivalent statutory bodies for Scotland and Wales are Historic Scotland and CADW: Welsh Historic Monuments.

Most towns have local amenity societies. A directory is held by the Civic Trust, which also acts as a link between the work of the building preservation trusts who apply revolving funds to conservation projects. The Civic Trust administers an awards scheme to bring attention to the most successful conservation projects. In recent years the Trust has given particular attention to projects combining environmental and economic regeneration in run-down towns and cities. It also works with voluntary organizations to tackle some of the environmental problems of inner-city areas. The Civic Trust has regional offices, and comparable work is undertaken by the Scottish Civic Trust and the Civic Trust for Wales.

The key to success in fighting to save a building or structure, or in gaining approval for a scheme of adaptation, is to make best use of the planning process and gain the support of the relevant officers in local authorities and English Heritage, rather than to launch a proposal or campaign out of the blue. The *Municipal Yearbook* lists the key officers in planning departments. The complex structure of English Heritage is unravelled in a 'family tree' printed in issues of their *Conservation Bulletin*.

There are a number of books which explain the planning procedures and bodies involved in conservation work, the most useful being by Pearce (1989), Ross (1991), Suddards (1988) and Cambridge County Council (1984). The Association of Conservation Officers has emerged as an articulate body for representing the interests of conservation within local government; topical issues are considered in its journal *Context*.

The national pressure groups exert a remarkable influence over the future of threatened buildings and, if convinced of the worth of a cause, will channel their energies towards important buildings or causes. The Georgian Group, the Victorian Society, and the Thirties Society were all established following the loss of key buildings; they tend to be at their most effective when fighting for the retention of churches, houses or major public buildings by recognized architects. They combine casework over applications to demolish or alter listed buildings with visits, lectures and publications. The Twentieth Century Society deals with any structures built after 1914.

The Ancient Monuments Society extends its charity to any listed building under threat and spends most of its time at public inquiries. The Society for the Protection of Ancient Buildings is the oldest of the amenity societies, its manifesto having been drawn up by William Morris. The society specializes in advising on repairs, producing technical pamphlets and running courses. Save Britain's Heritage is less of a membership organization than a media-conscious pressure group that aims to find alternative uses for historic buildings at risk. Reports are produced on individual buildings, on such diverse building types as chapels, factories and swimming baths, or on towns that are suffering from inappropriate planning policies. The Association for Industrial Archaeology fights to preserve industrial buildings, monuments and machinery.

The National Trust is less of a pressure group and more of a long-established and revered institution that holds some of Britain's finest country houses and landscapes in trust. The Trust is becoming more involved in urban and industrial sites, having recently taken into care a Victorian middle-class villa for example. It is often worth developing contact with the appropriate regional director and historic buildings representative.

The responsibility for conservation in Ireland is vested in the Office of Public Works; some monuments are owned or held in guardianship by the Commissioners of Public Works. Other buildings are listed in a Register of Historical Monuments. In Northern Ireland the Department of the Environment (NI) has responsibility for historic buildings and monuments.

The conservation lobby has gained a comparable strength in the United States. Reflecting the scale of the country, activity tends to focus at city or state level, many historical societies owning a range of museums and historic houses and proving able to draw in major sponsors for special exhibitions and projects. The American Association for State and Local History promotes the work of regional and local societies through publications, training programmes and research.

The National Trust for Historic Preservation is more directly involved in urban conservation than its British counterpart. The emphasis, since its establishment in 1949, has been to increase public awareness and promote public involvement in the preservation of buildings and districts. It coordinates preservation efforts and provides advice, as well as maintaining a variety of properties. There are six regional offices.

The range of federal programmes was cut back during the Reagan era. The bodies of most direct significance to conservation are grouped within the US Department of the Interior. The nation's national historic sites and national parks are administered by the National Park Service, which also identifies national historic landmarks. The Interagency Resources Division keeps the National Register of Historic Places, reviewing nominations from state historic preservation offices.

The Advisory Council in Historic Preservation reviews federal projects affecting properties in the National Register of Historic Places. The Conservation Foundation is the only national organization that relates the high level of American awareness of nature conservation to the protection of urban areas. There is a plethora of associations covering different aspects of the built environment, including the amenity-conscious Partners for Liveable Places and the more historicist Victorian Society in America.

The network of local preservation activity is complex, varying from one state to the next. A historical preservation office may be in the form of a state's division or department, vested in the historical society or linked to parks and recreation. The major cities such as Chicago and New York have Landmarks Commissions which work to protect designated buildings and areas. The pattern of preservation organizations is equally unpredictable; they may be titled alliances, leagues, trusts or councils. For an introduction to the network of American preservation organizations, refer to Maddex (1985).

The infrastructure of conservation activity in Canada shares some features of American practice. Canada Parks Service has designated a series of historic sites; meanwhile Heritage Canada Foundation is a non-profit organization more interested in sites of historical than high architectural importance. The approach to area conservation as well as museum preservation and interpretation varies between states. In Australia the main onus lies on the state, each having a heritage commission. The National Trust and National Parks Services play an important role in some areas of conservation activity such as industrial archaeology.

European countries differ in the extent to which conservation is delegated to regional as opposed to national level. Some see a greater proportion of activity amongst volunteers. The national system of protection in Denmark, run by the National Agency for Physical Planning, is supplemented by local listings by several provincial cities, in collaboration with the National Agency and the National Museum. In Italy the listing of buildings has been slow at a national level; progress has been strongest through the commitment of provinces such as in Milan and Bologna. In some countries responsibility is largely devolved to provinces. The provincial offices of conservators of monuments take a key role in Poland. In Belgium responsibility has been divided between Flemish and Walloon authorities since 1975; this division is mirrored by most of the voluntary organizations.

The individual *Länder* in Germany are independent as regards cultural affairs and have their own approach to conservation. States develop lists of monuments, distinguishing between those that are architectural, movable such as sculpture or painting, or archaeological. Each state has a body called the *Denkmalschutz* which is responsible for the care of monuments. Conservation in Switzerland tends to concentrate on the cantonal and municipal level.

Southern European countries are likely to have a ministry of culture that oversees both building conservation and museum administration. The Portuguese Institute of the Cultural Heritage is responsible for the preservation and conservation of historic buildings, while the protection of monuments in Turkey is administered by the Ministry of Culture. In Greece conservation activity is concentrated within the Ministry of Culture which conserves sites, buildings and artefacts; the Ministry of Urban Planning lists buildings and sites. France shares this characteristic through the work of its Historic Monuments Administration.

The legislative structure may make a fundamental distinction between the protection of buildings in private and in public ownership. In Sweden publicly owned buildings gained the possibility of protection by an Act of 1920, and ruins and buried sites in 1942, while private buildings could only be protected after legislation was enacted in 1960. The system is run by the Central Office of National Antiquities.

The International Council on Monuments and Sites (ICOMOS) aims to further the conservation and protection of groups and buildings; it has a network of national and international committees. In recent years its most widely publicized work has been the designation of world heritage sites, including Durham Castle and Cathedral, the Ironbridge Gorge, the Statue of Liberty and Yosemite National Park.

Buildings: conservation techniques

Anybody involved with architectural conservation in England needs to be aware of the range of grants available from English Heritage and the conditions with which any application must comply. An introduction to the funds available for listed buildings, ancient monuments and conservation areas is provided in Chapter 12 by Anthony Streeten. Broadly parallel systems of funding and advice for outstanding buildings, ancient monuments and conservation areas are offered in Scotland and Wales by Historic Scotland and CADW: Welsh Historic Monuments. It is always advisable to discuss any project informally with an inspector before making an application. From 1 April 1991 the Conservation Group of English Heritage has been organized on a regional basis, north, midlands and south, following the model of the London division. The regional directors are based at Fortress House, in London.

The Department of the Environment, the Scottish Office and the Welsh Office administer grant schemes for deprived inner-urban areas; projects may incorporate aspects of building conservation. Other relevant schemes include derelict land grants and the special grants programme of the DoE, the latter being aimed towards voluntary organizations. The highest levels of grant-aiding are channelled through the urban programme linked to inner-city partnership authorities or urban programme authorities. The urban programme in Scotland is administered through the Industry Department for Scotland, and for Wales by the Welsh Office. The Welsh Development Agency assists in environmental improvement programmes in urban areas with several funding schemes.

The urban development corporations have not generally had a very positive image in terms of conservation. However they are able to grant-aid to conversion and restoration projects for buildings to 50 per cent of costs, and some have backed museum and related heritage projects.

Low-interest loans are made available to charities and preservation trusts, for feasibility studies or for the cost of purchasing historic buildings, from the Architectural Heritage Fund.

The European Community has a variety of funds that may be applicable to architectural conservation projects. Many of the schemes, such as the pilot conservation projects (architectural heritage), have a fixed timespan, but a variety of programmes are available especially in areas of high unemployment: contact the European Commission in Brussels.

For technical advice concerning conservation it may be worth contacting the Association for Studies in the Conservation of Historic Buildings, who organize meetings and site visits as well as producing a newsletter and journal.

The Association for Preservation Technology, a Canadian-American association of professional preservationists and curators, has a leading role in disseminating technical information relating to building conservation.

Museums: defining and recording the resource

English Heritage also have a scheme for encouraging adequate standards of storage for excavation archives. Historic Buildings and Monuments (Scotland) have a rescue archaeology programme, grants normally being channelled through an officer within a museum. In the following section, information concerning many of the bodies grant-aiding museums is drawn from Farnell (1990).

The major source of funds for museum purchases is the National Heritage Memorial Fund, which can give grants or loans to purchase or preserve land, buildings or objects. The sums usually have to be combined with other sources of funds. The Purchase Grant Fund (Arts) is administered by the Victoria and Albert Museum for the Museums and Galleries Commission to help finance purchases in the area of the arts by museums. The National Museums of Scotland have a corresponding scheme.

Many different types of collections are the subject of trusts or societies, which can provide advice or contacts. Examples are the Maritime Trust, the British Aviation Preservation Council, the Costume Society, the Furniture History Society and the Ephemera Society.

Most museums now show a strong commitment to documentation, and the Department of National Heritage has funded a range of projects to advance the documentation ethic. The area museum councils and the Scottish Museums Council have also been active in the field of documentation; the latter can assist with the costs of introducing documentation systems.

The main body concerned with advising museums concerning documentation is the Museums Documentation Association, which has recently taken on a more entrepreneurial flavour, undertaking much of its work on a consultancy basis. The National Museums of Scotland have become a centre of expertise for documentation.

A variety of groups are advancing the cause of museum documentation in North America. The Art Information Task Force is evaluating descriptive standards and investigating options for the interchange of information through computer systems. The Computer Interchange of Museum Information Project is working towards a common standard for the communication of museum information, with the support of the Museum Computer Network, active in both the United States and Canada.

Museums: legislation and institutional context

The Museums Association undertakes programmes of training, publications, professional support, research and information to enhance the standards of museums and represent the needs of museum professionals. Founded in 1889, the Association provides a forum, partly through its annual conference and periodic meetings, for the exchange of ideas. The structure and work of the Association has formed a model for comparable bodies in many other countries, most of which produce publications and a directory: examples are the American Association of Museums, the Canadian Museums Association, and the Art Museums Association of Australia. For France and Germany one should contact the Association Générale des Conservateurs des Collections Publiques de France and the Deutscher Museumsbund.

In some European countries the national museums may be administered within a ministry of culture, and be linked more closely with policies concerning architectural conservation than in Britain. In Poland the museums, as well as historical monuments, are managed by the Ministry of Culture and Art. Sweden has possibly the most distinctive approach to museology in Europe, many museums arising from the tradition of people collaborating to research their own history and present it in the form of books and exhibitions. The Samdok project encourages curators to document contemporary life.

The International Council of Museums produces a quarterly magazine, conference proceedings and an annual bibliography. The British committee is termed ICOM UK.

A range of international organizations are affiliated to ICOM including the Association of European Open Air Museums, the International Confederation of Architectural Museums and the International Congress of Maritime Museums.

Different types of museum have their own national organizations. One of the most active in Britain is the Association of Independent Museums, which provides publications and meetings for museums of charitable trusts, company and private status. Advice on the constitution of a museum trust or trading company can be gained from the Charities Aid Foundation.

Two different types of forum assist the museum professional at a regional level. The area museum councils were developed from 1959 to promote closer collaboration between museums and to distribute government funds via the Museums and Galleries Commission. The regional federations of British museums and art galleries date back to the inter-war period and provide a forum for staff to discuss matters of shared interest. The *Museums Yearbook*, produced by the Museums Association, lists the councils and federations and their senior officers and members.

Museums: conservation techniques

Museum professionals frequently need to obtain advice concerning specific conservation problems, especially if they cannot turn to an in-house team of conservators. The area museum councils, major local authority museums, or national museums can often assist on an informal basis. There are specialist groups who can advise concerning certain types of material, for example the Institute of Paper Conservation. The Association of Independent Museums organizes courses on aspects of conservation, while the Ironbridge Institute arranges an annual seminar on the conservation of paint finishes. The appropriate standards and techniques for conserving industrial objects and machinery are less clearly defined. Curators have typically to chase assistance on an *ad hoc* basis, maybe to the relevant department of the Science Museum or to the British Engineerium or Dorothea Restoration.

Monies are being channelled from a variety of sources into improving conservation facilities within museums. The Department of National Heritage can support improvements to ventilation and lighting of galleries as part of conservation measures. The Museums and Galleries Commission (MGC) has a capital grants scheme to help museums improve or extend their accommodation for conservation and storage facilities. This scheme is complemented by the work of the Conservation Unit of the MGC; funds are available for conservators to attend conferences, for training, internships and publications. The MGC also administers the Preservation of Industrial and Scientific Material (PRISM) Fund on behalf of the Science Museum. PRISM grants used to be applicable to the purchase of artefacts of technological or scientific significance; they are now concentrated towards conservation work for collections held by museums. The scheme covers England and Wales; the National Museums of Scotland have a parallel fund.

The Northern Ireland Museums Advisory Committee has been established to advise and support improvements in museums and galleries in Ulster. The Scottish Museums Council offers grants for conservation and documentation as well as development planning. The Council of Museums in Wales has the remit of grant-aiding the training of conservators and initiatives concerning the care of collections. The Conservation Bureau supports the work of conservators in Scotland with advice and grant-aiding, in particular for training and publication.

The area museum councils also administer schemes to advance standards of museum conservation. Most expect grants to be matched by some contribution from other sources. The precise theme of the projects that might be eligible for aiding varies between the different councils: some support laboratory or studio work, others improvements to storage and display conditions, or training for staff.

The United Kingdom Institute for Conservation (UKIC) organizes meetings and training courses on aspects of conservation and produces a newsletter and an annual journal. *The Conservator* and *Conservation News* are edited and produced by UKIC, while the international group IIC publishes *Studies in Conservation*. The American Institute for Conservation of Historic and Artistic Works produces a quarterly newsletter.

The Getty Conservation Institute, based in California, organizes an international and interdisciplinary programme in conservation, supplemented by field projects, conferences and publications.

The International Centre for the Study of the Preservation and Restoration of Cultural Property (ICCROM) produces publications and runs conservation courses at its base in Rome and in other countries. The subjects embrace both architecture and museum collections.

Useful addresses

Australia

Art Museums Association of Australia, PO Box 284, Kingston, ACT 2604

Museums Association of Australia, Museum of Victoria, 328 Swanston Street, Melbourne 3000, Victoria

Belgium

European Commission, JD XVI, Rue de la Loi 200, B-1049 Brussels

Canada

Association for Preservation Technology, PO Box 2487, Station D, Ottawa, Ontario K1P 5W6

Canadian Museums Association, 280 Metcalfe Street, Suite 202, Ottawa, Ontario K2P 1R7

Computer Interchange of Museum Information Project, CIMI Project Manager, 5659 Merkel Street, Halifax, Nova Scotia B3K 2J1

Heritage Canada, 306 Metcalfe Street, Ottawa, Ontario K2P 1S2

Parks Canada, Research Division, 1600 Liverpool Court, Ottawa, Ontario K1A 1G2

France

Association Generale des Conservateurs des Collections Publiques de France, Palais de Louvre, 75041 Paris

ICOMOS, 75 Rue de Temple, 75003 Paris

International Council of Museums (ICOM), Maison de l'Unesco, 1 rue Miollis, 75732 Paris, Cedex 15

L'Inventaire General, Hotel de Vigny, 10 Rue du Parc-Royal, 75003 Paris

Germany

Deutscher Museumsbund, 14–16 Colmanstrasse, D-5300 Bonn 1

Ireland

Irish Architectural Acrchive, 63 Merrion Square, Dublin 2

Office of Public Works, 51 St Stephen's Green, Dublin 2

Italy

International Centre for the Study of the Preservation and the Restoration of Cultural Property, 13 Via di San Michele, 1-00153 Rome

Norway

International Congress of Maritime Museums, Bard Koltveit, Norsk Sjofartsmuseum, Bygdoynesv 37, 0286 Oslo 2

Sweden

Internatioanl Confederation of Architectural Museums, Joran Lindvall, Swedish Museum of Architecture, Skeppsholmen, S-111 49 Stockholm

UK

Ancient Monuments Society, St Andrew by the Wardrobe, Queen Victoria Street, London E4

Architectural Heritage Fund, 17 Carlton House Terrace, London SW1Y 5AW

Association of Conservation Officers, Secretary, 151 Leahurst Road, Hither Green, London SE13 5LW

Association of European Open Air Museums, Christopher Zeuner, Director, Weald and Downland Open Air Museum, Singleton, Chichester, Sussex PO18 0EU

Association of Independent Museums, Honorary Secretary, Andrew Patterson, Hotties Science and Arts Centre, St Helens, Merseyside, WA9 1LL

Association for Industrial Archaeology, Ironbridge Gorge Museum, Ironbridge, Telford, Shropshire TF8 7AW

Association for Studies in the Conservation of Historic Buildings, Honorary Secretary, Margaret Davies, 20a Hartington Road, London W4 3UA

British Aviation Preservation Council, Sercretary, Don Storer, Stone Wharf, 2 Dale Road, Coalbrookdale, Telford, Shropshire, TF8 7DT

British Architectural Library, Royal Institute of Bristish Architects, 66 Portland Place, London W1N 4AD

British Engineerium, Nevill Road, Hove, East Sussex BN3 7QA

CADW: Welsh Historic Monuments, Brunel House, 2 Fitzalan Road, Cardiff CF2 1UY

Charities Aid Foundation, 48 Pembury Road, Tonbridge, Kent TN9 2JD

Civic Trust, 17 Carlton House Terrace, London SW1 5AW

Civic Trust for Wales, Empire House, Mount Stuart Square, Cardiff CF1 6DN

Conservation Bureau, Scottish Development Agency, Roseberry House, Haymarket Terrace, Edinburgh EH12 5EZ

Conway Library, Courtauld Institute of Art, Somerset House, The Strand, London WC2R 0RN

Costume Society, Honorary Secretary, Kensington Palace, London W8 4PX

Council for British Archaeology, 112 Kennington Road, London SW11 6RE

Council of Museums in Wales, 32 Park Place, Cardiff CF1 3BA

Department of the Environment, 2 Marsham Street, London SW1 3EB

Department of National Heritage, Government Offices, Great George Street, London SW1P 3AL

Dorothea Restorations Ltd, New Road, Whaley Bridge, Stockport, Cheshire SK12 7JQ

English Heritage, Fortress House, 23 Saville Row, London W1X 2HE

Ephemera Society, 12 Fitzroy Square, London W1P 5HQ

Furniture History Society, c/o Department of Furniture and Interior Design, Victoria and Albert Museum, London SW7 2RL

Georgian Group, 37 Spittal Square, London E1 6DY

Historic Buildings and Monuments Branch, Department of the Envirnoment for Northern Ireland, 5–33 Hill Street, Belfast BT1 2LR

Historic Scotland, 20 Brandon Street, Edinburgh EH3 5RA

ICOM UK, Secretary, C. R. Hill, Natural History Museum, Cromwell Road, London SW7 5BD

ICOMOS UK, 10 Barley Mow Passage, Chiswick, London W4 4PH

Industry Department for Scotland, New St Andrews House, St James Centre, Edinburgh EH1 3TA

Institute of Advanced Architectural Studies, King's Manor, York YO1 2EP

Institute of Field Archaeologists, Metallurgy and Materials Building, University of Birmingham, Edgbaston, Birmingham B15 2TT

Institute of Paper Conservation, Leigh Lodge, Leigh, Worcester WR6 5LB

Ironbridge Institute, Ironbridge Gorge Museum, Ironbridge, Telford, Shropshire TF8 7AW

Maritime Trust, 2 Church Street, Greenwich, London SE10 9BG

Museums Documentation Association, 347 Cherry Hinton Road, Cambridge CB1 4DH

Museums and Galleries Commission, 7 St James Square, London SW1Y 4JU

Museums and Galleries Commission and Victoria and Albert Museum Purchase Grant Fund, Victoria and Albert Museum, London SW7 2RL

National Heritage Memorial Fund, 10 St James Street, London, SW1A 1EP

National Monuments Record Centre, Royal Commission on the Historical Monuments of England, Kemble Drive, Swindon SN2 2GZ

National Museums of Scotland, Chambers Street, Edinburgh EH1 1JF

National Trust, 36 Queen Anne's Gate, London SW1H 9AS

National Trust for Scotland, 5 Charlotte Suqare, Edinburgh EH2 4DUY

Northern Ireland Museums Advisory Committee, Museums Development Officer, 181a Stranmillis Road, Belfast

PRISM Grant Fund, Science Museum, Exhibition Road, South Kensington, London SW7 2DD

Public Record Office, Ruskin Avenue, Kew, Richmond, Surrey TW9 4DU

Royal Commission on the Ancient and Historical Monuments of Scotland, 54 Melville Street, Edinburgh EH3 7HF

Royal Commission on Ancient and Historical Monuments in Wales, Crown Buildings, Plas Crug, Aberystwyth, Dyfed SY23 2HP

Save Britain's Heritage, 68 Battersea High Street, London SW11 3HX

Scottish Civic Trust, 24 George Square, Glasgow G2 1EF

Scottish Museums Council, Country House, 20–22 Torphichen Street, Edinburgh EH3 8JB

Society for the Protection of Ancient Buildings, 37 Spital Square, London E1 6DY

Standing Conference of Archaeological Unit Managers, c/o County Planning Department, Shire Hall, Gloucester GL1 2TN

Tiles and Architectural Ceramics Society, Department of Visual Studies, Leeds Polytechnic, Calverley Street, Leeds LS1 3HE

Twentieth Century Society, 58 Crescent Lane, London, SW4 9PL

United Kingdom Institute for Conservation, c/o The Conservation Department, Welsh Folk Museum, St Fagans, Cardiff

Victorian Society, 1 Priory Gardens, London W4 1TT

Welsh Office, Urban Affairs Division, Cathays Park, Cardiff CF1 3XX

USA

Advisory Council on Historic Preservation, 1100 Pennsylvania Avenue NW, Suite 809, Washington DC 20004

American Association of Museums, 1225 Eye Street NW, Suite 200, Washington DC 20005

American Association for State and Local History, 708 Berry Road, Nashville, Tennessee

American Institute for Conservation of Historic and Artistic Works, 3545 Williamsburg Lane NW, Washington DC 20008

Art Information Task Force, Thomas J. Watson Library, Metropolitan Museum of Art, 1000 Fifth Avenue, New York, NY 10028–0198

Conservation Foundation, 1717 Massachusetts Avenue NW, Washington, DC 20036

Friends of Cast Iron Architecture, 235 East 87th Street, New York, NY 10128

Friends of Terracotta, 771 West End Avenue, Apartment 10E, New York, NY 10025

Getty Conservation Institute, 4503 Glencoe Avenue, Marina del Rey, California 90292–6537

Historic American Buildings Survey and Historic American Engineering Record, Heritage Consevation and Recreation Service, 440 G Street NW, Washington, DC 20243

National Park Service, PO Box 37127, Washington, DC 20013–7127

National Trust for Historic Preservation, 1785 Massachusetts Avenue NW, Washington ,DC 20036

Partners for Liveable Places, 1429 21st Street NW, Washington, DC 20036

Victorian Society in America, 219 South Sixth Street, Philadelphia, PA 19106

References

CAMBRIDGESHIRE COUNTY COUNCIL (1984) *A Guide to Historic Buildings Law*

FARNELL, G. (1990) *The Handbook of Grants*, Museum Development Company, Milton Keynes

MADDEX, D. (1985) *All About Old Buildings: the Whole Preservation Catalog*, Preservation Press, Washington, DC

Municipal Yearbook, Municipal Journal Ltd, London

Museums Yearbook, Museums Association, London

PEARCE D. (1989) *Conservation Today*, Routledge, London

ROSS, M. (1991) *Planning and the Heritage,* Spon, London

SUDDARDS, R. W. (1988) *Listed Buildings: the Law and Practice of Historic Buildings, Ancient Monuments and Conservation Areas*, Sweet and Maxwell, London

SECTION THREE

FUNDING AND OPERATIONS MANAGEMENT

20

Financial management

Brian Griffiths

In a competitive and cost-conscious environment, good financial management is crucial to the health and viability of all organizations. Financial management is sometimes looked upon as one of the least attractive management tasks, yet it is one which it is dangerous to ignore. The perceived unpopularity of the subject often results in neglect of this vital area until attention is unavoidable, by which time it is sometimes too late.

In the private sector, profitability, a positive cash flow and the need for financial control speak for themselves. In the public or not-for-profit sector, profit or viability has historically sometimes been of secondary concern, particularly where subsidy has removed the requirement for financial self-sufficiency. However, the last decade has shown the determination of the government to apply private sector principles and working practices to public sector institutions, and the late 1980s and early 1990s has seen a confirmation of these policies through the advent of compulsory competitive tendering and the requirement to measure performance in terms of efficiency and effectiveness.

Every business, be it a private or a not-for-profit organization, needs a clear strategy, a statement which points the way forward for the foreseeable future. In financial terms this strategy will not only anticipate development and spending requirements but also plan for providing the monies necessary to fund the development. A strategy may plan for growth, consolidation or perhaps even survival if operating in a difficult business environment.

Business plan

A key element of a forward strategy and perhaps the expression of that strategy is the business plan, whether it be to negotiate loans or mortgages for business start-up, recapitalization, development, expansion or when applying for grant-aid. The purpose of the business plan is to state the reasons for the existence of the business, the role it is filling, the evaluation of competition, the marketing strategy and the justification of its proposals (evaluated financially). A good way to undertake an assessment of the business and its competitors is by way of a SWOT (strengths, weaknesses, opportunities and threats) analysis. In this exercise the strengths and weaknesses of the organization are examined, together with the opportunities it has for the future and the threats to its existence or strategy for the future. Typically strengths might be regarded for example as reputation, locality, customer care and quality of service. Weaknesses might be poor decor, lack of staff training or the age of interpretative displays. Similarly opportunities may be regarded as expansion, diversification or specialization, whilst threats may well come from competition or lack of finance.

Any prospective lender or grant-aid body will need the answers to certain basic questions as a forerunner to an examination of exact financial requirements. At what stage is the organization now? In which directions does it wish to move? Has it the resources to achieve its ambition? What research has been undertaken to justify the ambitions? How will the organization benefit? Is the project worthwhile?

If the answers to these key questions are satisfactory, the next stage will seek to clarify further matters. What is the total cost of the project? What loans are required? What financial input is provided by the organization? Where is the proof that this finance is available? What security is available to the lender? Are the profits sufficient to meet the commitments? If approved, when and how are the finances required?

Part of the business plan will also be a cash flow analysis, which estimates the flow of money into and out of the business. It is a projection of expenditure and income, usually on a monthly basis and covering a minimum of the next twelve trading months. A full cash flow analysis will include every conceivable item of expenditure, including loan repayment and every source of income. The totals of expenditure and income are calculated on a monthly basis and when complete should be a very comprehensive and realistic assessment of the likely finances of the project or organization for the forthcoming twelve trading months. It should be noted here that it is very likely that any new project which relies for its viability on income may well find that this income is low in the first few months of the project, and the projections should reflect this. On this basis the net expenditure will be high until income begins to flow and the initial surge of setting-up costs begins to level out. A comparison of monthly funding needs with the loan agreement or overdraft facility will determine whether sufficient funds are available to meet demand until the business begins to produce the income required, initially to cover costs and later to reduce the overdraft requirement.

As a general guideline, when anticipating expenditure and income, the principle should always be to estimate expenditure high and income low and not vice versa. Above all, the vital requirement in any financial projection should be realism. History is littered with bankrupt businesses which were not realistic in their financial forecasting. In addition, this sense of realism will be appreciated by financial institutions or grant making bodies when approaches are made for support or raising funds.

Budgets and financial control

The execution of a business plan requires strict and effective financial control to record commitments of expenditure and receipt of income, to analyse this cash flow in order to keep the business viable and to control the business by using the information which the financial system provides. The best method of controlling the efficiency of any business is by watching and controlling expenditure.

A budget is a plan which estimates future spending and income. In simple terms, a budget can be prepared by:

Defining the goals of the whole organization and each section or facility for the next financial year.
Calculating the anticipated costs of providing the service. Costs will include every conceivable need such as salaries, wages and related contributions (NI, superannuation), heating, lighting, maintenance, uniforms, training, materials, advertising, printing, purchase of stock for resale, exhibitions etc. In addition, if major capital expenditure is anticipated in later years, a regular annual reserve of, say, one-fifth of the anticipated costs set aside over a five-year period should be included in order that the whole of the spending does not have to be borne in one financial year. It is also vital that the costs of any loan repayments including an adjustment for fluctuating interest rates, are not overlooked as these may have a major effect on the budget.

Estimating the likely income over the period from all sources, including grant-aid, fund-raising, admissions, catering, retail sales, concessions and voluntary contributions. Estimating should always assume high expenditure and low income within the parameters of the budget. When working to this principle the budget should not be caught out by unanticipated price rises, or disappointed by income falling short of the anticipated level.

In making budget calculations, all available information should be used in order for the estimates to be as accurate as possible. For example, when calculating staff costs it is necessary to consider and decide the staffing rota and costs not only over a year or even a season, but also at peak and quiet times. It may be the case that the Easter holiday requires a full staffing contingent, which may be reduced in the quiet period until Spring Bank Holiday, for which a full contingent is again necessary. The record of the working rota or visitor numbers for previous years can be used to project the likely staffing requirements for given periods. (Staff costs estimates must also provide for annual pay increases and inflation on an appropriate percentage scale.) The same principles can be applied to all other areas of spending. Similarly the record of income received during given periods in previous years will be a strong indicator of realistic expectancy for the forthcoming year.

Realistic assessments of likely spending needs and income receipts are essential. There is a tendency for managers, when under pressure, to make the budget 'add up' and meet the required targets, to overestimate income. This seems to be particularly so after a very wet and unsuccessful season, when the opinion is often 'it surely can't be that bad again next year' and inflated income is assumed. Unfortunately, it *is* often that bad again next year and income falls below anticipated levels. To compound this further, if all spending plans and estimates are based on improved weather and increased visitors, it is likely that the spending commitment is made before the income is realized. Conversely, of course, a particularly good summer is unlikely to be repeated, so a realistic budget will allow for the probability of poorer weather and hence perhaps fewer visitors in the following years. Indeed, if no new attractions are provided, and there is no additional spending on advertising or in marketing, there is no justification for projecting any increase in visitor numbers over the previous year: to do so may be a recipe for disaster.

When total expenditure is calculated and the total income is deducted the remainder is the net expenditure, i.e. the total sum of money required to operate for the next financial year. If the estimated net expenditure is above that prepared for, but is nevertheless felt to be necessary, under no circumstances should the estimated income figures be increased in order to reduce the net expenditure. On the assumption that the income figures have been calculated realistically and conservatively, there will be no justification in increasing them. Cost reductions in expenditure must therefore be identified and made. The reductions must be real and be acted upon, not merely shown in the budget to make the figures appear favourable.

It is not sufficient to plan and calculate the budget accurately; it is also necessary to create a system which will show the amounts actually spent at any particular times and what is already committed to be spent but not yet paid out. In terms of salaries or wages, it is known exactly what will be spent over the year from the budget calculations, including overtime and rota payments. Unless there is any increase or decrease in these working arrangements the monies should be regarded as committed and set aside, not to be used for any other purpose. Similarly, known commitments on energy bills, maintenance contracts and any other area of known spending commitments which are unavoidable should be regarded as unavailable for other use. It is essential that official orders are used for *all* spending and a record kept not only of the amount paid against each order but also the amount still to be paid against that same order. A good example of the need for such a system would be in the ordering of cleaning materials, where perhaps one order would be made at the start of each year for a regular supply to be delivered and paid for monthly. Thus a total order value of £1200 could be interpreted in financial terms as a spending of say £200 at the end of the second month and a false impression given that there is a surplus of £1000 available to be spent on other items. The fact is that the £1200 worth of supplies will be delivered, received and paid for unless a positive move is made to alter the arrangement with the supplier, and in reality the whole of the £1200 is committed and therefore unavailable to spend on any other items.

If the budget has been calculated originally on a monthly basis, it is possible to compare spending commitments with spending expectations cumulatively at the end of each month. Similarly, if accurate records are kept of income, it will not be a problem to compare income actuals with income expectations. In net expenditure terms it will now be easy to look at the budget as regularly as necessary and compare actual performance with budgeted performance. If expenditure is on target but income is down, an early decision may be needed to cut certain non-essential areas of spending in order to bring the net figure back into line. Alternatively, if spending is down or on target yet income is higher than expected, there may be an opportunity to spend on something which had not been budgeted for because it was unanticipated or likely to be too costly.

Good budgetary control is one of the main ingredients of good management, because it is a quick and easy way to 'take the temperature' of the business and will provide the financial information so essential for continued viability. The advantages of budgetary control can be summarized as follows:

(1) It clarifies the aims and policies of business and helps it translate its policies into programmes.
(2) It clarifies the priorities of the manager and increases awareness of his responsibility.
(3) It improves control of the vital finances in the business, by comparing actual performance with planned (budgeted) performance.
(4) It helps development of corporate strategy by focusing the minds of management on vital areas of operation.
(5) It helps improve efficiency by showing which resources are used in which areas of the operation and helps assess how well or inefficiently they are being used.

In order to be effective the spending plans which are contained in a budget need to be:

Realistic for all the reasons previously mentioned.
Comprehensive by including every conceivable demand.
Comprehensible and capable of being understood by all who need to implement or are affected by them.

A budget, which must of necessity be a financial forecast, does not predict what will happen. It only attempts to foresee the result if certain things happen or are made to happen. It is not sufficient therefore to prepare a budget and assume that it does not need attention, monitoring or possibly revision at a later date in the light of changing circumstances. It is fair to assume that any budget which is prepared, from necessity, some months before the start of a financial year is unlikely to be totally accurate, as situations and demands change over time. It is, however, the margin of error which will dictate the success or failure of the budget and ultimately, perhaps, of the organization itself.

Pricing and admissions policies

Every business, be it commercial or non-profit, working in today's very competitive environment, needs to pay close attention to its pricing policies. On the face of it this appears quite straightforward: a price is set and the subsequent income collected. Successful businesses will, however, examine their prices extremely carefully and consider all criteria to ensure that maximum income is achieved whilst maintaining market share and viability. In the case of not-for-profit organizations, particularly, there are many key questions and issues which need to be tackled, including for example, whether a charge should be made for entrance or for the use of particular facilities.

The issue of charging may be a political one and not always susceptible to rational argument. A case for charging might suggest that:

(1) Many programmes of facilities could not be provided if income did not accrue.
(2) Any profits could help the facility to be improved.
(3) Where sponsorship, plural funding or partnership is a possibility, income generated by charging may encourage private developers to invest, so freeing funds for other purposes.
(4) Charging can encourage a more caring attitude by users.
(5) Charging may be a valuable mechanism to reduce overusage of the facility at peak times.
(6) It is unreasonable to expect the tax payer to entirely underwrite a facility which may only be used by a proportion of the population who contribute to it.

Conversely, it may be argued against charging that:

(1) A facility provided from community funds should not require members of that community to pay a second time to visit or use it.
(2) Charging may exclude those who are unable to pay.
(3) Managers will ignore financially non-viable developments in favour of those which generate an income. Not charging will prevent raising income becoming more important than providing the service or facility which the community requires.

If it is finally decided by those responsible that charges need to be made, there are further key questions to be asked when considering the objective of making a charge and what needs to be achieved. For example:

(1) Is generating income of main concern and, if so, how much income is needed to be viable? Does the facility have to pay for itself entirely or can it be part subsidized from elsewhere in the budget – perhaps by a grant-in-aid subvention from a local authority or the government?
(2) How important is efficiency? Does the organization need to be concerned about cost, or income, or profit per visitor? How important is this efficiency? What level of efficiency does the organization wish or need to achieve?
(3) Is the organization committed to equal opportunities for all? Should only those who pay get the service, or is it considered that those 'more in need' should receive more preferential treatment or prices?
(4) How important is value for money to the organization? Is the primary concern the one-off visitor, or is there a dependence on making people want to come back for more?

The answers to these key questions will all have to be considered when deciding the pricing policy. For example, if financial survival is top priority then perhaps efficiency and income generation will be the main concern. Alternatively, if the quality of a visit is deemed to be more important than financial returns then value for money will be the main consideration.

Even after tackling these fundamental areas there are even more issues to be resolved before prices can be set, for example:

(1) How feasible and economic is it to collect fees?
(2) Would the benefits of low or even free admission result in increased retail and catering income?
(3) How will the prices compare with those of competitors?
(4) What price do visitors expect to pay?
(5) What prices rises will they tolerate?
(6) If it is decided to give concessions to those with special needs or to the disadvantaged, who will be included and what discounts will they receive?

The granting of concessions or discounts to some users will invariably either leave the organization open to criticism if certain groups are excluded or cost money if all likely qualifiers are included. Perhaps the only advice that can be given is to make a decision as to which groups, if any, will be allowed concessions and stick to that decision. Many organizations, particularly those in the private sector, have made a policy decision that no concessions will be allowed in any circumstances. Critics will be only too pleased to highlight this fact, yet it is perhaps understandable that management do not wish to be making individual decisions between, say, various charities, when it could be felt that to open the doors for one group may well open the floodgates for many others.

The issues of the retail mark-up and profit margins are ones on which it is impossible to generalize as the aims and intentions of organizations differ so markedly. It is important, however, that all the key issues mentioned previously are satisfied and that a sound policy decision is made on the absolute aim of the income producing enterprise. If these income areas are essential for the future of the business then the aim would be to maximize profit without alienating customers, i.e. setting prices according to what the market will stand. It should always be borne in mind that in some situations and with some products the souvenir of the stay, or the value of a good cup of tea, may perhaps be as important as the individual financial profit on each item. There will therefore be conflicting needs and priorities within each organization, but the important thing to remember is that attention to detail is again vital, to ensure that the income is doing the job that is required of it.

These general policies on evaluation of fees and charges can be applied to any areas where income is involved, be it in admission, retailing or catering services. The important question to be asked repeatedly is whether or not the service provided is of high quality and reflects the fees charged.

Value-added tax

The matter of value-added tax is one which needs to be paramount when charges are set, income received and banked, and invoices paid. The penalties for non-declaration or non-submission of VAT returns are severe. Returns are made quarterly and it is sound advice that returns should never be late, as one late submission will result in a warning, but subsequent submissions can result in surcharges at the very minimum. In order to help cash flow, businesses which are dependent largely on seasonal trade can choose to claim back VAT either on receipt of the invoice or on subsequent payment, which may be some weeks later.

As a guide, at the time of writing the areas which will mainly affect leisure outlets are classified as follows:

(1) An organization with an annual turnover of £45,000 and above must register.
(2) Entrance fees, if the visit is *not* deemed to be educational, are chargeable to VAT.
(3) Books, newspapers, food and children's clothes are not chargeable.
(4) Souvenirs, gifts and adults' clothes are chargeable.
(5) All confectionery, crisps, food and drink prepared and/or sold on the premises are chargeable.

It should be noted that these points are for very general guidance only and the advice of HM Customs and Excise should be sought at all times to ensure compliance with the law. The VAT inspectors have the legal right to enter premises and inspect trading records at will, and the importance of seeking expert advice on the matter of VAT cannot be over-emphasized.

Retail outlets

A vital area of trading which is often not given the time and attention needed is that of retail (shop) management. In many heritage businesses the management of retail outlets has traditionally been of secondary importance, yet the increasing demands of viability and profitability make retail sales a major item in many budgets. Successful shop sales may make the difference between a viable and a non-viable business, but in order to establish and maintain an efficient retail outlet the resources (finance, premises and manpower) have to be made available and managed correctly.

Efficient use of financial resources cannot be achieved without an awareness of the implications of setting up, stocking, holding stock etc., and the effect they will have on the budget. It is very important to know, therefore:

(1) How much stock should or can be bought
(2) How much stock has been ordered, received and paid for
(3) What percentage mark-up is needed to be profitable
(4) What percentage mark-up the market will stand
(5) Which items will need reordering and with what frequency
(6) How much stock is in hand and what is its value
(7) Which items are slow moving and why
(8) Is income from sales all that it could or should be
(9) Is the shop making a profit, and if so how much

(10) What can be done to improve performance

A further examination of purchasing methods and principles should also be undertaken prior to orders for supplies being issued. The problem of bulk buying is always a difficult area to evaluate. In managerial terms, it is sometimes felt that bulk purchases early in a season remove the need to effect repeat orders at busy times and also that the advantages of discounts are sufficiently attractive when needing to maximize profit. These advantages of bulk buying may, however, not be as clear-cut when analysed in more detail. For example:

(1) Can the business afford the initial capital outlay?
(2) Will that money be needed for anything else in the future?
(3) Will the product deteriorate easily?
(4) Is there sufficient suitable storage space, bearing in mind that to keep the goods in good condition needs a room which is clean, dry, warm etc.?
(5) Are the discounts offered substantial and is the saving per item likely to affect selling prices and profitability?
(6) Is it possible that products will become obsolete before they are all sold?
(7) Can it be virtually guaranteed that all of the product will be sold within a specified period?

The classic mistake when bulk buying, particularly when related to point 6 above, is in relation to the printing of information leaflets and guide books. Because products are used very much as a marketing tool as well as a source of income, the tendency is often to produce them in large quantities to take advantage of the large discounts offered in most print runs. In reality, however, it is very difficult to assess the product and the information needed perhaps two or three years in advance. If after the first year it is decided to change the dates of the season or the opening hours or the admission prices, or if there are now additional facilities to offer, the information in the leaflet or guide book is out of date and the product becomes virtually unsaleable; yet it has tied up a great deal of the budget and continues to cost money in storage, until the almost inevitable decision is made to write off its costs.

If such issues are looked at in the light of the introduction to this chapter, it can be seen how easy it is to identify areas of financial inefficiency and bad practice in the management of retail outlets.

Contracting out

An element of financial management which has recently become increasingly important is the contentious and difficult issue of contracting out of services. If the principles behind compulsory competitive tendering are accepted, the contracting out of services traditionally provided in-house should allow a more efficient, competitive and cost-effective service. However, it should always be remembered that the customer will assume that the service is being provided by the site operator and will be almost certainly unaware of and unconcerned by the fact that a contractor is involved. Any poor standards displayed by the contractor will therefore inevitably reflect on the museum and not on the contractor. It is essential therefore when considering contracting out a service that a system of control is included in the contract document. Areas of control should always include the quality of the product or service, the prices to be charged and the hours during which the facility should be available. In addition, there may well be other key aspects which it is felt are vital to the image of the establishment, such as recruitment and training of staff, uniforms to be worn, length of hair and customer care standards.

Preparation of the contract document is a matter which is best dealt with by a legal expert, but it is vital that it is totally comprehensive and suits the needs of the organization. It should always provide for a situation where the contractor can be removed without undue delay if the conditions of the contract document are not adhered to.

Unless it is a requirement of a governing body's standing orders that the lowest tender must be taken, the acceptance of a contract is, at the end of the day, a matter of preference for a particular contractor. There are, however, important areas which should not be overlooked:

(1) The financial inducements offered to the organization need to be realistic, achievable and attainable.
(2) The contractor should have a proven track record in providing a similar service.
(3) References should always be taken up, initially by telephone and followed up in writing.
(4) The credibility of the referees should be established.
(5) The financial standing of the contractor and, where appropriate, of the directors of the contracting company should be checked.

Perhaps the most difficult part of any contract lies in the controlling of standards and the monitoring of performance when the contract is operational. This control and monitoring procedure is absolutely vital. It is not acceptable to let a contract and assume that the conditions will be met at all times. Frequent inspections need to be made and customer research carried out to ensure that the image of the facility is enhanced and not damaged by the service provided by the contractor.

Monitoring: the use of information

In every business the assessment and evaluation of income received is often given low priority. Many organizations regard it as sufficient to merely bank income as it is received without noting the source of or checking the accuracy of the figures. It has been noted previously that every item of income or expenditure should be allocated to the relevant budget area, in order that the information can be used for budgetary control and cash flow purposes. It is advisable therefore to ensure that an adequate system of control is established so that, for example, every visitor receives a numbered entrance ticket and every sale is recognized by the provision of a receipt, in order that the money received from staff at the end of the day can be checked. A careful record should be made of the dates and the amounts of income received and banked, for later reconciliation and evaluation against expectancy. In addition, the possibility of staff dishonesty must be guarded against. Each organization will have its own individual requirements, but a comprehensive system of monitoring income needs to be established in all cases, not only to monitor the income flows but also to confirm that the money banked balances with the money received. The issuing of a numbered entrance ticket and a receipt for all purchases is therefore a mandatory requirement. It is generally accepted that there is no foolproof system which will prevent losses, but the insistance on certain basic rules being followed at all times, and a frequent inspection that this is indeed taking place, will hopefully be sufficient to deter all but the most determined.

As a general rule, a manager is only as good as the information he has to work with. Although many modern businessmen regard gut feeling as an important part of decision making, it is highly dangerous to make decisions without the information needed to make a valued and rational assessment of the situation and the alternative decisions possible. Data are not information; data are merely a collection of facts and figures. It can often be seen that the difference between a good and an average manager is the ability to convert those data into meaningful information on which to base a decision. The data can come from a number of sources and can be easy, difficult, expensive or inexpensive to collect. Modern cash registers or tills can often provide a mass of data which, for example, will not only show the amount of money received that day but also split the income into the hours taken, the staff members receiving the money and the items which were sold. In addition, they will also provide data on each item of stock showing, for instance, number sold, number remaining and VAT content. These data are provided in large quantities daily, yet are often only used for bank and VAT reconciliation purposes. They can, however, be transformed into useful information on how well or badly certain stock items are moving, which hours of the day provide highest or lowest takings, which members of staff appear to be selling more than others, which popular stock items must be reordered to ensure continuity and availability, and the effects on certain ranges if their display positions are altered.

Similarly, a computerized entry facility can show peak and quiet visitor flows of each hour during each day, the visitor make-up of adults, children, OAPs, disabled etc. and the differences on days of special events. Alternatively, some of this information can be gathered manually at the entrance gate, though this is likely to be expensive in staff time and not as accurate and comprehensive as an electronic system.

The whole problem of data provision needs to be looked at realistically and objectively. In reality, the technology is available to provide more data than the average facility could ever wish for or use. The questions which need to be asked, therefore, are likely to centre around the amount of data needed, the amount which is available given any financial constraints, and the amount which the manager has the time and inclination to interpret into useful and meaningful information which he has the resources to act upon. Used correctly, the information available to the manager should allow for better control over the organization by more efficient use of staff and resources through correct allocation to duties and responsibilities in peak times and more meaningful deployment at quiet times.

The Data Protection Act now dictates the information which can be stored on computer and the uses to which that information can be put. Registration under the Act is mandatory if certain information of a personal and/or financial nature is kept in relation to any person, including employees, members, financial supporters etc., and it is highly recommended that expert advice is taken if any such information is held or is likely to be held on a computer system.

Security

The issue of security is very relevant to many areas of every facility and has a particular application to overall financial management. It applies not only to computers but also to responsibility for purchase orders, safe keys etc., apart from the obvious problem of ensuring safety of cash.

In many leisure facilities it is likely that the daily reconciliation and banking of income is carried out at an unsociable hour, and sometimes it is not possible to restrict access to the money to the same staff continuously. There will be times when, for example, certain staff with the responsibility for ensuring the security of the money are unavailable for any number of reasons. The issue then arises of which staff will hold keys to the safe. It is obviously not prudent to issue keys without control as any losses are then difficult or impossible to trace. Every organization should always know:

(1) how many safe keys exist;
(2) how many people have access to them;
(3) where they are kept;
(4) who is responsible for them.

The opportunities for staff, if they are so inclined, to divert money away from the bank account for which it is intended are considerable. There are certain basic rules which should be followed:

(1) Do not allow staff to mix their own money with that of the organization under any circumstances. In order to achieve this it is necessary to ensure an adequate cash float at the commencement of each shift.
(2) Do not have staff keep on their person, in their cash box or till, more than they have to at any given time.
(3) Always ensure that there are adequate arrangements for surplus cash to be removed from collection points and stored in a safe at regular intervals throughout the day.
(4) Always ensure that the person collecting this surplus cash does so within a controlled system and that all cash handovers are signed for by both the person handing over and the person receiving the money, so ensuring that any subsequent losses can be traced back to their origin.
(5) Never leave cash unattended for a second, for that is all the time it takes for it to disappear.
(6) At the end of each shift or each day, always deduct the cash float from the takings first and then reconcile the balance with the amount due.
(7) Always record all movements of cash and keep all records accurate and up to date.

It is noticeable that in most businesses there is a regular and predictable time and route taken when banking money in, say, a bank night safe. This regularity and predictability is in itself a potential security problem. It is always a good idea to vary the time, route, person and transportation of money to make theft more difficult. If large amounts are involved it may well be worth considering a specialist cash collection company to ensure security.

Staff members, if challenged on any discrepancies, will always point to the working conditions prevailing at the time of the loss, and in many cases they may well have a valid point. It is therefore for the manager to assess, for example, the suitability of the staff, the technology, the systems and the working environment, to cope with the pressure times of high demand. It is suggested that the manager therefore assesses each loss according to its nature, source and size and also the value of the loss as a percentage of the total receipts. For example, a loss of £50 in entrance receipts on a day when £2000 was taken is of much less significance in percentage terms than the same loss on a day when £500 is received. It is important that a manager, though officially insisting on a 100 per cent return, accepts a percentage loss according to circumstances and keeps this level of percentage loss to himself to avoid the impression that employees can afford to be less diligent on busy days.

Auditing

Most businesses employ a method of auditing to check that all expenditure has been sanctioned, all income has been banked and all administrative systems and requirements have been met. A system of internal auditing can be carried out by authorized and trained personnel working within the organization, which will ensure that all is in order and that internal rules and regulations have been followed. A further audit is carried out at the end of each financial year by a team of auditors from outside the organization, who have the authority to examine any financial document to ensure accuracy, prudency and security. With this in mind the importance of accurate, comprehensive and up-to-date record keeping cannot be overstressed.

Conclusions

To summarize, financial management is an area of the manager's work which, though sometimes regarded as onerous, can play a crucial role in dictating the success or failure of any business. The increasing calls for efficiency and effectiveness demand that close scrutiny and attention is given to this subject. The increasing freedom of choice available to and used by the consumer is already having significant effects on interpretative and information services, and financial efficiency is perhaps the first step on the ladder to ensuring continuing effectiveness and value for money in museums.

Bibliography

ARNOLD, J. and HOPE, T. (1983) *Accounting for Management Decisions* (2nd edn), Prentice-Hall
BROMWICH, M. and BHIMANI, A. (1989) *Management Accounting: Evolution not Revolution*, Prentice-Hall
BROULES, J., COOPER, J. and ARCHER, S. (1983) *Financial Management Handbook* (2nd edn), Prentice-Hall
COOK, S. and SLACK, N. (1984) *Making Management Decisions*, Prentice-Hall
LYLES, R. I. (1982) *Practical Management Problem Solving and Decision Making*, Chartwell-Bratt
SPRAGUE, R. H. JR. and CARLSON, E. D. (1982) *Building Effective Decision Support Systems*, Prentice-Hall
TAYLOR, D. E. and SINGER, E. J. (1983) *New Organization from Old*, Institute of Personnel Management
WILD, R. (1977) *Concepts for Operation Management*, Wiley

Case study 20.1

Business plans and budgets: Quarry Bank Mill, Styal

Stephen Feber

At Quarry Bank Mill, strategy and tactics are separated in two closely related documents: a corporate plan and a business plan. The corporate plan is concerned with issues of cultural and educational development; it has a five-year perspective. The business plan is concerned with a three-year perspective and shows how the organization intends to fulfil these wider objectives. The former is essentially strategic, therefore, and the latter tactical. The budget is a numerical expression – usually on an annual basis – of the policies embodied in the business plan.

The business plan shows how the corporate plan can be realized in the markets in which the museum finds itself. When, for example, the labour market changed with the cessation of the Manpower Services Commission programme, the strategic objectives of the museum remained the same but the speed with which they could be realized changed. The tactical response to loss of grant support was a greater diversion of resources into commercial activities which would produce a long-term benefit to the Mill's finances, but a short-term reduction in cultural service.

In showing how the cultural and educational purposes of the museum can be sustained over time, the business plan demonstrates how management intend to balance certain critical ratios. Paramount is the relationship between the long-term work of collections management and scholarship and the drawing up of new exhibitions and education programmes which interpret the research and development activity and communicate it to the public. Where the proportion of earned income is high the need to be in the market and to compete for audience with other attractions is also high. The plan must pay careful attention to market share, to sustaining it and developing it.

Contents of the plan

The plan has three components. It says where the institution is, where it wants to go and how to get there:

Audit Description of the institution; description of the institutions' strategic position.
Outcome The market; the cost of entry; the cost of maintenance of market share including development projects.
Means The cost of development; the management team and history; the timetable.

A business will require a further component:

Business indicators Rate of return to investors; risk assessment.

In reality the Quarry Bank Mill business plan contains a number of individual plans for different departments and projects, but the basic approach is the same and the individual section plans are summarized in a single master document. The *description* of the institution, department or project will include an assets audit, in terms of collections and buildings, land, stocks, people and other resources. The *strategic position* is an assessment of the distinctive competence that the museum has and where it has an advantage over its competition. The *market analysis* seeks to understand the existing or future market for the section or institution, showing penetration rates for different sectors of the market and the costs and benefits of that market share. The *cost of development* and the *timetable* are functions of a new project. The *management plan* looks at the strength of the team and asks whether they can deliver the business plan on budget and on time. *Risk assessment* is important to the heritage attraction as much as the normal commercial business.

The plan then describes the acquisition and management assets, be they land, buildings, exhibitions or exhibits.

Creating the plan

Ownership by the managers who will have to deliver the plan is vital. At Quarry Bank Mill in the first instance the corporate plan was written with wide consultation between staff, volunteers and trustees. Once agreement had been reached at this level, detailed discussion of the pace and form for fulfilment of the corporate plan took place. In essence this internal audit looked at all aspects of the Mill listed above – strategic position, market and so on. The business plan seeks to maintain the distinctive competence that the Mill has, which the corporate plan describes as being 'the premier museum in the UK for the understanding of textiles and textile history'. This purpose is fulfilled in a number of exhibitions and education programmes. The broad areas which these exhibitions and programmes are to cover are described in the corporate plan.

Example: education in the corporate plan

The corporate plan, under the education section, calls for support for learning following school visits, i.e. in the family of the schoolchild. Analysis of the audience composition to the Mill showed that family groups were under represented in the audience compared with other attractions, and the business plan called for an increase in the audience.

The following steps were undertaken:

(1) The non-visiting public were surveyed with the particular objective of discovering why family groups did not come to the museum.
(2) A marketing plan was devised and costed on the basis of the survey, which included promotions and new print.
(3) A temporary exhibition programme was designed to appeal to children.
(4) New facilities, e.g. baby changing room, were provided.
(5) New children's menus were introduced in the restaurant.

We thus set a target for an increase in an audience segment and allocated budget for it in both revenue and capital terms. Through ticket sales we had a way of monitoring the outcomes. The scheme was introduced in 1990–91.

This element of the business plan therefore has a cultural as well as a financial benefit. In that it required a redirection of resources, it necessitated agreement between managers that this was a correct shift in expenditure. Agreement at this level of planning is difficult to achieve without agreement on the overall values represented in the corporate plan.

The budget: managing the plan

The organizational plan is made up of a number of smaller plans. In the example, children's menus formed part of the catering department's plan, which obviously included other elements, e.g. an increase in functions business.

It is important to understand the distinction between budgets and targets. The budget is a numerical expression of policy; it sets limits on the acquisition of assets which will be used with appropriate resources to support actions. The budget says what management, prudently and slightly pessimistically, believes it can achieve. It is in the meeting of these figures that the organization is able to achieve its cultural objectives. Higher targets may be set by management; their achievement is to be regarded as a bonus, not a necessity. Once set, budget figures are unalterable.

Management information

It is assumed that the organization keeps legal books of account and that the financial accounting system is set up with professional advice, either on a manual system for a small organization or on computer for larger ones. Whilst such systems are standardized, management accounting systems are not and are tailor-made to suit the management systems and departmental structures of organizations. The construction of the Mill management accounts may be instructive.

The Mill operating trust runs a working cotton mill as a museum, the apprentice house as a museum, a shop, a snack bar and a restaurant. In addition, since the Mill manufactures textiles there is a textile design and production unit. These departments are split into three: cultural, commercial and overhead. The cultural departments are further divided between mill, apprentice house, mill education and apprentice house education. Commercial departments are shop, catering and textiles, whilst the overhead departments are engineering, finance and administration, marketing and PR, and development. Each department, including the overhead departments, have income as well as expense codes, and each is budgeted to produce a gross margin, either positive or negative. Gross margin is defined as sales minus labour and materials. For example, the catering department may operate on a sales figure of £250,000 per annum. In normal circumstances this would yield a gross profit of £70,000 to £80,000, the total being made up of one-third wages, one-third materials and one-third profit.

Management information on this basis is produced each month for each department for each individual item of expenditure. The manager gets a monthly set of figures and a cumulative set. A profit and loss account is produced for each department. Quarterly summaries are produced, with pre-payments and accruals – showing expenditure incurred but not yet paid. From these quarterly figures a cash flow is produced which is a latest forecast for the year. Each manager is therefore able to see the performance of his or her own department, with variances, and is also able to make a comparison against the prior year. In addition, the manager is able to see the performance of the whole organization and therefore to understand how total performance against budget may affect planned spending for capital investment. It may be impossible to wash up more than a certain volume of cups by hand: a dishwasher may be called for.

Assessing performance

Overheads

A limited degree of internal recharging is used in the Mill system. Food and shop purchases are recharged to departments but general overheads such as lighting, engineering and cleaning expenses are not charged back. The cost of maintaining a system of precise allocation outweighs the benefits.

Earning money

Prices should be raised until price resistance is met. It may be difficult to raise total spend per head and the objective therefore is to get the spend in the most profitable way.

Shops

Museums shops vary enormously, but the golden rule is that the shop should be managed (as should the catering facility) to be an attraction in itself. The commercial elements should add to the mass of the attraction, not merely feed off the main body of visitors attracted to the cultural elements of the operation. Indeed, properly developed, a shop can add audience, especially if it specializes and gains a reputation for its speciality.

In general, stock lines should reflect the nature of the attraction and it is common to have items in sympathy with collections or exhibitions. In addition many organizations have developed a strong image or identity which can be applied by manufacturers to unbranded items. The value of uniqueness and identity is high, as the National Trust have proved.

A great deal of retailing success is down to the individual managers, and this should not be fettered by a restrictive cultural policy. The shop should be returning 40–42 per cent gross margin. If it is not doing so then it must be achieving a lower margin knowingly. It is perfectly acceptable to take a lower overall margin because a proportion of the stock is, say, academic publications; it is not acceptable to make a lower margin because of poor stock selection or pricing.

A classic problem in museum shops is over-stocking. The manager or manageress is easily tempted to carry large stocks of an item to obtain good discounts or to reorder frequently because of sloppy stock control. Such practices are to be stamped on. A good, well applied, manual stock control system with a quarterly stock take plus the discipline of holding no more than 2–3 months' stock for most lines is desirable.

The shop should be sited at the entrance/exit to the museum and should be accessible to customers without them having to enter the museum.

Catering and functions

Again, catering should be managed to be a positive draw for visitors. Catering is a far more difficult business to get right than retailing, but it should always be approached from the position that it will make money; but how much? Beware of becoming ambitious with food; there is much profit to be made from simple sandwiches, soup, tea and coffee and ice cream. Above the simple snack level, management are well advised to consider bringing in a carefully selected contract caterer. There are many ways of striking a deal on catering, but the expected 40 per cent gross margin figure may well fall and it is normal to agree a fixed fee or guaranteed return. The disadvantage of the approach is lack of control over food quality and service. The risk, however, of running catering can be considerable and management must be certain that they have adequate systems of control in place before embarking on ambitious food and beverage provision. It is quite possible to spend heavily on capital equipment and new staff and make less profit than from the old tea and biscuits snack bar.

Space

At the audit stage of the planning cycle, space should be keenly assessed. Many institutions now profit from using galleries or other areas within the museum for functions and events. Again, careful market research is essential, and proper literature, since the heritage attraction will be competing with hotels and other venues. Normally, the heritage attraction scores highly in terms of uniqueness and this is a strong selling point.

Conclusion

An essential element of making money is good control and management information, especially in a situation of rapid growth. Information systems need to be designed to meet the needs of managing the organization. Where the ratio of earned to unearned income is high, for example, the organization will have an entrepreneurial flavour and it is essential that the interconnectedness of each part of the operation is revealed through the information systems.

Case study 20.2

Fund-raising in the smaller museum

Christopher Zeuner and Richard Pailthorpe

Fund-raising remains one of the most discussed problems for museums in the independent sector and it has increasingly important implications for many heritage attractions.

The first question must be to decide who is to be responsible for the fund-raising activity. Is it to be a function of the friends of the museum? Is a fund-raising firm to be employed? Should the museum employ a member of staff with special responsibility to undertake the work, or should the task be part of the museum director's responsibilities? Each of these approaches has merit but one essential must be taken into account. Success in fund-raising depends to a large extent on commitment and understanding of the institution for which funds are being sought.

The decision to use a professional firm of fund-raisers will need to be addressed. It is a well developed service that has been successful for many organizations, especially the caring charities. Its success in the museum field is more varied. Perhaps the best advice to give is to interview a number of well known firms who offer the service, but before doing so prepare your own campaign, list your own contacts, look carefully at your own available man-power and compare this with the service on offer from the professionals. If your conclusion is that a professional will add to your success, go ahead, but be prepared to work just as hard as if you were alone. A professional fund-raiser who does not make this clear to you at the outset is either a magician or not giving you the whole picture!

Before any fund-raising scheme should be allowed to start, a museum must have a well worked out development programme. It is essential to know exactly what it is that funds are needed for and what the costs of a project are going to be. To put it simply, know what you want to do, how much it will cost and how long it will take to achieve, and do not be tempted to take the broader path by offers of a pot of gold. The following are the main sources of funds:

(1) Funds raised by direct appeal from: (a) charitable trusts, (b) companies, either as patronage or sponsorship, (c) grant from local and central government, (d) friends membership schemes, (e) individual donations and legacies.
(2) Funds raised through the earning capacity of the museum: (a) through trading, (b) through special events or linked to a sponsorship deal, (c) through the selling of services and special products.

Most museums are registered charities and are able to benefit from the considerable funds generated by grant-giving trusts. There is a wide variety of such trusts, some very large with national interests and others whose funds are much more limited and in some cases restricted to local or regional activity. Nearly all trusts have a published policy declaring their areas of support. A number of directories are available, but a good one is the *Directory of Grant Making Trusts* published by the Charities Aid Foundation. This is just one of a number of useful publications produced by the Foundation.

Each trust will have a correspondent. Make contact with the correspondent, discover when the trustees meet to decide on applications, how they like the material presented and what is the scale of their support. It is of little use asking a trust that usually gives grants of £500 for a donation of £5000. The building of confidence between the grant-giving body and the museum can greatly enhance its chances of assistance in the future.

Over the last decade museums, like many other institutions, have been encouraged to look increasingly towards business sponsorship for financial assistance. The economic recession of the early 1990s has made it increasingly difficult for the business community to respond in the way that had been envisaged. To encourage new sponsors into the field the government introduced a business sponsorship incentive scheme whereby government funding is available to match sums given by a sponsor.

Many museums have a local or regional profile and will inevitably look towards their own local business community for support. Local companies and branches of national companies receive numerous appeal letters from all organizations engaged in social and cultural activity. If a direct contact is not available, only a special and well presented project will be considered. It is therefore advisable to target appeals to those organizations where one might have a contact or where there is a connection between the museum and the businesses concerned.

There is a distinct and important difference between a sponsorship deal and patronage. Most local and regional museums benefit from patronage. Sponsorship is a two-way deal that requires the museum to offer something in return. This may be in the form of exposure in the media, or privileged entertaining opportunities, or permanent exposure in an exhibition. Before trying to achieve a sponsorship deal, decide exactly what you can offer in exchange. If the conclusion is that there is little to offer, you will not raise funds in this way; if you are unhappy about allowing privileged use of your museum or gallery, do not offer it. It is very important when dealing with sponsorship to know the people at the other end of the telephone, or whose desk your letter is falling on. In large companies there may be a special department dealing with sponsorship. Find out who to approach and if possible try to arrange a meeting. Problems and opportunities are much more easily dealt with face to face.

Currently, a government scheme administered by the Association for Business Sponsorship of the Arts (ABSA), through the Department of National Heritage, encourages companies and businesses to sponsor by way of a matching pound-for-pound grant to new sponsors in the field of arts and museums. A company or business already sponsoring in the arts may still qualify for a BSIS award, but at a reduced rate. Further details can be obtained from ABSA.

Sometimes an element of gifts in kind can enter into a sponsorship negotiation, and awareness of the problems and opportunities this source of assistance can present is worth consideration. Gifts in kind can be a very cheap way for a company to give assistance: printing, legal services, management advice, building materials – the list is a long one.

The vast majority of funding for the development of the independent sector has, in practice, come from the public sector in one form or another. The sources of public sector funding are numerous and changing and an officer responsible for fund-raising must keep an eye open for the opportunities. The tourist boards have played an important role in providing capital funding, but in England at least, the funds are no longer available. Special schemes for development in areas of high unemployment, grants in the countryside for conservation and recreation and museum-oriented grants from area museum services and the Museums and Galleries Commission are examples. How should these be approached?

All grant-giving bodies have a procedure that must be followed. In most cases a form will be required and it is essential to complete these forms correctly. When considering a wide range of applications, committees can only judge your case on your application. Make it good and concise. Make sure that your financial information is plausible. We may run our museums on a daily basis with a little hope and a lot of luck, but this will not impress the decision makers.

It is of course possible to tailor your application to fit a source of funds, and indeed the current grant-giving policy of a major organization may indeed alter your priorities. In some cases this is the intention of the granting body. The Museums and Galleries Commission's concentration on the funding of collection care is intended to influence what museums are actually doing. Look for these policies and respond to them.

Most museums have a friends' organization. The constitutional relationship between the friends and the museum will vary and, in some cases, the museum will be owned and run by the friends. Whatever the formal relationship, the friends are a major source of potential fund-raising effort. They are also one of the ways in which a museum can forge a link with the community it serves. The friends of a museum are, in many cases, the major regular fund-raising body of a museum. This will be primarily through annual subscriptions and covenants from both private individuals and corporate bodies. Friends will, in return for their annual subscription, obtain concessions such as complimentary admission, newsletters and opportunities to join in activities and events organized by the museum or the friends. Many friends are also volunteers at the museum and are much involved with perhaps the daily running. It is also advantageous for friends to pay their subscription through a covenant that attracts tax relief.

Friends' organizations will also raise money through traditional means such as raffles, social occasions, sponsored rides or walks, auctions and craft fairs. Further information can be obtained from the British Association of Friends of Museums (BAFM). Museums can also benefit considerably from legacies, and the benefits of this form of giving can be brought to the attention of members of the friends and local solicitors.

Capital funding presents museums with their greatest difficulties. Conventional methods have already been mentioned, but other unusual examples undertaken by museums include a catering facility financed through a mortgage granted at a discretionary rate of interest by a building society and funded by the revenue derived from the catering concession. A loan note or issue of debentures could also be an effective way of securing funds. Legal advice must be taken before embarking on such schemes. They are complicated, but can help to raise capital for development, or reduce seasonal borrowings.

A fund-raising programme in most museums will be a long-term responsibility. It will therefore need to be organized in such a way that its management and development become part of the museum's regular activity. It should be structured to involve all sections of the museum. The best people to sell the attractions of the museum are its leading people, both paid and unpaid. These may not be the best people to make the opening approach. Sometimes an existing donor can be enlisted to approach others to join. In other cases the constant search for connections in the right places is the key to a successful start in raising funds. The opened door is, however, the start. Trustees must play a leading role in this task. Successes will depend on well researched sensible proposals, made at the right time, to the people with the power or responsibility to make the decision.

Useful addresses

Association for Business Sponsorship of the Arts, 2 Chester St, London, SW1X 7BB

British Association of Friends of Museums, Honorary Secretary, E. F. Cass, 548 Wilbraham Rd, Manchester, M21 1LB

Charities Aid Foundation, 48 Pembury Rd, Tonbridge, Kent

Foundation for Sports and Arts, PO Box 20, Liverpool, L9 6EA

National Heritage Memorial Fund, 10 St James's Street, London, SW1A 1EF

21

Developing a training strategy and plan

Robert Scott

Why have a strategy?

Individuals, and the organizations for which they work, benefit from the enhancement of their skills and knowledge through training. However, training has to be directed to the actual needs of both the individual and the organization. It is all too easy to assume that simply by providing training, benefits will automatically occur. In reality, misdirected training will prove counter-productive, leading to wasted expenditure and a loss of morale. Conversely training that is carefully tailored to the needs of individuals and the organization will increase both competence and confidence. To ensure that training is relevant requires a strategy that is devised for the entire organization, that enjoys the confidence of everybody associated with it, and which is reviewed and updated on a regular basis.

Who should be trained?

Organizations involved in the care and presentation of heritage come in many forms, from very large national bodies employing hundreds of people to small voluntary groups. Most organizations have a governing body, paid employees, and volunteer supporters. A training strategy needs to take account of the requirements of all three groups. It should also be based on the assumption that every person who is active on behalf of the organization can benefit from training. Even if, for example, a senior manager is the most highly qualified in his or her particular field, the pace of change will require an updating and probably also a broadening of their skills. A volunteer who spends a few days from time to time working for the organization might be thought not to require training, but when the potential for damage to the material cared for by the organization or to its reputation are considered, the need for training and supervision become clear.

Corporate planning

The development of a training strategy cannot take place in isolation. Unless the objectives of the organization are clearly defined, and a business (or corporate) plan has been formulated with identified existing and future developments, targets and resources, a training strategy is worthless. A corporate plan which identifies the future direction of the organization is a prerequisite for the planning of training initiatives. Training has to be directed at raising the level of skills, knowledge and competence of individuals in such a way that it contributes both to individual development and the overall performance of the organization. The development of a corporate plan, and its updating, is a process that should provide an opportunity for all individuals to contribute towards, thereby producing a document that draws on a wide spread of knowledge and experience, and which commands support throughout the organization.

Creating a positive climate for training

Training will not succeed if individuals feel that they are being forced to accept it against their will, or if they feel that 'being sent on a course' is a way of highlighting their inadequacies. It is essential that a training strategy is developed against a widespread acceptance of its benefits throughout the organization. There are many ways in which this can be achieved. The leadership of the director and senior managers is essential; they must be prepared to acknowledge that they themselves have areas where improvements can be made. It may prove difficult to persuade old-fashioned, authoritarian managers to acknowledge that there may be room for improvement in their performance, but it is essential that they do. Trustees too must not simply pay

lip-service to the idea of training; they must be prepared to support the allocation of resources to training
in the annual budget review. The topic of training
should be fully discussed with all employees both on
a departmental level and through such bodies as trade
unions, professional associations, and a joint consultative committee if such exists. Volunteer bodies such as
friends should also be fully consulted.

Once there is broad support for training it is then
possible to devise a policy that can succinctly express
the organization's commitment to training. The training policy should be endorsed by all the key representative bodies in the organization, and adopted as
official policy by the trustees. By the time that this
careful preparation phase has been completed, training (which may initially have been seen by some as a
threat) should be recognized for the value it places
upon individuals and their contribution to the success
of the organization.

Role of the trustees: development of a training policy statement

The principal responsibility of the board of trustees will
be the adoption of a training policy statement. The
training policy statement will clarify the organization's
position on training and development, provide guidelines on staff responsibilities towards training, and ultimately provide a framework within which detailed
training and development plans can be formulated in
a systematic way to contribute to the success of the
organization.

In adopting such a training and development policy
the trustees recognize that staff training and development are an investment in the future and an essential
part of its overall business strategy. It will also be
apparent that the trustees attach great importance to
the training and development of each member of staff
and, in agreeing that training should be managed on a
continuous basis, will provide appropriate opportunities and facilities for training and encourage staff to
share the responsibility for their own learning and
progress.

The statement should include paragraphs on the
following.

Objectives of training

(1) To maintain a fully skilled and efficient workforce,
able to respond flexibly to meet current and future
objectives as outlined in the organization's corporate
plan.
(2) To ensure that staff have the necessary skills and
knowledge to perform their job effectively.
(3) To enable staff to acquire new skills and knowledge
to increase job satisfaction and assist career development.
(4) To ensure that staff understand the organization's
procedures and objectives.

Scope of training

The purpose of training is to develop the skills, knowledge and attitudes of employees. As development is a
continuing process, training can take place at any level,
in any job and at any stage of an individual's career.
The main training activities should then be listed (see
the types of training listed later in this chapter).

Responsibility for training

The statement will define the responsibilities of the
director and senior managers in establishing a training
culture throughout the organization. The director will:

(1) ensure that forward plans identify organizational
changes which may result in the need for training
and development;
(2) assist with the development and approval of training
policies and plans, setting training priorities in line
with overall objectives and, where appropriate,
regional/national trends;
(3) assist with the monitoring and evaluation of training
policies and plans;
(4) ensure that adequate resources are allocated to training and development activities;
(5) give active support to training activities and promote
the concept of continuous self-development for staff.

All managers/supervisors are responsible for ensuring
that staff under their control have the necessary qualifications, skills and knowledge to perform their duties
efficiently and effectively. They will give regular and
ongoing attention to the continuous development of
their staff by discussing needs, preparing and updating
personal developments plans, coaching, and introducing changes which make learning easier and/or more
effective.

Management involvement in the training process
will be:

(1) to induct new employees;
(2) to identify staff training needs;
(3) to formulate training plans and programmes in conjunction with the training officer;
(4) to select staff for training and brief them;
(5) to carry out on-the-job training;
(6) to give support to the transfer of learning from off-
the-job training to the workplace;
(7) to ensure that the benefits of training are dissemi-
nated to other employees;
(8) to ensure employees are kept up to date with occu-
pational developments and new techniques etc.;
(9) to evaluate the results of training;
(10) to identify organizational/departmental changes
which may result in the need for training and development.

The training officer will play a central, supporting and
coordinating role, identifying training needs, planning,
implementing and evaluating training, and managing

the organization's training resources. He/she will work closely with managers, advising, training and supporting them in carrying out their training responsibilities.

The training officer will:

(1) provide guidance on the training policy and procedures;
(2) assist managers to identify training needs and priorities;
(3) assist with the formulation of departmental training plans;
(4) develop an annual corporate training plan;
(5) design and/or organize specific training programmes, using the most appropriate training methods etc.;
(6) promote training activities;
(7) evaluate the effectiveness of training activities;
(8) ensure effective utilization of the organization's training resources, including the budget;
(9) maintain full training records;
(10) be proactive in identifying current and future training areas, e.g. due to organizational change, or new legislation;
(11) periodically review the training policy statement.

A major aim of the trustees will be to ensure that training and development become an integral part of the organization's culture – a corporate responsibility. All staff, therefore, share the responsibility for their personal development. Everyone should take the initiative over their own training, raising issues with their managers, helping identify their own learning needs and making proposals.

Identification of training needs

A training need can arise when there is an observed or anticipated shortfall between actual performance and desired performance. Examples of when this may happen are:

(1) upon recruitment of new employees;
(2) upon alteration of a post's duties and responsibilities;
(3) upon the promotion of a member of staff to a new position.

All employees have a responsibility to identify their own training needs in conjunction with their manager. Managers will discuss such training issues with the training officer, as he/she will be able to assist with the identification of training needs and advise on the most suitable programme of on-the-job and/ or off-the-job training.

A training needs analysis

Once the training policy has been formulated and endorsed by the governing body, the next stage is the production of the training plan itself, which will provide a blueprint for all the training and development activity for the organization for the forthcoming year. The corporate plan will have established a number of targets and objectives for the organization, and the purpose of the plan will be to provide the training to be available to equip staff to meet this challenge. An integral part of the process of formulating the plan will be the carrying out of a training needs analysis which will identify the strengths and weaknesses in the organization. Whilst it is possible to carry out a training needs analysis internally, assistance from an external agency may sometimes be required. Two possible sources of advice are training consultancies and local authority personnel departments. Financial support may also be available from a number of areas including government agencies (in the UK, training and enterprise councils should be approached).

Staff development scheme

One of the most effective approaches to the implementation of a training needs analysis is by way of a staff development scheme. The overall aim of such a scheme is to provide a means for the systematic review of all staff in order to motivate and develop them to their full potential for the benefit of themselves and the organization. Each member of the organization, from the director down, will require his/her own personal development plan (PDP). The information contained in the PDPs forms the basis of the organization's training plan. In order to produce an effective training plan which accurately reflects the needs of staff, it is essential that managers are able to understand their role and fulfil their responsibilities within the staff development scheme.

Personal development plans are agreed between the member of staff and their manager/supervisor. There can be four stages in the preparation of a PDP: preparation; first interview; reflection; and second interview.

Preparation

The member of staff will be briefed on the aims and objectives of the staff development scheme, the stages involved, the benefits for the individual and the organization. All staff should be aware of departmental and corporate objectives.

First interview

This will be the first face-to-face session between the manager and the member of staff. The manager will:

(1) express the confidentiality of the meeting;
(2) explain the staff development scheme and the purpose of a personal development plan;
(3) ensure the individual understands the role of the department in relation to the organization's corporate objectives;

(4) review the individual's previous PDP and decide whether points need to be updated or carried forward;

(5) gather information about the individual's needs and wants;

(6) make sure an accurate summary of the individual's needs is made;

(7) agree a time and venue for the next session.

Reflection

The manager should have the opportunity to reflect on the content of the session and consider the needs that have been identified and any that have not. The manager will also consider possible solutions – training and development opportunities that may be available both within and outside the organization. It is essential that resource implications should be considered at this stage and whether the needs/wants identified are achievable or indeed practical.

Second interview

The manager will:

(1) reiterate the needs identified in the first interview, and ask whether there should be any changes or additions;

(2) identify and discuss any further needs, perhaps omitted from the first interview;

(3) agree priorities among the needs and wants identified;

(4) agree learning objectives for each of the needs and wants identified;

(5) discuss development opportunities available, i.e. workshops, short courses, on-the-job training;

(6) draw up an agreed personal development plan for the next twelve months to meet the needs identified and ensure that there is commitment to its achievement.

A questionnaire developed for use in the identification of individual training needs for an individual's personal development plan is enclosed as the appendix to this chapter. *Table 21.1* shows an example of the future training and development needs identified and incorporated in a personal development plan.

Development of the training plan

As already stated, the identification of training needs is the key element in the formulation of the organization's annual training plan. However, there are a number of other stages which have to be carried out during the course of the year, which are described below together with approximate timings.

Stage 1: corporate objectives (September)

The director will formally address all members of staff at the beginning of the cycle in September, outlining the organization's priorities and objectives for the forthcoming year as incorporated in the corporate plan. The importance of the staff development scheme as a means of developing staff in order to achieve these objectives will also be highlighted.

Stage 2: departmental objective setting (September/October)

Every head of department will meet the director in September/October to agree the following:

(1) primary aims of the department;

(2) departmental objectives for the forthcoming year, in line with the corporate plan;

(3) the resources required to achieve these objectives.

Stage 3: initial evaluation of the current training plan (October)

In October the training officer will meet each head of department to evaluate the extent to which the current training plan has met the department's training and development needs so far. This also affords both parties the opportunity to discuss priority training areas to be addressed in the next training plan.

Stage 4: personal development plans

Managers' PDPs (November)
Personal development plans are produced in October/November for senior managers and departmental heads and are agreed between the manager concerned and either the director, the training officer or an external training consultant.

Staff PDPs (December)
Personal development plans are then agreed between members of staff and their managers/supervisors during November/December.

Stage 5: PDPs forwarded to training officer (middle of December)

By the middle of December, managers will forward a copy of their own PDPs and those of their staff to the training officer. It is *essential* that the training officer receives *all* PDPs to enable a comprehensive document reflecting the needs of all staff to be produced.

Stage 6: production of draft training plan (January)

The training officer collates the information contained within the PDPs, analysing the stated demand for various training areas and methods. S/he then prioritizes the above, considering a range of training methods, in order to maximize the level and variety of training activity provided within budgetary constraints.

Table 21.1   Future training and development needs identified as part of a personal development plan (PDP)

Needs identified (long/short term)	Personal learning objectives	Time constraints	Agreed action	Success criteria
Role change	To clarify role and work within the boundaries of that role	Corporate Plan implementation	Meet and discuss with the director Have more involvement with museum committees	Positive feedback from the director
Management skills: human resources, financial and business administration	To develop further management skills in the areas of human resources, finance and business administration	Paternity leave	To get accepted on to the MBA course	Complete the MBA course to satisfaction of course tutors and gain qualifications
Hostile interviews	To become more confident and able to deal with various interviews		Joint workshop with director Attend internal personnel procedures course	To feel more confident when faced with interviews Gain positive feedback from personnel/director
Computer awareness	To be aware of new and updated systems and understand the benefits to the organization of using computer systems	Diary pressure	Receive training from the finance manager on new financial package Visit external computer company	Gain broader knowledge of systems available and to be aware of appropriate systems
Lively writing and public speaking	To develop the ability to adjust my style to various situations		Attend and host an internal support workshop Write other articles for internal training	Feedback from delegates Feedback from the director and personnel manager

Stage 7: allocation of resources (beginning of February)

The training officer and the director discuss and agree priority training needs to be met by external training (which is often costly). Resources are allocated to both internal and external courses and the training budget is agreed.

Stage 8: presentation of training plan to managing body (February)

The director presents the draft training plan to the managing body for approval in February.

Stage 9: presentation of training plan to senior managers (April)

The training officer will discuss the content of the training plan with senior managers, affording them the opportunity to comment on how effectively it meets the training needs within their department. The training officer outlines the resources allocated departmentally and discusses the implications of the training plan in that department.

Stage 10: operation of the training plan (April onwards)

The training officer will implement and monitor the training plan with the support of managers and staff throughout the organization. Specific programmes of training will be designed and delivered internally, and approved external courses will continue where appropriate. Many other training initiatives will take place, e.g. workshops, coaching and open days, and managers will be expected to ensure that necessary on-the-job training is carried out for their staff.

Types of training

There is a variety of training which the organization, depending on its size, will want to provide. Obviously resources are a factor in what can or cannot be provided. It is perhaps more cost-effective where possible for an organization to provide courses in-house or to link up with organizations of a similar size in a joint exercise. Some of the most useful types of training are described below.

Induction training

Each new entrant should be provided with information and instruction about their job and department by line management. The aim of this training is to enable the newcomer to adjust as quickly as possible to the new working environment and to achieve effectiveness in the shortest possible time.

Supplementary induction training can be organized centrally by the personnel and training section to encompass the wider aspects of induction, such as the structure and functions of the organization as a whole.

Skills training

The nature of an individual's existing and possible future duties and their level of responsibility determine the skills and knowledge which need to be acquired and the timing of any training activities. Generally, the following factors should be taken into consideration: previous experience; level of competence and expertise; motivation; and learning ability.

Skills can be thought of in two categories: first, skills required by a wide range of employees, e.g. report writing, public speaking, interpersonal and communications skills and supervisory and management skills; and secondly, skills more specific to a particular occupation. Managers are responsible for ensuring that their staff have the necessary occupation skills.

The methods of meeting identified needs for skills training also fall into two categories: on-the-job training methods include instruction, coaching, counselling, special projects, directed reading and deputizing. Off-the-job training methods include seminars, lectures, conferences, visits to study other projects, and short courses/workshops. These may be organized in-house by the training officer or by employing external training providers/organizations.

Qualific_tion training

Managers should assess the need for qualified employees and counsel staff on which qualifications are either essential or desirable at particular stages of their careers.

Training for promotion/development

This is to develop skills necessary for future development. Suitable training methods include deputising, special projects, directed reading and courses.

Management training and development

Effective management is another factor vital to any organization's success. Management training and development is therefore an essential part of any training programme. As already discussed, each manager and his/her deputy will have their own personal staff development profile which will be reviewed annually, i.e. a training and development programme specifically tailored to their individual needs.

Areas of management skills training include delegation, time management, public speaking, report writing, meeting skills, communications and interpersonal skills. Short courses, work-based programmes and coaching/counselling are suitable training methods.

More general developmental work may be carried out through the use of group dynamics techniques to deal with such areas as team building, developing corporate, collaborative skills, and preparation for change.

Professional and occupational updating

All staff have a need to keep up to date with new developments in their occupations and to have an appreciation of the legislation which affects their work. These needs are usually met by short courses, seminars or conferences.

Training the trainer

All managerial/supervisory staff have specific training responsibilities and may therefore require training to fulfil their duties. Short courses and coaching are two methods commonly used.

Health and safety

The organization will have a legal responsibility to provide information, instruction and training in safe working methods and procedures. Managers will establish and maintain a programme of training appropriate to meet departmental needs by introducing standards of performance and providing instruction on the safe handling of equipment and where appropriate chemicals. In support of this it may be possible to run in-house courses in health and safety appreciation or to seek assistance from external agencies or local companies.

First aid training

This is another area where it is essential that professional training should be provided for staff.

Volunteer training

All volunteer workers will receive induction and health and safety training in addition to a programme of on-the-job training relevant to their work (or the work in hand).

Appendix

Museum of Science and Industry: Staff Development Scheme

Identification of individual training needs for your personal development plan (PDP)

(1) What are the key tasks which comprise your current job?

(2) What skills and knowledge do you feel are required for you to perform your current job satisfactorily?

(3) Which of the skills and knowledge identified in 2 above do you feel yourself to be:

   (a) more than competent in

   (b) competent in

   (c) need further development in?

(4) What do you consider to be your strengths in dealing with other people?

(5) What do you consider to be your weaknesses in dealing with other people?

(6) Do you experience any problems in your current job which you feel could be overcome by training? If so, what are they?

(7) (a) The following developments are likely to affect our section/department during the forthcoming year:

   (b) What training do you feel you will need to enable you to deal with these developments effectively?

(8) Are there any areas of your current job you would like to develop?

(9) What skills and knowledge do you possess which you could use to assist other staff in their training and development (and thereby increase your own development)?

(10) How would you like to see your career develop in the future?

(11) What training and development do you need to enable you to fulfil your career goals?

(12) What is your preferred learning style?

(13) Any other comments:

        Signature: ....

        Manager's signature: ....

        Date: ....

Case study 21.1

Changing a culture: the English Heritage custodian training programme

Jonathan Griffin

The training courses instituted for English Heritage custodians were probably the most significant single initiative in changing the historic properties in the care of English Heritage into places where visitors were welcomed. Their aim was not just to train staff in new techniques but to change the culture of the whole properties group.

English Heritage was created in 1984 out of the Department of the Environment. About 150 properties were staffed with a custody force which contained a large proportion of former service personnel. This balance reflected the historical recruitment policy which emphasized security, both of the monuments and of money, as the first priority. Visitors were admitted to properties on payment of a fee, anecdotally tolerated rather than welcomed. The custodian uniforms reflected this priority, consisting of a dark blue, police-style uniform with a peaked hat and dark tie.

The priorities of English Heritage were different. Its brief was to improve the presentation and marketing of its properties. For the custody staff this meant a simple change to put the welcome of visitors first and security second. The task was to introduce this change through training and other techniques.

The first stage was the introduction of new outfits. In itself this was not a training item, but it was an important outward and visible sign of the change of culture, reminding custodians of their new role. The term 'outfits', rather than 'uniforms', was a conscious effort to distinguish the new approach and a style guide was produced to support the change. There was some dissonance between the maintenance of high standards of presentation and the supportive nature of training provision, but this was gradually resolved as line management took responsibility for monitoring standards.

To get the training itself under way required a specialist, and Allyson Roose Clarke was recruited. Clarke had been part of the British Airways 'Putting People First' campaign, perhaps the most famous of recent customer care programmes, before becoming training manager for Air New Guinea. Over the next five years she was primarily responsible for developing all the new custodian training as well as contributing to the development of the new visitor service culture.

Clarke's first task was to carry out a needs analysis across the custody workforce. This highlighted the fact that many of the custodians actually wanted to enthuse about their properties to a wider world but had been discouraged from so doing by the attitudes of the Official Secrets Act which had governed thinking when English Heritage was part of the Department of the Environment. The custodians themselves came from a cross-section of backgrounds. The core attitudes and skills were those of the former services personnel, but there was also a selection of former teachers and professionals. The analysis was very much management led but helped to suggest priorities and a phased programme of training.

The training itself developed into three stages, each spanning a period of about eighteen months. The first courses were entitled 'Customer Service and Display' (CSD). These dealt with elements of customer service from body language and interpersonal interactions to the principles of merchandise display. The training was held away from the workplace in hotels and used conventional techniques of discussion groups, plenary sessions, flip charts, case studies and videos.

Many of the elements of these early courses now seem simplistic, but it would be wrong to underestimate the impact of holding courses at all. Prior to the creation of English Heritage there had been no training and custodians almost never met each other unless they took a day off to visit a neighbouring property. Travelling managers turned up to inspect and audit; there were no business targets to achieve. Each property had been isolated and there was no common culture. Bringing staff together in unfamiliar surroundings to meet each other and hear about new ideas must have been disorientating for the staff concerned, but it helped to start the grapevine buzzing and to begin the culture change.

To support the culture change a series of conferences was introduced. Twice a year, in the spring and autumn, representatives of each property were brought together to one of four regional conferences to hear the marketing news for the year or to review the successes or failures of the past season. Progress with these conferences was uneven. Some staff were more willing to accept the new approaches than others, and dissent occasionally surfaced at these events. Gradually mutual trust was established thanks largely to a number of influential converts.

The aim was to put all permanent staff through the CSD courses, but staff turnover and the need to maintain the initiative meant that many missed out on this early stage and came in at the second, 'Product Information and Promotion' (PIP) stage. This concentrated on how to make the most of presenting and marketing a property in the local area. It dealt with product knowledge about English Heritage and about the local properties, and taught how to deal with the local media. This last was important because the move from the Department of the Environment had brought with it a freedom which the civil service mind had never allowed, and custodians were now being actively encouraged to promote their properties to the local press.

Clarke could not carry out all the training herself as she had done for the first courses, and so a consultant supported her in providing PIP training, more as a spare pair of hands than in an advisory role. Meanwhile Clarke herself started to develop a series of mentor training courses. These were designed for a limited number of key staff who could act as trainers in the local area, supporting and monitoring progress on seasonal staff recruited only for the season, or to induct new permanent staff if there was no space on major courses. In due course many of these key staff became first-line managers when staff structures were revised in 1990.

The last stage of the training programme, by now some four years old, was a 'Connections' course, so called because it sought to make a connection between the two earlier modules. This was unashamedly revision but it brought together the earlier elements. The format allowed staff to talk about what they had learned at first hand and how they had applied the techniques in practice. By now the proportion of female custodians had increased and the culture was sufficiently established to make these into lively sessions between people who knew each other well.

By 1989, after five years' work, it was becoming clear that the major culture change had been effected. A new custodian management structure was introduced, with five regional custody managers each with around four group custodians reporting to them. There were now effective and active managers located in each of the five regions, and the time had come to pass the responsibility for training across to these managers.

One group which had not been well accommodated in the previous courses was the band of seasonal and new staff who worked only for the summer season each year. They had to absorb the culture by osmosis, which was possible at some of the larger properties but impossible at some of the smaller ones where they might be the only person on site at any one time. This group was the remaining priority.

The final part of the jigsaw was completed when Clarke brought together the five regional custody managers into a team to script their own national training package or presentation kit which they could use with their new group custodians in a series of annual induction courses for new and returning seasonal custodians. The latter course was inevitably named the RSC (returning seasonal custodians) course. This package is still in use and is updated annually by the regional custody managers (who are now called visitor services managers).

Running in tandem with all this work was a series of specialist courses on subjects like firefighting, safety and security, merchandising and first aid. The core of the visitor service culture change was however the CSD, PIP and Connections courses used in conjunction with the conferences. All these were developed in close cooperation with managers to meet the business objectives.

Training is never finished but should be constantly refreshed. However, in so far as this programme of courses set out to change the culture and attitudes of a large group of dispersed staff, it could be described as complete. The programme was successful because there was a clear vision of what was required, with management commitment to this, and because the very existence of training spoke of an employer who demanded change but also assisted employees in equipping themselves with the new skills necessary to meet the fresh demand.

The change was dramatic and led to very greatly increased levels of customer satisfaction and income to English Heritage. At its heart was the simple priority that the job of the custodians was to welcome customers to their property, to entertain and inform them while they were there, and to send them away with a greater appreciation of the property and of the importance of the heritage. It is a tribute to the staff and to Allyson Roose Clarke that this was achieved.

22

Visitor and user-services

Gordon Riddle

Visitor expectations and management commitment

Poor visitor services will inevitably lead to comprehensive complaints:

Dear Sir

I was unfortunate enough to bring my family to visit your property yesterday. Once we eventually managed to negotiate the myriad of confusing signs and locate the car park, there were no vacant spaces and we were forced to leave the car in a muddy overflow area. After a lengthy walk up an equally muddy path, which was not appreciated by my elderly mother, we made use of your toilet facilities which, to say the least, were in a disgusting condition. The tearoom was only marginally better. Uncleared tables, a long line of people at the counter, very indifferent service and lukewarm tea did nothing to dispel our growing disillusionment with your establishment. I did ask to see the person in charge but I was told that he was having a day off and that no one was available to deal with my complaints.

Having travelled quite a distance, we decided to press on and visit the house and gardens. The restoration work on the buildings was a joy to behold and the gardens were superbly kept; it's just a pity that these standards are not extended to the facilities for the people who pay good money to view and enjoy them. I shall certainly not be back, and will have great difficulty in recommending your property to any of my friends.

Yours in anger

. . . .

There is no excuse whatsoever for this nightmare scenario. Once the decision has been made to open a heritage property to the general public, high standards of conservation management must be matched by high standards of visitor management.

Great strides have been made since the Second World War, with the National Trust, the National Trust for Scotland, commercial institutions, private trusts and individuals opening a huge range of heritage sites for public enjoyment. These established operations are well past the pioneer stage in developing techniques for receiving and presenting their properties to visitors. A wealth of expertise is there to be tapped, including many recently formed freelance professional consultancies.

Mechanisms now exist to obtain advice for visitor management and to provide finance for facilities and services. Organizations such as Scottish Natural Heritage and English Nature can award grants for specific projects. Where heritage sites play a key role in local tourism strategies, requests to tourist boards and local government can also be helpful.

The clientele has also changed. Within Britain increased mobility, affluence and recreation time have generated a huge number of 'heritage' devotees from all sectors of society. This has been encouraged by heightened awareness of heritage owing to media coverage and in-house publicity machines. Many visitors are well informed and discerning, and visit heritage sites all the year round, not just during holiday periods. They often have their favourite local sites with which they form a very strong attachment and which they visit on a regular basis.

Visitors' expectations today are very high and centre on a combination of value for money and quality of experience. In the quest to meet these expectations many diverse factors are involved, from the conservation and presentation of the site through to the provision of basic facilities, and a total approach is required.

This chapter will draw heavily from experiences at Culzean Castle and Country Park, a National Trust for Scotland property on the coast of South Ayrshire. As well as having a Robert Adam designed Castle, open to the public since 1945, the spectacular 225 ha coastal estate was declared Scotland's first country park in 1969. In many ways it is an ideal example, as well over 300,000 people visit the property annually, posing problems in balancing the primary conservation needs of the heritage site with the needs of visitors. At Culzean the commitment to the visitor is encapsulated in some of the objectives in the property management plan: 'The provision of facilities for all sections of the community, including the disabled, catering for the day visitor, the passing tourist and the local repeat visitor'.

A ten-year development plan to improve existing facilities and five-year plans for both environmental education and interpretation further emphasize the approach. Appropriate staffing levels and a strategy to provide for the large influx of people have become established, based upon the pattern of usage and visitor profile. Strong links with the US National Park Service (NPS) have had a major influence at Culzean, including the setting up of a Ranger Service, the design of the Visitor Centre and the provision of a comprehensive interpretative programme.

Visitor reception: first impressions

The success, or otherwise, of a visit to a heritage site is often determined by the visitor's first impressions. No matter how spectacular or attractive the initial impact of the stately home, designed landscape or industrial scene, if the visitor has had navigational difficulties due to poor signing, or suffered in a long queue, frustration will be the overriding emotion. Compound this with poor facilities and a frosty welcome from bored or harassed staff, and negative responses are guaranteed.

Liaison with the appropriate road authority is important in order to locate standard heritage directional signs as far out from the property as possible and at all potentially confusing intersections. The main entrance should be positively and tastefully signed and be as welcoming as possible. If the site is in an urban setting, with mainly pedestrian access, a clear and concise explanation of what is offered, with prices, should be posted at or near the entrance to avoid misunderstanding and allow choice. In a rural situation, where inevitably access is vehicular, a series of simple, unambiguous signs, spaced at regular intervals before a pay point or car park, gives the driver time to absorb the information, facilitate decision making and prevent unpleasant surprises. Designed into the traffic system should be the option to turn back without totally disrupting the traffic flow. There will always be those who change their mind for whatever reason. If the price is reasonable and the appetite whetted by the information and the general appearance of the entrance, this should help to minimize the number of doubters.

The second phase of visitor management relates to the provision of basic facilities on arrival and first contact with staff. A car parking area within easy reach of toilets and a refreshment point are expected today, particularly when the travelling distance to the property is lengthy. Parking spaces specifically allocated for the disabled and elderly near the facility are necessary, as is a clearly defined bus park. A painted line along the front of the bus park helps drivers align their buses when reversing. Free-standing signs can be very useful on busy days to assist staff in directing parking, but they regularly fall victim to reversing vehicles!

There is little doubt that toilet facilities come in for the greatest scrutiny. All visitors are experts on this subject, and the impression given by regularly checked, clean and well laid out toilets is lasting. The extra facility of a changing room for mothers with babies is always appreciated. (Facilities for the disabled visitor will be discussed later.) The refreshment point, whether it be a tearoom, kiosk or restaurant, is often next on the agenda and the same principles apply. Judgement is swift if cleanliness, lack of service, poor-quality fare and value for money are below par. Problems related to toilets and refreshment points will surface very quickly and complaints will inevitably follow.

At some point, visitors will make their first contact with staff, and again the first impression will be crucial. A curt answer, a glare or, worst of all, being treated as an unwelcome intrusion, will evoke a predictable response. All members of staff, no matter which position they hold within an organization, must be attuned to giving visitors a cheerful welcome, an accompanying smile and an offer of help if appropriate.

The aim of the initial stages is to make visitors comfortable in the environment by minimizing difficulties and getting them into the correct frame of mind to make full use of the resource.

Visitor reception: orientation and information

Questions such as where to go, what to see and what to do, now confront the visitor. In most instances, management employs a combination of methods to convey the information: manning by staff, automation, signs or displays. Out-of-hours provision must be addressed if the opening hours, both daily and seasonal, are not restricted. There is little doubt that face-to-face contact with a member of staff, assisted by the tools of the trade, is the most productive way to orient visitors and convey the information which will be of most benefit to them. The flexibility of the human touch is more likely to cater for individual needs.

Normal practice is to site a reception area at a point where maximum visitor contact is guaranteed. Facilities can vary considerably, from the minimal desk format, with a member of staff carrying out a multitude of tasks such as selling tickets or recruiting new members of the organization, to the purpose-built visitor centre information area with all the modern technical aids. Knowledge of the visitor profile and a clear idea of objectives are essential in the planning of this critical interface with the general public.

The Culzean Country Park information area at the Visitor Centre was designed in the early 1970s and was influenced by the US National Park Service, which has vast experience in this field and achieves a very high standard in visitor reception. Culzean has a high percentage of return visitors compared with first-time visitors, and a balanced approach has been adopted to satisfy both categories. The information receptionist at the desk welcomes and responds to a wide range of questions. The model of the property and a map of the local area are also equally valuable to both types of visitor, as is the range of free and saleable publications and up-to-date information boards.

The regular clientele is specifically catered for by updated wildlife boards, details of events and activities, a series of different topical displays and three new audio-visual programmes annually. An events board shows at a glance the activities arranged for the next seven days and a new events brochure is published each year. In addition to the standard guide book a series of leaflets on different subjects like bird life, the shoreline, geology and scenery and on the Visitor Centre itself offers the regular visitor a choice. Having the flexibility to rearrange the reception area is very advantageous, as it can give an immediate impression of a new interesting development or theme. The role of the receptionist in removing dated information and adding fresh material is also a high priority in everyday management.

The standard guide book and a separate audio-visual programme both give the first-time visitor an overview of the property, and the 'rogues' gallery' of staff photographs not only identifies personnel but illustrates the diversity of disciplines in the Culzean team. By employing different techniques the aim is to maximize the amount of information available to the wide spectrum of visitors to the property.

The types of information at any property can be categorized as follows:

Geographical orientation   A model and/or maps will show the extent of the property, its character, the main locations of interest and the system of access. Some form of handout with a map is essential.

Ground rules   It is very important to explain clearly the ground rules for visitors in order to minimize conflicts and sources of disappointment. The Country Code is an obvious example on countryside properties, but restrictions on photography in big houses, fishing bans on waterway systems, rules for dog owners, smoking and many other issues are relevant to the visitor. If possible, it is desirable to explain the *raison d'être* behind the ground rules rather than to confront the visitor with negative signs.

Activities for visitors   The interests of visitors vary considerably, from those who wish to be relatively independent to those who thrive upon highly organized activities. The range

of options should be explained in a colourful, exciting and meaningful way, for example using leaflets, posters and displays. In Culzean, the activities include a guided walks programme, evening talks, major events, Castle tours, and a Young Naturalists' Club for the six- to sixteen-year-olds. For those who wish to explore the old estate on their own, information is provided on the system of woodland walks which link the most interesting features of the property. A colour-coded time planner can help visitors organize their stay and maximizes the time spent on activities which interest them most.

Services available   These can include the availability of wheelchairs (see section on facilities for the disabled), the location of public telephone, and the hire of bicycles, cameras and Walkmans. Any specialist provision, such as a ranger naturalist service or environmental education programmes for schools, should be highlighted.

Local information   There is always a demand for information relating to local transport, accommodation, catering and other major attractions in the area. Good liaison with other organizations can have reciprocal benefits. Daily weather forecasts and tide times are also appreciated.

Immediate information   Details of current work on or near the property which could cause inconvenience – a road being closed, power being off for a period, a room closed for repair or decoration, the danger of thin ice on ponds – should be prominently displayed. A-boards are very useful in this type of situation.

In unmanned situations, whether at the entrance to a building or at a car park, there are many ways in which the information listed above can be dispensed, and technology is constantly developing to improve existing techniques. Leaflet dispensers, sealed information panels, directional signs and encapsulated orientation maps are standard methods used to overcome the problems of delivering information. A new product called porcelain enamel, which is being tested by the USNPS, could, because of its indestructible qualities, replace the embedded fibreglass or metal displays in the future. The threat of vandalism is a constant and expensive one and this new material could play a key role in overcoming the problem.

A Caramate projector with slides and captions sited behind glass in a building can be used to introduce people to the property and can operate out of hours. Similarly, a computer screen at a window can dispense useful information in three- or four-minute programmes. Both methods allow flexibility and the material can be changed regularly.

No matter what the technique, the aim is to give visitors a range of information which will enable them to organize and appreciate their stay at a heritage site, no matter how brief. Having been given a realistic view of what might be experienced, they can then choose their options and maximize the time they have available. However, do not swamp the visitor with so much information about the site that the element of surprise is lost.

Facilities and furniture

One of the dilemmas which must be faced is how to integrate all the facilities and ancillary structures to accommodate the visitor without, at the same time, radically devaluing the very resources which people have come to appreciate. A sensitive, sympathetic approach based upon sound predictions of visitor pressure and requirements can enhance the property rather than diminish it, but constant monitoring with a fully financed maintenance budget will be required to preserve and even improve standards.

The stately home or castle

The problems of visitor access are much more acute and difficult to resolve in a stately home or castle where the original architect had a very different remit. Rooms, stairwells and servants' turrets were not designed with visitor flow or tour routes in mind, and the wear and tear on original floor coverings is often unacceptable. The hundreds of valuable artefacts and furnishings pose security limitations, while heating and lighting can adversely affect old fabrics. It is indeed a great challenge to allow thousands of feet to tread where once only the privileged few, supported by their entourage of servants, enjoyed an enviable lifestyle.

Notwithstanding these restrictions, whenever possible determined efforts must be made to resist the temptation to herd people through room after room in closely controlled roped-off channels on a strip of robust floor covering. This does little to excite the imagination and certainly hastens boredom in children. Manning a room with staff or installing discreet surveillance equipment does allow more flexibility, but sometimes decisions must be taken which sacrifice authenticity for practicality. The management of the saloon in Culzean Castle is a classic example.

This unique and incredibly beautiful round drawing-room was designed by Robert Adam to combine eighteenth century elegance with wild natural scenery. Its function was entertainment, and furniture was restricted to chairs arranged round the perimeter. Family and guests mingled on the exquisite circular carpet and walked over to admire the seascape of the Firth of Clyde, the Mull of Kintyre and Arran as the waves crashed on the rocks below. Unfortunately, by the time the Castle came into the care of the National Trust of Scotland, the carpet was well worn and certainly could not have withstood the pressure of hundreds of thousands of visitors. Until a few years ago, the room was viewed from a roped-off area by the door, and visitors could not enjoy the essential atmosphere of one of Adam's most inspiring creations (*Figure 22.1*).

Figure 22.1 Restrictions in the saloon at Culzean Castle prior to recarpeting and opening the room to the public

A management decision was taken to remove the old carpet and replace it with an exact copy, made locally in Irvine, but with a cut pile which can withstand hard wear rather than the old flat loop pile which is difficult to reproduce today. Now there is no need for druggets and ropes on stands. Visitors can promenade in the room, wonder at the original watercolour ceiling above their heads, and gaze out at the west coast scenery in all its moods. It is a very special experience.

The freedom to explore and fully appreciate the saloon, the armoury and the magnificent oval staircase breaks up the tour and adds immeasurably to the enjoyment factor. If visitors can be involved at any time in practical activities, such as using pieces of equipment or taking part in historical tableaux this adds greatly to the end product (*Figure 22.2*). Good interpretative practice is essential. The staging of an exhibition, whether permanent or temporary, can add considerably to the variety and interest. Restoration work, which takes place at most heritage sites, fascinates people and, with the use of display boards, can bring alive otherwise uninteresting corridors or lobbies.

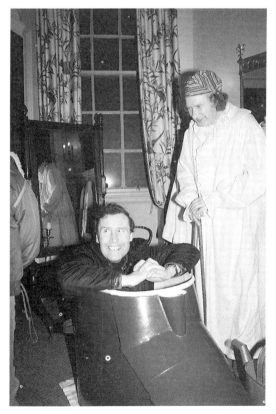

Figure 22.2 Involvement of visitors breaks up the tour, and staff in period costume can add to the interest and enjoyment

Provision of extra facilities, such as toilets, refreshments and a shop, in a stately home or other major building, often hinges upon space capacity and what priority is given to income and aesthetics. Problems can arise with people gaining access to the interior through these facilities, rather than the normal tour routes, and steps must be taken to deter this. These facilities are most often located at the end of a tour near the exit, which ideally should be separate from the entrance to avoid congestion and confusion. If a tearoom is provided, toilets are a legal requirement, but in most cases toilets are located away from the house near the car park.

Visitor centres

The same constraints exist for visitor centres because these can have an enormous impact on a site. No matter how well designed, a new purpose-built centre will never completely blend in and will always be out of time with its surroundings. Although a more expensive option, the adaptation of existing buildings is often the answer. Some compromise will be necessary, but the converted building has the advantages of being historically and visually acceptable and less likely to provoke controversy.

The need for a large Visitor Centre at Culzean Country Park to accommodate the anticipated surge in visitor numbers was solved by converting the clifftop Robert Adam farm complex (*Figure 22.3*). The buildings were ideally placed at the bottom of the inward traffic route and had long ceased to be an efficient working unit owing to changes in farming methods and to mechanization. The sympathetic conversion resulted in a range of facilities for visitors and the restoration of the outer façade of this important building. There are now numerous examples all over Britain of this type of conversion, and fortunately expertise is readily available in many of the disciplines which are critical to this work.

Disadvantages do exist, however, with this approach. The most striking at the Culzean Country Park Visitor Centre is the flow problems caused by Adam's T-shaped wings. Both in the restaurant and in the exhibition, people must retrace their steps as no circular routing is possible. Heating can also be an expensive item and the shape of rooms is often not compatible with modern usages.

A purpose-built centre, with its lack of internal constraints, can obviously overcome these negative aspects and can be tailor-made for visitor reception and interpretation. This enormous bonus must be weighed against the twin challenges of exterior design and siting, both of which may create unwanted criticism and a blot on the landscape. Use of local materials, a sympathetic design which blends with the style of other buildings on the property and good screening can successfully overcome the problems.

Figure 22.3 The Culzean Home Farm converted into the Visitor Centre with adequate space for visitors in the immediate vicinity

Whichever option is chosen, a new complex or converted buildings, one of the key considerations is the optimum management of space both in the centre and in its immediate surroundings. The US National Park Service pioneered the visitor centre principle and it has proved to be an important role model in the field of visitor management. The components of visitor centres are now well established, and all or a combination of the following are included: car parks, toilets, refreshment points, shops, information areas, exhibitions, auditoriums, staff work areas, education or children's rooms.

Experience has shown that flexibility is an incredibly important factor. The emphasis may well change as staffing levels increase; certain operations, such as education, may expand; and visitor patterns of use may change.

It is dangerous to become locked into a finite use for a room or area, making change difficult and expensive. Building a utility space, or incorporating multi-purpose rooms into a complex, will pay dividends in the fullness of time. The large Stone Barn in one wing of the Culzean Visitor Centre is a case in point. This area lacks fixtures, other than lighting and heating, and is used regularly for conferences, young naturalists' indoor meetings, a wet weather picnic area for schoolchildren, a venue for the maintenance of park furniture in winter, registration for the fun run, temporary exhibitions, staff social evenings and so on.

Outdoor furniture

Visitor centres are not the only facilities which can enhance a visit and at the same time assist management. Numerous types of outdoor furniture and resources can help the visitor with orientation, recreation, access and education. Great care must be taken not to end up with a plethora of styles, colours and materials which are visually confusing and unaesthetic. A standard house style can be most effective and clean on the eye. If this discipline is accepted the creeping sickness of masses of different temporary signs and structures can be avoided.

In Culzean, this was adopted from the start in the Country Park. The result is one style of picnic table, two styles of litter bins, two types of sign, three types of pathway, two standard colours (other than natural wood and preservatives) and very few major new structures. Every attempt is made not to deviate from this.

The only major recreational structure which has been built is the well screened adventure playground. A commercial climbing net (the Spider's Web next to the Giant Spider) is the only exception to wooden structures. The siting is very important and the noise factor must be taken into consideration, but there is little doubt that it is a winner with younger clientele. Safety is a key factor in the design.

Picnic sites are equipped with tables and litter bins. The policy for the latter is only to locate them at points where people congregate in numbers, and not to spread them throughout the property (*Figure 22.4*). Similarly, seats and benches are only sited at major honeypots or on well used routes. Other facilities, such as drinking fountains for human use, are provided at honeypots, and a dog drinking bowl is available at the Visitor Centre.

It is always difficult to balance the need for signs with their obvious impact upon the site. In Culzean, there is a standard green directional sign (other than official road traffic signs) with white lettering or illustrations. The signs are made on site using staff labour and Eurotext lettering. This cuts down the time and cost factor in producing signs and allows quick replacement if necessary. A different material is used for interpretative signs, for example at the deer park. A combined directional and interpretative sign still retains the green and white livery and has been well received by visitors (*Figure 22.5*). Other properties adopt different styles: Brodick Country Park on Arran, another National Trust for Scotland property, has routed signs with a different colour combination. Uniformity within the property is the goal.

Miles of pathways allow the visitor to explore Culzean's eighteenth century landscape. In the gardens, pea gravel is used on path surfaces, while the general estate path system has fine, hard-wearing crushed whinstone chips as a base. Chipped bark is laid on selected well drained woodland routes to give a more natural surface. In all types of path, good drainage will cut down maintenance work.

Figure 22.5 A combined directional/interpretative sign in Culzean livery

Figure 22.4 Picnic areas are concentrated at major honeypot areas at Culzean

Boardwalks are sited over wet areas such as marshes, or sensitive areas such as the dunes, to allow access to the beach. Stiles are built to allow visitors to negotiate fences. Most types of countryside furniture are well documented now and many are on the open market. In Scotland, the Scottish Natural Heritage's display area at Battleby is well worth a visit and its team can give valuable advice. Non-pedestrian access can often pose problems. Horse riding was initially a conflict area at Culzean until a permit system was introduced, clear guidelines were given to riders and designated routes were worked out. Unfortunately a maverick can cause immense damage in a very short time.

Structures, such as sampling platforms for pond dipping or hides for bird watching, are important resources for educational work but can again offer more options for the general visitor as well. Fortunately, although organizations like the RSPB give excellent guidelines for building hides, there are always local variations due to terrain. The individuality of each property is precious. No one wants to see exactly the same design of structure at every place they visit. A good example of this is the treetop walkway at Culzean. The structure at Landmark Carrbridge, though serving the same purpose, is totally different in style and size. The Culzean structure stands over 12 m high and is so well hidden that despite its scale, and its location near a main car park, the majority of visitors do not even see it. Because of the obvious safety aspect, only ranger-led groups use this facility. The Carrbridge structure is not as high and is open to the public. *Vive la différence!*

The maintenance of visitor facilities is often a problem as manpower and financial resources can fall short of what is required. It is no good installing a facility and hoping that future maintenance will take care of itself. Systems must be introduced to monitor and deal with the never-ending lists of unglamorous jobs. These fall into two main categories: large-scale planned programmes of work, like the out-of-season upgrading and repair of pathways and car parks; and the absolutely vital response to the hundreds of stitch-in-time tasks which arise on a daily and weekly basis.

Vandalism, erosion problems and minor repairs, however mundane, must be addressed quickly as their cumulative effect can cause speedy deterioration (*Figure 22.6*). The attitude 'we'll do it at the end of the season' or 'it'll heal in the fullness of time' is criminal, and will lead to a decline in standards. Having a store of resources with stockpiles of materials, such as pathway surfacing, paint, wood and wire, speeds the response time, which can be long if materials need to be ordered. A pot of paint held in readiness can counter the visual impact of a damaged sign quickly and effectively. Using natural materials, at hand on the property – for example thorns for blocking off unwanted tracks – can also help ground to reinstate quickly by providing a safe microclimate. Respond

Figure 22.6 Verge damage and other unsightly problems must be addressed urgently to minimize impact

quickly to the small jobs and the quality of the property will remain high; the big jobs usually get done anyway.

Management systems

The smooth running of visitor services relies heavily upon well organized day-to-day management procedures. These encompass the timetabling of the visitor facilities, staff organization, communication, booking systems, security and emergency procedures. In Culzean decisions related to opening times, costs and staffing levels are taken nine months in advance of a season to facilitate the production of promotional material which is circulated in January.

Group visits are very popular and can be significant at certain times of year. For example, without school groups on weekdays, and Sunday school trips on Saturdays in May and June, these months would be fairly quiet in visitor terms. The booking system is the key management tool in spreading the load, controlling large numbers of visitors, easing the pressure on the property and organizing staffing resources (*Figure 22.7*). This planning routine, in turn, will inevitably improve the quality of the visit. Schools and tour operators are targeted with the booking form and relevant information sheets and, from their response, the groups are timetabled to suit their individual requirements. The end product is a weekly sheet which is circulated to all departments comprehensively detailing the logistics of each group's visit.

Communication of this nature within the staff structure is vital as there is nothing worse than having to face the public not knowing what is happening. Staff should be fully conversant with policy matters relating to dealing with the public. Regular staff meetings, to convey information and receive feedback, staff circulars, notice boards and an open channel for individuals to seek information or guidance, should be built into the system of daily management. No member of the

Figure 22.7 The booking system at Culzean involves allocation of bus parking

team should be isolated within the team, and even if someone is at an outpost of the property, telephone or radio contact should be established. Efforts should be made to visit the post daily. In Culzean, the radio system has proved invaluable in speeding up operations and improving communications between departments and individuals.

Even with a carefully planned framework worked out in the pre-season and well tried daily routines, there is still a high responsive element to deal with on a daily basis and there must be a mechanism to address this. There must be a rapid feedback of information to a person in authority who can make positive decisions. The onus is on the manager to monitor operations, whether on a personal basis or through heads of departments. Facilities opening late, toilets not cleaned properly, litter left unpicked, paths blocked, out-of-date posters, positions unattended, all spell out one thing: poor monitoring and a resultant decline in standards.

Reaction to visitor complaints and comments must be limited to a well defined, clearly laid down procedure. Someone in authority must be available to deal with dissatisfaction. Staff passing the unfortunate visitor from pillar to post, saying it has nothing to do with them, will only exacerbate the situation. All this should be ironed out in staff training and reinforced throughout the season.

Procedures should also be well honed to deal with security or emergency situations for the benefit of both the property and the people visiting. The range of incidents which can occur is daunting, from minor first aid to full-scale emergencies, and staff must be trained to take quick action with confidence. The disastrous fire which devastated the National Trust house at Uppark in Hampshire has concentrated the minds of many organizations and individuals, and one positive outcome has been the widespread introduction of emergency procedures in heritage properties.

The format adopted by the National Trust for Scotland, after close consultation with the National Trust, is to undertake a property appraisal, followed by the production of an emergency plan with training arrangements built in. These arrangements will then be monitored and reviewed at regular intervals. This should result in a coordinated, well rehearsed reaction if the occasion arises. Detector and alarm systems, fire practices, first aid provision, staff safety notice boards, accident recording process, health and safety regulations, safety officers, snatch squads, priority listing of artefacts, site familiarization for emergency services etc. will all be embraced in these procedures. Preventing or reducing damage to the property and its historic contents is obviously a priority, but safeguarding the lives of the public and staff must always come first. The Health and Safety at work etc. Act 1974, the

Food and Environment Protection Act 1985 and the Control of Substances Hazardous to Health (COSHH) Regulations 1988 are also applicable and should be consulted regularly and implemented whenever necessary.

Security can be another major headache, whether it concerns protecting a valuable collection, combating vandalism against vulnerable ancillary buildings away from busy areas, or handling cash. Expensive electronic surveillance systems and high-profile staffing are often the answer, but there are many common-sense precautions which can reduce the risks: restrictions on the carrying of large bags in houses; collection of cash at frequent but irregular intervals, avoiding easily detected patterns; having a strict key system (master keys can be convenient, but are potentially disastrous) and a thorough locking-up procedure; limiting the operation of the security system to a core team of key personnel; and strict control of entrances and exits. Out-of-hours security can be assisted by a good relationship with the local police, who will patrol if manpower allows, by staff living on site and by security lighting.

It must never be forgotten that although it is day 90 of the season for staff, for the visitor it may be day one. Smooth, effective, daily operations will have a lasting impression.

Managing numbers

At any heritage property there will be a number of days in the season when, owing to exceptional weather, public holidays or major events, visitor pressure will exceed normal levels. A general strategy for managing large numbers is an early priority in the master plan for any property open to the public and must take on board these pressure situations. The control of car parking more often than not is the most important element.

At Culzean, the choice was either to concentrate parking at one location near the entrance and have an internal transport system from there, or to spread the load throughout the property. The latter was chosen and three distinct zones evolved offering the visitor a range of options. Four honeypots were developed in a linear pattern, parallel with the coastline, at the Visitor Centre, the Castle vicinity, the Walled Garden and Swan Pond. At each area car parking spaces on hard standing and a range of facilities were provided. A second zone served by well signed, well maintained pathways encouraged the more adventurous to explore the cliffwalk, the old railway line and the woodland garden. The remainder of the property, wooded glens, rocky shoreline and policy woodland, was there for the most adventurous to step off the beaten track. As 80 per cent of visitors confine

themselves to the honeypots, the bulk of people management is concentrated there.

On many days, the car parking capacity is exceeded and an overflow system was developed using nylon mesh to reinforce the surface of selected sections of the field adjacent to the Visitor Centre (*Figures 22.8, 22.9*). On busy days, the field is used at short notice to accommodate the extra vehicles, while for most of the year it is still a productive and unobtrusive piece of Ayrshire pasture.

One of the traps which must be avoided is to chase visitor numbers at the expense of the property. It takes a brave person to decide to close the gates or door when the property's threshold has been reached, but the option must never be discounted. If roadways are involved, police cooperation must be sought, and in fact this will often defuse a situation. The alternatives of damage to the property, irate visitors and low staff morale due to extra pressure are not desirable. The trick is to anticipate the peaks and take appropriate precautions, such as extra staffing, increased stocking of refreshment points and adequate change for pay points. Even if the day does not quite match up to the expected blitz, at least the public won't suffer.

Figure 22.8 Overflow car park areas can be provided by reinforcing field surfaces near facilities

Figure 22.9 Overflow car parking on a busy event day

The running of major events, especially if outdoor, is a risky business owing to the unpredictability of the weather. At Culzean, the Classic Vehicle Show or Country Fair can attract as many as 12,000 people and that adds up to several thousand cars. A comprehensive operation order for the day must be produced and distributed to staff and volunteers alike and should include the timetable of events, tasks and responsibilities, car parking strategy, general background information and a map of operations (*Figure 22.10*). The car parking strategy at Culzean for major events was designed following problems of massive queues, and consists of a new road to take vehicles off the traffic route to a six-lane pay point where they can be processed quickly. The vehicles are then guided into two large fields which are kept in permanent pasture to take the cars. Mobile toilets are usually needed to supplement existing facilities for the event days. A volunteer pool is essential on these days for stewarding. One of the great benefits of major events is that very often a clientele which would not normally be attracted can be introduced to the property.

Figure 22.10 Operation orders are vital when dealing with large numbers of visitors on event days

The link: staff

Well trained, enthusiastic and committed staff are one of the shrewdest investments in a property budget. The quality of staff reflects the property and its organization. The welfare of visitors is the responsibility of all the team, and communication skills should be taken into consideration in the selection of all staff. Induction training at the beginning of the season, with monitoring and upgrading of individual needs as the season progresses, should have a strong element of customer care on the agenda. Staff should be encouraged to respond positively to visitors at all times and should be readily identifiable, whether by uniform, badges, costume or even vehicle signing, for security, safety, information and interpretative functions. This link between the property and the visitor is the catalyst for success or failure.

Special needs groups

Within the visitor profile for any property there are several segments, like the disabled, the elderly, foreign visitors and even children, which have special needs. In most cases they do not want to be singled out for special attention; they simply want to enjoy the property like anyone else with no fuss. The philosophy everywhere should be to integrate the requirements of these groups into the facilities and services as a matter of course. If management is unclear about the problems, then it should go to the horse's mouth. Get into a wheelchair or push one round, accompany disabled or elderly people round the facilities, and you will begin to understand their difficulties.

Many organizations now have booklets or leaflets outlining the information which disabled people will find useful when visiting properties. Some projects, such as inserting lifts or providing unisex toilets for the disabled, can be expensive – especially if the facility has been operating for some time. Designing them into new complexes is easier. However, there are many simple inexpensive things which can be done to make life easier: doors or paths being wide enough for wheelchairs; lay-bys on paths; avoiding strong springs on doors or gates; avoiding gravel surfaces and tight corners; putting audio enhancement facilities in auditoriums; taking into consideration colour combinations of signs for those suffering from colour blindness; adapting picnic tables; having wheelchairs available (and also repair kits and pumps); and putting in ramps. The list is endless. Special interpretative facilities, such as braille trails for visually impaired visitors and tape recorded tours for visitors with learning difficulties, can add enormously to the enjoyment and appreciation of a site.

Staff training must include practical advice on face-to-face contact with the disabled. Offer help but step back if not required; talk to the person in the wheelchair, not the attendant; maintain eye contact by kneeling or bending down; assist lip reading by not standing with the light behind you. If a guide dog is in harness it is working, so do not distract it. Disabled people expect to pay and should not be singled out as needy.

The elderly appreciate good access and comfort too. Convenient parking, well placed seating, level walking surfaces and a policy of allowing cars to drop off less mobile passengers as near to the door of the facility as possible, all help to make a visit more enjoyable. Pace is all-important and the elderly and infirm should not be hurried unless in an emergency.

Translation sheets and signs, with a member of staff fluent in at least one other European language, are highly desirable if foreign visitors feature at the property, and will assume greater importance as the European Community evolves. Finally, the needs of children are often ignored despite the fact that they comprise at least a third of all visitors, and of all the clientele can generate more repeat visits. Too often displays, signs, information and interpretation are out of reach or in language which they have difficulty understanding. An investment in good facilities for children will reap high rewards.

Summary

(1) The conservation of the heritage site comes first but visitor needs should not be a poor second.
(2) Heritage properties should be available for all sectors of society and should cater for all abilities and disabilities. A strategy for visitor management is essential.

(3) Visitors expect high standards of reception and presentation and the aim must be to give a quality experience through good facilities and services.
(4) First impressions are critical: get off to a good start and build from there.
(5) Give visitors a range of information which will enable them to organize their visit and appreciate the property.
(6) The smooth running of visitor services relies heavily upon well organized daily procedures. The ability to respond quickly and effectively to visitor needs and pressures is vital.
(7) Major projects tend to get done, but the ultimate quality of experience depends upon attention to detail in the thousands of small jobs.
(8) Well trained, enthusiastic and committed staff are one of the shrewdest investments.
(9) Accessibility is the main requirement of disabled persons. They simply want to enjoy the property like everyone else with no fuss.
(10) The provision of good facilities for children will reap high rewards.

Finally, with the improvement in services should come a very different kind of letter from that presented at the beginning of the chapter:

Dear Sir

Having visited your establishment today, I was most impressed by the superb facilities and your friendly, helpful staff. They certainly matched up to the quality of the site. We had plenty to occupy us during the visit and you can be assured that we will be back.

Yours

. . . .

23

Managing volunteers: a partnership approach

Sue Millar

> Staff in other museums complain that volunteers take so much time to instruct that it is easier to do the job oneself. That is not our experience: we love them.
>
> *Private View*, Dulwich Picture Gallery Newsletter

Such contrasting views on the involvement of volunteers in museums and heritage organizations highlight the importance of good management procedures and practices. The question of volunteers has the ability to stir extremes of emotion amongst paid staff in museums and heritage organizations: people either love them or hate them. This chasm, in which the cult of personalities can readily dominate and volunteers are perceived as organizational outsiders, is also acknowledged by volunteers. Dawn Muirhead, the first Honorary Secretary of the British Association of Friends of Museums (BAFM), writes: 'You can have a stunning museum with divine collections but a dragon of a Director: the Friends creep along desperately trying to find a dragon for a Chairman to keep their end up, but it takes a dragon to know another, and the Director is paid, the Chairman is honorary, so dragons think twice before becoming Chairmen' (1991, pp. 2–3).

A positive attitude to the partnership between the volunteer and the heritage organization that combines both a recognition and an understanding of the nature of the volunteer contribution to the particular heritage organization is essential for effective policy planning and policy implementation. Volunteers are a vital resource in heritage management. 'Gifts of time' from volunteers provide a counterbalance to the otherwise daunting cost of conservation, the critical issue in heritage management, in all but the most specialized university museums and privately owned collections. Properly managed by paid staff, or self-managed, volunteers offer valuable human resources and a financial asset that extends beyond direct help in the organization to influence in the community.

The successful management of volunteers requires a heritage site manager or director (paid or unpaid) to

have a grasp of both the practical issues associated with the recruitment and retention of volunteers and the reasons how and why volunteer involvement is integral to the ethos and energy of the heritage movement. Therefore, in the first half of this chapter the nature of the relationship between the volunteer and heritage conservation is examined. The range of tasks undertaken by volunteers in heritage organizations of varying size and with different organizational structures is reviewed. The significance of the volunteer contribution to heritage organizations is explored alongside a consideration of the role of support groups such as Friends' associations and national organizations concerned with volunteering in the heritage field: the British Association of Friends of Museums (BAFM), the British Trust for Conservation Volunteers (BTCV), and the National Association of Fine and Decorative Arts (NADFAS) Volunteers (NVs). The second half of the chapter focuses on the procedures that a heritage/museum manager, director or curator, who is involved in managing volunteers, should consider in order to formulate volunteer policy and practices tailor-made to the needs of the particular heritage organization.

Volunteers and heritage conservation

Community identity, closely allied to the need for individual identity, is at the philosophical core of the huge expansion in the number of countryside, woodland and archaeological trusts, independent local history and transport museums, canal and railway preservation societies, and Friends' associations in the United Kingdom over the past 25 years. Heritage sites and museums are a dynamic force in adjusting to the process of change in society. Until now, however, the social uses of museums and heritage organizations have been underplayed and undervalued, although they were noted in the Miles Report, *Museums in Scotland* (1986). Community involvement in conservation matters rather than just the enthusiasm of volunteers has been the main impetus behind the rapid growth in charitable trusts. Nearly all independent museums, upward of 1100 at the present time, are charitable trusts. Two-thirds of local history museums have opened since 1970 and 88 per cent of the current industrial museums were not in existence before that date.

Two examples from opposite parts of the United Kingdom reveal a local community's search for its own identity. At Ilchester, the World War II air station close by was an incentive for newly arrived residents in this Somerset village to create an educational resource. It was the result of three years' preparation and planning, a loaned collection, and a rota of twenty volunteer steward helpers with a subcommittee of four administered by the Town Trust. Springburn, Glasgow, has a museum created for the specific purpose of giving a historical perspective to help residents of the existing community cope with change following the devastation and demoralization caused by the closure of the British Rail works. It has no permanent displays. Neither museum is acceptable from the point of view of the Museum Registration Scheme. But, it could be argued, the value of such heritage organizations is in the immediacy of their response to the specific needs of a community at a particular time of great change through a tangible continuity with the material culture of the past, and not the longevity of the organization itself.

Communities of interest bring together like-minded people as volunteers across local, regional, national and international boundaries. The large industrial and transport museums and the Association of Railway Preservation Societies are examples. They were established at the very moment the working machinery and ways of life they now depict became obsolete; at the time when there was a major shift away from traditional heavy manufacturing industry towards the service sector; and at the time when there were dramatic changes in the retail sector reflected by the demise of individual grocers, butchers and ironmongers and the growth first of supermarkets and then of hypermarkets. Beamish North of England Open Air Museum, County Durham; the Weald and Downland Museum, West Sussex; and Ironbridge Gorge Museum, Shropshire – the self-proclaimed 'Birthplace of the Industrial Revolution' – are amongst the best known examples of this type of museum. Local members of the Friends Association were the pioneers in the growth and development of Ironbridge Gorge Museum Trust

and established branch associations world-wide, in Birmingham, London and the USA.

In addition to campaigning through formal groups such as Friends' associations, volunteers frequently set up informal pressure groups in support of the preservation of particular sites they perceive to be in imminent danger of destruction. The archaeological remains of the Rose Theatre on the south bank of the River Thames in London, a famous venue for Shakespeare's plays in the sixteenth century, were saved from property developers' excavators and bulldozers in the late 1980s. Success was entirely due to the active interest of members of the theatrical profession and to general public indignation and concern for our national heritage, heightened by wide-scale media coverage. Expert advice was sought from English Heritage.

Friends associations are responsible not only for spearheading the creation of new heritage organizations but also for sustaining the development of existing ones through practical help, fund-raising initiatives and promoting good relations with other people in the local community. Above all, Friends' associations benefit the individual member. They provide the opportunity for people with similar interests to get together; they offer cultural enrichment – to use an American phrase that has no equivalent this side of the Atlantic – through talks and visits; and they enable people to become involved in a project that will enhance the quality of life for other people both now and in the future. For many, Friends' associations give a sense of purpose to their own lives and a personal identity with a cause that is perceived as 'a good thing' within the local community. Conservation by museums and heritage organizations represents stability and continuity amidst society in a constant state of flux around the globe. Friends associations are growing in number and unity world-wide.

Volunteers and heritage management

Volunteers undertake an enormous range of activities. Volunteers engender enthusiasm and offer dogged persistence to secure the preservation of new heritage sites and initiate new projects within existing heritage organizations. Volunteers provide the underpinning for the development of an expanding range of functions at heritage sites. Behind-the-scenes volunteers undertake a large number of jobs, from such mundane and necessary activities as stuffing envelopes for mailings and digging ditches to giving professional legal and financial advice requiring experience and expertise. Many volunteers are actively involved in curatorial and conservation work. They document and research museum collections, catalogue and record trees in historic gardens, clean old books and repair damaged footpaths. Frequently, volunteers provide the human face of a heritage organization as managers, guides, room stewards or countryside wardens. Individuals may be members of governing bodies, management committees or trustees, but may also, on occasions, volunteer to do some litter picking or be a car park attendant. Groups of supporters or Friends' which are primarily involved in fund-raising and public relations activities in the community may also have members who are hands-on volunteers within the organization.

Recent research on volunteers in museums and heritage organizations revealed that 'The nature of the partnership between volunteers and paid staff will vary according to the size and type of management structure in the organisation and the differences in the nature and value of the collections. These two factors affect both the range of museum functions undertaken by volunteers and the degree of responsibility they have within each' (Millar, 1991). Consequently, the experience for a volunteer working in the same resource area can be very different. Documentation is an example. Volunteers working in the Archives Section of the Tate Gallery are required to have a high level of accuracy. They do tasks such as sorting and filing exhibition catalogues; this can be somewhat monotonous, but the congenial environment compensates. Whitby Pictorial Archives is staffed almost entirely by volunteers and presents a marked contrast. The work of the project teams is far wider ranging and includes pictorial research, the maintenance of an oral history archive, and dealing with enquiries into family history as well as filing and documentation.

The National Trust not only is the largest voluntary conservation body in Europe but also has been extraordinarily successful in appointing skilled paid staff and applying modern management techniques to gain over 2 million members and recruit and retain volunteers, now numbering some 20,000 overall. In recent years regional volunteer coordinator posts have been established throughout the Trust in England and Wales. Administrators are responsible for organizing room stewards at each property, and wardens undertake parallel responsibilities in the countryside. Large-scale volunteer involvement within the Trust combined with the employment of qualified paid staff as volunteer managers gives rise to questions of ownership. As a counterpoint to greater professionalism at regional level, Friends' associations are emerging spontaneously at individual sites throughout England and Wales. At Wimpole, Cambridgeshire, there are separate Friends' associations for the house and the farm. This situation illustrates the problems that arise from the expansion of an organization accompanied by an emphasis on cost-effectiveness and efficiency when that organization is a charitable trust and has depended on members' direct involvement for its initial growth and development.

The same pattern is familiar in many smaller museums, archaeological and countryside trusts in the United Kingdom which expand to the point where the appointment of paid professional staff is essential. As a result of this cycle of growth, volunteers often feel a vacuum and sense a loss of identity once responsibility for decision making has shifted to paid staff. Robert Logan, Chairman of the Friends of Glasgow Art Gallery and Museums Association, writes: 'An abiding memory of the British Association of Friends and Museums (BAFM) Conference at Bristol was the message from the Museum Director who would not be able to keep the doors open without Friends. In the melting pot of our movement it is not always so. Professionals resent the possessive attitude of those who have grown up with a collection – a vicarious ownership; their career jostlings make them impatient with those who are in with the bricks' (1991). Insensitivity to the origins of the organization on the part of paid professional staff, combined with a failure to manage change – including an ability to delegate their own control over the day-to-day running of operations – on the part of the trustees, can lead to the kind of personality cults and clashes referred to in the introduction.

Volunteers and heritage resources

The heritage provides an inspiration for people to volunteer and, in turn, the service given by volunteers is an invaluable resource in operations management at heritage sites. Cultural or heritage volunteering has developed separately from other forms of volunteering. People attracted to volunteer in this field are motivated primarily from a commitment to the heritage resource. The chance to pursue a special interest or hobby, meet like-minded people, stave off loneliness, use their expertise, offer a service to the community, add to their own knowledge in a life-long education or begin a career in the heritage sector are other factors that motivate people to volunteer. Each has a personal agenda. Large numbers of retired people work in museums and heritage organizations. This is atypical of the national picture of volunteering generally. *The 1991 National Survey of Voluntary Activity in the UK* (Lynn and Davis Smith, 1991) found that people aged 35–44 were the most likely to volunteer, with those over 75 least likely. Enthusiasts – mainly men – provide practical help at industrial and transport museums. Guiding in art galleries and at historic houses, however, is undertaken principally by women.

One-third of the total workforce of 25,000 in museums comes within the voluntary category according to *Museums Matter*, a report from the Museums and Galleries Commission (1992). This is in line with the shift in the balance from statutory to voluntary bodies within the museum and heritage sector and the continuing involvement of volunteers in local authority and national museums. Above, the wide range of functions undertaken by volunteers was discussed. Volunteer initiative, volunteer enthusiasm, volunteer expertise, volunteer skill, volunteer time and volunteer fund-raising abilities play an important role in successful heritage management. They provide valuable human and financial resources. The impact of the quality and quantity of volunteer activity in museums, uncovered and recognized during extensive research throughout the United Kingdom in 1989–90, led to the conclusion that 'Volunteers are a significant part of the museum community. In a majority of museums high public expectations and high professional standards cannot be met as far as the care of and access to collections are concerned without volunteer help' (Millar, 1991, p. 3).

Yet, few museums or heritage organizations in this country keep a record of volunteer hours worked, or give this a monetary value. The National Trust recorded just under 1 million volunteer hours in 1989. In the Mercia region a total of 134,130 hours were worked and rated at £410,200. At the Smithsonian Institution in Washington DC, some 5252 volunteers in the fiscal year 1989 provided services in excess of some $6 million. In the United States, however, the volunteer as well as the institution has a vested interest in recording the hours that s/he has contributed to the organization: tax relief is provided as an incentive for volunteering.

Management practices relating to volunteers in museums and heritage organizations in the United Kingdom, with some notable exceptions such as the National Trust, fell behind the growth of volunteer involvement during the 1980s. Volunteering is based on the principle of reciprocity. Volunteers do not come free. Until recently, procedures were often piecemeal and *ad hoc* rather than explicit and formalized. This situation is changing. In 1992, volunteer policy planning was the focus of the Association of Independent Museums' annual conference and funding from The Carnegie UK Trust was agreed for training managers of volunteers. A course concentrating on expanding leadership skills and team building relating directly to standards of competence is being developed by the Museum Training Institute.

Volunteers and national organizations

The development of national organizations of volunteers reflects a change in the status and public profile of volunteering within heritage organizations and museums over the past twenty years, alongside an increase in the numbers of charitable trusts. In turn, such organizations help to raise the standards and expectations of volunteers. The need for a central

body to define policy and coordinate the activities of dispersed groups with common aims is part of the move towards increased professionalism, greater specialization, and recognition by the heritage movement as a whole that volunteers and paid staff must work in partnership.

The publication *Museums Among Friends* (Heaton, 1992) identifies five prominent charities connected with museums at national level: the National Art Collections Fund (NACF), founded in 1903, with 35,000 members which help museums acquire works of art; the National Campaign for the Arts; the National Association of Decorative and Fine Arts, founded in 1968, with 67,000 members, an educational focus, and some 3000 NADFAS Volunteers; National Heritage (not to be confused with the newly formed Department of National Heritage), founded in 1971 as a lobbying body with 900 members; and the British Association of Friends of Museums (BAFM), founded in 1972 as the umbrella organization for 225 Friends' groups, currently with around 165,000 members. The publication acknowledges both the tangible benefits offered to museums by Friends' associations in terms of volunteer time and fund-raising initiatives, and also the intangible benefits they offer through links with the community. The report recommends enlarging the present membership, endorses the appointment of two paid staff and suggests combining with National Heritage on publications. 'BAFM should expand its services to members, raise its profile on volunteers and do more to promote the interests of museums generally' (Heaton, 1991, para. 5.13). The impact of the report is yet to be digested. Therefore, BAFM's responsive and supportive current role rather than the more forceful and dynamic one envisaged for the future is outlined here.

British Association of Friends of Museums (BAFM)

Apart from a consistent, but somewhat low-key, campaigning role designed to achieve greater recognition and financial support for museums, BAFM offers members a wider regional and national forum for social gatherings and educational activities including lectures and tours. Advice is available on approaches to fund-raising and public relations. Friends see themselves as advocates of paid professional staff. Insurance is available for Friends who become actively involved in the day-to-day work of the museum. *Are You Insured?* was published in 1990.

The Association is run by a council whose members represent groups in the regions, corresponding approximately to those covered by the Area Museums Councils. Member groups receive a yearbook, renamed *Museum Visitor* in 1991, a regular broadsheet, and the newsheet of the World Federation of Friends of Museums (WFFM). An annual award is given for the most interesting and best presented newsletter. The Friends of the National Maritime Museum, Greenwich, received this in 1991.

British Trust for Conservation Volunteers (BTCV)

The British Trust for Conservation Volunteers was initially established to undertake nature conservation work. The need for training was recognized at an early stage and courses on group leadership, habitat management and practical work techniques were developed. Trained volunteers fell small trees to thin overgrown and derelict woods, clear away scrubby growth (such as rhododendron), reintroduce coppicing regimes, and plant trees to replace old timber that has passed its prime. Advice on the role of volunteers in woodland management is given in a BTCV publication *Woodlands*. Another booklet, *Waterways and Wetlands*, emphasizes the suitability of the work for volunteers of all ages. 'It is curious how much enthusiasm people display for getting really wet and muddy in a good cause!' (Pettigrew, 1985).

NADFAS Volunteers (NVs)

NADFAS Volunteers, run by the National Association of Decorative and Fine Arts Societies, place an equal emphasis on training and procedures, but generally stay clean. Their largely preventive conservation work covers the refurbishment of books, ceramics, silver, arms, armour, furniture and textiles: library work and paper conservation; the indexing, cataloguing and recording of church contents and trees in historic gardens; and the making of replica furnishings and costume. Members undertake voluntary work for a range of heritage organizations including museums, libraries, historic houses and the National Trust.

The reputation for reliability and high standards developed by NADFAS Volunteers is based on carefully formulated procedures and training organized centrally. NV group leaders receive a starter pack which includes details on insurance, specialist information on starting a library conservation project, and forms for formalizing and regulating procedures. They visit the museum or historic property to discuss the task with the director, curator or owner and then report back to the NV chairman for approval. Checks on such matters as health and safety conditions, the reimbursement of expenses and provision of materials are made before the project begins. Leaders also ensure that members receive the right conservation advice and training in advance. Indemnity forms, signed by the employer, provide indemnity for NADFAS against third-party claims at work. A handbook gives heritage managers comprehensive information on the services and procedures offered by NADFAS Volunteers.

Why is a volunteer policy needed?

A volunteer policy:

(1) is part of good resource management linked to the process of corporate planning;
(2) provides openly acknowledged parameters between heritage managers who are paid and volunteers, or between volunteer managers, other volunteers and paid staff;
(3) provides information on the recruitment of volunteers and gives recognition to the volunteer involvement.

Heritage organizations of all sizes need a volunteer policy if volunteers are involved in day-to-day operations management. The policy has to be tailor-made to meet the requirements of the particular heritage organization and designed to take account of the potential pool of volunteers in the region. The large number of retired professional people in SE and SW England makes careful selection both a desirable and a viable option. The sparse population in certain areas of NE England and Scotland means that there must be a great emphasis on training to maximize the abilities of available volunteers within the community.

Volunteer policy planning

The start of the planning process involves a review of existing volunteer resources and helps an organization to understand who does volunteer, who might volunteer, and whether their skills and talents are being used fully and effectively. In larger organizations, this is followed by a consideration of the benefits of a volunteer coordinator. The process is completed with the presentation of a policy statement, procedures and practices in a handbook or manual.

A policy review

Consultation at the review stage gives coherence to the formulation of a volunteer policy and eases its implementation. At the same time, the principle of reciprocity – central to the ethos of volunteering – is maintained. Some or all of the following participants should be included: volunteers, paid staff, the volunteer organizer, trade union representatives and members of the membership or Friends' association.

The steps to be undertaken in a volunteer policy review are outlined below (Millar, 1991). They take account of the needs of heritage organizations in both the independent and public sectors. Calculations concerning the number of volunteers required, the space needed, a breakdown of the costs and details of supervision and training arrangements are common concerns for all heritage organizations. Essentially, the questions to ask here are: how do - or how will - volunteers help the heritage organization achieve its goals? Is their contribution effective? In practice:

(1) Explore the ways in which the volunteer contribution interlocks with the management plan and organizational structures.
(2) Examine and define areas where volunteers work and the tasks undertaken. Are these core or supplementary activities?
(3) Calculate/estimate the numbers of volunteers working/required.
(4) Investigate the supervision arrangements in relation to the line management structure of the organization and staff time: curator/manager, volunteer coordinator.
(5) Examine procedures and practices: recruitment, induction and training.
(6) Look at potential supply: density and employment profile of surrounding population, accessibility of site, demographic trends.
(7) Assess the resources: office/common-room space, transport, equipment, workspace for special projects, expenses and training.
(8) Explore funding requirements and funding sources: Friends, sponsorship.
(9) Formulate a volunteer policy through consultation between curators/managers, volunteers, the volunteer organizer, members of the Friends' association and, if appropriate, trade union representatives.

A volunteer policy review is critically important as part of the management of change. For those heritage organizations in the process of expansion or contraction, transition to charitable trusts status, or starting to supplement direct funding or grant-in-aid with engendered income and sponsorship, a review can pinpoint where changes are needed in terms of the volunteer contribution to meet fresh goals and new challenges. It is more difficult for individual volunteers to see a decision that involves a change in, or the complete removal of, their status as a personal slight if the change in the direction of volunteer policy is the result of a review.

Increasingly, the care of customers alongside the care of collections is recognized as part of a heritage organization's core activity. The growing awareness of the role of heritage organizations within the community (as discussed earlier), the changes in funding from government and local authority sources, and the consequent pressure on funds from sponsorship and charities, mean that visitor numbers and visitor income are of paramount importance. As a result of a review, heritage managers employing both paid and unpaid staff, therefore, may find themselves asking: 'Are volunteers the best means of service delivery?' If so, the profile of volunteers within the organization, volunteer training requirements and the coordination of the volunteer contribution may need both a higher priority and a sharper focus.

A volunteer organizer

For all heritage organizations there are immense advantages in employing a volunteer organizer or volunteer coordinator on a paid or unpaid basis. In small voluntary trusts this will be the manager/curator. Fragmentation of the volunteer effort can present problems even within a small informal group. Maintaining good communications and ensuring that volunteers receive up-to-date information is difficult when people come in on a rota system only once a week or once a fortnight, at weekends, or for a week once or twice a year. Up to seven volunteers are sometimes needed to offer services equivalent to one full-time member of staff.

The quantity of volunteers and the array of disjointed timetables mean that a high level of organization is essential. The supervision of particular tasks can still be done by individuals on the paid staff, or project leaders, once the parameters for the work have been negotiated between the volunteer organizer, the manager/curator or team leader, and the volunteer. A volunteer organizer or coordinator can encourage teamwork and foster positive working relations through providing training, setting aside time to talk to people, offering encouragement and praise and, if necessary, carrying out disciplinary procedures.

The essential question here is: does the heritage organization need a volunteer coordinator (paid or unpaid) to assist with the transfer of policy into action? The tasks associated with volunteer coordination are as follows (Millar, 1991):

(1) liaison between volunteers and paid staff;
(2) public relations, Friends, open days, editing a newsletter/journal;
(3) programme planning;
(4) job design and job descriptions, with curators/managers;
(5) preparing a recruitment and skills register;
(6) induction and training;
(7) organizing supervision and reporting arrangements for volunteers;
(8) organizing volunteer support and development, including clerical help, access to a telephone and career paths;
(9) organizing volunteer records and evaluation/appraisal procedures;
(10) offering recognition to volunteers through the personal touch, awards and social gatherings;
(11) negotiating disciplinary/dismissal proceedings.

Handbook or manual

A looseleaf manual will assist the integration of volunteers within the management framework of the individual heritage organization. The essential question here is: does the heritage organization need a manual/handbook in which to assemble and coordinate relevant information in looseleaf form for easy updating? This would include details on some or all of the following (Millar, 1991):

(1) information on the organization, its background, aims and objectives;
(2) policy statement on volunteers;
(3) details on volunteer programmes, including job descriptions and application forms;
(4) volunteer agreement;
(5) recruitment, induction, training procedures;
(6) codes of practice, e.g. health and safety, disciplinary procedures;
(7) insurance;
(8) reimbursement of expenses;
(9) discounts at the shop;
(10) information on the Friends' or membership association.

How does a heritage manager recruit and retain volunteers?

The enhanced status of volunteering and demographic trends indicate that there will be increased competition for volunteers in the 1990s. A reduction in the number of 16–19-year-olds and a middle-age bulge by the year 2000 mean that heritage organizations will need to offer an attractive package to volunteers if they want to recruit and retain good people.

Recruitment

One person, either the heritage manager or the volunteer coordinator, should follow the recruitment and selection procedures through from advertisement to appointment. Far from deterring prospective volunteers, careful selection procedures encourage commitment and give the volunteers the chance of greater job satisfaction and a sense of their worth to the organization. The selection process includes the following.

Advertising
Informal networking – word of mouth advertising – can be extremely effective. The dangers are, however, that current volunteers will recruit in their own image. If volunteering in heritage organizations is to be made attractive to a wider audience, then new, innovative recruitment methods are needed. Advertising on local radio, in the local newspaper, at youth clubs, job centres, and in the specialist newspapers of ethnic minorities and people with disabilities, are other ways of reaching different people who might be interested in becoming volunteers.

Job description
A job description (*Figure 23.1*) gives specific information on the scope and remit of a particular task. The job title, principal purpose, duties and responsibilities of the post are described together with an indication about the potential it offers for the development of the individual volunteer appointed. Details of the desired skills, knowledge and/or experience that are expected

Practical Workday Coordinators

The task This post requires people to draw up regular lists of workdays on our reserves with the help of the Conservation Officer. Some liaison with our reserve wardens will also be necessary. The schedules produced then have to be distributed to all our practical volunteers. Volunteers are also needed to load up the van for the Sunday workday, preferably on the preceding Friday

Requirements A chance to put your organizational skills to good use! A knowledge of practical conservation would be useful. Some experience of word processing would be helpful, although training could be provided.

Time involved The production and posting of the workday schedule takes about half a day, although complications can make the job a little longer. This would be done every two or three months. The loading of the van would be once a week and take about an hour each Friday prior to a workday. Again this job could be shared amongst several people.

Location All work is currently based at Trust Headquarters. However, some of the more specialist tools may have to be collected from other stores in the future.

Figure 23.1 Avon Wildlife Trust job description

from the person who applies for the job, alongside clarification of lines of accountability, are also necessary. The job description is separate from a volunteer agreement.

Application form
The main purpose of an application form is to obtain information from potential volunteers to make effective placements. A well designed application form, however, can provide the basis for a skills register and record keeping: it can also help subsequently with evaluation procedures. Apart from basic personal data, space can be provided for information on time available, skills and expertise, interests, preferred areas of work and recruitment checks, e.g. referees.

Interview
The interview is a two-way learning process. Even at those heritage sites and museums placed in locations where volunteers are at a premium, the interview is important. It may be formal or informal. It provides an opportunity for the person interested in volunteering to find out about the place, the staff and the other volunteers, as well as details of the nature of the work on offer. Careful selection and matching of the volunteer's interests, skills and enthusiasms to an

available job creates the foundation for an effective, cooperative team.

Recruitment checks

If the person is suitable, references can be taken up together with other recruitment checks. If a candidate is rejected, a letter of thanks saying s/he will be informed of future opportunities is important in maintaining good community relations. Checks that may be carried out, in addition to taking up references, include an investigation into a volunteer's driving licence and insurance status, health and past offences. One argument against such action is that excessive red tape can discourage volunteers. Frequently, however, the reverse is true. The volunteer is reassured by the care taken by the organization, thus demonstrating that s/he is suitable to hold a position of responsibility.

Equal opportunities

If the heritage organization has an equal opportunities policy this affects not only recruitment procedures but also health and safety, insurance and training matters. The aim is one of positive action in promoting equal opportunities in practices and service provision for all – volunteers as well as paid staff. A commitment to anti-racism and anti-sexism, therefore, can be asked of volunteers. Conversely, procedures to deal with sexual harassment are available for use by volunteers and paid staff alike.

Volunteer agreement

Once a volunteer is recruited, a letter of appointment can be sent out. Some heritage organizations also send out a welcome letter together with a written agreement outlining conditions of service to be signed by the volunteer. This is not a contract since contracts of employment are legally binding and cannot be used in relation to the appointment of volunteer staff.

The agreement can include the following information:

(1) clarification of the volunteer's role, tasks and time commitment;
(2) details of the position/person to whom the volunteer is accountable;
(3) information on personnel practices, that is details of induction, training and support, procedures for illness and holidays, grievance or disciplinary procedures;
(4) insurance provision;
(5) expenses allowable and arrangements for payment;
(6) health and safety procedures;
(7) working arrangements and conditions;
(8) expectations of the volunteer, namely punctuality, courtesy commitment, regular attendance, a satisfactory performance of the agreed task and a willingness to undertake training;
(9) specify a trial period, e.g. six months, and request a period of notice in the case of resignation.

When a volunteer signs an agreement before starting work, there are two-way advantages. If the volunteer proves unsuitable for reasons of absenteeism, or an inability to execute a particular task, the appointment can be reviewed. Equally, if the heritage organization does not fulfil its obligations, a volunteer is in a position to file a complaint. Termination of the agreement is a last resort. In this case, however, a period of notice built into the agreement and a fixed-term letter of appointment are helpful.

Recognition and support

The scant attention paid to stimulating and sustaining volunteer involvement in many heritage organizations is out of keeping with the rising demand for the services of volunteers. A good staff development policy offers opportunities for volunteers to develop interests and skills alongside paid staff. Training programmes, regular appraisal of work in progress and a deliberate policy of recognition through rewards and social gatherings provide the necessary ongoing system of support and encouragement. Moreover, they are fundamental to maintaining high, professional standards of service within heritage organizations. Grievance procedures and disciplinary measures ensure that when a problem does occur it can be dealt with quickly and effectively.

Induction

Introducing new volunteers to their surroundings can be done through a formal tour and talk about the organizational structure of the museum and how their own contribution fits in. An induction pack is provided by some organizations. A warm welcome is critical to a successful volunteer input. This introduction should be followed by a briefing on fire, safety and security procedures on the one hand, and information on social activities on the other.

Training

Most volunteers have no knowledge or previous experience of the tasks they agree to do, and paid staff find supervision time prohibitive. *Ad hoc* on-the-job training has, in the past, led to resentment and frustration on both sides. This situation is changing.

The cost of training, however, is frequently ignored in any review of resources necessary for the implementation of a volunteer policy. Induction, on-the-job training, in-service training and refresher courses are essential if the volunteer contribution is to be effective within the organization and also a satisfying experience for the volunteer. Standardization is difficult. The variety of heritage sites and management structures, as well as the different ways in which volunteers interlock into the activities of paid staff or operate on a self-management basis, mean that training programmes are ideally custom-made.

Attaching a volunteer to an overloaded manager or curator can hinder work in progress rather than offer training opportunities. However, if this aspect of the manager/curator's work is built into his/her job description and time is allocated for this task – for example, one morning a week – then such specific, tailor-made training can be extremely effective.

Core training, moreover, is also part of risk management and safety procedures. A court of law would not be critical of a volunteer displaying a lower standard than a paid person in a particular field, but guidance on the degree of reasonable skill would be expected. This includes: the safe handling of special tools and equipment; hazard awareness training; and ensuring a volunteer understands her/his own limitations and when to seek assistance.

Appraisal

Trust is essential to cooperation. On the one hand, volunteers may see the appraisal process as threatening rather than as a useful planning tool which gives them a stake in the organization. On the other, acknowledgment of progress can make people feel proud and successful. It also visibly demonstrates the importance of volunteer work. Appraisal and performance reviews show that volunteers are accountable both externally and internally – to funding bodies and other staff. This helps to reduce the risk of volunteers being viewed as marginal to the organization. People need to be reassured that the focus is developmental and not judgemental. Volunteer self-appraisal can take the form of a written report.

Rewards

The main difference between volunteers and paid staff is that the former are rewarded through personal satisfaction and not through money. Volunteers, by the very nature of their motivation, need positive and regular demonstration that their efforts are appreciated. A friendly welcome, social gatherings, announcements of special achievements in the newsletter or local press, and above all 'thank you' , are the kind of reward volunteers are seeking. Special facilities including car parking, crèche, discounts on meals and goods bought in the shop are an added bonus. The National Trust gives volunteers a card for 40 hours work which offers them free admission to Trust properties and a 10 per cent discount in the shop.

Resignations

Disciplinary procedures and dismissal

This is an area in which heritage organizations appear reluctant to exert authority. There is an embarrassment about what are considered to be difficult and sensitive areas. Nevertheless, they need to be addressed. Volunteers frequently expect more flexibility than paid staff in terms of defining their hours and workload. The need for flexibility has to be balanced with the need

for accountability. In the first instance, if a volunteer's performance is unsatisfactory, the reasons should be discussed and agreement reached on whether an alternative task would be more suitable.

Dismissal is never easy. If disciplinary measures have failed, however, or if a person's performance is irredeemably inadequate, it may be in the volunteer's and the organization's best interests to terminate the appointment. Recalcitrant or disruptive attitudes can affect the morale of others. Once the decision has been taken, the matter needs to be dealt with speedily. There is no legal redress for the unjust dismissal of a volunteer.

Grievance procedures

Volunteer workers have every right to make complaints or criticisms on any matters which cause them concern. This includes disagreement over duties, aspersions cast on character or allegations of dishonesty. In the first instance, they should raise the matter with their supervisor who should advise them of the complaints procedure. All complaints and grievances should be considered carefully and investigated fully, objectively and in a confidential manner.

Common causes of grievance and high turnover are a lack of support, direction and control in the work situation, poor treatment and poor working relations. The hostility of paid staff can aggravate problems, and conflicts can arise between personal and organizational goals. Frequently, there is either too much work, or too little work, or too many difficult tasks. A lack of resources to accomplish goals leads volunteers to feel that they are not meeting expectations. When money is not a motivating factor, recognition is all-important. Volunteer coordinators or supervisors will soon learn to recognize the warning signs, including poor performance and indifference.

Turnover

Good volunteers are accountable, but even good volunteers do not stay forever. Volunteers may choose to leave for any number of valid reasons such as family commitments, moving away from the area, or because they are no longer fit and well. Recognized procedures help volunteers feel that they are leaving legitimately without being put under pressure or treated as 'defectors'. The volunteer should be thanked for her/his services.

Legal and financial considerations for heritage managers

Insurance

Employer liability insurance does not automatically cover volunteers, although some insurers – for policy purposes only – are prepared to regard volunteers as employees. This means that they will cover the legal liability of the heritage organization for volunteers as well as employees under the organization's employer's liability policy. A suitable premium basis would have to be agreed. Agreeing to regard volunteers as employees for policy purposes, however, does not alter their legal status.

Employers in heritage organizations also need to insure for public liability to cover employees and the public using the premises, or acting on their behalf. But, from the heritage organization's point of view, it is preferable to treat the volunteers as employees and to arrange for the legal liability to be handled under both the employer's liability and public liability policies.

All insurance arrangements, including any personal accident cover, should be made clear to volunteers when they join the organization. It is particularly important to inform volunteers whether they are to be treated as employees as far as employer liability and public liability cover are concerned. Other insurance considerations relate to the museum's buildings, furniture and fittings, vehicles and collections.

For a full discussion of employment law and liability as it affects volunteers see Millar (1991).

Out-of-pocket expenses

Volunteers, as an important component of the organization's staff resources, have a right to claim out-of-pocket expenses. People who give their time and skills free should not, in addition, be required to spend their own money. Retired people on fixed incomes, and unemployed people, generally cannot afford to have their income prejudiced. Arrangements for claims and payment need to be simple, flexible and fully publicized.

The Inland Revenue (IR) and Department of Social Security (DSS) have stated that the reimbursement of expenses to a reasonable level will not threaten benefit or tax liability. This may include travel on a mileage basis (at a rate which is agreed as reasonable, and not necessarily the total sum claimed if a large mileage has been incurred) or actual public transport costs. In addition, it may include the cost of subsistence, e.g. light refreshments, a main meal and overnight accommodation when necessary.

The distinction between unpaid voluntary work and paid voluntary work is defined by the DSS leaflet FB26 (91). Paid voluntary work involves small payments such as out-of-pocket expenses and a little pocket money. A paid volunteer is treated as a part-time worker. Out-of-pocket expenses paid for travel and subsistence are considered earnings if they exceed the actual earnings disregard. They are then set against benefit or incur tax liability.

Conclusion

Heritage managers steeped in the knowledge of the background to a partnership approach to managing volunteers (as discussed in the earlier sections of this chapter) and equipped with information on how to formulate a tailor-made volunteer policy with proper procedures and practices relevant to volunteer involvement within her/his particular heritage organization (as detailed in the later sections) will nevertheless, at times, find themselves frustrated. Even the harnessed energy and enthusiasm of volunteers can be a daunting prospect for paid staff struggling with such awesome tasks as controlling miniscule budgets, landslides or the pile of paper in the in-tray. At such moments it is difficult to put theory into practice.

Yet, at such tired times, it is especially important to remember that without the 'gifts of time' from volunteers in fund-raising initiatives, as formal or informal pressure groups, as ambassadors in the local community and as hands-on helpers, the majority of heritage sites and museums in the United Kingdom would not be able to maintain the extraordinarily high professional standards of visitor care and collections care that we have come to expect. Dwindling financial support from central and local government and growing competition for grants and sponsorship bring the significance of volunteers as valuable human and financial resources in heritage management to centre stage. Volunteers deserve good management through a partnership approach. The future of effective heritage management in the 1990s is dependent, in many ways, on volunteer involvement.

References

HEATON, D. (1992) *Museums Among Friends*, HMSO

LOGAN, R. (1991) *Museum Visitor*, BAFM Yearbook

LYNN, P. and DAVIS SMITH, J. (1991) *The 1991 National Survey of Voluntary Activity in the UK*, Voluntary Action Research, Second Series, paper no. 1, Volunteer Centre UK

MILLAR, S. (1991) *Volunteers in Museums and Heritage Organisations: Policy Planning and Management*, HMSO

MUIRHEAD, D. (1991) 'Who goes there, friend or foe?', *Museum News*, no. 56

MUSEUMS AND GALLERIES COMMISSION (1986) *Museums in Scotland: Report by a Working Party*, HMSO

MUSEUMS AND GALLERIES COMMISSION (1992) *Museums Matter*, London

PETTIGREW, W. (1985) *Involving Volunteers in the Environment*, Volunteer Centre UK

Case study 23.1

Volunteers at The Boat Museum, Ellesmere Port

Tony Hirst

Volunteers appear in some role in virtually all museums, whether it be a tiny village museum or a major national museum that has a friends organization. For a very large number of museums, particularly in the independent sector, it would be difficult for them to exist without a contribution from volunteers.

A group of volunteers must be managed like any other organization; it is really no different in the need for good management, except that the rewards are psychological rather than fiscal. Satisfaction and enjoyment are two key factors in motivating volunteers. Any group, even if it only has a few members, should be set up in a formal way. Even the smallest operation, if it wishes to continue past the enthusiasm of the founders, must formulate some method of bringing in others. Proper organization will enable the objectives to be not only set but followed. It will also help to perpetuate the organization beyond the enthusiasm of the founders who at some time or another will leave or die.

Many groups form companies limited by guarantee and then seek charitable status. The first protects the members, as long as they have carried out their duties reasonably, from any major financial liabilities which may be incurred. Charitable status enables them to attract donated money with tax benefits to the society and the benefactors. It does, though, require a clearly defined set of objectives for the organization.

The status of company and charity ensures that the finances of the organization are properly organized (for larger organizations audited accounts are required by both Companies House and the Charity Commission) and that the officers, chairman, secretary, treasurer etc. of the organization are properly elected by the members and have to report on their actions to the membership. Both give the organization credibility to the outside world.

Managing volunteers is in one major aspect different from running an organization employing staff. The latter can select the right person to match a job specification, but with volunteers the specification has to be tailored to those involved. Failure to match the two can be fatal, leading to poor-quality work being undertaken, a loss of enthusiasm and a gradual drifting away of members.

Good communications are probably the most difficult function in any organization, be it volunteer or professional. Most volunteer organizations have three principal methods of communication. The first is verbal, whether it be at meetings of members, by face-to-face meetings, or over the telephone. As far as transferring information, this is the best way. It is limited, though, to a small proportion of the membership, i.e. to those that turn up at meetings or are specifically contacted. The second is written communication through minutes of meetings. These are essential, but again they are usually distributed to a limited number of members; they are rather formal, abbreviated and specialist in their nature.

The third form of communication is the newsletter, which fills a vital role in developing and holding together a volunteer organization. Direct verbal communication is probably only regularly possible to 10 per cent of the membership, but 100 per cent must be kept informed of what is happening in order to retain their enthusiasm. Well laid out in a professional manner, clear, typeset, illustrated and with a good content, a newsletter can look and be very effective at a modest cost. A bullish enthusiastic content can have a dramatic effect on the organization. Clearly defining how members and others can help, telling them the time, date and purpose of meetings, and when other activities are to take place are key messages and keep people involved. Who the officers and personalities of the society are should be clearly identified in the newsletter with photographs so that new members recognize them. Ensure that the production takes place to a regular pattern of predetermined dates. An investment in this activity will repay itself many times. In this way the majority of the membership will know what is going on and what they can participate in. They will feel involved and grow to expect the arrival of the newsletter on a particular day. People get very upset if the magazine they regularly read is not available when expected. A society member is just the same. To encourage others to join and support the organization, information about its activities must be promoted beyond its own membership. This is equally as important as communicating with the membership, and can be adequately achieved by further distribution of a good newsletter.

On the assumption, which is probably the majority case, that there is a volunteer organization separate from that of the museum itself, the following is given as guidance on how to achieve the most for and from both organizations. I believe that each organization has a different role in achieving a common objective, that of improving the operation of the museum. Mixing roles can lead to uncertainty, confusion, lack of achievement and satisfaction. The role of the volunteers must be precisely defined and agreed with the director of the museum. Each organization must know what it is responsible for achieving and be able to progress with it without interference. Targets for volunteers should be set, based on what can be achieved within the resources that are available in people, skills, finance and equipment. The end of a project must be capable of being seen with the resources at hand. People will soon become disillusioned if they cannot see progress.

If their work is on a project basis, for instance the restoration of a large object, volunteers should be able to progress independently except for the control of specifications and standards, which ultimately must be the responsibility of the museum staff involved. Where volunteers are helping in some routine function, i.e. guiding or catering, they should be organized by a member of the museum staff, so that there is a common brief for its staff members involved in the same or similar activities.

It is well worth while the museum giving the responsibility for organizing volunteers to a member of staff, who should also be responsible for training. This is not just with regard to the content of the tour, but should include aspects of health and safety, fire procedures and the topical subject of customer care. The absence of training is all too evident in some volunteer organizations!

The trainer needs to understand the skills and aspirations of the volunteer. Volunteers should be asked to complete a questionnaire about themselves. Based on this and discussions, training and work activities, satisfying the aspirations of the volunteer can be organized. It is well worth keeping a card index of active members, their skills, their training and the activities that they have been involved in.

Training sessions involving half a dozen or so volunteers can be organized. This enables them to meet others in the same situation and learn from each other, which can be a big factor in gaining confidence. To many, becoming involved with a society can be a nerve-wracking experience; considerable effort should be expended to overcome this and give them confidence to continue.

It is just as important that volunteers know how the museum itself works, who is who, their responsibilities and the museum's objectives. It is also essential that they know about the collections. All these topics can be coordinated by the museum trainer.

The trainer must work very closely with the volunteers' own organization, who should ensure that a new member knows about their own organization as well as the museum's. New members should have a warm welcome, be introduced to others and shown around, quickly being given some productive tasks that they are able to undertake, possibly in conjunction with a well established member. It should never be assumed that they will know how to do something.

Even what seems a simple task to those regularly involved may be difficult to understand by a newcomer. Confidence needs to be built up. Regular communication between organizer and in particular new volunteers is essential to ensure that they are enjoying themselves and getting the satisfaction they expected from being a member and that they do not have problems.

The museum staff should work to give the volunteers some status. Use name badges with the museum logo, the volunteers' first names and surnames, and what they are, e.g. 'volunteer guide' may be justified. Uniforms or overalls may be required and can be provided, possibly embossed with the museum logo.

There can be other perks for volunteers such as free admission for his or her family to the museum; free admission to other museums on a swap basis; organized outings, possibly to other museums; and meeting people in similar circumstances at these establishments. Parties, particularly at Christmas and other social events, are always appreciated, as are discounts in the museum café and shop. Every small item helps to create a feeling of belonging and being special; the museum becomes *their* museum.

I mentioned earlier the organization to which the volunteers belong, which may be constituted as the museum's friends. To succeed this group must have a good set of officers with well defined objectives. It is important that one person is not overloaded with responsibilities.

There are six key positions in any volunteer organization, from which a number of other posts emanate. These are the chairman, the treasurer, the working party organizer, the membership secretary, the communicator and the secretary. Each has a specific role and between them they should form the team who run the organization.

Chairman This person should lead, guide and inspire the organization in line with its objectives. S/he should coordinate the activities of all other officers of the society. This person should be the principal means of communication to the main museum and other organizations. Communication between the volunteer society and the museum is critical and is best achieved on major policy matters through the chairman and the director of the museum.
Treasurer The treasurer should control all the society's finances. The objective should be to maximize the income with various sales activities, donations, memberships etc. while controlling the expenditure within the resources of the organization. The treasurer should produce, in consultation with other officers, a budget to be operated for a period, with which income and expenditure should be regularly compared. The treasurer should be responsible for the payment of all bills and invoices.
Work or activity organizer This person should organize all work programmes in conjunction with the museum staff. The person should ensure that the necessary resources are available to undertake these programmes and that adequate

instruction is given to members of what is required from them and of particular features, objects or other items that must be conserved. Ensure that new and existing members receive adequate training and instruction in the relevant activities.

Membership secretary   The responsibility for recruiting and maintaining members to ensure that their aspirations in joining the society are met lies with the membership secretary. S/he should endeavour to communicate regularly by some means with all members.

Communicator   This person should produce a good-quality, regular newsletter for members and others to act as a quality advertisement for the society. Ensure that people who may be of benefit to the society receive copies and that regular press releases relative to the society are distributed to the media to generally build up an image of the society to the world at large.

Secretary   The secretary records the activities of the society, be it at meetings or other places, and answers all correspondence to the society. The secretary should carry out all the statutory activities relating to the company.

From these six positions, tasks may be delegated through others for particular aspects of the work.

One sometimes hears of museum professionals complaining about the volunteers in their museum. This may be from genuine bad experiences but, when effectively managed, a volunteer society can be a great asset to any museum and should be encouraged. If each organization's role is defined and they *are* effectively managed, both can work in harmony with an effect that is greater in sum than the output of the two organizations working alone.

24

Information systems

Terry Robinson

Controlling the information resource

To say we live in an information age is to ignore the extent to which previous generations have manipulated and used information. But it is helpful to reflect on the enormous extent to which we have, during this century, come to recognize information as a vital resource. It now pervades every aspect of our life, from fighting battles and controlling weapons to the more humdrum aspects of happier existences, such as controlling the food stocks in supermarkets. Some commentators believe we have lived through an information revolution, akin to the great agricultural and industrial revolutions: it is a concept with some validity.

The revolution has been both made possible and in turn stimulated by developments in electronics. We can now build machines that will store and process at great speed huge volumes of highly detailed information and communicate it to other machines or to human users. This has put enormous power at our disposal, and with that has come danger: to confuse, to frustrate and to waste money and vast amounts of time.

We refer to this wizardry as *information technology* – the use of electronic machines (computers and the links between them) to store, recombine, distribute and present information.

Data and information

Information is data made meaningful. An item of data is normally one small isolated fact, often a statement of quantity or of the presence or absence of an attribute. To make sense it needs to be set in a context, which can either be one or more other items of data or an existing context already understood by the recipient of the data; in other words,

data only become information when they match the information needs of the recipient. Upon this concept hangs much of what follows: we want to control and exploit information technology so that it helps the process of heritage management rather than gets in the way. In other words, we want the technology to give us information that we can understand and use.

IT hardware

Computers fall into three main types:

Mainframe Large computers used for corporate business; buying and managing a mainframe is only cost-effective for large business applications. This was the earliest type of computer used for commercial purposes; for many applications their use has been superseded.
Minicomputer On a smaller scale than a mainframe but possessing many of the same properties; technological advances enabled the processing power of mainframe computers serving more modest applications to be built into a much smaller box. They are, however, designed for a large group of users to share in commercial applications. They are often put to work in networked groups.
Microcomputer A machine small enough to sit on a desk-top and therefore be available for individual use at work or for home applications. The most significant development in computers in the last decade has been the enormous growth in the use of one type of microcomputer, the personal computer or PC.

These categories are cited for purposes of clarity. In fact, the boundaries between them are increasingly blurred. It is becoming easier, by virtue of the relentless drive by the technicians to pack more power into smaller, cheaper boxes, for small enterprises to become active IT users at a proportionately higher level.

In addition, the remaining important item of IT hardware is the electric wiring and signal control systems developed to link a group of computers together through various types of computer network.

Planning information systems and the way they will exploit information technology is a complex process. The way business practice uses information is evolving and this, coupled to the high speed of development of IT systems themselves, means information systems planning has to aim at a moving target from a moving platform.

In terms of hardware alone, the most basic component, the silicon chip, has increased in power ten times every seven years, and over the same period it is reckoned that computer systems become four times more powerful in terms of processing and storage. Furthermore, every year, any given machine can be designed to occupy 20 per cent less space without any loss of computing or storage power.

IT software

When watching a film on video, you are using the video cassette recorder as the hardware; the tape in the cassette is the software. Similarly, in computing, the box or machine containing the wiring, semiconductors and other fixed circuitry is the hardware. On its own, switched on and with electric power running through it, it represents no more than a capability: it can do nothing. In order to carry out any information processing, it has to receive instructions, either direct from the user through some type of input device such as a keyboard, or through a program of instructions electronically coded, known as software.

It is the computer's capacity to receive and respond to a large variety of different and changing instructions that raise it above the orbit of ordinary automated machines repetitively carrying out single tasks. There is, however, a growing number of machines which blur the boundary between automatic task performer and computer. Many modern machines have a small computer installed to govern their performance according to different circumstances. For example, sophisticated computers are now used to fly aircraft, control trainee pilots' flight simulators, control surgical and medical equipment such as scanners, and, more domestically, to control washing machines, compact disk players, video tape recorders, cameras, musical keyboards, telephones and the family car.

More significant than the development in IT hardware has been the rapid evolution of IT software programs, made more usable because they mimic more closely the logic, thought processes and language of the human mind. It is now standard for corporations and businesses to manage their financial and business affairs on information systems that employ IT software programs especially written to match their particular business needs. Large corporations are rich enough to be able to employ specialists to analyse their business requirements and build IT systems to meet their own particular needs.

Increasingly, however, standard software packages are available on the open market which have undergone continuous development financed by the returns from selling to a huge user market. They incorporate many years of thorough feedback and testing and resulting improvement so that the functionality of the package now caters elegantly for a large variety of non-expert users.

All these applications are potentially useful to managers of the heritage. The more commonly available packages are as follows:

Word processors allow a computer to work like a super-smart typewriter, allowing correction of mistakes, editing of text, trial of different text layouts, storage and easy updating of text, the use of a variety of design features in the finished document and the incorporation of simple mathematical calculations, diagrams etc.

Spreadsheets do for mathematical figures what word processors do for text: they process numbers. They provide a standard matrix on which can be set calculations to reflect the relationship between different sets of numbers, so they can be used for the automatic calculations of accounts, forward plans, historic progressions etc. They normally possess the capability to present sets of figures in the form of graphs and charts.

Databases are electronic filing systems, which can hold huge amounts of information. Provided that they are properly planned before they are created, they can allow retrieval of individual items of information in a large variety of different groupings to demonstrate relationships and give evidence of causes and effects.

Desk-top publishers allow the user to manipulate text, figures, page layouts and different design characteristics on a computer quickly and much more flexibly than using physical materials.

Project management packages are useful in situations where a large number of different resources and inputs are required to achieve an overall outcome. They help in predicting where log-jams may occur, where resources are crucial and where coordination is needed.

Computer-aided design and mapping systems at their most sophisticated allow testing of the configuration and design of new structures and systems before any physical prototypes are constructed at all. Packages are also available to process maps and plans and allow for their easy storage and updating.

Geographical information systems are complicated databases that allow for the geographical distribution of attributes to be recorded, analysed and recombined. These systems, which are still developing rapidly, have enormous capacity to lead users to new insights on the combination of physical, natural and other features that exist in geographical relationships to each other: they are of great potential benefit to heritage managers.

Graphics packages provide the user with the ability to draw diagrams and pictures, normally with colouring capabilities, to combine work, store it and revise it.

Most of these packages are delivered with a sophisticated set of functions that are ready to run. Also available to users are computer languages, whereby users can develop the functionality of the package, or indeed write their own software to make the computer perform functions that they themselves have designed: BASIC is one such language.

Developments in software

There is also a class of software that provides the interface, making the software understood by the hardware of the computer, known as computer operating systems. Some of the commoner standards which are becoming more widely adopted to make systems produced by different manufacturers work alongside each other include:

MS-DOS, the most widely used operating system for IBM-type PCs.
MS Windows, a graphical user interface that delivers the same basic functionality as MS-DOS but makes it more intuitive for the non-specialist user to control the computer, without requiring knowledge of the operating system's own language and syntax.
Apple Macintosh, operating on a different standard but enjoying a large market following because of its high degree of user-friendliness.

Large corporate organizations that use IT, most notably the Government, are in a powerful commercial position to enforce from manufacturers better compatibility and standardization to allow a broader spread of applicability between IT hardware and IT software products. The end point of this trend towards what are known as 'open systems' is the ability of any computer hardware and software products to work together. One of the industry standards that is emerging for this is the UNIX operating system.

Business benefits of information technology

Information technology on the one hand can be exploited and controlled, or on the other hand can be tolerated and toyed with. It can help keep an organization in business and evolving or, conversely, it can become a major impediment to an enterprise's ability to deliver the goods. Wise managers will understand this and be canny and forward-looking in their plans to use information technology.

Computers are machines designed to store and rearrange information. Because of their capabilities and the uses to which they are put, any organization wanting to benefit from IT has to decide in detail the business applications it will serve. Detailed prescriptions have to be drawn up of who will use computers and how both they and the information they deliver will be used. All these considerations have to be worked through in

advance of decisions on whether and how to computerize functions.

It is normal to expect to spend 80 per cent of the establishment costs of a computer system on the design work. This uses brain, pencil and paper and often long hours of analytical discussion and brokerage (the logical design process). It has to be complete before anyone physically implements the system, that is programs a computer to carry out the allotted task. It is essential that this method, dubbed the information systems approach, is taken if IT is to be properly used as a servant of the organization rather than a domineering, illogical and often cranky tyrant.

Processing information electronically delivers two key capabilities:

(1) the ability to handle large volumes of data (because of the high speed of processing);
(2) the ability to forge and put on display complex linkages between items of data, and furthermore to display large numbers of such links.

These capabilities make possible certain jobs that are impossible, uneconomic or unmanageable using the human mind alone. In nearly all cases the difficulty of doing the job without a computer will be due to the huge volumes of data involved or the complex nature of the linkages. To this end, computers have been used for improving efficiency:

(1) to produce higher speed
  (a) in retrieving information
  (b) in restructuring information;
(2) to produce greater accuracy in terms of
  (a) precision of numbers
  (b) reliability of mathematical processes
  (c) opportunities for integration of different processes or information;
(3) to work with lower quantities of data by
  (a) enabling the use of a smaller sample size
  (b) data sharing
  (c) highlighting duplicated, redundant or inconsistent information.

IT has also been used to make businesses more effective by:

(1) improved control of the business through
  (a) focusing of attention where it's needed
  (b) better monitoring and tracking of business
  (c) easier diagnosis of problems
  (d) better forecasting of future trends and events;
(2) improved understanding of the business by revealing
  (a) patterns and correlations
  (b) sensitivities
  (c) probabilities
  (d) the significance or non-significance of certain trends;
(3) better communication within the business through
  (a) connection between people
  (b) translation of information

(c)   presentation to make information understandable;
(4) greater influence of information due to its
   (a)   reliability and validity
   (b)   flexibility for reuse and re-presentation in
different ways.

As IT moves deeper into the heart of the organization's business, it becomes more and more an influence on the strategic directions taken by the business. It can have a profound influence on an organization's ability to evolve and compete, adapt to changing circumstances and exploit new opportunities.

Information technology can enable an organization to offer new services and new ways of operation. It can both change boundaries and responsibilities within the organization and enlarge the scope of the organization's business, taking it into new areas of activity and opportunity. Information technology can make possible integration with external businesses: a number of mergers with organizations have taken place because an IT opportunity made the merger decisive and possible. Information technology can also provide the means to greater cooperation between organizations as it can itself act as a catalyst for change by leading people to new insights, exposing requirements, problems or opportunities that were not hitherto apparent. Crucially, information technology can greatly strengthen strategic decision-making and improve management's confidence to take big decisions by its clearer presentation of options, more reliable information, which allows greater objectivity, easier access to the history of past decisions and better evidence of what given expenditure actually buys in business terms.

Computers cannot think, be creative or reach new insights themselves. They cannot be inventive, but they can aid the human mind to work with a much better quality of information and understanding to reach better decisions.

Burnt fingers for the unwary

Sophisticated and elegant presentation of information is now available from a large number of computer software packages that can be bought across the counter. This makes the acquisition of a computer seductive: it is also very easy to forget the amount of dull, detailed analysis and planning that had to be done by someone to make the thing work that way.

It is a common mistake to underestimate badly the amount of detailed analysis and design work that has to be done to get an IT system to do what the user wants. This misconception is, to some extent, fuelled by the computer industry itself. Also frequently forgotten is the expense and time of training staff in using new IT systems and in changing their working procedures to accommodate and exploit them. Failure to understand

this results all too frequently in disappointment, disillusionment, demoralization and damage to progress and prospects.

The answer is not to handle information technology with kid gloves but instead to adhere to the strict disciplines involved and undertake the necessary exertion to make it perform as required. What happens to the hapless folk who do not do this? They run an almost certain risk of one or more of the following unpleasant experiences:

(1) buying computer systems that 'don't work', meaning they do not do what the user wants them to do;
(2) wasting enormous amounts of time and energy trying to coax a poorly designed system to work in the user's favour;
(3) trying to run a business using information technology that gets in the way, rather than assists the enterprise.

Most businesses with IT experience will be able to cite experiences of such suffering. A confident understanding of the business that you want to do and a willingness to define it in detail should guide your decisions in investing in IT. This approach should help you resist any temptation to pre-empt your understanding of business requirements with fixed longings about a given IT product that you imagine will meet your needs. This approach, coupled to a willingness to use good advice, will be valuable proof against a fairly voracious IT industry that wants to sell you boxes and gadgets.

Experts on every side

These messages are sometimes received with more scepticism in the 1990s because of the advent of the personal computer, designed to serve the needs of an individual user. A proportion of PC users appears to believe that possessing the expertise to make one computer serve one master gives you the necessary understanding to make a corporate computer system serve the business needs of a corporate body with a large number of different users with different needs. It is common experience to be able to buy a software package for a PC, install it in less than an hour, and have it running and doing what you want almost straight away: implementing IT systems for corporate use is a much more complex process.

The current vogue for IT deployment in organizations is the use of locally applied systems, serving local needs but implemented using standards of software and data compatibility that allow widespread exchange, use and amalgamation of information for corporate needs. The technology that makes this sharing of information possible is the sophisticated telecommunications network hardware and the software that controls it.

The emergence and further evolution of fourth-generation languages that can use everyday English to program computers, and the development of computer system design tools, are gradually making the business of analysing user needs more approachable by the non-specialist. The logical conclusion of this is that it should one day be possible to buy systems that will make packages for corporate business use as easy to install and configure as PC-based systems. The trend is towards greater self-service and self-sufficiency in the normal non-specialist computer user. Exclusively technical IT departments with specialist analysts and programmers are, to most opinion, on the way out. Computers and the ability to control them will become more and more an accepted and expected part of the everyday business life of most people. An organization which has got to this level of IT maturity is in an advantageous position. No one has claimed to be there yet.

Uses of IT in heritage management

Given all that has gone before about ensuring that information system requirements are well understood before investments are made in information technology, the following applications of IT in heritage management are notable:

Financial management systems There exist a large number of commercially available ready-made packages on which to carry out the normal processes of managing the finances of an enterprise. Many are in use in heritage management organizations, such as museums, national parks and government bodies like English Nature. Larger organizations have been able to afford to have systems custom-built to meet their own needs. The Countryside Commission is currently working with a commercial body, ACT Info, to build an integrated financial and management information system (IFMIS) on which to run its financial business. It is intended that this product will become available on the open market.
Personnel management There are a number of ready-to-use packages that store and retrieve key information about employees' status, entitlements etc. and their skills and capabilities, which organizations with more than a handful of staff or volunteers will often find it worthwhile investing in.
Office automation tools Electronic mail, with a networked set of personal computers or terminals, allows the sending of typed messages from one terminal to another. Electronic diaries can be used to fix meetings, control time expenditure, inform on the availability of colleagues etc.
Databases have enjoyed a large number of applications in:

(1) Catalogues of collections and collection documentation. The royal households have worked with BIS Information Systems to produce a system on which to catalogue the royal household collections. BIS has now made this commercially available for use as a general catalogue database.
(2) Environmental features. The characteristics and special conservation requirements of parts of an area.

(3) Management agreements. The details, conditions, areas affected, financial commitments etc. involved in agreements for owners to manage land in certain ways to meet environmental conservation requirements.
(4) Rights of way. Some highway authorities are computerizing their register of rights of way to make it easier to update and easier to retrieve the information. Some implementations employ a geographical information system.
(5) Registers of users of areas. For instance, a register of boat owners of a fragile area.

Word processors These are enormously useful for an organization which has to keep a set of publications up to date or when parts of publications need to be incorporated into other documents. The task of updating, for instance, a visitor guide book to an area is much reduced when the old copy exists as computer code which can simply be updated.
Spreadsheets These help in analysing and presenting financial and other arithmetic information. They can also make possible better cost or other projections of future trends or activities.
Desk-top publishers Using these, heritage organizations have been able to provide high-quality newsletters and publications, performing with ease their own layout and illustration work at quite acceptably low costs.

For those organizations involved in environmental management which have to deal with visitors, IT applications again are strongly relevant. For instance:

Computer-based displays in museum and other exhibitions allow a high degree of reactiveness and programmed learning on the part of the visitor.
Counters or behavioural response records allow a visitor's use and attention to a museum or other exhibition to be recorded and analysed.
Statistical packages can be used in analysing the results of surveys such as questionnaires or postal surveys.
Computerized tills can also give market information and stock control information in shops and retail outlets.
User recognition devices, such as 'smart cards', can be used where a large number of regular users or members exist and the manager can benefit from more accurate information of the type of use being made of a resource, such as timing a visit, length of stay, products bought etc.

In general, the current status of IT development means that any environmental management organization will be using IT in a way very similar to any organization working in a totally different sphere. At its current state of play, the use of IT in business has made us all much more aware of how common and universal basic business practice is, no matter what business an organization may be in.

In the future, however, some developments may become more exploited by environmental organizations than by other sectors. For instance, the digitization of images allows computer-based records to be made of text-based documents, photographs and other graphic images, maps and some objects. This could be highly relevant to organizations that want to establish electronic catalogues of document collections etc. Particularly important will be some of the developing systems that can, through linkage to large databases, scan text and recognize and abstract passages relating to certain required subjects. Retrieval of text from historic documents could be made easier by this means. Text scanners themselves, without the ability to recognize and abstract, can be important in reading text off paper and converting it to computer code for word processing or desktop publishing. Multi-media systems are also a developing field, where data from a number of disparate sources, such as video disks, audio recordings and digitized images, can be assembled for a purpose; they are likely to find a role in managing large resources of information on the environment or in information and interpretation.

Also extremely important is the developing field of geographical information systems. They are able to analyse, overlay and present information that exists spatially in a way that can re-present to the user relationships that are not apparent without the use of this aid. Their usefulness in heritage management is only just beginning to be understood. They are expensive to install and manage but, like all IT, their price is falling. Geographical information systems occupy a complex field of IT application, and are still fast developing. Heritage organizations are able to quote good and bad examples of using GIS. The Association for Geographic Information, which is seeking to establish some standardization in this area, promotes beneficial and efficient use of the technology and has acted as a force to make available good advice in this area.

Off-the-peg or bespoke?

The pitfalls and difficulties in designing and implementing systems to meet defined user needs are set out earlier in this chapter. As the years go by, more and more good software becomes available in ready-made packages over the counter. It is a good rule to buy off-the-peg wherever possible. It is almost always cheaper and, unless your system development is extremely good, is likely to result in an IT system that meets the needs of users more satisfactorily than a home-made system. The general rule of thumb is that if an existing system meets 80 per cent of your needs, it is not worth going through the agony of developing your own system purely to meet that extra 20 per cent.

IT security

Competitors or those seeking to do an organization down will often make for a computer system, either to get hold of the information it contains or to deny the information to the organization that owns it because that information can be the key to power.

Some people attack IT systems for fun: they like to outsmart them. Others do it for money to gain commercial or other advantage. It is quite clear, with environmental management organizations often seeking to change people's behaviour against their self-interest, that environmental information can become crucial to some of the power struggles that take place. This is quite apart from its commercial sensitivity as part of the process of running the environmental organization's business. Attacking computer systems is a thriving area of criminal activity. Organizations can guard against it. IT security can be highly sophisticated and costly. Some major safeguards can, however, be put into place by quite simple expedients.

Unauthorized access to the computer system should be prohibited by siting the actual equipment in places where it is not easily accessible. Access to a terminal should be by the use of a password, available only to authorized users, and which they keep secret to themselves; most systems now incorporate as standard the option to bar access from people who do not use a password.

Some computer systems are damaged, or the data they contain are corrupted by computer viruses – hidden programs which bona fide programs can 'catch'. They are written out of malice or mischief. Cheap diagnostic packages are available on the market to detect viruses and these should be used, together with a strict rule that no computer software, including data held on floppy disks, can be loaded into a computer unless it has first been run through the virus checking system.

Sensitive data can be kept secure by not leaving them stored on any computer. Most systems allow for the storage of data on a removable floppy disk; these can be locked away in safes. This again will only work if a strict rule is applied not to store sensitive information on the resident storage medium of the computer, normally known as the hard disk.

Computer security is sensible to apply to a reasonable degree. Good advice and publications exist on the topic, and any organization using computers should adopt security practices appropriate to the sensitivity of the information held and the vulnerability to its loss or disclosure to unauthorized people.

Legislation

A number of laws exist governing the use of IT, and any individual or organization storing and processing information electronically needs to be aware of them. There are guidelines but as yet little actual legislation concerning the conditions under which organizations can require employees to use IT. These include sitting and lighting conditions, length of time without a break that can be spent at a computer, protection from low-level radiation, eye strain and muscular disorders from repetitive movement.

The most significant of legislation is the Data Protection Act 1984, which anyone keeping records of individuals on an electronic storage system needs to know about and abide by. In essence, the Act provides that people storing such information make every reasonable effort to ensure its accuracy; do not disclose it to third parties without the permission of the subject to whom the information refers; and make the information available for inspection by subjects who want to check its accuracy.

More recent is the European Directive on Access to Environmental Information. This does not refer solely to electronically stored information. It provides that any organization which holds information relevant to the environment or the way it is managed must make it available to any member of the public who requests it. Organizations that make information available may levy a reasonable charge to cover their costs in delivering the information, but no more. Organizations do not have to disclose information affecting individuals, nor do they have to disclose information that is incomplete or in the process of being finalized. For instance, draft research reports, unfinalized sets of numerical data and draft policies do not have to be disclosed.

Willing buyers

This chapter has attempted to give an overview of the applicability of information technology to managers of the heritage. It has set out the extent to which IT may be applicable and of benefit to organizations, pointed out the pitfalls and the ways in which information technology can become a hindrance to an organization's activity and progress, and suggested ways of safeguarding against these pitfalls.

In the final analysis, those who wish to benefit from information technology must remember that IT products and services to make them work are on sale from highly commercial companies, some of them very profitable. Their prime purpose is to sell gadgets, kit and programs and make a profit. Often they do this best by getting alongside the users and trying to help them make the best purchase and invest wisely to get the best out of IT. But they still have to make a sale, and that is why there is plenty of experience from those who have bought IT and then regretted it.

Be in control, know what you want, and do not be dazzled by the often impressive performance of systems that may be demonstrated or that other people may show off. You should then become one of the large and growing population of people who benefit from this astounding and revolutionary technology.

SECTION FOUR

INTERPRETATION AND PRESENTATION

25

Heritage interpretation in Britain four decades after Tilden

David Uzzell

The display of artefacts and ideas in museums and exhibitions has undergone a radical transformation over the past four decades. While ranks and rows of glass cabinets of gemstones, butterflies or Etruscan pots with minimalist labels can still be found in many museums, there has been an attempt to engage and sustain more effectively the interest of visitors. Many exhibitions now try to help the visitor to understand and appreciate the meaning and significance of the displayed object by a variety of interpretive media. When the Natural History Museum opened in 1881, it presented an impressive but static collection of objects that were expected largely to speak for themselves. Nowadays the same museum recognizes the need to encourage and facilitate learning actively, and emphasis is placed on the importance of interpretation and interaction to maximize understanding.

There have been several reasons for this shift. The desire to enhance the educational effectiveness of displays has been a strong motivation. Equally, there has been a wish to make exhibits more attractive and appealing to a wider audience. Educational and stylistic motivations, however, have not been the only justification. The reduction in state subsidies for public sector museums and the consequent pressure for financial self-sufficiency have been a further motivation. Museums are increasingly subject to commercial competition from other tourism and leisure attractions.

Of course, these radical changes to the communication of information and the creation of attractive and engaging learning environments have not been limited to museums. It has been a notable feature of recent years that interpretation has been embraced by the tourism, leisure and public relations industries. Interpretation has been regarded as a novel way of pepping up tired tourist attractions. It has even been used as a way of selling everyday commercial products such as pottery, glassware or whisky. Stevens (1989) has argued that heritage has been sucked in by tourism,

public relations and marketing professionals, redefined, reconstituted and repackaged to become an exercise in trivia. Allied to this has been the interpretation of that heritage. As Stevens writes, 'Technological wizardry, media consultants, innovative presentations, audio animatronics – these are the buzz words to switch on the lights in tourist board offices around the world.'

Changing displays, changing philosophies

Changing displays and presentation styles does not simply enhance educational effectiveness. The way in which artefacts are presented says something about our relationship to those artefacts. What has changed over the years has been the way we think about our relationship to these objects. This change does not simply date from the recent shift to a more interpretive presentation style. This is best illustrated by an example from South Africa.

In his wide-ranging book *A Social History of Museums*, Hudson (1975) discusses the professional and realistic glass-fibre diorama of Bushmen that is on display in the South Africa Museum in Cape Town. The excellence of the presentation, though, has given rise to criticisms and accusations of racism. Presenting Bushmen in a similar way to butterflies suggests there is no real difference between the two: 'Both are the white man's specimens' symbols of his power and freedom to collect what pleases him'. If there were dioramas in South African museums that presented the white European in a similar way then perhaps the displays would be more acceptable. Has it been the nature of South African society that alerts us to this inconsistency? Does not this type of contradiction exist elsewhere but remains 'invisible' because it is part of our taken-for-granted world? The exhibition designers at the South Africa Museum have used, interestingly and courageously, the Bushmen exhibition as a device to tell the public about changes in museological presentation styles over the last 70 years.

In the earliest displays, Bushman casts were used to illustrate the typical physical characteristics of Bushmen. The message conveyed was that these people were a primitive anthropological type occupying a low position on the evolutionary scale. The display was later changed so that the figures were grouped according to geographical region and language to show the supposed links between physical type, language and culture. By the 1970s, the theoretical stance that informed the display had changed again. It was appreciated that the Bushman way of life was never static and had to be presented as part of a wider and developing social and political process.

In a review of the exhibition in *The Cape Times* in February 1925, a reporter wrote: 'The value of the Bushman casts lies in their absolute impartiality, their pure unadulterated "objectivity". They are the Bushmen themselves without the gloss of "interpretation" or extraneous adornment.' No presentation, of course, is free of interpretation. The way in which people, objects and ideas are presented says something about the way we think about these things and our relationship to them. Unfortunately, this is too often forgotten by many interpreters, who believe that without their intervention, the environment will remain devoid of meaning. Even when interpreters have cast their spell, it should not be assumed that the public will only go away with the intended message.

This was well illustrated during a research study undertaken by the Countryside Commission for Scotland (Lee and Uzzell, 1980). Visitors to three farm open days were asked about their attitudes to farming and the countryside. On two of the farms the visitors, having had the farm interpreted for them, saw farming as a modern technical science-based British industry, which has trade union involvement, does not make large profits and involves long hours of work. On the third farm, visitors came away with completely the opposite impression. They saw it as an old-fashioned and traditional activity undertaken by gentlemen farmers who were as much interested in leisure pursuits as work, from which large profits were made, and where there was no trade union activity in what was a minor British industry. The interpretation provided by the farm open day organizers was similar in terms of its agricultural information and messages at all three farms. The reason for the different responses can be understood by both what was and was not interpreted. There was some emphasis at the third farm in the interpretation of high-income leisure activities, such as pheasant shooting and riding. A light aircraft and a vintage car were next to the refreshment stall in a barn, although they were not accessible to the public. The laird walked around the estate most of the afternoon in plus-fours with a shooting-stick. It must be remembered that although the farm open day organizers tried to interpret the farm and its activities in a positive way using conventional media, the social, economic and physical environment itself was simultaneously conveying messages that either reinforced or contradicted the intended story. People are constantly interpreting the environment around them in order to make sense of it. People try to make the world about them more meaningful by drawing on their repertoires of experience.

Rummaging in the interpretive toy cupboard

This is not to devalue the role of interpretation. It is, though, to question the unchallenged assumption that simply by interpreting time or place, visitors will have an enhanced understanding of the meaning and significance of the object of interpretation. The first major exhibition evaluation study undertaken in the Department of Psychology at the University of Surrey was *Interpretation in Visitor Centres* (DART/University of Surrey, 1978). This research concluded that visitor centre exhibitions were fairly effective means of interpreting the countryside as measured by the recall of information after a short period. A detailed examination of the findings, however, revealed that the recall level of post-visit respondents was quite low. Furthermore, there was very little difference between the post-visit knowledge recall scores of those visitors who were visiting the centre for the first time and those who were on a repeat visit. In other words, even those visiting the exhibition for a second or third time were not able to recall significantly more information from the displays.

It was also found that the increase in knowledge levels varied considerably between centres. As no significant differences were found in visitor profiles between each centre, this suggested that visitor centre variables were responsible for these differences. The most important factors were the interpretive themes of the exhibition, the spatial layout of the displays, the interpretive media used and the general atmosphere. Visitors learnt most at those exhibitions that had historical and human interest themes. These are themes for which visitors have pre-existing cognitive structures or schemata that readily allow them to assimilate new information. This may not be so for themes focusing on subjects such as geology or ceramics. Visitors also learnt more where the interpretation was presented sequentially. This applies both to the subject matter and the spatial layout. Historical themes and presentations have an obvious advantages here as material is invariably chronologically presented with one idea developing from the previous one. A spatial organization of displays that minimizes competing claims on the visitor's attention, such as exhibitions that route people along a corridor, is also more successful than those that allow uncontrolled and often random movement between displays.

Visitors are particularly attracted to and benefit from interpretation that is animated, whether it is an audio-visual presentation, an interactive exhibit or the use of live animals for demonstrations. However, the message is more important than the medium in increasing visitors' understanding of a site or subject. It is the subject matter of the exhibition, not the display technique, that is the critical factor. This is quite an important finding for three reasons. First, it strengthens the argument that at the heart of good interpretation lies good research. The more interpretation research that is undertaken, the greater the choice of material that can be drawn upon to provide the most stimulating themes and stories. This has knock-on effects because the greater the range of stories, the more interpretive media options will be available. Secondly, it reasserts the role of the interpretive planner at a crucial stage in the design process. It also challenges the undue influence, if not supremacy, of the exhibition designer in dictating the form and content of displays. Finally, it challenges the supposed critical role of the media in accounting for enhanced learning.

In their enthusiasm to attract the public there has been a tendency for interpreters to run to what Don Aldridge calls 'the toy cupboard' at the first opportunity. Insufficient consideration is often given to what is the best interpretive medium for the job. Once, interpretation meant leaflets and exhibition panels (also known as books on the wall) and maybe an audio-visual programme. The range of interpretive media now used is not only considerably more varied but increasingly technical: computer simulations, personal stereo guided tours, rides augmented with sounds and smells.

The power and pervasiveness of the toy cupboard syndrome should not be underestimated in interpretation. There is little doubt that much interpretation has been media-led. In other words, the decision has been taken about 'how' a subject is to be interpreted before the decision as to 'what' is to be interpreted. If it were not for the increasingly expensive nature of technology-driven interpretative media then we would witness even more of this as fashions (and budgets) dictate provision. The tyranny of the toy cupboard is not limited to technology-dominated interpretation.

Knowing the past

One claim made for interpretation is that it opens a window on the past. It enables us to identify with those who have gone before us and to see the world as they saw it. This is attempted by a variety of interpretive means, ranging from the passive, such as exhibitions and audio-visual presentations, through to three-dimensional evocations such as historic displays, role playing or first-person interpretation. This has been perfected to a fine art at places such as Old Sturbridge Village and Charleston in the United States. Interpreters not only research in detail the characters and extended family and friends they are portraying, but dress in period costume, speak in the contemporary language and to all intents 'live' in the seventeenth and eighteenth centuries. This is not without its problems. Should actors, say, pretend to be eighteenth century sheep farmers conveying bemusement as banks of camcorders focus on their unshaven cheeks? Or should they provide a dispassionate and reflective commentary on what life was like? This raises many important issues. How can we know the past? Whose past are we interpreting? Even if we can deceive ourselves into believing that we can know the past, how do we re-create or re-present it?

Writers such as Hewison (1987) and Wright (1985) quite justifiably question whether we can truly access the past. Lowenthal (1985) puts forward a number of seemingly insuperable obstacles for us that firmly challenge the notion that we can know the past. What is now known as the *past* was not what anyone experienced as the *present*. There is a sense in which we know the past better than those who experienced it. We have the benefit of hindsight and we know the outcome of the story: 'Knowing the future of the past forces the historian to shape his account to come out as things have done' (Lowenthal, 1985). Equally, though, no historical account can ever capture what is the infinite content of an event. Most of the information generated by an event – whether it is at the individual or group level, or whether it is cognitive, affective or behavioural information – is not recorded: that which is recorded is also only a record of the past. Furthermore, we can only verify accounts of the past through other accounts. Historical knowledge, however well authenticated, is subjective and is subject to the biases of its chronicler who is susceptible to the psychological processes of selective attention, perception and recall. To confound matters even more, selective attention, perception and recall affect what we, the chronicler's audience, make of this historical interpretation. Despite sincere attempts at authenticity, neither those who provide interpretations of the past nor those who receive them can avoid loading them with their own twentieth century perspectives. We cannot re-create the past or provide a 'truly authentic experience', since visitors' perceptions of the past will be influenced by their present-day attitudes and values.

One of the greatest difficulties faced by museum curators is the problem of selectivity. What should museums choose to collect and to display? Having chosen what to say about their collections, how should they present or re-create the past? There is a need to be more objective, to establish contexts for the objects on display, to show the past as a process and to make connections with present-day issues. This is particularly relevant in the interpretation of industry. Nostalgia is not the route to producing an objective approach to the past. The interpretation of industrialization often alternates between images of heroic inventors, philanthropic owners and satanic mills. Steering a safe course, many museums tend to concentrate on evocative or large artefacts while presenting an idealized view of living and working conditions. The public are offered 'slices of the past' mixed up with actual relics. They may not learn very much from this.

It is necessary, therefore, when interpreting the past to relate it to the industrial present. We, of course, may not be any more objective about the present. The coincidence of the past and the present, however, forces the presenter and the audience to ask critical questions about industry and society. Laenen (1986) argues:

> Most museums present the past in isolation from the present, forgetting that the present is a continuation of the past, and that the present is tomorrow's past. It is most important to demonstrate that continuity. One way to make the past relevant to the public is to trace the links with the present and to point up the strands of cultural continuity . . . The challenge lies in devising ways of bridging the gap between past and present. The reason some museums fail is that they deal with the past in isolation or deal with particular subjects in isolation from real life.

Whose past is it anyway?

There is one issue in interpretation which interpreters and educators seldom regard as problematic: 'whose interpretation?' Interpreters rarely seem to come clean and admit that the interpretation of a place, event or phenomenon is precisely that – an interpretation. In other words, the past as presented is one interpretation among many possible interpretations. Stories are told as if they are *true*, as if there is only one way of understanding. From our earliest days at school we are taught to believe in the world of facts, in which there is one truth, one reality. This is how myths are created. Telling the story of the industrialization process is invariably undertaken within a capitalist framework, although there are other perspectives on history that might lead one to tell a different story with different emphases and draw different conclusions. Interpretation is ideological; stories are told which reflect the values and interests of different groups in society.

Wallace (1987) points out that the re-presentation of history has taken a dramatic turn in recent years. A decade or so ago, the focus of the industrial museum was on industrial processes, objects and entrepreneurs. In some places in recent years this has shifted to the universe of the working classes, their experience and

their economic, social and political organization. Wallace, however, strikes a note of concern: 'I am beginning to fear that the old tyrannies of artefact and place may have been replaced by new tyrannies of shop floor and boarding house.' There is a need to paint a broad canvas. Entrepreneurs and workers were entrepreneurs and workers, but they were also people experiencing life in the complexity of its social, economic, cultural and political dimensions.

Re-creating or reconstructing the past

When considering how best to interpret the past, two approaches have dominated interpretive thinking. These can be called the re-creation and the reconstruction approaches.

Blists Hill at Ironbridge Gorge Museum, for example, adopts the *re-creation approach*. On this site the intention is to represent a typical east Shropshire mining community at the end of the nineteenth century. The history of the buildings, collections and work processes is interpreted by costumed demonstrators. The attempted creation of an authentic atmosphere of the past in this way attracts large numbers of visitors.

The re-creation approach has advantages as well as disadvantages, and raises certain questions in relation to authenticity and objectivity. It brings the past to life; it has high emotional appeal; it is attractive to the uncommitted and disinterested; it encourages identification with the characters; it allows for the creation of a sense of nostalgia. The presentation of 'slices of the past' permits the packaging of vignettes of our heritage that is fashionable, reassuring and attractive to tourists and visitors. A re-creation approach enables an engaging presentation of historical artefacts.

In some respects, the arguments against a re-creation approach are more fundamental and persuasive. The sheer volume of visitors attracted to the site may destroy the supposed authentic atmosphere and the suspension of disbelief that is essential for its effectiveness. A community is not fixed in time and the notion of change and process, which is the essence of history, cannot be conveyed by simply re-creating a past era. This becomes especially problematic when we try to freeze-frame a particular period or year. It is almost impossible to look at the past except through our late twentieth century eyes and laden down with a highly influential set of cultural baggage. A re-creation approach offers romanticism, not interpretation. The result of this is the production of myths, not objectivity. Inevitably, this must question the educational value of the experience.

The *reconstruction approach* is arguably a more objective approach to the presentation of history. This model sees no need to maintain an authentic atmosphere or offer visitors a 'slice of the past'. It would entail, for example, showing aspects of domestic and working life from different periods rather than adhering strictly to the 1890s period and introducing comparisons with today. Where doubts and gaps about some aspects of history exist, these are revealed to visitors. Instead of presenting the past as a closed system that is 'nice' to look at, a variety of interpretive methods can make visitors aware of the compromises that have to be made in the telling of any historical account. This might include explaining why certain aspects of everyday life cannot be presented as they existed in the nineteenth century because of health and safety regulations, or because certain raw materials are no longer available. Reconstruction can aid objectivity by highlighting doubts about the past rather than pretending to dubious certainties.

A reconstruction approach relates the story presented to the visitor's own experience by creating a channel between past and present. This reduces the risk of culture/values conflict. The visitor is not simply a voyeur of the past, but becomes part of the continuing story. Educationally, a reconstruction approach has the advantage of teaching people to be more critical and analytical. It encourages the visitor to think about relationships and development, and not simply accept history as presented. Within this context a reconstruction approach offers an opportunity for innovative interpretation. This does not necessarily mean new presentation techniques such as hardware, but using more questioning and mentally stimulating material.

However, dispensing with nostalgia may result in museums being less popular with visitors. The notion of the 'suspension of disbelief' is no less applicable to interpretation as it is to film or other media. A reconstruction approach is more challenging and demanding. A consequence of this is that visitors may have to work harder to enjoy their visit. Furthermore, this approach requires constant change and reappraisal in terms of interpretation techniques. This will, at least, reflect the reality of the continually changing assessment and reassessment of the past, present and future that we all do daily.

Strategic considerations

The rationale behind this chapter has been to focus on a number of issues that are central to the effective presentation and interpretation of places, events and artefacts. The context of interpretation is as important as the interpretation itself. A recurring message throughout this book is that one cannot consider the provision of a service in isolation from all the other factors that go to make up the visitor experience. So it is for interpretation. If the interpretation is excellent, but other facilities such as car parking, signposting,

catering and toilets are poor, this will have a detrimental effect on visitors' image of the place. Apart from having an unsatisfactory experience, they will not recommend a visit to their friends, they will not make a repeat visit themselves and, most important, they will not be in a receptive frame of mind to grasp the concepts and meaning of the museum or site and leave with an enhanced understanding of the heritage. Unfortunately good interpretation will not compensate for poor facilities, but good facilities will enhance the interpretation.

Several years ago, I took a friend (and interpreter) from Australia to visit a museum that had received a national award for good interpretive practice. On arrival, my friend was immediately told that not only could he not use his video camera (without lights) in the museum, but he would also have to surrender it to the desk and collect it when leaving. No explanation was given as to why filming was not allowed except that it was against the rules. The museum's response said something about how the management saw their visitors. Clearly, visitors were regarded as untrustworthy and not to be relied on to refrain from taking film or photographs. When we asked who would be responsible and liable for any damage to the equipment while it was in the museum's possession, this was just shrugged off. This was not a good start to a visit and was hardly guaranteed to put us in the receptive frame of mind to appreciate and enjoy the theme of the museum. Furthermore, it coloured, perhaps irrationally and unreasonably, our view of the organization that runs the museum. Was the attitude displayed at the shop window of the industry indicative of this particular world as a whole?

Another issue that usually receives scant attention is the impact of interpretation on the place or object being interpreted or the community in which it is situated. It is believed, presumably, that as the aim of interpretation is to educate the public to protect the resource, then it can be safely assumed that the interpretation itself will not have any unintended damaging consequences. The influx of large numbers of visitors can, however, greatly affect communities. This is even more the case where the gap between wealth, culture and class makes meaningful dialogue impossible. In the Third World, tourism has caused serious environmental damage. Excessive hotel developments have led to the destruction of ecosystems from mountainsides to the beach shore, where tourists' demands for water have had precedence over farmers' needs and where pollution has destroyed the very environmental qualities which tourists have sought (Cohen, 1978). In addition, the social pathologies created in the wake of international tourist movements have been equally devastating and well reported: drugs, drunkenness, prostitution and economic exploitation. No less significant are the psychological consequences for the host population such as the loss of self-esteem, shifts in sex roles, loss of privacy, feelings of embarrassment, stereo-typing and the hardening of in-group/out-group dif-ferences. Contrary to the notion that 'travel broadens the mind' and brings people from different nations and backgrounds together leading to greater intercultural empathy and understanding, most research evidence suggests that antipathy and resentment are often all that is exchanged (Pearce, 1982; Krippendorf, 1987).

Interpretation is used as a 'soft' management tool to aid the conservation of both the natural and the built heritage. So too should it be at the forefront of strate-gies to protect the cultural heritage and prevent the eradication of cultural traditions. The antagonisms that have arisen through insensitive tourist incursions have sadly been equally apparent in interpretive situa-tions. Interpreters are constantly telling the visitors how welcome they are and how much they want to reveal *their* community to the visitor, their guest, so that they can go away with a better understanding and sense of place. Many people in such communities resent this open-house invitation as tourists peer in through windows, have a presence in every public place and disregard the social, spiritual and symbolic spaces that assume meaning and significance for the inhabitants and their ancestors (Upitis, 1989). Interpre-tation ought to assist in the breaking down of these barriers, but there is little evidence to suggest that this is the case. If anything, it is the contrary.

Greenwood (1989) cites the example of how an important public ritual, the Alarde, which commem-orates the Basque victory over the French in the siege of 1638, has taken place annually for the past 350 years in the streets of Fuenterrabia in Spain. Traditionally the whole town has been involved in its preparation and re-enactment. It has been produced by the local people for the local people as part of an important cultural ritual. It has a strong symbolic function because dur-ing the siege young and old, rich and poor, merchants and fishermen stood together in an act of solidarity against an outside force; it serves to affirm courage and identity. Through the agency of the govern-ment's tourism ministry it was quite quickly trans-formed into an event that is performed for tourists to see. Consequently, the local people became cynical and disaffected and stayed away. They will not now participate. The government tried to overcome this by paying people to perform, but this only served to accentuate the alienation of the local people from their cultural past.

Smith (1989) cites the example of tourists who come to gaze on the fishermen and hunters of Alaska to experience what life for Eskimos is *really* like. When the fishermen bring in seals to butcher, this is seen as raw native culture and something to be experienced. For the Eskimos it is a source of tiresome questioning and endless posing for photographs. The Eskimo women put up barriers to give them privacy and eventually some felt forced to hire taxis to take the

carcasses home and butcher them in private. Again, what started out as a communal activity involving local cooperation and socialization was transformed if not destroyed by tourists keen to have an 'authentic native cultural experience'.

It is not the purpose of this chapter to focus unduly on the context of the visitor experience, except to stress that it is no less important an issue in relation to interpretive facilities and services than any other aspect of heritage, recreation and tourism provision. There are other strategic issues that should inform the planning, design and management of interpretive provision even more directly. They are general prin-ciples of good practice that we can identify based on research and experience over many years to enhance the interpretive provision and increase visitor satisfaction.

Principles of good interpretive practice

The need for a clear concept

It is too easy for managers of museums and heritage sites to assume that the visitor can 'read' and under-stand their site in the same way that they do. Too often, managers make unreasonable assumptions about the knowledge level and experience of their visitors. This may result in interpretation starting from where the manager is or where he or she thinks the visitor is, rather than from where the visitor actually is. In other words, interpretation needs to build upon the pre-existing experience and knowledge levels of the visitor, even if that knowl-edge is incorrect. Visitors require and demand a sense of direction or orientation. Visitors need guidance about what to look at. They require a cognitive map which they can use to guide their journey through the re-presented past in a meaningful way that ties up with their own experience, a conclusion first drawn by the DART/University of Surrey (1978) study referred to earlier. Visitors cannot be assumed to recognize the significance and meaning of objects or places from the objects or places them-selves. This is especially true for overseas visitors who often arrive with a different cultural background and set of expectations.

At the risk of stating the obvious (but obvious to whom), visitors need to be told what is unique about the place they are visiting. Why is it significant and worthy of interpretation? A good example of this can be drawn from Risley Moss Visitor Centre in Warring-ton New Town. The Visitor Centre exhibition tells the story of the mossland and how its existence has influ-enced wildlife, conservation, industry, agriculture, transport and the lives and livelihoods of the people who lived on or near it. The exhibition opens with a panel that simply states 'What is mossland? A shallow saucer of clay holding a wet sponge of peat.' Underneath this panel is a clay saucer with peat in it. This image is used as a *leitmotif* throughout the exhibition to reveal the relationship between the geomorphological structure and social, economic and cultural development. If the visitor can understand this concept, then the remainder of the exhibition becomes that much more interpretable and meaningful. This is simple but effective.

In the absence of evaluation research it is difficult to know with what key concepts and understandings visitors leave a heritage site. It is suspected that many go away with collections of bits of information – much of it inaccurate and with no coherent pattern or structure such that they could articulate the story of the heritage, even in outline form. In short, statements of the obvious are essential. Devices such as analogy can provide the visitor with a familiar idea that they can use to understand a more complicated one. This will provide a framework or schema which visitors can then use to assimilate new information. The education pack for Hampton Court Palace was designed for school use and provides an excellent example of how this can be achieved. The architectural development of Hampton Court Palace was far from straightforward, extending as it did over at least three centuries. Telling the story of this is made even more complicated by the size and complexity of the building. To interpret the historical development of the Palace, the education pack uses the analogy of a sandcastle:

A Royal Sandcastle
One sunny morning a boy builds a large sandcastle on the beach with towers and a moat. In the afternoon his elder sister comes along and adds to it, making it bigger and even better. She builds on extra towers and decorates the walls with seaweed.

A few days later a third child finds the same sandcastle on the beach. It is still in good shape, but he has his own ideas as to what sandcastles should look like. He thinks of knocking it down and starting again, but he does not have enough time. So he changes only part of it. He takes off the seaweed and puts on some beautiful shells instead.

After that, one or two children wander past. Some add little bits to it, others just keep it looking tidy. Now you come to the beach and look at the sandcastle closely. You notice the parts the first boy built, which parts the second girl added, and what the third boy did to change it.

Think of Hampton Court as being like that sandcastle.

Now visitors have the sandcastle analogy it can be used to explain in more detail the subplots.

The need to know

There is a limit to how much the visitor can absorb. It is better that one key feature is interpreted and that the visitor understands its meaning and significance, than that ten features are interpreted which the visitor just ignores. What do visitors *need* to know (in an interpretive sense) about the heritage site to make their visit more interesting, stimulating, enjoyable and memorable?

An interactive and involving experience

The interpretation should be an interactive and involving experience. By interactive is meant that it should encourage visitor groups, especially family groups, to interact and learn from each other. There are now trail packs (e.g. at the Weald and Downland Museum in West Sussex) that encourage precisely this type of response: adults and children are given interpretive material that facilitates their learning from each other.

Strong human interest

Interpretation should have strong human interest themes. People are interested in people. Interpretation should focus on the human story. Architecture is not a particularly interesting subject for many visitors. If it is felt important to tell the story of the architectural history of a place, then it should be told through the people who were involved in commissioning, designing, constructing and using the buildings.

Interpretation should build on pre-existing knowledge

Interpretation should build on pre-existing knowledge and frameworks (or schemata) of knowledge. Interpretation should relate to visitors' own experience. If we do not know how visitors see and understand the heritage site then we need to do some research to find out. This will ensure the interpretation is relevant and meaningful, and builds on (or corrects) existing perceptions and information.

Different interpretation for different audiences

There is no such body as the general public. The so-called general public is made up of different audiences with different needs and different expectations. These should be acknowledged and planned for in order to ensure effective interpretation and conflict avoidance. Different groups (e.g. the elderly and children) will be looking for different experiences of which interpretation is an important part.

Interpretation should not be a substitute experience

Too often a visitor centre becomes the focus of the visit rather than the catalyst. It becomes a substitute for experiencing the object of interpretation itself. The objective of the interpretation is to *push* people out to explore the surrounding environment. Some visitors may be unable to venture far but the majority will. While exhibitions and other forms of interpretation are important, they should be only part of the experience on offer. Visitors ought to be encouraged to discover the environment that makes the site a unique place.

Hierarchies of interpretation

Interpretation should be provided at hierarchical levels to reflect the interests and comprehension abilities of different visitor groups.

Consumer-led interpretation

The interpretation should be consumer-led as well as resource-led. That is, a balance must be struck between interpretation that reflects the interests and needs of the visitor and the range of messages that the organization responsible for the interpretation wishes to communicate.

The principles of Freeman Tilden

Although Freeman Tilden wrote his book *Interpreting Our Heritage* in 1957, the principles he advocated for good interpretive practice are no less pertinent today than they were then. These include:

(1) Interpretation should relate to something within the personality or the experience of the visitor.
(2) Information, as such, is not interpretation. Interpretation is revelation based upon information. These are entirely different things. However, all interpretation includes information.
(3) The chief aim of interpretation is not instruction, but provocation.
(4) Interpretation presented to children should not be a dilution of the presentation to adults, but should follow a fundamentally different approach.

Sympathetic to local people

Any interpretation strategy must be sympathetic to the needs and interests of the local residents, for whom the visitors' heritage site may be their home. Everything should be done to ensure that any expected increase in visitors and tourists has a minimal effect on the daily lives of the inhabitants. Interpretation can be used for visitor management as much as visitor education, and advantage should be taken of the various interpretive devices to reduce the less acceptable consequences of tourism.

Orientation

Visitors need orientation to the site they are visiting to give them a mental map of the place. This will also help them in their appreciation of its structure and development. Orientation also enables visitors to understand the scale of the site and to plan their visit more effectively and enjoyably. This can be done by line drawings, axonometric drawings, artists' impressions, models and all the other imaginative techniques at the designer's disposal. If the site is very large, visitors can see from the outset that they will be unable to visit it all. They can plan which parts they will concentrate on and then visit the remainder on another occasion. This will ensure that they do not hurry through the interpretation and leave out some parts of the story altogether because they have run out of time.

A sequence of experiences

Selling a ticket to a heritage attraction is selling an experience. One duty of the heritage owner or manager is to plan and provide a sequence of interpretive experiences to interest, entertain and inform visitors from the moment they arrive to the time they leave. In this way, the whole visit can be considered as a potential interpretive experience from the themed restaurant to the themed children's play areas. However, a themed restaurant does not mean decorating the walls with cardboard shields and plastic muskets, or having miners' lamps dangling from the ceiling while simultaneously serving steak and chips or cod mornay. The food too can be themed using 'authentic' meals (i.e. reflecting contemporary cooking and diets). For those managers concerned about losing a profitable part of their income by only serving bread and cheese, a variety of dishes could be supplied ranging from what the miner had for lunch through to what the mine owner and his family might have eaten. In this way, the restaurant becomes a genuine part of the interpretive experience and adds an important dimension to their visit.

A variety of interpretive techniques

Interpretation can draw on a variety of techniques. These include permanent and temporary exhibitions, audio-visual presentations, demonstrations, costumed interpreters, trails, events, wayside panels, guided walks and talks, themed catering, themed children's play equipment and leaflets. The decision about which techniques to use should be determined by considerations such as what is being interpreted, for whom and for what purpose. In other words, the interpretation should be appropriate for the setting, the particular type of audience and the story the manager wishes to tell. The integrity of the site, its artefacts, buildings and setting, and the conservation work of the management must be preserved.

Be opportunistic

Advantage should be taken of opportunities that may present themselves for extending and consolidating the interpretive provision. This might include borrowing exhibits from other museums and exhibitions through-out the country if they are appropriate. Indeed, there is scope for developing an interpretive lending service. This would secure maximum use of exhibits and other interpretive material, extend the useful lifespan of any one exhibit and spread the word about the heritage site. This could be one innovative part of a distance learning package.

The right staff

All staff make a vital contribution to the visitor experience. Appointing staff of a high calibre is fundamental to the success of any project. A programme of staff training to instil a customer-oriented and customer-care philosophy is essential.

The way ahead

The rapid growth of interpretation as an activity from the 1970s onwards led to the often uncritical and unthinking development of visitor centres, exhibitions, panels and other media. Perhaps this was inevitable, as organizations wanted to prove that they were at the cutting edge, and whatever the neighbouring authority or attraction could do, they could do bigger, better and probably more expensively. Typically, visitor centres became institutional virility symbols with seemingly scant attention being paid to whether they were the most appropriate interpretive solution to a heritage site.

One way of ensuring that resources are used effectively and appropriately, and that the interpretation communicates to the target audience in a meaningful way, is to plan thoroughly the interpretation and ancillary facilities. In Chapter 26, an overview of the interpretive planning process, Brian Goodey begins by declaring that 'the interpretive plan is a highly regarded yet seldom executed activity.' For Goodey, planning is essential, and his chapter discusses in detail various approaches to interpretive planning. Assorted models of the interpretive planning process have been put forward in the past, typically with an ancestry in the urban planning paradigm of survey–analysis–plan. Goodey takes a much broader and innovative perspective, making the case for plans which reflect, amongst other things, institutional practice, the skills required and the spatial-temporal context of the place being interpreted.

The chapter order in many books on interpretation reveals tellingly the status of certain activities and their assumed importance in the planning of interpretive facilities and services. In Chapter 30, Roger Miles tackles one of those themes that is usually assigned to the closing section – evaluation. Miles demonstrates that evaluation is an essential part of interpretation at every stage of interpretive planning and implementation. It should be at the forefront of our considerations,

not just a luxury add-on to be undertaken if budgets, time and inclination permit. Evaluation is probably most effective when it is undertaken in-house, as it is likely to be more meaningful, educational and acceptable.

Miles begins his chapter with the assertion that although evaluation is a skill, it is nevertheless something that is done by all of us most of the time. Evaluation in interpretation may be more systematic and objective, but the end product of the evaluation process – making judgements about the strengths and weaknesses of interpretive provision – is something with which we all ought to be familiar. Evaluation also ought to be non-threatening. Miles discusses the purpose and value of different types of evaluation techniques and the different types of information they provide. One important message of his chapter is that evaluation should not be seen as something that is done by outsiders to check up on an organization. Assessment, evaluation, appraisal and audit have become familiar words in the management-speak of the 1990s. Evaluation is beneficial when it leads to the effective use of resources with improved quality of product to the ultimate satisfaction of visitors *and* staff. Evaluation is damaging when it is used as a threatening and judgmental device. Some evaluation may require the assistance of a professional evaluator. If this is not possible there is still much that can be done by interpretive staff. Miles highlights these areas and suggests further reading where evaluation skills can be acquired.

One always feels that the best writers on interpretation are those whose writing is an interpretation in itself. With many years of experience, Paul Risk fulfils this quality superbly in Chapter 27. His extensive knowledge, perceptive insights into interpersonal communication and elegant writing style produce a chapter on people-based interpretation full of ideas and imagination. Several authors argue that if interpretation is pitched at an average audience, the end result is average interpretation. At best, perhaps, one can only reach some of the audience most of the time, or most of the audience some of the time. Risk suggests that oral interpretation can overcome this problem. Interpersonal interpretation is 'a delicate and dynamic balancing act . . . a graceful ballet enabling the interpreter to touch, at some time during the presentation, the intellect and emotions of each age group, attainment level, occupation and interest'.

The issue of research and planning is the starting point for Giles Velarde in Chapter 28. He makes the point that there may be some circumstances where interpretation is unnecessary or an intrusion. We can all think of heritage sites that have been ruined by the wrong kind of media or simply the existence of interpretation. Velarde draws attention to the level of detail that is required in preparing any kind of interpretation media. He also makes the point that interpretive techniques cannot replace the pleasure to be found in the real thing. That ought to be the case, but it is questionable whether this is so for everyone. Couch potato culture is so rife that for some the image rather than the reality holds the greater fascination. Sitting in the audience during the recording of a BBC TV programme many years ago I was struck by the mesmeric effect that the TV monitors overhead had on some of the audience, although reality was being played out in front of them.

In Chapter 29, Graham Carter explores the differences and similarities between environmental education and heritage interpretation. The differences, he contends, are very significant. A failure to appreciate them can lead to an inadequate provision both for the formal education groups that are typically the target for environmental education and for the tourist and visitor, the recipients of heritage interpretation. Carter also raises the subject of ethics, an issue that is rarely discussed by interpreters either at conferences or in the few textbooks that exist (Sharpe, 1982; Grater, 1976). He argues that a balancing act has to be achieved in the presentation of educational material between on the one hand avoiding contentious issues and on the other falling prey to political propaganda and political correctness. This is inevitably a difficult issue.

The aim of this introductory chapter to the interpretation section of the manual has been twofold. First, it has sought to provide practical guidelines for the design and management of the full spectrum of heritage sites and museums. This advice is relevant for all who have a responsibility for the management of the natural and cultural heritage, whether in the public or private sectors. Second, and perhaps more importantly, it has identified many strategic and philosophical issues that need to be considered at the planning stage of any heritage facility or service.

This chapter finishes where it began. As the way in which artefacts are presented and interpreted says something about our relationship to those artefacts, so too is it important to recognize and articulate the philosophy that underlies our interpretive policy and practice. What are we trying to achieve? What assumptions lie behind our actions? What relationships are presumed by the interpretation? It is too easy to head straight for the interpretive toy cupboard without considering the nature of our relationship to the past. What assumptions underlie the different ways of presenting that past? Whose past is it? These question ought to be framed normatively as well. What do we want our relationship to the past to be and what should it be? Whose past should we represent? These are not just idle musings of purely academic interest, but fundamental to the practical implementation of any heritage project.

References

COHEN, E. (1978) 'The impact of tourism on the physical environment', *Annals of Tourism Research*, **5**(2), 215–237

DART/UNIVERSITY OF SURREY (1978) *Interpretation in Visitor Centres*, CCP 115, Countryside Commission, Cheltenham

GRATER, R. K. (1976) *The Interpreter's Handbook: Methods, Skills and Techniques*, Southwest Parks and Monuments Association

GREENWOOD, D. J. (1989) 'Culture by the pound: an anthropological perspective on tourism as cultural commoditization', in V. L. Smith (ed.), *Hosts and Guests: the Anthropology of Tourism*, University of Pennsylvania Press, Philadelphia, 171–185

HEWISON, R. (1987) *The Heritage Industry: Britain in a Climate of Decline*, Methuen, London

HUDSON, K. (1975) *A Social History of Museums*, Macmillan, London

KRIPPENDORF, J. (1987) *The Holiday Makers*, Heinemann, London

LAENEN, M. (1986) 'The integration of museums and theme parks: the example of Bokrijk', paper presented at *White Knuckle Museum: the Converging Roles of Museums and Theme Parks*, Ironbridge Gorge Museum, 15 May 1986; reproduced in D. L. Uzzell, L. Blud, B. O'Callaghan and P. Davies (eds), *Ironbridge Gorge Museum: Strategy for Interpretive and Educational Development*, report to the Leverhulme Trust, Ironbridge Gorge Museum Trust, February 1988

LEE, T. R. and UZZELL, D. L. (1980) *The Educational Effectiveness of the Farm Open Day*, Countryside Commission for Scotland, Battleby, Perth

LOWENTHAL, D. (1985) *The Past is a Foreign Country*, Cambridge University Press, Cambridge

PEARCE, P. L. (1982) 'Tourists and their hosts: some social and psychological effects of inter-cultural contact', in S. Bochner (ed.), *Cultures in Contact*, Pergamon, Oxford, 199–221

SHARPE, G. (1982) *Interpreting the Environment* (2nd edn), Wiley, London

SMITH, V. L. (1989) 'Eskimo tourism: micro-models and marginal men', in V. L. Smith (ed.), *Hosts and Guests: the Anthropology of Tourism*, University of Pennsylvania Press, Philadelphia, 55–82

STEVENS, T. (1989) 'The visitor – who cares? Interpretation and consumer relations', in D. L. Uzzell (ed.), *Heritage Interpretation: Volume I: The Natural and Built Environment*, Belhaven Press, London

TILDEN, F. (1957) *Interpreting Our Heritage*, University of North Carolina Press, Chapel Hill, NC

UPITIS, A. (1989) 'Interpreting cross-cultural sites', in D. L. Uzzell (ed.), *Heritage Interpretation: Volume I: The Natural and Built Environment*, Belhaven Press, London

WALLACE, M. (1987) 'Industrial museums and the history of deindustrialization', *The Public Historian*, **9**(1), 9–19

WRIGHT, P. (1985) *On Living in an Old Country: the National Past in Contemporary Britain*, Verso, London

26

Interpretative planning

Brian Goodey

The interpretative plan is a highly regarded yet seldom executed activity. John Hanna's (1974) definition states both the function and the aspirations of a plan, which is essential to a carefully managed facility:

> The official guideline for the resource management body which sets forth the policies concerning development, philosophy and operation of the interpretative program. The plan is a single unified design for the integration of the interpretative program into the total management objectives.

But a minority of facilities have determined a plan, and even fewer have adhered to the path thus described.

Several models are widely quoted in the British literature. These include Binks's (1983) *Interpretative Plan for Wirksworth, Derbyshire*, part of a pioneer small-town rejuvenation project by the Civic Trust. Its introduction summarizes the main purpose of such a document:

> *Interpretation* of the story of Wirksworth to visitors and residents alike involves drawing out the main threads of historical development, of the life of the community to-day, of the wealth of interest in the natural history and geology of the surrounding countryside, and relating them to features on the ground. Then by using a variety of techniques, interested visitors and residents can begin to understand and explore and see for themselves how the town and the urban community has evolved and works now.
>
> The purpose of this report is to identify the main threads of that story, to suggest the range of people who might be interested in it and to outline the facilities and techniques which would tell them about the town in the most effective and enjoyable way, and to suggest ways in which those facilities might be provided. (pp. 7–8)

The concept of an integrated presentation, a network for discovery, is an essential characteristic of interpretative planning (Goodey, 1992a). The plan must ensure the spatial and/or thematic linkage between often disparate elements which is the major contribution of interpretation (explored in Alfrey and Putnam, 1992, pp. 191–8).

Although interpretative plans and strategies have been commissioned and prepared over the past 30 years, the major period of sponsored development was in the 1970s. American summaries of practical experience (e.g. Putney and Wager, 1973; Hanna, 1974; Alderson and Low, 1976; Food and Agriculture Organization, 1976; and Sharpe, 1976) were available to inform development of British interpretative planning, largely through the work of the Countryside Commission (1977; 1979), initiated by Aldridge (1975), by Tillyard's (1979) strategy for Nottinghamshire, and the Commission's *Interpreting Tatton Park: Implementation of the Interpretative Plan* (1983).

Later Civic Trust plans, such as that by Touchstone Associates (1987) for Ilfracombe, and by Michael Quinion Associates (Civic Trust, 1986) for the Calderdale region of post-industrial Britain, added significantly to the planning methods adopted (see Jackson, 1992). Interpretative plans formed a major element in the many consultant reports on heritage sites produced in what now seem the boom years of the late 1980s.

Recognition of interpretation as an essential element of national heritage management in the UK has ensured that professionals now play a significant role in the range of national institutions. Indicative is the development of integrated site interpretation schemes (ISISs) as an element of the monument plans pursued by English Heritage for their diverse range of sites.

Whatever the scale of activity or the initiating agency, the key features of an interpretative plan remain those identified by the Countryside Commission for Scotland (1977) at the regional scale:

(1) to rationalize the work of private and public agencies involved in conservation and tourism;

(2) to provide a multi-disciplinary approach preceding physical plan making which stimulates the local community to articulate cultural values and perceived needs; and

(3) to provide an effective way to enhance the main physical and cultural features of localities, integrating them within wider cultural landscapes.

Planning and interpretation

The process of planning requires the systematic structuring of a path to the future. It is built upon best-guess estimates as to future scenarios, markets and techniques. However, it is initially generated by social constructions and aspirations as to the world we wish to inhabit – balanced against the image of a world which we expect to inhabit.

Johnstone (1991, p. 7) discussing planning in another emerging field, notes:

> The planning process is central to the whole concept of urban forestry and indeed any other form of resource management. It is not a one-off exercise carried out in isolation from the facts but a constantly changing and on-going process that is frequently revised in the light of changing circumstances. Put simply . . . (it) enables the urban forester to get on top of the situation and stay there.

At root, it is an exciting and demanding necessity which organizes thought, requires an effective assessment of resources and should unleash the creative urge that is basic to all interpretation.

Unfortunately, concepts of planning have become very muddled over the past decade. Environmental planning, which grew from the most positive, even utopian, stock early in the present century, is seen as restrictive by much of the British population, which has turned against a public process which ensured, and still maintains, many of the natural and built features which are the focus of interpretation.

One popular approach to interpretation, devised initially by Uzzell (1991), defines the subject within the parameters of *resources*, *themes* and *markets*. In discussing interpretative planning, three further terms come into play: *agencies*, *professions* and *funding*.

In terms of institutional practice, work context and the task as set, a useful distinction can be made between two kind of interpretative planning. *Internalized* interpretative planning focuses on a discrete task with parameters which may be defined by building and collection (as with a museum or gallery). *Externalized* interpretative planning must necessarily be integrated with other planning processes covering parallel or overlapping aspects of the appropriate environment.

Another useful distinction is between three types of interpretative plan, based on the nature of the space or the place being interpreted:

(1) the *novel* scheme, where the interpretation planned is the first for the site;

(2) the *remedial* scheme, where existing interpretative provision is revised because of changes in attitudes, collection, policy or market;

(3) the *generative* scheme, developed as part of a promoted facility which is often fairly discrete, and only loosely related to its context.

Planning literature is full of tree/box diagrams which suggest the optimum way of organizing a planning process. These tend to develop an other-worldliness which makes practical application difficult. I prefer to remind the reader that we all engage in planning, albeit on a limited scale. You would neither have arisen this morning, nor be reading this, had you not planned such personal actions. The continual short term planning in which we are all involved requires often unspoken answers to a series of questions such as the following:

(1) Where am I going?

(2) How do I get there from here?

(3) What do I achieve on the way?

(4) What resources, usually financial, do I gather and use to achieve the task?

(5) What actions and decisions of other people and groups need to be considered?

(6) Which services and agencies should I ensure are available?

(7) How many mid-course corrections should I cope with?

(8) How do I know when I have arrived at my goal?

The remainder of this chapter elaborates and illustrates the discussion so far. One warning should be given before proceeding further. Planning is a cooperative activity, involving many others. It requires the setting out of a sequence of clear statements for discussion and comment. To ensure success you must carry partners and agents with you, firing them with your enthusiasm, but also responding to their constraints and evaluation. For this reason alone, effective planning can be a painful but rewarding process.

The resources–themes–markets model

The resources–themes–market model (or more correctly, paradigm) has stood the test of time in a very wide range of interpretative contexts at all scales. Although it is an information gathering device, rather than a system model capable of prediction of itself, it has been used as the sole tool for determining the form and function of many heritage and leisure facilities.

A market town – the brown-signed 'historic market town' – provides a useful setting for detailing the paradigm (see Goodey, 1989; 1992b; Goodey and Parkin, 1990; 1991). Imagine a town set on restating its position once the required bypass has damaged high-street retailing. Such centres turn rapidly to heritage and tourism development. What is the process?

Resources

The initial resource focus will depend on the initiating local authority department: listed buildings and townscape on planning services, parks and events on leisure services, local collections on the museum services (see Murta, 1991). In addition, resources include local character and image, folk and vernacular culture, publications, performance traditions and outlets, and the town form itself (see Newcomb, 1979 for a useful exploration of such resources). Retail and customer care facilities are also an essential ingredient.

In each element, matters of location, form, condition, ownership, responsibility and availability must be collated and a resource inventory established using language and format which transcend official lists. In addition, the most significant *people* resource must be added. This will include established professional and amateur authorities on a range of local subjects, as well as volunteer enthusiasts, collectors and events organizers waiting to be harnessed in any community.

Themes

Am I the only interpreter who feels that the casual repetition of themes and stories trivializes the essence of the subject? Too often the search for themes and stories is a dismissive journey towards a banal marketing phrase which can be inflated to bursting point over a short campaign and then discarded.

Themes are the broad concepts containing the significant elements which define a unique local history and topography, a means by which fact and personality-strewn academic and popular knowledge can be organized for presentation within contemporary value systems. *Stories* are the specific strands which may be drawn from each theme in order to highlight the role of buildings, sites, features or individuals. They also imply an attractive structuring of evidence to involve the visitor and resident.

Theme identification requires interpretation of evidence, the nature of which will depend on interpreter, local culture, time and values. This function is previewed in Crawford's (1984, p. 5) introduction to the nineteenth century Arts and Crafts movement:

> Much of its fire was kindled, oddly enough, in the sad and colourful city of Venice, around 1850. Where others saw in its architecture only decaying stonework, or the sequence of European architectural styles with local variations, John Ruskin saw the whole history of the city: its building of a stable society against the odds in the Middle Ages; its peak of civic virtue at the end of the fourteenth century; the beginning of its spiritual decay while still a great power, in the fifteenth century; its decline into luxury and impotence. All this Ruskin saw, when he examined the fabric of Venice, as if he read it in a book. And when he looked at the naïve and spirited sculptural detail of its Gothic period, he seemed to see, just as clearly, the condition of the workmen who created it.

Themes and stories are only identified through research. There is really no escape from the investment in fundamental research by trained staff in excavating effective themes and stories from the mass of evidence available for each and every context. The following advice applies:

(1) Always collate themes from existing current publications, interpretative signs and other evident sources, then *question* each and every 'fact' thus gathered.
(2) Discuss preliminary ideas with a wide range of local professionals and enthusiasts. Railway and garden interests may never have met, but the cross-fertilization of ideas will be rewarding.
(3) Consider where, in national literature and primary sources, the town may be mentioned. Pursue any evidence of national or regional recognition in formal or popular history.
(4) For births, marriages and deaths, consider particularly human associations, however fleeting or recent. Such areas as football and TV personalities are seldom mined in the establishment of local themes.
(5) Develop a long list of themes – any town should provide at least 50 – which could be developed further.
(6) Consider which themes are supported by visible evidence, are not duplicated within the region, have relevance to contemporary life, and have the potential for strong visual or interactive presentation.
(7) Research deeper and wider in order to validate at least ten with new primary evidence. This process is itself often newsworthy.
(8) Order a final selection of up to five major themes and make a preliminary allocation of resources such as buildings or artefacts.
(9) Establish a group of stories for each theme, balancing a wide range of story types which will appeal to known market sectors within the population.
(10) Ensure that the theme-story package is rigorously assessed by a mixed group of local experts in various fields.

Without such a process, there is every danger that the themes and stories selected will lack the substance, or the contribution to place or collection, which ensures their comprehension by the visitor.

Markets

At the end of the present century it is difficult to escape the identification of visitors, users, customers or clients with the politically charged collective of the market. However much the reader experiences discomfort with the dominant role of the market in determining our understanding of or selectivity towards heritage, it is likely to dominate heritage definition and management into the next century.

At its most blatant, market orientation suggests that the lowest common denominator of public taste, previously applied to the pop single, newspaper or chocolate bar, is now accepted as arbiter when it comes to conservation and management of a national inheritance. Behind this sadly superficial skating-rink of public decision making lurks a very significant element of interpretative planning (Kotler, 1979 is useful in this regard). My own working definition of interpretation is 'adding value to the experience of place', which allows for the fact that such value may be expressed in both financial and cultural terms. Each requires that the intended audience for interpretative presentation be identified.

Although specialist market research facilities are available from a number of sources, these are seldom either sufficient or appropriate for local needs. They may well provide effective data on travel range, potential visitor structure for facilities and evidence as to educational and other specific markets.

What will require specific local knowledge, together with an insight into similar facilities or situations elsewhere, is the detailed projection of market segments and specific interest groups which might be drawn to the site. It may be useful to consider, especially, the role of local enthusiasts, specialist audiences and returnees, and the potential audiences for local education and for short-term presentation or events.

Inevitably, there has been a tendency to over inflate the potential market for facilities where many parties are attendant on the outcome of a feasibility or development study. Volume and potential income have come to dominate over the structure and specific needs of user groups. It is the latter which should preoccupy the interpretative planner.

Agencies, professions and funding

The resources-themes-markets paradigm tends to isolate the interpretative planner from the environment within which the plan must be developed – the real world rather than the ideal.

Analysis of resources, themes and markets can stimulate the development of a concept, but concept it will remain unless three further matters are considered. As identified here, these tend to be neglected either through site considerations, or because avoidance seems to provide an easier path to success. Not so!

Agencies

Organizations – official   and   voluntary – provide security to the member and, often, an annoyance to the outsider. The rule in any society must be that the subject for interpretation, and the location where it is to be interpreted, are already the concern of a wide range of usually non-interactive bodies before the interpreter first sets foot or word processor on the territory.

Consultation will be essential if the plan is to have any chance of success. The often tedious process ensures that interests are identified and incorporated within the process, but more important, that agency plans and knowledge bases are tapped. Returning to the market town, it is certain that the planning authority will have spatial and conservation plans for the area, that the highway authority may have changes in access and parking in view, and that sign schemes flaunting an idiosyncratic array of sites are planned. Local voluntary groups may have long-standing events programmes, publishing or exhibition intentions geared to future commemorations or funding activities.

National agencies may also have an essential role, representing, for example, the significance of historic figures or events. International or overseas bodies may equally lay claim to local figures who made their mark elsewhere. When it comes to specific cultural tradition or values, it is essential that ethnic and religious groups are involved.

In all consultations the interpreter seeks to explain the project's purpose and to solicit support at several stages: in the identification of themes, in the clarification of responsibilities, in the acquisition of artefacts, and in effective interpretation for the widest range of potential audiences. Being part of the interpretative planning process can ensure valuable publicity, finance and ongoing support from local and national communities.

Professions

Interpretation has not achieved the level of professionalization which allows easy and secure access to inter-professional debate. It is, in sociological terms, a subprofession, seeking recognition for an evolving range of skills which are too often subsumed within a broader professional title. This has two implications for interpretative planning.

First, the interpreter must always be sure to state clearly the purpose of a specific interpretative plan and the roles which he or she will undertake within the ensuing process. Is the interpreter a researcher, a story writer, an exhibition and display designer, a picture researcher, a graphic designer, an audio-visual expert, a retail planner, an events organizer, or just some of these? Job definition and personal skills will describe the precise role the interpreter plays, but it is important that this role is clearly identified in a specific project.

Secondly, the function of professional training as a shaper of attitude and function cannot be underestimated. Different professionals will view the world – and the subject or site – in different ways, and a major function of the interpretative planner is often to manage these perceptions, and the skills which adhere to them, to best advantage. Without giving the game away, it is evident that there are 'people professions' and 'place professions', 'design professions' and 'analysis professions', each of which can be drawn into a fulfilling role within the interpretative process.

In many recent projects there has been a tendency for interpretation to become dominated by one profession – commonly exhibition design or countryside management – which can lead to an imbalance in final presentation, and to the effective exclusion of ideas and audiences. So, know the cognate professions, their practices and potential.

Funding

Within the past decade, interpretation has moved from a charmed world of creative display to the hard-headed reality of financial viability.

Every interpretative initiative begins within implicit capital *and* revenue parameters which must be accepted as major determinants of plan form and outcome. Both research and design processes have the capacity for journeying great distances into the uncharted waters of expenditure, providing knowledge and ideas far in excess of those required by the project. Preliminary budget negotiation is a sobering experience for all involved, but does ensure that the role of both interpreter and plan are understood within a broader context. Sponsorship now plays a very significant role in interpretation, from the by-lined interpretative panel to the nationally promoted London exhibition.

A few key pointers are in order:

(1) Sponsors expect a positive association with the interpretative product. This has implications for content, values expressed, and promotional opportunities in design and retailing.
(2) Sponsorship support is likely to have as long a lead-in time as the interpretative planning process. Sponsors must identify with the initial concept rather than just with the final product.
(3) The sponsor must know the specific details of the project, the unique selling proposition, and the intended image.
(4) More important, the sponsor must share in the determination of the market segments to be targeted. Age, consumer type or locality may all be significant and detailed assessments will be required.
(5) Sponsorship represents another area of cooperation where consultation and regular contact are essential. The sponsor who feels part of a project's development is able to share this experience with others.

Although the comments above imply a commercial sponsor, readers will be aware that the majority of points also apply to national or local governmental sponsors, where the active participation of elected members is essential. Direction of sought-after public funding to your scheme merits public recognition for elected members.

Time and space parameters: internalized and externalized locations

The information gathered and structured under the headings above is of little value without both *temporal* and *spatial* frameworks within which to locate it. The planning process is a journey from here and now to there and then, and the journey must be structured as appropriate to the institutional framework within which you operate.

Time parameters

Time parameters are most likely to be structured by space availability or by seasonal operation. For example, the new display to be effected in a visitor centre between autumn closure and spring opening will require a planning period which starts at least *twelve months before* the Autumn closure. Practice suggests that there are a number of unfortunate rules associated with time management. Research and design development will both grow to fill double the time allocated. Essential consultation and script editing are amongst the matters which are regularly neglected in time planning. Consultees are always expected to return draft proposals within 24 hours. Matters of safety, fixing, and service supply are avoided until the last moment.

A week-by-week statement of plan stages from inception to opening, with roles clearly identified, activities linked in sequence and key decisions identified, will not prevent the faithful performance of established panic traditions in interpretation, but will help everyone back on the rails again. A wall chart and plan document are essential, even when the interpreter is single-handed and presumes a well-worn path to success.

Space parameters

The establishment of space parameters is less evident but equally important at the outset of many projects. There is, for example, a fundamental distinction to be made between the *internalized* and the *externalized* project. Broadly the former includes in-house exhibition design as for museums or other pay-boundary facilities, whilst the latter includes a wide range of open-air heritage sites such as historic landscapes, buildings, townscapes, and urban and countryside sites.

In the case of internalized locations, the majority of relationships to be achieved within the interpretative planning process are within known boundaries, and involve a potential team which will carry the majority of the process. The externalized location will have a much softer boundary with extensive consultation and diverse agency responsibility, both of which will extend the planning process. There will be less opportunity for effective teamwork and the interpreter will receive less personal support. The planning process within an internalized location may be shorter, but is potentially more volatile in terms of pressing interests. The externalized process must have more in-built flexibility.

Novel, remedial and generative plans

Another distinction between the intentions of interpretative plans is useful in identifying the skills required and the allocation of time within the planning process. Three basic types are suggested.

Novel plans

The novel situation is one where no previous professionally developed interpretation has been provided, but where the resources are evident and a general market has been identified. Examples would be the countryside location where interpretation is seen as a key feature of necessary visitor management, or a listed building which has been rehabilitated for public access. The required interpretative plan must build on latent resources and themes within the area, but has considerable freedom in the approach adopted. It should, of course, be operating in parallel with the physical and promotional development of the site or structure for public use, and must draw on the knowledge and skills of other professionals active on site.

Remedial plans

The remedial scheme is the most difficult, but increasingly frequent, requirement of the interpretative process. It is applied to facilities where changes in facilities, collections, markets or values suggest the need for substantial revision of a presentation. The starting point here is not a building or collection, but rather the recognition (by whom?) that change is required, and that the change must represent a substantial revision of what existed previously. Here the interpreter must balance a fundamental assessment of resources, themes, markets etc. with an assessment of the discarded, and the reasons for its rejection. The path to a future presentation will be littered with professional and public nostalgia and with expectations unlikely to be realized in a revised financial climate. It is particularly difficult to confront popular patterns of affection for local symbols, or to lead in the presentation of new values.

Generative plans

The generative scheme is the most appealing to the designer and has least connection to a specific location or place-related themes – as with the media-

dominated 'black-box' experience. Here the emphasis is on providing a coherent and stimulating environment which establishes its own sense of place, contributing to rather than drawing from the immediate environment. Interpretative planning here may have less to do with consultation, and more with involvement in design and experiment. Financial planning and constraints will feature more strongly.

Figure 26.1 Welcome on arrival as the front page of interpretation: Saranda, Albania, 1992

Figure 26.2 Rationalizing and pointing messages: ten messages in view on a heritage trail, Leicester, 1992

Figure 26.3 Integrating interpretation with building programmes: future railway museum, Gijon, Spain, 1992

Figure 26.4 Integrating interpretation with conservation programmes: Roman remains near Saranda, Albania, 1992

Figure 26.6 Capitalizing on existing signage: Sunderland, 1992

Figure 26.5 Ensuring first-person interpretation: Saranda, Albania, 1992

Figure 26.7 Recognizing existing tourism and visitor plans: South Shields, 1992

Figure 26.8 Inserting specific interpretative material: Tankersley, near Barnsley, 1992

Figure 26.9 Establishing themes in the landscape: Leiden Botanic Gardens, Netherlands, 1992

Figure 26.10 Sensitive fixed information which focuses the visitor: Utrecht, Netherlands, 1992

The interpretative plan: need I bother?

Although there is a literature of interpretative planning, it is neither lengthy nor profound. There have been some notable experiments in documentation and execution. The subject has featured in the key texts, and is much discussed as a necessity at professional meetings and seminars. Yet there is surprisingly little evidence as to its use.

The major reason for low visibility is that most practitioners develop proposals, programmes and products which reflect elements of the planning process without recognizing them as such. Most consultant reports identify the resources available, consider markets, assess the array of interpretative devices, and provide a phased programme of actions embracing management design and implementation activity.

The individual interpreter can only benefit from a rigorous approach to the task at hand. By identifying and validating intentions, assessing available resources (including time and assistance) and recognizing external programme constraints, we face up to the inevitable: that interpretation is a professional activity for which a client or employer is paying.

Specifically, the following benefits result from adopting a form of interpretative planning:

(1) Intentions and values are clearly identified at the outset.
(2) The brief is fully analysed and negotiated to fit within stated financial and time constraints.
(3) Resources, themes and markets are assessed at an early stage.
(4) Consultations with relevant agencies and professions are ensured and valuable cooperation is achieved.
(5) A realistic understanding of funding opportunities provides the setting for future work.
(6) The detailed planning document itself provides a sound basis for seeking financial support.
(7) The timed programme to achieve the plan, if agreed by all participants, provides a neutral management tool.
(8) The interpretative plan provides a clear statement of professional role for the interpreter.
(9) Associates can identify their opportunities and responsibilities within the broader team framework.
(10) There is more chance of achieving target dates for seasonal opening or provision.

All plans rely on those involved to follow the agreed path from here to there . . . unless the context changes radically. As is evident from the physical planning process, new circumstances (such as the growth in car ownership or national policy on out-of-town shopping centres) must lead to a reappraisal of original intentions. Mid-course corrections (rather than U-turns) are common and endorse the fact that plans are tools to serve us rather than to dominate our lives.

Without a professionally prepared plan for all significant activities, the interpreter is in danger of serving only as an adjunct to others who have such plans. The plan demands a responsible and measured approach to the task, but it also provides insurance and the basis for evaluation and assessment. More important, it provides the basis for personal professional development, and the much needed enhancement of the subject.

References

ALDERSON, W. T. and LOW, S. (1976) *Interpretation of Historic Sites*, American Association for State and Local History, Nashville, TN

ALDRIDGE, D. (1975) *Guide to Countryside Interpretation. Part One: Principles of Countryside Interpretation and Interpretative Planning*, HMSO for Countryside Commission and Countryside Commission for Scotland, Edinburgh

ALFREY, J. and PUTNAM, T. (1992) *The Industrial Heritage: Managing Resources and Uses*, Routledge, London

BINKS, G. (ed.) (1983) *Up Greenhill and Down the Dale: an Interpretative Plan for Wirksworth, Derbyshire*, Civic Trust and Centre for Environmental Interpretation, Manchester

CIVIC TRUST (1986) *Caring for the Visitor: the Calderdale Interpretative Strategy Study*, London

COUNTRYSIDE COMMISSION (1977) *Interpretative Planning at the Local Scale: a Guide to the Choice of Facilities and Media*, Cheltenham

COUNTRYSIDE COMMISSION (1979) *Interpretative Planning*, Advisory Series 2, Cheltenham

COUNTRYSIDE COMMISSION (1983) *Interpreting Tatton Park: Implementation of an Interpretative Plan*, Cheltenham

COUNTRYSIDE COMMISSION FOR SCOTLAND (1977) *Regional Interpretative Planning in Grampian*, Perth

CRAWFORD, A. (1984) 'The Arts and Crafts movement: a sketch', in *By Hammer and Hand: the Arts and Crafts Movement in Birmingham*, Birmingham Museums and Art Gallery, Birmingham

FOOD AND AGRICULTURE ORGANIZATION (1976) *Planning Interpretative Programmes in National Parks*, UN FAO, Rome

GOODEY, B. (1989) 'Small-town images: evocation, function, and manipulation', in F. W. Boal and D. N. Livingstone (eds), *The Behavioural Environment*, Routledge, London, 111–132

GOODEY, B. (1992a) 'Pubs, plots and parades', *Environmental Interpretation*, February, 6–7

GOODEY, B. (1992b) 'Interpretative planning as an integral element in place development: Spanish examples', *Interpretation Journal*, no. 50, 9–12

GOODEY, B. and PARKIN, I. (1990) *Environmental Audit for Broseley, Shropshire*, First Interpreters for Civic Trust UK 2000 and Bridgnorth DC, Coventry

GOODEY, B. and PARKIN, I. (1991) *Urban Interpretation* (2 vols) School of Planning, Oxford Polytechnic

JACKSON, S. L. (1992) *The Future Role of the Civic Trust in Urban Interpretation*, MA in urban design, Joint Centre for Urban Design, Oxford Polytechnic

JOHNSTON, MARK (1991) 'Planning the urban forest', *The Planner*, **6**(XII), 7–9

HANNA, J. (ed.) (1974) *Interpretative Skills for Environmental Communicators*, Texas A&M University, College Station, TX

KOTLER, P. (1979) 'Strategies for introducing marketing into non-profit organisations', *Journal of Marketing*, **43**, January

MURTA, S. M. (1991) *The Role of Interpretation in Urban Planning*, MSc in urban planning studies, School of Planning, Oxford Polytechnic

NEWCOMB, R. M. (1979) *Planning the Past: Historical Landscape Resources and Recreation*, Dawson, Folkestone

PUTNEY, A. D. and WAGER, J. A. (1973) 'Objectives and evaluation in interpretative planning', *Journal of Environmental Education*, **5**(1), 43–4

SHARPE, G. W. (ed.) (1976) *Interpreting the Environment*, Wiley, New York

TILLYARD, R. (1979) *Nottingham's Countryside – a Strategy for Interpretation*, Nottinghamshire County Council

TOUCHSTONE ASSOCIATES (1987) *Quiet Nature and Kinder Climate: Presentation Plan for Ilfracombe*, Touchstone Associates for the Civic Trust, Bristol/Stroud

UZZELL, D. (1991) private communication

Case study 26.1

The development and interpretation of Oakwell Hall Country Park, Batley, West Yorkshire

Catherine Hall

Kirklees Metropolitan Council have developed Oakwell Hall Country Park as a site under single management combining historic house, education and visitor attractions as well as over 44 ha of country park. Development under a single management has brought clear benefits in terms of direction and future planning as a unified site.

Development timetable

Oakwell Hall was acquired by Birstall Council in 1928 as a public museum surrounded only by its immediate gardens. In the early 1970s land sales of the adjacent farm and the closure of the Gomersal Colliery provided the opportunity to reclaim derelict land and create a country park. Large-scale landscaping works using derelict land grants followed, which included the development of an infrastructure of paths, bridleways and car parks. The old farm buildings were acquired: some were demolished, while the main courtyard complex was rebuilt and restored to provide a visitor centre, a shop and a display space as well as a large barn for events. Manpower Services Commission schemes were used to provide both park and building labour and to initiate interpretative and education projects on the site.

During the development phase of the park a team of officers from different sections met to coordinate the scheme. This included landscape architects from the Technical Services Directorate, staff from the Outdoor Division of Leisure Services, and the museum staff from Libraries, Museums and Arts. It was agreed at an early stage that the management of the site should be in the control of the Museums Service.

Significant grant-aid support was forthcoming for the project from the Countryside Commission, who were at that time prioritizing urban fringe country parks as important countryside gateway sites.

In 1985 the future shape and direction of the site were described in a development plan for the following five years. Policy and objectives for all Kirklees museums and galleries including Oakwell are reviewed and updated each year. A distinctive house style had by then been established to identify and provide a unity for the site.

Subsequent developments have included the creation of an equestrian area which is used both for horse shows organized by site staff and for local riders who hire the area by the hour.

Between 1986 and 1988 the historic house was closed for major repairs. Once it reopened, the results of several years of research into the likely appearance of a local gentry house of the late seventeenth century were implemented as a new interpretative strategy.

A Countryside Information Centre at the main car park, at some distance from the heart of the site, was built to provide toilet facilities and an information point for the dissemination of countryside access and conservation information. The structure opened with a temporary display in 1989 and a permanent exhibition opened in 1991.

Also in 1991 a pattern of seasonal admission charges was introduced to the historic hall. This serves both to generate income and to reduce usage over the summer months when visitor numbers could damage the fabric of this small house. Admission charges to the park are not made. For specific large scale events, however, there are parking charges which serve to discriminate in favour of those who arrive on foot or by public transport.

In 1992 the park was extended by a further 8 ha incorporating an area of grazing land to the north which was formerly part of the Oakwell estate. This land will be used both for the grazing of rare breed cattle owned by a local enthusiast and as the venue for sporting events, including mountain bike and hunter trials which have become an important part of the equestrian calendar. Funding for the extension has come from the Countryside Commission and the local authority's opportunity purchase budget.

Key site objectives

(1) To preserve and interpret Oakwell Hall as the Batt family home of the late seventeenth century.
(2) To promote and conserve the site's landscape and wildlife habitats for public enjoyment and education.
(3) To provide public events related to the historical and natural environment of the site.
(4) To provide opportunities for education work of all kinds relating to the site.
(5) To provide exhibitions, workshops and other interpretative media relating to the site and its associated history and environment.
(6) To provide opportunities for active public involvement in countryside skills and other related activities.

(7) To encourage understanding and enjoyment of the countryside.

Benefits of single-site management

(1) Clear objectives for all aspects of the operation of the site.
(2) Grant-aid bids coordinated and pursued.
(3) Clear image and house style for visitors.
(4) Public comments responded to quickly.
(5) Flexible, multi-disciplinary team.
(6) Clear line management.

Market research

Market research has remained important for the project since its early days when public consultation was encouraged following the initial plans for the park. Frequent site-based surveys and a household survey have been conducted to provide information on existing visitor profiles and local awareness. This information will help in increasing publicity effectiveness and setting priorities for future development.

At any one time, 75 per cent of Oakwell's visitors have visited the site before, whereas 25 per cent are first-time users. We know that several of the specialized events that we organize serve to reach a wide regional market.

Community involvement

Community involvement takes many forms including informal holiday activities and educational projects for children, membership of the Friends of Oakwell Hall, and the Oakwell Riders Club for horse riders using the park and its equestrian facilities. Conservation volunteers including BTCV groups also provide much needed support for conservation projects, and have to a large extent replaced MSC staff for project work in the park. A junior Watch group based at the site has been joined with the local authority's environmental group 'The Absolute Rubbish Club' to hold regular events at the site.

Interpretative provision

A wide range of interpretative techniques have been used at Oakwell, suited to the location and types of information being communicated:

(1) On-site information panels explain land use and country park management techniques, e.g. hedge-laying (*Figure 26.11*).
(2) Interpretative panels within the barn give a brief history of the site and the establishment of the park.
(3) A booklet gives the history of the house through time.
(4) Room panels inform visitors of both the room's use and the history of key objects in that room.

Figure 26.11 Families exploring Oakwell Hall Country Park on an interpretative trail

(5) Regular historical re-enactments as part of the events programme bring history to life and illustrate the lives of the people at Oakwell in the late seventeenth century.
(6) On Sundays in the summer the Oakwell Friends act as guides in the hall.
(7) Many of the frequent events at the site have strong interpretative or educational value, for example guided walks, workshops on environmental or historical subjects, and candlelight evenings in the historic hall led by curatorial staff. Even the very large events such as the annual country fair have clear interpretative objectives to communicate environmental information and encourage countryside access (*Figure 26.13*).
(8) Some interpretative techniques have been rejected to date, including tape guides for general visitors, as the site poses security problems for their use and storage. Other techniques used in earlier years have been abandoned as unreliable, i.e. simple tape/slide systems.

Figure 26.12 Schools costume visit

Figure 26.13 Learning the skills of turning wood on a pole lathe

Educational provision

In common with all of Kirklees' museums, Oakwell's events programme has a strong educational content. All staff are involved in the organization of these events; there is no separate education department.

Formal school provision is very well developed, with the site holding a Sandford Award. Between 1983 and 1991 the site benefited from seconded teachers from the Education Department of the authority. This post was ended as part of a package of cuts to discretionary services. Staffing is now provided by an assistant curator responsible for education, a part-time education assistant with support from a community curator, and casual staff. Schools' use of the site is operating at almost total capacity. The principles underlining schools' provision are as follows:

(1) Schools should be accompanied by a member of Oakwell staff. The educational provision involves access to the classroom and the use of replica materials, costume and toys (*Figure 26.12*).
(2) Differential changing rates apply to schools; Kirklees LEA Schools pay only a small administrative charge at present, with other schools bearing a much higher percentage of costs.

(3) School visits are usually restricted to a single class. Only one class uses the hall at a time, though there is scope and accommodation to take one historical and one environmental visit simultaneously.
(4) Demand is heavily skewed towards historical visits due to the inclusion of Tudors and Stuarts in the National Curriculum. Requests for environmental visits have declined considerably in comparison, but they will remain an important element of our visit offer to schools. In contrast informal environmental education with non school groups has increased in recent years.

Provision for visitors with special needs

A site such as Oakwell which incorporates both a grade I listed building and a park with numerous steep gradients creates many challenges for providing facilities for visitors with special needs. Both the main visitor centre and the countryside information centre incorporate RADAR accessible toilets and have level access. Staff from our disability access section have provided advice on improving facilities at the site.

In 1991 an access path of 0.5 km was created to link the countryside information centre and the main car park with the heart of the site. This path is at the limit of acceptable wheelchair gradients but was the only means of providing adequate access. It has been particularly well received by the many elderly visitors to the park and visitors with children in pushchairs who are a significant category of park users.

Re-evaluation of the site's wildlife garden had led to a new interpretative plan which incorporates level access to all areas including the pond dipped by educational groups. A series of interpretative panels have been used to provide an intensive experience of the park environments.

Projects at the site have included a successful two-week special needs theatre project for schools and adult groups. Future initiatives include a braille guide to the wildlife garden.

Case study 26.2

London's Tower Bridge

Richard Harrison

In 1991 the Corporation of London let a contract for the refurbishment of the visitor facilities on London's Tower Bridge as part of a broad-based programme of renewal of the Bridge in preparation for the centenary of its opening in 1994.

An integral part of the concept development and initial design process was the preparation of an interpretative plan for the very reasons set out in Chapter 26. In addition to describing the objectives of interpretation for a client who was not familiar with the process, the document contains:

(1) an assessment of the audience;
(2) a summary of the design objectives;
(3) an outline of the concept based on comprehensive details of the key themes and stories, which form an appendix to the plan;
(4) a summary of the resources available to the designers;
(5) a section on special needs which establishes guidelines for the use of language (written and spoken), publications, educational provision (with an appendix setting out the requirements in more detail), disabled provision, and facilities for non-English-speaking visitors.

What follows is a summary of the contents. Some of the sections are almost complete, others are summarized. The appendices are omitted.

The interpretative plan was accepted by the Corporation and formed the basis for detailed design. The concept has only been modified in detail, and Tower Bridge was reopened in September 1993.

Primary objectives of the project

These are:

(1) to develop a high-quality visitor attraction that educates and entertains and is relevant to visitors from all parts of the world;
(2) to develop a visitor attraction that will appeal to a wide base of visitors, notably family groups;
(3) to develop an attraction relevant to the National Curriculum and therefore to schools;
(4) to ensure a satisfactory return on capital invested.

What is successful interpretation?

A definition of interpretation

The art of presenting the story of a site to an identified audience in a stimulating, informative and entertaining way in order that the visitor leaves with an understanding of why it is important and with a sense of place.

Information as such is not interpretation; interpretation is revelation based on information.

Successful interpretation through key principles

Interpretation should:

(1) explore the 'how' and 'why' as well as the 'what' and 'when' of any particular piece of information;
(2) explore the options for an interactive and involving experience; visitors, both young and old, should be able to interact and learn from each other;
(3) have strong human interest themes; people are interested in people and the interpretation should focus on this;
(4) be provided at different levels to reflect the interest and comprehension abilities of different visitor groups;
(5) be consumer-led as well as resource-led; there should be a balance between interpretation which reflects the interests and needs of the visitor and the range of messages which the Corporation of London wishes to communicate;
(6) ensure that the visitor gains some new knowledge and is stimulated to know more;
(7) should recognize that there is a limit to how much a visitor can absorb;
(8) recognize how unobservant people are; visitors need guidance as to what to look at, what is significant;
(9) build on pre-existing knowledge; this will ensure that the interpretation is relevant and meaningful;
(10) provide an overall experience which stimulates all of the senses.

A strategic approach to interpretation

The starting point is:

(1) through careful and sensitive research to understand the key themes and stories to be communicated to visitors;
(2) understanding who the visitors are now and are likely to be in the future, their characteristics, interests, needs and level of knowledge;
(3) appreciating the resources available with which to communicate the stories, including the human resources which can be used to interpret to visitors;
(4) other factors which will influence the proposals, namely financial parameters, implications of status and dignity, planning and operational constraints etc.

It is from an analysis of these issues that a realistic and manageable visitor route, a logical story-line and a creative solution can be developed.

The audience

Total number of visitors

The total number of visitors is currently of the order of 500,000 a year. It is projected that this can be increased over several years to as many as 750,000. In common with most London attractions they are well spread out over the year but with peaks in the summer months.

Visitor segments

At present 70 per cent of all visitors are from overseas, with 30 per cent from the UK. A recent survey indicates that 80 per cent are on holiday in London. The largest groups of overseas visitors are German, Dutch, French, Spanish, Italian and Japanese. (It is anticipated that the American market will recover over the next few years).

Of the UK visitors, over half come in family groups.

Market objectives

The brief made it clear that the product (and future marketing) should have the following aims:

(1) whilst recognizing the importance of the world-wide market, to substantially increase the numbers from within the UK;
(2) within the UK market, to cater for the family group as a whole, including the children;
(3) to balance the requirements of the Bridge and the associated security issues with the needs and expectations of the visitors;
(4) to ensure the visitors receive a value-for-money experience and leave satisfied, eager to return and tell their friends;
(5) to provide the Corporation of London with the opportunity to promote its interests.

The visitor experience: the concept

Circulation

Under normal circumstances, groups of 25 will be taken in the lift to the second floor at regular intervals (not exceeding 10 minutes). If the queue becomes too long the staircase will be used; it will also be used if necessary for pre-booked parties. The displays are organized in such a way that these groups will stay together until they reach the engine room. The engine room is designed for free flow; it will also provide a holding space for visitors waiting to go into the final black-box presentation. Excluding time spent in the shop and café, the total visitor experience

is scheduled to last 72.5 minutes. This allows a dwell time of 4 minutes on each floor of the towers and a little longer on the walkways and in the engine room. Moving from one space to the other takes just over 15 minutes.

Overall concept

The story of the Bridge is a fascinating mix of history, human endeavour, engineering achievement and the creation of one of the world's most famous landmarks. By taking visitors back in time to the 1890s our aim is to tell this story in the words of those who were involved in its creation.

Lift and stairs access to second floor

Images of London from Tower Bridge.

North Tower: second floor

Story-line   The creation in the visitor's mind of an image of being on the Bridge as it is being prepared for the opening on 30 June 1894, and as part of achieving this to illustrate some of the key London events that have affected the Bridge since 1894 and changes in traffic patterns over and under the Bridge up to the present day.
Media   Audio-visual using familiar images and sounds to convey the visitor back 100 years.

North Tower: third floor

Story-line   The story of bridges crossing the River Thames, the role of the Bridge House Estate, why Tower Bridge was built and the lengthy debate over twenty years prior to the decision to go ahead with construction.
Media   'Harry', an animatronic figure, introduces a merchant from Butler's Wharf who presents the theme by means of a multi-visual presentation.

North Tower: fourth floor

Story-line   The story of the competition for the design of the Bridge, the rival designs and their designers, and the winning Horace Jones design. How late Victorian engineering skills and know-how were applied to the Bridge.
Media   'Harry' explains about the competition; visitors then meet the committee discussing the various schemes. Horace Jones (who died in 1887) appears as a ghost to defend his design.

Walkways: east and west

Story-line   The differences in the skyline of London between 1894 and today and the influences that have changed its so dramatically. To identify specific buildings and sites and learn something of their origins and history.

Media CDI (or similar) programme which enables visitors to identify key buildings, sites and features on the skylines, east and west. To obtain information on the use, history and internal details of the buildings and on associated people and events.

South Tower: fourth floor

Story-line The story of the people involved in the building of the Bridge from the designers to the navvies, who they were, the skills employed, their working conditions, the time it took to build the various elements, how much the Bridge cost, health and safety etc. There will be a focus on certain unusual skills, e.g. riveting using a hydraulic riveting tool, and the way in which the steelwork was erected. The civil and structural engineering methods used in the construction of the Bridge, the people involved and the skills and technology used, with particular reference to the use of steel and caissons (in the construction of the piers).
Media 'Harry' introduces the clerk of works who talks about the various elements of the story line from the roof space.

South Tower: third floor

Story-line The engineering story, the people involved, the engineering skills and techniques employed, with particular reference to the way in which the lessons of the (then) recent Tay Bridge disaster were learnt. The application of hydraulic power to the lifting process and how this worked, notably the way in which the bascules function, including the way in which the counterweights are housed in the Bridge piers. Also the operation of opening the Bridge and the systems used to achieve this.
Media Model of bascule chamber on 1:5 scale with audio-visual programme explaining the technology of the bascule.

South Tower: second floor

Story-line The people who used the Bridge at the time it opened. Who they were, what were the ships they sailed in, where they went and came from, the cargoes they carried, how they coped with passing through the Bridge, stories associated with them, what they thought of the Bridge. The people who crossed the Bridge, who they were, where they came from, where they were going and why, what they thought of the Bridge, their method of transport. What people in public life thought of the Bridge.
Media Sounds and images of the opening day.

Control room

Restored to its original function. The head watchman will explain to the visitor what he will do when the Prince of Wales officially opens the Bridge.

Engine room

Story-line How the surviving equipment operated and what its function was in the day-to-day operation of the Bridge.
Media Re-creation of a working atmosphere: people, steam, heat, smell. The operating parts of the equipment labelled for the benefit of guests to the opening. Film of bridge opening: live when possible. Interactive hands-on exhibits to explain the function of key elements of the equipment and the technology used. Displays of artefacts associated with the operation of the Bridge and no longer in use.

Bridge opening ceremony

Story-line In three parts:

(1) the story of the opening by the Prince of Wales, to emphasize the great sense of achievement felt by all concerned;
(2) to put the Bridge into the overall context of Victorian ingenuity and engineering achievement over the latter part of the nineteenth century, and the influence of the British Empire;
(3) Tower Bridge as one of the world's capital city landmarks.

Media A multi-media black-box presentation.

General

All the connecting staircases etc. will be themed, as will the retail and catering facilities.

Resources

It is very important that all known resources of material and information are used. The key ones are as follows:

Bridge The design and structure of the Bridge is a key resource in its own right. The ability to make full use of this must not be obscured by the displays themselves.
Bridge staff The Bridge Master and certain of his key staff have accumulated a wealth of information about the Bridge, some historical, some hearsay, but all important.
Tower Bridge collection of artefacts A wide range of material associated with the operation of the Bridge prior to the conversion to electricity has survived. This gives a useful insight into some of the details of Bridge operation.
Corporation of London Record Office All the archives associated with the Bridge are deposited with the Record Office. They include all the minute and account books,

drawings and daily log books. Other departments, particularly the City Engineers, may also have material.

Port of London Authority Has archive and other records related to the history of the Port of London, its docks and trade, on deposit with the Museum of London.

Museum of London Material related to the social history of London, and the docklands history in particular.

Special needs

Language

Spoken

The dwell time will determine the length of each piece of spoken commentary. This also effectively deals with the limited concentration span of many visitors. In order to ensure that the majority of visitors understand what is being said, it is important that the language should be that understood by twelve-year olds (tabloid newspaper).

The script needs to be specifically written as a piece of spoken text. Care needs to be taken about the length of phrases, words with hard consonants, avoiding alliteration and words which the reader may have difficulty in pronouncing.

The needs of the hard of hearing should also be borne in mind in terms of both language and the speed of delivery.

Written

The time it takes to read written material should be taken into account in preparing any copy.

The language requirement is as for spoken. Sentences should be kept short without making the style too stilted.

Whilst the amount of written material will be limited, there should be a hierarchy of text:

(1) thematic headings which flag the main story-line;
(2) headings which convey the main thrust of the story-line (20–30 words);
(3) supplementary information which provides more detail;
(4) captions to individual exhibits.

The size and style of type should reflect:

(1) the importance of legibility;
(2) the three levels of information;
(3) the needs of the partially sighted, particularly in the context of the distance of any written material from the eye.

Publications

The amount of detailed information provided to the visitor will be limited both by time and by the media used. It is proposed that this will be overcome by having a structured publications policy. This will also recognize that:

(1) many visitors, having been stimulated by their visit, like to have further reading to take home with them;
(2) the range of interest and need for detailed information varies considerably, from the student to young children.

Such a structured publications policy will include:

(1) an illustrated guide book available at the ticket desk, which will supplement both spoken and written material in the displays;
(2) a souvenir guide, a high-quality glossy publication with a high proportion of illustrations, which will have an important marketing function as well as being informative;
(3) a family guide designed to help the family group get as much as possible out of a visit to the Bridge;
(4) a series of fact sheets related to specific aspects of the Tower Bridge story, aimed primarily at the student and the visitor with particular interests.

Education provision

As indicated earlier, this forms an important part of our brief. Accommodation is being provided within the Bridge for use by schools and other educational groups, as are specific resources.

It is important that the detailed design and content of each exhibit recognizes the need for a balance between recreation and education which particularly takes into account the needs of schools.

People with disabilities

The Bridge was not designed with wheelchairs or the needs of people with disabilities in mind. Our overall plan for the presentation of the Bridge has taken their needs into account, including the provision of a lift from road level down to the engine room.

There are four groups of people we need to take into account:

(1) the wheelchair borne;
(2) the blind and partially sighted;
(3) the deaf and hard of hearing;
(4) the elderly and less mobile.

Their specific needs are:

(1) sufficient floor space for wheelchairs;
(2) displays visible and readable from a wheelchair;
(3) additional audio or reading material for the deaf;
(4) lighting levels and print sizes to take the partially sighted into account wherever possible;
(5) the opportunity wherever possible for the blind to touch;
(6) seating and places to pause for the elderly and less mobile.

Non-English-speaking visitors

A recent survey revealed that only 31 per cent of visitors in the vicinity of the Bridge were British. Of those interviewed, about half did not have English as their first language. Of these, only 6 per cent indicated they were unable to understand English commentaries or graphic panels. As this represents about 20,000 visitors, there is a clear need for language support. The use of infrared sourced foreign language versions of all commentaries using a wand is to be recommended.

27

People-based interpretation

Paul Risk

People-based interpretation will hereafter be referred to as *personal* interpretation: those kinds of interpretative activities and services which provide active, face-to-face contact between the interpreter and the site visitor. All other forms of interpretation will be relegated to the area of *non-personal* interpretation, and include all interpretation in which the interpreter is not physically present, such as self-guided activities, computer-assisted interpretation, exhibits, message repeaters, publications, etc.

Freeman Tilden (1984) has said that personal interpretation is the highest and best form of interaction, the most desirable and the best use of the visitor's time, although he cautioned that bad live interpretation is worse than nothing at all. This is still true and, in spite of the continued growth and development of high-tech, multi-media, non-personal presentations, most visitors are likely to continue to gain the greatest satisfaction from involvement with a live interpreter. However, with moving picture holographic projection, interactive computer enhancement, stereo sound and slick, professional media presentations on the horizon, the day may come when only the most polished communicators will take precedence over these technodramas. Perhaps this is even more reason for professional interpreters to realize the importance of fine honing their skills throughout their careers.

It is the intent of this chapter to touch on the highlights of personal interpretation, particularly as they relate to categories of some of the most effective techniques and styles. The interpreter is encouraged to examine each area, sift through its strong and weak points, and then try them out with whatever modification is required to make them his or her own.

Communication: the foundation of excellence

Before talking about specific interpretative forms, it is critical to emphasize that all interpreters trade upon their ability to communicate orally. Too often, talks, walks and tours exemplify less than the best in interpersonal communication skill. Stilted, dry and memorized, and presented with little or no enthusiasm and sparkle, the presentation drones endlessly and painfully on to a well deserved termination while visitors, reduced almost to a trance by boredom, drift aimlessly away before the conclusion of the programme or presentation.

Verbal and non-verbal components

The reasons for such mediocrity (or worse) are many, but tend to centre on lack of skill in presenting the spoken word, and failure to understand and utilize the non-verbal component inherent in all interpersonal communication.

Sixty-five per cent (some say higher) of interpersonal communication is non-verbal, represented by observing and responding to posture, body movement and position shifts, eye contact, facial expressions and even such transient and subliminal phenomena as eyebrow flashes. The vocal components, including pitch, rate and volume changes, so critical to establishing and maintaining credibility, represent a second set of vital parts of the symphony of effective personal interpretation.

Learned not born

Too often, interpreters and others assume the stance that speech communication is something with which we are born. Some, they postulate, 'have the talent' while other more ordinary mortals are doomed only to suffer along in mediocrity. Nothing could be farther from the truth! Tilden (1984), in his third principle of interpretation, stated that 'interpretation is an art . . . [and] . . . is in some degree teachable.' On the one hand, Tilden's statement may be intimidating to one who equates art only to master painters or musical virtuosos. The art of communication, of interpretation (and I use the two words as nearly synonymous), ought to terrify no one. It is the bread and butter of everyday interaction and clearly benefits from attempts to learn and improve it. Interpretation is merely explanatory communication, something we all do every day of our lives.

Greatest shortcomings

Probably the most important area deserving of attention by interpreters as they strive towards excellence is that of reading the audience, whether that be a single individual or a multitude in an auditorium or outdoor amphitheatre. Those who fail to see or respond to the numerous clues are doomed, sooner or later, to fail. Boredom, confusion, anger, resentment, appreciation, understanding, exhilaration and a multitude of other conditions can be clearly identified from non-verbal feedback provided by the face and body of the listener. The literature abounds in papers and books on this subject and it is not appropriate here to spend a great deal of time detailing this aspect of interpretation. The reader is urged strongly to become familiar with such literature (Knapp, 1972; Harrison, 1974; Bettinghaus, 1968; Makay and Sawyer, 1973; Malandro *et al.*, 1989).

Personal interpretation's many faces

Talks, role playing, demonstrations, informal interpretation, information duty, conducted activities and tours are the primary types of personal interpretation. They will be examined in some detail as to their strengths and weaknesses and the context in which they are most or least effective.

Commonalities

It may accurately be said that almost all forms of personal interpretation, even to some extent information duty, have three things in common. They have a beginning, a middle and an end, and this sequence from here on will be referred to simply as BME. Beginnings tell the visitor what we are going to do. Middles do it. Ends tell them what we did or summarize, often with a wrap-up including a philosophical 'think piece'.

The beginning must command attention by drawing visitors from their daydreams, conversations and other preoccupations. The middle, whether it be part of a talk, walk, demonstration or tour, is an interconnected series of stories each with its own BME. The end encapsulates, summarizes, concludes and puts the final glistening finish on the masterpiece of interpretative art.

Details on the basic logistics of the creation and format of interpretative programmes should be clearly in mind so that the interpreter can devote his/her time to the micro-manipulation required to produce a superb product. Several books are available which can provide information outside the scope of this chapter (Grater, 1976; Sharpe, 1982; Uzzell, 1989).

Talks

In general, talks are either illustrated or unillustrated. Included in this category could also be story-telling – almost an art in itself. Depending on the desires or budget of the agency, talks may be presented from start to finish by one person or may include a master of ceremonies (MC) or similar person who greets the audience, warms them up and then introduces the main speaker. There are advantages to both approaches.

Master of ceremonies format

In some parks operated by the United States Park Service, the MC welcomes the audience, makes announcements, leads songs, tells a few light stories or humorous, relevant anecdotes, and after perhaps fifteen minutes introduces the featured speaker.

An MC may enhance the presentation of a weak speaker by establishing rapport with the audience which puts them into an accepting mood. On the other hand, the MC tends also to warm the audience to himself rather than to the featured speaker. This may build a barrier between the audience and the featured interpreter, who must come on as a virtual stranger in an environment crafted by the MC. My preference is the solo approach, in which a single interpreter takes the programme from start to finish. He or she establishes the critical audience rapport and can therefore work with them with more finesse and success.

Formal versus informal talks

Formal talks tend to be those during which the interpreter generates all the information and the audience is a passive group of recipients. Informal talks, usually to small groups, enable members of the audience to ask questions or otherwise respond. The pros of the formal talk include the fact that the interpreter, by exercising near total control over the presentation, can sculpt the atmosphere and more clearly direct the audience's reaction. This is particularly important when a strongly emotional message is implicit in the interpretation and a specific outcome is desirable. The informal talk, by allowing visitors to interact and question, provides a more participative atmosphere conducive to an enhanced understanding of the topic. Talks, whether formal or informal, are generally used in heritage interpretation in settings such as visitor centres, lodges, auditoriums and classrooms, and the audience type tends to be dictated by the location of the talk site. The benefits of the different types of talks are that each draws a different client group, thus expanding the variety of people who are reached by the interpretative message.

Visitor centre audiences tend largely to be park or historic site visitors who are there of their own volition during a block of leisure time. They tend to be relaxed, motivated primarily by recreational interests, younger than middle-aged, less affluent and more apt to participate in active forms of interpretation. The setting is informal in terms of dress and demeanour.

Lodge or hotel talks are presented by the interpreter in an auditorium. For example, at Grand Canyon National Park in the United States, visitors to the North Rim Lodge attend talks in a rustic auditorium adjacent to the main lobby and opposite the formal dining room. The programme is presented in the evening and frequented by visitors who have just finished dining in a setting of silver, crystal and linen. These park visitors are often affluent, middle-aged or older, and tend to participate in the more passive forms of interpretation at the park.

Campfire programmes

A special type of talk with particular strengths, the campfire programme in the United States originated with those pioneer nature guides whose programmes ultimately became an integral part and almost a trademark of the National Park Service. Outdoor programmes are generally an hour to an hour and a half in length, incorporating projected illustrations or unillustrated, and conducted from dusk into dark. The campfire programme, where firewood is abundant, is a treasured part of the outdoor interpretative repertoire.

Campfire programmes are generally presented in an amphitheatre, seating being provided on rustic benches with a low stage and screen at the front from which the interpreter works and containing remote controls for lighting, sound and projectors. Images may be projected either from the rear of the seats or from equipment housed behind the screen itself (rear projection). When illustrations are used, combined with a public address system, the campfire programme allows very large audiences to be reached effectively.

Audiences at campfire programmes tend to be made up of young families, young singles or older people on fixed incomes, but most attenders participate in more active forms of interpretation including walks and hikes. Parks which provide campgrounds find that most of their campfire programme attendance comes from campers rather than lodge, hotel or motel clients, and the amphitheatre is usually placed in close proximity to the camping areas.

The outdoor atmosphere tends to heighten the visitor's relationship with and feeling for the natural environment and enables, where trees do not limit visibility too severely, specialized programmes such as night sky interpretation which is discussed below. The sight and fragrance of the fire is important in rekindling memories of other trips and picnics. Earlier and perhaps similar days of explorers and pioneers are brought to mind, and links with the historic and prehistoric past are easily made by the interpreter.

The campfire and its setting provide an interesting mixture of negative effects. The fire itself, as it has for eons, provides a magnetic attraction and focal point, drawing visitors from the surrounding area. However, children tend to play around them, throwing rocks into the embers, poking the glowing coals and burning wood with sticks, and pushing and shoving each other. If they are not requested to be seated with their families before the programme begins, they often become a distraction with their rowdiness. Campfire programmes, however, also seem to be activities at which parents drop off their children while the older family members do something else. Because of that, the instruction to please sit with your families at the commencement of the programme may be useless. Some park areas, because of such problems and liability concerns, have had to ask that no unescorted children below a certain age attend these programmes.

Parks located close to cities are sometimes heavily used by weekenders, who come not to involve themselves with the park but rather to wax their cars, play their audio equipment at maximum volume, entertain themselves with card games and drink heavily. Not infrequently, those who have over-indulged in alcohol end up at the campfire programmes, often seated at the rear, from which vantage point they heckle (light-heartedly or not) the interpreter and those around them. At Lassen Volcanic National Park in California, adjacent to both Redding and Red Pluff, the author has had drunks roll empty beer cans down the amphitheatre's sloping aisles while accompanying this game with rude remarks. This is only one of several reasons why many park agencies in the United States and Canada ban the use of alcoholic beverages within their boundaries.

Children, often in spite of the fact that they are sitting with parents, shine flashlight beams on the screen. Before the programme, they play light tag, chasing each other's beams. If this isn't quickly discouraged at the start of the programme, the interpreter can be assured of continued activity of this type, with lights flashing across slides and the speaker's face!

Although there are more opportunities for problems at campfire programmes than any other types of talks, the benefits far outweigh the liabilities and these programmes can reach a very large segment of the public visiting the park.

The fire itself may be used as an interpretative tool. If ignition is postponed until the audience arrives, the interpreter (wearing a suitable microphone) can build and light it while explaining the wood type, the placement and the differences between tinder, kindling and fuel. Holding up a single match with which to light the blaze, and soliciting the audience's assessment of the interpreter's fire-building skill, lends an element of fun to the process. Also, the members of the audience who have just failed miserably in trying to light their own campfire can get some needed advice. The author, prior to the evening programme, watched one park visitor, who already had a stock of over a dozen burned-out matches to his credit, try to light a 100 mm log by applying a burning match to its end. Meanwhile, he wondered out loud why the logs from the supermarket at home would ignite with a single match and these wouldn't! The ones from the store are usually made from compressed wood chips with a flammable binding agent, very unlike a natural log.

Songs around the campfires are traditional, and lighten and enhance the atmosphere at the programme. They should be selected to reflect the theme of the talk and magnify the overall interpretative effect of the evening's presentation. Announcements and subjects of concern with safety, conservation or weather are made at the beginning of the presentation, and should be skilfully woven into the fabric of the programme rather than standing alone as an awkward addition.

Illustrations used are most often slides, but a number of park agencies project movies as well. It is the author's opinion that interpreters serving as moving picture projectionists represent a poor use of resources and, except in very unusual circumstances, this ought not to happen. Slides, skilfully sequenced and presented, accompanied by an interpreter's well crafted and presented narration, can transport the visitor visually to any place desired. They may see seasonal changes, micro and macro views of minerals, animals and plants, great panoramas or views from space. The programme should be executed so that the interpreter presents a talk which happens to be illustrated, never a series of illustrations about which one talks! Visuals are a mighty tool when used properly.

Night sky interpretation at campfire programmes

The sky overhead represents a great interpretative asset, but one which is rarely used by most interpreters. At amphitheatres with project capability, slides of constellations can be shown and a laser pointer or halogen bulb pointer used to indicate the actual celestial phenomena overhead. Sky lore of ancient, early and native peoples can be used to great advantage to enhance the programme. Night sky talks, because of their need for complete darkness, often begin following a regular campfire programme. The distance from the interpreter to the audience poses a significant but not insurmountable parallax problem for the use of the pointer. The view from the audience makes the point beam appear off-centre to the constellation or object in the sky. However, the members of the audience can be provided with sky charts and encouraged to bring red-lensed flashlights with which to view the charts. The red light does not destroy night vision. (The interpreter can also provide red acetate composition covers which can be cut with scissors to fit visitors' flashlights). The foregoing, combined with the image on the screen, makes viewing and accurately identifying the parts of the night sky successful and very enjoyable. Telescopes may be set up to enable informal observation following the programme, and visitors should also be encouraged to use binoculars.

Night sky interpretation as well as other kinds of sky interpretation is growing in popularity as more and more interpreters learn about and implement it.

Unillustrated talks

From time to time, talks at amphitheatres, auditoriums and other locations are not illustrated. Unillustrated amphitheatre talks usually occur because electricity or projection equipment are not available. In any case, unillustrated talks can still be very effective, particularly if objects and items can be substituted for illustrations. The interpreter can bring a bag of tricks containing the items needed to enhance the presentation. For example, arrowheads, spear points, food plants or pieces of clothing could be used as examples in an otherwise unillustrated talk on native people.

A major benefit of an unillustrated presentation is that the interpreter is not limited to locations where projection capabilities exist, and programmes may be taken to remote camp sites or marginally developed areas. Unillustrated talks are often delivered at locations catering to very small groups of people, and the interaction possible under those circumstances enables a more tailor-made presentation which may meet the needs of the visitors better than a 'canned' talk. Unillustrated talks lend themselves particularly well to the story-teller's art, and a skilled interpreter can assist visitors in experiencing a rich voyage of the imagination. When combined with the intimacy of a small group seated around a fire, as well as the tranquility, isolation and darkness at a remote location, an unillustrated talk may weave magic impossible under other conditions.

Off-site, off-season interpretation

Most interpretation takes place on site in the park, museum, house or other location operated by the heritage agency. Owing to budgetary limitations, scheduling problems or lack of desire on the part of the interpreter or the agency, the opportunity to leave the confines of the park or other heritage site is too seldom utilized.

Schools offer one of the most fertile grounds for taking interpretation to those who both need to know and are thirsting for what we can bring. In Florida's Everglades National Park, interpreters regularly take programmes to the schools in the area, with the result that many children who otherwise would never have contact with national parks philosophy are becoming enlightened. Environmental issues of great concern to the Everglades area and southern Florida are usually the subject. Poster, art and essay contests for schoolchildren provide a competitive setting in which the students not only participate with enthusiasm but also demonstrate profound understanding of complex ecological principles.

Parks and environmental education centres are, in some cases, taking their shows to schools, city parks and playgrounds by way of converted buses and trailers. Initial cost can be high, but used vehicles are often available for quite reasonable sums of money. Buses with seats removed and replaced with exhibits, laboratory tables and other equipment, or smaller trailer exhibits with special interpretative programmes, ply the streets of cities and other areas. Often, in order to maximize their contact, multilingual interpreters travel with these mobile centres. This is especially important to inner-city areas where diverse cultural groups are found who speak only their native non-English language.

Research and interpretation

In several national parks in the United States a unique and innovative programme of involving the general public in ongoing research is taking place. In one area, monarch butterflies, which migrate across the United States, are tagged and their routes plotted by participating visitors who are trained by park biologists and interpreters. In another, water quality testing is carried out. Some states use their biologists and interpreters working cooperatively with the public to conduct bird migration observations and studies. The combined effect of interpretation with the greater depth of understanding brought about by the hands-on experience of the participants greatly magnifies the enjoyment and learning which take place. In addition, volunteers assisting in the research provide a greatly needed bolstering of the paid interpretative and biologist staff, enabling significantly more to be accomplished than would be the case if only employees were involved.

Mass media and interpretation

Radio and television offer great opportunities for innovative interpretative programming. It may be stretching things to call this personal interpretation since there is no face-to-face contact between the live interpreter and the visitor. But the presentation is live and can be vital in every sense of the word. Radio and television stations in the United States are required by law to provide a certain amount of free public service time. Parks, nature centres, environmental education centres, museums, historic sites and related agencies utilize this time by using their best communicators to provide coverage of the widest type. A major segment of society seldom stirs from the familiar confines of their home. They span a wide demographic range in terms of education, age and income. Radio and television often form their only contact with the world as a whole. The horizons that open for them via these high-tech transmission media are limitless. Witness the great number of nature programmes which take us from the cold of Antarctica to the sweltering tropical rainforests, and from the depths of the oceans to the peaks of the highest mountains. A special kind of rapport can develop between the interpreter and the audience via the media. Strong bonds grow in which members of the audience feel they know the interpreter they see or hear regularly in their home or car.

Role playing: first person versus third person

Role playing may, in large part, be categorized as first person or third person with modifications or variations on this theme. Historical or cultural interpretation utilizes role playing to the greatest extent in an effort to present a living representation of a past event. It is, in fact, often called 'living history' interpretation, and takes the form of a costumed or uniformed interpreter pretending to be a nameless person from the past, a particular historic personage or even, in the case of one Canadian park, a dinosaur or other prehistoric animal.

Comparing first- and third-person interpretation, it is apparent that some sacrifices must be made in both cases. First-person interpretation may represent the greatest opportunity for dealing with the emotions. It is strong on essence and weak on detailed information. The flavour of the period, the characteristics of speech and dress as well as of family, community and social behaviour, are well presented, limited only by the accuracy and talent of the interpreter. Names, details of military movements, global perspectives and other minutiae are absent. The visitor's understanding of events is limited to the perspective of the individual being portrayed. Third-person interpretation substitutes the 'I am, I did' approach for the 'on the 4th of April 1567, troops under the command of' or 'they were, they did' style of presentation.

Both first and third person have their place and may be implemented to interpret the same historic event as a means of showing it from different perspectives. The visitor who is a United States Civil War buff or historian may be so immersed in the fine details of the event that first-person interpretation will be too superficial. On the other hand, the average visitor may want a lighter touch on historical detail and be thrilled by the first-person portrayal.

First-person costumed interpretation in any form is not easy, but portraying a person who actually existed is most difficult. The in-depth research necessary to understand the entire character of the person portrayed, and to represent that accurately, is critical. In order to carry it off, the interpreter must be a special person, both a highly qualified communicator and an accomplished actor. Often hours of practice are required to master the nuances of the presentation.

(1) Hal Holbrook, an actor from the United States, has played and toured in a presentation entitled 'Mark Twain Tonight'. Holbrook comes on stage haltingly, assuming the mannerisms of Mark Twain in his old age as he recites many of Twain's most notable writings. One is struck by the impression that Twain is alive before our eyes.

(2) In a Canadian national park, the first Royal Canadian Mounted Police constable killed in the line of duty returns. At an evening campfire programme hosted by an interpreter in the traditional present-day uniform of Parks Canada's interpreters, the visitors are welcomed and the programme begins. Several moments later, as darkness has fallen and the only illumination is the light of the campfire, a voice from the still darkness is heard to hail the group. He announces himself as the long-deceased constable and, accompanied by the measured clip-clop of his horse's hoofs, he walks into the firelight attired in the flat-brimmed hat, red coat and gleaming boots of the Mounties. After telling much of his history to a hushed audience, he excuses himself and he and his horse melt back into the darkness.

(3) On the flanks of Mount Rainier, in the state of Washington, the author leads a group of visitors through pitch dark forest depths on an activity purported to be a nature walk. In night so deep one could not see a hand before the face, the line of visitors clings to each other's belts or coats as they feel out the trail beneath their feet, warning those behind with muffled explanations ('root', 'rock'). Suddenly, a visitor sees a flicker of light in the blackness. 'What is that?' she queries. 'I don't know,' the interpreter answers. 'It can be nothing. Ahead is only the long-deserted Longmire cabin.' 'But,' his voice hesitates, 'the Longmires have been dead for years and years.' Without sound, the small group slowly approaches a rustic cabin, now obviously illuminated from within by a flickering light. Without warning the door creaks open to reveal an aged, white-haired woman rocking in her chair as she

knits by the light of a solitary candle. 'Come on in,' her thin voice squeaks. 'I thot I heerd folks a'comin'. I'm old Ma Longmire and ye're welcome here.' Then, costumed young interpreter Karen Sprague goes on, before an entirely rapt audience, to enact a decrepit Ma Longmire as she recites her recollections of the earlier days of Mount Rainier National Park.

The opportunities for creativity in role playing are limitless and the dividends are of great value. In this lies much of the magic of interpreting historic events. One of the most exciting possibilities for the historical interpreter lies in the involvement of visitors themselves in the re-enactment of the past.

(1) In a tiny community in the state of Maine, visitors themselves may enrol to become a part of the historical past. They live in eighteenth century housing, taking the part of those who actually occupied this tiny village and whose tombstones they've seen in the cemetery. For an entire weekend they work, eat and live in the past, experiencing history in a way few will equal.

(2) At the Jefferson National Expansion Memorial in Missouri, often known simply as 'The Arch' at St Louis, the National Park Service interprets from the time of President Thomas Jefferson and the Louisiana Purchase to the present. Like the spokes of a wheel radiating through islands of light, the museum unfolds year after year in floor to ceiling exhibits enlivened by interpreters in present-day uniforms or period costumes. At one location, an interpreter wheels out a museum table containing the clothing and equipment of a mountain man. He does not, however, hold up a single item and interpret it. Instead, he selects a volunteer visitor from the audience who, accompanied by the interpreter's narration and with some initial shyness and hesitancy, dons one by one the articles of clothing. With each addition to his costume the volunteer seems to stand a little taller until, entirely garbed from the past, he 'becomes' a mountain man himself – a rejuvenated relic alive before our very eyes.

(3) At a castle in England, visitors are escorted through dark candle-lit corridors by ominously hooded monks to share their meagre meal, only to be interrupted by the king's troops who, pounding at the door, force their way into the dining hall. A transformation occurs and a medieval feast is laid on, the only eating utensil a short dagger at each visitor's place. Meat, mead and other foodstuffs, brought by young maidens, appear on the table. Music and jolliment round out the festive step back in time.

Demonstrations

Many historical sites provide demonstrations of skills, crafts and activities from the period interpreted. Typical are tin-, silver- and blacksmiths, watch and clock makers, weavers and dyers, glass blowers, coopers, fletchers and gunsmiths, to name only a few. Visitors watch master craftspeople ply their trades and may even be able to purchase items being produced. Where health laws permit, visitors may taste foods prepared as they were during the historic period interpreted. Again, visitor participation can add to the atmosphere.

The most positive aspect of demonstrations is the opportunity to watch crafts, often long obsolete, being performed. The demonstrators also help to perpetuate knowledge which otherwise would be lost. Demonstrations are attractive to visitors in many ways. There is something mesmerizing about watching brittle glass glow golden with sodium flame, melt, droop, then expand with blown breath. With a touch here and a push there from molten glass rod or graphite prod, a work of unsurpassed beauty emerges. When that very object is available to the visitor for purchase, a souvenir has its birth which will, from then on, refresh memories of the visit.

Demonstrations have their own set of problems. Often craftspeople, skilled as they may be in their work, are far less comfortable in the role of interpreter. It is not unusual to find that they are somewhat surly in their demeanour – as they probably were in real life. The best a visitor can expect is a grunt or nod of the head in response to questions. Sometimes, although the craftsperson wants to communicate, he or she is either too shy or too soft-spoken to be effective in that role. In this case, it may be desirable to have one of the other interpreters interpret or narrate for them.

At Lassen Volcanic National Park in northern California, Mrs Lamar (Bu-nu´-key-me´noor, 'woman whose name means the sunset'), an Atsugewi Indian, sits dressed in buckskin on the ground by the visitor centre at Manzanita Lake. Her legs bend gracefully to one side so that her feet may be decorously placed beside her. She works with a partially completed basket made of spruce root fibres and reminisces about bygone days and her family. As the interpreter assigned, I sit beside her and we talk. As I try to say her Indian name and stumble miserably over the glottal stop at '-key', she laughs that she has an ugly name. 'But,' she allows, 'sister had *really* ugly name. Ka-rot´-a-me´noor!' ('Green grasshopper woman'). Wearing a suitable microphone of great sensitivity to pick up her very soft voice, I sit for an hour quietly talking with her about leaching acorn meal to make it sweet (a staple in her early diet), catching trout by dextrously inserting a little finger in a gill and flipping it out of the stream, and experiences with Sasquatch ('big foot'). Equally quiet, park visitors sit or stand around us eavesdropping with great respect and interest, while this tiny, vital, humorous woman shares her life with us.

Point duty

Certain especially significant or interesting locations in parks, recreation areas and cultural sites become focal points where visitors congregate. These may be appropriate locations at which to station an interpreter on point duty. The responsibility here is to perform what might be called spontaneous or informal interpersonal contact. For example, at Grand Canyon National Park in Arizona, approximately 50,000 people pass through the south entrance gates daily during peak summer months. A minute percentage of this huge number go to the amphitheatres provided or attend talks and walks. So, interpreters are regularly scheduled at several heavily visited view points along the canyon rim where most, if not all, visitors stop to view this wonder.

It has been suggested that in North America less than 50 per cent of park visitors partake of any form of interpretation. The majority leave with only a marginal understanding of the heritage site's story or its relevance to them. The interpreter on point duty performs the very important function of meeting the needs of many of these people. However, it is important to recognize that while the presence of a uniformed interpreter may be an invitation for communication to some, many are hesitant to approach.

Therefore, a vital responsibility of the interpreter is to recognize point duty as more than a passive, boring ordeal of waiting for visitors to initiate contact. A warm, cordial greeting given by the interpreter actively sets the scene for interaction. Inquiry about the visitor's home location or length of trip can lead into discussion and provide the opportunity to suggest alternative places to see and things to do which can enhance their visit. An important consideration is that interpersonal contact, no matter how brief, accomplishes several important things. It demonstrates that the visitor is appreciated and respected and presents a positive image of the agency. Visitors are more likely to participate in other, more formal, interpretative programmes as a result of this initial contact. Point duty is too often viewed as a frill of little importance by supervisors and a required but not enjoyed part of the day by interpreters, when in reality it can be exciting and fruitful to both the interpreter and the visitor.

Information duty

The visitor centre, information desk, entrance station or other location usually offers visitor services by providing directions, information on facilities, road conditions, brochures and other help. Too often interpreters and other personnel assigned this responsibility fall into providing curt, cryptic responses. 'Are there rest rooms in the building?' asks a visitor. 'Yep!' shoots back a disinterested employee. The answer ought to have been, 'Yes, they're down the hall to your right', rather than waiting for the frustrated visitor to painfully extract every morsel of desired information. Information duty, like point duty, presents a wonderful opportunity, especially when demand is not too high, to engage visitors in conversation and provide informal but valuable interpretation.

Non–interpretative interpreters?

Heritage sites and agencies abound in personnel who can be important interpretative resources but who are not used often enough. Although interpreters are sometimes involved in protective activities, in most areas these responsibilities are delegated to specialists, sometimes called law enforcement officers, rangers or wardens. Their everyday duties can be grist for the interpreter's mill. Some of the best attended, most exciting and enlightening programmes the author has witnessed were those with a protection theme.

At Grand Canyon National Park's South Rim, the evening amphitheatre programme has been under way for 12 minutes. The interpreter is just concluding announcements when, to the surprise and delight of the audience, a helmeted head rises from behind the 6 m screen and a search and rescue ranger climbs over the top and rappels down to the stage. Demonstrations, narrated by the interpreter, of climbing and rescue technique, including Jumar ascensions of a nearby Ponderosa pine, a Tyrolean traverse (from tree to tree) with a rescue litter, and slides of actual emergencies, comprise the rest of the programme.

One of the keys to the effectiveness of this approach is the element of surprise. Also, visitors are attracted in great numbers to programmes dealing with the excitement of emergency services. Visitors who would never attend a naturalist programme will come to presentations dealing with protection. When planned correctly, environmental messages and other important information can be skilfully woven into the fabric of the programme, reaching an entirely new audience.

At Grand Canyon's North Rim, a similar scenario unfolds. As announcements are concluding, a siren can be heard in the distance. Ignored by all, the sound draws closer until it is obvious that an emergency vehicle is approaching the campground. The interpreter pauses as all heads turn toward the approaching fire truck, its lights flashing. Wending its way through the campground (and attracting a myriad of hitherto uncommitted visitors) it rushes up to the amphitheatre; the crew leaps off, unreels a hose line and, with a whoosh and a huge cloud of smoke and steam, extinguishes the interpreters campfire!! The audience, at first hushed and awed, now breaks into laughter and the crew chief of the fire control team takes over the microphone to do a programme on firefighting. Demonstrations with the hose and fire tools, and a slide talk of actual fire scenes, complete the evening for a now standing room only crowd.

Conducted activities

Walks, tours and hikes; boat, raft and canoe trips; horse, mule and bike expeditions are all examples of conducted activities. They each offer a different set of opportunities and attract different kinds of visitors. Conducted activities allow maximum interaction between the interpreter and the visitor and also pose their own special challenges. A major controlling factor, too frequently exceeded, associated with conducted activities is the number of visitors. Outdoor walking tours led by a single interpreter can almost never be handled effectively for more than 35 people. The lag time imposed in moving a long line of people, the difficulty in positioning everyone around a small point of interest, the challenge of making oneself heard by all and the tendency of small groups of people towards the rear of the group to carry on their own distracting conversations, are all reasons to keep the group small. In a large group, interaction with the visitors drops off in direct proportion to the number of people on the activity.

Children on walks can be a problem, and Tilden (1984) suggests that we ought to provide interpretation specifically designed for them. In the author's experience, it is almost always children accompanied by their parents who run in dangerous areas, throw rocks and sticks, pick flowers or do other things of a disruptive or dangerous nature. However, much if not most of this can be discouraged by covering, in a positive, reinforcing manner at the start of the walk, suggestions that children stay with their families and not involve themselves in dangerous or environmentally degrading behaviour. (Although it sounds a bit abrasive in this short paragraph, a smile, a diplomatic delivery and a bit of humour can accomplish this goal without putting anyone off.)

The pace, within reason, of a conducted activity, particularly of walks and hikes, should be set according to the slowest person in the group. Otherwise, slower visitors will be left behind and tend to miss part of the message when stops are made along the trail. In the worst case, visitors may be endangered by separation from the main body of hikers.

Cemetery walks

Cemeteries offer a unique kind of interpretative opportunity and as such deserve special mention. In the United States, during the 1800s, cemeteries were often focal points for pleasant family outings and picnics on Sunday afternoons.

Often beautifully landscaped and carefully maintained, cemeteries provided an escape from less tranquil city settings. For this reason, we still find many communities in which the governmental organization responsible is called a department of parks, recreation and cemeteries.

Cemetery art provides interpreters with a rich resource. In the United States, inscribed designs on tombstones vary from the death heads, skeletons, imps and angels of death of the 1700s through cherubic faces with wings, flowers severed in their prime, and hands pointing heavenward of the latter 1800s to lambs, winged angels, willow trees and ornate columns of the more recent past. The artistic changes evidence a transition from early Calvinistic religion to a more hopeful philosophy or a more recent religion. The tombstones themselves provide lessons in geology from their composition. Epitaphs illuminate personal and religious philosophy, goals and aspirations, occupations and causes of death, and their patterns demonstrate epidemics and war.

A small group of visitors, led by a park interpreter, crosses the railroad tracks adjacent to a historic cemetery in Ohio. It is dusk, and there are several lit lanterns providing subdued illumination for the group. The interpreter has set the necessary tone of reverence and respect before leaving the visitor centre, and now pauses briefly to tell the story of an individual who was killed crossing the tracks here and whose ghost has been seen along the roadbed near this location. The tour progresses into the cemetery where, the oblique lighting from the lanterns casting shadows and enhancing the engravings on tombstones, stories are quietly told and a step is taken into a past which suddenly becomes not so distant and strange.

Hikes versus walks

In general, a hike is more arduous and of greater length and duration than a walk. Hikes are best suited for interpretation where relatively long distances must be covered, such as a trip to the summit of a mountain. Generally, interpretive stops are less frequent on a hike, allowing individuals to immerse themselves in the experience. Rest stops are ideal locations for interpretation, and permit visitors to sit during the presentation. These stops also enable information conversation between the interpreter and the visitors, and between visitors.

Walks, often of a maximum length of 2.5 km, are leisurely paced and generally not too fatiguing for older people or those whose physical condition is less than ideal. Stops not to exceed 10 minutes are interspersed along the route, carefully chosen to permit their alignment with a theme and carefully interwoven with smooth transition statements. Questions are usually solicited and an easy flow of information takes place in both directions.

Pedestrian tours

Walking tours are conducted at museums, historic homes, forts, castles, caves and even cemeteries. Like talks, they have a beginning, middle and end (BME)

with discrete stops carefully interconnected. They can be very rewarding both for the visitor and for the interpreter, but also have the potential for becoming one of the dullest, most uninteresting interpretative forms. In the worst situation, the interpreter falls into what has been called the 'museum guide syndrome'. Formulas, clichés and pure information rather than interpretation are parroted in a monotonous voice by an interpreter who long ago has lost all enthusiasm for the job.

The reasons for this all too frequent situation are numerous, but one of the most important is that the contents of museum, historic home, fort, castle, cave or even cemetery change very slowly, if at all. The interpreter finds it increasingly difficult to maintain spontaneity or excitement and falls into a repetitive pattern requiring little energy. In short, he or she goes into an automatic, unthinking mode which is guaranteed to generate the same response in the visitor. The cure for this is to interpret the sequence of items or objects in varied order or to change the route in minor or major ways. Wording should be varied and increased interaction with the group encouraged.

Vehicular tours and trips

Trams and buses are frequently used to transport and interpret for visitors. They are especially useful in heavily visited areas where crowding from private vehicles is a problem, where great distances must be covered or where dangerous animals pose a threat to the visitor. As visitation continues to increase in heritage sites throughout the world, we will see a growing need for and use of vehicular interpretative tours. Trams are usually owned and operated by the heritage agency. Buses are often owned by a concessionaire or company which runs tours to and through the site.

In many cases, the tram or bus driver doubles as the interpreter by speaking into a microphone attached to the vehicle by a flexible mounting, worn around the neck or attached to the clothing by a clip. This approach permits maximum utilization of a single interpreter and can be very effective, but poses several distinct problems. The driver's attention may be diverted from traffic hazards by concentration on interpretation and/or the interpretative message may be affected adversely because the driver must devote too much attention to traffic safety. Even under the more ideal conditions of a tour through a botanic garden or similar site on a road shared only by occasional pedestrian traffic, the driver/interpreter's back is to the audience, permitting no eye contact, with only periodic glances in the mirrors to obtain feedback from the listeners. Attention tends to wander; visitors strike up conversations of their own; continuity breaks down.

A better arrangement is when a second person acts as the interpreter. Still using a microphone, the interpreter can then turn to face the passengers from time to time as well as devote uninterrupted attention to points of interest along the route. However, interpretative effectiveness on tram and bus tours, even under the best of circumstances, seems to be diluted in direct proportion to the distance form the driver/interpreter. The author, as an interpreter with the county of Los Angeles, California, drove and interpreted from a tram at Descanso Gardens divided into three trailers with a total of about 70 passengers. Even though there were speakers under the seats on each trailer, those beyond the half-way point were noticeably less involved than those at the front.

Boat tours may take place, as in Lowell, Massachusetts, along old power canals which once directed the flow of water to drive power looms for the fabric industries of the city, or on large vessels plying the inland passage to Alaska as is the case with the US Forest Service and National Park Service. They too reach another segment of the heritage thirsty public. They also suffer from some of the same weaknesses as tram and bus tours. In the case of the larger vessels, the interpreter may speak from the bridge and be entirely out of view of the passengers. A better approach is that used on vessels travelling to Isle Royal National Park on Lake Superior in the United States. The interpreter during much of the trip roams informally around the vessel talking with visitors. The formal talk takes place in a large lounge, enabling the interpreter to face the audience and build better interpersonal bonds.

Canoe and raft trips

A very special opportunity exists for interpreters on canoe and raft trips. In New Jersey, a county park system leads what might be called canoe caravans. Several canoes float leisurely down a stream while an interpreter speaks from the lead canoe. A particularly relaxed tone is established because the stream is slow-flowing and the canoes drift with the current.

Each bend has the possibility of revealing something new and unexpected and provides a spontaneous and unscheduled format. If there is a drawback to this, it is that a guaranteed structure to the float trip is not possible. However, a skeleton or foundation framework of static information provides necessary stability around which serendipitous occurrences can be allowed to weave themselves.

Conclusions

This chapter has not been, and neither was it intended to be, an exhaustive description of how to carry out every detail of each of the multitude of variations of talks and conducted activities. Rather, it was intended to highlight more generally some categories in the vast array of interpersonal interpretative techniques with an eye towards emphasizing some of the more important generalizations associated with them. Although

weaknesses and strengths inherent in them have been presented, weakness for one is often a strength for another. The aim of this chapter, then, is to stimulate the interpreter or budding interpreter to think, to explore and to learn to exult in the opportunities and challenges of the career of interpretation. It is intended, as Freeman Tilden (1984) encouraged, not just to instruct but to provoke.

Simply put, effective people-based interpretation is based on a short but critical premise: people like people who like people (PLPLP), and find particularly attractive those who combine this trait with a clearly demonstrated love of their area and ability to communicate. It is vitally important that the interpreter is able to put herself in the place of the visitor. Whether the listeners are small children, teenagers, mature adults or senior citizens, the interpreter must approach them from their level of experience and personality. Successful oral interpretation is a delicate and dynamic balancing act which cannot be targeted merely at an average member of any audience. Rather it is a graceful ballet enabling the interpreter to touch, at some time during the presentation, the intellect and emotions of each age group, attainment level, occupation and interest. Not only is this possible, it is part and parcel of the very sinew which binds and maintains the integrity of interpretation. The opportunities represented by this seemingly grandiose statement are at once mind-boggling and exhilarating in the highest degree.

Interpretation, particularly personal, live, people-based interpretation, can change lives. Formal education and life experiences unfortunately do not at present prepare people to make wise environmental decisions. 'Environment', for far too many of us, means only 'nature' or those things of biology – birds, bees and buffalo.

Our environment is in fact global or universal, and until we realize this and frame our appreciation, concerns, desires and requirements in a context that considers all living and non-living things in the universe as interrelated and mutually necessary for wholeness, our decisions in so-called environmental matters will be distorted by personal and cultural myopia and limited by a tunnel-visioned egocentrism. A vitally important role in people-based interpretation is to bridge the educational gap for the general public, not just for special groups enamoured and therefore limited by special interests such as a particular bird or tortoise or relic plant population. Interpreters must be what the author has for years referred to by the acronym JOATAMOM (pronounced Joet´-a-mom). They must be jacks of all trades and masters of most, and truly recognize and accept their roles as guardians of and spokespeople for our heritage. It is my most fervent desire that interpreters or, perhaps more important, those considering careers in interpretation, strive and look forward to becoming real contributors to the quality of existence

not just on this tiny globe but in the universe. May
they all become JOATAMOMs.

References

BETTINGHAUS, E. P. (1968) *Persuasive Communication*, Holt,
Rinehart and Winston, New York, London

GRATER, R. (1976) *The Interpreters Handbook*, Southwest
Parks and Monuments Association

HARRISON, R. P. (1974) *Beyond Words: an Introduction to
Nonverbal Communication*, Prentice-Hall, Englewood
Cliffs, NJ

KNAPP, M. L. (1972) *Nonverbal Communication in Human Interaction*, Holt, Rinehart and Winston, New York, London

MAKAY, J. J. and SAWYER, T. C. (1973) *Speech Communication
Now! An Introduction to Rhetorical Influences*, Charles E.
Merrill, Columbus, OH

MALANDRO, A., BARKER, L. L. and BARKER, D. A. (1989)
Nonverbal Communication, Random House, New York

SHARPE, G. W. (1982) *Interpreting the Environment*, Wiley,
New York

TILDEN, F. (1984) *Interpreting Our Heritage*, University of
North Carolina Press, Chapel Hill, NC

UZZELL, D. (1989) *Heritage Interpretation. Vol. 1: The Natural
and Built Environment. Vol. 2: The Visitor Experience*,
Belhaven Press, London, New York

Bibliography

CROSS, D. (1991) *Please Follow Me . . . : The Practical Tourist
Guide's Handbook* (4th edn), Wessexplore Tourist Service

HAM, S. (1992) *Environmental Interpretation: a Practical Guide for
People with Big Ideas and Small Budgets*, North American
Press

Case study 27.1

Bringing history alive: special events at English Heritage

Jonathan Griffin and Howard Giles

The programme of special events at English Heritage properties was started in 1985 and has developed to a point at which it is a major part of the promotional activity each year. While the main reasons for the programme have moved over time, the central thinking has not changed markedly. The programme responds to the old marketing saw that one should find ways of constantly re-presenting one's product.

In 1984, when English Heritage was founded, the properties were not well presented. The budgets available had meant that there were few modern exhibitions, there was little information for visitors, and the publications were fairly academic. There was also a rudimentary marketing effort with little in the way of advertising or promotion. Unlike a transient product such as a play, concert or festival, the properties were always there and the public were given few reasons as to why they should visit.

A review of the options for improving presentation highlighted the growth in the use of costumed interpreters which has been sweeping the USA. Historic attractions in North America were increasingly using first- or third-person interpretation (fully in role or costumed only) to bring history alive for their visitors. This suggested a more imaginative approach to interpretation for English Heritage than had so far been used in the UK.

The use of costumed interpreters offered a relatively quick and easy way of achieving two objectives. It could rapidly increase the level of explanation at properties and so avoid the high cost and long gestation periods necessary for exhibitions and displays. It could also give the marketing a boost by providing the all-important short-term promotional message which could be used to present a reason to make a visit: the call to action.

The analysis showed, however, that it would be economically impossible to provide costumed actors or interpreters at all properties or even at a range of the larger ones, without a very significant investment in recruitment and training. There were also questions about the degree to which the naturally reserved British would accept a technique which required a spontaneous interaction with a stranger.

An alternative was to make use of the major untapped cost-effective resource of historical re-enactment societies. If someone could coordinate their efforts into a coherent programme, then it would be possible to provide short-lived activities at a range of properties and so achieve the presentation and marketing objectives, albeit for much shorter periods. A small team was put together in 1986 to create and manage such a programme, under Howard Giles who had experience of re-enactments and was at the time working on other presentation projects. Having in-house experience significantly shortened the inevitable learning curve. In the first year there were three events, mostly held in the pouring rain.

In the early years there were some experiments with large-scale events such as the major battle re-enactments by the American British Brigade who visited in 1987. Although they helped to establish a high profile for the programme, they proved very resource hungry and were prone to much greater financial risks than a broader programme of less high-profile events. An alternative solution was used in 1988 when a package of activities was combined and taken to properties along the south coast of England to mark the anniversary of the Spanish Armada. This saved set-up costs and yet, by touring, ensured maximum coverage.

Initially there were few good-quality amateur re-enactment groups available. Whether as a result of cause or effect, the number and quality of groups have increased over the last few years, as has the breadth of the displays they offer. Many now provide very detailed and historically sincere presentations of particular periods and events. Many of their members travel thousands of miles each summer to participate in displays with fellow enthusiasts. Professional groups are used sparingly as they tend to be expensive, but they are used for small events where there is considerable reliance on a few individuals, or for activities such as falconry and story-telling for which the skills are less readily available from amateur groups.

When setting the programme each year, the aim is to maintain a mix of activities ranging across historical periods, theme and activity; music, song, dance, plays and picnics are all included as well as military, civilian and child-oriented events. In the early days, some critics were concerned that the programme consisted mainly of battles and other military re-enactments. This was partly a function of the property portfolio of English Heritage which favoured castles, but was also influenced by commercial factors and the groups of performers available. As military-oriented societies have broadened their displays to include camp followers, so their displays have moved away from physical conflict towards the re-creation of drill manoeuvres, off-duty and civilian life.

The symbiosis between the growth of re-enactment societies and the English Heritage events programme has continued behind the scenes. Early in 1992, English Heritage was pleased to be involved in the creation of the National Association of Re-Enactment Societies (NARES). This brought together many of the major societies to discuss current concerns and to share experiences. This was a significant move as some of the societies had occasionally shown mutual suspicion, making multi-society displays difficult to coordinate. The creation of NARES has helped to change this and mutual cooperation is now the norm.

It was a compliment to Howard Giles and his team that many living history groups have adopted the English Heritage authenticity guidelines for their displays. These standards were developed over time and go into minute detail about anachronisms such as the use of rings, spectacles and watches. They also set very high standards for replica clothing. The benefit has been an all-round improvement in authenticity standards, not only at English Heritage events but at other shows too.

The events are often referred to disparagingly as jousts. While perhaps sometimes historically correct, the term is used pejoratively to discuss something more akin to a Disney film than an attempt at authenticity. It is sometimes difficult to make this subtle but important difference clear in promotional material. Where possible the existence of, and adherence to, authenticity standards is used to demonstrate that these are authoritative displays within the constraints of the twentieth century, and not fantasy history.

Experience has also led to other improvements. In the past the re-enactors were left to create their own story-lines and displays. These did not always put the needs of the visitor first. As displays became larger, often involving several groups, so carefully planned display scenarios have been developed, often orchestrated by walkie-talkies carefully disguised from the eyes of the audience. Perhaps the most complicated of these was the superb re-enactment of the Battle of Hastings in 1991, which involved no fewer than five re-enactment groups, 300 infantry and 35 full mounted cavalry, and which lasted for over 45 minutes. There was a real thrill in seeing a re-created combat on the very spot where it actually happened.

Over the years the emphasis of the programme has shifted from pure interpretation to marketing and commercial objectives as pressure has increased on English Heritage resources generally. But these pressures have not excluded very small events or enhancements. The most famous of these delights is the medieval music of Hautbois, a husband and wife duo who travel around the properties making music, working with schools and charming all with whom they come into contact. Often the first a visitor knows of their presence is the sight of the Hautbois tent, the beat of a drum or the grind of a hurdy-gurdy.

Measurement of the programme is an important part of the annual review. Each event is assessed on its ability to attract additional visitors and income, and for its success in attracting extra publicity for the property and for English heritage. This is used in planning the future year's programme.

By 1993 the programme had grown to include over 200 events on 50 different themes at 70 properties. Titles are self-explanatory: The Fury of the Norsemen; Roma Victrix – Romans and Celts from the Fall of Maiden Castle; Everyday Life in the Time of Richard III; Life in a Medieval Household; Music and Archery from the Age of Henry VIII; The Bard's Best Bits; The Civil War Comes to Kenilworth Castle; Falconry; Story-telling; Three Comic Interludes; Milling Day; Fourth National Longbow Championship; and even A Grand Catastrophe.

Although, in the initial stages, the programme tried to concentrate only on activities which were historically relevant to the properties in question, in recent years teddy bears' picnics and commercial craft fairs have been included where the properties can be effectively used as sympathetic backdrops.

The programme is now an integral part of the marketing effort. It provides an important reason to visit and, despite the occasional thunderstorm, earns its keep and is a vital source of new members. More importantly, it also achieves another objective, for the number of visitors to properties with events goes up, not just on the day itself, but in the weeks following. It is not clear whether these extra visitors are people who have visited the event coming back for another look on a quiet day, or whether it is a different group of people who have heard that the property is an interesting place to visit. Either way, the events programme is managing to persuade more people to discover the beauty, fascination and interest there is in the built heritage which is all around us; and that is the true aim of English Heritage.

Case study 27.2

Illustrations and observations from Wigan and Beamish

Peter Lewis

Let us begin with a seeming heresy. I do not believe that people-based interpretation is necessarily the highest or the best form of interpretation in museums. Nor is it always the most desirable and the best use of the visitor's time. This may appear to be a strange comment from the past Director of Wigan Pier and the present Director of Beamish, given that both institutions use either professional actors or trained interpreters as their principal means of informing visitors.

People are neither better nor worse than labels, interactive computers, publications or any of the other means employed by museums and their designers. They are, however, different. People do not, despite the fears of some museum professionals, challenge the integrity of artefacts or debase the principles of collection management. People are of particular use to certain kinds of museums, especially those concerned with social history. In other kinds of museums or galleries the use of people can be at least inappropriate, and at worst infuriating.

At Wigan in 1985, my colleagues and I built a complex which included a small museum which attempted to explain what life was like in that part of Lancashire in 1900. Some tableaux combined objects and machinery with static life-sized models. In one area we created a slide and sound display which told the story of a local pit disaster. The images were striking; the voices were disembodied. In other locations we decided that we needed people: no other medium would work as effectively. Thus, in the schoolroom or the colliery cottage, visitors met people in costume who spoke to them in the first person, who guided them through lessons or in paying their respects to a bereaved family. In other open areas actors playing the parts of market traders, mill workers or travelling salesmen spoke to visitors as they moved around the museum. All of these different techniques worked well but only after extensive training and experiment. Seven professional actors, controlled by a resident artistic director, formed a company. Each actor had a minimum contract of twelve months, the minimum period that I believe is needed to give a sense of purpose and time to develop skills.

We quickly learned to recruit a specific kind of actor, one drawn more naturally into the world of theatre-in-education than that of the West End stage or of television commercials. In order to achieve a high standard the company needed to be a permanent one rather than one from outside brought in for special performances. The missionary zeal of a museum-based acting company had to be acknowledged. The skills of acting, particularly in confined spaces without the boundaries of curtains or a proscenium arch, are every bit as professionally valid as those of curators. The intensity of regular performance and the consequent exhaustion was immediately apparent. Actors had to be carefully rotated, rested and moved around. They needed the challenge and the refreshment of a wider variety of roles than we had originally planned. Like trainee teachers they had to build up a resistance to child-borne illnesses. Scripts were not sacrosanct. A core script was only a starting point. They had to be free to adapt, within the bounds of historical accuracy and good taste. A repertory system evolved. They performed in the first person and established an important contact with visitors who needed the security of prior information. 'When we enter the classroom, I expect you to stand until told to sit and work' . . . 'It's very good of you, friends and neighbours of the family, to come and pay your respects to my late father.'

At Beamish, though the interpretative staff are not the product of acting schools, the same basic rules apply. Local residents, well trained and highly motivated, people the many period buildings of this open-air museum site. They wear costume appropriate to their status and role and speak with their own distinctive idiom and accent, in either the third or the first person, as appropriate to visitors' needs. Some staff are permanent; others are seasonal. Many return each year. All receive training before Easter and their performances are monitored daily by area supervisors and the Keeper of Interpretation, a senior member of the curatorial staff. Until four years ago interpretation staff were under control of the museum's marketing department. After some debate they became the responsibility of the curatorial team. This enhancement of their role was, and still is, intellectually important. It reinforced the museum's belief that the interpreters are there to provide both education and entertainment, not merely the latter. An additional bonus of curatorial supervision is that it brings curators daily into contact with visitors and staff. The use of costumed interpreters also obviates the need for uniformed security staff. There are no peak-capped warders at Beamish. Indeed, it is important that there is a clear distinction between interpreters and other staff. Admissions, retailing and catering staff should *not* wear period costume. The visitor needs to understand that all the people in costume have a specific interpretative role. The costume is not some nostalgic decoration.

The principal criticism of people-based interpretation is that, unlike labels or fixed forms of information, the performance can be variable or even erratic. This is a matter for management. When the system works, it works well. Complicated or subtle information can be conveyed both quickly and competently by people. The dangers inherent in personal interpretation are positive virtues. We, as audiences, don't expect safety in the theatre, cinema, concert hall or opera house. Why should we in a museum? People are a means of avoiding artistic blandness or neutrality. They can, in the original meaning of the word, be *provocative*, able to draw out or stimulate thought from visitors.

There exists at Beamish a second form of interpretation, one not building based. We regularly create events, repeated throughout the year, which move across the site. Our own staff, plus members of the Friends of the Museum, local dramatic societies and students create suffragette rallies, election hustings, temperance meetings or chapel anniversary celebrations. These are difficult to organize but eminently worthwhile. They enable the museum to engage topics for a few days that are not sustainable throughout the year. They provide variety and also allow the museum, by the use of historical precedents, to comment or provoke opinion on modern topics. This is a valid part of *interpretation*, well sustained by the strands of meaning that form that word and principle.

An interpreter, my dictionary tells me, is not only one who, in a neutral sense, translates one language, one jargon or one technique to another. More importantly, it is one who helps to explain or make clear. The most archaic meaning is perhaps worth rediscovery. An interpreter, I understand, is a 'descendant of Mercury, a special messenger who makes known the will of the gods' – or even, dare it be said, the thoughts of that lowest level of the pantheon, the museum director. It's her role – or his – to decide what level or tone of personal interpretation is acceptable within her or his own culture. Much of the North American style outlined in Chapter 27 by Paul Risk might, as yet, seem gauche or 'over the top' to northern European visitors. Public tastes change; people's background knowledge of their own history and heritage alters, or may be warped by other cultural activities like period films, plays or historical novels. The personal interpreter is one increasingly valuable way of constantly updating both material and its presentation.

Case study 27.3

The Young National Trust Theatre

Sally Woodhead

The Young National Trust Theatre (YNTT), sponsored by Barclays Bank PLC, is the National Trust's professional theatre-in-education company. Established in 1977, the YNTT tours nine National Trust properties each year with participatory, history-based productions. It also runs 'Performing Arts in Trust' residences: site-specific theatre projects which use a National Trust property as the focus for creative work across the performing arts (*Figure 27.1*). In an average season the YNTT works with over 7000 schoolchildren.

The aims of the YNTT's artistic policy are as follows:

(1) to introduce children to important elements in their common cultural heritage, using National Trust properties as a tangible and evocative resource;
(2) to give children a greater understanding of historical issues;
(3) to create theatre-in-education programmes which work across the performing arts to give children hands-on experience of drama, music and dance;
(4) to develop theatre-in-education productions with a high regard for historical accuracy;
(5) to link productions to the National Curriculum whenever appropriate;
(6) to encourage, whenever practically possible, the involvement of children with special needs in productions;
(7) to act as a means of welcoming young people to National Trust properties and as an incentive for them to return in the future.

How we meet our objectives

The hallmark of the YNTT's work is participatory theatre. The children are asked to join the production with a role which they have been preparing in school (this preparation will often also involve the making of

Figure 27.1 Lanhydrock 'Performing Arts in Trust' residency (courtesy of the National Trust)

a basic costume). The nature of the role will vary depending on the historical theme and the dramatic structure of the piece, but in all cases it should enable the child to take on the function of a person from the past: for example, a nineteenth century philanthropist, a pupil from a village school in 1927 or a member of a village community in 1558. The aim is to give children a dramatic function which they are able to combine with their own intellectual and emotional experiences of the 1990s to help them understand the motivations of people in the past. The experience of working in role is most successful when the children are familiar with the historical context through good preparation in school.

Once the actors have helped the children to feel secure in the production, it is structured so that they are able to participate in a number of activities relevant to the plot, to meet characters who represent different political, religious or personal points of view on the issues in question, and eventually to make a decision based on their experiences within the show. This decision will sometimes dictate the outcome of the play. The children work as a full group (65 maximum) and in subgroups, both inside and outside the house (*Figure 27.2*). Performances take place when the house is both closed and open to the public.

From its inception, each production is a carefully researched venture. The Artistic Director carries out detailed research into the period in question before writing the piece. Actors are expected to continue this research into their own character during rehearsal and throughout the tour. A *Teachers' Resource Book* complements each production and includes many primary sources. A briefing course is run at each venue by the Artistic Director so that teachers are in tune with the aims and objectives of the piece.

YNTT productions link in well with the requirements of National Curriculum history core study units for the 7–11 and 12–14 age groups. The YNTT's work is particularly useful in the teaching of history AT 2 which looks at interpretations of history. It also supports history AT 1, 'knowledge and understanding of history'. The work is closely allied to English AT 1 with its emphasis on speaking and listening skills. The inclusion of dance, music and costume making ensures that a performance is truly a cross-curricular experience (*Figure 27.3*).

Figure 27.2 Young National Trust Theatre at Polesden Lacey, Surrey (photo: Homer Sykes)

Figure 27.3 An endless maze, Osterley, 1992 (photo: Kim Williams)

Successful interpretation

We believe that the company's work is an interesting example of good practice in people-based interpretative work in historic buildings. Through the powerful learning tool of theatre, the YNTT's work is a valuable resource for giving schoolchildren a greater understanding of history and a way of encouraging them to build a personal link with their heritage. Teachers' evaluation of the company's work is extremely positive. This is borne out by long waiting lists for places and a high percentage of repeat bookings. Experts in the field of history through drama are also supportive of the work.

Details and acknowledgements

For more details on the YNTT please contact: Sally Woodhead, Administrator YNTT, Sutton House, 2–4 Homerton High Street, Hackney, E9 6JQ; telephone 081 986 0242; fax 081 985 2343.

For details on the National Trust's other education work please contact: Patricia Lankester, Education Manager, The National Trust, 36 Queen Anne's Gate, London, SW1H 9AS; telephone 071 222 9251; fax 071 222 5097.

The YNTT is sponsored for £450,000 for the 1989-95 seasons by Barclays Bank as part of its wide-ranging programme of community support.

28

Design-based interpretation

Giles Velarde, with a contribution by Rosemary Allen

It is important not to ignore the role of designers as interpreters. Design is creative problem solving; the visual or design problems associated with communication were first confronted in the design of typefaces for printing. The evolution of the handwritten word to the printed word is not relevant here, but the more recent evolution in modern printing design and technology is worth studying and there are many books devoted to it. The evolution of various other communication techniques is relevant, as communication is clearly not restricted to the printed word.

In recent years designers have evolved, invented or pirated from other disciplines a huge variety of sometimes very complex means of bridging the gap between the source and the recipient of information. There is no such thing as good, bad, more or less effective techniques; they can only be evaluated in context and they cannot with any validity be compared with each other.

Any compilation of communication techniques is not a demonstration of the work of a designer; it is simply a list of the tools he uses. The techniques themselves are usually the work of skilled craftsmen and technicians responding to the problems defined and set out by designers. The work of the designer is the definition of the problem, the successful planning of the enterprise, the use, evolution and extension of communication techniques to create the most effective interpretation, and finally the detailed drawing up and supervision of the installation. Interpretation is of course simply a style or type of communication.

Exhibitions, displays and visitor centres are the usual vehicles for communication techniques, but there is always a primary decision to be taken: is an exhibition the most effective way of interpreting? There should be no inevitability about this. Exhibitions and visitor centres should not be allowed to spring up all over the place simply because nobody has given sufficient early thought to the problem. It must be allowed that many

heritage attractions should be left to speak for themselves. It should also be recognized that many heritage sites have been ruined by visitor centres and many an exhibition has been mounted that did nothing at all for the subject it was supposed to interpret. There are places, and there should be no fear of recognizing it, from which the interpretative designer and his sponsor should be firmly excluded. It is therefore obviously sound practice for a designer to be consulted early enough for him to have some input into the decision whether or not to proceed, and it is to be hoped that he will be sufficiently professional not to recommend a design solution simply because he needs the work.

Assuming that due thought has been given to the above, it is possible to go on to discuss the techniques currently at the disposal of the designer. It is necessary to advance cautiously into this area. There are dangers. The first is the word 'currently', which clearly implies the most modern, and in today's world the most modern will be out of date before this pen leaves the paper. The second danger is to assume that the most modern is the best. This is certainly not so; the best solution to any problem is the most suitable one, even if it is 500 years old. The third danger is listing these things at all. There is a real risk of sponsors demanding such and such a technique, a ride here, an audio-visual show there, simply because they like it and have seen it to be effective elsewhere. Effectiveness cannot be measured without a total understanding of the problem as it was originally presented, nor can it be measured by the local response of a solitary visitor. A technique, as will be demonstrated in Chapter 30, can only be evaluated successfully relative to individual contexts and a variety of visitor types. It is sadly recognized that some readers will pursue this list, select their favourite techniques and find a designer to execute their preconceived notions. This may all sound paranoid, but in the writer's experience and that of many other interpretative designers, one of the biggest problems can be the weaning of the sponsor from his or her ideas of the design solution, long before the problem has been properly defined. With the above three caveats in mind, it is possible to proceed timidly.

The printed word: labels, captions and graphic panels

It is important at this stage to make some kind of differentiation between label, a caption and a graphic panel. A label is the descriptive information alongside an object or view. A caption is generally part of a graphic panel and is a piece of descriptive text or the short explanation of an illustration or photograph. A graphic panel is a board containing interpretative text, supported by illustrations.

Because heritage design is largely involved with place, any associated written information is generally exposed at least to touch and as often as not to the weather. It is frequently unsupervised, as is the case with wayside panels and direction signs. The simplest approach to communication of a handwritten label, still to be found in small rural or provincial museums, is therefore best avoided. The same applies to typewritten labels. Clearly printed labels are best, and it is important to remember that these should be of a size and style that can be read relative to the object or view they interpret. It is also important to remember that interpretation is not the place for a qualitative description. Phrases such as 'this beautiful room' or 'this delightful view' are subjective and should be avoided. The visiting public is not travelling about the country to be told what is beautiful; they should be given the concise relevant information and be allowed to make up their own minds.

Economical writing will not only be less condescending; it will also be shorter and therefore more likely to be read. It will also be more likely to be read if it is in short paragraphs. It is dangerous to make rules, but a metre square panel should not generally contain more than 100 words of descriptive text, together with 12- to 24-word picture captions as and where necessary.

Another aspect of the written material is that it should be as jargon-free as possible. In this regard the 'interpreter' designer is useful, as his ignorance of the subject in detail can help the sponsor to avoid text that the designer does not understand. The designer is in fact the interpreter between the source of the information and the visiting public. Yet by 'understanding' the subject the designer can perform an almost journalistic function, assisting in the production of information readily understood by the visitor. There are in fact professional script-writers and, if in doubt or on adequately funded projects, it is well for such people to be employed. They can only work effectively if they are part of the interpretative team, working with both the source of the information and the designers of the presentation.

In any means of communication the disabled must be considered, and they are dealt with in several chapters in this manual. It is dangerous however to forget the minor and much ignored disabilities of the middle-aged and elderly. Bifocal spectacles present a real problem for the wearer if the graphic design of written information panels or labels is inadequate. A typeface which is too small and too distant for the bottom lens is probably going to be too small for the top lens at any distance.

Most labels and captions are printed and then reproduced photographically for use. This is because the photographic papers and plastics are more durable and more easily handled and bonded than ordinary paper. Another advantage is that the photographic negative can be kept for producing replacements, and it also means that colour can be used. Screens for screen printing are made photographically, and methods of bonding printed information into plastic or metal panels usually involve photographic or screening processes. These last techniques are improving and modifying all the time. Some hand techniques can be both very durable and visually appropriate for certain circumstances. Etched laminated plastics come into this category, as do engraved or carved wood and cold (resin-based) or hot castings. Clearly such durable treatments have evolved for use out of doors and unsupervised.

The spoken word: recorded commentaries and descriptions

There are several ways of transmitting such communications, but it is necessary before discussing the means to examine the production. No matter how mellifluous, articulate and cheap the resident academic might be, it is essential always to use professionals for reading commentaries, and professionals to record them. If a project of any sort is to include a sound commentary, this is usually produced first, and then such images as are to be used are matched or timed to it at a later date. A commentary could be drafted by the subject specialist, but it is wise to have it rewritten by a professional script-writer and then checked and approved by the specialist. The reason for this is that the written and spoken word are very different; a writer who is trained to write for actors will understand breathing and timing and will avoid tongue-twisters. It is best to employ an actor to speak the lines rather than a commentator or radio/TV journalist. The latter can be used but actors usually have a far more realistic impact; it is after all their job to imitate reality successfully. If the commentary is produced in a recording studio it will have all the advantages one might expect: multiple tracking for stereo and signal impulses (to activate special effects etc.), ease of re-recording of copying, good and relevant acoustics – and, where necessary, easy dubbing of background sound effects or music.

It is a truism that in every area of exhibition production it is by far the best practice to employ the relevant professionals. When amateurs are used for commentaries it is painfully obvious – even more irritatingly so when warding or museum staff have to listen to the same grisly recording hour after hour, day after day. This human consideration is highly relevant in the choice of sound replay systems and is one of many factors involved in the decision to use either headphones or loudspeakers.

Sound is a very potent creator of atmosphere, and often without the spoken word the right sound can be marvellously evocative. Simple, effective but possibly corny examples are bird sounds in a rural setting or a hubbub of voices in a reconstructed street scene. A tape created by actors and special-effects experts of a battle overlooking a battlefield (Battle, near Hastings) is a striking example. The means of conveying the sounds are many and, along with most other special effects, are continually evolving.

Sound for the individual

This can be conveyed on a cassette tape in a hired or bought personal stereo (it is possible to buy a simple personal stereo for under £10). These systems use either a simple headset or a hook-on ear jack. The other methods currently in use are the buried induction loop and the infrared transmitter/receiver. These provide sound specific to the area into which they are carried by the visitor (Bayeux Tapestry). All these systems have their advantages and disadvantages. The advantage of the cassette (unless it is switched off by an impulse on leaving one area, to be switched on by the visitor when joining another) is that it is under the control of the wearer. The advantage of the loop/infrared system is that a visitor, and therefore the visitor flow, can be controlled by the programme. These latter systems are generally contained in a baton about 300 mm long with a small individual speaker at the head, and the baton is held to the ear by the carrier as he/she walks around the site. The cassette is pocketed, clipped on or shoulder hung and is stopped and started by the visitors as they progress through the tour, indoor or outdoor, described on the tape. There are numerous permutations of these systems: one advantage common to all is that different languages can be supplied and indeed different levels of information, for instance for children and adults. The disadvantage of all of these individual systems is that if the individual using them is hard of hearing or simply brutish, the loud squeaking emanating from them can be pretty irritating to the visitors, with or without their own sound system. Theft is avoided on

the hired cassette system by supplying players whose motors operate at a different speed from those of normal players, rendering both the cassette and the player useless under other circumstances.

Clearly these individual systems are ideal for large sites, campuses and exhibitions but they can also be used in auditoriums, especially if choice of languages is to be offered (D-Day, Bayeux). Another system of individual sound is the use of telephone handsets alongside specific exhibits. Anything up to four handsets could be provided around an exhibit. They too could offer a choice of languages and academic levels or types of description. Such handsets are vulnerable to vandalism on some inner-city or unsupervised sites, but the sound can be recorded into solidstate or CDs and be very durable.

Group sound

If this is adjacent to an exhibit or view, it should be localized using special speakers and sound absorbing surfaces to avoid too much irritating sound spillage. Again, this is an area of rapid development. Generally group sound should be in some kind of auditorium. With the right loudspeakers, top-quality replay systems and professionally made recordings, these can be as effective as the best theatre systems. Since most heritage sites seem to cater for groups of 50 people (a coachful) or less, this translates to five rows of ten seats or stools and does not require a great deal of space. The length of programmes designed for such audiences is important and is relative to the comfort of the auditorium. It is dangerous to expect visitors to stand up unaided and pay attention for more than three or four minutes. If a simple or crude leaning rail is provided then perhaps eight minutes are acceptable; with stools, up to twelve minutes; and with luxury seating, as long as is required. The real controlling factor is how long it is wise or feasible to keep the visitor in one place. Luxury seating is likely to be a bad idea, as it might encourage a visitor to go through the programme more than once or even to nod off. If it is comfortable, dark and unsupervised, then anything could happen.

Replay systems for the above

Solid-state systems are currently in use for short sound tracks. They are very reliable, are expensive and give an instant repeat facility, as opposed to all types of tape system which have to rewind to the nearest start point of the programme, sometimes quite a long time. CDs are also very dependable and give almost instant replay; they are currently cheaper than solid state. Tapes and tape players cost little and are still widely available, but they are not as reliable or durable as solid state and CDs which, with proper maintenance, are more or less indestructible.

Images

Having discussed words, both printed and spoken, it is time to discuss images as a means of communication. In future paragraphs, images and words will be mixed, but it is important at this stage to consider images separately as they are of real value on their own in the process of communication.

Still images

The commonest methods of reproducing still images are identical to those used for reproducing the printed word; in other words, photographically based techniques. For outdoor use photographs, which fade rapidly in direct light, would be changed into screened images using durable coloured inks, although they would lose quite a lot in quality in this process. Such reproductions, screened on to special materials, can be bonded into cold or hot plastic finishes.

On panels containing a number of still pictures, it is wise not to mix colour and black and white, as each shows up the weakness of the other.

The importance of multiple printed images on a panel as a communication medium is best discussed relative to their placement and their relationship to each other. The pictures should be chosen to create a coordinated panel. Most photographs taken by professionals are well composed in that they draw the eye to the focal or important part of the picture. A panel should also be well composed and it is the job of the graphic designer to do just that. Pictures of vessels or animals are often directional and they can be used to lead the eye and the visitor along a path of information; so can a panel. One-off panels should clearly be sited at a place and height where they can be seen easily. They should be oriented horizontally rather than vertically to allow for the maximum number of people to see them at one time.

The majority of pictures will need captions, but many groups of pictures can tell a story without text: 'before' and 'after' photographs, line diagrams or photographs of stages of construction – there are many examples. It is a sublime and proper means of communication to use such sequences with perhaps a simple explanatory heading or short introductory text. It is dangerous to assume that words are always necessary. They are not.

A back-lit transparency is another means of presenting a photographic image. This produces probably the best result but is limited in use to indoors and low-light areas. The light boxes and the complexity of detailing around them are generally too risky for use long term and out of doors, but there are exceptions, generally exploited and maintained by the advertising industry (see section below on Rotosigns) who can probably afford it.

Another category of printed image is the giant blow-up. Again these start off as a photographic negative. Greatly enlarged photographs can be mounted on to walls or boards, and there is effectively no limit to their size. The photograph is printed on to rolls of coated paper approximately a metre wide by limitless length so there will always be joins at regular intervals. Another technique (Scanachrome) starts with a transparency of the image required. This is read by a computer and transferred to a roll of almost any sort of fabric using a series of tiny paint guns controlled by the computer. The advantage of this technique is that it can produce a large image on to non-reflective materials and on to fabrics which can be stretched or hung over voids. The disadvantage of all blow-ups is the degraded image which appears at normal viewing distance as a series of dots. Such blow-ups are best used to create atmosphere and effects, and are optimally viewed under these circumstances from many metres away.

It is often the case that a number of images are required in the same confined space. There are several established techniques for doing this, though designers and technicians are always coming up with new methods, and some are pretty crude. The most effective methods are as follows.

Back-projected slides

A number of slides, generally contained in a full Kodak carousel (i.e. 80 slides or an even fraction of that number, repeated to avoid blank spaces and prolong the life of the slides) are projected from behind on to a ground glass or plastic screen. There is some loss of picture quality and slides do fade if they are continually recycling through the system. The best thing is to use a projector with automatic lamp change, and, using a visitor response system, to show the slides only when there is someone there to see them.

A disk-fed TV monitor

Laser vision disks, designed and made only for industrial uses, hold an astonishing number of images which can be used either as stills or as frames for a moving image or film. In this context the image will inevitably be TV shaped; the images are good by contemporary TV standards but not as good as slides.

Rotosign

This system of French design uses a number (depending on the size of the unit) of top-quality transparencies taped into a sandwich of clear and opal plastic film. This is then wound on to drums and mechanically rolled past the back-lit viewing aperture, stopping a short time for each exposure. Transparencies of course give the best possible image, but complex mechanical devices are prone to break down if they are not regularly supervised and maintained.

Rotagraphics

These are metal frames containing a large number of three-sided bars like Toblerones; these are laid flat whilst an image is glued on to each of the three sides. Of necessity the images are cut at each division, which produces a severely degraded image, but with simple images or at a great distance this does not really matter. The bars are revolved mechanically and the effect can be quite dramatic, producing three totally different images in the same place.

Other systems for producing a variety of large images in one place do exist, but they come and go with recessions in the advertising industry and are generally too expensive for humble heritage and museum folk.

Moving images

Under normal circumstances the best place for a moving image is in the cinema or on the TV at home. In recent years, as means of communication have proliferated, film and TV have been used more and more in heritage centres, exhibitions and museums. It is very important to remember that they should only be used as a carefully considered part of the type of simple story that a heritage centre can tell. They should not be the 'be all and end all' of such communication. If they are, then the visitor centre might seem hardly necessary and TV advertising or programming should have been the communication option selected in the first place.

In the heritage circumstances, reality is far better than a movie of it. People will always stop and watch a film, but that does not necessarily justify its use: most men will stop and watch a pretty girl taking her clothes off but that does not justify such activity for selling cars. Movement attracts the eye and a film or programme, whilst attractive to some, is precisely the reason others left home to visit a heritage site.

The same time restrictions apply to moving images as apply to slide and audio sequences. Moving images can be produced and shown on film, but there are so many disadvantages to this in comparison with TV screen or projection that it is hardly worth considering. The disadvantages are that film fades and breaks and projector lamps go, projectors break down without continuous and careful maintenance, and continuous loops of film are complex and expensive. The only real advantage is the first-class picture quality. A TV screen is quite good enough for most circumstances and, if fed by a disk player, is so reliable that it is worth adapting the circumstances to suit is use.

Under very controlled lighting conditions TV projection is of value; the projectors are large and costly, but as reliable as a TV set and they use the same source. They have a comparatively limited viewing angle for the screen and certain screen materials are better than others. White emulsion paint gives the widest viewing angle but special screen materials give a sharper image.

They are best used under stable and fairly dark circumstances. Dealers will happily give demonstrations of such equipment and it is best to have a good-quality light meter handy when testing, so that comparisons of circumstances can be made. It is possible to project on to a very large screen providing there is sufficient viewing distance; if too short, all that can be seen is lines. In reality they are at their best in a purpose-designed auditorium.

If a TV screen with programme is placed in a display or a corner of a room, it will draw a crowd and that crowd will form an obstruction. The old designer's maxim, 'if in doubt, leave it out', is a healthy point of view.

Auditoriums

Whilst a hierarchy of communication has been discussed so far, it is pointless to avoid the fact that there is sometimes a genuine need for an auditorium for a slide show, film or multi-screen TV show of one sort or another, or indeed for a series or sequence of shows. Clearly the specific circumstances will dictate the type and duration of the show, but there are standards and specifications designed originally for the use of architects, which should be studied. These relate to safety precautions, viewing angles and heights, and circulation, exits and entrances.

Slide shows are almost always cheaper than films to produce and can be very effective. Again, they must be professionally done at every stage: scripting, acting, special effects, photography, programming and timing. There are many excellent production companies for such shows and, when mixed with imaginatively designed auditoriums with revolving seating, disappearing screens, laser shows, dry ice, and first-rate sound effects coming through first-rate sound systems, they can be a powerful (but expensive) attraction in their own right. The public generally refers to them as 'films' though of course they are not. They do however require a sophisticated approach to maintenance.

Films, either normal or animated, are familiar to all of us and we all have a point of view about them. Because they are commonplace they are less of an event than an audio-visual show but imaginatively presented they too can be most effective. Existing films can of course be hired or purchased, but to make a film especially costs a great deal of money – many times the cost of an audio-visual show.

Film, and more especially TV, is widely recognized as being the most powerful means of communication, but it cannot replace the pleasure to be found in the real thing. An actual dungeon, burial mound or eighteenth century room will have a charm and an atmosphere that cannot be captured artificially. It is dangerous to mix the two too closely: the real space of distance and time is needed between reality and its filmed interpretation and this should be given careful consideration in the design and layout of the visitor attraction. There are, however, some mixtures that can be most attractive. Two ingredients, sound and two-dimensional images, have already been discussed. The third, most appropriately, is the third dimension.

Models, reconstructions and dioramas

There has always been a peculiar charm to models. Everybody is stopped in their tracks by a well made miniature of reality; railway sets, doll's houses, toy soldiers, dolls, model boats and cars all have the power to attract and hold our attention. There are many psychological explanations for this phenomenon but the simple truth is that we generally like them and they make us feel good. The manipulation of these simple responses is therefore common sense provided that there is the money, skill and time to do it properly and effectively.

Models

These are familiar to all of us; the better the model, the more powerful the message and the longer the time spent looking at it. Small-scale models of large events such as battles (the Battle of Hastings, at Battle) can, when related to the actual scenery they interpret, be most effective. The days of the fragile model of this type are gone and first-class reproductions, painted in durable paints and cast in glass-reinforced plastic, will only need the simplest weather protection. Larger-scale models such as cut-aways of mills or castles will generally be more fragile, often being made from the actual materials used in the constructions they represent, and they should be well lit in showcases. Preferably they should be viewable from 360 degrees and a slow revolve can often enhance their display, but it should be made possible to stop the revolve for close, detailed examination.

Working models
These take the attraction of a model one stage further, for miniature and precise movement is even more fascinating than the static model. All models are costly and working models obviously even more so. They are generally so skilfully engineered that they give very little trouble, but anything with moving parts needs careful maintenance. Some models are activated to demonstrate natural phenomena; a model in the late lamented Geological Museum tilted up sections of the earth's crust under Britain to show its structure.

Interactive displays
These are more appropriate to the museum context but there may well be occasions when some kind of visitor participation and interaction, other than the

occasional button, is considered to be a useful part of an interpretative display. Interactives are a special subject in their own right, but personal studies of the Exploratory in Bristol and the Launch Pad at the Science Museum in London are worth while. They are not new; the Science Museum was using them in its basement in the 1930s and the Deutsches Museum in Munich probably ten years before that. In the second half of this century they have really taken off as a means of communicating the complexity of science and nature. Formative work was done by James Gardner at Evoluon, Philips Industries' permanent exhibition at Eindhoven in Holland. The Exploratorium in San Francisco and the Ontario Science Centre in Toronto shortly followed. The Ontario Science Centre's travelling Science Circus was clearly the inspiration for Launch Pad. There are companies which specialize in the design and production of interactive displays.

Reconstructions

This is the name given to skilfully constructed, full-size models of places or events. The most common sort of reconstruction is that of an interior scene – a chemist's shop, a peasant's living quarters, a Bronze Age tomb. The more exact the briefing information and the more skilled the construction, the better it is. When figures are included in the reconstruction, care has to be taken to ensure that they are of the highest quality. Many a reasonable reconstruction has been ruined by window dummies that have been begged or borrowed from a local shop. They are made for a completely different purpose and should *never* be used. The best advice is to use a first-rate sculptor to produce accurate figures. If a good-quality figure is beyond the project budget, then do not have a figure at all, or use a simple wicker or wire frame to carry any clothing that is important and relevant to the display.

Animated figures
Whilst talking of figures it makes sense to mention what Walt Disney called animatronics – animated figures. These are always very expensive, so there is no point in embarking on a project that is to involve them until guide prices have been sought. A full-size, full-height figure with moving arms, hands, hips, lips, eyes and head (but at least one anchored foot) is the most expensive of all. A seated figure that only moves arms, head and lips is probably half the price, simply because it is much easier to make. All of them involve sophisticated mechanical and electronic programming technology. There are two or three different types of animated figure, so it is best to shop around for the one that suits the purse and the purpose best. Of course miniature figures can be used but unfortunately reducing the size of the technology is only likely to increase the cost. Sound tracks for animated figures are again

usually made first and the models' movements are synchronized to the track.

Dioramas

These can, when well made, be a very effective form of miniaturized reconstruction, giving a sometimes marvellous impression of three-dimensional space and reality. They consist of a painted view, with all the drawn perspectives you might expect from a painting, but painted on to a relief model of the scene with modelled false perspectives. The fact that they are three-dimensional creates the illusion of reality very powerfully. They can be built with actual reality in the foreground, before the false perspective begins. For instance it is possible to look through an actual window on to a completely modelled and painted interior or exterior.

A simple form of diorama is called a flat-plane diorama. This uses a series of flat cut-outs of painted reproductions of interiors or exteriors which reduce in size while moving further from the eye of the visitor, in exactly the same way as a set for a ballet or opera is constructed from 'flats'. Another attractive way of achieving a three-dimensional image is with glass paintings. Here a series of images is painted on separate sheets of glass and placed one behind the other; the images are painted on the reverse side. With skilful painting and lighting, the end result can convey depth in a subtle and effective way.

All dioramas, in employing a false perspective, demand fairly precise viewing positions. They are generally constructed around an eye (or horizon) level of approximately 1.64 m; if a child, a shorter adult or a wheelchair-bound person is to get the same effect as the average adult, then clearly a ramp or step must be constructed to facilitate this.

Pepper's ghosts

Using slides and cross-fade it is relatively easy to show one image, perhaps 'before', merging into another 'after' image. It is more complex but still possible to do this in three dimensions using a Pepper's ghost. This consists of one skilfully made model remaining static in one position, face on to the viewer, whilst another model, exactly matching but of a period say 300 years later, is superimposed over it. This can only be accurately demonstrated with a diagram (see Designing Exhibitions), but it uses the common phenomenon where it is possible to see into lit rooms at dusk and virtually impossible to see into them unlit in bright daylight. If half-silvered glass is placed at an angle of 45 degrees in front of a model with no light upon it, all that will be seen is the reflection in the glass; if the model is brightly lit, the glass will disappear. Needless to say skilled craftsmen are once again needed for such magic displays and they are not cheap.

Holograms

These can be used in displays. They are expensive and as yet static. Moreover, since they comprise a photograph, a subject is needed in the first place; it is sadly not possible to conjure up a lovely three-dimensional image from nowhere.

Mixed media

The printed word, the spoken word, sound effects, still images, moving images, models, reconstructions, dioramas, holograms, lasers, lighting and special dry ice smoke effects can of course all be used together or in various combinations at the same time. The end result will be some kind of show or activity with a beginning and an end – theatre, in fact, but not quite. The French started it with *son et lumière*, which used a real place, actors' voices, music and stunning lighting to create an impression of life at this or that certain time in the place's history. Now, with laser projections and superb sound systems it is possible to carry such events even further into the realms of fantasy or reconstructed fact. Needless to say we are in the hands of the professional producers again, and quite rightly. Consequently things will become expensive, but if the end result is a marvellous piece of interpretation and a profitable enterprise, then who can complain?

In recent years an old fairground delight has been updated and brought effectively into the heritage shopping bag: a ride.

Rides

These come in quite a few shapes and sizes. In the heritage world the daddy of them all is the ride at Jorvik, in York. Here, after an initial approach into the basement of a fairly ordinary office block, visitors climb into an electric vehicle which carries them through ten minutes of Viking village reconstruction, in-car sounds and localized smells, but no real movement except from the car. It has proved a very effective and popular display. The visitor quits the village, leaves the car, visits an archaeological dig, a small museum, a shop and emerges into the sunlight. This is all pretty straightforward, but the first of its kind in Britain. Other companies and heritage centres have tried the same with varying degrees of success. There are different sorts of vehicle which can be hung from monorails, controlled through wires laid on the floor as at Jorvik, or go up hills using rack and pinion systems. They can be boats in shallow water-filled channels or run on rails. They can travel through reality or a mixture of media and special effects; they can be frightening, factual or fantastic. However, they are not cheap. It is really necessary to debate whether they are the right answer to the interpretation problem; they can be a very real answer to the disabled visitor and, as they are controlled by the programme and not by the visitor, they can contain commentaries, sound effects and even a small TV monitor.

Massive revolves and turntables can achieve a similar result, perhaps by revolving seated visitors past a series of displays or views, or revolving a series of exhibits past the visitors. In all these circumstances the visitor stays still, sitting down, and that should be considered as the best advantage of such systems. Their gimmick value is powerful, as is clearly demonstrated by Jorvik which has had very many more visits than the subject itself actually warrants, but in other places where they have been used for their gimmick value they have failed completely.

As with most devices the best practice is to visit sites where they are used and do some serious evaluation of their effectiveness.

Maintenance

This is probably the most important word in the whole of this chapter, but it must necessarily be left to the end. Absolutely none of the devices, gadgets, gimmicks or effects mentioned so far in this chapter is worth using if there is not a sufficient maintenance team built into the management structure of the visitor centre or whatever. The simplest picture will be vandalized or will fade in ultraviolet light, captions will be picked off, displays will be tampered with, and bulbs will fail in lighting or projectors. Models will grind to a halt, seats will collapse, signs will get nibbled by deer, laminated glass showcases will haze, vehicles will break down, models will get dusty, and so on. A sufficient maintenance team is a primary consideration. Its members should be carefully selected and then trained on the actual site before the project opens to the public. Facilities for them should be built into the structure in the form of workshops, access passages and traps. Stores and ongoing staffing, training and promotion programmes must be considered from the earliest moment. If the project cannot afford such staff, limit the project to a size and complexity that can be minimally maintained. Maintenance staff can be hired for off-the-shelf items such as projectors and TVs, but anything especially made for a project will need an engineer who understands and knows it. It is often possible to build a maintenance clause into a manufacturing contract, but it is unfair to expect a manufacturer in the south-east to be able to be in the north-west at a moment's notice. A working exhibit that is not working is worse than no exhibit at all.

Conclusion

Interpretative communication, in the peculiar circumstances presented by heritage projects, should not be treated as a simple matter of sticking up labels here and wayside panels there. Unless it is considered thoughtfully by all involved, we will remain in the Dark Ages. There is a danger of assuming that the sophisticated techniques increasingly available to us will solve the communication problems on their own. They cannot.

The first level of concise communication was dealt with in the previous chapter; nothing can improve on direct person-to-person explanations. This chapter has dealt with the second and third levels. The second level must be the printed and the spoken word. These two methods should not be mixed, for there is very little point in saying to a visitor what he can see printed in front of him. However the printed word or the spoken word can be mixed with the third level, images; and these, as has been seen, can range from the simplest diagram to the most sophisticated three-dimensional model.

This chapter deliberately separated the techniques into these levels of communication in order to emphasize that interpretative design is a thoughtful and considered process. Too often design is seen as a decorative assembly job with artistic people having to be controlled by the cool pragmatism of the client. The very opposite is often the case. But the truth of the matter is that without mutual respect for the roles played by each individual in the production process, what usually results is a hotchpotch; if this sometimes achieves success it will be far more by luck than judgement.

All the designers in the field would be happier if that were not the case. They would prefer to work with other dedicated professionals, to produce results that satisfy all the requirements set out in a concise and well written brief.

Interpretative publications in museums and heritage attractions

Rosemary Allen

Interpretative publications vary dramatically in their sophistication, size and use. They range from photocopied A4 sheets of closely spaced typescript to full-colour print work, folded or bound. Some material is designed for repeated use and may be protected through cold sealing or encapsulation, whilst other material is specifically designed to be taken away and retained by the visitor.

The interpretative publication can never offer the experience, interaction or aesthetic satisfaction of an exhibition, but it does have the obvious advantage of being an optional extra which moves with or guides the visitor, and which can be easily targeted to meet a range of different needs.

Brevity may be the soul of wit as far as exhibition graphics are concerned, but a visitor who goes away without the information for which they were looking will be a frustrated and disappointed one. This situation must be avoided, and a leaflet or fact sheet may be the answer to providing detailed information without cluttering an exhibition. Information offered in this way (like the exhibition itself) should be targeted at specific groups. Some may be far-reaching and some may overlap, but the distinctions should be clear. This can mean producing material with enlarged type size for the visually impaired, translations into languages other than that of the exhibition text, special educational material for schools, work sheets or quizzes for children, information categorized under different areas of special interest, and so on.

Printed material will also offer additional opportunities for publicity and provide a vehicle for an attraction's corporate identity. Anything which is carried away by a visitor and left in another place will disseminate information about the attraction and, if well designed and produced, improve its public perception and raise its profile. A visitor attraction which capitalizes on all facets of its presentation will be keen to ensure that publications are used to maximum advantage. Every item should be clearly identified as a product of the attraction, and carry credits where appropriate, as well as a contact telephone number and location and, if possible, details of opening hours and access arrangements.

Some types of publication will be the sole method of interpretation. These often take the form of a guide, trail or map and can be particularly effective in a historic building, or on a site where graphics or other methods of communication are considered obtrusive or inappropriate. For this type of arrangement, landmarks or reference points of some sort are essential. A guiding sheet at Skipton Castle some years ago used line drawings of details of the architecture itself and gave instructions such as 'turn right immediately you go through the carved door'. Although sometimes confusing, this approach added an element of fun to the tour.

Other trail guides simply have maps or plans which, when clearly and simply presented, work extremely well. They have distinct advantages over fixed orientation points, which the visitors are seemingly expected to commit to memory before finding their way. Marker posts or plaques which identify strategic positions or buildings, and offer additional information, will greatly enhance a guide of this sort.

Publications are almost always most effective when they take this two-pronged approach, building on an exhibition and carrying its ideas out beyond the confines of the attraction, as do some geological or archaeological trails. Exhibitions may include, like some at the Science Museum in London, special indicators which show that more information is available on particular topics or issues. 'Food for Thought', a permanent exhibition about food production, its trade, transport, use and consumption, included a series of numbered apples amongst its graphics and structures which related to the teachers' pack which was designed to accompany it. These provide meeting points for split groups, and enable teachers to prepare in the classroom and then quickly locate the areas they wanted to highlight in a large free-flow exhibition space.

The design of interpretative publications, like the content, will reflect the audience at which they are directed. This is clearly distinguishable in the difference between an information sheet directed at an adult audience and a teachers' pack for classroom use. Illustrations may be sophisticated or stylized in the former and deliberately simplistic and easily recognizable in the latter. Type sizes are likely to be larger when directed at a younger reader and the typeface selected for legibility rather than style.

A high-quality full-colour catalogue, which is an important work of reference and a popular souvenir in a London art gallery, will be a stark contrast to a set of A4 sheets in a local museum, produced specifically for classroom use and with photocopying in mind. Both may be successful in their own right, and if well designed offer equal benefits in publicity and enhanced reputation to their producers as well as responding to the needs and desires of their audiences.

Whatever the style, size or type of publication it will only be as useful as it is accessible. Lack of thought as to how publications are displayed, dispersed or sold often detracts from their benefits. Some museums adopt a policy of charging nominal fees for information to discourage misuse. There can be no doubt that freely available printed material will result in increased litter problems if on the one hand it is of an ephemeral nature and is perhaps not worth keeping, or if on the other there is inadequate provision for waste paper disposal.

Increased concern these days about green issues and the use of paper means an increased responsibility for museums and heritage attractions in sensitivity over its use. The institution will have its own concerns over environmental issues, but in addition there should be an awareness that many visitors may be alienated by a perceived waste of resources. Recycled papers should be used as far as possible and all printed material should be stored and displayed with care. Appropriately managed leaflets, guides and information sheets, housed in dispensers or racks, will not only enhance their appearance but will also encourage respect and correct use.

The cost of publications will of course be a further consideration. That the cost is an ongoing one may sometimes be forgotten. Since much of the cost of print production is in generating artwork and origination, it is usually more economic to reproduce it in large quantities. Runs of fewer than 1000 copies often won't cost any less, and this is generally considered to be a minimum economic run. A print run of, for example, 10,000 of the same piece of print would considerably reduce its unit cost. Storage facilities and available money for investment in print will be governing factors in decisions about production quantities. Fluctuations in paper costs will have an influence on future reprint costs, although generally they will be cheaper than the initial costs, particularly if origination has been retained by the printer. If the publications are to be dispersed by post, the cost of postage itself can be high and should not be overlooked. It is prudent to check the weight of a finished publication in the form of a dummy before production, as a slight reduction in the weight of paper used throughout may put it into a lower postage bracket. A unit saving of 10p on a quantity of 5000 or 10,000 represents a total saving of between £500 and £1000.

The most successful interpretative publications are those that are considered and appropriate to their purpose, responding in content and design to those for whom they are produced. At worst they may be perceived as tatty, unnecessary, a waste of paper and a potential cause of litter problems. At best they are an invaluable asset, giving satisfaction to the visitor, expanding the attraction's contact with its public by increasing access to information and collections, enhancing the attraction's reputation and increasing its opportunities for publicity.

Bibliography

BELCHER, M. (1991) *Exhibitions in Museums*, Department of Museum Studies, University of Leicester

BROOKLYN CHILDREN'S MUSEUM (1989) *Doing it Right: a Guide to Improving Exhibit Labels*, American Association of Museums, Washington, DC

KAVANAGH, G. (1991) *Museum Languages: Objects and Texts*, Leicester University Press, Leicester

KENNEDY, J. (1990) *User Friendly: Hands-On Exhibits that Work*, AST Centers, Washington, DC

KENTLEY, E. and NEGUS, D. (1990) *Writing on the Wall*, National Maritime Museum, London

VELARDE, G. (1988) *Designing Exhibitions*, Design Council, London

WITTEBORG, L. P. (1992) *Good Show! A Practical Guide for Temporary Exhibitions*, Smithsonian Institution, Washington, DC

Case study 28.1

Audio-visuals at Hellfire Corner, Dover Castle

Jack Lohman and Simon Rice-Oxley

Audio-visual production occupies a particularly crucial role in the interpretation of the network of tunnels beneath Dover Castle. For years this underground world, within the famous White Cliffs of Dover, was Britain's best kept secret. In 1986 its ownership passed from the Home Office to English Heritage and the complex was officially taken off the Secrets List. Today the tunnels form an essential part of any visit to Dover Castle, where visitors can explore the full span of British history from a Roman lighthouse and an Anglo-Saxon church to an observation station from the last war. Ninety per cent of visitors to Dover Castle make their way to Hellfire Corner – the official name given to the tunnels.

The tunnels have an important history that goes much further back than their marketed Second World War image. They were initially constructed by the Royal Engineers in the Napoleonic period in response to a threatened French invasion. During the First World War they were used by the Admiralty for storage at a time when the entire British fleet was assembled in Dover harbour. With the fall of France in June 1940, Dover found itself in the front line. A German invasion was expected daily and, amongst the frantic preparations to counter this, the secure tunnels beneath the castle assumed greater importance. What in 1939 had been a purely naval headquarters, with liaison officers from the Army and the Air Force, ultimately blossomed in 1943 into a combined headquarters for all three services. Extra accommodation was built at an upper level which was used as a hospital and dressing station. A further level incorporated a central operations room. In May 1940 Operation Dynamo, the evacuation of Dunkirk, was masterminded from the operations room within the tunnels. After the war, fear of Russian intentions and the three-minute warning of a nuclear attack at the height of the Cold War prompted the Home Office to transform the tunnels into a regional seat of government – intended to function during and after a nuclear attack which it was assumed would have destroyed London and central government.

In 1984 the Home Office abandoned the Dover tunnels after removing virtually all the equipment, leaving some 8km of empty passages. It was agreed at an early stage that the tunnels should be presented to the public without reconstructions or imaginative tableaux but left much as they were found. This approach would allow visitors to share a sense of discovery as they explored the tunnels. It was left for

audio-visual programmes to reconstruct the interiors and provide the trigger for visitors' imagination. It is not often that audio-visual producers have the opportunity to take full responsibility for the interpretation of a historic site from calculating the maximum operational length of programme through to programme production. Hellfire Corner is unusual in that it relies heavily on the audio-visual interpretation to generate visitor satisfaction.

A 13 minute introductory programme is presented in twin cinemas carved out of the natural chalk rock (*Figures 28.1, 28.2*). The cinemas are set up to run in tandem to cope with some 230,000 visitors a year. As

Figure 28.1 Hellfire Corner, Dover Castle: filming the tunnels for the introductory programme

Figure 28.2 Hellfire Corner, Dover Castle: filming the tunnels for the introductory programme

visitors take their seat in the cinema, they are aware of the bare rock in front of them. This transforms into a screen as the invisible gauze stretched in front of it picks up the images from the video projector. The introductory programme outlines the story of the tunnels using archival material and computer-generated maps. Rare photos interpret the interior of the tunnels and provide the framework for the visit.

Half-way through their tour, prior to entering the Dunkirk Operations Room, visitors see a second programme on the story of Dunkirk. This allows visitors to rest and pause before continuing as well as contributing to their understanding of this highlight in the tunnels' story.

The wealth of research archive material dictated the use of audio-visual. Archival footage and stills were traced to sources in England and Germany. Through strategically placed newspaper advertisements, photographs taken by individuals during the war were discovered, as were lost plans of the complex. This was supplemented by information from civilian and service personnel who served in the tunnels in the Second World War and could be traced. The material allows the story of the tunnels to be pieced together and presented in a documentary approach and allows for the tunnels to take on a clearer significance. Both programmes play an important role in peopling the tunnels and, by using contemporary newsreel and war footage, an image of restless, round-the-clock activity can be presented – in contrast to the empty passages the visitor encounters. The programmes offer an opportunity to set the mood and atmosphere for the visit. This is carefully controlled through sound production and choice of image to create an emotional response in the visitor. The use of a contemporary poem set to a sequence of a gun barrel on a destroyer at the close of the introductory programme creates a reflective response in the visitor and delivers a message that this is not just a historic entertainment but a collection of vital memories.

The elegant and seamless programmes bear little trace of the scars of mediation and transformation which marked the progress of their production. The views and opinions of veterans and specialists needed to be presented in a clear and accessible language. The holding power of images needed to be tested with real visitors to see which best interpreted the subject and offered the most effective connection with the past. Similarly music production was tested with visitors to see which sounds might contribute to a heightened awareness and emotional reaction. Towards the end of the programme, Vera Lynn's voice is deliberately used to provoke such a reaction. Whilst Hellfire Corner is a historic attraction, the interpretation sets out to react with visitors.

Such programme production also has its dangers. It is easy to fall into a nostalgia trap and offer visitors simply a flavour of the past. As the main communications vehicle, the programmes needed to interpret. This required careful analysis of the interpretation of the tunnels, and visitors' reaction to them and to the proposed messages. Given the nature of the subject, there is also a great danger of being nationalistic and potentially offending a major part of the audience. Great care was taken to adopt a suitable tone and to test messages and images with foreign visitors.

The use of audio-visual programmes within natural underground environments presents serious technological problems. Dusty and damp conditions even at steady temperatures throughout the year create short-circuits and attack the most robust equipment. All programmes are relayed from a centrally located control room which houses the video disk players. Video projectors are housed within the cinemas in dust-free cases designed to keep the damp out. A maintenance contract with a local firm ensures operational readiness and uninterrupted service.

The programmes were produced by The Visual Connection (TVC) Ltd. The cost of the programmes was £25,000, and the cost of the hardware was also £25,000. The equipment used included a Sony LDP 1500P video disk player, an Imager 160 projector and a Sony PVM 2730Q monitor.

Case study 28.2

Audio-visuals at the Museum of Tolerance, Los Angeles

Jack Lohman and Simon Rice-Oxley

Built for $50 million, the Museum of Tolerance presents one of the grandest and most ambitious uses of audio-visual media in a museum environment. The project was funded and developed by the Simon Wiesenthal Center, a human rights organization named after the famous Austrian Jew who helped to bring more than 1000 Nazi criminals to justice. Given the sensitivity of the subject, the research required and the innovatory approach, it took almost four years to develop and produce the audio-visual within the 26 sections of the Holocaust exhibit.

The strong technology-led audio-visual and interactive approach to the presentation of the Holocaust subject was chosen to appeal to a particular target audience, mainly California teenagers for whom the Holocaust is as unreal as the Second World War itself. In the main, the museum addresses that generation, but the messages are pitched to have a much wider appeal. An earlier design suggestion put forward a museum with a cineplex – multiple cinemas – each addressing separate issues such as justice

or stereotypes. This was rejected as too passive in favour of a more interactive and audio-visually led approach.

The museum occupies some 2300 m^2 on one floor of an eight-storey purpose-built block. The Holocaust experience is made up of 26 distinct areas themed along a winding exhibition path. Themes follow the story from Berlin between the wars to the revelations of mass murder and genocide in 1945. The experience is designed to cope with self-guiding groups of 15–20 people pulsed every 10 minutes. Tours are calculated to last 45 minutes. Sound and light guide the visitor through the show. As the documentary in one section stops, the following area lights up, encouraging visitors to move on.

In the initial sections of the museum, audio-visuals are used to create a documented atmosphere and to accompany dioramas. A café street scene in Berlin offers a carefully modelled tableau with figures of typical Berliners at tables (*Figure 28.3*). Typical conversations are heard. Lights then dim on the tableau

Figure 28.3 Museum of Tolerance, Los Angeles: presenting the past and the future in the Berlin café scene

and the audio-visual slide projection takes over to project what fate has in store for these characters in the future: a respectable GP ends up as a doctor in the Auschwitz concentration camp, and so on. By combining these two techniques, using technology to describe the future, a fusion is created that allows visitors to feel themselves as observers rather than actually an integral part of the scene. In another section dealing with the rise of Nazism, six video projectors are set up to run simultaneously to re-create the mesmerizing effect of the Nuremberg rallies and offer a powerful dimension of the Führer. The impact is overwhelming. Each screen measures 2.75 m by 1.8 m. Together the screen works in 8.25 m blocks, imposing on visitors the group response to the rally.

Further sections of the exhibition draw the visitor into the story and create a calculated response often shocking and provoking. By the end of the exhibition the interpretation creates a distinct uncomfortable feeling for the visitor. Two doors, one marked 'Able Bodied' and the other 'Women and Children', both lead into a sinister concrete chamber where monitors play the archival footage taken by the Allies in 1945, while the audio accompaniment plays the testimonies of the survivors. The combination of design, programme and audio creates a strong message with a psychological punch guaranteed to break the hardest of cynics (*Figure 28.4*).

The sections are woven together chronologically and interactively. On entering, visitors take a plastic card with a passport photo and the name of a child. This becomes the passport to the tour. At intervals within the exhibition there are opportunities for the card to be entered into an interactive computer to allow visitors to discover what is happening to their adopted infant. At the end of the exhibition visitors receive a computer printout of the history of their child which includes in most cases the date of disappearance. This feature complements the main

display and acts as a secondary interpretative and educational tool.

Throughout the museum design process an emphasis was placed on using audio-visuals in new and unusual combinations. This was seen as important in sustaining interest and offering a challenge to the square television format (*Figure 28.5*). A section dealing with the Wannsee Conference of 1942 illustrates this approach. It consists of a conference table strewn with papers and minutes as if the protagonists have just left. Visitors hear the dialogue of the participants, cold dispassionate voices which rubber stamp the Final Solution. Images are synchronized to float over the table to illustrate what their decision meant in human terms. The contrast between the detached and matter-of-fact voices and the archive material creates an uncomfortable response in visitors.

No Second World War attraction today can afford to ignore the wealth of documentation and available contemporary footage. The large archives dictated the medium. Archival material was sourced in Germany, Holland and America, supplemented by material from the Imperial War Museum, London. The material dictated the serious and accurate 'documentary' approach. The use of a British voice, that of John Hedges, for the narration provides documentary clout for the American audience.

The creative process, whilst considerably more complicated than the creation of programmes for most museums, is typical in bringing together museum designers and programme producers to the project team. At an early stage the team interacts and evolves developing ideas in tandem. Where there is a strong dependence on technology and a need for an effective interpretative strategy, this close cooperation delivers the most creative solutions. The museum designers on this project were James Gardner 3d Concepts Ltd.

Audio-visual media communicate with impact. Compared with many museums, especially those that

Figure 28.4 Museum of Tolerance, Los Angeles: the Final Solution. Archival footage is presented in a concrete chamber with survivors' testimonies as commentary

Figure 28.5 Museum of Tolerance, Los Angeles: the prelude to war presented on three dominating screens

deal with Jewish themes such as the Diaspora Museum in Tel Aviv, the Museum of the Holocaust is high-tech. The hardware becomes quite noticeable when in the evening all the monitors are turned off. Dozens of blank video screens, rows of video monitors, interactive computers and mute loudspeakers line the exhibition route. Operation of all systems in the museum is accomplished by pressing a single start button. The show control is delivered from a computerized system. There is no requirement for museum maintenance personnel to be on hand since all exhibits are either programmed or initiated by the visitor.

Audio-visual programmes are an important interpretative vehicle. The programmes are intended not simply as information points but to contribute to heightened awareness and changing attitude response in visitors. The experience cannot re-create the past or a truly authentic atmosphere, but it can provide a provocative catalyst. This is particularly significant given the acceptability of war today.

The programme was produced by the Visual Connection (TVC) Ltd, London at a cost of £160,000, excluding copyrights which were cleared by the client.

Case study 28.3

Interpretation for persons with a disability

Sir John Cox

Many major charities concerned with disability have complained over the years that there are few museums, historic houses, art galleries, gardens, cathedrals etc. which have made provision for persons with disabilities. In many cases access is difficult and interpretation of venues by guides and/or other techniques is often inappropriate. There are at least 6 million persons who are disabled in the UK who would benefit from an improvement in this situation.

Interpretation

An audio tour guide can help to make so many visitors sites much more accessible and enjoyable for persons with a disability. A listen and touch tour for persons with visual impairment gives a great deal of pleasure. For people with a learning disability there is now sufficient experience and knowledge to produce a tour which is fun, informative and attention keeping. These tapes have been called basic language tapes.

A shortened specially designed tape or an audio-visual tape slide programme can be produced in order that a person with a physical disability, i.e. in a wheelchair, who is unable to cover the whole site may enjoy the visit despite the limitations of access without feeling left out. A slide tape programme is particularly valuable for visits to houses without lifts for viewing upstairs. The family does not have to deny themselves their fun; they can be assured that their member in a wheelchair is seeing the slides and sights and hearing the dialogue that they themselves are hearing upstairs.

Those persons with a hearing impairment can enjoy the full sounds of an audio tour with the use of a personal induction loop. This sits neatly over the head and, when plugged into the personal stereo or sound stick, can be used without headphones. This facility has brought a great deal of enjoyment to people who felt they were being left out. A person with a hearing impairment is probably on the most lonely island of all.

Tapes for the visually impaired

Script-writers for tapes for those with a visual impairment (VIP) need to be specially trained. The best solution is for the script to be written by a person who is visually impaired. William Kirby is such a person. He lectures, he writes, he is a consultant to many museums on adaptations for those with a visual impairment, and he is Chairman of the Museum and Gallery Disability Association (MAGDA). The remainder of this section is Kirby's description of his work at Shugborough Hall, one site that has taken access for the disabled seriously.

The aim was to give the maximum amount of safe and independent access: physical access to the house and the route through it, and educational access to the style of the building, its story and its people. Most visually impaired visitors will be accompanied, but some with good mobility skills will wish to visit alone. Nevertheless, the aim was to give all visually impaired people in both categories the maximum amount of independence. The work of the blind consultant was based on the fact that he could gain a good perception of the Shugborough story by studying the available literature, including the existing Soundalive audio guide for sighted and able-bodied people, and a raised version of the plans of the house – all this in advance of the visit.

The building and the route of the tour were surveyed. All physical problems, such as obstacles, hazards, changes of level and changes in floor texture, were noted; recommendations about the removal or adaptations of these hazards were made to the Curator, where this could be done; and the difficult areas were described in the tape. Information is the best way to compensate for lack of sight. The overall shape of the house and then the individual rooms was described. This was to give a feeling of security, but also a perception of how the house worked and of the style of architecture: so reference was made to the tactile plans and to a raised image of the façade of the house.

The shape and size of individual rooms were described, using 'paces' – with an explanation that these are not sighted people's strides, but the kind of paces that visually impaired people take. The route was followed with a senior guide. It is important to be accompanied by a guide who is aware of the policies of the house – or, in this case, the National Trust. Junior guides or attendants can be very knowledgeable about the history, but one's companion for the research survey must be aware of educational, interpretative and curatorial policy.

Notes were taken on a pocket tape recorder, noting objects which might be touched with gloved hands, and objects which might be seen by people with partial sight: the blind consultant had a little peripheral vision.

The consultant asked about the colour schemes of the rooms.

Often one can avoid such phrases as 'now look at . . . ' by substituting 'here such and such can be seen . . . '. But one need not be nervous about saying 'now take a look inside this room' when one means 'now go and stand in this room while I tell you about it'. Visually impaired people like to hear about the colour of objects because they can see a little or can remember colour; and even if they have never seen colour it is found that they like to hear about such phenomena, especially where the references can trigger an imaginative response.

It is important to indicate pauses in the tape to allow people to walk from one place to another, to indicate where they should stand – or where they might sit, if possible – to listen to long pieces of narrative. Ways should be considered of how to allow companions to know what the tape is saying, and the easiest and safest is to lend them their own cassette player and tape. One should avoid asking companions to read out information panels as some companions are diffident about reading out in public.

So the blind consultant's perception of Shugborough Hall was full, and he tried to convey this perception. In one sense a blind person's view of a house like Shugborough will be as limited as his or her view of everyday life, but the difference is that it can be enhanced by the commentary of the historian.

Sound guides for people with learning difficulties

Colin Crowther is the author of 23 sound guides and numerous educational materials for charities including many on themes around people with learning difficulties (PWLDs). The following is Crowther's description of such sound guides, again with reference to Shugborough Hall.

Sound guides for people with learning difficulties (PWLDs) aim to increase physical and intellectual accessibility for people who would otherwise feel intimidated or left out of places of interest to all members of society. The immediate aim is to enhance their enjoyment, but the ultimate aim is to give people with learning difficulties a greater sense of belonging to the mainstream of our society.

Sound guides are needed for PWLDs to provide a quality of opportunity and resources. We need sound guides on machines which are easy to operate so that able-bodied persons and PWLDs use the same machine. We need sound guides that are written in the appropriate language within the user's conceptional and experiential framework. Sound guides are needed to allow PWLDs the pleasure of visiting at

their own pace: dialogue is carefully timed and directions must be very simple.

At the start of the process of preparing a guide, the writer asks the custodian for the single overriding impression or message that the custodian wishes the visitor to carry away. This provides the theme and a yardstick against which to judge the final script. The writer uses all research material which is available and works out the route with the custodian. It should be the same route as the normal adult visitor enjoys. It is important to have visual pointers to guide the visitor from one stopping point to the other.

The custodian describes what should be enjoyed at each stopping place, its history and significance. This is where it is important that the writer has experience of working alongside PWLDs so that he can sift the most interesting aspects and disregard other aspects which will not be understood. Where there is a long row of family portraits in a room, the PWLD may not be interested in the name and story of each portrait, but attention can be drawn to a particular family member who is essential to the story of the place, and only that person's portrait will be described. Where successive generations have had significant impact on the history of the venue, the story of each generation will be told in that room where the inference is more clearly marked.

The author separates his material into three areas:

Narration   The need is for a simple story-line illustrating the agreed theme to be followed throughout.
Direction   The need is for another voice to describe to the visitor how to get from one stopping point to another.
Dramatization   The need is to draw attention to enliven the most important events by re-enacting them in dramatic dialogue and sound effects. For instance, at Shugborough, how Admiral Anson made the voyage which allowed him to build Shugborough is re-created dramatically. The most significant collection at Shugborough is of Chinese objects, so the story of the Admiral's visit to China is also dramatized.

Personalization is important. Where the venue is a family home or has a link with a living person, every attempt is made to involve that person in the guide. So at Shugborough, Lord Lichfield is heard to recount stories of his memories of the various rooms.

The completed script is tested using an experienced teacher. Does it make sense? Does it hold interest and attention? Is it easy to follow?

The curator must approve the script. It is also important that he should point out any *objects d'art* which are moved from time to time. Problems can arise when the client wants to use the PWLD script for a popular family sound guide or for people for whom English is a second language. Very often the basic language script is very much enjoyed for these additional purposes but they must *not* take precedence over the prime intention, which is to interest

PWLDs. Very often there needs to be some fairly hard bargaining when the client/curator does not know the ability and interest of PWLDs but insists on changing the script.

Voices are particularly important and must not by either age or accent alienate the listener. Most users of these sound guides are young people and they need to identify with the narrator and director as friends. Actors therefore need to be young with classless accents, very clear delivery and lots of enthusiasm.

Conclusion

It is important that people with learning difficulties should feel wanted and have the experience of being valued, catered for and welcomed as equals. Their confidence in society grows and they benefit out of all proportion to the costs of producing these tapes. If anyone has a particular interest in developing guides and wishes for more information, they should write to: The Lord Rix, CBE, DL, Chairman, Libertas Charity Group, 61 Webbs Road, London, SW11 6RX.

Case study 28.4

Verulamium Museum

Sam Mullins

> One of the best and most enjoyable interpretational museum displays I have ever seen.
>
> Judge's citation from 'Interpret Britain' Awards, 1992

By 1987, the displays at Verulamium Museum had become rather long in the tooth, a judgement reflected in a fall of visitor numbers by over 50 per cent in the preceding decade to around 55,000 a year. Opened in 1939, on the site of Roman Verulamium in modern St Albans, the museum displayed nationally important collections of Iron Age and Roman materials, most notably mosaic floors and wall paintings as well as a comprehensive record of everyday life in the city from AD 50 to 450: glass, coins, ceramics, metalwork and stone. Despite a chronological treatment, the style of display was typological and consequently difficult for all but specialist visitors. For the interpreter this comprehensive collection consisted, with a few notable exceptions, of small pieces – broken, fragmentary or severely corroded.

Following an unsuccessful feasibility study for a commercially funded Roman Experience at Verulamium, an in-house solution was advanced. In broad terms our objective was to open up everyday life in a Roman city for a general audience, and in particular for the high proportion of schools using the museum visit as part of course work. The displays were above all to be artefact based, to offer an opportunity for hands-on and active participation, to include at least as many artefacts as previously shown and to be about Verulamium as a place, not a generic treatment of Roman Britain.

The chosen means of achieving these objectives were arrived at through a number of visits to other displays, including Saffron Walden, Ipswich and the Museum of London. Two visits stood out: those to the Natural History Discovery Centre at Liverpool Museum and the Archaeological Resource Centre in York. Both curators and designer were attracted to the busy atmosphere and active learning processes fostered at both places. We would seek to include similar features (accessible storage, database information, hands-on areas) *within* the gallery, rather than one step away. We would combine the best of such ideas for public access with the virtues of 'traditional' archaeological display and with evocations of Roman rooms based on our outstanding of wall paintings and mosaics.

The design partnership named Objectives was chosen, largely on the basis of an excellent working relationship fostered during the redisplay of the

Museum at St Albans. Coordination and graphic work was provided by our in-house museums designer. All were involved from the earliest possible stage in the evolution and sharpening of the brief.

The use of reconstruction drawings was essential if both the size and changes in the city over time were to be effectively conveyed. A sequence of ten newly commissioned illustrations form the introduction to Verulamium, displayed together with headline text and selected key artefacts, setting the chronological and thematic scene for the visitor (*Figure 28.6*). The sequence runs from the pre-Roman Iron Age, through the arrival of the Romans and the revolt of Boudicca, to the rebuilding of the city and then its decline in the middle of the fifth century.

The real thing, the original artefacts, are used at every possible point. In a series of reconstructed rooms, based on large sections of Roman wall paintings, replicated items are all based on the collections or other evidence and actual items are displayed close to the replicas in sloping cases, with accessible drawers beneath.

We had as an objective that the new displays should show at least as many artefacts as the old galleries. This set quite a challenge as the old cases had been densely packed. The objective was met both through the imaginative use of limited space, and by making the storage drawers beneath the

Figure 28.6

cases accessible to all visitors. The drawers are secured with locked glazed tops and the artefacts within them are mounted in plastazote forms in Perspex boxes to avoid damage from the repeated opening and closing of the drawers (*Figure 28.7*). This solution was neat as it also serves a second major feature of the brief, that of enhancing public access. It gives visitors the opportunity to start making decisions about what they would like to see and whether they would like to see more.

The displays were to combine large, well lit, authoritatively labelled showcases with hands-on work spaces and simple databases accessed by touchpads. For example in the section on trade, the visitor can see a representative selection of coins found at Verulamium. To avoid dominant labelling of such small objects, the groups of coins are labelled on a computer monitor. Replicas for touching are also next to the coin cases, one replica gold aureus being shown with the equivalent silver denarii and bronze sestertii. The graphic panels use clearly written text and cartoon illustrations to describe the striking of a Roman coin and why coins are useful to archaeologists as dating evidence. Finally, on the worktop nearby, real coins can be manipulated under a magnifying video camera to see at ×25 magnification their mint marks, changes in emperor's representations, pictorial reverses etc. (*Figure 28.8*). This brings together the accessibility and activity of the Liverpool and York displays into the museum gallery itself, an integral part of the interpretative process.

An interpretative exhibition of any length must have pace: it must draw visitors along and repeatedly arouse interest. The nine areas which make up the exhibition each approach their subject in a different way: lighting, floor and wall finishes change from section to section, and each area has something different to do. This pulls the visitor through in an active way, stimulating interest and suggesting that

Figure 28.8

there is always something good to come. There is no set route, just the attraction of the next section drawing visitors along. The limited use of sound effects has a similar purpose, providing context or background as well as drawing visitors through. At Verulamium great care has been taken to make the sounds authentic: the Roman theatre sounds are the epilogue from a play by Plautus, the description of the baths is by Lucretius, and the temple sounds are based on the excavated evidence from Verulamium's triangular temple.

First-person interpretation is a developing feature at Verulamium. Schools can book a session with Marcus Allius of the XIIII Legion (a re-enactor) or a handling session with a curator or supply teacher. Volunteer guides are present on the weekends and offer short topic talks on Roman roads, the Boudiccan revolt, Sir Mortimer Wheeler etc. This takes place in a lecture room off the gallery. Within the gallery a short video is 'narrated' by a wealthy Roman, aged 50 and proud possessor of a richly decorated lead coffin, excavated in 1989. He describes the forensic evidence gleaned from his remains and how his facial features have been reconstructed to give the only known face of a Romano-Britain. Short narrations of a Roman play, an afternoon at the baths and a ritual at the triangular temple are also accessible by push-buttons.

Figure 28.7

Since the reopening of Verulamium to the public in September 1991, visitor numbers have risen from 55,000 to nearly 90,000 per annum. Schools' use has more than doubled, the number of schools using Verulamium in a year rising from 320 to over 800. A visitor survey undertaken in the months after opening suggests a high degree of visitor satisfaction: 95 per cent expressed an interest in repeating their visit, 83 per cent felt Verulamium compared favourably with other museums and 87 per cent thought the admission charge good value for money. This survey information accorded closely with front-of-house impressions of very satisfied customers. Outside interest in the interpretative methods at Verulamium has been great: our video won a British Archaeological Award, our marketing a 'Come to Britain' Award from the BTA, and our interpretation an 'Interpret Britain' Award from the SIBH. In fact, high visitor numbers have proved a problem since 1991, exposing further the inadequacies in visitor facilities, which are to be addressed in the next phase of refurbishment: a new entrance and visitor centre. These, however, are the right sort of problems to have.

29

Heritage interpretation and environmental education

Graham Carter

In discussing the relationship between heritage interpretation and environmental education, no attempt will be made to define either term. It is assumed that those who have read thus far will already have a clearly defined personal view of the philosophies, skills and concepts encapsulated in heritage interpretation, while environmental education is constantly redefined to meet the personal academic and political needs of the individual. It is likely, therefore, that there will be considerable divergence between the views of individual readers and that of the author of this chapter. Readers should therefore be perhaps aware that the author is a middle-aged, middle-class, white, male, British academic ecologist, professional educator and accidental interpreter in the leisure industry whose political preferences comprise a woolly mixture of traditionally left-wing and right-wing philosophies. This viewpoint definition is essential if only to emphasize that the opinions expressed are individual and not intended to represent universal truth.

Interpretation versus education?

It is an unfortunate fact of life that, increasingly, sites which are used for environmental education have been previously submitted to the loving attention of the heritage interpreter, particularly in Western Europe and North America. Although good heritage interpretation can make some contribution to environmental education, in an ideal world the two would not mix. The co-location of opportunities for interpretation and education is the result of many different influences, some philosophical, some purely pragmatic.

In over-populated countries the pressure on the so-called 'natural' environment is heavy. Where the majority of the land is in private ownership, opportunities for public access are reduced further. Much of the land in 'public' ownership has achieved this status because of its particular aesthetic or scientific value, and thus becomes a destination not only for the public who wish to enjoy the beauty of the surroundings, but also for educational groups whose studies require first-hand investigation of the environment. In an effort to conserve these precious areas, site managers attempt to control, manage, direct and limit public access with the laudable aim of preventing visitors from destroying that which they come to enjoy. Thus a series of environmental honeypots is created. Within these honeypots, site managers provide the basic facilities required by the visitor: shelter, catering, toilets. These facilities are as desirable for environmental education students as for recreational visitors. For a variety of reasons, explored later, site owners and managers may then feel it necessary to interpret the site so that interpretation and education opportunity are collocated.

Within the broadly defined built environment, the pressures are rather different but the net result is the same. Any area with a long history of human settlement has a multiplicity of historic sites, ranging from neolithic workplaces to World War II pillboxes and 1960s power stations. With the growth of population, urbanization and industrialization, the increase in the number of historic sites has probably been more nearly exponential than linear. At the same time, public perception of what may be described as historic has broadened, and the urge to preserve has become indiscriminate. Under the influence of sentiment, nostalgia, local pride, tourism development, commercialization and desperation, there has been a surge to preserve everything from the past and describe it as heritage, particularly if it is an industrial site which is no longer required and for which there is no alternative future use. At the same time, under the influence of social historians and politicians, the accepted subject area of environmental education has been broadened (quite justifiably) to incorporate increasing emphasis on the built environment. Driven by the need for either public accountability or commercial viability, many of the most interesting heritage sites have also received the attentions of the heritage interpreters while remaining important destinations for the environmental educator. Thus, once again, there is coincidence of interest between the two fields of activity. And yet there remain fundamental differences and potential conflicts between good practice in heritage interpretation and good practice in environmental education.

Audiences

At most locations there is, or perhaps should be, a major difference between the target audiences for interpretation and education. Good environmental education is closely targeted but to a wide range of audiences. Each group will normally comprise a fairly narrow age band, at a particular level of educational development, pursuing a specific area of the curriculum, with clearly defined objectives for their visit, which may or may not accord to the National Curriculum. The target audience for heritage interpretation, however, is that undefinable body known generally as the public. The nature of this public audience will vary considerably from site to site, and even within the audience the motivation for the visit will vary enormously. The owners or operators of a site may honestly believe it to be of national or international significance. However, some visitors will be there because it is somewhere to take the children. For others, it will represent a destination at which to point their expensive technological toy, the motor car. Others will come to satisfy their general intellectual inquisitiveness, while for others the site may explore a subject in which they have a deep personal interest. Some may visit as a result of heavy television promotion, and others as a result of peer group pressure.

The interpreter, after careful visitor research, will find it impossible to cater for the individual needs of the general public and will settle on a mean level of interpretation, catering not to the lowest common denominator but to the average visitor. At the best sites, this basic provision will be supplemented by access to more specialist information and services for those who discover a desire to pursue the subject in greater depth. This averaged presentation is usually unsuitable for, and should be ignored by, environmental education students.

Levels of knowledge

Visitor surveys at any site will probably reveal that the bulk of the visitors have no specialist knowledge of the site and its subjects. This assessment will dictate that the majority of the interpretative activity should therefore be aimed at the intelligent beginner. One outcome of this is that interpretation is usually (but not universally) superficial. In contrast to this, environmental education groups have a clearly defined knowledge base and level of attainment, and site visits are designed to add new information and concepts to pre-existing knowledge. Thus, unless the site happens to offer an introduction to a totally new area of knowledge, much of the pre-prepared interpretation may well be irrelevant.

Episodic or integrated?

The nature of a site visit should also differ fundamentally for the general visitor and the educational group. There are comparatively few general visitors who pursue their interest in a subject through a carefully coordinated series of site visits which escalate in intellectual challenge. For most of the visitors, the time spent at a heritage site is episodic – a 30-minute cultural fix. It is simply a constituent of a varied recreational experience which may also include driving along rural lanes, walking on the beach, enjoying a traditional English cream tea, and leisure shopping in a themed supermarket, all perfectly acceptable elements of a recreational day. However, the episodic nature of the interpretative experience has a definitive effect on the interpreter's approach to the audience. Interpretation will probably be planned to ensure that the average visitor staying for the average period can gain sufficient experience from the site to feel that their visit was worthwhile, or, in more commercial terms, that magic phrase 'value for money'.

The objectives of a site visit for the environmental educator are completely different. Environmental education is a through-life process and any single site visit will represent the addition of a limited body of knowledge to that already acquired by the student. Its function will be to assist in the long-term formulation of concepts, attitudes and ethics. This will mean that, on site, the environmental group may well wish to study just one topic or aspect in much greater depth than that which is acceptable to the general public, and those site operators who are serious in their wish to provide for environmental education must cater to these more specific needs.

Heritage interpretation and environmental education could not be said to be as different as chalk and cheese, since the basic constituents, namely the sites, remain the same. However, the difference is probably more akin to that between instant mash and seed potatoes. Interpretation has been grown, harvested, boiled, mashed, freeze-dried, weighed out in portions, stored in long-life packs, and presented in carefully designed and eye-catching packages. It is thus instantly available in acceptable form to the average visitor. Environmental education is the seed potato which needs to be planted, tended and nurtured over a long period to produce a fresh, satisfying and individual result.

Organization and individual

There is a marked difference in focus between heritage interpretation and environmental education. The former is almost entirely site-specific and designed to meet the needs of the management. In general, the content of the interpretation will be controlled by the site and the techniques and objectives determined by management. The objectives may be purely pragmatic within the well known visitor destination sequence: persuade them to come, persuade them to come in, show them something, give them a ride on/ in something, persuade them to eat something, sell them something, and let them out happy at the end of the experience. Practical objectives may be linked to intellectual objectives, such as helping visitors to understand important historical or environmental concepts linked to the site. Alternatively, objectives may be political (see 'The hidden agenda' below).

In contrast to this, objectives in environmental education have to be much more closely related to the student and his or her needs. This means that visits by environmental groups need much careful pre-planning. Preliminary visits by group leaders and discussions with site management and interpreters therefore become a vital ingredient in the planning of a worthwhile educational experience.

Differing time lines

By the sheer nature of its sites and subject matter, much heritage interpretation is related to the past, with purely contemporary reference being limited to justification for the current conservation of the site. There is, of course, absolutely nothing wrong with this. Indeed, there is a view that an understanding of history aids social coherence and cultural identity. It is certainly true that new nations which lack a clearly identifiable national history seek to create one, which can be particularly difficult when a nation's boundaries were determined by pencils and rulers wielded by previous invaders and colonizers. Environmental education, on the other hand, is looking to the future. It seeks to use an understanding of the past and present, to assist students in reaching a personal view of the future needs of society and the environment.

Human and non-human

Don Aldridge would argue that all interpretation includes reference to people – the human factor – and that without the human perspective, interpretation is impossible. While the majority of site interpretation refers to a greater or lesser degree to the interaction between people and their environment, the principle itself remains debatable. Nevertheless, it represents a distinct contrast to general environmental education. In general environmental terms, the human race is a comparatively recent influence on the planet and many of the basic concepts of geology, meteorology, ecology etc. can be studied totally independent of the human factor. Indeed, it is important that these concepts should be understood as an aid to judgements on the effects of interaction between people and their environment.

Avoiding the issue

Interpreters are under enormous pressure to avoid consideration of any critical or contentious issues. These pressures may be self-generated owing to their own enthusiasm for a particular subject, or may result from outside pressure. Such pressure may come from the academic establishment, employers, political paymasters or commercial sponsors – or from a general feeling that the visitors need to be informed and entertained, but not challenged. Very few professional interpreters are prepared to tell lies, but most of us are willing to at least be economic with the truth or adopt a strictly neutral tone. Examples abound at international, national and local level. Untrammelled population growth, for example, remains a major threat to future survival of the human race. However, because it is a political and religious hot potato, international conservation agencies are soft-pedalling on this particular issue. Increased energy consumption in the developed world results in increased pollution and rapid depletion of fossil fuel resources, yet a government in the 1990s can privatize energy production with the aim of increasing efficiency, controlling prices through competition, and reducing state intervention. It ignores the fact that such privatization leads inevitably to a reduction in research capacity, to a lack of national energy policy and to a total lack of commitment to energy conservation. At a more local level, interpreters will deplore the use of pesticides and fertilizers and the development of monoculture, while failing to point out to the visitor the inevitable rise in food prices which would follow reduction in their use. Moreover, in the undignified rush to capitalize on the commercial value of the heritage, few will stop to ask whether we actually need to preserve yet another fine example of yet another steam engine in yet another pumping station on yet another derelict sewage plant.

The hidden agenda

As well as avoiding major issues, interpretation is often used for subtle propaganda to meet the requirements of owners and managers. The interpreter may be required to present a positive view of the Countryside Commission, English Heritage, English Nature, British Nuclear Fuels or any other statutory or commercial body.

Environmental education on the other hand has a responsibility to provide broad-based accurate information on the environment and the effect of people thereon. The overall aim of environmental education is to produce an adult population which is sufficiently well informed to allow individuals to arrive at their own personal environmental ethic. It must be said, however, that in recent decades even environmental education has been showing an increased tendency towards political propaganda and this trend is to be deplored. It is likely, however, that this trend will increase as the environment becomes more of a political issue and a more marketable commodity, and it is essential that interpreters and educators alike remain constantly aware of the inherent dangers in their professional activity.

Thus far, we have considered predominantly the divergence in needs between heritage interpretation and environmental education. It may be worth considering briefly whether there is in fact any common ground between the two disciplines and, if so, whether this can be exploited.

Educational influences

In the UK at least, education is in turmoil. The Education Reform Act (1988) and the introduction of the National Curriculum present both barriers and opportunities to the operators of heritage sites. In purely commercial terms, the education sector has been recognized as a very important part of the market for heritage activities. This is amply demonstrated by the fact that many sites with little intrinsic educational value have manufactured educational materials in order to generate and justify group visits. Within the defined National Curriculum, environmental education is identified as a cross-curricular theme, together with others which may be of potential value to the heritage interpreter. These include economic awareness and political and international understanding. Moreover, individual subjects within the core curriculum present outstanding possibilities for site visits by educational groups. To take but a single example, the history curriculum at key stage II (7–11 years) includes such subjects as: invaders and settlers; Britain since 1930; Tudor and Stuart times; Victorian Britain; exploration and encounters; together with supplementary units spanning ships and seafarers; food and farming; writing and printing; houses and places of worship; land transport; and local history. Many of these subjects can obviously be pursued on sites which are already interpreted for the general public.

Better than nothing

At the most basic level, it may be said that both interpretation and education on a specific site are better than nothing. They should both make the site more accessible to the visitor and, although the interpretative materials may not be exactly aligned to the educational needs of visiting groups, they should still give those groups access to material and information not readily obtainable from the site itself.

Common skills

Both interpretation and education employ similar skills. They require the ability to synthesize and analyse; to select relevant themes; and to choose the most appropriate media for transmission of message. The fact that the themes and media may be different for the two groups is a credit to the skill of the interpreter rather than a failing.

Interpretation as an educational resource

With more advanced students, on-site interpretation can itself provide an invaluable resource for educational activity. Students of English, history, art and design, media studies, environmental education, all can learn from critical assessment of both message and media chosen in interpretative display.

Educational visits to heritage sites

Heritage site operators have widely divergent views on educational groups. Some regard them simply as till fodder to be processed with maximum efficiency and minimal disruption to normal operation. Others wish to communicate their enthusiasm for their site and subject to a younger generation but have no idea how to achieve the objective. Finally, there are those who have a serious commitment to education and are prepared to invest in a professional service.

It should be clear from what has been said earlier that those who are seriously interested in environmental and other education should not expect visiting educational groups to rely solely on the interpretative materials provided for the general public. Once this basic principle has been accepted, then heritage sites can become very worthwhile destinations for environmental education. The degree of specialist provision for environmental education will depend, not only on the degree of commitment of the site operator, but also on the popularity of the site, the specific subject areas covered, and financial resources. Adequate educational provision can be made at a variety of levels of investment. Some possibilities are outlined below. However, it must be stressed at this early stage that whatever level of investment is selected, education is a sufficiently serious subject to warrant professional attention, even if resources do not permit the employment of permanent education staff. The preparation of educational materials, facilities and resources should be undertaken by experienced educators, even if they are retained only on a short-term consultancy basis.

Teacher materials

In planning visits, teachers can benefit from the provision of additional materials. These can provide detailed historic background notes on the site and its inhabitants. They can also include suggestions for activities both at school before and after the visit, and on site during the visit. They should highlight links between the site and schools' curricular needs, possibly in a variety of subject areas. It may also be worth while considering the provision of illustrative material for use in the classroom. Where school groups operate unsupervised by site staff, the provision of suggested routes and trails with suitable teacher annotations may also be of value.

Student materials

It is impossible to produce perfect worksheets, workbooks, assignment cards or student guides for any site. The needs of visiting groups are diverse, the amount of background work which they have done varies, and each teacher will probably have slightly differing objectives for the visit. That being said, materials prepared for students can help the teacher to judge activities which are possible on site and suggest possible lines of enquiry. These materials should be simple, flexible and inexpensive. Unless they are seen by the site operator as an important source of revenue, it is preferable that they should be produced copyright free for educational use, to allow individual teachers to copy and adapt the materials to suit the needs of their own specific class.

Education spaces

The educational effectiveness of a site visit can be greatly enhanced by the provision of separate education spaces for use by visiting groups. The aim is not to isolate the group from the environment but to provide an opportunity for specifically targeted displays and for introductory talks at an appropriate level and on an appropriate theme for each group.

Handling materials

One of the main aims of educational visits is to give students first-hand experience of a site and its artefacts. However, in the interests of conservation and good visitor management, interpretation often places barriers between visitors and objects. This educational disadvantage can be overcome by the careful selection of objects which can be handled and closely examined by visiting school groups. Herein lies one of the major advantages of a separate educational space, as this allows materials to be made available to students under supervision and away from the general public.

Professional staff

The best quality of provision for visiting school groups can be made by the appointment of professionally qualified and experienced educators. Successful organizations should regard this appointment as a commitment to the community and education. However, large and successful sites should also be able to justify it on purely economic grounds, should this be the yardstick by which they make their judgements.

Special opening

Some sites find it worthwhile to open specifically for educational groups at times when members of the general public are not admitted. This is usually a device adopted by small sites whose normal opening is seasonal, but educationally it has considerable advantages. It means that the staff on duty can orient themselves to the needs of the visiting students without trying at the same time to cater for the needs of the general visitor. Visiting groups are able to progress through the site at their own speed, and concentrate on those aspects which are most relevant. Moreover, particularly on small sites, the general public are not obliged to step round or over students engrossed in their own work.

Separate sites

Finally, managers of large sites might like to consider the possibility of providing separate sites for use by interpretation and education. This device would allow for the provision of the 'instant mash' heritage fix for the general visitor, while allowing serious environmental students to pursue a more heuristic line of enquiry.

Conclusion

In summary, it is probably sufficient to say that heritage interpretation and environmental education are different processes with different objectives aimed at different audiences. However, many heritage interpretation sites can be of great value to environmental educators. If this opportunity is to be exploited then the provision for environmental education within the site should be different to that for heritage interpretation.

Bibliography

CORNELL, J. B. (1979) *Sharing Nature with Children*, Ananda Publications

HOOPER-GREENHILL, E. (1991) *Writing a Museum Education Policy*, Department of Museum Studies, University of Leicester

HOOPER-GREENHILL, E. (1991) *Museum and Gallery Education*, Leicester University Press, Leicester

LUNN, J. (1988) *Proceedings of the First World Congress on Heritage Presentation and Interpretation*, Alberta, Canada, Heritage Interpretation International (see especially section 'On Education and the Young')

PITMAN-GELLES, B. (1982) *Museums, Magic and Children: Youth Education in Museums*, AST Centers, Washington, DC

Case study 29.1

The Bancroft Villa Thriller

Marion Blockley

The interpretation and presentation of open-air sites and monuments is one of the most direct and effective means of communication between archaeologists and their public. This case study summarizes a recent successful collaboration with children to interpret an oasis of historic landscape within a new city.

The Bancroft Roman Villa was excavated between 1973 and 1986. Its site and some visible remains now survive within a public open space in Milton Keynes. During 1989 a scheme was implemented to commemorate the Villa in its setting as a landscape feature for the Milton Keynes Year of the Environment. The scheme has its limitations since it incorporates a genuine Roman stone-lined fish-pond and replica Villa foundations. The foundations are a too faithful copy of the excavated remains and are assumed to be genuine by most visitors, according to a formative evaluation carried out in the park. The footings were laid out from the excavation plan on a raised platform above the site of the original building. where colourful mosaics had once covered the floors of the Villa a carpet of grass was sown. Interpretation panels were erected and appropriate Roman plants were grown in the re-created formal garden.

Bringing the site to life: the community action approach

Once the Villa had been interpreted in a concrete form, it was clear there was a need for a more imaginative management policy. It was not enough merely to reconstruct the walls and produce leaflets and interpretation panels and assume that communication had been achieved. There was a need to promote the site to the public and to give it a focus within the community. A few months after the site was officially opened, rubbish began to fill the pond, graffiti appeared on the interpretation panels and plants were uprooted. In a sense the traditional interpretation methods had failed because they were imposed on a community without consultation or collaboration. The site had become merely another example of a paternalistic authority designating appropriate historical or artistic features for its fledgeling community. The most direct way of reaching a community is through its children. At the same time involving local schools in interpreting the site fulfils the educational objectives to which many archaeology units and museums now aspire. Also, the Bancroft Villa is the only publicly accessible Roman site in Buckinghamshire.

The Bancroft Villa Thriller

After discussion with teachers and the local theatre-in-education group, 'Interaction', the author devised the Bancroft Villa Thriller project. It was a new departure for the Milton Keynes Archaeology Unit, using enquiry, art, drama and creativity to inspire children. The project was motivated by and based on primary evidence: potsherds, burnt tile fragments, burnt stone and bones from the site.

The emphasis was on active learning, finding out, handling and questioning the evidence in an exciting and stimulating way. Children were encouraged to use and develop their skills through exploration, investigation, knowledge and understanding. In effect, they became archaeologists, using all the deductive and recording skills used by the professionals. The guiding principle behind the project was that children should be enabled to understand processes rather than absorb facts by rote. Looking at things is good practice, but it is dangerous to think of observation as an end in itself, rather than as a vehicle to promote further enquiry. As a detective searches for clues to solve a crime, so the children searched for clues on site to solve the mystery of the villa (*Figure 29.1*).

Down by the stream the children walked in a grassy meadow with a rich variety of flowers. This had once been the site of a Roman kitchen garden producing herbs and cooking ingredients. Pine kernels, plums, mustard, cabbage and elderberries had all once grown there. The children were able to find living specimens of plants which had grown there since Roman times, as shown by the identification of pollen grains and seeds in the soil – and even to taste the pine kernels.

Walking up the hill to the site of the Roman farm, the children searched for objects on freshly landscaped ground which might provide clues to the history of the site. They placed their finds in polythene bags, clearly labelled to show their find spot, ready for further study at school. On the surface of the recently disturbed topsoil they found fragments of pottery, roof tile, cement, burnt stone, plaster, oyster shell, bone and mosaic tesserae.

The children were totally absorbed by this, making genuine discoveries for themselves. One even found a Roman whetstone. Many rapidly distinguished between natural and man-made objects. Some objects were more difficult. How do you distinguish between Roman and modern land drain or concrete? Why can't you be sure? Mere confirmation of identification was

Figure 29.1 Looking for clues on site (photo: Marion Blockley)

not enough; the children began to question the evidence.

Eyes glued to the ground, engrossed in searching for clues, the children moved to the Roman fish-pond set in a re-created Roman garden. During the archaeological dig, it had been emptied of rubbish thrown into it over 2000 years. Now new rubbish was rapidly filling it up. How could lager cans and chocolate wrappers give us clues about the people who visited the site today and how they used it? The children soon realized how easy it was to date litter, and how archaeologists interpret it. They also commented on people's eating habits and attitude to litter.

The young archaeologists interpreted evidence they found on the site (some of it planted by the author in the rooms of the pastiche Villa, much of it genuine finds from systematic walking over disturbed ground adjacent to the Villa). They also considered the evidence found by archaeologists during their excavations: part of the marble statue of Mercury; a wooden wheel, symbol of the Celtic god Taranis; five mosaic floors; and the remains of two bodies in a mausoleum on the hill. Whilst recording the layout of the building and plotting their finds, the children

noted technical discrepancies between the Villa as excavated and as reconstructed.

The children's story

Throughout the project the children learnt how to research, to collaborate, to reason and to question. They were encouraged not to think in terms of right or wrong answers, but always to be aware of alternatives. Through discussion they were asked to debate which were the most likely alternatives. Gradually they began to understand the limitations of the evidence and how subjective interpretation can be.

Each child (250 children took part in the project) wrote their version of what might have happened at the Villa. Why did it burn down? Who were the people in the mausoleum on the hill? The children became the interpreters of the site, the adults the enablers. From all the stories, a script for a performance was prepared. The Archaeology Unit interpreted the Villa's history in a lengthy report; the children interpreted it by writing, designing and performing a play of their own.

The performance

For six weeks leading up to the performance, community artists and the author visited each of the five schools to help sift the evidence and produce costumes, props and craftwork. One school produced a faithful replica of the smallest mosaic (*Figure 29.2*). As the excitement mounted more and more families visited the site of an evening, guided by their knowledgeable and enthusiastic eight- and nine-year-olds. On a trip to Cirencester Museum, fascinated adults were observed eavesdropping on the children explaining the workings of Roman underfloor heating systems. One teacher reported that her parents had never come across such enthusiasm and commitment amongst their offspring. Local TV and radio followed the project with great interest, which reinforced the children's sense of pride in their own work. Their status within the local community was raised still further when the project was featured in the inaugural week of Radio 5 (August 1990) with a follow-up programme one month later.

The media coverage increased the profile of the site within the local community. Local residents came and cleared away rubbish; no more plants were uprooted. Community groups, pensioners, the parent and toddlers club and the residents' club adopted aspects of the project and the site, and took responsibility for them. Thankfully the afternoon and evening of the performance day were hot and sunny, and the dramatic fire-show finale went off with the right balance of excitement and control (*Figures 29.3, 29.4*).

Figure 29.2 Piecing together the replica mosaic on site (photo: Marion Blockley)

Figure 29.4 The god Mercury and attendants (photo: Marion Blockley)

Postscript

The Villa Thriller took place in the summer of 1990. Since then the site has been continuously used by local schools as a resource for the National Curriculum. The methods pioneered during the project have been adopted for use by individual teachers, and a 'Romans' resource pack based on the Bancroft Villa has been made available for loan to schools through the Buckinghamshire County Museum Service.

The Roman garden is now used by residents from both sides of the park as a place to sit and talk. In the past, individuals from the estates on either side of the park did not generally mix, a common problem in new town communities. The park rangers have even reported a pleasing decrease in vandalism. Green artworks created by the children were left in the park to represent their view of the special hidden places beyond the Villa, where evidence of man had also been found.

The author circulated a questionnaire to the residents of Bancroft Park before and after the event to evaluate its impact. Before the event there was mild disinterest in the Villa site, and few had visited it;

Figure 29.3 Mourners at the Mausoleum (photo: Marion Blockley)

whereas after the event 80 per cent were enthusiastic. Many felt aggrieved that they had not been consulted about the original interpretation proposals (which were rejected because of the anticipated impact on residents). The majority were in favour of more imaginative interpretation at the site in the form of both events and more substantial long-term interpretation. A large number lamented the removal of the mosaics from the site (although they appreciated their conservation needs) and favoured some form of representation of them *in situ*.

In summary, the main virtue of the Bancroft project was that rather than buying in an off-the-peg living history performance, the project was produced by the children (and families) of the local community. The process of producing and understanding the interpretation enabled locals to see their familiar park in a new light:

Very often we do not appreciate our everyday surroundings until we learn that someone else values them. Now when I walk my dog I feel I've made a special contribution to our park. (Bancroft park resident)
I found it! It's a piece of mosaic and I found it! It's got straight sides like a maths cube. Oh – and this is a bit of broken land drain: it's Victorian so it is only about 100 years old. But this has been here for 2000 years – that's 20 lots of 100 years. And I'm the first to find it since the Romans! (Frances, aged 8)

30

The evaluation of interpretative provision

Roger Miles

My aim in this chapter is to provide a straightforward account of evaluation as it is practised in interpretative work (Loomis, 1987; Miles *et al.*, 1988; Screven, 1990). I attempt to answer the main 'what', 'why', 'when' and 'how' questions about evaluation, and to indicate the strengths and weaknesses of the various approaches that are now being used. It is not possible to deal with all the technical skills and knowledge required in the more highly specialized areas such as survey design, sampling methods and statistical analysis. Readers are referred to the literature cited for this information, with the firm suggestion that an expert should always be consulted if there are any doubts at all about the practice of these disciplines. There are nevertheless many areas where valuable evaluation can be carried out with minimal training and with low-cost techniques, and there is no reason why these should not be widely adopted and used to improve the quality of interpretation.

What is evaluation and why do we do it?

To evaluate is to assess the worth of things. And this is something we do throughout our waking hours with everything we come into contact with, from the egg we eat for breakfast to the museum we visit in the afternoon to the letter we write to the tax inspector in the evening. In every case we are assessing how good or bad something is, and we carry out this *informal* sort of evaluation throughout our lives. When, however, we talk about the evaluation of interpretative provision, we have in mind something that goes beyond the formation of personal, and possibly idiosyncratic, views. Rather, we are thinking about the formation of objective judgements about how good things are, by subjecting them to careful scrutiny through special methods and skills,

guided by a knowledge of what to look for. In this way *formal* evaluation can detect strengths and weaknesses that would otherwise go undetected; and if things have gone wrong it may be able to give constructive suggestions concerning what we should do to put things right. In other words, evaluation, in assessing the worth of things, aims to provide information to guide our actions.

What, in the context of interpretative planning, are the 'things' we have been talking about? Well, they are virtually everything that we do, or produce, in providing interpretation. They include activities such as tours, lectures, workshops and lessons, as well as more material things such as exhibits, guide books, audio guides, worksheets, maps and signposts. All of these can be evaluated to inform our decision taking. Our things might also include marketing activities and service in shops, restaurants, toilets and so on, though these are not aspects of interpretation I shall stress in this chapter. But we shall include among our things the plans for our interpretative activities, as well as the objects and activities that we provide. In fact evaluation of plans, before any practical action and therefore large sums of money are committed to them, is one of the most important uses of evaluation.

When we carry out informal evaluation in our daily lives (e.g. how good is this fried egg?), we generally form our judgements against criteria that are based on experience, although these may be understood rather than openly stated. In the same way, the evaluation of interpretation can be carried out against targets. This is called goal-oriented evaluation. However, unlike daily informal evaluation, the targets must be clearly and openly stated at the planning stage, lest we move the goalposts after the ball has been struck, and are tempted to declare our interpretation a failure or success as we see fit. Targets should be phrased as aims and objectives at the planning stage, and can cover most aspects of visitor behaviour and learning. The results of goal-oriented evaluation typically help us to decide whether to go with what we've got or make changes.

Evaluation can, however, be goal free, at least with respect to the interpretative planner's stated intentions. In such cases we evaluate an activity (e.g. a lecture) or an object in action (e.g. an exhibit) to find out what is happening. Evaluation judgements are made from the information collected without reference to any original aims and objectives. The assumption is that what is really happening is of at least as much interest as what was planned to happen. And that if we concentrate exclusively on what was planned to happen, we may overlook some significant outcomes from our interpretation, such as unforeseen but nevertheless worthwhile learning. Goal-free evaluation is also used when conducting a needs analysis, e.g. to discover where to concentrate further evaluation effort.

The biggest danger in deciding to undertake formal evaluation is that we do it for the wrong reason. Evaluation should always be done with a clear purpose in mind. It should not be done simply because others are doing it. We should be clear what information we are setting out to collect, and this should not be to confirm what we already know. Evaluation should not be done to confirm decisions that have already been taken or to settle old scores. But it can give invaluable knowledge of the audience, cheer staff on with feedback on their work, and provide information to help the planning, running and revision of all types of interpretation.

The best safeguard against the dangers noted above, when embarking on evaluation, is to prepare a written brief or, if an external consultant is involved, a proposal. This should outline the purpose of the study, who will do it and how, and how the results will be analysed and used. A proposal, and often a brief too, should also clarify the time, personnel and money needed to complete the project. The only exception to this advice is when evaluation is carried out by the person or team responsible for the interpretation as part of the design process (see section below on formative evaluation).

When and what to evaluate

Interpretation is a continuous process from first conception to opening and interaction with real visitors. There are many ways of chopping up and describing this continuum. Here I shall simply divide it into three stages: planning, production and running. Evaluation can take place at each stage. Evaluation *before* the production stage, i.e. during planning, is called front-end evaluation. Evaluation *during* the production stage is called formative evaluation. And evaluation *after* production, i.e. once the interpretation is up and running, is called summative evaluation. We shall deal with these three types of evaluation separately.

Front-end evaluation

We have already noted that data can be gathered to help judge the worth of plans before large sums of money are committed to carrying them out. This is front-end evaluation, and the focus of attention is the target audience for the proposed interpretative provision. The basic question we are asking is: how well will the planned piece of interpretation work for this audience? And the question is important, because if we can get a project off on the right lines at this stage, its further management is largely a matter of keeping it on the rails through to completion, with no need to backtrack or revise major planning decisions.

The data used in front-end evaluation may be extrapolated from general sources, e.g. visitor surveys carried out at the interpretative site, and national surveys of the target population; or they may be obtained specifically in relation to the proposed piece of interpretation. The first will provide demographic information (i.e. factual information about the mix of the sexes, age, distance travelled, socio-economic group, education and so on), while the second will illuminate the audience's existing knowledge and misunderstandings of the subject, and its expectations and likely commitment. Specific studies can also be used, e.g. to try out the proposed content of the interpretation and test the acceptability of the proposed media of communication. The aim is to gather the maximum amount of information, whether from general or specific sources, and whether from new or already published work. It may not be possible to collect all the information you would like, but even a little accurate information about the target audience is better than none, and it is always worth checking to see what information already exists.

The data assembled in these ways are used to review plans and improve them. They can help in defining the target audience, giving a starting point for the communication (i.e. the visitor's existing knowledge), revealing misunderstandings that have to be removed before communication can succeed, suggesting the effort that must be put into motivating the audience to attend, fixing the circulation space to be provided (e.g. for family groups as well as single visitors) and so on.

One of the dangers of this approach, and one of the criticisms most commonly levelled against it, is that it can lead to giving audiences only what they think they want: 'pandering to the lowest common denominator' as the critics more colourfully put it. Any interpretation with a serious educative function must aim to go beyond what the visitors already know, or think they know. In this context, front-end evaluation can be seen as an effort to find a suitable starting point for connecting the interpretative message to the visitor's familiar world, and thus to improve the interpreter's chances of success.

Formative evaluation

Formative evaluation, also known as prototyping or developmental testing, is carried out on mock-ups or prototypes, and is most commonly employed in the production of exhibits, maps, signposts and worksheets, where the physical form of the interpretation lends itself to this approach. The aim is to improve communicative quality by repeated trial until satisfactory results are obtained.

Formative evaluation may be carried out in a room specially set aside for this activity, or in a public space such as an exhibition gallery of a museum. The mock-up is quickly and cheaply made, using, wherever possible, nothing more elaborate than cardboard, photographs and machine-printed or hand-printed text. It is important that mock-ups and prototypes are kept as simple as possible consistent with their purpose, for they are put through a rapid succession of revisions in response to the audience's reactions.

There are two ways of evaluating mock-ups and prototypes, called cued and non-cued testing. In cued testing, a small representative sample of volunteers (not more than 25, often as few as 10, per test cycle) are individually asked to study the mock-up or prototype as long as they like. They are then asked a few questions, generally with the help of a questionnaire, designed to reveal how well the interpretation works as a piece of communication. For this reason, e.g. in the case of an exhibit, the interview normally takes place within sight of the mock-up or prototype (so it is not a test of the respondent's memory), and the questionnaire is based on asking the volunteers to explain in their own words what the interpretation is saying. Parallel procedures are adopted in the case of maps, signposts, worksheets and so on, all directed at gaining some insight into what needs to be done to improve the communication potential of what is to be provided.

In non-cued testing the mock-up or prototype is left out for the audience to see and its reactions are unobtrusively recorded. The aim here is to gain some insight into the motivational power of the designs, and thereby improve them (e.g. by altering the wording of titles). Here, as with cued testing, the question arises as to how long the testing cycle should be continued, given that we can never know when we have achieved the best possible results. The answer is, in fact, extremely pragmatic. Formative evaluation is continued until we have arrived at a satisfactory level of interpretative performance in the light of the time and money available. We then stop and move on to the next problem.

We have looked so far at the formative evaluation of the material objects of interpretation, such as exhibits. However, it is perfectly possible to put events through a similar trial-and-error cycle – often known as a dry run – and to use the resulting information to revise the content of the activity, or its staffing or its organization.

As I have just described it, formative evaluation is a highly pragmatic activity, and not surprisingly there are many pitfalls associated with it. These can be overcome with a little care. It is important that mock-ups and prototypes remain rough and ready productions, requiring only a few hours to prepare. If too much effort and money are invested in them there is a reluctance to modify them or to accept they do not work, and the notion of a fast trial-and-error cycle is undermined. Designers (and others) are often reluctant to believe that a rough and ready mock-up – say a poster representation of a three-dimensional exhibit – can provide valid information. But an enormous amount of practical experience, as well as formal studies (Griggs and Manning, 1983), shows that they can do just that. On the other hand, formative evaluation should not be devoted to just any ideas that come up for consideration. The danger here is that the trial-and-error cycle becomes an endless process of rejecting errors without any real progress. Mock-ups and prototypes should embody well thought out ideas that have been carefully developed in the light of the best experience and practice of interpretation. In this way, formative evaluation can get to grips with real communications problems, rather than dissipate its energy on poor designs.

Once a satisfactory design has been achieved through formative evaluation, it should not be spoilt by later changes. While spraying a car blue or green may not affect the performance of the engine fitted at the beginning of the production line, changes of this magnitude can completely destroy a piece of communication. It is important with printed material, for example, to guard against unfortunate changes in type size or in the relationship of text to illustrations.

It is time now to acknowledge the limitations of formative evaluation. These are mainly that it gives incomplete information. Mock-ups, prototypes and dry runs can give a strong indication of how attractive and communicative a piece of interpretation will be, but they cannot tell us with complete certainty how it will work in its final form under real conditions. For this we need summative evaluation. And for some media of communication (e.g. multi-screen audiovisuals) it may be impossible to produce a satisfactory mock-up with the resources available. But the argument for formative evaluation is that it gives *some* useful information, and this is better than no information at all. The value of this information is that it comes before money and reputations have been irreversibly committed to the final product.

Summative evaluation

In some ways the advantages and disadvantages of summative evaluation are the reverse of those of formative evaluation. Summative evaluation is done with the fully developed piece of interpretation under real conditions with a real audience. This means that all the extraneous environmental factors such as crowding, fatigue, noise and competing attractions (including the exit in museum galleries) can be taken into account, and the evaluator has a wider range of techniques to draw on, with better samples and a more powerful range of statistical techniques to analyse the results. These are reasons why professional evaluators often prefer summative evaluation. On the other hand, it can be too late: a case of bolting the stable door after the horse has gone, for all the money may have been spent with none available to put mistakes right. And if critical, summative evaluation can be a blow to the self-esteem of the people planning, producing and carrying out the interpretation, who might reasonably think 'once bitten, twice shy' when next asked to cooperate in the evaluation of their work. Summative evaluation needs, therefore, to be handled with great sensitivity, though we should not forget the real fillip that a tough but favourable report on a successful project can give.

Goal-free evaluation is much more typical of summative than of formative evaluation. Goal-oriented evaluation is, however, equally important. Summative evaluation uses these approaches to study how people feel and are motivated by a piece of interpretation, as well as how successful it is as a piece of communication. The results of summative evaluation can be used to report back to sponsors on how well the project turned out; to decide whether to continue or discontinue, expand or contract, an activity; as a basis for revision; and to guide the next project. If the results of summative evaluation are to form the basis of revision then it is clearly a good idea to keep back some of the budget for this work. Up to 10 per cent of the budget is sometimes recommended, but whether this is feasible in the present world may be open to doubt.

A notable canard with summative evaluation is the notion that it is possible to measure learning by comparing random pre-interpretation and post-interpretation samples of the audience. Whilst in theory this is perfectly feasible, in practice it fails because the approach does not take into account people's motivations and behaviour in an informal setting, and the great demands this approach to evaluation places on the human memory. A more satisfactory approach is to carry out cued testing on the definitive piece of interpretation, so as to gain an idea of its potential to teach factual information, given a suitably motivated audience.

How to collect evaluation data

There are basically two ways of finding out what happens when people encounter interpretation. We can *observe* what they do; and we can *ask* them what they feel or think about the interpretation, or what they have learned from it. This second method, which involves carrying out surveys, is also used to gather background information about the audience, e.g. demographic data. As we look at these approaches in more detail, you should bear in mind that normally three factors influence the choice of data-collecting methods: the *type* of information needed, *why* it is needed (or what will be done with it), and the *means* available to collect it.

When collecting data by observation we must first decide exactly what items of behaviour to observe. These items must be unequivocally specified so that behaviour can be consistently and accurately quantified, not only by you but by someone else as well. Moreover, the observations and the time frame in which they take place must be capable of categorization, and of being recorded, because this is the only way they can be made to yield useful information.

What sort of behaviour are we talking about? Well, it includes a wide variety of items that might be relevant to our purpose: sitting, walking, reading, interacting with others, interacting with the interpretation and so on (see Diamond, 1986, for some real-life examples). Two particular measures derived from observing visitor behaviour have been used in evaluation, and these are worth noting for their wide applicability:

Attraction   The ratio of the number of people stopping at a piece of interpretation for five seconds or more to the total number passing by.
Holding   The time spent at the interpretation given that the person has stopped.

The observer may remain hidden during the collection of data. This is called unobtrusive observation. Or the observer may be a participant in the interpretative experience and known to the audience, just as an anthropologist is known to the society he or she is studying. In this case the observer is obtrusive. Unobtrusive observation is simpler and does not require extensive training. It is important, of course, that the people being observed remain unaware of the observer's presence. Participant observation is potentially a richer source of data because the behaviour is observed at close quarters, but the danger is that the people being observed do not behave naturally in the presence of the observer.

Unobtrusive recording of behaviour can be carried out by machines (e.g. video recorders and tape recorders) as well as by people. The advantage of 'permanent' records on tape is that they can be analysed, and checked by a second evaluator, at leisure. Inevitably though, questions of ethics arise. Is taping a conversation so very different from tapping a telephone? At all events the audience should be aware of the intention to observe or record (which may affect their behaviour), individuals should not be identified in the records, and the tapes should be wiped as soon as the behavioural data have been extracted. Some indirect methods are, however, less problematic, such as recording wear patterns in carpets or nose-prints on glass. But these methods yield relatively poor data, and they have hardly been used in evaluating interpretative provisions.

Observation is generally used in evaluation to gain descriptive information on what is going on. It is generally combined with surveys to obtain a more complete picture. A more detailed account of observational methods is given by Hutt and Hutt (1970) and Bechtel and Zeisel (1987). Surveys provide descriptive information about how people think and feel, which is obtained by asking questions. It is usual to distinguish between quantitative work, which lends itself to analysis, and qualitative work, which does not because it is generally less formally organized. Both approaches have a part to play in evaluation, and the best results can often be obtained by combining the two.

The minimal aim of quantitative surveys is to provide objective results summarized in descriptive statistics (range, averages, standard error), though analytical statistical techniques are often used as well. The data must, therefore, be carefully collected using standard questionnaires. These questionnaires may be filled in by the respondents themselves, i.e. they are self-administered, or they may be filled in by an interviewer (and are therefore often called interview forms) in a face-to-face interview. The questionnaire is essentially the same in both cases. However, a self-administered questionnaire is limited to preset questions and written responses, whereas an interview form can allow the interviewer to ask for explanations.

Surveys need to be carefully planned, and there are a number of stages to negotiate successfully if the work is to be done properly. The golden rule is that it is better to do nothing than to conduct an ill conceived and badly planned survey giving inaccurate data that result in people unwittingly taking wrong decisions. This does not mean that surveys are particularly difficult to plan and conduct. They are, in fact, largely a matter of common sense. But for the reason just given, professional advice should be sought if doubts arise at any stage. A good source for anyone starting in this field is Fink and Kosecoff (1985).

Writing a questionnaire means making decisions about its length (how much time will respondents be prepared to give?), the types of questions to include and how they will be ordered, and how the responses will be recorded. Payne (1951) is a fund of good advice by an experienced practitioner in this area. Once written, it is essential to pilot a questionnaire before using it in a real survey. This will tell you whether it is usable in practice, and indicate whether it is *valid* in the sense that it records what it is supposed to record and *reliable* in the sense that it *consistently* records what it is supposed to record.

For most purposes, surveys must be carried out on samples of the group of people or population we are interested in, such as the visitors to an interpretative site. Only rarely do we have the resources to question everyone in the group, as happens in a census. It must be stressed that results obtained from non-representative samples can be quite meaningless. For example, self-completion questionnaires left out for visitors to pick up and return can only tell us about the subgroup of visitors who pick up and return forms, not about visitors as a whole. In fact, the two groups may differ in many ways other than in their form-filling behaviour. A simple random sample is often all that is required, and there are a number of straightforward techniques that can be used to obtain them. Hood (1986) suggests:

> First estimate how many interviews you need to acquire in a day or week, based on your previous attendance for a similar period of the year. Then station interviewers at designated locations, usually exits, where they count off visitors (every fifth or tenth, etc.) to meet your desired sample size.

A similar method can be used with postal surveys, by counting off addresses on a list instead of visitors at exits, to obtain the desired sample size. Telephone surveys are, however, more difficult, and professional advice should always be obtained. In drawing a sample of visitors (e.g. to an interpretative site) you should take into account fluctuations in the characteristics of the audience from one part of the day or week to another, and from season to season. A sample of unaccompanied visitors on weekdays may, for example, be strongly misleading if most visitors come in family groups at weekends.

The size of the sample has been mentioned above. It needs to be big enough to be representative of the group of people that the survey is concerned with. The size can be determined statistically to give the desired degree of accuracy in the results. But for many purposes Hood's (1986) rule of thumb will suffice: sample 10 or 20 per cent of the audience, using the lower percentage for a larger audience (e.g. 10 per cent for 5000 people). Usually 300–400 responses are satisfactory for general visitor surveys, and this number of returns is satisfactory for postal surveys too.

In concentrating on the mechanics of designing and conducting surveys, we must not overlook the vital role of the interviewer. It is important for this person to strike the right, friendly relationship with the respondent during the interview, to be thoroughly familiar with the questionnaire, and to follow the wording and sequence of the questions exactly. No difficult skills are required, and a small amount of training and practice in these matters can do much to ensure success.

Turning now to qualitative surveys, these tend to generate a lot of information, and to capture a much richer human response than quantitative surveys; but they are time consuming (particularly in comparison with self-administered questionnaires) and the results are often difficult to organize or summarize in a coherent way. Qualitative results are more subjective than quantitative results.

Qualitative surveys include both individual and group interviews. In both the aim is to have the participants respond in their own words to open-ended questions, so they can clearly express their understanding of the subject being researched. These views may be drawn forth in informal conversations, or they may be elicited on the basis of a carefully prepared guide, which includes the topics to be discussed and questions to be asked. Wolf developed the *informal conversation* approach in the interpretative world under the rubric 'naturalistic evaluation' (which also includes observation). Wolf's (1980) paper is a good introduction to this approach, which is especially sympathetic to individual differences among the people being interviewed. The main criticisms are that – even more than other qualitative methods – it is time consuming, produces data that are difficult to analyse, and depends a lot on the subjective judgements of the interviewer.

A more planned approach to qualitative work is the *unstructured interview*, which makes use of an interview guide but allows the interviewer to take the topics and questions in any order, and to probe and explore responses in any way that seems appropriate. The main advantage of this approach is that it is more systematic than informal conversations, requires less interviewing skill, and makes better use of the time available. A third method uses a *structured interview* with a standardized, open-ended interview form, similar to a quantitative questionnaire. It uses a fixed sequence of questions with limited scope for the probing and exploration of responses, but the responses are still open ended in contrast to quantitative work, as they comprise the words of the persons interviewed. Standardized interviews are especially valuable when several interviewers are involved, as some uniformity of approach can be achieved, and the results more readily combined.

Group interviews are also known as focus groups. They have been used in commercial market research for many years to test consumers' attitudes, and are now finding a place in interpretative planning, particularly in front-end evaluation. A focus group comprises eight to ten people who have been carefully chosen to mirror a segment of the target audience. Several focus groups may be needed to obtain the range of responses needed. The interviews take place in a quiet, comfortable room – generally with refreshments available – and last from one to two hours. The conversations are normally recorded for detailed analysis later. It is quite acceptable for the interpretative planners to sit in on the focus groups, either in the room or behind a one-way mirror if a fully equipped interview room is available. The participants should be asked to agree to this, and it is important not to break the relaxed atmosphere if the interview is to go well. The interview is normally conducted with the help of an interview guide, i.e. it is unstructured.

Focus groups allow for a more free-wheeling exploration of the audience's feelings, about plans or existing interpretation, than do more highly structured quantitative surveys. It helps that individuals can test out their views against those of the other members of the group. But focus group interviews cannot tell us about the views of the audience as a whole. Only quantitative work on representative samples can do this. Ideally, then, focus groups results should be followed up with quantitative work.

On the face of it, qualitative studies are easier to carry out than quantitative studies. But this is a mistaken view because it underestimates the great skill required to conduct informal interviews so that they yield the required information. It also underestimates the difficulty of analysing qualitative data. For these reasons qualitative work is best left to professional evaluators, though readers interested in developing their own skills will find help in Sommer and Sommer (1980), Taylor and Bogdan (1984), Patton (1988) and Krueger (1988).

Table 30.1 indicates how the main ways of collecting data are normally utilized in each of the three types of evaluation. There is no single best way of doing evaluation, but some methods fit better at one stage than at others. In reading this table we should bear in mind that it is better to evaluate early (front-end and formative evaluation) rather than late (summative evaluation), when resources and reputations have been irreversibly committed; that it is better to use a range of methods rather than one, because each has it strengths and weaknesses; that some methods are more suitable for beginners and non-professional evaluators than others, notably simple quantitative surveys, cued testing and unobtrusive observation; and that the work is only worth doing if it can be done well. I can do no better than end this section with Hood's (1986) advice:

For the beginning researcher, it is advantageous to choose a method whereby the information can be easily recorded, analysed and interpreted. Usually this means an approach that asks definitive questions, uses a paper record and involves analysis of the data by calculator or computer.

Table 30.1 Typical methods of collecting evaluation data

Method	Front-end evaluation	Formative evaluation	Summative evaluation
Observation			
Unobtrusive		x	x
Participant			x
Quantitative surveys			
Interview	x	x	x
Self-administered	x		x
Qualitative surveys			
Informal conversation (naturalistic)	x		x
Unstructured interview (with individuals)	x	x	x
Structured interview (with individuals)	x	x	x
Focus group (unstructured interview)	x		x

Who does the evaluation?

So far in this chapter I have tried to indicate where professional help should be used. But there are many opportunities for the interpretative planner to carry out, or be involved in, evaluation. Ideally, these should not be seen as optional but grasped as real opportunities to be involved. Evaluation works best when everyone in the interpretative team is committed to it, and to acting on the results that come out of it. Opportunities for involvement are not difficult to find in planning interviews, carrying out straightforward surveys, sitting in on focus groups, and making unobtrusive observations. But in particular the team should be responsible for formative evaluation (with or without the help of a professional evaluator), so that this becomes a natural part of designing effective interpretation, rather than an opportunity for outsiders to comment on how well, or otherwise, the team is doing.

References

BECHTEL, R. B. and ZEISEL, J. (1987) 'Observation: the world under a glass', in R. B. Bechtel, R. Marans, and W. Michelson (eds), *Methods in Environmental and Behavioral Research*, Van Nostrand Reinhold, New York, 11–40

DIAMOND, J. (1986) 'The behavior of family groups in science museums', *Curator*, **29**(2), 139–154

FINK, A and KOŚECOFF, J. (1985) *How to Conduct Surveys: a Step-by-Step Guide*, Sage, London

GRIGGS, S. A. and MANNING, J. (1983) 'The predictive validity of formative evaluation of exhibits', *Museums Studies Journal*, **1**, 31–41

HOOD, M. (1986) 'Getting started in audience research', *Museum News*, **64**(3), 24–31

HUTT, S. J. and HUTT, C. (1970) *Direct Observation and Measurement of Behavior*, Charles C. Thomas, Springfield, IL

KRUEGER, R. A. (1988) *Focus Groups: a Practical Guide for Applied Research*, Sage, London

LOOMIS, R. J. (1987) *Museum Visitor Evaluation: New Tool for Management*, American Association for State and Local History, Nashville, TN

MILES, R. S., ALT, M. B., GOSLING, D. C., LEWIS, B. N. and TOUT, A. F. (1988) *The Design of Educational Exhibits* (2nd edn), Unwin Hyman, London

PATTON, M. Q. (1988) *How to Use Qualitative Methods in Evaluation*, Sage, London

PAYNE, S. L. (1951) *The Art of Asking Questions*, Princeton University Press, Princeton, NJ

SCREVEN, C. G. (1990) 'Uses of evaluation before, during and after exhibit design', *ILVS Review*, **1**(2), 36–66

SOMMER, R. and SOMMER, B. (1980) *A Practical Guide to Behavioral Research: Tools and Techniques*, Oxford University Press, Oxford

TAYLOR, S. J. and BOGDAN, R. (1984) *Introduction to Qualitative Research Methods: the Search for Meanings*, Wiley, New York

WOLF, R. (1980) 'A naturalistic view of evaluation', *Museum News*, **58**(1), 39–45

Bibliography

ALT, M. B. (1980) 'Four years of visitor surveys in the British Museum (Natural History)', *Museums Journal*, 10–19

ALT, M. B. and SHAW, K. M. (1984) 'Characteristics of ideal museum exhibits', *British Journal of Psychology*, **75**, 25–36

BORUN, M. (1983) *Planets and Pulleys: Studies of Class Visits to Science Museums*, AST Centers, Washington, DC

BORUN, M. (1980) *What's in a Name? A Study of the Effectiveness of Explanatory Labels in a Science Museum*, AST Centers, Washington, DC

MELTON, A. W., GOLDBERG, N. and MASON, C. W. (1936) *Experimental Studies of the Education of Children in a Museum of Science*, American Association of Museums, Washington, DC

SERRELL, B. (1990) *What Research Says About Learning in Science Museums*, AST Centers, Washington, DC

TAYLOR, S. (1992) *Try It! Improving Exhibits through Formative Evaluation*, AST Centers, Washington, DC

UZZELL, D. L. (1988) 'The interpretative experience', in D. Canter, M. Krampen and D. Stea (eds), *Ethnoscapes*, Gower, London

UZZELL, D. L. (1989) *Heritage Interpretation: Volume II: The Visitor Experience*, Belhaven Press, London

UZZELL, D. L. (1992) 'Les approches socio-cognitives de l'évaluation sommative des expositions', *Publics et Musées*, **1**(1), 107–123

Case study 30.1

An evaluation of the provision of drama in the Science Museum, London

Sandra Bicknell

It is the brave evaluator who looks at first-person interpretation. A review of the visitor studies literature quickly shows the dearth of work that goes anywhere near assessing the impact of people as part of a museum's work with its visitors. However, in October 1992 the Science Museum in London initiated a study of the provision of drama in our galleries.

This study is proving fascinating and I have used it to illustrate evaluation methods and approaches. At the time of writing we are still some months from producing the final report. This case study therefore concentrates on the process of evaluation and what we are expecting to gain from the work.

Drama in the Science Museum

One of the interpretative provisions at the Science Museum is the use of professional actors on the galleries. The actors provide a means of portraying both fictitious and 'real' characters from the history of science and technology. In general, the approach is non-intrusive. Visitors are welcome to join in, or they can walk by: the choice is theirs.

Gallery drama in the Science Museum began in a modest way in 1987 with a single actor portraying Ben, the driver on *Puffing Billy*. Initially the presentations were monologues, with the actors speaking in role from a basic script. Developments have included the use of duologues (two actors in character), theme days (a group of actors playing a number of roles around a single theme, such as transport), workshops and small-scale plays. By 1992 the company of actors, Spectrum Drama and Theatre Projects, had grown to some twenty actors performing over twenty roles as part of a daily programme. In fact, in 1992, there were over 1000 performances with a potential audience of well over half a million visitors.

There are many intentions for this provision, including giving a human face to the Museum, enlivening the visit and entertaining the visitors. The performances are also hoped to provide a memory trigger for a gallery, or specific object, as well as communicating information: the complexity of the issues, a historic context and an overview. The drama also provides a unique opportunity for debate both amongst the visitors and between the visitor and the actor.

What do we want to know?

When doing any evaluations in the Science Museum we ask ourselves the following. What is it we want to know? Why do we want to know this? How are we going to find out? What are we going to do with the information when we do know?

Let me start by answering – at least in part – the first of these questions: what do we want to know? We want to know if the drama meets its own stated aims but we also want to know how our visitors react to such presentations. Therefore, the study is both goal oriented (does it meet the stated aims?) and goal free (letting the visitors' responses guide the assessment of the data gathered).

The goals of the evaluation are to establish what happens when visitors encounter the actors, to define the strengths and weaknesses of the medium and to assess how well it can meet its objectives.

Why do we want to know this?

The Museum's drama is seen by many of the Museum's staff as an excellent way of providing context for the artefacts in our collections. However, the provision of such first-person interpretations has been perceived as demanding of resources. There is some debate, within the Museum, as to the effectiveness of drama as a communication medium. The provision will continue in the Museum but we are looking for weaknesses and strengths in the use of this sort of interpretation. Our aim is to provide information that will help staff to make informed decisions – based on quantitative and qualitative data – to enable appropriate developments to the drama provision in the Science Museum.

The report will also focus on goals for future development of drama in the Science Museum and will recommend actions to enable the achievement of these goals.

How do we collect the data?

For this study an independent firm of consultants who specialize in qualitative work was contracted to carry out in-depth research. An initial brief was sent to the company, the Susie Fisher Group, outlining our expectations of the work and the financial and staff constraints to the project. In liaison with in-house staff the evaluation scenario was developed and a proposal document submitted. This document identified timescale, costs, staffing and methodology, including the sampling strategy. The result was a mix of quantitative and qualitative work, structured and unstructured interviews, focus groups, naturalistic work and observational work both unobtrusive and as participant observers.

Trying to understand the interaction between visitors and the drama roles in the Science Museum is complex. Using a standard communication model with a sender, a medium of communication and a receiver, we began to develop the evaluation scenario. The sender is the Museum or, more accurately, the Museum's staff. Some of the issues important to the senders are the need to maximize the effectiveness of the communication, its comprehensibility, and the accuracy of the information being presented. The medium is the actor, the actor's script, the staging of the presentation and the locality of the performance. All of these factors, and others, contribute to the outcome for the visitors – the receivers.

In general, museums attract heterogeneous audiences. With the drama provision at the Science Museum we have identified a number of audiences whose views we felt to be crucial to helping us to understand the strengths and weaknesses of the drama presentations. These key audiences are: adults, teachers, parents, children in family groups, children in school groups and non-participants. What these people gain from the drama will be influenced by many factors such as their willingness to take part and their prior knowledge.

A general strategy was developed by the Susie Fisher Group which firstly involved observing four of the drama performances. The observers were asked to note what was happening during the performance. These observations were augmented by the commissioning of video recordings of the performances. The recordings were also used to compare the actual performances with the scripted versions.

Group discussions – focus groups – were used to gather greater detail about the audiences' views of the drama. Four formal groups were used: a school group with children aged eight to nine years, a group of teachers, a group of adults without children and a group of the actors. In addition two families, who were visiting the Museum, were joined by one of the researchers for the duration of their visit.

Another method used was to ask teachers, with school groups who had booked to take part in one of the Museum's drama theme days, to take a Dictaphone with them into the galleries. The teachers were given a prompt sheet of issues we were interested in, but it was left to them to tell us whatever they wished.

The qualitative methods outlined above were used to help us to formulate the questionnaire, the quantitative aspect of the evaluation. One-to-one interviews were used to provide quantitative substantiation of key visitor attitudes to the drama presentations. Just over 200 five-minute interviews were conducted. The questionnaire was designed to be used with both children (aged six and above) and adults, as well as with participants and non-participants; a quarter of the sample were non-participants. The effectiveness of the questionnaire was tested by piloting it prior to bringing in professional interviewers to collect the actual survey data. Six of the drama roles were targeted for interviews.

The data were then put on to a computer database for analysis (we use a statistical analysis package designed for use on a personal computer, SPSS/PC). The sampling strategy and subsequent analysis have allowed us to compare responses from a series of roles, from non-participants and participants, from children and adults and between female and male visitors.

What will we do next?

The information from any evaluation is only as useful as its application. To me the purpose of all evaluation is to initiate change, or at least to provide for potential change, in a constructive and focused way. Evaluations should not be used as a confirmation of the status quo.

This evaluation study will be used to develop the Science Museum's drama provision. The data will allow us to gauge the most appropriate presentation style for the various audiences. The study will guide us in the maximization of communicating with the visitors, show us how best to keep the interpretation accurate, provide us with an idea about what is special about drama as compared with other interpretative tools, and inform us of the effect of such presentations on visitors. In general terms, having made an assessment of the worth of the drama provision to our visitors we can then focus on developing the enterprise to be even more worth while.

The evaluation of the drama provision at the Science Museum can be viewed as an example of all three of the production stages for evaluation work described in Chapter 30: front-end, formative and summative evaluation. It is a summative evaluation in that it looks at the end result: assessing the drama in terms of both its stated objectives (goal oriented) and the visitors' reactions (goal free). It is formative in the sense that the data may identify areas with potential for improvement. Strictly speaking, formative work should involve an iterative process of testing and amending and the drama provision is continually going through this process, although in an informal way. The evaluation can also be viewed as a piece of front-end work – work that will help us to develop future dramatic presentations. It will provide us with information about the target audiences, their existing knowledge, their misconceptions, their expectations, their feelings towards the drama and their interest in the general idea of drama in museums. The evaluation also provides us with information about the medium itself, whether it is an effective means of communication. All of these factors will help us to further develop the use of drama in the Science Museum.

From the preliminary analysis we have received an overwhelming thumbs-up for the drama. Over 200 visitors were interviewed and over 90 per cent of them felt that the actors made the museum exhibits come to life and more memorable, and that they told them more about an exhibit than a label. As one visitor expressed in a letter to the Director: 'We were really entertained and enthralled by Bridie McPherson on the Glasgow tram. It really brought history alive to the children, and they remembered nearly all that she told them.'

SECTION FIVE

MARKETING

31

Selling the heritage product

Kenneth Robinson, with contributions by Marion Wertheim and Grahame Senior

Marketing is the process of delivering products to customers. In the case of heritage attractions, the principal difference is that the products are at fixed locations and the customers have to be persuaded that the product is one that they are prepared to travel to and to buy. Success in selling the heritage product is fundamental to most heritage attractions and sites, whether the primary purpose is curatorial, economic or both.

Curatorship implies the care, conservation and interpretation of assets. Curatorial objectives are, of course, not exclusively the concern of those with formal curatorial responsibility. Even those owners who open their houses with some reluctance realize that visitors who understand and appreciate what they visit and see will treat it with greater care and derive more satisfaction. Visitor satisfaction is the aim. The most effective means of achieving this satisfaction is by engaging the interest of the visitors, conveying information to them about what they see, to ensure that they derive value for money if an admission charge is made.

Perhaps the objectives may, on the other hand, be primarily economic: seeking to achieve optimum levels of income by attracting and satisfying visitors.

Marketing is the process by which these curatorial and economic objectives can be selectively accomplished. The marketing process involves a number of interrelated aspects, which could be called the steps in the marketing process. Within this chapter, the process is summarized under four stages:

(1) setting marketing objectives through strategies and targets;
(2) market research;
(3) promotion;
(4) evaluation.

This process is not limited in its application to the grand plan of attracting visitors to heritage sites. It is equally valid as a system of objectives, appraisal, action and evaluation for many aspects of management.

Setting marketing objectives: strategies and targets

Among those who have not been trained in marketing or are unfamiliar with how the process can be applied, there is often a suspicion that marketing is synonymous with selling and commercialism – that in following marketing techniques, basic curatorial and idealistic objectives must inevitably be distorted and comprised. This fallacy has fortunately diminished in recent years, during which time the number of visitor attractions in the United Kingdom has increased faster than the level of public demand and available leisure spending, leading to greater competition between heritage sites. This competition has created the need to utilize more sharply focused management skills. The marketing process does not prescribe the objectives of owners or managers, but is a means by which defined objectives can be achieved.

Very few heritage sites have a clear social and interpretative mission – a clear objective to provide access to their historic assets for socially and demographically defined individuals within their catchment populations. An exception occurs in respect of general aspirations to attract educational groups. However, consideration of the process described in this chapter will demonstrate that marketing techniques can be used precisely – to attract and satisfy particular target segments of potential visitors from the whole population, if this is a required objective.

For most heritage sites, however, which are open to the public in general with some added educational provision and possibly with some special arrangements for minority and special interest groups, the fundamental marketing proposition is simple. Are there sufficient potential visitors in the catchment area who can be persuaded to buy the product in its present form? Or, does the product have to be modified to attract the required number of type of potential visitors?

Matching the heritage product to its potential market

The thought that what is offered to visitors might be varied, so as to attract more of them, is often considered intimidating – but this need not be so. From the point of view of the basic heritage assets at a site – buildings, artefacts, historic connections and ambience – the product is not merely a matter of what these asset ingredients are, but is critically dependent on how they are presented, and the experience and level of enjoyment that the visitors receive.

Defining the image and product presentation

No steps should be taken towards interpreting heritage sites, or indeed in deciding which elements of a site should be interpreted and to what extent, without a clear analysis of the demographics of future customers.

As each year goes by and the competition in the UK visitor attractions market increases, it will become increasingly difficult for heritage sites to ignore their customer profile when determining the way in which their assets are presented to visitors. It may no longer be adequate merely to publicize what exists, or has been developed and interpreted to reflect the enthusiasms of those most closely involved with a project and most knowledgeable about its subject. Who will the users be? What are their characteristics, expectations and needs?

The second, but closely related, aspect of matching a product to its potential market is concerned with the image that is chosen for its product. Again, this should not be devised in isolation, or merely using the obvious and logical elements such as the established name of a property or location, its subject and theme names. The image of a heritage attraction must of course be dependent on, or compatible with, its intrinsic historical aspects, its location and its theme.

The overall image of a heritage attraction is an amalgam of its name, logo, content, promotional message and location. These questions are further reviewed in a later section which discusses promotion in greater detail. Suffice it to say that for marketing techniques to be most effectively applied, the image of a heritage product should be specifically defined to ensure that it will be attractive and informative to the selected target customers, if the effect of marketing activity is to be optimized.

Consequently, where the existing form of a product cannot attract the selected potential visitors or adequate numbers of potential visitors, whichever is the case, a key aspect of the marketing process is to define who

the potential customers will be – and, by appraisal, to decide how best the heritage aspects of the property can be presented to appeal to those potential customers and what, therefore, the promotional image should be.

It has been traditional in many heritage attractions to treat visitors as if they were a more or less homogeneous group. In fact, the total is always divisible into different groups or market segments. The usual segmentation of the potential visitor market for heritage attractions is by the following user types, which are useful in selecting marketing and promotional media:

(1) local residents;
(2) day visitors from regional catchment area;
(3) domestic visitors staying in hotels, guest houses and caravan parks etc. (commercial accomodation) or with friends and relatives;
(4) overseas visitors in commercial accommodation or with friends and relatives;
(5) education groups.

From a promotional point of view, the analysis of potential visitors into these categories can be used to guide how the heritage assets can most effectively be interpreted and presented and the promotional messages which need to be developed to match the different perceptions, motivations and needs of these market segments. This analysis is an essential foundation for effective marketing activity.

Having defined who the potential visitors will be and how the assets of the product are to be interpreted and presented to them, it will be essential to analyse available promotional media which will reach the target customers and then to design advertisements which reflect the product and its image for different forms of advertising and promotional media. This part of the process is, then, a question of defining how many visitors are required (or how many can be accommodated if capacity is a limiting factor) and who they are, if specific social targets are involved.

Once the numerical and social targets have been established, it is essential to consider whether the existing product can be promoted to attract the desired audience. If it cannot, then the assets of the product must be carefully considered to decide what features or themes can be presented on the basis of the intrinsic assets and their history, so as to attract the required number and/or types of visitors. The presentation is not merely a question of physical presentation and interpretation on site, but also how it is reflected in all aspects of the image of an attraction.

Pricing strategy

Whether the primary objective of admitting visitors to an attraction is curatorial or financial, the criterion for success is the same: visitors must receive good value for money if they are to be satisfied. Accordingly, pricing strategy is an essential element of the marketing process.

Determining value for money

What constitutes good value for money is dependent on many factors. One is whether a visit matches visitors' expectations: this can be affected by various aspects such as the accuracy of the promotional image and the quality of interpretation and visitor management within a site. A second factor is whether all aspects of the visit are satisfactory: no matter how good most of a visit may be, visitor satisfaction can be seriously marred by matters of detail or small disappointments.

However, the most important aspects in determining value for money are:

(1) the intensity of the visitor experience;
(2) the length of time a visitor stays in an attraction (length of stay);
(3) the *demand*.

Length of stay and intensity of experience

The length of stay and intensity of experience are inversely proportional. The most intensive visitor experiences, such as riding in a simulator or watching an audio-visual show, may sustain (at 1993 levels) a payment of £2–£3 per adult for a few minutes. At the other end of the scale, a visit to a historic site with few remaining features and little interpretation may not engender satisfaction at an admission charge of £1 per adult even if a comprehensive visit to a site takes an hour or more.

Demand

The third of the key elements, demand, is particularly interesting as demand can be stimulated solely through marketing. Demand can justify a higher payment and sustain satisfaction where, without such demand, this would not be possible. An extreme example of demand-supported value was the initial visitor interest and the admission charge to see the remains of part of the hull of the *Mary Rose*. The recovery of the *Mary Rose* was an extraordinary *cause célèbre*, involving national television and newspaper coverage months before the lifting of the hull, with Prince Charles taking a direct interest and diving on the hull. There was a sequence of archaeological finds. This continuous media interest fuelled the enthusiasm of the public to visit and pay handsomely for the privilege of seeing the relatively scant remains of the wooden hull – originally subject to an admission charge separate from that for the excellent accompanying exhibition of finds. In the case of the *Mary Rose*, the demand was, from the outset, created by the media attention, rather than being purchased through promotion. Nevertheless, demand and expectation can sustain higher prices even though, subsequently, visitors must still at the end

of their visit be satisfied that they have received value for money.

To charge or not?

For some heritage organizations, whether it is acceptable to charge the public for admission is considered a crucial question. It may be assumed they should have access to cultural and historical assets in the ownership of public authorities, as of right. It is no part of this chapter on marketing techniques to suggest whether it is right or wrong to charge for admission; that is entirely a matter for those responsible for the assets. It is, however, appropriate to reflect that the sometimes vexed question of the application of admission charges need never simply be a question of whether to charge or not.

For a number of years in the USA, many major museums and public institutions have operated voluntary contribution systems, in lieu of an enforced admission charge payment at a fixed level. The voluntary systems vary tremendously. At their simplest and least lucrative they are merely contribution boxes supported by notices requesting a contribution – but so placed that they can easily be avoided. In other locations a contribution box is placed at the point of entry, with staff available to observe and to press the conscience of those visitors considering whether or not to make the voluntary contribution. At a further level of encouragement, staff occupy 'pay boxes' alongside individual turnstiles; badges are given to visitors who have paid, thereby identifying those who have not; and, in some cases, a voluntary contribution is recommended, occasionally with a minimum contribution. Whatever may be considered of the ethics of these methods, they provide an opportunity to solicit contributions which may be an acceptable alternative to some heritage attractions to the introduction of fixed charges.

However, when charges are made there is no reason why they have to be made for all visitors or that they need apply at all times. Even those who believe local residents or British citizens should have a right of access without charge, generally believe that it is acceptable that tourists should be charged and thereby contribute to the upkeep of the heritage that they so greatly appreciate and for which they expect to have to pay for access.

There is no reason why admission charges cannot be introduced and monitored to ensure that certain categories of visitor may be admitted without charge or that any visitors who come at certain times of the day, or on specified days, or out of the main season, can be admitted free of charge whilst all others pay.

Establishing the level of admission charge

It is of course a question of policy as to what the level of admission charge should be. Where charges apply, is it intended that commercially justifiable levels of charge will be applied, or will they be subsidized? Is it merely a question of ensuring that all visitors receive good value for money?

Price can be used as a means of controlling demand. Conservation and protection of fragile heritage assets can be a motivating factor in setting a relatively high admission charge, which has the effect of reducing visitor numbers and therefore reducing pressure on the core heritage assets. The intensity of the experience however has to be increased, by improving what is shown or how it is presented, if value for money is still to be achieved at the higher price level. Can one accept the elitist social impact of limiting access to those who can afford to pay fairly high prices?

Setting the level of charge is frequently assumed to be a conjectural and subjective matter. It is a decision that is vital to the success of a business and is often made by those whose subjective judgements are least well informed. Many a boardroom disagreement, or year-end appraisal of performance against budget, will turn on whether or not admission charges have been set at the right level.

The tendency of the visitor attractions business to set prices generally no more frequently than once each year is a further weakness. It is a strange stricture – although the operation of fixed rates is necessary for pre-booked groups of visitors, particularly those arranged through the travel trade where commitments may have to be firmly made months in advance. Most other consumer products expect to vary selling prices according to market forces and supply and demand. Why not so at heritage attractions? The strait-jacket of once-a-year revision could usefully be discarded, although this would require caveats in promotional material for properties that chose to publicize prices, as the length of time that promotional material is in circulation is uncontrollable.

Where value for money is the prime criteria for establishing admission price, there is no reason for uncertainty as to what the right level should be. All visitor attractions experience some degree of 'turn-around': visitors who approach the pay point but choose not to go in for various reasons. In town centre sites and at sites where the number of visitors attracted on impulse is high, the degree of turnaround is usually quite high. Where there is plenty to do outside the paying area, a high turnaround percentage also applies. At rural sites where there is little alternative activity, the turnaround percentage may be quite low. Nevertheless, it is variable and the final decision is strongly influenced by the admission price – when an individual or a group of visitors considers whether or not to pay to go in.

A visitor's perception of value for money also varies directly as the admission charge changes. Accordingly, it is possible to survey the number of visitors entering a site and compare this number with the proportion who actually choose to pay to go in – and at the same time measure value for money by survey – at several different price levels. It can immediately be measured how the perception of value for money varies by price and what effect it has on the turn-around percentage. It then becomes a simple matter to determine what percentage of arriving visitors at a given admission price will produce the optimum result, bearing in mind the subsequent spending of visitors within a site on other aspects such as retailing and catering. If visitors do not pay to come in, the subsequent spending does not arise.

Pricing strategies are very much a part of the marketing process, in terms of the structure of prices that is set by visitor category (adult, child, senior citizen etc.) and by special enhanced-value tickets (family tickets, season tickets, friends/members etc.). Traditionally, child admission prices were set at half adult rates. Senior citizens were generally charged at the same level as children. At most leading heritage sites, this is no longer the case. Most senior citizens are no longer impoverished. Many have savings and private pensions to supplement their income from the state pension and they are increasingly likely to seek heritage outings. Whilst most heritage sites still have some concessions for senior citizens, it is usual for them now to be priced somewhere between the adult and child price.

Similarly, child prices in general have risen above half adult price. This has been greatly encouraged by leisure and theme parks where the child price is frequently virtually the same as the adult price. However, at many heritage sites, items of interest and enjoyment for children are limited, and some heritage sites, particularly historic houses, do not seek to encourage more family groups and children. In such cases the child price may be maintained at a fairly high level.

Whilst having to acknowledge the senior citizen qualification age at the level established by the state, there are otherwise no real industry standards concerning age definitions between adults and children or student rates where these apply, or the age below which children are admitted free of charge. The most important aspect from a marketing point of view is to consider the objective: to attract given numbers or target segments of visitors, and to use pricing policies so as to optimize the products that are offered to these visitors. The price and the product are inextricably related. For consumers, one reflects the other. The price is part of the product offer.

Price variations may be used as part of the visitor management methods employed at a heritage site, or as a part of the marketing process. In visitor management terms this is usually achieved by offering price incentives by season, by day of the week or even by time of day. Vouchers may also be used to encourage visitors to come when they would not otherwise do so or to encourage them to come at specific times. Unless the objective is to influence the timing of a visit, all such schemes should be treated with great caution.

In reality, few heritage sites have real capacity problems. Despite the extreme seasonality of the tourism business, seasonal peaking has reduced greatly over recent years. Bank holiday crowds are no longer exceptional and demand is not so highly peaked in the school summer holidays as used to be the case. The problem with many price incentive schemes is that they are introduced without associated arrangements to monitor and evaluate their effect. Very often such schemes are considered to be successful, because of the number of people who use them. However, if the visitors would have come anyway without using such price incentive schemes at times when they could have been accommodated, then shifting them by price incentives, or merely encouraging them to use an incentive when they would have paid full price, is in reality a loss. This can be tracked by survey, but from experience it rarely is.

Family tickets are often promoted at the point of entry but not advertised away from the site. Where this policy is followed, it is obvious that any family aware of the family ticket will purchase one on arrival; hence the sales of family tickets look good in numerical terms. Do people who purchase family tickets report significantly better value for money than families on days when family tickets are not on offer, if checked by survey? If not, then does the proportion of families who turn around and do not pay for admission on days when family tickets are not in operation justify the loss from full price admission that occurs on the days when the family ticket is in use? Surveys can prove the acceptability of such schemes.

However, even if family tickets are promoted they can actually lead to a direct loss of income. Most family tickets offer admission for two adults and between two and four children at slightly less than the full price for two adults and two children. Where family tickets are in operation and are publicized, it is noticeable that the number of families with three and four children increases. It is highly likely that some parents bring children of other families with them, and two or more adult admissions are lost. This applies more often in attractions where there is a considerable amount for children to do than in adult-oriented heritage attractions. All schemes must be evaluated to ensure that their effect is successful, by whatever criteria are established.

Market research

Marion Wertheim

Role and definitions

Market research (MR) is an essential ingredient in the development of marketing strategies. If the important marketing objectives defined earlier in this chapter are to be met, attractions must recognize the many individual market segments which need to be targeted in different ways and may have to be satisfied with variants of the visitor experience provided. This is where market research has its place: it provides market data and consumer feedback to use whilst developing and monitoring effective marketing strategies.

A. H. R. Delens, who was explaining the uses of market research to British businesses as long ago as 1950, defined it as 'a matter of plain common sense. It is to the manufacturer (service provider) what military intelligence is to the general, and as such can be described as the intelligence tool of management.'

Market research is concerned with all aspects of marketing. More technically, MR can be defined as the systematic study and evaluation of all factors bearing on any business operation which involves the transfer of goods or services from a supplier to a consumer. Thus MR is a support service to help managers limit their risks, providing information to be used alongside their own experience and flair.

Scope of MR in heritage management

There is a wide scope for useful MR in the marketing of heritage attractions. Visitors experiences are the main 'products' on offer and they will have been produced as a result of strategic policy decisions. Market research information is relevant to all marketing factors which relate to the sale of these products and also to the matters of policy which are determined by the market for these products.

The scope of market research for heritage attractions can, therefore, be broadly summarized as follows.

The market in terms of consumer profile and behaviour

(1) Studying the consumers who constitute markets.
(2) Evaluating the potential of visitors as different categories (segments) of consumer.
(3) Analysing their attraction visiting habits and the factors which influence their choices/activities.
(4) Understanding the strengths and weaknesses of competing products.

Marketing strategies and product development

(1) Guiding managers to present heritage assets which are appealing to, welcomed by and accepted by the market.

Successful communication with target markets

(1) Assessing which forms of advertising and publicity can most cost-effectively promote the product both to consumers themselves and to those who may influence them, such as travel trade intermediaries and educationalists.
(2) Determining the most cost-effective information distribution channels.

Major types of tourism surveys for heritage management
Thus the most frequently encountered types of research survey in the heritage attractions market are:

Market surveys and feasibility studies These assess market size, structure, trends and likely demand for a particular development.

Market awareness and attitude surveys These examine issues such as what existing and potential customers know about an operation, whether or not it appeals to them, how well advertising communicates with them, and what it would be necessary to do to encourage them to come.

Customer surveys These can be conducted whilst a customer is captive, or as an after-sales follow-up survey. They can establish who is there, why they are there, what they have done since they arrived, together with what they feel about their experience, and the value for money it represents. It can cover both an attraction/operation as a whole and individual facets/facilities within this. As well as monitoring current customers, it can be most instructive to talk to lapsed customers and to turnarounds, i.e. those who come as far as the door but leave without entering.

Product development This focuses either on changes already made (and attitudes to these amongst those who have experienced them) or on possible future changes. The latter can be examined at various stages right from concept (a simple statement of what might be done) to actual experience of a finished/semi-finished product (such as a visit to a redesigned exhibition area or special event).

Advertising testing and tracking Here image and awareness measures are taken before and after an advertising campaign has run, to determine its effectiveness. Changes in awareness indicate the appropriateness of the media strategy adopted, whilst shifts in image reflect on the creative approach.

Performance monitoring

(1) Measuring customer satisfaction levels for all aspects of the visitor experience.
(2) Providing benchmarks and targets for staff performance.

Preparing a market research brief and evaluating proposals

Market research surveys are normally commissioned from professional market research agencies. In Britain it would be wise to select an agency run by a member of the Market Research Society (MRS), a professional body with some 6500 members involving over 400 market research agencies which adhere to strict codes of conduct. A free list of agencies is available from the MRS as well as an inexpensive *Guide to the Practice of Market and Survey Research*. Similar professional bodies exist in most developed countries.

Whilst many valuable ongoing relationships exist between clients and market research agencies, it is common for clients to invite three or four agencies to submit tenders. Increasingly, financial controllers insist on a tendering procedure.

It is good practice for a client to provide a research brief to which an agency can respond with a research proposal. The main features of each are listed below.

The client's research brief

There are a number of specialist market research agencies with considerable experience of conducting research for heritage attractions. But market research agencies, however experienced, are experts in research and *cannot* be expected to know the finer details of the potential client's current business or his plans for the future. Furthermore, if several agencies are to submit tenders, they must all do so on the same basis.

A written research brief, preferably followed by a person-to-person discussion, should provide the following information:

(1) the background to the problem or marketing strategy which has given rise to the need for a market research survey, with an indication of the way in which the results will be used;
(2) the specific objectives of the research or, in simple terms, the question areas which the survey results are required to answer;
(3) the timescale in which the project is to be completed;
(4) an indication of the likely budget available.

The agency's research proposal

Market research agencies do not normally charge for the preparation of a research proposal, but they can take several days of work to complete for a larger project. As the proposal of the successful tenderer will be the blueprint document for the research project, enough time must be allowed for agencies to put forward thoroughly thought out and creative proposals.

In order that proper evaluation of different proposals can be made by the client, a research proposal should cover the following aspects:

(1) a demonstration that the research brief has been clearly understood;
(2) details of an appropriate and realistic methodology for conducting the survey work;
(3) the proposed method of presenting the survey results to the clients and the form in which it will be presented;
(4) the experience and qualifications of executive members of the agency's project team and their individual roles in the project;
(5) how fieldwork interviews are to be organized and supervised, with details of quality control checks proposed;
(6) related experience in terms of previous projects and clients, preferably with names of clients who can be contacted for a confidential reference;
(7) the timescale for the project, stage by stage;
(8) a clear statement of the cost and conditions of contract, such as payment terms, copyright and provisions for delays occasioned by circumstances outside the agency's control, such as bad weather or labour strikes.

Main MR techniques for heritage management

Analysis of internal records

An analysis of admissions, preferably through computerized tills, enables management to monitor visitor trends and flows on a continuous or at least regular basis. This simply requires the entry of code numbers according to ticket type and date/time information when tickets are used. This enables daily admission data to be analysed by such factors as:

(1) time of day;
(2) day of week;
(3) season;
(4) category of visitor ticket: adult, child, family, reduced rate (e.g. senior citizens, students), educational, complimentary, season, special promotion group.

Whilst it is not reasonable to ask ticket office staff to question visitors in any details, some extra information to help target marketing can be asked of visitors and noted. Good examples would be origin of visitor (local, other nationals, overseas visitors); party size and composition; and method of transport used to arrive.

Analyses of shop and catering receipts, in parallel with admission ticket analysis, will paint a comprehensive picture of visitors and their behaviour on site. However, such data do not show which visitors do what, their socio-economic group, their age, and so on.

Feedback from sales visits

If sales staff are calling on travel agents or company travel departments, they should be encouraged to take note of any comments, criticisms or suggestions made, and to relay these back in a usable form, preferably in written memos. If any information can be obtained on competitor tactics or performance, this could also be of value. However, all such information must be treated as subjective rather than objective.

Desk research and secondary sources

For basic information on tourism (both national and regional) and on numbers of paid admissions to main attractions, the best direct sources of data are the British Tourist Authority and the English Tourist Board (BTA/ETB) and the regional tourist boards. Their publications include the following:

Tourism regional fact sheets Published yearly for each individual region; available free or at a nominal sum from ETB and the regional boards.
Regional tourism studies Most English regions, and some resorts also, have commissioned market studies in recent years. Summaries of these may be available for sale or reference.
English Hotel Occupancy Study This is published monthly, with an annual summary: available from ETB.

Sightseeing A yearly analysis of use and marketing activity of attractions for visitors, available from ETB.
British Tourism Survey A summary of main domestic tourism trends, available from ETB.

BTA/ETB can supply a full list of their own publications.

In addition to tourist board publications, there are a wide variety of books on tourism, marketing, market research, advertising and other business skills. Local reference libraries can advise you on what is available.

A further source of reference is provided by trade journals. Magazines such as *Leisure Management* and *Caterer and Hotelkeeper* publish occasional detailed reviews and specialist surveys. These reports will be listed in the index sections in the magazines, and back numbers can usually be found in reference libraries.

Joining an appropriate trade association will give access to its own publications, and these too can be a valuable resource. It may also be possible to buy copies of existing commercial market research surveys, provided these have been carried out on a syndicated basis, i.e. they are owned by the research company who can then sell them to anyone interested.

In addition to all these specific elements, it is important to take account of general social and economic trends in terms of population structure, change in use of leisure time, and disposable incomes, for example. These can be found in government publications (such as those for the General Household Survey) or from commercial reports published by organizations such as Mintel, Keynote and the Economist Intelligence Unit (again available via reference libraries). At a lighter level, it is essential to keep in touch with the developing mood of consumers via press and TV. It is also vital to be aware of the current school curriculum.

Whilst some desk research exercises may be carried out in response to a particular issue, operators will need to consider running others on a continuous basis. For example, market volume and market share data may be obtained every month or quarter.

Observations

Valuable information can be obtained simply by:

(1) Monitoring competitors' advertising, promotions and brochures, and the exposure of these in comparison with one's own. This would include examining how widely and how well brochures are displayed in hotels, tourist information centres etc.
(2) Reading news items on competitors, together with company reports, and reviews in the financial press.
(3) Attending relevant trade shows, to see what others in the same industry are doing.
(4) Observing the behaviour of visitors at one's own sites (and possibly also at competitor sites). Do visitors seem purposeful or confused? Are they actually entering the gift shop? And so on.

Questionnaire-based research

Questionnaire-based research involves a visitor (or non-visitor) being asked direct questions. These are usually designed to provide specific and objective information for the attraction operator in relation to questions such as:

(1) What are the perceived strengths and weaknesses of the product?
(2) To whom is the product thought to be intended to appeal, and to whom does it appeal?
(3) Does the product represent good value for money?
(4) How could the product be improved?

There are two broad types of personal interview, usually referred to as qualitative and quantitative. These are described in detail in the following sections.

Qualitative questionnaire-based research

Qualitative research may be carried out with individuals, with couples, with families or with groups of four to ten people at a time. It involves a skilled interviewer working through a series of pre-selected topics, which he/she can cover in any order intended to mirror an atmosphere of an informal conversation or discussion. The objective is to develop a detailed understanding of why people behave as they do, of what they really would like/need and of their views, both of existing operations/attractions and of possible new developments. Replies are obtained in the consumer's own words and the interviewer can modify the initial topics guide, if this proves helpful.

Qualitative research is particularly useful:

(1) Before the start of a large-scale (quantitative) project, to make sure that all relevant issues are included in the main stage of work, and that the right consumer language is used to describe them. Experts are not always best placed to understand the worries or priorities of customers, who may be operating from a very different base of knowledge, interest, confidence etc. It is all too easy (without qualitative research) to construct a questionnaire which, whilst being very logical and sensible, nevertheless misses out underlying attitudes of vital importance.
(2) To form a sound basis for developing new products. Propositions can be checked with the consumer at an early stage before too much investment has been put into them, and further consumer work will then ensure that the potential is realized to the full.
(3) To help assess and improve advertising communications.
(4) To assist in the design of brochures, making sure they are clear, contain all the information the customer requires etc.

Qualitative research, however, by its very nature is indicative and not definitive. It involves only relatively small numbers of people (for reasons of cost) and, however carefully these are selected to be repre-sentative of bigger groups, any hypotheses which emerge must be checked on larger numbers of people before they can be accepted as being statistically valid. Although qualitative research on its own can indicate at an early stage which of a number of possible new visitor experience developments might be of most interest (and therefore should be pro-gressed further), the actual *numbers* of people who might eventually visit such a development will have to be assessed via a quantitative study.

Focus groups

It has already been noted that qualitative research can include discussions amongst small groups of people (from four to ten participants). This technique draws together people who are strangers to each other but who have something in common (possibly visiting a particular resort/attraction) and who then spend one or two hours sharing experiences and opinions.

The advantages of this method are twofold. First, it obtains information from people more quickly (and therefore more cheaply) than would one-to-one inter-views. Secondly, it encourages creativity, and may help to provoke detailed examination by an individual of his/her own motivations. Comments from one group member may spark off thoughts from another.

Group discussions are especially useful for develop-ing a general understanding of a product's strengths and weaknesses or when dealing with new product development. They are less useful for probing, for example, individual day trip destination decision pro-cesses (when it may be necessary to examine a specific sequence of events in considerable detail). They may also not be practical in certain circumstances, for exam-ple if the target market is too thinly spread or if it consists of trade rivals who might be reluctant to dis-cuss issues in front of competitors.

It is not usually practical to hold a group discussion during the course of an individual's visit or stay (at an attraction or hotel) as few people are willing or able to allocate one or two hours at short notice. Focus groups are therefore usually held off site and can involve users and/or non-users of a particular travel or tourism pro-duct. They are usually designed to be reasonably coherent in terms of the age and social background of their members, to ensure a relaxed and balanced communication during sessions.

In-depth interviews

In-depth interviews may take place with individuals or with couples or family units (in circumstances where a decision may be made by a family rather than an individual). They provide an ideal forum for examin-ing any topic involving sequential actions, e.g. the decision process, the booking process, a visitor experi-ence at a site.

Such interviews can sometimes take place on site but this depends on having suitable facilities available (a conveniently located private room) and on fitting in with the visitor's own timetable (interviewing guests just after arrival at a hotel or at breakfast, catching people at a coffee break in a visitor attraction). Alternatively they can, like focus groups, take place off site: this is obviously necessary anyway for work with non-visitors.

Analysis and reporting
In general, all qualitative research will be tape recorded, unless this proves impractical in on-site studies. Tapes are subsequently transcribed and these transcripts are carefully analysed, noting for each topic by whom and in what context it has been mentioned.

Reports on qualitative research do not usually contain numbers. They will however, when relevant, indicate where opinions seem to be held by the majority or by a minority, and whether these appear to relate to particular types of people (in terms of age, region, sex, lifestyle, family circumstances or other possible defining factors). General comments will probably be interspersed with specific verbatim quotations, which give the data more life.

A verbal presentation of the findings, allowing a detailed interchange between client and researcher, will normally prove most valuable.

Quantitative questionnaire-based research

Quantitative research is the process of obtaining the response of a large enough number of people of a particular type to be confident that the replies they give are a 'true' indication of the opinions of the whole group from which they are drawn.

The sample
When carrying out a quantitative survey, it is vital that care and attention are given to:

(1) Selecting the most appropriate set(s) of people to whom to pose questions, e.g. the target market for a product or service, existing users/non-users of the product, the population as a whole etc.
(2) Defining this set (these sets) of people as closely as possible (in terms of attitudes, behaviour, socio-demographics, for example), such that it is possible to set down in writing the exact characteristics of the sample who will eventually need to be interviewed.
(3) Estimating how many people are likely to fall within a set and deciding the precision with which answers to questions are required from the set. For example, is it enough to know that about half of those interviewed say they may visit X, or does success/failure depend on being confident that over 50 per cent of the target market will visit rather than just 48 per cent? Issues such as this will determine just how many interviews need to be carried out.

Sometimes, although the views of a number of different sets of people have been sought separately, it may

also be helpful if these can be combined together to provide a wider picture of opinions held. Depending on the nature of the subgroups involved, such an amalgamation may sometimes be done very simply. In other cases, data may need to be *weighted* to provide a 'true' picture of the market as a whole. For example, if a number of equal-sized regional samples had been asked about a specific tourist attraction and it was also wished to look at a national sample, then it would be necessary to weight the regional data before combining them. The views of a sample from a densely populated area like the north-west of England would need to be given more emphasis than those coming from more sparsely populated areas such as mid Wales or East Anglia. This would be done statistically, based on the relative populations of the areas.

Survey types
Quantitative research can be bought in several different ways:

Ad hoc surveys An *ad hoc* survey is tailor-made to meet a specific client's needs. This is the most flexible but most expensive type of research.
Omnibus surveys These operate on, and are named after, the principle of a bus. A survey is run at regular (weekly, fortnightly, monthly, twelve monthly) intervals by a research company, and it is possible for any client to book questions (seats) on this at a laid-down rate. Omnibus surveys are available both amongst the public as a whole and (on a less frequent basis) amongst specific target groups such as hotel users, travel agency staff, motorists and young people. The general style of these surveys makes them most suitable for obtaining answers to fairly straightforward questions. In this context they can be a relatively inexpensive way of quickly and easily obtaining access to a large number of people. Purchase of a question includes data analysis (with access to full demographic profiles of those being interviewed).
Syndicated research Here, either several clients group together to commission a particular *ad hoc* project, agreeing to share the costs between themselves, or a research agency sets up a survey on a particular market and then offers participation and/or the results to interested parties. In the first case, data would only be available to an operator if it was one of the original sponsors. In the second case, an operator could either joint a syndicated survey from the start, receiving basic data and possibly adding its own confidential questions, or simply buy basic data after the project was complete. Either way of operation allows data about minority markets to be collected in an affordable manner.

Many projects are best served by a combination of *ad hoc* survey with omnibus survey or syndicated research.

Data collection techniques
However a survey is funded, there are a number of different ways in which data can be collected. Four main techniques are available:

(1) personal interviews on site, in homes or in the street;
(2) telephone interviews;

(3) self-completion on-site surveys;
(4) postal surveys.

Omnibus surveys are usually carried out personally or by telephone (since they rely on a relatively quick provision of answers to clients). *Ad hoc* and syndicated surveys may use any of the above techniques. The choice between the various options will be based on factors such as:

(1) nature, size and spread of target group(s);
(2) availability of a mailing list;
(3) type of questions it is wished to ask;
(4) length of interview;
(5) how quickly results are needed;
(6) cost constraints.

Some of the relevant issues are illustrated in the following:

Personal interviews Personal interviews, particularly for fixed-site locations like museums, other visitor attractions and transport termini, remain a highly effective way of collecting both factual and attitudinal information. However, they may prove expensive off site, particularly with widely spread or difficult-to-reach samples. If personal interviews are carried out on site there are a number of specific issues which must be taken into consideration. It is necessary to decide, for example, how visitors should be selected (whether randomly or to meet preset criteria); how many interviews should be carried out at particular times of day and on particular days of the week; where on-site interviewers should work; which member of a couple or group should be asked to answer for the group as a whole; and whether interviews are to be restricted to those who can speak English, or whether foreign language questionnaires and/or interviewers are required.

Telephone interviews Because personal interviews are expensive, tourism research is frequently conducted by means of telephone surveys, now that telephone ownership is so widespread. These can be particularly useful for reaching decision makers and for influencing people like teachers or tourism ground handlers, and also for small groups of consumers who may live anywhere in the country. However, they do have some problems. For example, school trip organizers may already be over-researched, and a telephone interviewer is easily assumed to be a salesperson who is just claiming to be doing a survey. It may prove hard work to obtain interviews with these sets of people..

Self-completion on-site surveys On-site self-completion questionnaires, where the recipient ticks boxes and/or writes in his own answers, are increasingly used for continuous monitoring of customer profiles and attraction option ratings. Whilst these used to be implemented only by the very largest tour operators, far more companies are now introducing such monitoring programmes.

Postal surveys Postal surveys (also self-completion, but sent to the recipient's own home/office) on tourism subjects can attract good response (far greater than sometimes achieved on more mundane matters). A well designed postal questionnaire with an attractive free prize draw incentive could even result in 60–75 per cent response rates, and be statistically reliable. However, this technique may only be useful if a mailing list (of users and lapsed users of a product, for example) already exists.

Questionnaire design
Whatever the survey type and technique selected, and however well the sample is chosen, a study can only be as valuable as the questions it asks. The characteristics of *good* questionnaires are that they should be:

(1) clear and unambiguous;
(2) easy and quick to understand;
(3) simple to respond to;
(4) relevant to the respondent.

In designing the questionnaire it is necessary to ask:

(1) Will the respondent have a reasonable chance of understanding the question?
(2) Will the respondent, having understood the question, be willing to answer it?
(3) Will the respondent, having understood the question and being willing to answer it, have a reasonable chance of being able to answer it?

The choice of words is very important. Take the words 'dinner' or 'tea', which have different meanings for different social classes and in different parts of the country. By using the phrases 'midday meal' and 'evening meal', it is possible to clarify exactly what one is talking about.

Aspects of design which help the questionnaire flow include:

(1) avoiding unnecessary repetition of questions;
(2) avoiding complicated filtering and referring back to earlier questions;
(3) inserting suitable linking statements between questions;
(4) using respondent-involving activities (e.g. card sorting or self-completion scales) which may help to make a long interview seem shorter;
(5) varying the type of question used to avoid boredom and to prevent a response style developing;
(6) using open-ended questions to allow respondents a chance to speak and express an opinion;
(7) not asking impossible questions.

From the point of view of the interviewer, all instructions as to how to proceed through the questionnaire must be clearly given. Interviewers need to be told which answers should be probed or explored in depth.

Once a questionnaire is prepared, it is always advisable to do a number of pilot interviews to check that the questionnaire is working properly. It is vital that respondents, interviewers and clients all understand exactly the same thing from each question. It is also important to check how straightforward the progress between questions is for the interviewer (to avoid errors in recording data) and how long a total interview takes.

Following such a pilot survey, any problems identified will be resolved before a final version of the questionnaire is prepared.

Data analysis

Data recording techniques
As an interviewer asks questions, the answers may be recorded in a number of ways. Usually face-to-face interviews involve entering answers on paper, either by circling numbers (for questions where consumers are asked to pick one of a number of pre-selected answers) or by writing in comments verbatim (when consumers are asked to express opinions in their own words).

Telephone interviews may be similarly recorded on paper, or a computer-assisted telephone interview (CATI) system may be adopted. This utilizes the fact that telephone interviews are usually conducted from a specifically equipped centre, with individual interviewing booths. All these booths are linked directly to the centre's computer. Interviewers work from a screen display of questions and enter answers (both pre-selected and free response) directly from a keyboard. As each answer registers, the next relevant question will come up on screen automatically.

A version of the CATI system has been developed for personal interviews (CAPI). Interviewers enter answers directly into a portable (e.g. lap-top) computer for subsequent unloading via a modem or a disk. This method is not yet widely used, owing to the expense of the current computer equipment and the additional interviewer training necessary. However, it is likely to increase in use in future years.

Coding
However data are initially recorded, a coding operation has to be performed on verbatim, free-response comments before they can be handled by the computer. This involves examining a proportion of all the comments made (for each open-ended question), identifying the key elements of these, listing the elements (to form a code frame) and assigning numbers to each element. Each time a particular comment is made it will then be identified to the computer by the special number assigned to it.

This identification of key elements may be carried out entirely by hand or it may use computerized word count facilities as an aid. However, the final structure must always be decided by the executive running the project as it is necessary to understand which issues are of particular interest to the client.

Data entry
Data from CATI systems may have gone directly to the computer, but data from paper (plus all coded free-response answers) will generally be either punched on to cards, or entered directly on to the computer by a keyboard. In big surveys, optical document reading is a useful option: the computer is given a template of the questionnaire and scans data directly off completed paper versions to match this pattern.

Computer analysis
Once all data are on the computer they can be analysed in any way that is required. Subgroups can be examined separately or combined with weighting, if necessary.

Data for each subgroup will be presented in total and can also be split up to show the opinions of, for example, particular age groups, those with or without children, repeat versus first-time visitors, and those who particularly liked or disliked the product. The precise splits to be applied will depend on the client's needs.

Presentation of findings
At the end of a project, the client will always receive a full set of computer tables and would normally also request an interpretative report. The latter would either be a brief summary of the main results and their implications, or a much more detailed examination of findings on a question-by-question basis. If appropriate, the report could also include relevant results of qualitative and desk research, or could make comparisons with earlier survey results, pointing out any apparent trends.

On any major *ad hoc* project, a verbal presentation would usually take place. This offers an opportunity for a client to obtain an overview of the results, to discuss specific points of interest with the research team in person, and to explore actions to be taken in the light of survey findings.

Promotion

Grahame Senior

Getting the point across

Start by knowing what you want to say and to whom. The purpose of promotion is to get the right people to do exactly what we want them to do by telling them the things they would like to hear. The art of persuading effectively is working out what to say and how to say it. The key discipline in promotion is *effective communication*: that is, getting the point we need to make across and making it stick.

The previous section dealt with market research. This essentially is the starting point of all effective communication – an objective starting point. Find out who your actual and potential customers are by analysing all existing visitor data. Decide whom you wish to attract and know what you need to say. Make sure you understand what it is that will make your message relevant and credible to the right target market. That is why research is so important in defining exactly who is the right target market group for your product. Having defined the market, you can then measure the effectiveness of all your communication and improve all aspects of promotion through constant checking with research.

Communicating well and using the right media

In the good old days, promotion was either *above the line* (advertising in recognized media such as television, posters or press) or *below the line* (direct promotion through non-media methods such as PR, offers, messages on product packaging, vouchers and mailings). To match in with those simple times, the marketing services community was split between specialists in above the line (advertising agencies) and specialists in below the line (PR and promotion consultancies).

Nowadays it is nowhere near so simple. We are all much clearer on the need for a fully coordinated approach to communication and promotion, and an effective promotion strategy that needs to work *through the line*. It is very important to remember that many potential visitors will be exposed to more than one form of communication. The cumulative effect of your messages and the media delivery of these messages must be carefully planned. That means that from the very outset of initial brand concept right through to the design of a brochure or even pricing communication, we need to organize all aspects of our communication to meet the requirements of the target market.

Advertising agencies have tended to become less simplistic and more like total communication companies, and advertisers have come to expect this. Whether you use an agency or work direct, you need to ensure that all your promotion is targeted to build the most cost-effective cumulative impact. Assembling your portfolio of communication and promotion requires an understanding of the function of all the facets of marketing.

Planning promotions

Taking the range of activities for a typical promotional requirement, let us examine the items that need to be considered. I will deal with these initially in principle and then demonstrate how they work in practice by taking a single case history – that of Hampton Court Palace.

A menu of the components of a promotional portfolio would be as follows:

Mission statement or proposition This is the starting point of effective communication and again should be aimed at the target market. It is a short paragraph which takes the essence of the property and describes how it fits in with the current needs of the market-place. This then becomes the reference point for all other forms of communication and promotion.
Research Analyse all available data about your market and use them to understand who you are aiming at. Get to know your actual and potential visitors really well.

Target market definition Describe the main market or markets for your property using demographic and geographic parameters. That is, define the people you are aiming to address.
Brand and product concept This is the main description of the way in which the property is named and described in the quintessential offer to the consumer. Many historic properties have an existing name. The way in which that name is designed and the graphics that are used to enhance it, together with the way it is described, should all be judged against the intended target market. There is a world of difference in the way heritage attractions should be presented to a mainly overseas or UK tourist audience of once-only visitors and to a local UK repeat business audience. The fundamental name style and description are so important that it is well worth researching them.
Media plan and schedule Setting a media plan is vital and you must consider the media in their true role – that of a communication pipeline between yourself and your market.

Choosing media above the line

The effectiveness of the media pipeline depends on two main factors: the value with which it delivers the eyes and ears of the right market (usually measured in cost per thousand), and the authority of the editorial environment which makes the message credible. Advertising a heritage property in *The Independent* is likely to be more credible and persuasive for the right market than a similar message in *The Sun* or *The Daily Sport* (even though the cost per thousand is higher!).

It is at the start of media planning that the value of having clearly defined target markets expressed in one of the known demographic languages (Acorn, Mosaic etc.) really starts to work for you. The details of the audiences of all the major media from posters to television programmes are expressed in terms of their demographic audience.

The choices of media are very wide, but you should always have your target audience in view. Some media can be very selective, like printed material for newspaper inserts; some may be partially selective, like papers which allow you to put your advertisement in just one geographic edition (avoiding wastage); and others may be very rigid, like papers where you have to buy the full circulation.

In the following I have described the majority of media but concentrated on those which are likely to be relevant to heritage properties.

Television
This is the most intrusive medium of all, with a combination of real impact, colour and movement and, of course, huge audience volumes. It is often thought of as very expensive, but careful use of the rate card with a very specific message at specific holiday times can yield real benefits. A ten-second spot repeated five or six times over a holiday weekend can do wonders. Because advertising time is bought regionally, wastage is reduced and the message can be delivered to exactly

the right catchment area. Production need not be expensive if a combination of good photography and clear messages is used.

Radio

This has many of the same benefits as television but of course a much lower audience level. It is even more regionally targetable and again can deliver very rapid response in terms of visitors. There are many successful case histories of radio campaigns for heritage properties. The 24-hour programming means it is very important to select the segmentation of your spots to ensure that you have the right audience profile for your product. It is particularly useful for promoting special interest exhibitions or events.

National press

This is one of the most effective means of attracting a specific audience. The press tends to be demographically fairly well segmented and thus can represent very cost-effective buying in terms of cost per thousand of a target audience. Because most national press can also be bought regionally this also avoids wastage. One of the most effective ways of using the national press is by inserting leaflets (which can be run-ons from an existing piece of print) in specifically targeted editions. These have very high impact and cut out wastage both regionally and demographically. Features of historic relevance are also very important as the editorial content of a newspaper can make a huge difference to the impact of an advertisement.

Local/regional press

The same rules apply as for national press. As a generalization, regional press is more expensive in cost per thousand terms than national press and is less demographically targeted. It does, of course, tend to offer very good coverage geographically – particularly through free distribution newspapers. Again these tend to be best used as a vehicle for inserts rather than space advertising as this delivers both impact and minimal wastage.

Outdoor advertising

Posters, whether in strategic sites or in transport stations, can be very effective in terms of directional information and also marketing special events or exhibitions. Posters can be bought with careful attention to geodemographic and demographic targeting. They also have very high audience levels in terms of cost per thousand and they have the great benefit of transmitting 24 hours a day. In practice, most individual operators should attempt to buy on a specific site basis rather than going for packages: the latter are more suitable for the larger London-based operation. It can take a number of years to build up an effective portfolio of sites, but the right sites with the right message are probably the single most effective media form.

Direct mailing and distribution

This is a very important media area for operators because of the opportunity to use existing print material in a highly targeted way. Direct mailing can be effective in communicating with an enthusiast market, but direct distribution is more cost-effective for new visitor recruitment. The key to effectiveness is careful selection of the right postcodes for your target audience.

Specialist magazines and guides

These are a very effective source but need to be carefully evaluated to get the right target audience for your property. Careful evaluation of the competitive advertisers as well as the readership is necessary. Cost per thousand is usually quite high in comparison with such media forms as the national press. The larger-circulation magazines (e.g. *Radio Times* or *Reader's Digest*) can be used most cost-effectively by treating them as an extension of your national press and aiming for regional targeting. They can also be used for inserting leaflets to good effect.

Choosing media below the line

Below the line are three main traditional areas of activity: public relations, sales promotion and direct mail.

Exactly the same principles of targeting the message to the market apply. The most important rule is to ensure that the approach below the line is integrated with the approach above the line. Thus you gain greater cumulative impact. If, for instance, advertising posters are presenting a property as possessing special architectural characteristics, then PR and sales promotion messages should reflect this.

At the same time, if within the overall marketing plan the *general* character of a property is being presented by a brand concept, then both PR and direct mailing can be used to stage temporary exhibitions, presentations and events in a very cost-effective way below the brand umbrella. This must always be done, of course, within the context of the creative style and character that has been set for the property.

Direct marketing promotions

One of the most effective areas of promotion for historic and heritage properties is the careful use of direct marketing allied to the overall advertising campaign. Promotional print is often the most targeted of all media forms. Advertising your property in the press, guide books etc. can be used to present the general character and basic proposition of the property, e.g. in the case of Hampton Court Palace, the concept 'Royal History by the Thames'.

Underneath this umbrella, different specific propositions can be made to different market groups using direct marketing techniques with promotional print. Some individuals will be interested in the history of the royals as people, some will be interested in political history as a dimension, some will be interested in architecture and the arts. Different leaflets and even posters can be used to reflect the activities and the appeal of a property to each one of these market groups – underneath the overall concept. The property can be marketed to the total audience, and different events or promotions carried to the different audiences via leaflets.

The key trick in terms of effective communication is to build up over time a database of the different visitors by different types of exhibitions and events. Then you can profile and analyse this demographically and aim at the communication in terms of not only the message but the media delivery at each target group. I will cover this in more detail when we look at the specific example of Hampton Court Palace.

Because of the relatively low budgets most historic properties can afford, direct marketing is a very valuable method. By spending the majority of money against the most susceptible groups, it is worthy of a high priority in planning an annual marketing campaign.

The analysis of differential profiles of visitors at different times for different events and in different groupings is one of the most important ways of getting closer to your target market. To persuade someone effectively, it is important to know them well.

Sales promotion

This is the technique of improving business through offers, incentives, competitions, promotional campaigns with vouchers etc. Sales promotion is an effective way of harnessing other people's promotional opportunities to aid your own. Sales promotion can be very effective if you are promoting to families for days out via the leaflet promotions of a transport operator like British Rail or National Express, for instance.

If you are aiming to attract overseas visitors, on the other hand, a promotion with retail outlets like Scotch House, Harrods, Fortnums etc. can be equally valuable. Local retail outlets – particularly the leisure-oriented ones like sporting youth shops – can be very helpful. This technique can be made even more effective by banding together with other properties and offering a choice or collection to the consumer.

As in every other branch of marketing communication, it is a question of horses for courses. Pick the right business partner with the right target market – one who is seeking to attract the same target market at the same time.

Facts

One final word on PR: *use facts*. So often press releases and stories tend to be a reprise of the marketing or product intentions of the retailer or operator. They work much better when specific facts are released.

The trick in getting better coverage with the right impact is to ensure that the facts themselves are targeted to be of interest to the market. Journalists will simply not print policy statements and general puff about any enterprise. They will almost always give some coverage to something of genuine factual interest presented credibly as news.

One of the most effective forms of PR targeting is to ensure that it is presented around human stories. The selection of the right human interest can be the most effective way if getting the targeting right.

Media budgeting

In summary, selecting the right media is a question of assessing the critical factors for your property based on the coverage of the right market; the impact of the publication; the longevity/lifespan of message; the suitability of media forms for your message; and the absolute cost.

To illustrate costing, two typical media budgets are shown. The first (*Figure 31.1*) is for a small individual heritage attraction in a rural environment, with an annual budget of £20,000. The second (*Figure 31.2*) is for a larger historic property with a constantly changing exhibition throughout the year in a metropolitan area, with an annual budget of £85,000.

Obviously you need not only to plan your schedule against the demographic profile of a medium, but also to take into account the regional bias. The principle is 'fish where the fish are'.

Media planning can be a very complex and highly specialized business. In essence, viewing your media exposure as a pipeline to the right market at the right price will give you a good rule of thumb.

One of the most important media forms for heritage properties is of course the different types of printed material. The brochure, simple leaflet, door-to-door

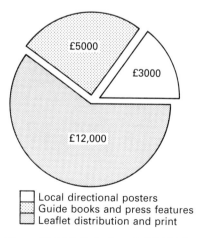

Local directional posters
Guide books and press features
Leaflet distribution and print

Figure 31.1 Media budget of £20,000 for a small heritage attraction in a rural area

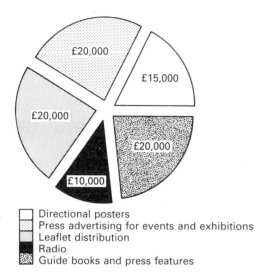

Figure 31.2 Media budget of £85,000 for a large historic property in a metropolitan area

distribution piece or mailing pack are all media forms. They should be viewed in exactly the same way – judged by the audience they can deliver.

After the medium: the message

In exactly the same way that your selection of media – press, leaflets, posters, etc. – is governed by the efficiency with which it delivers the audience, the message should also be judged by the efficiency with which it makes the point. Effective promotional headlines are those which get the right market to do the right things.

If the principle of judging media is known as 'fish where the fish are', then the principle for the message is 'use the right fly'. Getting the right creative message is a question first of communicating the very existence of the property; secondly, of communicating the character and the facilities it offers; and thirdly, of engendering a desire to visit in the market. The rule of producing an effective communication message is a three-part one:

(1) it *is* (existence);
(2) I *know* what it is and what it offers (relevance);
(3) I *want* to go there (desire).

Again, it should always be remembered that the style and presentation of the message must be judged against the preference of the desired market group. It is possible to ensure that the planning of the design style, the presentation of the property (history led, architecture/heritage led, exhibition led etc.) and the style of copy

are all carefully aimed and targeted at the identified potential visitors.

I believe it is essential when taking any significant new departure from the creative approach that is currently being used to research various alternative concepts and propositions with a market group selected from the right target market individuals. It is only by taking this approach that the full power to convince and persuade inherent within any piece of promotional communication can be unleashed.

Case history: Hampton Court Palace

The work carried out to improve visitorship to Hampton Court during the late 1980s is a good example of an integrated campaign aimed at promoting better business for a historic property.

The background
Whilst Hampton Court may be a famous name and well know to many, it actually does require a very specific trip from central London for most visitors (who are UK or foreign tourists). It is not in the high-traffic areas like the main central London attractions with a large volume of passing potential visitors. It is also the case that its superb parkland setting with free access can be something of a deterrent to people to pay and actually go inside, when they can enjoy the visit and the views free of charge.

In 1988, Hampton Court Palace set out to develop marketing activities and undertake promotion to improve visitorship. Naturally this had to be done in a manner in accord with the status and dignity of the property.

Starting out
The first step was to carry out research to find out visitor totals and variations and analyse the current situation and get a view as to the different market profiles. This was done through a series of direct interviews, group discussions and profiling evaluation carried out in Acorn language. The visitor tracking studies undertaken by Palace staff in recent years were also invaluable in coming to understand the pattern of visitors. The point was to get a view of who visited the Palace, who did not and, most importantly, *why* not.

The branding concept
Once all this had been evaluated, the work started on developing a creative concept which would present the Palace effectively.

The first stage was to decide what to call it. Most people call it 'Hampton Court', and the first objective was to generate a better understanding of the existence of the *Palace* itself. We wanted visitors inside rather than simply going for a walk.

A logo was designed and the concept proposition 'Royal History by the Thames' was selected and fine tuned by research against target market groups ranging from overseas visitors to upper-middle-class people who lived within day trip distance of the Palace.

Advertising messages
Again through research, a series of campaign concepts was developed. One was a general presentation of the Palace with its famous west front which was used for posters and leaflets aimed at overseas and once-only visitors.

To back this up a series of leaflets covering special exhibitions and specific events in the Palace was also produced. This was aimed at the other main market group: those families – in particular middle-class education families (Acorn groups J and B) – who would take a specific interest in visiting such properties.

Planning the media
Media selection became an important priority. Having defined the existence of two main target market groups (once-only casual visitors, and families with the potential for repeat visits), it was necessary to find a way to approach both cost-effectively.

Posters selected by Acorn, and leaflets distributed either through press insertion or by door-to-door delivery, became the main media. Low wastage, high targeting and specific communication were critical to the media selection. By careful management and distribution during winter 1989, the programme was successful in significantly improving visitorship to the Palace during that winter season.

It is a credit to the consistency of the very professional team handling Hampton Court Palace marketing that the discipline of building the database and measuring and evaluating the consumers has continued. This has led to a whole series of specifically targeted initiatives aimed at improving visitorship by carefully selected groups during low-demand periods. Examples of this material are shown in *Figures 31.3–31.5*. Without going into great detail, PR activity, and promotional activity using business partners with particular emphasis on British Rail, were also used to good effect. It all added up to an effective promotional concept in the fully integrated campaign.

Summary: principles of effective promotion for heritage properties

(1) Get rid of subjectivity and concentrate on *objectivity*. Don't think about what you want to say, think about what the market will want to hear.
(2) Get to *know the market* and allow facts to challenge and change assumptions. Measure your visitorship, bring in industry data, and compare and contrast. Build up a specific picture of who has been and who currently is in the market for your product. Have a clear view of your position *vis-à-vis* the competition and be quite objective in defining what are your unique properties. Emphasize these.
(3) If at all possible, use one of the accepted *demographic languages* to describe your market. This has two great advantages: first, it allows you to be clear and objective; and secondly, it allows you access to published data on media marketing trends, promotional opportunities etc.
(4) Plan creative messages and media delivery against a *specific market* – not the general market. Remember the principle of 'fish where the fish are' (media) and 'use the right fly' (creative message).

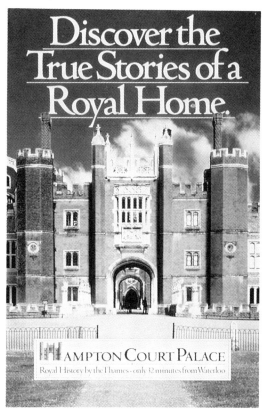

Figure 31.3 New logo and concept line

Figure 31.4 Overseas and general interest visitors

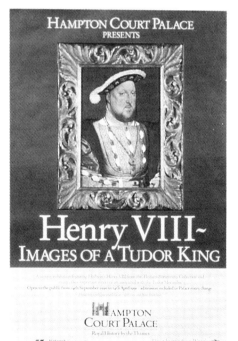

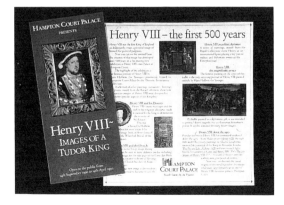

Figure 31.5 Examples of special interest leaflets and posters targeted at the domestic market

(5) Collect, record, analyse and evaluate all advertising responses, customer comments, differences in visitorship patterns etc. and build a management *information system* on a common basis which allows you to see the way business is changing. Evaluate what the competition is doing also: remember that you are not alone!

(6) Wherever possible, try to work out situations in which your market is the same as someone else's target market. This will allow you to do a partnership marketing and *cut the cost* of getting your message across.

(7) Talk to your customers: *keep in touch* with their views about your communication as well as your product, and try to develop the message in tune with their observations. However, do not chop and change too rapidly: maintain consistency and have faith in your researched message.

(8) Remember you are not alone. Seek out and *share information* with similar operators and ensure that you keep in touch with trends and developments.

(9) *Keep it simple*, particularly with PR. Remember that the current market is accustomed to thinking in 'sound bites'. If your message takes longer then a single sentence to communicate, cut it down.

(10) Make each pound spent work twice for you: once for specific objectives and a second time to spread the *common image and concept* of your property. Even a small budget with consistent communication can create a really strong impression on the consumer.

(11) *Setting the budget* can be very difficult and should always relate back to an objective evaluation of what you are trying to achieve. An optimum target for visitors to maximize your returns can be achieved by spending the right promotional money at the right time. It is only by trial and error and keeping accurate records of results that you can judge how much more business a leaflet drop or an advertisement will bring you. Budgets must be set against quantified objectives. Aim to measure and judge what different promotional budgets will yield based on known experience. Over time, that becomes quite accurate.

In conclusion, always go back to the basic rules and judge all aspects of your promotion from the point of view of the audience it is intended to impress. Fish where the fish are (media), use the right fly (creative) and present it correctly (proposition). It is, as they say, easy when you know how!

Evaluation

The essence of the marketing process is that it involves setting targets in terms of the type and number of visitors to be attracted, based on market research and using carefully defined promotional methods to put the promotional image in front of the prospective visitors in a persuasive way, at times when they are likely to respond. Marketing also involves very considerable promotional expenditure. In addition, there are the costs of presentation and interpretation, and related market research.

The most successful heritage sites (in terms of visitor numbers and income) have very substantial marketing budgets. It is usual for the marketing budgets to be the largest item of variable expenditure. At most the heritage attraction overheads of the visitor business are relatively fixed and do not vary in relation to the number of visitors who attend. The marketing budget may vary between nil and more than £2 per visitor, by choice.

It is absolutely fundamental to the marketing process that the success in achieving the identified objectives, and the cost-effectiveness of marketing activity, should be continuously or regularly evaluated. The outcome of the evaluation should be a reappraisal of the marketing programmes and their refinement, to more effectively achieve the defined objectives.

Evaluation and performance measurement has, of course, to be undertaken against the background of variation in national economic circumstances, international tourism volume and tourist expenditure. It must take account of weather. A knowledge of how performance relates to the performance of appropriate other competitor businesses in the catchment area is also important.

Most heritage businesses maintain relatively poor numerical records, principally only for accounting purposes. Cash is probably recorded more accurately than the number of visitors by visitor categories. Visitor characteristics, types, origins, motivations and activities are probably not recorded at all, unless by survey. The expenditure and activity patterns by different types of visitors may not be known unless survey data are compared with accounting data. Swiftly produced accurate data, consistently prepared on a year-to-year basis, are essential for adequacy of marketing evaluation. Some key ratios can be defined and regularly recorded or computed. Most numerical criteria required for marketing evaluation purposes can quite easily be incorporated into routine procedures so that they do not require significant additional effort or staff expense to generate.

The most important criterion is that the data required for marketing decision making are coordinated with accounting and other records. They must be prepared using common definitions, so that accounting and management records can be directly related to market research data.

A key question faced by all businesses is to establish the marketing budget; this is a question addressed in the section on promotion. However with accurate evaluation, marketing expenditure can easily be seen not as a cost but as an investment. So long as it can be *proved* that every additional £1 of marketing expenditure generates the required return from admissions and other income, its investment will not be in question. Unless it can be proved that it does so, its expenditure must be questioned.

Competent marketing is an essential element of heritage attractions, in an increasingly competitive consumer market-place. Its use may be unreasonably resisted or resented. Marketing is a technique. It is a servant, not a master. Appropriately applied, it will serve well.

Acknowledgement

I am indebted to Marian Wertheim for her sage remarks on market research.

Case study 31.1

Warwick Castle

Martin Westwood

The product that all owners and managers of heritage properties should be aiming to provide is a satisfying and rewarding experience for all visitors. As with all businesses, satisfied customers are the key to future success either through word of mouth recommendation to others or as repeat purchasers. It is, therefore, of paramount importance that the quality of experience is such that the satisfaction of the customer is ensured. Owners, managers and staff must all dedicate themselves to this fundamental aim in order to maximize the potential of the establishments which they manage. A less than determined approach will produce an experience which falls short of visitor expectation and will surely jeopardize the success and future staying power of the enterprise.

Those of us who work in the so-called heritage industry are immensely fortunate. We work in beautiful surroundings in an industry whose assets or raw materials are unrivalled in any other country of the world. The sheer diversity, breadth and cultural significance of the collections contained in our historic houses and museums must be the envy of all civilized countries. Fortunately our civil wars came early, so the great collections of more recent generations have not been dissipated; nor have we as a nation suffered the rapacity of invading armies.

This vast wealth of buildings, collections, grounds and gardens is hugely advantageous to our tourism industry. It provides the backbone for this country's appeal to leisure visitors from overseas, and the *raison d'être* for a thriving (and unique) outings business for the resident population, as well as colouring significantly the content of the packages of the increasingly popular short-breaks market. Nor should it be forgotten that a popular attraction devolves considerable economic benefit on the local host community in terms of accommodation, shopping and transportation. The establishment's employees' wages and its purchasing of goods and services locally also contribute in some measure. Not only will revenue be generated but often the provision of services and amenities for local residents, which otherwise would not be available, is triggered.

The tourism attraction business is relatively young. Its pioneers have become household names and its success has been spawned by post-war affluence, the ability for most families to own and use a motor car and the wide availability of air travel to this country from overseas. Forecasters tell us that these trends will continue and, therefore, for the entrepreneurial owner there are potential sources of revenue which would have been undreamt of a generation or so ago.

The benefits, however, will only accrue if the experience the visitors receive matches their expectations and represents good value for money. It is vital, therefore, that both managers and operative staff understand that they themselves and their attitudes to their customers and their work are as much a part of the presentation as the assets and collections they present to their patrons. It is the staff members of any establishment who will make it live for their visitors. It is people who drive businesses, not the inanimate assets, however prized the latter may be. The presentation and interpretation of a site, therefore, depend greatly on the zeal and commitment of all staff members to do the very best for their customers in terms of both their creature comforts and the aesthetic appreciation of a collection or a unique environment.

Presenting an establishment in terms of its physical and comfort aspects begins not at its doors or gates but on the approaches to it. Clear road or pedestrian signing is important in helping the potential patron arrive at the premises in a relaxed state of mind with a subliminal feeling of welcome. A friendly acknowledgement from an alert member of staff on the periphery of the site will further that impression. Toilets (of a clean and hygienic standard) are essential close to the entry point. Visitors expect them: they may have travelled a long way, and lack of provision will undoubtedly get things off on the wrong footing. We should care for our guests as we hope to be treated ourselves.

Good signing directing visitors to the main entrance point from car parks is an obvious necessity, and clear site plans and descriptions of what is to be seen at the property are vital in the conversion of the prospect into a paying customer. Once through the main reception area, clear signing throughout the site, perhaps the provision of a site plan for each guest on the purchase of a ticket, clearly defined pathways and walking areas, set the tone for the rest of the visit. Litter control requires a helpful response from the visitor: a litter-free environment will be largely self-promoting provided that adequate litter bins are available. By the same token the right signals that the establishment is cared for by those who own it will certainly be respected by the vast majority of visitors and, if it can be demonstrated to visitors that the proprietors are mindful of their welfare also, then a rapport can be built up automatically which serves the ends of both purveyor and consumer.

If unsightly scaffolding is shrouding part of the building, a neat notice describing the reason for the situation and an apology will be read and appreciated by visitors. Good walking surfaces outside and inside, clear warning signs where there are possible dangers, clear warnings if some areas are considered unsuitable for the very young or very old, clear signs for restrictions stating the reason why the restriction is imposed, and so on: this attitude of care is recognized by visitors and contributes to their perception of a safe customer-oriented environment, adding further to their impression of welcome.

We have all become increasingly aware in recent years of the responsibility that the Health and Safety at Work Act places upon us. It is difficult to imagine that any organization with the welfare of its clientele in mind can fail to train its staff in this vital area by inculcating a safety culture so that constant vigilance by everyone on site minimizes the risk of injury to both visitor and staff.

All the foregoing really comes under the broad heading of customer care. Let us not kid ourselves that this concept is simply about a broad smile and the Anglicized version of 'Have a nice day.' It is far more than that. Fundamentally it is about 'doing as you would be done by' (to paraphrase Kingsley) and it involves getting down to some real basics and using some common sense. It ought to be second nature to us all. Sadly it isn't and the reason for giving the topic a good airing here is that all of us fall down on any aspect of it regularly. Only constant monitoring by a committed management and staff can hope to ensure the kind of standards to which we should all aspire. If we get it right then our enterprise gains significantly.

The presentation of the establishment itself and its collections, grounds and gardens is naturally of the greatest significance to the visitor. A litter strewn site with an obvious lack of care in its maintenance, where other visitors are able to wander or picnic at will without restriction, is a recipe for a bad visit. We should not be shy about guiding visitors, by whatever subtle means we choose, to where we would like them to go. This is for their benefit and enjoyment as well as that of others.

Wonderful vistas may be ruined, quiet contemplation disrupted and eager study curtailed by a lack of sensitivity to what makes the establishment work as a satisfier for visitors. We should always be aware of the effect that lack of control of visitor movements can have. Where queues form (as they do at most popular establishments) they should be ideally managed by a steward, who can turn a potential irritation into a bonus for the visitor by perhaps describing the things that will be seen and giving confidence that the wait is well worth while.

Visitors to historic houses and similar establishments are expecting to see something quite special or spectacular. This expectation will be diminished if the general standards of housekeeping are poor. The finest old master painting will not look its best in or be able to compensate for a setting where paintwork is chipped, curtains are tatty, upholstery is threadbare and carpets are worn through. It is essential that situations like this are not allowed to occur. Commitment to regular maintenance and constant monitoring is the unavoidable requirement for running a site properly.

Most historic houses are at a disadvantage when compared with museums in that they are not able to move the collection round or add to it from store or elsewhere. Museums can add material and mount special presentations. They promote these to attract repeat visits. It will be difficult for a historic house faced with a static situation to stimulate repeat visits when the overwhelming impression from previous visitors is that they can cross this one off the list as done!

Larger houses add extra features fairly regularly, but this is not so easy for smaller establishments where resources are limited. A picture rescued from the attic, restored and on special show for a limited period is unlikely to add incremental visits unless it is quite outstanding (in which case one assumes it would have been a major feature of the house to begin with). A route might well be for the establishment to concentrate on quality to gain the reputation of being a gem for its catering service, immaculate grounds and so on.

One area where a house can also score very highly is in the way the site is interpreted for the visitor. The interpretation of heritage sites, tour centres and special parts of the countryside, to name but a few areas for this specialism, has become quite an industry in recent years. It recognizes that what the visitor seeks in return for his admission fee is an experience which can be greatly enhanced by receiving information in a form which heightens his appreciation and pleasure.

There is a whole range of interpretative techniques and it is not possible to go into them in any detail here. My experience comes from my long association with Warwick Castle and the techniques we use there to interpret a highly complex building and its history to our visitors. Earlier in this case study the point was made about people being essential vehicles in the forming of the product – a satisfying experience. In the main show areas of Warwick Castle the communication of information to visitors is by human beings – our guides and room stewards – and we believe it is by far the most satisfactory way of interpreting the building, its contents and its rich history.

Time spent with a guide can often be the most rewarding aspect of a visit. This is because they are trained not only to become fully conversant with the subject matter relating to the Castle, but also to develop background knowledge so that the aspects relating to the Castle can be put in context. The curator's policy is to provide new insights and information about various aspects of the Castle on a regular basis so that the guides do not develop a stereotyped patter but rather can share their knowledge with visitors. It is not possible to cover everything in a short talk or guided tour: there is simply too much of interest. It must be remembered also that the vast majority of visitors do not have a large canvas of knowledge. It would be all too easy to become elitist in one's approach: this is not what is required. One or two examples will illustrate. On viewing the plaster death mask of Oliver Cromwell in the Great Hall one visitor was heard to remark to her companion, 'Well, I don't think he was feeling particularly well when that was taken.' Another time a guide was asked, 'On what occasion would he have worn that?' One lady was convinced that the guests represented in the Royal Weekend Party (our acclaimed presentation by Madam Tussaud's) had, as she put it, 'dedicated their bodies'; and one gentlemen, when asked by his son what pot-pourri was, described it as 'that there incest'. It is really the anecdotal comments that get most of our visitors' imaginations going, along with the pleasure they feel at being in such rich surroundings. There really is little merit in a guided tour where glib patter and paucity of information, owing to the need to get you round quickly, is the only 'experience' offered.

As one small boy many, many years ago at the Castle, admiring a ladder up against the wall outside, remarked to the companions that he had just accompanied on a rather tedious tour of the interiors: 'This ladder is believed to be of the late seventeenth or early eighteenth century and we are told it is a particularly fine example for the period.' Rather than articulating a list of dates, artists, craftsmen etc. the experience of the state rooms can be brought to life for visitors by guides who can gauge their audience and interpret what they see accordingly. Naturally guides cannot be provided everywhere, and in the remoter parts of the Castle various exhibits and rooms are interpreted with written labels or illustrative panels – a standard approach. Gardeners are encouraged to share their knowledge with visitors. In a technologically sophisticated age we believe that personal contact adds value to our product and will continue to do so in the future.

From the interpretation and presentation of the site it is now necessary to turn to the presentation or promotion of properties to potential customers. What is the image that will attract custom? Our approach here must be guided by a clear understanding of our potential visitors' needs. All tourist attractions operate in a highly competitive market and, although what most heritage properties have to offer appeals to the connoisseur and the well informed, it has to be said that were houses to rely on this segment of the market they would quickly become a burden on the state's resources.

The bulk of visitors to heritage properties visit for an entertaining and informative experience. They do not expect to have to work too hard (they are at their leisure, after all), to be lectured too intently or to pursue an enforced course of study. Few come for a purely educational experience. This does not mean that in the promotional message the reverence or dignity of the site should in any way be vilified; rather we should be aware that in order to succeed well the image of a visit (which in most cases could look extremely dull) has to be presented as something that is inherently pleasurable. Again I have to turn to the Warwick Castle case.

The image we actively promote is that of an establishment which is vibrant, alive, a place where something is always happening and there is something new to discover. We continually market editorial to get this image across and see it as a major plank in the platform of our success in recent years. Like several other leading historic houses we have a strapline which positions our facilities at the pinnacle of our market niche: Warwick Castle – the finest medieval castle in England. This could be described as the establishment's unique selling proposition, and self-evidently is of enormous value in marketing terms. Other descriptions could be used. For example, Warwick Castle was described by Sir Walter Scott as 'the most noble sight in England' and 'that fairest monument of ancient and chivalrous splendour'. Such phrases are capable of conveying instantly the prestige of the site and its 'must see' quality.

If a small country house has the finest 'rococo picture frames' in Britain it would be best to find something else to say. The word 'rococo' will be known by many but will probably be understood by only a very small section of the population – and will be found interesting by an even smaller number of people. In order to achieve patronage the offer has to appeal, however strongly the uniqueness of items of specialist interest is felt by owners and managers to fulfil that task.

Ensuring that the image appeals to potential users requires considerable skill and information. In developing material to promote an establishment, if research has been done to discover the likely response that the attraction will enjoy, whom it will attract, from where and so on, then success will be all the greater since the promotional message will be honed and properly targeted. Time (and money) spent on research (like reconnaissance) is rarely wasted.

The basic proposition to the potential audience will be succinct. In the case of Warwick Castle, we have: Warwick Castle – the finest medieval castle in England – open every day (except Christmas Day). This covers the simple questions 'where?', 'what?', 'why?' and 'when?'. The disclaimer is always small: it is a courtesy, earning nothing. This promotional image can now be filled with or supported by strong visual images, preferably with little text, majoring on the breadth and variety of attractions that a visit to

Warwick Castle offers. Different aspects can be highlighted to attract selected market segments either in the same or in separate advertisements or printed items within a family of printed material.

In the Warwick Castle case we deliberately ensure that the tone of the copy is not academic, since through it we are aiming to influence the potential patron by getting across the fact that it is a place that everyone can enjoy. It is not merely the preserve of the highly talented but has interest and delight for all through its broad spectrum of facilities.

The process of defining the promotional image is, therefore, of great importance to the enterprise and is to a large degree the key in determining the success of its marketing activities. It demands time, careful refinement, and often significant investment in expertise.

By the same token the typefaces, the logo, and the whole communication in whatever medium should have a cohesive style and branding, so that the corporate message is constantly working in the market-place. The same style should obtain on all company communications, letterheads, invoices, external signs and so on. The constant impression should be one of high quality, giving a professional organized feel which will persistently promote confidence in the enterprise and its selling proposition. In order to achieve this standard the design element will be critical. Good design is expensive: it is probably the best investment that can be made since it will carry the company message forward in the best possible light. Confidence will not be instilled into potential customers by poorly designed, cheaply printed material on poor-quality paper, or by an erratic promotional image with constantly changing messages and styles.

An excellent way of instantly carrying the brand is the logo. Companies can spend a fortune on this. We are all aware of the British Telecom and Kingfisher cases. The most striking logo in the heritage business, which in my judgement is outstanding, is that of Beaulieu (Hampshire), into which the owner's colours, the name and a feeling of there being high quality and a good experience are cleverly designed. Many establishments rely on a suitable type style and perhaps a line drawing or the owner's coat of arms. There is considerable competitive advantage in a logo that expresses the totality of the proposition, but it is not easy to achieve.

We all need confidence to purchase a product of any description. The reasons that persuade us to do so will be either the recommendation by a purchaser whose taste and judgement we respect, or exposure to the offer by way of printed material or other media, which promote confidence that it will live up to expectations or our own previous experience. Ultimately what persuades us to visit an attraction will be the confidence that our status as individuals will be enhanced by investing in a satisfying and rewarding experience for ourselves and for those for whose opinion of us we have regard. This is the real product we are selling. High quality presentation, both in the media and on site, will be critical to a positive decision to visit, repeat the purchase and refer.

Reference

DELENS, A. H. R. (1950) *Principles of Market Research*, Hillman, Frome, Somerset

Index